THE COMPACT READER

SHORT ESSAYS BY
METHOD AND THEME

TENTH EDITION

THE COMPACT READER

SHORT ESSAYS BY METHOD AND THEME

Jane E. Aaron

Ellen Kuhl Repetto

Bedford/St. Martin's
A Macmillan Education Imprint
Boston • New York

For Bedford/St. Martin's

Vice President, Editorial, Macmillan Higher Education Humanities: Edwin Hill
Editorial Director, English and Music: Karen S. Henry
*Publisher for Composition, Business and Technical Writing, and Developmental
    Writing:* Leasa Burton
Executive Editor: John E. Sullivan III
Developmental Editor: Sherry Mooney
Production Editors: Annette Pagliaro Sweeney; Louis C. Bruno, Jr.
Publishing Services Manager: Andrea Cava
Production Manager: Joseph Ford
Project Management: Books By Design, Inc.
Director of Rights and Permissions: Hilary Newman
Senior Art Director: Anna Palchik
Text Design: Janis Owens
Cover Design: John Callahan
Composition: Jouve
Printing and Binding: RR Donnelley and Sons

Manufactured in the United States of America.

0   9   8   7   6   5
f   e   d   c   b   a

For information, write: Bedford/St. Martin's, 75 Arlington Street, Boston, MA
02116   (617-399-4000)

ISBN 978-1-4576-3297-6

Acknowledgments

*Text acknowledgments and copyrights appear at the back of the book on pages
427–29, which constitute an extension of the copyright page. Art acknowledgments and copyrights appear on the same page as the art selections they cover.
It is a violation of the law to reproduce these selections by any means whatsoever
without the written permission of the copyright holder.*

helping them to form and express their own ideas before they read the essay itself.

■ *Headnotes about the author and the essay* place every selection in a context that helps focus students' reading.

■ *Gloss notes* explain allusions, historical references, and specialized vocabulary that students may not understand without help.

■ *Detailed questions* after each essay guide students' analysis of meaning, purpose and audience, method and structure, and language. A question labeled "Other Methods" highlights the writer's interweaving of methods, showing students how the rhetorical modes might be fluidly combined.

■ *Writing topics* after each selection give students specific direction for their own work. Among these, "Journal to Essay" topics help students build their journal writing into finished essays, "Cultural Considerations" topics lead students to consider similarities and differences among cultures, focused "Research" topics prompt students to expand their understanding of a subject by locating and synthesizing sources, and "Connections" topics encourage students to make thematic or rhetorical links to other selections in the book.

A Thoroughly New Edition

Developed with the input of dozens of teachers who use or have used *The Compact Reader* over three decades, the tenth edition has been completely overhauled and updated to meet the interests and needs of today's students.

Engaging New Readings

Half the selections are new to this edition. Seventeen new essays and eleven new paragraphs in Part Two touch on engaging themes that invite students to laugh, to reflect, and to explore. Ranging in subject from politics and culture to media and advertising, the new readings present a mix of real student writers, remarkable new voices, and requested classics. For instance:

■ Student Jessica Sayuri Boissy, in "One Cup at a Time," draws on her Japanese heritage to explain a Zen concept that can help bring inner peace to her stressed-out peers.

■ In a paragraph from *Denial*, popular writer Jonathan Rauch recalls the confusion engendered by his first kiss.

- Brian Doyle breathlessly imagines the perfect environmental article, in "How to Read a Nature Essay."

- In "The Border on Our Backs," Mexican-born scholar Roberto Rodrí-guez takes issue with the dehumanizing effects of immigration reform.

In recognition of the rising importance of visual literacy and source-based writing in composition courses, four of the essays now include images such as cartoons and photographs, and four student models are documented in MLA style. The readings also reflect several new themes chosen for their capacity to capture students' imaginations: Growing Up (Chapter 5), Considering the Natural Environment (Chapter 10), Pursuing Happiness (Chapter 12), Investigating the Working World (Chapter 13), and Discussing Social Issues (Chapter 14).

A Contemporary Guide to Reading and Writing

A highlight of the fresh readings is a new set of thematically related selections supporting Part One's overview of critical reading and writing:

- *A recent, accessible new essay for analysis.* Edward P. Jones's "Shacks" examines the author's struggles as a disoriented college freshman and anchors a more pointed sample of close reading to show students how asking a series of questions about a work can help them reach a critical understanding of its elements and its writer's strategies.

- *A new student-annotated photograph* in the discussion of reading visuals looks at the experience of successful female cadets at the traditionally male US Military Academy at West Point.

- *A new student essay-in-progress,* by Nicole Lang, models what college students are increasingly asked to do in beginning composition courses. Both analytical and argumentative, her essay "Foundations" questions Jones's assumptions and articulates Lang's own assessment of the purpose of a college education.

The chapters in Part One also include a new section on talking and listening as a discovery tool; stronger coverage of shaping a thesis, with a new checklist for drafting effective thesis statements; and a reorganized discussion of revision that prioritizes developing ideas and simplifies the key concepts of unity and coherence.

More Attention to the Nuts and Bolts of Grammar

Chapter 4, "Editing," has been reworked and clarified to provide students with the necessary tools for taking their writing beyond the first-draft stage. With a new emphasis on grammar and punctuation, the chapter now explains not only nuances of craft but also common sentence-level issues, such as fragments, run-ons, and awkward pronoun references. Simple explanations, multiple examples of weak and revised sentences, and a boxed editing checklist are complemented by Focus boxes in the introductions to the rhetorical methods. Newly expanded with detailed explanations and multiple examples, these boxes continue to highlight those elements of language and usage especially relevant to each method — such as verbs in narration, parallelism in comparison and contrast, and tone in argument and persuasion.

A New Take on Argument

Chapter 14, "Argument and Persuasion," now grounds students in the fundamentals of *ethos*, *pathos*, and *logos* and more clearly outlines the processes of inductive and deductive reasoning. Updated and expanded to center on a more flexible theme — Discussing Social Issues — the chapter concludes with a new three-essay casebook focused on questions of immigration reform.

A Practical Approach to Researched Writing

The updated Appendix, "Working with Sources," includes more discussion of the varied purposes of research, a new section on asking questions, additional tips for finding and evaluating online sources, a clarified explanation of the relationship between MLA in-text citations and a works-cited list, and up-to-date documentation models, with new entries for literary sources. A new sample research essay, "Women and Children First" by student writer Jarrod Ballo, argues a solution to homelessness (prompted by reading Barbara Lazear Ascher's "The Box Man") and illustrates the elements of source-based writing. Because academic writing often draws on and synthesizes sources, many of the essays in Part Two are now accompanied by clearly labeled "Research" topics that encourage students to investigate compelling issues in the library or online.

A Newly Integrated Glossary of Terms

To help students find the information they need and understand what they find, the Glossary has been substantially expanded and better integrated with the text itself. Key terms throughout the book are now printed in boldface, signaling to students that detailed explanations are provided in the back of the book. The entries themselves function as an informal index and guide, defining and illustrating more than a hundred terms with specific cross-references to fuller discussions in the text.

Fresh Writing Topics

The suggestions for writing at the end of each chapter have been refreshed as well, with anywhere from five to fifteen new ideas for writing with the method and three new or revised prompts for writing about the theme.

Additional Resources

Bedford/St. Martin's offers an abundance of resources that help you and your students get even more out of *The Compact Reader* and your course. To learn more about or to order any of the following products, contact your Bedford/St. Martin's sales representative, e-mail sales support (*sales_support@bfwpub.com*), or visit *macmillanhighered.com/compactreader/catalog*.

Value Packages

You can add value to your course by packaging *The Compact Reader* with a Bedford/St. Martin's handbook or any other Bedford/St. Martin's title for a significant discount.

Multimedia Supplements

LAUNCHPAD SOLO FOR READERS AND WRITERS offers skill-specific practice with interactive modules on reading, writing, research, and grammar. Each module tracks learning through a variety of activities—including a pre-test, an adaptive LearningCurve quiz, and a post-test—and offers several multimedia study aids to help students develop mastery.

THE POPULAR I·SERIES presents multimedia tutorials in a flexible online format: *ix: visualizing composition 2.0* helps students practice key rhetorical and visual concepts for multimodal composition, and *i-claim: visualizing argument* offers six multimedia tutorials, an illustrated glossary, and a wide array of multimedia arguments.

PORTFOLIO KEEPING, Third Edition, by Nedra Reynolds and Elizabeth Davis, provides all the information students need to use the portfolio method successfully in a writing course. *Portfolio Teaching*, a companion guide for instructors, provides practical support for you and your writing-program administrator.

RE:WRITING 3 offers online resources with videos and interactive elements to engage students in new ways of writing. You'll find tutorials about using common digital writing tools, an interactive peer review game, Extreme

Paragraph Makeover, and more—all for free. Visit *bedfordstmartins.com/ rewriting*.

Instructor Resources

Because you have a lot to do in your course, Bedford/St. Martin's makes it easy for you to find the support you need and to get it quickly.

RESOURCES FOR TEACHING THE COMPACT READER, available bound into the instructor's edition of the book or as a downloadable PDF on the instructor tab of the online catalog (*macmillanhighered.com/compactreader/catalog*), aims to help you integrate the text into your course and use it in class. It includes an overview of the book's organization and chapters, ideas for combining the reader with other course materials, sample syllabi, and varied resources for each selection: teaching tips, content and vocabulary quizzes, and detailed answers to all the critical-reading questions.

TEACHINGCENTRAL (*macmillanhighered.com/teachingcentral*) offers the complete list of Bedford/St. Martin's print and online professional resources in one place. You'll find landmark reference works, sourcebooks on pedagogical issues, award-winning collections, and practical advice for the classroom—all free.

BITS (*bedfordbits.com*) collects creative ideas for teaching a range of composition topics in an easily searchable blog format. A community of teachers— leading scholars, authors, and editors—discuss revision, research, grammar and style, technology, peer review, and much more.

Acknowledgments

Many instructors helped to shape this edition of *The Compact Reader*, offering insights from their experience and suggestions for improvement. Many thanks to Karen Amano-Tompkins, Harbor College; Barbara Bonallo, Miami Dade College; HoneyLou Bonar, Hastings College; Naomi Carrington, CSU Northridge; Rebecca Chalmers, University of Mary; Gregory Chandler, Mount San Antonio College; Karin Cooper, Saddleback College; Tamera Davis, Northern Oklahoma College; Ember Dooling, St. Joseph High School; Lynnell Edwards, Spalding University; Jonathan Elmore, Beaufort County Community College; Agnes Fleck, College of St. Scholastica; Michael Given, Stephen F. Austin State University; Chad Greene, Cerritos College; Jessica Hasson, Moorpark College; David Hatz, Chula Vista High School; Mary Heider, Coker College; Pamela Kraft, Ohio University–

Chillicothe; Tamara Kuzmenkov, Tacoma Community College; Annie Liu, Fullerton College; Paulette Longmore, Essex County College; Elaine Lux, Nyack College; Kara Lybarger-Monson, Moorpark College; Terry Mathias, Southeastern Illinois College; Elisabeth McLaren, College of Southern Nevada; Pam Monder, Community College of Vermont; Rebecca Mooney, Bakersfield College; Nancy Padilla, Alhambra High School; Paul Pelan, Curry College; Rebecca Portis, Montgomery College; Mary Rohrer-Dann, Pennsylvania State University; Jasna Shannon, Coker College; James Slama, Los Angeles Southwest College; Kimberly Tolson, Walla Walla Community College; and Tammy Tucks-Bordeaux, Peru State College. Special thanks to Kim Sanabria, Eugenia Maria de Hostos Community College, whose contributions to the seventh edition continue to influence the book's content and features.

The always wonderful people at Bedford/St. Martin's once again contributed greatly to this project. Our friends Joan Feinberg, Karen Henry, Steve Scipione, and John Sullivan provided encouraging leadership and good ideas. Sherry Mooney proved to be an enthusiastic and invaluable new editor, helping to conceive the book's features, select readings, shape new material, solve problems, and smooth frayed nerves. We are grateful also to Jen Prince for her assistance and creativity. Janis Owens created the book's striking new interior design, John Callahan gave us a beautiful cover, and Annette Pagliaro Sweeney, Louis Bruno, and Nancy Benjamin deftly shepherded the manuscript through production on a demanding schedule. Deep and happy thanks to all.

CONTENTS

PART TWO
SHORT ESSAYS BY METHOD AND THEME   59

5 ▶ NARRATION
GROWING UP   61

9 ▶ CLASSIFICATION
SORTING FRIENDS AND NEIGHBORS   178

13 ▶ CAUSE-AND-EFFECT ANALYSIS
INVESTIGATING THE WORKING WORLD   295

THE COMPACT READER

SHORT ESSAYS BY METHOD AND THEME

PART ONE

A COMPACT GUIDE TO READING AND WRITING

1

READING

This collection of essays has one purpose: to help you become a better reader and writer. It combines examples of good writing with explanations of the writers' methods, questions to guide your reading, and ideas for your own writing. In doing so, it shows how you can adapt the processes and techniques of others as you learn to communicate clearly and effectively.

Writing well is not an inborn skill but an acquired one: you will become proficient only by writing and rewriting, experimenting with different strategies, listening to the responses of readers. How, then, can it help to read the work of other writers?

- *Reading introduces you to new information and ideas.* People routinely share facts, observations, discoveries, varieties of behavior, and ways of thinking in writing. Reading what others have to say lets you learn about subjects and perspectives that would otherwise remain unknown to you, gives you knowledge worth exploring further, and can spark ideas for your own writing.

- *Reading gives you insights on your own experience.* Many of the essays collected here demonstrate that personal experience is a rich and powerful source of material for writing. But the knowledge gained from reading can help pinpoint just what is remarkable in your own experience. Such insight not only reveals subjects for writing but also improves your ability to communicate with others whose experiences naturally differ from your own.

- *Reading exposes you to a broad range of strategies and styles.* Just seeing how widely these vary—as much as the writers themselves—should assure you that there is no fixed standard of writing. It should also encourage you to find your own strategies and style. At the same time, you will see that writers do make choices to suit their subjects, their purposes, and especially their readers. Writing is rarely easy, even for the pros; but the more options you have to choose from, the more likely you are to succeed at it.

- *Reading makes you sensitive to the role of audience in writing.* As you become skilled at reading the work of other writers critically, discovering intentions and analyzing choices, you will see how a writer's decisions affect you as audience. Training yourself to read attentively and critically is a first step to becoming a more objective reader of your own writing.

Reading Attentively

This chapter offers strategies for making the most of your reading—in this book and elsewhere. These strategies are reinforced in Chapters 5–14, each of which offers opportunities for careful reading with two paragraphs, one student essay, and two professional essays. Each chapter also introduces a method of developing a piece of writing:

narration	process analysis
description	comparison and contrast
example	definition
division or analysis	cause-and-effect analysis
classification	argument and persuasion

These methods correspond to basic and familiar patterns of thought and expression, common in our daily musings and conversations as well as in writing for all sorts of purposes and audiences: blogs, social-networking sites, and online discussion boards; college papers, lab reports, and examinations; business memos and reports; letters to the editors of newspapers; articles in popular magazines.

As writers we draw on the methods, often without thinking about it, to give order to our ideas and even to find ideas. For instance, a writer narrates, or tells, a story of her experiences to understand and convey the feeling of living her life. As readers, in turn, we have expectations for these familiar methods. When we read a narrative of someone's experiences, for example, we expect enough details to understand what happened, we anticipate that events will be told primarily in the order they occurred, and we want the story to have a point—a reason for its being told and for our bothering to read it.

Building an awareness of such expectations can sharpen your skills as a critical reader and as a writer. A full chapter on each method explains how it works, shows it in action in annotated paragraphs, and gives advice for using it to develop your own essays. The essays in each chapter provide clear examples that you can analyze and learn from (with the help of specific questions) and can refer to while writing (with the help of specific writing suggestions).

To make your reading more interesting and also to stimulate your writing, the sample paragraphs and essays in Chapters 5–14 all focus on a common subject, such as travel, popular culture, or diversity. You'll see how flexible the methods are when they help five writers produce five unique pieces on the same theme. You'll also find a springboard for producing your own unique pieces, whether you take up some of the book's writing suggestions or jump off with your own topics.

Reading Critically

Much of the reading we do every day is superficial: we skim a newsfeed, magazine, or Web site, noting headings and scanning visuals to get the gist of the content before settling on what catches our interest. But such skimming is not really reading, for it neither involves us deeply in the subject nor engages us in interaction with the writer.

To get the most out of reading, we must invest something of ourselves in the process, applying our own ideas and emotions and paying attention not just to the subject matter but to the writer's interpretation of it. This kind of reading is **critical** because it looks beneath the surface of a piece of writing. (The common meaning of *critical* as "negative" doesn't apply here: critical reading may result in positive, negative, or even neutral reactions.)

Critical reading can be enormously rewarding, but it takes care and time. A good method for developing your own skill in critical reading is to prepare yourself beforehand and then read the work at least twice to uncover what it has to offer.

▶ Preparing

Preparing to read need involve no more than a few minutes as you form some ideas about the author, the work, and your likely response:

- *What is the author's background, what qualifications does he or she bring to the subject, and what approach is he or she likely to take?* The biographical information provided before each essay in this book should help answer these questions; many periodicals, Web sites, and books include similar information on their authors.

■ *What does the title convey about the subject and the author's attitude toward it?* Note, for instance, the quite different attitudes conveyed by these three titles on the same subject: "Safe Hunting," "In Touch with Ancient Spirits," and "Killing Animals for Fun and Profit."

■ *What can you predict about your own response to the work?* What might you already know about the author's subject? Based on the title and other clues (such as headings or visuals), are you likely to agree or disagree with the author's views? *The Compact Reader* helps ready you for reading by providing a two-part feature before each selection. First, quotations from varied writers comment on the selection's general subject to give you a range of views. And second, a journal prompt encourages you to write about your thoughts on the subject before you see what the author has to say. By giving you a head start in considering the author's ideas and approach, writing *before* reading encourages you to read more actively and critically.

▶ Reading Actively

After developing some expectations about the piece of writing, read it through carefully to acquaint yourself with the subject, the author's reason for writing about it, and the way the author presents it. (Each essay in this book is short enough to be read in one sitting.) Try not to read passively, letting the words wash over you, but instead interact directly with the work to discover its meaning, the author's intentions, and your own responses.

One of the best aids to **active reading** is to make notes on separate sheets of paper or, preferably (if you own the book), on the pages themselves. As you practice making notes, you will probably develop a personal code meaningful only to you. As a start, however, try this system:

■ *Underline, bracket, or check passages* that you find particularly effective or that seem especially important to the author's purpose.

■ *Circle words* you don't understand so that you can look them up when you finish.

■ *Put question marks in the margins* next to unclear passages.

■ *Jot down associations* that occur to you, such as examples from your own experience, disagreements with the author's assumptions, or connections to other works you've read.

When you have finished such an active reading, your annotations might look like those below. (The paragraph is from the end of the essay reprinted on pp. 9–11.)

I learned, once the world became larger than Sandra Walker and me and Worcester, Massachusetts, that we are born with few tools with which

True? to build our little shacks of life and we are born ?
with even less knowledge of how to use those
tools. I don't know what I would have done if I
✔ hadn't had it in me to write those letters, those
stories, to Sandra. I was able to crawl into Decem-   *Like a*
ber, and I woke up one day and knew, without a   *toddler*
Why? letter from Sandra, without anyone telling me so,
that wherever in the universe Sandra Walker would
end up I would not be there with her. I made peace
with that, and I think I had a sense that I wasn't   *So he grew*
◀─ *up, but just*
really eighteen anymore, but fast going on twenty.   *a little bit?*

To answer questions like those in the annotations above, plan to reread the essay at least once. Multiple readings increase your mastery of the material; more important, once you have a basic understanding of a writer's subject, a second and third reading will reveal details and raise questions that you might not have noticed on the first pass. Reading an essay several times also helps you uncover how the many parts of the work—for instance, the organization, the tone, the evidence—contribute to the author's purpose.

▶ Using a Reading Checklist

When rereading an essay, start by writing a one- or two-sentence summary of each paragraph and image—in your own words—to increase your mastery of the material (see p. 389). Then let the essay rest in your mind for at least an hour or two before approaching it again. On later readings, dig beneath the essay's surface by asking questions such as those in the checklist for critical reading on the next page. Note that the questions provided after each essay in this book offer more targeted versions of the ones presented here. Answering both the questions in the checklist

---

CHECKLIST FOR CRITICAL READING

- *Why did the author choose this subject?*
- *Who is the intended audience?* What impression does the author wish to make on readers?
- *What is the author's point?* Can you find a direct statement of the thesis, or main idea, or is the thesis implied?
- *What details does the author provide to support the thesis?* Is the supporting evidence reliable? complete? convincing?
- *How does the author organize ideas?* What effect does that arrangement have on the overall impact of the work?
- *What do language and tone reveal about the author's meaning, purpose, and attitude?*
- *How successful is the work as a whole, and why?*

---

and the questions for individual readings will ensure a thorough analysis of what you read.

Analyzing a Sample Essay

Critical reading—and the insights to be gained from it—can best be illustrated by examining an actual essay. The annotated passage on page 7 comes from "Shacks" by Edward P. Jones. The entire essay is reprinted here in the same format as other selections in this book, with quotations from other writers to get you thinking about the essay's subject, a suggestion for exploring your attitudes further in your journal, a biographical note on the author, and an introductory note on the essay.

We tell ourselves stories in order to live.   —Joan Didion

Almost all good writing begins with terrible first efforts. You need to start somewhere.
                                                              —Anne Lamott

As you become proficient . . . your style will emerge, because you yourself will emerge, and when this happens you will find it increasingly easy to break through the barriers that separate you from other minds, other hearts—which is, of course, the purpose of writing, as well as its principal reward.
                                          —William Strunk, Jr., and E. B. White

JOURNAL RESPONSE   Reflect on your experiences with writing—whether for school, for friends, or for your own purposes. Does writing come naturally to you, or do you struggle to express your thoughts? How so? What do you expect to gain from taking a writing class in college?

Edward P. Jones

Born in 1950, Edward P. Jones has been hailed as a major voice of Southern litera-ture. Although his childhood in Washington, DC, was marked by poverty and insta-bility, Jones showed an early love for reading and won a scholarship to the College of the Holy Cross. He completed a BA in 1972 and went through a brief period of homelessness before obtaining a clerical job with *Science* magazine and publishing his first short story in *Essence*—both in the same week. Jones went on to earn an MFA from the University of Virginia, and for eighteen years he edited tax news-letters during the day while writing fiction in his spare time. His tales of urban life—collected in *Lost in the City* (1992) and *All Aunt Hagar's Children* (2006)—have won popular and critical acclaim, and his novel *The Known World* (2003), about black slaveholders, was awarded the Pulitzer Prize and the National Book Critics Circle Award. Now a professor of English at George Washington University, Jones has also taught at Princeton, the University of Maryland, and the University of Virginia. He lives in Arlington, Virginia.

Shacks

In this essay written for a special "Starting Out" issue of the *New Yorker* in 2011, Jones reflects on a life lesson he stumbled across in his first semester of college. By engaging in an eager yet futile effort to build a romance, Jones discovered a talent he hadn't known he had.

In my first months as a college freshman, I cared more than anything about   1
a young woman with whom I'd gone to high school—Sandra Walker, a
thin, brown-skinned woman who might not have been pretty enough for
the rest of the universe but was more than pretty enough for me. She was at
college in Atlanta and I was in Worcester, Massachusetts. I had never kissed
her, for she was true to someone else. I don't think I'd even so much as
touched the back of her hand, but I cared for her, and the only way I knew
how to express what I felt at that point in my life was to write letters, and
write letters I did. Three and four and five a week I wrote. All of them were
more than five pages long and many went to fifteen pages—so thick once
they had been folded that I had to reinforce the envelopes with tape. I had
always written legibly, but the fear was so great that Sandra Walker might
not be able to decipher even one syllable I had written that I began printing
everything, and to this day the only cursive writing I do is my signature.

   Things like that get in the blood, and they become who you are. I   2
never received a strongly positive response from Sandra, but the crumbs,
the letters sharing with me only the minutiae of her life, were enough to
keep me writing—September and October and November. There wasn't
much beyond the crumbs. Imagining as best I could what a young woman
at the front door of the rest of her life might want to hear from a young
man, I put all the hope I had into each letter, using the limited language
of an eighteen-year-old who knew books of mathematics but not much
else. It is amazing the little shacks of life we can build when it seems that
so much is at stake. Before it was all over, the letters—from what I can
remember, for I have not seen any of them since the day I sent them off—
became grand and fanciful creations about some marvelous future that
Sandra Walker and I could have. It was a world of fiction, of course, a
place conjured up in my imagination, because, as my mother could have
told Sandra, I could barely take care of myself and would not have known
what to do with, first, a girlfriend, and then a wife and all the children we
were supposed to have.

   But I was alone in the wilderness in Worcester, away from Washing-   3
ton, DC, my home, for the first time, and I needed some shack of life. I
know now that had I been someone who knew only how to paint pictures, I would have done that. I would have made my case with painting
after painting, wrapping them with care and sending them off to Atlanta.
Or if I had known how to carve little figures in wood I would have carved
Sandra and me and our happy future in oak or maple or whatever wood I
could salvage in Worcester. Or I would have weighed poor Sandra down
with volumes of poetry or tapes of songs with her name in every title.

   I learned, once the world became larger than Sandra Walker and me   4
and Worcester, Massachusetts, that we are born with few tools with which

to build our little shacks of life, and we are born with even less knowledge of how to use those tools. I don't know what I would have done if I hadn't had it in me to write those letters, those stories, to Sandra. I was able to crawl into December, and I woke up one day and knew, without a letter from Sandra, without anyone telling me so, that wherever in the universe Sandra Walker would end up I would not be there with her. I made peace with that, and I think I had a sense that I wasn't really eighteen anymore, but fast going on twenty.

Even read quickly, Jones's essay would not be difficult to comprehend: the author draws on a story from his time as a college student to make a point about talent. In fact, a quick reading might give the impression that Jones produced the essay effortlessly, artlessly. But close, critical reading reveals a carefully conceived piece whose parts work both independently and together to achieve the author's purpose.

One way to uncover the underlying intentions and relations in a piece of writing is to answer a series of questions about the work. The following questions proceed from the general to the specific—from overall meaning through purpose and method to word choices—and they parallel the more specific questions located after the essays in this book. Here the questions come with possible answers for Jones's essay. (The paragraph numbers can help you locate the appropriate passages in "Shacks" as you follow the analysis.)

▶ Meaning

What is the main idea of the essay—the chief point the writer makes about the subject, to which all other ideas and details relate? What are the subordinate ideas that contribute to the main idea?

Jones states his main idea near the end of his essay: "[W]e are born with few tools with which to build our little shacks of life, and we are born with even less knowledge of how to use those tools" (paragraph 4). As we mature, he is saying, we discover our talents and desires and learn what to do with them. (Writers sometimes postpone stating their main idea, as Jones does here. Perhaps more often, they state it near the beginning of the essay. See p. 23.) Jones leads up to and supports his idea by narrating an episode from his own life—his obsessive writing of letters to a woman he longed for during his first semester of college (1–2)—and by contemplating other ways he might have approached her (3), to reach a larger truth. The story is developed with specific details from Jones's memory (such as the bulk of the envelopes, 1), with descriptions of the raw talents he had (such as written expression, persistence, and imagination, 1–2), and with examples of the talents he lacked (such as taking care of a family, 2, or painting and carving, 3).

▶ Purpose and Audience

Why did the author write the essay? What did the author hope readers would gain from it? What did the author assume about the knowledge and interests of readers, and how are these assumptions reflected in the essay?

Jones seems to have written his essay for two interlocking reasons: to show, and thus explain, that we all feel an inherent need to do something constructive with our lives—to find our "shacks"—and to argue gently that individual talents must be identified and developed before they can be used to full advantage.

Jones assumes that his readers, like him, are people who have gone to college, people to whom the emotional turmoil of the first semester will feel familiar. He comments, for instance, on the doubts of "an eighteen-year-old who knew books of mathematics but not much else" (2), the reality that he "could barely take care of [him]self" (2), and the loneliness of being away from "home . . . for the first time" (3). But he also expresses hopes of being "at the front door of the rest of . . . life" (2) and reveals an imagination full of "grand and fanciful creations about some marvelous future" (2), taking pains to show (with some hint of embarrassment) the lengths to which he practiced his only skill—letter writing—to try to secure his desires.

At the same time, Jones seems to expect that readers of the *New Yorker*—with that magazine's emphasis on culture and the arts—will be aware that he is now an established fiction writer and therefore will grasp that his youthful letters, the "stories" (3) he conjured and sent out, built the foundation for his future life. However, readers who do not recognize this point are still likely to understand and appreciate his main idea.

▶ Method and Structure

What method or methods does the author use to develop the main idea, and how do those methods serve the author's subject and purpose? How does the organization serve the author's subject and purpose?

As writers often do, Jones develops his main idea with a combination of the methods discussed in this book. His primary support for his idea consists of narration (Chapter 5)—a story about letter writing as a means of romance. The narrative is developed with description (Chapter 6), especially of the letters Jones wrote (as in paragraphs 1–2), and with classification (Chapter 9) and examples (Chapter 7) of the forms of expression he might have tried if he had the talent (3). Jones relies on division or analysis (Chapter 8) to tease apart the elements of his messages to Sandra Walker, and he uses comparison and contrast (Chapter 11) to show the differences between his letters and her responses (2). In addition, he draws on definition (Chapter 12) to give meaning to the "shacks" metaphor that shapes the essay (title, 2–4). (See "Language," below, for further discussion of Jones's figures of speech.)

While using many methods to develop his idea, Jones keeps his organization fairly simple. He does not begin with a formal introduction or a statement of his idea but instead starts right off with his story, the inspiration for his idea. In the first paragraph he narrates and describes his efforts to connect with a former high school classmate by writing letters to her. Then, in paragraph 2, he explains why he persisted despite her unresponsiveness and suggests that those letters may have served an as-yet undiscovered purpose in his life. Still delaying a statement of his main idea, Jones contrasts his writing with other forms of communication, which he sees as talents different from his own (3). Finally, he relates his awakening to the truth of his situation and zeroes in on his main idea (4). Although he has withheld this idea until the end, we see that everything in the essay has been controlled by it and directed toward it.

▶ Language

How are the author's main idea and purpose revealed at the level of sentences and words? How does the author use language to convey his or her attitudes toward the subject and to make meaning clear and vivid?

Perhaps Jones's most striking use of language to express and support his idea is in his **figures of speech**, creative expressions that imply meanings beyond or different from their literal meanings (see p. 54). As is often the case, you may need to puzzle over some of his words before you can fully understand their meaning. This is particularly true of Jones's central metaphor, "shacks of life" (title and paragraphs 2–4). A **metaphor** is a figure of speech that compares two unlike things by saying one is the other: in this case, Jones equates physical shelters and the goals that people create to shape their existence. The **connotations** of the word "shack" add more layers of meaning: shacks are simple structures, often temporary or unstable, and they tend to be associated with people of limited means. Jones's idea, it seems, is that a person doesn't need much to build a life, just enough "tools" (4)—a metaphor for skills or talents—to give it purpose.

The essay includes several other inventive figures of speech. In paragraph 2 alone Jones uses metaphors such as the behaviors "that get in the blood," the "crumbs" offered by his female correspondent, and "the front door of the rest of her life"—separate from, but cleverly echoing, the "shacks" metaphor. Calling the small city of Worcester, Massachusetts, a "wilderness" (3) is **hyperbole**, or deliberate exaggeration, suggesting the author's emotional isolation more than the physical reality of place (and again, echoing the "shacks" metaphor). And finally, the last paragraph depends on contrasting **images** of infancy (captured in the words "born" and "crawl") and adulthood (not "eighteen anymore, but fast going on twenty") to reinforce Jones's admission that his maturation and understanding were incomplete.

Jones's ideas gain additional impact with **parallelism**, the use of similar grammatical form for ideas of equal importance (see pp. 50–51). For instance, every sentence of paragraph 3 except the first uses the phrase "I would have," building rhythm and stressing the young man's desperate need to communicate. The balanced phrase "those letters, those stories" (4) clarifies that his missives were an early form of fiction writing. Similarly, the **repetition** of "we are born with" (4) emphasizes both the author's lingering immaturity and his point that raw talents in their infancy must be nurtured in order to thrive.

These notes on Jones's essay show how a reader can arrive at a deeper, more personal understanding of a piece of writing by attentive, thoughtful analysis. Guided by the questions at the end of each essay and by your own sense of what works and why, you'll find similar lessons and pleasures in all of this book's readings.

Reading Visuals

Much of what you read will have a visual component—a photograph, perhaps, or a drawing, chart, table, or graph. Sometimes these images stand alone, but often they contribute to the overall meaning and effect of a written work. Some essays in this book, in fact, include visuals: William Least Heat-Moon's "Starrucca Viaduct" (p. 102) features a historic photograph of the author's subject, Scott Adams's "Funny Business" (p. 156) reprints a classic *Dilbert* comic strip, David Brooks's "People Like Us" (p. 196) includes a political cartoon to illustrate a point, and Jessica Sayuri Boissy's "One Cup at a Time" (p. 288) incorporates Japanese calligraphy.

Like written texts, visual texts are composed. That is, the people who create them do with images what writers do with words: they come to the task with a purpose, an audience, and a message to convey. You can and should, therefore, "read" visuals actively. Don't simply glance over images or take them at face value. Examine them closely and with a critical eye.

Reading visuals critically draws on the same skills you use for reading written works closely. The checklist for critical reading on page 8 can get you started. Determining who created an image, why, and for whom will help you tease out details that you might have missed at first look. Examining each element of a visual composition—such as the placement and arrangement of objects, the focus, and the uses of color, light, and shadow—will give you a greater appreciation of its intent and overall effect. Notice what first captures your attention, where your eye is drawn, and how different parts of the image interact to create a dominant impression. Finally, if the visual accompanies written text, such as an essay or advertisement, ask yourself what it contributes to the writer's meaning and purpose.

Consider, for example, one student's notes on a photograph of a college classroom. The picture was taken by photographer Damon Winter and was included in "The Women of West Point," a 2014 *New York Times Magazine* photo essay about female students at the elite military academy. The woman facing the camera is Brigade Commander Lindsey Danilack, the top cadet of her graduating class.

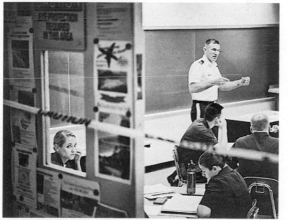

Wall splits image in half— gender divide?

Window highlights her—but also keeps her isolated.

Teacher is in military uniform.

Male students have their backs to the camera.

Staring right at us. She looks bored, or maybe annoyed.

Is that caution tape? Why?

Damon Winter/*The New York Times*/Redux

As Winter's photograph demonstrates, visual images can pack many layers of meaning into a condensed space. Learning to unpack those layers is a skill worth cultivating.

2

DEVELOPING AN ESSAY

Analyzing a text as shown in the preceding chapter is valuable in itself: it can be fun, and the process helps you better understand and appreciate whatever you read. But it can make you a better writer, too, by showing you how to read your own work critically, broadening the range of strategies available to you, and suggesting subjects for you to write about.

The essays collected in this book are accompanied by a range of material designed to help you use your reading to write effectively. Every reading is followed by several detailed questions that will help you read it critically and examine the writing strategies that make it successful. Accompanying the questions are writing topics—ideas for you to adapt and develop into essays of your own. Some of these call for your analysis of the essay; others lead you to examine your own experiences or outside sources in light of the essay's ideas. Chapters 5–14 each conclude with two additional sets of writing topics: one group provides a range of subjects for using the chapter's method of development; the other encourages you to focus on thematic connections in the chapter.

To help you develop your writing, *The Compact Reader* also offers several tools that guide you through composing effective essays. This chapter and the next two (on revising and editing) offer specific ways to strengthen and clarify your work as you move through the **writing process**, the activities that contribute to a finished piece of writing. This process is presented as a sequence of stages: analyzing the writing situation, generating ideas, focusing, shaping, revising, and editing. As you'll discover, these stages are actually somewhat arbitrary because writers rarely move in straight lines through fixed steps. Instead, just as they do when thinking or talking, writers continually circle back over covered territory, each time picking up more information or seeing new relationships, until their meaning is clear to themselves and can be made clear to readers. No two writers work in exactly the same way, either. Still, viewing the process in stages does help sort out its many activities so you can develop the process or processes that work best for you.

Complementing the general overview of the writing process in Part One of this book are the more specific introductions to the methods of development in Part Two—narration, comparison and contrast, definition, and so on. These method introductions follow the pattern set here by also moving through stages, but they take up the particular concerns of each method, such as organizing a comparison or clarifying a definition. (See the inside back cover for a guide to the topics covered.)

Getting Started

Every writing situation involves several elements: you communicate a *thesis* (central idea) about a subject to an *audience* of readers for a particular *purpose*. At first you may not be sure of your idea or your purpose. You may not know how you want to approach your readers, even when you know who they are. Your job in getting started, then, is to explore options and make choices.

▶ Considering Your Subject and Purpose

A **subject** for writing may arise from any source, including your observations or reading, a suggestion in this book, or an assignment from your instructor. In the previous chapter, Edward P. Jones's essay on his first months of college demonstrates how an excellent subject can be found by examining one's own experience. Whatever its source, the subject should be something you care enough about to probe deeply and to stamp with your own perspective.

This personal stamp comes from your **purpose**, your reason for writing. The purpose may be one of the following:

- *To express* the thoughts and emotions triggered by an amusing, revealing, or instructive experience.
- *To explain* a subject so that readers understand it or see it in a new light.
- *To persuade* readers to accept an idea or opinion or to take a certain action.

A single essay may sometimes have more than one purpose: for instance, a writer might both explain what it's like to have a disability and try to persuade readers to respect special parking zones for people with disabilities. Your reasons for writing may be clear to you early on, arising out of the subject and its significance for you. But you may need to explore your subject for a while—even to the point of writing a draft—before you know what you want to do with it.

▶ Considering Your Audience

Either very early, when you first begin exploring your subject, or later, as a check on what you have generated, you may want to make a few notes on your anticipated **audience**. The notes are optional, but thinking about audience definitely is not. Your topic and purpose, as well as your thesis, supporting ideas, details and examples, organization, style, tone, and language—all should reflect your answers to the following questions:

- *Who will read your writing?*
- *What impression do you want to make on readers?*
- *What do readers already know about your subject? What do they need to know?*
- *What are readers' likely expectations and assumptions about your subject?*
- *How can you build on readers' previous knowledge, expectations, and assumptions to bring them around to your view?*

These considerations are crucial to achieving the fundamental purpose of all public writing: communication. Accordingly, they come up again and again in the chapter introductions and the questions after each essay.

▶ Generating Ideas

Ideas for your writing—whether your subject itself or the many smaller ideas and details that shape what you have to say about it—may come to you in a rush, or you may need to hunt for them. (You may also need to do some research to learn more about your subject or to gather support for your ideas. See the Appendix.) Writers use a variety of discovery techniques, from jotting down thoughts while they pursue other activities to writing concentratedly for a set period. Here are a few techniques you might try.

Talking with Others

When you write, you essentially join a conversation on a subject: you add to what other writers have said with your own thoughts. So it makes sense that one of the best ways to generate ideas for writing is to talk with other people. Speaking and listening will give you new insights into a subject and reveal connections that you may not have found on your own. That is why much of your time in class will be spent discussing what you read. To get the most out of those conversations, follow these guidelines:

- *Be prepared.* Do the assigned reading, and jot down your thoughts and questions before class. If you will be discussing one of the essays in this book, you can use the questions that accompany the essay to help prepare your notes.

- *Pay attention.* When others speak, listen. Even if you disagree with people or detect flaws in their reasoning, respect their points of view. Ask questions, and try to express their thoughts in your own words to better understand them.

- *Build on each other's ideas.* The purpose of discussion is to discover new perspectives and to find common ground, so feel free to add your own thoughts to what others have to say.

As you discuss readings and exchange ideas with others, you'll almost certainly discover new ways of thinking about a subject. Write those ideas down. Later, you can explore them further using the other techniques described in this section.

Journal Writing

Many writers keep a **journal**, a record of thoughts and observations. Whether in a paper notebook or a digital file, journal entries give you an opportunity to explore ideas just for yourself, free of concerns about readers who will judge what you say or how you say it. Regular journal entries can also make you more comfortable with the act of writing and build your confidence. Indeed, writing teachers often require their students to keep journals for these reasons.

In a journal you can write about whatever interests, puzzles, or disturbs you. Here are just a few possible uses:

- *Prepare* for a class by taking notes on the assigned reading.
- *Record* summaries of classroom discussions.

- *Analyze* a situation that's causing you problems.
- *Imitate* a writer you admire, such as a poet or songwriter.
- *Explore* your reactions to a movie or television program.
- *Confide* your dreams and fears.

Any of this material could provide a seed for writing, but you can also use a journal deliberately to develop ideas for assignments. One approach is built into this book: before every essay you will find several quotations and a suggestion for journal writing—all centering on the topic of the essay. In responding to the quotations and journal prompt preceding Edward P. Jones's "Shacks" (p. 9), for example, you might examine your attitudes toward writing, recount a particular episode from your own first months of school, or consider your reasons for taking a writing class. One student, Nicole Lang, wrote this journal entry in response to the material preceding Jones's essay:

> Does writing come easily to me? No! I mean, I have no trouble commenting on somebody's Facebook post or sending out a tweet to my friends, but papers for school? Nightmare! Writing is HARD. I don't feel like I have anything to say and then if I do think of something I just get stuck. Who cares what I think? I guess that's the point of this class. To learn, right? But I wouldn't be here if it wasn't required, that's for sure.

Writing for herself, Lang felt free to explore what was on her mind, without worrying about correctness and without trying to make it clear to external readers what she meant by words such as *nightmare* and *stuck*. By articulating her mixed feelings about writing, Lang established a personal context in which to read Jones's essay, and that context made her a more engaged, more critical reader.

Lang used journal writing for another purpose as well: to respond to Jones's essay *after* she read it.

> Interesting that writing letters (who writes letters anymore?) helped Jones get through a difficult time in college. And I like the idea of "little shacks of life," that we don't need all that much to be happy—but aren't most of us in college because we want something better than a shack? Sure, Jones's shack apparently led him to a career as a writer, and it's nice that his infatuation with Sandra turned into a defining moment of his college experience, but not everyone is so lucky.

As this entry makes clear, Lang didn't come to any conclusions about writing or about Jones's essay. She did, however, begin to work out ideas that would serve as the start of a more considered critical response later on. (Further stages of Lang's writing process appear throughout the rest of this chapter and in the two chapters that follow.)

Freewriting

To discover ideas for a particular assignment, you may find it useful to try **freewriting**, or writing without stopping for a set amount of time, usually ten to fifteen minutes. In freewriting you push yourself to keep writing, following ideas wherever they lead, paying no attention to completeness or correctness or even sense. When she began composing an essay response to "Shacks," Nicole Lang produced this freewriting:

> In the context of Jones's essay, it seems like college is an extension of high school. If that's true, then why go to college at all? College is expensive. Really expensive. But it's practically required for a good job so you have to come up with the money somehow. Loans! Jones was lucky he got to spend three months daydreaming. Who can afford that now? Not everyone can waste an entire semester building "shacks"—postponing reality. For a lot of us being an adult is not something that can be put off.

Notice that this freewriting is rough: the tone is informal, as if Lang were speaking to herself; some thoughts are left dangling; some sentences are shapeless or incomplete; some ideas are repeated. But none of this matters because the freewriting is just exploratory. Writing rapidly, without pausing to rethink or edit, actually pulled insights out of Lang. She moved from being vaguely uneasy with Jones's essay to developing an argument inspired by it. Then, with a more definite focus, she could begin drafting in earnest.

Brainstorming

Another technique that helps to pull ideas from you is **brainstorming**, listing ideas without stopping to judge or change them. As in freewriting, write without stopping for ten or fifteen minutes, jotting down everything that seems even remotely related to your subject. Don't stop to reread and rethink what you have written; just keep pulling and recording ideas, no matter how silly or dull or irrelevant they seem. When your time is up, look over the list to identify the promising ideas, and discard the rest. Depending on how promising the remaining ideas are, you can resume brainstorming, try freewriting about them, or begin a draft.

Using the Methods of Development

The ten methods of development discussed in Part Two of this book can also help you expand your thinking. Try asking the following questions to spark ideas about your subject:

- **Narration** (Chapter 5): What is the story in the subject? How did it happen?
- **Description** (Chapter 6): How does the subject look, sound, smell, taste, and feel?
- **Example** (Chapter 7): How can the subject be illustrated? What are instances of it?
- **Division or Analysis** (Chapter 8): What are the subject's parts, and what is their relationship or significance?
- **Classification** (Chapter 9): What groups or categories can the subject be sorted into?
- **Process Analysis** (Chapter 10): How does the subject work, or how does someone do it?
- **Comparison and Contrast** (Chapter 11): How is the subject similar to or different from something else?
- **Definition** (Chapter 12): What are the subject's characteristics and boundaries?
- **Cause-and-Effect Analysis** (Chapter 13): Why did the subject happen? What were or may be its consequences?
- **Argument and Persuasion** (Chapter 14): Why do I believe as I do about the subject? Why do others have different opinions? How can I convince others to accept my opinion or believe as I do?

The kinds of questions suggested by these methods can open up perspectives you may not have considered; they can also help you begin to focus and shape your thoughts. As you explore your subject and begin to draft, you might use the methods singly, with one dominating in an essay, or in combination, with different methods supporting varied aspects of your subject. Whether taken individually or together, each method provides a direction that can help you achieve your particular purpose for writing.

Forming a Thesis

Have you ever read a newspaper or magazine article and wondered, "What's the point?" Whether consciously or not, we expect a writer to *have* a point, a central idea that he or she wants readers to take away from the work. We also expect that idea to determine the content of the work—so that everything relates to it—and we expect the content in turn to demonstrate or prove the idea.

Arriving at a main idea, or **thesis**, is thus an essential part of the writing process. Sometimes it will occur to you the moment you hit on your subject—for instance, if you think of writing about the new course registration system because you want to make a point about its unfairness. More often, you will need to explore your thoughts for a while—even to the point of writing a draft or more—before you pin down just what you have to say. Even if your thesis will evolve over time, however, it's a good idea to draft it early because it can help keep you focused as you generate more ideas, seek evidence, and organize your thoughts.

▶ Identifying Your Main Point

A thesis is distinct from the subject of an essay. The subject is what an essay is about; the thesis captures a writer's unique understanding of one aspect of that subject. In the case of "Shacks," for example, the subject is college, but Jones's thesis—that struggling with self-expression can help young adults discover their talents and ambitions—makes a strong point that readers may not have contemplated on their own. In the essay draft that appears at the end of this chapter, student writer Nicole Lang takes the same subject—college—but she makes a completely different point: that contemporary students cannot afford to take their education for granted.

The distinction between a subject and a thesis is evident throughout this book. Each chapter of readings focuses on a single subject—such as travel, the environment, or work—yet the individual paragraphs and essays demonstrate the writers' unique perspectives on particular aspects of those general topics. The readings in Chapter 5, for instance, all center on the subject of youth, but no two writers take the same approach. Michael Ondaatje writes to capture the mystery of a snake that seemed immortal; Jonathan Rauch recalls the awkwardness of his first kiss; Annie Dillard uses a memorable incident to explain the thrill of misbehavior; Langston Hughes writes about a church revival to make a point about innocence and faith; and student writer Lauren Fulmore reflects on the consequences of a runaway imagination.

To move from a general subject to a workable thesis for your own writing, keep narrowing your focus until you have something to say about the subject. For example, one writer decided to write about family but quickly discovered that the topic is too broad to work with. She then narrowed the subject to adoptive families, but even that covered too much territory. As she continued to tighten her focus, she first thought to discuss adopted children who try to contact their birth parents, then considered explaining how adoptees can locate the necessary information, and finally decided to discuss how legal and other barriers can impede adoptees' efforts to find their birth parents. In a few steps, the writer turned a broad subject into a manageable idea worth pursuing. The process isn't always simple, but it is a necessary first step in finding a working thesis.

▶ Drafting and Revising a Thesis Sentence

Once you've narrowed your subject and have something to say about it, the best way to focus on your thesis is to write it out in a **thesis sentence** (or sentences): an assertion that makes your point about the subject. Edward P. Jones states his thesis near the end of his essay "Shacks" (p. 9):

> [W]e are born with few tools with which to build our little shacks of life, and we are born with even less knowledge of how to use those tools.

Jones's thesis statement, while poetic, nonetheless ties together all of the other ideas and details in his essay; it also reflects his purpose in writing the essay and focuses his readers on a single point. All effective thesis sentences do this: they go beyond generalities or mere statements of fact to express the writer's unique perspective on the subject. Notice the differences in the following sentences that Nicole Lang considered for her response to "Shacks":

ANNOUNCEMENT OF TOPIC   In this essay, I will discuss the purpose of going to college.

STATEMENT OF FACT   Many college students take out loans to finance their education.

GENERAL STATEMENT   Not everyone has the time or resources to dedicate an entire semester to building "shacks" and postponing reality.

EFFECTIVE THESIS SENTENCE   For those who struggle just to pay for the opportunity, a college education has to serve the more concrete purpose of preparing for employment.

> ## CHECKLIST FOR AN EFFECTIVE THESIS
>
> - *Have you narrowed your subject to a focused topic?* Can that topic be managed in the space and time available for your writing project?
> - *What main point do you want to make about your topic?* Can you express that point as a debatable assertion or a unique perspective? Be sure that your thesis does more than announce your topic, repeat a fact, or make a broad generalization. Instead, use the opportunity to explicitly state your opinion or articulate your fresh idea.
> - *What is your purpose for writing?* Your thesis should make it clear to readers whether you intend to express your thoughts and feelings, explain a point or concept, or persuade them of an idea.
> - *Does your thesis control the content of your essay?* Check that every subpoint and supporting detail in your draft supports your main idea.
> - *Where, if at all, will you state your thesis?* It may help readers to know the point of your essay from the start, or they may be more receptive to your main idea if you withhold it until the end. If you choose not to state your thesis outright, readers should nonetheless be able to recognize your controlling idea without difficulty.

The first sentence identifies the topic of the paper, but gives no indication of the writer's purpose or perspective. The second sentence merely expresses a fact, not a main idea worth developing in an essay. The third sentence offers an opinion, but because it's a very broad assertion that few would dispute, it fails to capture readers' interest or make a significant point. The final sentence, however, makes a strong assertion about a narrow subject and gives readers an idea of what to expect from the rest of the essay.

Because the main point of an essay may change over the course of the writing process, the thesis sentence may also change, sometimes considerably. The following examples show how the writer discussed earlier moved from an explanatory to a persuasive purpose between the early stages of the writing process and the final draft of her adoption essay.

WORKING THESIS   Adopted children can contact their birth parents, although sometimes the process is difficult.

REVISED THESIS   Adopted children often need persistence to locate information about their birth parents.

FINAL THESIS   Laws and traditions unfairly hamper adopted children from seeking information about their birth parents.

The first two sentences identify the subject of the essay, but they are broad and bland, and neither clearly focuses on the writer's interest: the impediments to obtaining information. In contrast, the final sentence makes a definitive assertion and clearly conveys the writer's persuasive purpose and opinion. Thus the sentence lets readers know what to expect: an argument that adopted children should be treated more fairly when they seek information about their birth parents. Readers will also expect some discussion of the "laws and traditions" that hamper adoptees' searches, what is "unfair" and "fair" in this situation, and what changes the writer proposes.

Commonly in academic writing, the thesis sentence comes near the beginning of an essay, typically at the end of the first paragraph, where it serves as a promise to examine a particular subject from a particular perspective. But as Edward P. Jones demonstrates by stating his thesis at the end, the thesis sentence may come elsewhere as long as it controls the whole essay. The thesis may even go unstated, as some essays in this book illustrate, but it still must govern every element of the work as if it were announced.

Organizing

Writers vary in the extent to which they arrange their material before they begin drafting, but most do establish some plan. A good time to do so is after you've explored your subject and come up with a good stock of ideas about it. Before you begin drafting, you can look over what you've got and consider the best ways to organize it.

▶ Creating a Plan

A writing plan may consist of a list of key points, a fuller list including specifics as well, or even a detailed formal outline—whatever gives order to your ideas and provides some direction for your writing.

As you'll see in later chapters, many of the methods of development suggest specific structures, most notably description, narration, classification, process analysis, and comparison and contrast. But even when the organization is almost built into the method, you'll find that some subjects demand more thoughtful plans than others. You may be able to draft a straightforward narrative of a personal experience with very little advance planning. But a nonpersonal narrative, or even a personal one involving complex events and time shifts, may require more thought about arrangement.

Though some sort of plan is almost always useful when drafting, resist any temptation at this stage to pin down every detail in its proper place. A huge investment in planning can hamper you during drafting, making it difficult to respond to new ideas and even new directions that may prove fruitful.

▶ Thinking in Paragraphs

Most essays consist of three parts: the introduction and the conclusion (discussed in the next section) and the **body**, the most substantial and longest part, which develops the main idea or thesis.

As you explore your subject, you will generate both ideas that directly support your thesis and more specific examples, details, and other evidence to support these ideas. In the following informal outline for Nicole Lang's first draft (pp. 29–30), you can see how each supporting idea, or subpoint, helps to build her working thesis:

> WORKING THESIS   Not everyone has the time or resources to dedicate an entire semester to building "shacks" and postponing reality.
>
> SUBPOINT   Many students are already adults.
>
> SUBPOINT   Other students are in school specifically for job training.
>
> SUBPOINT   A lot of students take on significant debt and will need jobs with good incomes to pay it off.

Lang uses specific evidence to develop each subpoint into a paragraph. In essence, the paragraphs are like mini-essays with their own main ideas and support. (See pp. 33–37 for more on paragraph structure.)

When you seek a plan for your ideas, look first for your subpoints, the main supports for your thesis. Use these as your starting points to work out your essay one chunk (or paragraph) at a time. You can sketch the supporting details and examples into your organizational plan, or you can wait until you begin drafting to get into the specifics.

▶ Considering the Introduction and Conclusion

You may not know for sure how you want to begin and end your essay until you're drafting or revising. Still, it can be helpful to consider the introduction and conclusion earlier, so you have a sense of how you might approach readers and what you might leave them with.

The basic opening and closing serve readers by demonstrating your interest in their needs and expectations:

- The **introduction** draws readers into the essay and focuses their attention on the main idea and purpose, often stated in a thesis sentence.

- The **conclusion** ties together the elements of the essay and provides a final impression for readers to take away with them.

These basic forms allow considerable room for variation. One essay may need two paragraphs of introduction but only a one-sentence conclusion, whereas another essay may require no formal introduction but a lengthy conclusion. How you begin and end depends on your subject and purpose, the kind of essay you are writing, and the likely responses of your readers.

Specific strategies for opening and closing essays are suggested in each chapter introduction and in the Glossary under *introductions* and *conclusions*.

Drafting

However detailed your organizational plan is, you should not view it as a rigid taskmaster while you are drafting your essay. **Drafting** is your chance to give expression to your ideas, filling them out, finding relationships, drawing conclusions. If you are like most writers, you will discover much of what you have to say while putting your thoughts into words. In fact, if your subject is complex or difficult for you to write about, you may need several drafts just to work out your ideas and their relationships.

▶ Writing, Not Revising

Some writers draft rapidly, rarely looking up from the paper or keyboard. Others draft in fits and starts, gazing out the window or doodling as much as writing. Any method that works is fine, but one method rarely works: collapsing drafting and revising into one stage, trying to do everything at once.

Write first; then revise. Concentrate on *what* you are saying, not on *how* you are saying it. You pressure yourself needlessly if you try to produce a well-developed, coherent, interesting, and grammatically correct paper all at once. You may have trouble getting words down because you're afraid to make mistakes, and worrying about mistakes may distract you from exploring your ideas fully. Awkwardness, repetition, wrong words, grammatical errors, misspellings—these and other more superficial concerns can be attended to in a later draft. The same goes for considering your readers' needs: like many writers, you may find that attention to readers during the first draft inhibits the flow of ideas. If so, postpone that attention until the second or third draft.

If you experience writer's block or just don't know how to begin, start writing the part you're most comfortable with. Writing in paragraph chunks, as described on page 27, will also make drafting more manageable. You can start with your thesis sentence—or at least keep it in view as a reminder of your purpose and main idea. But if you find yourself pulled away from the thesis by a new idea, let go and follow, at least for a while. If your purpose and main idea change as a result of such exploration, you can always revise your thesis accordingly.

▶ Nicole Lang's First Draft

Some exploratory work by student Nicole Lang appears on pages 20 and 21. What follows is the first draft she subsequently wrote on the purpose of college. The draft is very rough, with frequent repetitions, wandering paragraphs, unsupported ideas, and many other flaws. But such weaknesses are not important at this early stage. The draft gave Lang the opportunity to discover what she had to say, to explore her ideas, and to link them in rough sequence.

In Edward P. Jones's essay "Shacks," he writes about his first semester of college. He recalls writing three to five letters each week to his high school crush, Sandra Walker, in the hopes that she would come to love him. Unfortunately, his attempts to win Sandra's affection were met with little enthusiasm. This experience gave him something important that helped him get through a difficult time of adjustment for students entering college, but when he says, "It is amazing the little shacks of life we can build when it seems that so much is at stake," I can't help but wonder what was really at stake for Jones. Not everyone has the luxury to indulge in three months of emotional growth, to look for talents they may not even know they have. Not everyone has the time or resources to dedicate an entire semester to building "shacks" and postponing reality.

Jones seems to think of college as an extension of high school. A place to grow up, if just a little. That may be true for some people. But adulthood cannot be put off for many students.

A growing number of college students are adults over the age of 25. Getting a degree will give them the skills they need for a better job and prove to employers that they can work hard. Jones's understanding that his infatuation with Sandra turned into a defining moment of his college experience is nice, but he doesn't represent the financially burdened students of today.

Writing doesn't come as easily to me as it did for Jones. While I struggle, I understand the importance of the education I am receiving. Its important to find a career path that feels meaningful and fulfilling. But it is also important to find a job that can give you economic stability that will outweigh the significant cost of the degree. Although it would be nice to discover ourselves while we're here, it all comes down to time and money.

Jones's "shack" in college led him to a successful career as a writer, but not everyone is as lucky. Our shacks are different, and some are built later than others. For students who struggle just to pay for the opportunity, college serves the more concrete purpose of preparing us for employment—and that's OK.

3

REVISING

▶

The previous chapter took you through the first-draft stage of the writing process, when you have a chance to work out your ideas without regard for what others may think. This chapter describes the crucial next stage, when you actively consider your readers: revising to focus and shape your meaning.

Revision means "re-seeing." Looking at your draft as your reader would, you cut, add, and reorganize until the ideas make sense on their own. Revision is not the same as editing. In revising, you make fundamental changes in content and structure. **Editing** comes later: once you're satisfied with the revised draft, you work on the sentences and words, attending to grammar, punctuation, and the like (see Chapter 4). The separation of these two stages is important because attention to little changes distracts from a view of the whole. If you try to edit while you revise, you'll be more likely to miss the big picture. You may also waste effort perfecting sentences you'll later decide to cut.

Reading Your Own Work Critically

Perhaps the biggest challenge of revision is reading your own work objectively, as a reader would. To gain something like a reader's critical distance from your draft, try one or more of the following techniques:

- *Put your first draft aside for at least a few hours—and preferably overnight—before attempting to revise it.* You may have further thoughts in the interval, and you will be able to see your work more objectively when you return to it.

- *Ask others to read and comment on your draft.* Your teacher may ask you and your classmates to exchange drafts so that you can help each other revise. But even without such a procedure, you can benefit from another person's responses. Keep an open mind to comments, and ask questions when you need more information.

- *Make an outline of your draft* by listing what you cover in each paragraph. Such an outline can show gaps, overlaps, and problems in organization. (See also p. 27.)

- *Read the draft out loud.* Speaking the words and hearing them can help to create distance from them.

- *Imagine you are someone else*—a friend, perhaps, or a particular person in your intended audience—and read the draft through that person's eyes, as if for the first time.

- *Print a double-spaced copy of your draft.* It's much easier to read text on paper than on a screen, and you can spread out printed pages to see the whole paper at once. Once you've finished revising, transferring changes to the computer requires little effort.

Looking at the Whole Draft

Revision involves seeing your draft as a whole, focusing mainly on your purpose and thesis, the support for your thesis, and the movement among ideas. You want to determine what will work and what won't for readers—where the draft strays from your purpose, leaves a hole in the development of your thesis, does not flow logically or smoothly, digresses, or needs more details. (See the revision checklist on p. 39.) When rewriting, you may need to cut entire paragraphs, condense paragraphs into sentences, add passages of explanation, or rearrange sections.

▶ Purpose and Thesis

In the press of drafting, you may lose sight of why you are writing or what your main idea is. Both your purpose and your thesis may change as you work out your meaning, so that you start in one place and end somewhere else or even lose track of where you are.

Your first goal in revising, then, is to see that your essay is well focused. Readers should grasp a clear purpose right away, and they should find that you have achieved it at the end. They should see your main idea, your thesis, very early, usually by the end of the introduction, and they should think that you have proved or demonstrated the thesis when they reach the last paragraph.

Like many writers, you may sometimes start with one thesis and finish with another, in effect writing into your idea as you draft. In many cases you'll need to rewrite your thesis statement to reflect what you actually wrote in your draft. Or you may need to upend your essay, plucking your thesis out of the conclusion and starting over with it, providing the subpoints and details to develop it (such was the case for student writer Nicole Lang, whose revised response to Edward P. Jones's "Shacks" appears at the end of this chapter). You'll probably find the second draft much easier to write because you'll know better what you want to say, and the next round of revision after that will go even more smoothly.

▶ Development

Part of establishing that your draft fulfills your purpose is making sure that your thesis is fully developed. When you **develop** an idea, you provide concrete and specific details, examples, facts, opinions, and other evidence to make the idea vivid and true in readers' minds. Readers will know only as much as you tell them about your thesis and its support. Gaps, vague statements, and unsupported conclusions will undermine your efforts to win their interest and agreement.

Consider, for example, the following paragraph from Nicole Lang's first draft (pp. 29–30):

> Jones seems to think of college as an extension of high school. A place to grow up, if just a little. That may be true for some people. But adulthood cannot be put off for many students.

Lang felt she had a good point about adult students, but on reviewing her draft she realized she hadn't backed up her **generalization** with any evidence. So in revision she added an example from her personal experience:

> Jones seems to think of college as an extension of high school. A place to grow up, if just a little. That may be true for some people. But adulthood cannot be put off for many students. For example, my cousin Robert is 29 years old and he has a young child and a job that barely pays the bills. He takes nite classes at a community college so he can qualify for a better position, he does not have time at this stage in his life to dream about "some marvelous future." His shack is his son, and so he spends his time making a better life for himself and his family.

Notice that Lang's revised paragraph, while better developed and more convincing, contains several errors of grammar, punctuation, and spelling. That's fine; she'll attend to those details when she edits (see Chapter 4).

Development begins in sentences, when you use the most concrete and specific words you can muster to explain your meaning (see p. 53). At the level of the paragraph, these sentences develop the paragraph's topic (see "Focus on Paragraph Development" on p. 184). Then, at the level of the whole essay, these paragraphs develop the governing thesis.

The key to adequate development is a good sense of your readers' needs for information and evidence. The list of questions on page 18 can help you estimate these needs as you start to write; reconsidering the questions when you revise can help you see where your draft may fail to address, say, readers' unfamiliarity with your subject or possible resistance to your thesis.

The introduction to each method of development in Chapters 5–14 includes specific advice for meeting readers' needs when using the method to develop paragraphs and essays. When you sense that a paragraph or section of your essay is thin but you don't know how to improve it, you can also try the discovery techniques given on pages 18–22 or ask the questions for all the methods of development on page 22.

▶ Unity

When a piece of writing has **unity**, all its parts are related: the paragraphs build the central idea of the whole essay, and the sentences build the central idea of each paragraph. Readers do not have to wonder what the essay is about or what a particular passage has to do with the rest of the piece. Revising for unity strengthens your thesis by ensuring that every paragraph centers on your essay's main idea.

Consider Nicole Lang's revised draft on page 40. Her thesis sentence states, "For those of us who struggle just to pay for the opportunity, a college education has to serve the more concrete purpose of preparing for employment," and each paragraph clearly develops this idea, highlighting who those struggling students are, why they're in college, and how they expect to pay for it. This unity is true of Lang's revised draft but not of her first draft, where she opened with a lengthy summary of Jones's "Shacks." Some summary is helpful, of course, but the details blurred Lang's focus on today's college students and their goals. Recognizing as much, Lang condensed her discussion of "Shacks" to a single sentence when she revised. Deleting the distracting details also helped Lang clarify her introduction and her own purpose in writing.

Following the introduction, the body **paragraphs** of an essay are almost like mini-essays themselves, each developing an idea, or subpoint, that supports the thesis (see p. 27). In fact, a body paragraph should have its own thesis, called its *topic*, usually expressed in a **topic sentence** or sentences. The rest of the paragraph develops the topic with specifics.

In this paragraph from the final draft of Nicole Lang's "Foundations" (pp. 56–57), for example, the topic sentence is underlined:

> <u>Students in more traditional schools need to keep their eyes on the real world, too.</u> The typical college graduate will start out owing nearly $30,000 in loans (Olsen). While it is important to find a career path that feels meaningful and fulfilling, it is just as important to earn an income that will outweigh the cost of higher education. We therefore need to focus on academic programs that will directly benefit our job prospects and help us repay our debts. With limited resources, most of us cannot afford shacks into which we can retreat—at least not yet.

Notice that every sentence of this paragraph relates to the topic sentence. Lang achieved this unity in revision (see pp. 40–41). In her first draft, she focused the opening sentences of this paragraph on herself:

> Writing doesn't come as easily to me as it did for Jones. While I struggle, I understand the importance of the education I am receiving.

If you look back at the full paragraph above, you'll see that Lang deleted these sentences and substituted a final one that focuses on the paragraph's topic: the need for students to plan for life after college.

Your topic sentences will not always fall at the very beginning of your paragraphs. Sometimes you'll need to create a transition from the preceding paragraph before stating the new paragraph's topic, or you'll build the paragraph to a topic sentence at the end. Sometimes, too, you'll write a paragraph with a topic but without a topic sentence. In all these cases, you'll need to have an idea for the paragraph and to unify the paragraph around that idea, so that all the specifics support and develop it.

▶ Coherence

Writing has **coherence** when readers can follow it easily and can see how the parts relate to each other. The ideas develop in a clear sequence, the sentences and paragraphs connect logically, and the connections are clear and smooth. The writing flows.

Coherence starts as sentences build paragraphs. Writers can draw on several devices to achieve coherence, including **repetition** or restatement of key words, **pronouns** such as *they* and *them* to substitute for nouns, and

parallelism, the use of similar grammatical structures for related ideas. (See "Focus on Coherence" on p. 153 and "Focus on Parallelism" on p. 244.) Every paragraph you write will require some devices to tie the sentences together.

One of the most useful devices for achieving paragraph coherence is a liberal use of **transitions**, words and phrases that clearly link the parts of sentences and whole sentences. Transitions may indicate time (*later, soon*), place (*nearby, farther away*), similarity (*also, likewise*), difference (*in contrast, instead*), and many other relationships. Check all your paragraphs to be sure that each sentence connects with the one before and that readers will see the connection without having to stop and reread.

Transitions work to link ideas between paragraphs as well as within them. When the ideas in two paragraphs are closely related, a simple word or phrase at the start of the second one may be all that's needed to show the relation. In each example below, the underlined transition opens the topic sentence of the paragraph:

> <u>Moreover</u>, the rising costs of health care have long outpaced inflation.
>
> <u>However</u>, some kinds of health-care plans have proved much more expensive than others.

When a paragraph is beginning a new part of the essay or otherwise changing direction, a sentence or more at the beginning will help explain the shift. In the next example, the first sentence summarizes the preceding paragraph, the second introduces the topic of the new paragraph, and the third gives the paragraph's topic sentence:

> Traditional health-care plans have <u>thus</u> become an unaffordable luxury for most individuals and businesses. The majority of those with health insurance <u>now</u> find themselves in so-called managed plans. Though they do vary, <u>managed</u> plans share at least two features: they pay full benefits only when the insured person consults an approved doctor, and they require prior approval for certain procedures.

Notice that underlined transitions provide further cues about the relationship of ideas.

▶ Organization

Although transitions help alert readers to movement from one idea to another, they can't achieve coherence by themselves. Just as important is an overall **organization** that develops ideas in a clear sequence and directs readers in a familiar pattern:

- A **spatial** organization arranges information to parallel the way we scan people, objects, or places: top to bottom, left to right, front to back, near to far, or vice versa. This scheme is especially useful for description (Chapter 6).

- A **chronological** organization arranges events or steps as they occurred in time, first to last. Such an arrangement usually organizes a narrative (Chapter 5) or a process analysis (Chapter 10) and may also help with cause-and-effect analysis (Chapter 13).

- A **climactic** organization proceeds in order of climax, usually from least to most important, building to the most interesting example, the most telling point of comparison, the most significant argument. A climactic organization is most useful for example (Chapter 7), division or analysis (Chapter 8), classification (Chapter 9), comparison and contrast (Chapter 11), definition (Chapter 12), and argument and persuasion (Chapter 14), and it may also work for cause-and-effect analysis (Chapter 13).

The introduction to each method of development in Chapters 5–14 gives detailed advice on organizing with these arrangements and variations on them.

When revising your draft for organization, try outlining it by jotting down the topic sentence of each paragraph and the key support for each topic. The exercise will give you some distance from your ideas and words, allowing you to see the structure like a skeleton. Will your readers grasp the logic of your arrangement? Will they see why you move from each idea to the next one? After checking the overall structure, be sure you've built in enough transitions between sentences and paragraphs to guide readers through your ideas.

▶ Tone

The **tone** of writing is like the tone of voice in speech: it expresses the writer's attitude toward his or her subject and audience. In writing we express tone with word choice and sentence structure. Notice the marked differences in these two passages discussing the same information on the same subject:

> Voice mail can be convenient, sure, but for callers it's usually more trouble than it's worth. We waste time "listening to the following menu choices," when we just want the live person at the end. All too often, there isn't even such a person!

For callers the occasional convenience of voice mail generally does not compensate for its inconveniences. Most callers would prefer to speak to a live operator but must wait through a series of choices to reach that person. Increasingly, companies with voice-mail systems do not offer live operators at all.

The first passage is informal, expresses clear annoyance, and with *we* includes the reader in that attitude. The second passage is more formal and more objective, reporting the situation without involving readers directly.

Tone can range from casual to urgent, humorous to serious, sad to elated, pleased to angry, personal to distant. The particular tone you choose for a piece of writing depends on your purpose and your audience. For most academic and business writing, you will be trying to explain or argue a point. Your readers will be interested more in the substance of your writing than in a startling tone, and indeed an approach that is too personal, casual, or hostile could put them off.

Tone is something you want to evaluate in revision, along with whether you've achieved your purpose and whether you've developed your thesis adequately for your audience. But adjusting tone is largely a matter of replacing words and restructuring sentences, work that could distract you from an overall view of your essay. If you think your tone is off base, you may want to devote a separate phase of revision to it, after addressing unity, coherence, and the other matters discussed in this chapter. (For additional information, see "Focus on Tone" on pp. 340–41. For advice on sentence structures and word choices, see Chapter 4 on editing.)

Using a Revision Checklist

The following checklist summarizes the advice on revision given in this chapter. Use the checklist to remind yourself what to look for in your first draft. But don't try to answer all the questions in a single reading of the draft. Instead, take the questions one by one, rereading the whole draft for each. That way you'll be able to concentrate on each element with minimal distraction from the others.

Note that the introductions to the methods of development in Chapters 5–14 also have their own revision checklists. Combining this list with

---

CHECKLIST FOR REVISION

- *What is your purpose in writing?* Will it be clear to readers? Do you achieve it?

- *What is your thesis?* Where is it made clear to readers?

- *How well developed is your essay?* Where might readers need more evidence to understand your ideas and find them convincing?

- *How unified is your essay?* How does each body paragraph support your thesis? (Look especially at your topic sentences.) How does each sentence in the body paragraphs support the topic sentence of the paragraph?

- *How coherent is your essay?* Do repetition and restatement, pronouns, parallelism, and transitions link the sentences in paragraphs?

- *Does the overall organization clarify the flow of ideas?* How does your introduction work to draw readers in and preview your purpose and thesis? How does your conclusion work to pull the essay together and give readers a sense of completion?

- *What is the tone of your essay?* Is it appropriate for your purpose and your audience?

---

the one for the method you're using will produce a more targeted set of questions. (The guide inside the back cover will direct you to the discussion you want.)

Nicole Lang's Revised Draft

Considering questions like those in the revision checklist led student writer Nicole Lang to revise the rough draft we saw on pages 29–30. Lang's revision follows. Notice that she changed her thesis statement to reflect what she had written and added supporting details for several points. She also came up with a title that helped her focus her main idea, revamped the introduction, tightened many passages, improved the coherence of her essay, and wrote a wholly new conclusion to sharpen her point. She did not try to improve her style or fix errors at this stage, leaving those activities for later editing.

Foundations

In Edward P. Jones's essay "Shacks," he ~~writes about his first semester of college.~~ He recalls writing ~~three to five~~ letters ~~each week~~ to his high school crush/ ~~Sandra Walker, in the hopes that she would come to love him. Unfortunately, his attempts to win Sandra's affection were met with little enthusiasm.~~ ~~This experience gave him something important~~ and discovering a sense of purpose that helped him get through a difficult time of adjustment for students entering college/ But when Jones mentions our ability to find structure when ~~but when he says,~~ "It is amazing the little shacks of life we can ~~build when it seems that~~ " think about what so much is at stake," I can't help but ~~wonder~~ is at stake for college students today. ~~what was really at stake for Jones.~~ Not everyone has the luxury to indulge in three months of emotional growth, to look for talents they may not even know they have. ~~Not everyone has the time or resources to dedicate an entire semester to building "shacks" and postponing reality.~~ For those of us who struggle just to pay for the opportunity, a college education has to serve the more concrete purpose of preparing for employment.

Jones seems to think of college as an extension of high school. A place to grow up, if just a little. That may be true for some people. But adulthood cannot be put off for many students. For example, my cousin Robert is 29 years old and he has a young child and a job that barely pays the bills. He takes nite classes at a community college so he can qualify for a better position, he does not have time at this stage in his life to dream about "some marvelous future." His shack is his son, and so he spends his time making a better life for himself and his family.

A growing number of college students are adults over the age of 25. They come from a wide variety of backgrounds and enroll for a number of reasons and they all understand the demands of a tough job market in a down economy. Getting a degree will give them the skills they need for a particular ~~better~~ job and prove to employers that they can work hard. ~~Jones's understanding~~

~~that his infatuation with Sandra turned into a defining moment of his college experience is nice, but he doesn't represent the financially burdened students of today.~~ Such vocational training is important and deserves respect. Those in more traditional schools need to keep there eye on the real world, too. ~~Writing doesn't come as easily to me as it did for Jones. While I~~ The average student will graduate owing nearly $30,000 in student loans (source). ~~struggle, I understand the importance of the education I am receiving.~~

Its important to find a career path that feels meaningful and fulfilling. But it is also ~~important to find a job that can give you economic stability~~ necessary to earn an income that will outweigh the ~~significant~~ cost of ~~the degree. Although it would be nice to discover ourselves while we're here, it all comes down to time and money.~~ higher education. This means we need to focus our time and effort on academic programs that will directly benefit our job prospects and put us in a position to repay our debts. With limited resources, not everyone can afford shacks they can retreat into. At least not yet.

~~Jones's "shack" in college led him to a successful career as a writer, but not everyone is as lucky. Our shacks are different, and some are built later than others. For students who struggle just to pay for the opportunity, college serves the more concrete purpose of preparing us for employment—and that's OK.~~

Jones makes a good point that a successful life depends on some kind of structure. To be truly sturdy, however, any structure requires a solid foundation. That's what college provides. We should certainly hope to discover ourselves and our hidden talents while we're here. But for financially burdened students the realities of higher education all come down to time and money. We have to be practical even as we dream.

4

EDITING

▶

The final stage of the writing process is **editing** to clarify and polish your work. In editing you turn from global issues of purpose, thesis, development, unity, coherence, organization, and tone to more particular issues of sentences and words. The primary goal of editing is to ensure that your finished draft adheres to standard English grammar and usage. The formal language of US academic and business writing, **standard English** follows well-established expectations regarding sentence structure, punctuation, and vocabulary—the "rules" of writing—such as those addressed in this chapter.

Editing requires that you gain some distance from your work so that you can see it objectively. Try these techniques:

- *Work on a clean copy of your revised draft.* Edit on a printout rather than on the computer: it's more difficult to spot problems on a screen.

- *Read your revised draft aloud* so that you can hear the words. But be sure to read what you have actually written, not what you may have intended to write but didn't.

- *Try reading your draft backward sentence by sentence.* You'll be less likely to get caught up in the flow of your ideas and thus more likely to catch errors.

- *Keep a list of problems that others have pointed out in your previous writing.* Add this personal checklist to the one on page 55.

Checking Grammar and Punctuation

The first goal of editing is to express your ideas as clearly as possible, without sentence errors that might distract, confuse, or annoy readers. The guidelines here can help you catch some of the most common mistakes:

sentence fragments, run-on sentences, comma splices, lack of agreement, awkward pronoun reference, problems with modifiers, and shifts in person, tense, or voice.

▶ Sentence Fragments

A complete sentence has both a subject and a verb and expresses an entire thought. In contrast, a **sentence fragment** is a word group that is punctuated like a sentence but lacks a subject, lacks a verb, or expresses just part of a thought. Experienced writers sometimes use fragments deliberately, but unless you're very certain of what you're doing, make sure each sentence is complete by adding the necessary verb or subject or by attaching the word group to a nearby sentence:

> FRAGMENT   The price of oil unpredictable and rising.
>
> COMPLETE   The price of oil is unpredictable and rising.
>
> FRAGMENT   Consumers are warming up to alternative heating systems. Such as heat pumps and solar panels.
>
> COMPLETE   Consumers are warming up to alternative heating systems, such as heat pumps and solar panels.

Note that if you use a colon to introduce a list or a quotation, it must be preceded by a complete sentence. If it is not, remove the colon (before a list), replace it with a comma (before a quotation), or rewrite the first part of the sentence:

> FRAGMENT   Three newer options include: wind turbines, outdoor furnaces, and pellet stoves.
>
> COMPLETE   Three newer options include wind turbines, outdoor furnaces, and pellet stoves.
>
> COMPLETE   Three newer options are becoming common: wind turbines, outdoor furnaces, and pellet stoves.
>
> FRAGMENT   Local homeowner Marisol Gutierrez says: "Fossil fuels cost too much, both financially and environmentally."
>
> COMPLETE   Local homeowner Marisol Gutierrez says, "Fossil fuels cost too much, both financially and environmentally."
>
> COMPLETE   Local homeowner Marisol Gutierrez explains the appeal of such alternatives: "Fossil fuels cost too much, both financially and environmentally."

▶ Run-on Sentences and Comma Splices

An **independent clause** can be punctuated like a sentence because it contains a subject and a verb and expresses a complete thought. Two independent clauses in a row, however, need to be clearly separated. If the clauses run together with nothing between them, they create a **run-on sentence**. If they run together with only a comma between them, they create a **comma splice**.

RUN-ON   Pellet stoves are especially popular suppliers can't keep up with demand.

COMMA SPLICE   Pellet stoves are especially popular, suppliers can't keep up with demand.

You can correct run-on sentences and comma splices in several ways:

- *Punctuate each clause as its own sentence.*

- *Insert a semicolon* (and maybe a conjunctive adverb such as *however, therefore,* or *moreover*) before the second clause.

- *Separate the clauses* with a comma along with *and, but, or, nor, for, so,* or *yet.*

    EDITED   Pellet stoves are especially popular. Suppliers can't keep up with demand.

    EDITED   Pellet stoves are especially popular; suppliers can't keep up with demand.

    EDITED   Pellet stoves are especially popular; therefore, suppliers can't keep up with demand.

    EDITED   Pellet stoves are especially popular, and suppliers can't keep up with demand.

▶ Subject-Verb Agreement

The subject and verb in a sentence should match in grammatical form. Use singular verbs with singular subjects and plural verbs with plural subjects. Watch especially for the following situations.

- *When a group of words comes between the subject and the verb,* be careful not to mistake a noun in that word group (such as *pellets* below) for the subject of the sentence:

    MISMATCHED   The use of construction waste to make wood pellets contribute to their appeal.

MATCHED   The use of construction waste to make wood pellets <u>contrib-utes</u> to their appeal.

- *With compound subjects* (joined by *and*), use a plural verb:

    MISMATCHED   <u>Low carbon emissions and the renewability of sawdust</u> adds to the belief that pellets are environmentally friendly.

    MATCHED   Low carbon emissions and the renewability of sawdust <u>add</u> to the belief that pellets are environmentally friendly.

▶ Pronouns

A **pronoun**—*I, you, he, she, they, it,* and so forth—refers to or replaces a noun in a sentence. Imprecise and mismatched pronouns are common in casual speech, but they can be distracting in writing. When you edit, aim for formal usage.

- *Check that pronouns have clearly stated antecedents.* An **antecedent** is the noun to which a pronoun refers. Rewrite sentences in which the reference is vague or only implied:

    VAGUE   Text messaging while driving is dangerous, but <u>it</u> doesn't deter everyone.

    CLEAR   Text messaging while driving is dangerous, but <u>the risk</u> doesn't deter everyone.

    IMPLIED   Despite numerous studies showing that distracted driving causes accidents, <u>they</u> keep typing.

    CLEAR   Despite numerous studies showing that distracted <u>drivers</u> cause accidents, they keep typing.

- *Match pronouns and the words they refer to.* Singular nouns and pronouns take singular pronouns; plural nouns and pronouns take plural pronouns. The most common error occurs with singular indefinite pronouns such as *anybody, anyone, everyone, nobody,* and *somebody.* We often use these words to mean "many" or "all" and then mistakenly refer to them with plural pronouns:

    MISMATCHED   <u>Everyone</u> must check in before <u>they</u> can vote.

    MATCHED   <u>Everyone</u> must check in before <u>he or she</u> can vote.

    MATCHED   <u>All students</u> must check in before <u>they</u> can vote.

▶ Modifiers

A **modifier** is a word, phrase, or clause that describes another word (or words) in a sentence. Confusion arises when modifiers are positioned or punctuated incorrectly.

- *Make sure that modifiers clearly modify the intended words.* Misplaced and dangling modifiers can be awkward or even unintentionally amusing:

  MISPLACED I watched as the snow swirled around my feet <u>in amazement</u>.

  CLEAR   I watched <u>in amazement</u> as the snow swirled around my feet.

  DANGLING <u>Enjoying the quiet of the forest</u>, <u>the crack</u> of a hunter's rifle startled me out of my reverie.

  CLEAR   Enjoying the quiet of the forest, I was startled out of my reverie by the crack of a hunter's rifle.

- *Punctuate restrictive and nonrestrictive modifiers appropriately.* A modifier is *restrictive*, or essential, when it limits the word or phrase it modifies. If removing the modifier would change the fundamental meaning of the sentence, that element should not be set off with punctuation:

  RESTRICTIVE   The fashion magazines <u>*Vogue and GQ*</u> have been accused of setting unrealistic beauty standards by altering photographs to hide models' flaws.

  A modifier is *nonrestrictive*, or nonessential, if it adds information to a sentence that would still make sense without it. Writers use commas, parentheses, or dashes to separate a nonrestrictive element from the rest of the sentence:

  NONRESTRICTIVE Fashion magazines, including *Vogue* and *GQ*, have been accused of setting unrealistic beauty standards by altering photographs to hide models' flaws.

  NONRESTRICTIVE Fashion magazines (including *Vogue* and *GQ*) have been accused of setting unrealistic beauty standards by altering photographs to hide models' flaws.

  NONRESTRICTIVE Fashion magazines—including *Vogue* and *GQ*—have been accused of setting unrealistic beauty standards by altering photographs to hide models' flaws.

Note that the same modifier might be restrictive or nonrestrictive, depending on the writer's intended meaning:

RESTRICTIVE   The students who expressed optimism did well on the exam.

NONRESTRICTIVE   The students, who expressed optimism, did well on the exam.

In the first sentence above, the phrase *who expressed optimism* identifies which students did well. The commas in the second sentence indicate that the writer is referring to the entire group of students; the phrase adds information about their attitudes. Both sentences are correct, but their meanings are different.

▶ Shifts

As you edit, check that your use of pronouns and verbs is consistent. Straighten out any unnecessary shifts in person, tense, or voice.

- *Person.* Don't shift needlessly among the first person (*I, we*), second person (*you*), and third person (*he, she, they*):

  INCONSISTENT   We were frightened, but you had to stay calm.

  CONSISTENT   We were frightened, but we had to stay calm.

- *Tense.* Don't shift needlessly between the present tense and the past tense of verbs:

  INCONSISTENT   The tornado siren howls so loudly it rattled the walls.

  CONSISTENT   The tornado siren howled so loudly it rattled the walls.

- *Voice.* Don't shift needlessly between the active voice and the passive voice of verbs (see the next page for an explanation of voice):

  INCONSISTENT   The police told us to leave our belongings behind, and we were advised to notify family members.

  CONSISTENT   The police told us to leave our belongings behind, and they advised us to notify family members.

For more help avoiding shifts, see "Focus on Verbs" on page 69 and "Focus on Consistency" on page 212.

Making Sentences Clear and Effective

Clear and effective sentences convey your meaning concisely and precisely. In editing you want to ensure that readers will understand you easily, follow your ideas without difficulty, and stay interested in what you have to say.

▶ Conciseness

In drafting, we often circle around our ideas, making various attempts to express them. As a result, sentences may use more words than necessary to make their points. To edit for conciseness, focus on the following changes:

- *Put the main meaning of the sentence in its subject and verb.* Generally, the subject should name the actor, and the verb should describe what the actor did or was. Notice the difference in these two sentences (the subjects and verbs are underlined):

    WORDY   The use of calculators by students is sometimes why they fail to develop math skills.

    CONCISE   Students who use calculators sometimes fail to develop math skills.

- *Prefer the active voice.* In the active voice, a verb describes the action done *by* the subject (*We grilled vegetables*), whereas in the passive voice, a verb describes the action done *to* the subject (*Vegetables were grilled*, or, adding who did the action, *Vegetables were grilled by us*). The active voice is usually more concise and more direct than the passive:

    WORDY PASSIVE   Calculators were withheld from some classrooms by school administrators, and the math performance of students with and without the machines was compared.

    CONCISE ACTIVE   School administrators withheld calculators from some classrooms and compared the math performance of students with and without the machines.

- *Delete repetition and padding.* Words that don't contribute to your meaning will interfere with readers' understanding and interest. Watch out for unneeded repetition or restatement, and avoid empty phrases that add no meaning:

WORDY   Students <u>in the schools</u> should have ample practice in math skills, <u>skills</u> such as long division and work with fractions.

CONCISE   Students should have ample practice in math skills, such as long division and work with fractions.

WORDY   <u>The nature of</u> calculators <u>is such that they</u> remove the drudgery from math but can also <u>for all intents and purposes</u> interfere with the development of important cognitive skills.

CONCISE   Calculators remove the drudgery from math but can also interfere with the development of important cognitive skills.

For additional advice on reducing wordiness, see "Focus on Conciseness" on page 304.

▶ Emphasis

Once your sentences are as clear and concise as you can make them, you'll want to ensure that they give the appropriate emphasis to your ideas. Readers will look for the idea of a sentence in its subject and its verb, with modifiers clarifying or adding texture. You can emphasize important ideas by altering the structure of sentences. Following are the most common techniques.

- *Use subordination to de-emphasize what's less important.* Subordination places minor information in words or word groups that modify the sentence's subject and verb:

    UNEMPHATIC   <u>Computers</u> can manipulate film and photographs, and <u>we cannot trust these media to represent</u> reality. [The sentence has two subject-verb structures (both underlined), and they seem equally important.]

    EMPHATIC   <u>Because</u> computers can manipulate film and photographs, we cannot trust these media to represent reality. [*Because* makes the first subject-verb group into a modifier, de-emphasizing the cause of the change and emphasizing the effect.]

- *Use coordination to balance equally important ideas.* Coordination emphasizes the equality of ideas by joining them with a comma and a coordinating conjunction (*and, but, or, nor, for, so,* or *yet*):

    UNEMPHATIC   Two people may be complete strangers. A photograph can show them embracing.

    EMPHATIC   Two people may be complete strangers, <u>but</u> a photograph can show them embracing.

■ *Use the ends and beginnings of sentences to highlight ideas.* The end of a sentence is its most emphatic position, and the beginning is next most emphatic. Placing the sentence's subject and verb in one of these positions draws readers' attention to them. In these sentences the core idea is underlined:

> UNEMPHATIC   With computerized images, <u>filmmakers can entertain us</u>, placing historical figures alongside today's actors.

> EMPHATIC   <u>Filmmakers can entertain us</u> with computerized images that place historical figures alongside today's actors.

> MORE EMPHATIC   With computerized images that place historical figures alongside today's actors, <u>filmmakers can entertain us</u>.

■ *Use short sentences to underscore points.* A very short sentence amid longer sentences will focus readers' attention on a key point:

> UNEMPHATIC   Such images of historical figures and fictional characters have a disadvantage, however, in that they blur the boundaries of reality.

> EMPHATIC   Such images of historical figures and fictional characters have a disadvantage, however. <u>They blur the boundaries of reality</u>.

▶ Parallelism

Parallelism is the use of similar grammatical structures for elements of similar importance, either within or among sentences:

> PARALLELISM WITHIN A SENTENCE   Smoking can <u>worsen heart disease</u> and <u>cause lung cancer</u>.

> PARALLELISM AMONG SENTENCES   Smoking has less well-known effects, too. <u>It can cause</u> gum disease. <u>It can impair</u> blood circulation. And <u>it can reduce</u> the body's supply of vitamins and minerals.

The second example above shows how parallelism can relate sentences to improve coherence (see pp. 35–36).

To make the elements of a sentence parallel, repeat the forms of related words, phrases, and sentences:

> NONPARALLEL   Harris expects dieters to give up <u>bread</u>, <u>dairy</u>, and <u>eating meat</u>.

> PARALLEL   Harris expects dieters to give up bread, dairy, and <u>meat</u>.

NONPARALLEL   Harris emphasizes self-denial, but with Marconi's plan you can eat whatever you want in moderation.

PARALLEL   Harris emphasizes self-denial, but Marconi emphasizes moderation.

NONPARALLEL   If you want to lose weight quickly, try the Harris diet. You'll have more success keeping the weight off if you follow Marconi's plan.

PARALLEL   If you want to lose weight quickly, choose the Harris diet. If you want to keep the weight off, choose Marconi's plan.

For more examples of editing for parallel structure, see "Focus on Parallelism" on page 244.

▶ Variety

Variety in the structure and length of sentences helps keep readers alert and interested, but it also does more. By emphasizing important points and de-emphasizing less important points, varied sentences make your writing clearer and easier to follow.

Consider, for example, the two passages below. The first is adapted from "How Boys Become Men," an essay by Jon Katz. The second is the passage Katz actually wrote.

UNVARIED   I was walking my dog last month past the playground near my house. I saw three boys encircling a fourth. They were laughing and pushing him. He was skinny and rumpled. He looked frightened. One boy knelt behind him. Another pushed him from the front. The trick was familiar to any former boy. The victim fell backward.

VARIED   Last month, walking my dog past the playground near my house, I saw three boys encircling a fourth, laughing and pushing him. He was skinny and rumpled, and he looked frightened. One boy knelt behind him while another pushed him from the front, a trick familiar to any former boy. He fell backward.

Katz's actual sentences work much better to hold and direct our attention because he uses several techniques to achieve variety:

■ *Vary the lengths of sentences.* The nine sentences in the unvaried adaptation range from three to thirteen words. Katz's four sentences range from three to twenty-two words, with the long first sentence setting the scene and the short final sentence creating a climax.

- *Vary the beginnings of sentences.* Every sentence in the unvaried adaptation begins with its subject (*I, I, They, He, He, One boy, Another, The trick, The victim*). Katz, in contrast, begins the first sentence with a transition and a modifier (*Last month, walking my dog past the playground near my house . . .*).

- *Vary the structure of sentences.* The sentences in the unvaried adaptation are all similar in structure, marching like soldiers down the page and making it difficult to pick out the important events of the story. Katz's version emphasizes the important events by making them the subjects and verbs of the sentences, turning the other information into modifying phrases and clauses.

For more strategies and examples, see "Focus on Sentence Variety" on page 124.

Choosing the Best Words

The words you choose can have a dramatic effect on how readers understand your meaning, perceive your attitude, and respond to your thesis.

▶ Denotations and Connotations

The **denotation** of a word is its dictionary meaning, the literal sense without emotional overtones. A **connotation** is an emotional association the word produces in readers. Using incorrect or inappropriate words will confuse or annoy readers.

Using a word with the wrong denotation muddies meaning. Be especially careful to distinguish between words with similar sounds but different meanings, such as *to/too/two*, *their/there/they're*, *it's/its*, and *lose/loose*, and between words with related but distinct meanings, such as *reward/award* and *famous/infamous*. Keeping a list of the new words you acquire will help you build your vocabulary and improve your spelling.

Using words with strong connotations can shape readers' responses to your ideas. For example, consider the distinctions among *feeling, enthusiasm, passion,* and *mania.* Describing a group's *enthusiasm* for its cause is quite different from describing its *mania*: the latter connotes much more intensity, even irrationality. If your aim is to imply that the group's enthusiasm is excessive, and you think your readers will respond well to that characterization, then *mania* may be the appropriate word. But words can backfire if they spark inappropriate associations in readers.

Spell checkers and auto-correct functions can't catch words that are spelled correctly but used incorrectly. Consult a dictionary whenever you are unsure of a word's spelling or meaning. For connotations, you'll find a wide range of choices in a thesaurus, which lists words with similar meanings. A thesaurus doesn't provide definitions, however, so you'll need to check unfamiliar words in a dictionary.

▶ Concrete and Specific Language

Clear, exact writing balances abstract and general words, which provide outlines of ideas and things, with concrete and specific words, which limit and sharpen.

- **Abstract words** name ideas, qualities, attitudes, or states that we cannot perceive with our senses of sight, hearing, touch, smell, and taste: *liberty, hate, anxious*. **Concrete words**, in contrast, name objects, persons, places, or states that we can perceive with our senses: *toaster, red-faced, screeching, smoky*.
- **General words** name groups: *building, color, clothes*. **Specific words** name particular members of a group: *courthouse, purple, boot-cut jeans*.

You need abstract and general words for broad statements that set the course for your writing, expressing concepts or referring to entire groups. But you also need concrete and specific words to make your meaning precise and vivid by appealing to readers' senses and experiences:

> VAGUE The pollution was apparent in the odor and color of the small stream.

> EXACT The stagnant stream smelled like rotten eggs and ran the greenish color of coffee with nonfat milk.

Concrete and specific language may seem essential only in descriptions like that of the polluted stream, but it is equally crucial in any other kind of writing. Readers can't be expected to understand or agree with general statements unless they know what evidence the statements are based on. The evidence is in the details, and the details are in concrete and specific words. (See also "Focus on Concrete and Specific Language" on p. 97.)

▶ Figures of Speech

You can make your writing concrete and specific, even lively and forceful, with **figures of speech**, expressions that imply meanings beyond or different from their literal meanings. Here are some of the most common figures:

- A **simile** compares two unlike things with the use of *like* or *as: The car spun around like a top. Coins as bright as sunshine lay glinting in the chest.*

- A **metaphor** also compares two unlike things, but more subtly, equating them without *like* or *as: The words shattered my fragile self-esteem. The laboratory was her prison, the beakers and test tubes her guards.*

- **Personification** is a simile or metaphor that attributes human qualities or powers to things or abstractions: *The breeze sighed and whispered in the grasses. The city squeezed me tightly at first but then relaxed its grip.*

- **Hyperbole** is a deliberate overstatement or exaggeration: *The dentist filled the tooth with a bracelet's worth of silver. The children's noise shook the rafters.*

By briefly translating experiences and qualities into vividly concrete images, figures of speech can be economical and powerful when used sparingly. Be careful not to combine them into confusing or absurd images, such as *The soccer players danced around the field like bulls ready for a fight.*

In trying for figures of speech, we sometimes resort to **clichés**, worn phrases that have lost their power: *ripe old age, hour of need, heavy as lead, thin as a rail, goes on forever.* If you have trouble recognizing clichés in your writing, be suspicious of any expression you have heard or read before. When you do find a cliché, cure it by substituting plain language (for instance, *seems endless* for *goes on forever*) or by substituting a fresh figure of speech (*thin as a sapling* for *thin as a rail*).

Using an Editing Checklist

The checklist on the opposite page summarizes the editing advice given in this chapter and adds a few other technical concerns. Some of the items will be more relevant for your writing than others: you may have little difficulty with variety in sentences, but may worry that your language is too general. Concentrate your editing efforts where they're needed most, and then survey your draft to check for other problems.

CHECKLIST FOR EDITING

- *Where do sentences need editing for grammar and punctuation — so* that, for instance, sentences are complete; subjects and verbs agree; pronouns are used effectively; modifiers make sense; commas, colons, and semicolons are used appropriately; and tense is consistent?

- *Is each sentence as concise as it can be?*

- *How well have you used sentence structure, variety, parallelism, and other techniques to emphasize ideas and hold readers' interest?*

- *Have you used the right words?* Where can you clarify meaning with concrete and specific words or with figures of speech?

- *Where might spelling be a problem?* Look up any word you're not absolutely sure of. (You'll still have to proofread a spell-checked paper; spell checkers don't catch everything.)

Nicole Lang's Editing and Final Draft

The following paragraph comes from the edited draft of Nicole Lang's "Foundations." Below that, Lang's full final draft appears with notes in the margins highlighting its thesis, structure, and uses of the methods of development. If you compare the final version with the first draft on pages 29–30, you'll see clearly how Lang's revising and editing transformed the essay from a rough exploration of ideas to a refined, and convincing, essay.

EDITED PARAGRAPH

~~Those~~ (*Students*) in more traditional schools need to keep ~~there~~ (*their*) eye~~s~~ on the real world, too. The ~~average student will graduate~~ (*typical college graduate will start out*) owing nearly $30,000 in ~~student~~ loans (~~source~~) (*Olsen*). ~~Its~~ (*While it is*) important to find a career path that feels meaningful and fulfilling, ~~But~~ it is ~~also necessary~~ (*just as important*) to earn an income that will outweigh the cost of higher education. ~~This means we~~ (*We therefore*) need to focus ~~our time and effort~~ on academic programs that will directly benefit our job prospects and ~~put us in a position to~~ (*help us*) repay our debts. With limited resources, ~~not~~ everyone can (*most of us cannot*) afford shacks ~~they~~ (*into which we*) can retreat ~~into. At~~ (*—at*) least not yet.

FINAL DRAFT

Nicole Lang
Professor Binari
English 100A
19 September 2014

Foundations

Edward P. Jones, in "Shacks," reflects on his first semester of college. He recalls writing letters to his high school crush and in doing so discovering a sense of purpose, a "shack," that helped him get through a difficult time of adjustment. But when Jones wonders at our ability to find structure when "so much is at stake" (10), I can't help but think about what is at stake for college students today. Unlike Jones, not everyone has the luxury to indulge in three months of emotional growth, or to look for talents they may not even know they have. For those who struggle just to pay for the opportunity, a college education has to serve the more concrete purpose of preparing for employment.

> Brief summary of Jones's essay

> Author's name in text and page number in parentheses refer to "Works Cited" at end of paper

> Introduction establishes point of contention with Jones

> Thesis statement

Jones seems to think of college as an extension of high school—a place to grow up, if just a little (11). That may be true for some people. But for many students, adulthood is not something that can be put off. For example, my cousin Robert is twenty-nine years old and has a young child and a job that barely pays the bills. His shack is his son. He takes night classes at a community college so he can qualify for a better position, and he does not have time to dream about "some marvelous future" (10). Instead, he spends his time actively constructing a better life for himself and his family.

> Classification: types of college students

> Example of adult student

My cousin is not unusual. A growing number of college students are adults over twenty-five. They come from a wide variety of backgrounds and enroll for a number of reasons, but they all understand the demands of a tough job market in a down economy. They also understand that getting a certificate or a degree will give them the skills they need for particular jobs and prove to employers that they can work independently. Such vocational training is important and deserves respect.

> Classification: types of college students

> Cause-and-effect analysis: why adult students go to college

Students in more traditional schools need to keep their eyes on the real world, too. The typical college graduate will start out owing nearly $30,000 in loans (Olsen). While it is important to find a career path that feels meaningful and fulfilling, it is just as important to earn an income that will outweigh the cost of higher education. We therefore need to focus on academic programs that will directly benefit our job prospects and help us repay our debts. With limited resources, most of us cannot afford shacks into which we can retreat—at least not yet.

Jones makes a good point that a successful life depends on some kind of structure. To be truly sturdy, however, any structure requires a solid foundation. That's what college provides. Although we should certainly hope to discover ourselves and our hidden talents while we're here, for financially burdened students the realities of higher education all come down to time and money. We have to be practical as we build on our dreams.

Classification: types of college students

Name in parentheses identifies source of supporting point

Cause-and-effect analysis: why students need to consider future income

Conclusion extends Jones's metaphor and restates Lang's thesis

Works Cited

Jones, Edward P. "Shacks." *The Compact Reader: Short Essays by Method and Theme*. 10th ed. Ed. Jane E. Aaron and Ellen Kuhl Repetto. Boston: Bedford, 2016. 9-11. Print.

Olsen, Elizabeth. "Student Loan Debt Burdens More Than Just Young People." *New York Times*. New York Times, 12 Sept. 2014. Web. 15 Sept. 2014.

"Works Cited" begins on a new page and gives publication information for Lang's sources (see pp. 394–405)

PART TWO

SHORT ESSAYS BY METHOD AND THEME

5

NARRATION

▶

GROWING UP

You narrate every time you tell a story about something that happened. **Narration** helps us make sense of events and share our experiences with others; consequently, it is one of the longest-standing and most essential methods of communicating. You can use narration to entertain friends by retelling an amusing or scary experience, to summarize a salesclerk's actions in a letter complaining about bad customer service, to relate what went wrong in a ball game, or to persuade skeptics by means of several stories that the logging industry is sincere about restoring clear-cut forests. Storytelling is instinctive to the ways we think and speak; it's no surprise, then, that narration should figure into so much of what we read and write.

Reading Narration

Narration relates a sequence of events that are linked in time. By arranging events in an orderly progression, a narrative illuminates the stages leading to a result. Sometimes the emphasis is on the story itself, as in fiction, biography, autobiography, some history, and much journalism. But often a narrative serves some larger point, as when a paragraph or a brief story about an innocent person's death helps to strengthen an argument for stricter handling of drunk drivers. When used as a primary means of developing an essay, such pointed narration usually relates a sequence of events that led to new knowledge or had a notable outcome. The point of the narrative—the idea the reader is to take away—then determines the selection of events, the amount of detail devoted to them, and their arrangement.

Though narration arranges events in time, narrative time is not real time. An important event may fill whole pages, even though it took only minutes to unfold; a less important event may be dispensed with in a sentence, even though it lasted for hours. Suppose, for instance, that a writer wants to narrate the experience of being mugged in order to show how courage came unexpectedly to his aid. He might provide a slow-motion account of the few minutes' encounter with the muggers, including vivid details of the setting and of the attackers' appearance, a moment-by-moment replay of his emotions, and exact dialogue. At the same time, he might compress events that merely fill in background or link main events, such as how he got to the scene of the mugging or the follow-up questioning by a police detective. And he might entirely omit many events, such as a conversation overheard at the police station, that have no significance for his point.

The point of a narrative influences not only which events are covered and how fully but also how the events are arranged. There are several possibilities:

- A straight **chronological order** is most common because it relates events in the sequence of their actual occurrence. It is particularly useful for short narratives, for those in which the last event is the most dramatic, and for those in which the events preceding and following the climax contribute to the point being made.

- The final event, such as a self-revelation, may come first, followed by an explanation of the events leading up to it.

- The entire story may be summarized first and then examined in detail.

- **Flashbacks**—shifts backward rather than forward in time—may recall events whose significance would not have been apparent earlier. Flashbacks are common in movies and fiction: a character in the midst of one scene mentally replays another.

In addition to providing a clear organization, writers also strive to adopt a consistent **point of view**, a position relative to the events, conveyed in two main ways:

- Pronouns indicate the storyteller's place in the story: the first-person *I* if the narrator is a direct participant; the third-person *he, she, it,* or *they* if the writer is observing or reporting.

- Verb tense indicates the narrator's relation in time to the sequence of events: present (*is, run*) or past (*was, ran*).

Combining the first-person pronoun with the present tense can create great immediacy ("I feel the point of the knife in my back"). At the other extreme, combining third-person pronouns with the past tense creates more distance and objectivity ("He felt the point of the knife in his back"). In between these extremes are combinations of first person with past tense ("I felt . . .") or third person with present tense ("He feels . . ."). The choice depends on how involved the writer is in the events and on his or her purpose.

Analyzing Narration in Paragraphs

Michael Ondaatje (born 1943) is a poet, fiction writer, essayist, and filmmaker. The following paragraph is from *Running in the Family* (1982), Ondaatje's memoir of his childhood in Ceylon, now called Sri Lanka, off the southern tip of India.

After my father died, a grey cobra came into the house. My stepmother loaded the gun and fired at point blank range. The gun jammed. She stepped back and reloaded but by then the snake had slid out into the garden. For the next month this snake would often come into the house and each time the gun would misfire or jam, or my stepmother would miss at absurdly short range. The snake attacked no one and had a tendency to follow my younger sister Susan around. Other snakes entering the house were killed by the shotgun, lifted with a long stick and flicked into the bushes, but the old grey cobra led a charmed life. Finally one of the old workers at Rock Hill told my stepmother what had become obvious, that it was my father who had come to protect his family. And in fact, whether it was because the chicken farm closed down or because of my father's presence in the form of a snake, very few other snakes came into the house again.

Annotations (right margin):
- Chronological order
- Past tense
- Transitions (underlined)
- Point of view: participant observer
- Purpose: to relate a colorful, mysterious story

Jonathan Rauch is a contributing editor of *The Atlantic* and a senior fellow at the Brookings Institution. Born in 1960, he did not realize he was gay until after he was out of college. The following paragraph is condensed from his digital memoir *Denial: My Twenty-Five Years without a Soul* (2013), an exploration of his confused youth and early adulthood.

I knew what the world expected of me. Be a man! I Past tense was curious, <u>too</u>, <u>and of course</u> it was high time for me to get my feet wet. <u>So, on a moonlit night</u>, Mary and I Transitions (underlined) walked through the desert to the banks of the canal and stood close together, <u>and there</u>, with the dry breeze tickling us, we drew ourselves into a stiff embrace, <u>and</u> I kissed her. <u>And</u> kissed her. I kissed her, it seemed, for a long, long time. <u>Specifically</u>, when I say I "kissed" her, I Point of view: direct participant put my lips against hers <u>and</u> pressed them there <u>and</u> wagged my head gradually from side to side the way movie lovers do. Mainly I experienced difficulty breathing. My thoughts were a hundred miles away, pondering the situation with a puzzled detachment which I knew <u>even at that moment</u> to be ludicrous. I was conscious <u>after a while</u> that I was bored and felt much as you might Chronological order while waiting for a bus or an elevator. I might as well have been kissing the back of my own hand, or a doorknob. I felt oddly like a TV alien earnestly trying to understand what kissing means to earthlings, <u>except</u> that on TV, the alien who kisses the girl falls in love despite himself—such is the power of the kiss—<u>whereas</u> I was still as mystified as ever. <u>Eventually</u>, Mary and I Purpose: to express the confusion of gay adolescence took our lips apart and walked home. We probably tried it only once or twice again after that. I concluded that kissing was overrated.

Developing a Narrative Essay

▶ Getting Started

You'll find narration useful whenever relating a sequence of events can help you make a point, sometimes to support the thesis of a larger paper, sometimes *as* the thesis of a paper. If you're assigned a narrative essay, probe your own experiences for a significant or interesting situation, such as an argument involving strong emotion, a humorous or embarrassing incident, a dramatic scene you witnessed, or a learning experience. If you have the opportunity to do research, you might choose a topic dealing with the natural world (such as the Big Bang scenario for the origin of the universe) or an event in history or politics (such as how a local activist worked to close down an animal research lab).

Explore your subject by listing all the events in sequence as they happened. At this stage you may find the traditional journalist's questions helpful:

- *Who* was involved?
- *What* happened?
- *When* did it happen?
- *Where* did it happen?
- *Why* did it happen?
- *How* did it happen?

These questions will lead you to examine your subject from all angles. Then you need to decide which events should be developed in great detail because they are central to your story, which merit compression because they merely contribute background or tie the main events together, and which should be omitted altogether because they are irrelevant to the story or might clutter your narrative.

While you are weighing the relative importance of events, consider also what your readers need to know in order to understand and appreciate your narrative.

- *What information will help locate readers in the narrative's time and place?*
- *How will you expand and compress events to keep readers' attention?*
- *What details about people, places, and feelings will make the events vivid for readers?*
- *What is your attitude toward the subject*—lighthearted, sarcastic, bitter, serious?—and how will you convey it to readers in your choice of events and details?
- *What should your point of view be?* Do you want to involve readers intimately by using the first person and the present tense? Or does that seem overdramatic, less appropriate than the more detached, objective view that would be conveyed by the third person or the past tense or both?

▶ Forming a Thesis

Whatever your subject, you should have some point to make about it:
Why was the incident or experience significant? What does it teach or
illustrate? If you can, phrase this point in a sentence before you start to
draft. For instance:

> I used to think small-town life was boring, but one taste of the city made
> me appreciate the leisurely pace of home.

> A recent small earthquake demonstrated the hazards of inadequate civil
> defense measures.

Sometimes you may need to draft your story before the point of it becomes
clear to you, especially if the experience had a personal impact or if the
event was so recent that writing a draft will allow you to gain some
perspective.

Whether to state your main point outright in your essay, as a thesis
sentence, depends on the effect you want to have on readers. You might
use your introduction to lead to a statement of your thesis so that readers
will know from the start why you are telling them your story. Then again,
to intensify the drama of your story, you might decide to withhold your
thesis sentence for the conclusion or omit it altogether. Remember, though,
that the thesis must be evident to readers even if you don't state it explicitly: the narrative needs a point.

▶ Organizing

Narrative essays often begin without formal **introductions**, instead drawing the reader in with one of the more dramatic events in the sequence.
But you may find an introduction useful to set the scene for your narrative, to summarize the events leading up to it, to establish the context for
it, or to lead in to a thesis statement if you want readers to know the point
of your story before they start reading it.

The arrangement of events in the body of your essay depends on
both the order in which they occurred and the point you want to make.
To narrate a trip during which one thing after another went wrong, you
might find a strict chronological order most effective. To narrate your
experience of city life, you might interweave events in the city with contrasting flashbacks to your life in a small town, or you might start by relating one especially memorable experience in the city, drop back to explain
how you ended up in that situation, and then go on to tell what happened afterward. To narrate an earthquake that began and ended in an
instant, you might sort simultaneous events into groups—perhaps what

happened to buildings and what happened to people—or you might arrange a few people's experiences in order of increasing drama. Narrative time can be manipulated in any number of ways, but your scheme should have a purpose that your readers can see, and you should stick to it.

Let the ending of your essay be determined by the effect you want to leave with readers. You can end with the last event in your sequence, or the one you have saved for last, if it conveys your point and provides a strong finish. Or you can summarize the aftermath of the story if it contributes to the point. You can also end with a formal **conclusion** that states your point—your thesis—explicitly. Such a conclusion is especially useful if your point unfolds gradually throughout the narrative and you want to emphasize it at the finish.

▶ Drafting

Drafting a narrative can be less of a struggle than drafting other kinds of papers, especially if you're close to the events and you use a straight chronological order. But the relative ease of storytelling can be misleading if it causes you to describe events too quickly or to write without making a point. While drafting, be as specific as possible. Tell what the people in your narrative were wearing, what expressions their faces held, how they gestured, what they said. Specify the time of day, and describe the weather and the surroundings (buildings, vegetation, and the like). All these details may be familiar to you, but they won't be to your readers.

At the same time, try to remain open to what the story means to you, so that you can convey that meaning in your selection and description of events. If you know before you begin what your thesis is, let it guide you. But the first draft may turn out to be a search for your thesis, so that you'll need another draft to make it evident in the way you relate events.

In your draft you may want to experiment with **dialogue**—quotations of what participants said, in their words. Dialogue can add immediacy and realism as long as it advances the narrative and doesn't ramble beyond its usefulness. In reconstructing dialogue from memory, try to recall not only the actual words but also the sounds of speakers' voices and the expressions on their faces—information that will help you represent each speaker distinctly. And keep the dialogue natural sounding by using constructions typical of speech. For instance, most speakers prefer contractions such as *don't* and *shouldn't* to the longer forms *do not* and *should not*; and few speakers begin sentences with *although*, as in the formal-sounding "Although we could hear our mother's voice, we refused to answer her."

Whether you are relating events in strict chronological order or manipulating them for some effect, try to make their sequence in real time and the distance between them clear to readers. Instead of signaling sequence with the monotonous *and then . . . and then . . . and then* or *next . . . next . . . next*, use informative **transitions** that signal the order of events (*afterward, earlier*), the duration of events (*for an hour, in that time*), or the amount of time between events (*the next morning, a week later*).

▶ Revising and Editing

When your draft is complete, revise and edit it by answering the following questions and considering the information in the Focus box below.

FOCUS ON VERBS

Narration depends heavily on verbs to clarify and enliven events. Weak verbs, such as forms of *make* and *be*, can sap the life from a story. Strong verbs sharpen meaning and engage readers:

> WEAK   The wind made an awful noise.

> STRONG   The wind roared around the house and rattled the trees.

> WEAK   The pounding rain was alarming to us.

> STRONG   The pounding rain alarmed us.

Verbs in the active voice (the subject does the action) usually pack more power than verbs in the passive voice (the subject is acted upon):

> WEAK PASSIVE   Shelter was sought in the basement.

> STRONG ACTIVE   We sought shelter in the basement.

While strengthening your verbs, also ensure that they're consistent in tense. The tense you choose, present or past, should not shift:

> INCONSISTENT   As the water slowly rose, we held a conference to consider our options. It takes only a minute to decide to evacuate.

> CONSISTENT   As the water slowly rose, we held a conference to consider our options. It took only a minute to decide to evacuate.

See page 48 for a discussion of passive versus active voice and page 47 for advice on avoiding shifts.

- *Is the point of your narrative clear, and does every event you relate contribute to it?* Whether or not you state your thesis, it should be obvious to readers. They should be able to see why you have lingered over some events and compressed others, and they should not be distracted by insignificant events and details.

- *Is your organization clear?* Be sure that your readers will understand any shifts backward or forward in time.

- *Have you used transitions to help readers follow the sequence of events?* Transitions such as *meanwhile* or *soon afterward* serve a dual purpose: they keep the reader on track, and they link sentences and paragraphs so that they flow smoothly. (For more information, see p. 36 and the Glossary under *transitions*.)

- *If you have used dialogue, is it purposeful and natural?* Be sure all quoted speech moves the action forward. And read all dialogue aloud to check that it sounds like something someone would actually say.

A Note on Thematic Connections

All the authors in this chapter saw reasons to articulate key events in their youths, and for that purpose narration is the obvious choice. Michael Ondaatje, in a paragraph, recalls his stepmother's inability to kill a cobra, perhaps because it embodied his dead father (p. 63). Jonathan Rauch, in another paragraph, remembers the awkwardness of his first kiss (p. 64). In essays, Annie Dillard recounts the ecstasy of being chased by an adult for pelting his car with a snowball (next page), while Langston Hughes pinpoints the moment during a church revival when he lost his faith (p. 76). And Lauren Fulmore's narrative explores the ways children's stories colored her perceptions of family (p. 81).

We wove a web in childhood, / A web of sunny air.   —Charlotte Brontë

When she was good, / She was very, very good, / But when she was bad she was horrid.   —Henry Wadsworth Longfellow

Go directly—see what she's doing, and tell her she mustn't.   —*Punch*

JOURNAL RESPONSE   In a short journal entry, reflect on a time you misbehaved as a child. Was it exciting? scary? How did the adults in your life react?

Annie Dillard

A poet and essayist, Annie Dillard (born 1945) is part naturalist, part mystic. Growing up in Pittsburgh, she was an independent child given to exploration and reading. After graduating from Hollins College in the Blue Ridge Mountains of Virginia, Dillard settled in the area to investigate her natural surroundings and to write. Dillard demonstrated her intense, passionate involvement with the world of nature and the world of the mind early in her career with *Pilgrim at Tinker Creek* (1974), a series of related essays that earned her a Pulitzer Prize. Dillard's prolific output since then has spanned several genres, including poetry in volumes such as *Tickets for a Prayer Wheel* (1974) and *Mornings Like This* (1995); essays collected in *Teaching a Stone to Talk* (1982), *The Writing Life* (1989), and *For the Time Being* (1999); literary criticism in *Living by Fiction* (1982) and *Encounters with Chinese Writers* (1984); and, most recently, a novel, *The Maytrees* (2007). In 1999 she was inducted into the American Academy of Arts and Letters. Dillard now lives in North Carolina and is professor emeritus at Wesleyan University.

from *An American Childhood*

In her autobiography, Dillard's enthusiasm for life in its many forms colors her recollections of her own youth. This story of being chased, a self-contained chapter from *An American Childhood* (1987), narrates a few minutes of glorious excitement.

Some boys taught me to play football. This was fine sport. You thought up   1
a new strategy for every play and whispered it to the others. You went out
for a pass, fooling everyone. Best, you got to throw yourself mightily at
someone's running legs. Either you brought him down or you hit the

ground flat out on your chin, with your arms empty before you. It was all or nothing. If you hesitated in fear, you would miss and get hurt: you would take a hard fall while the kid got away, or you would get kicked in the face while the kid got away. But if you flung yourself wholeheartedly at the back of his knees—if you gathered and joined body and soul and pointed them diving fearlessly—then you likely wouldn't get hurt, and you'd stop the ball. Your fate, and your team's score, depended on your concentration and courage. Nothing girls did could compare with it.

Boys welcomed me at baseball, too, for I had, through enthusiastic practice, what was weirdly known as a boy's arm. In winter, in the snow, there was neither baseball nor football, so the boys and I threw snowballs at passing cars. I got in trouble throwing snowballs, and have seldom been happier since. 2

On one weekday morning after Christmas, six inches of new snow had just fallen. We were standing up to our boot tops in snow on a front yard on trafficked Reynolds Street, waiting for cars. The cars traveled Reynolds Street slowly and evenly; they were targets all but wrapped in red ribbons, cream puffs. We couldn't miss. 3

I was seven; the boys were eight, nine, and ten. The oldest two Fahey boys were there—Mikey and Peter—polite blond boys who lived near me on Lloyd Street, and who already had four brothers and sisters. My parents approved of Mikey and Peter Fahey. Chickie McBride was there, a tough kid, and Billy Paul and Mackie Kean too, from across Reynolds, where the boys grew up dark and furious, grew up skinny, knowing, and skilled. We had all drifted from our houses that morning looking for action, and had found it here on Reynolds Street. 4

It was cloudy but cold. The cars' tires laid behind them on the snowy street a complex trail of beige chunks like crenellated castle walls. I had stepped on some earlier; they squeaked. We could have wished for more traffic. When a car came, we all popped it one. In the intervals between cars we reverted to the natural solitude of children. 5

I started making an iceball—a perfect iceball, from perfectly white snow, perfectly spherical, and squeezed perfectly translucent so no snow remained all the way through. (The Fahey boys and I considered it unfair actually to throw an iceball at somebody, but it had been known to happen.) 6

I had just embarked on the iceball project when we heard tire chains come clanking from afar. A black Buick was moving toward us down the street. We all spread out, banged together some regular snowballs, took aim, and, when the Buick drew nigh, fired. 7

A soft snowball hit the driver's windshield right before the driver's   8
face. It made a smashed star with a hump in the middle.

Often, of course, we hit our target, but this time, the only time in all   9
of life, the car pulled over and stopped. Its wide black door opened; a man
got out of it, running. He didn't even close the car door.

He ran after us, and we ran away from him, up the snowy Reynolds   10
sidewalk. At the corner, I looked back; incredibly, he was still after us. He
was in city clothes: a suit and tie, street shoes. Any normal adult would
have quit, having sprung us into flight and made his point. This man was
gaining on us. He was a thin man, all action. All of a sudden, we were
running for our lives.

Wordless, we split up. We were on our turf; we could lose ourselves in   11
the neighborhood backyards, everyone for himself. I paused and considered. Everyone had vanished except Mike Fahey, who was just rounding
the corner of a yellow brick house. Poor Mikey, I trailed him. The driver
of the Buick sensibly picked the two of us to follow. The man apparently
had all day.

He chased Mikey and me around the yellow house and up a back-   12
yard path we knew by heart: under a low tree, up a bank, through a hedge,
down some snowy steps, and across the grocery store's delivery driveway. We smashed through a gap in another hedge, entered a scruffy backyard and ran around its back porch and tight between houses to Edgerton
Avenue; we ran across Edgerton to an alley and up our own sliding wood-
pile to the Halls' front yard; he kept coming. We ran up Lloyd Street and
wound through mazy backyards toward the steep hilltop at Willard and
Lang.

He chased us silently, block after block. He chased us silently over   13
picket fences, through thorny hedges, between houses, around garbage
cans, and across streets. Every time I glanced back, choking for breath, I
expected he would have quit. He must have been as breathless as we were.
His jacket strained over his body. It was an immense discovery, pounding
into my hot head with every sliding, joyous step, that this ordinary adult
evidently knew what I thought only children who trained at football
knew: that you have to fling yourself at what you're doing, you have to
point yourself, forget yourself, aim, dive.

Mikey and I had nowhere to go, in our own neighborhood or out of   14
it, but away from this man who was chasing us. He impelled us forward;
we compelled him to follow our route. The air was cold; every breath tore
my throat. We kept running, block after block; we kept improvising, backyard after backyard, running a frantic course and choosing it simultaneously, failing always to find small places or hard places to slow him down,
and discovering always, exhilarated, dismayed, that only bare speed could

save us—for he would never give up, this man—and we were losing speed.

He chased us through the backyard labyrinths of ten blocks before he   15
caught us by our jackets. He caught us and we all stopped.

We three stood staggering, half blinded, coughing, in an obscure hill-   16
top backyard: a man in his twenties, a boy, a girl. He had released our jackets, our pursuer, our captor, our hero: he knew we weren't going anywhere. We all played by the rules. Mikey and I unzipped our jackets. I pulled off my sopping mittens. Our tracks multiplied in the backyard's new snow. We had been breaking new snow all morning. We didn't look at each other. I was cherishing my excitement. The man's lower pants legs were wet; his cuffs were full of snow, and there was a prow of snow beneath them on his shoes and socks. Some trees bordered the little flat backyard, some messy winter trees. There was no one around: a clearing in a grove, and we the only players.

It was a long time before he could speak. I had some difficulty at first   17
recalling why we were there. My lips felt swollen; I couldn't see out of the sides of my eyes; I kept coughing.

"You stupid kids," he began perfunctorily.   18

We listened perfunctorily indeed, if we listened at all, for the chew-   19
ing out was redundant, a mere formality, and beside the point. The point was that he had chased us passionately without giving up, and so he had caught us. Now he came down to earth. I wanted the glory to last forever.

But how could the glory have lasted forever? We could have run   20
through every backyard in North America until we got to Panama. But when he trapped us at the lip of the Panama Canal, what precisely could he have done to prolong the drama of the chase and cap its glory? I brooded about this for the next few years. He could only have fried Mikey Fahey and me in boiling oil, say, or dismembered us piecemeal, or staked us to anthills. None of which I really wanted, and none of which any adult was likely to do, even in the spirit of fun. He could only chew us out there in the Panamanian jungle, after months or years of exalting pursuit. He could only begin, "You stupid kids," and continue in his ordinary Pittsburgh accent with his normal righteous anger and the usual common sense.

If in that snowy backyard the driver of the black Buick had cut off our   21
heads, Mikey's and mine, I would have died happy, for nothing has required so much of me since as being chased all over Pittsburgh in the middle of winter—running terrified, exhausted—by this sainted, skinny, furious red-headed man who wished to have a word with us. I don't know how he found his way back to his car.

Meaning

1. What lesson did Dillard learn from the experience of the chase? Where is her point explicitly revealed?

2. In paragraph 2 Dillard writes, "I got in trouble throwing snowballs, and have seldom been happier since." What exactly is Dillard saying about the relationship between trouble and happiness? Do you think she is recommending "getting in trouble" as a means to happiness? Why, or why not?

3. If you do not know the meanings of the following words, try to guess them from the context of Dillard's essay. Test your guesses in a dictionary, and then use each word in a sentence of your own.

crenellated (5)	compelled (14)	perfunctorily (18, 19)
translucent (6)	improvising (14)	redundant (19)
embarked (7)	labyrinths (15)	exalting (20)
impelled (14)	obscure (16)	

Purpose and Audience

1. What seems to be Dillard's purpose in this narrative: to encourage children to get into trouble? to encourage adults to be more tolerant of children who get into trouble? to do something else?

2. In her first paragraph, Dillard deliberately shifts from the first-person point of view (using *me*) to the second (using *you*). What is the effect of this shift, and how does it contribute to Dillard's purpose?

Method and Structure

1. Why do you think Dillard chose narration to illustrate her point about the difference between children and adults? What does she gain from this method? What other methods might she have used?

2. In this straightforward narrative, Dillard expands some events and summarizes others: for instance, she provides much more detail about the chase in paragraph 12 than in paragraphs 13 and 14. Why might she first provide detail and then pull back from it?

3. How does the last sentence of paragraph 2—"I got in trouble throwing snowballs, and have seldom been happier since"—serve to set up the story Dillard is about to tell?

4. OTHER METHODS Dillard makes extensive use of **description** (Chapter 6). Locate examples of this method, and analyze what they contribute to the essay as a whole.

Language

1. How would you characterize Dillard's **style**? How does the style reflect the fact that the adult Dillard is writing from a child's point of view?

2. What does Dillard mean by calling the man who chases her "sainted" (paragraph 21)? What is her attitude toward this man? What words and passages support your answer?

3. Consider Dillard's description of cars: traveling down the street, they looked like "targets all but wrapped in red ribbons" (paragraph 3), and their tires in the snow left "a complex trail of beige chunks like crenellated castle walls" (5). What is the **dominant impression** created here?

Writing Topics

1. JOURNAL TO ESSAY   Write a narrative essay about the incident of misbehavior you explored in your journal entry (p. 70). Use the first-person *I*, strong verbs, and plenty of descriptive details to render vividly the event and its effects on you and others.

2. Write a narrative essay about a time you discovered that an "ordinary adult" knew some truth you thought only children knew. What was that truth, and why did you believe until that moment that only children knew it? What did this adult do to change your mind?

3. Though Dillard focuses on a time when no harm was done, the consequences of throwing snowballs at moving cars could be quite serious. Rewrite the essay from the point of view of someone who would *not* glorify the children's behavior—the man driving the Buick, for instance, or one of the children's parents. How might one of these people narrate these events? On what might he or she focus?

4. CULTURAL CONSIDERATIONS   Childhood pranks like throwing snowballs at cars are tolerated more in some cultural groups than in others. In a narrative essay, retell an event from your childhood when you felt you were testing the rules of behavior in your culture. Make your motivations as clear as possible, and reflect on the results of your action.

5. CONNECTIONS   Annie Dillard and Alaina Wong ("China Doll," p. 246) share an exuberant attitude toward their childhoods, at least toward the small portions they describe in their essays. But Wong focuses on a concrete, specific object, while Dillard focuses on an event. Write an essay examining the effects each essay has on you, and why. What techniques does each writer use to create these effects?

Nothing is more restful than conformity.　　　　　　—Elizabeth Bowen

We all try to be alike in our youth.　　　　　　　—Ethel Alec-Tweedie

This above all: to thine own self be true, / And it must follow, as the night the day, / Thou canst not then be false to any man.　　—William Shakespeare

JOURNAL RESPONSE　When have you experienced a powerful desire to think, look, or act like others, especially your peers? Write a journal entry about your experience.

Langston Hughes

A poet, fiction writer, playwright, critic, and humorist, Langston Hughes described his writing as "largely concerned with depicting Negro life in America." He was born in 1902 in Joplin, Missouri, and grew up in Illinois, Kansas, and Ohio. After dropping out of Columbia University in the early 1920s, Hughes worked at odd jobs while struggling to gain recognition as a writer. His first book of poems, *The Weary Blues* (1925), helped seed the Harlem Renaissance, a flowering of African American music and literature centered in the Harlem district of New York City during the 1920s. The book also generated a scholarship that enabled Hughes to finish college at Lincoln University. In all of his work — including *The Negro Mother* (1931), *The Ways of White Folks* (1934), *Shakespeare in Harlem* (1942), *Montage of a Dream Deferred* (1951), and *Ask Your Mama* (1961) — Hughes captured and projected the rhythms of jazz and the distinctive speech, subtle humor, and deep traditions of African American people. He died in New York City in 1967.

Salvation

A chapter in Hughes's autobiography, *The Big Sea* (1940), "Salvation" is a simple yet compelling narrative about a moment of deceit and disillusionment for a boy of twelve. As you read Hughes's account, notice how the opening two sentences set up every twist of the story.

I was saved from sin when I was going on thirteen. But not really saved.　1
It happened like this. There was a big revival at my Auntie Reed's church. Every night for weeks there had been much preaching, singing, praying, and shouting, and some very hardened sinners had been brought to Christ, and the membership of the church had grown by leaps and bounds. Then

just before the revival ended, they held a special meeting for children, "to bring the young lambs to the fold." My aunt spoke of it for days ahead. That night, I was escorted to the front row and placed on the mourner's bench with all the other young sinners, who had not yet been brought to Jesus.

My aunt told me that when you were saved you saw a light, and 2 something happened to you inside! And Jesus came into your life! And God was with you from then on! She said you could see and hear and feel Jesus in your soul. I believed her. I have heard a great many old people say the same thing and it seemed to me they ought to know. So I sat there calmly in the hot, crowded church, waiting for Jesus to come to me.

The preacher preached a wonderful rhythmical sermon, all moans 3 and shouts and lonely cries and dire pictures of hell, and then he sang a song about the ninety and nine safe in the fold, but one little lamb was left out in the cold. Then he said: "Won't you come? Won't you come to Jesus? Young lambs, won't you come?" And he held out his arms to all us young sinners there on the mourner's bench. And the little girls cried. And some of them jumped up and went to Jesus right away. But most of us just sat there.

A great many old people came and knelt around us and prayed, old 4 women with jet-black faces and braided hair, old men with work-gnarled hands. And the church sang a song about the lower lights are burning, some poor sinners to be saved. And the whole building rocked with prayer and song.

Still I kept waiting to *see* Jesus. 5

Finally all the young people had gone to the altar and were saved, but 6 one boy and me. He was a rounder's son named Westley. Westley and I were surrounded by sisters and deacons praying. It was very hot in the church, and getting late now. Finally Westley said to me in a whisper: "God damn! I'm tired o' sitting here. Let's get up and be saved." So he got up and was saved.

Then I was left all alone on the mourner's bench. My aunt came and 7 knelt at my knees and cried, while prayers and songs swirled all around me in the little church. The whole congregation prayed for me alone, in a mighty wail of moans and voices. And I kept waiting serenely for Jesus, waiting, waiting—but he didn't come. I wanted to see him, but nothing happened to me. Nothing! I wanted something to happen to me, but nothing happened.

I heard the songs and the minister saying: "Why don't you come? My 8 dear child, why don't you come to Jesus? Jesus is waiting for you. He wants you. Why don't you come? Sister Reed, what is this child's name?"

"Langston," my aunt sobbed.   9

"Langston, why don't you come? Why don't you come and be saved?   10
Oh, Lamb of God! Why don't you come?"

Now it was really getting late. I began to be ashamed of myself, hold-   11
ing everything up so long. I began to wonder what God thought about
Westley, who certainly hadn't seen Jesus either, but who was now sitting
proudly on the platform, swinging his knickerbockered legs and grinning
down at me, surrounded by deacons and old women on their knees praying. God had not struck Westley dead for taking his name in vain or for
lying in the temple. So I decided that maybe to save further trouble, I'd
better lie, too, and say that Jesus had come, and get up and be saved.

So I got up.   12

Suddenly the whole room broke into a sea of shouting, as they saw   13
me rise. Waves of rejoicing swept the place. Women leaped in the air. My
aunt threw her arms around me. The minister took me by the hand and
led me to the platform.

When things quieted down, in a hushed silence, punctuated by a few   14
ecstatic "Amens," all the new young lambs were blessed in the name of
God. Then joyous singing filled the room.

That night, for the last time in my life but one—for I was a big boy   15
twelve years old—I cried. I cried, in bed alone, and couldn't stop. I buried
my head under the quilts, but my aunt heard me. She woke up and told
my uncle I was crying because the Holy Ghost had come into my life, and
because I had seen Jesus. But I was really crying because I couldn't bear to
tell her that I had lied, that I had deceived everybody in the church, that
I hadn't seen Jesus, and that now I didn't believe there was a Jesus anymore, since he didn't come to help me.

Meaning

1. What is the main point of Hughes's narrative? What change occurs in
   him as a result of his experience?

2. What finally makes Hughes decide to get up and be saved? How does this
   decision affect him afterward?

3. What do you make of the connection between the title and the first two
   sentences? What is Hughes saying here about "salvation"?

4. If you are unfamiliar with any of the following words, try to guess what
   they mean from the context of Hughes's essay. Check the definitions in a
   dictionary, and then use each word in a sentence or two of your own.

   dire (3)   rounder (6)   deacons (6)

Purpose and Audience

1. Why do you think Hughes wrote "Salvation" as part of his autobiography more than two decades after the experience? Was his purpose simply to express feelings prompted by a significant event in his life? Did he want to criticize his aunt and the other adults in the congregation? Did he want to explain something about childhood or about the distance between generations? What passages support your answer?

2. What does Hughes seem to assume about his readers' familiarity with the kind of service he describes? What details help make the procedure clear?

3. How do dialogue, lines from hymns, and details of other sounds (paragraphs 3–10) help re-create the increasing pressure Hughes feels? What other details contribute to this sense of pressure?

Method and Structure

1. Why do you think Hughes chose narration to explore the themes of this essay? Can you imagine an **argument** essay (Chapter 14) that would deal with the same themes? What might its title be?

2. Where in his narrative does Hughes insert explanations, compress time by summarizing events, or jump ahead in time by omitting events? Where does he expand time by drawing moments out? How does each of these insertions and manipulations of time relate to Hughes's main point?

3. In paragraph 1 Hughes uses several **transitions** to signal the sequence of events and the passage of time: "for weeks," "Then just before," "for days ahead," "That night." Where does he use similar signals in the rest of the essay?

4. OTHER METHODS   Hughes's narrative also explains a process (Chapter 10): we learn how a revival meeting works. Why is this **process analysis** essential to the essay?

Language

1. What does Hughes's language reveal about his adult attitudes toward his experience? Does he feel anger? bitterness? sorrow? guilt? shame? amusement? What words and passages support your answer?

2. Hughes relates his experience in an almost childlike **style**, using many short sentences and beginning many sentences with *And*. What effect do you think he is trying to achieve with this style?

3. Hughes expects to "see" Jesus when he is saved (paragraphs 2, 5, 7), and afterward his aunt thinks that he has "seen" Jesus (15). What does each

of them mean by *see*? What is the significance of the difference in Hughes's story?

Writing Topics

1. JOURNAL TO ESSAY   Continuing from your journal entry (p. 76), write a narrative essay about a time when others significantly influenced the way you thought, looked, or acted—perhaps against your own true beliefs or values. What was the appeal of the others' attitudes, appearance, or behavior? What did you gain by conforming? What did you lose? Use specific details to explain how and why the experience affected you.

2. Hughes says, "I have heard a great many old people say the same thing and it seemed to me they ought to know" (paragraph 2). Think of a piece of information or advice that you heard over and over again from adults when you were a child. Write a narrative essay about an experience in which you were helped or misled by that information or advice.

3. CULTURAL CONSIDERATIONS   It seems that Hughes wants to be saved largely because of the influence of his family and his community. Westley (paragraphs 6 and 11) represents another kind of influence, peer pressure, that often works against family and community. Think of an incident in your own life when you felt pressured by peers to go against your parents, religion, school, or another authority. Write a narrative essay telling what happened and making it clear why the situation was important to you. What were the results?

4. CONNECTIONS   When Hughes doesn't see Jesus and then lies to satisfy everyone around him, he feels betrayed and pained. How does Hughes's experience differ from the one cheerfully reported by Michael Ondaatje (p. 63), in which a potentially deadly snake is said to be Ondaatje's deceased father, "who had come to protect his family"? Write an essay analyzing what elements these narratives have in common and any significant differences between them.

I didn't think much about the future when I was a child . . . but to the extent that I did imagine a future, it held an ever-widening range for my explorations—more hills and valleys, shorelines and dunes.

—Barbara Ehrenreich

You can't put a limit on anything. The more you dream, the farther you get.

—Michael Phelps

Adults are always asking children what they want to be when they grow up because they're looking for ideas.

—Paula Poundstone

JOURNAL RESPONSE   When you were a child, adults probably asked you, "What do you want to be when you grow up?" What did you reply? Write a journal entry in which you recall your childhood fantasies.

Lauren Fulmore

Lauren Fulmore was born in 1993 and grew up in woodsy Hampstead, New Hampshire, an hour or so north of Boston. As a high school student at Pinkerton Academy, she became involved with the Special Olympics and played basketball for a unified league that encourages interplay with special-needs athletes. She is studying nursing at the University of New Hampshire, where she plays club lacrosse and continues to work with people with developmental disabilities—while also supporting herself with a full-time job. Fulmore expects to graduate in 2016; she then plans to spend some time as a traveling nurse while she pursues her goal of camping in every national park before she applies to graduate school as a nurse practitioner.

Chasing Fairy Tales
(Student Essay)

Fulmore wrote "Chasing Fairy Tales" for her required first-year writing course in 2012, in response to a prompt asking for a story about a "moment of realization" in her life. The essay was subsequently selected for *Transitions*, the University of New Hampshire's annual collection of exceptional student writing. In an imaginative personal narrative, Fulmore recounts a series of adventures from her childhood to re-create the accidental discovery of a "magical" truth.

I grew up in a fairly stereotypical suburban household. My father was a con-   1
tractor and my mother a registered nurse. As the offspring of two working

parents, my elder sister and I were called upon to do the chores that my full-time employed parents' busy schedules did not allow for. It was no more responsibility than that of any other child my age: I was responsible for my own laundry, cleaning the dishes, and other fairly common tasks. However, to my overactive imagination and inclination toward drama, I felt as though I were a slave to my household. Often while "nursing bleeding hands" over the dishes or "laboring" over laundry I would picture myself as a character such as Cinderella, forced by her evil family to do all of the chores while they relaxed in leisure. In my fantasies I was always the victim of some type of switched-at-birth scenario in which my current "family" was holding me back from my true potential. It was this train of thinking that led to the phase in my life that my mother likes to call "the sneaky sevens."

It began one day after a particularly heavy load of chores. I had settled   2
into my favorite comfy laundry basket to do some daydreaming. Somewhere between fantasizing about my mystery parents and thinking about dinner, my seven-year-old logic realized that there was no reason for me to stay where I was. I was getting nothing done by feeling sorry for myself. If I was truly to fulfill my role as the heroine in the stories I had read, then sitting around doing laundry was not going to bring me any closer to my destiny. No, the time had come. I had talked myself into rebellion. So I devised my first escape.

The first step was preparation. With a handkerchief tied around an   3
old stick, I crafted my first bindle, just like I had seen in the old movies. I wrapped up a chunk of bread, a few slices of cheese, and an apple—just the essentials. I was sure this would last me the weeks I needed it to until I stumbled upon my real family. *Dear former family*, I began my attempt at a cordial last goodbye. I remember the combination of my chicken-scratch writing and the Hello Kitty notebook looking so juvenile. *I have left to find my true family. They will not make me do chores and I will be famous. Do not look for me, I'm not coming back.* Satisfied with my handiwork, I smudged my Lip Smacker glossed lips together and planted a child's attempt at a grown-up's kiss on the bottom of the note. It was perfect, like something out of *Gone with the Wind*. I then donned my hiking boots, embodying my inner Scarlett O'Hara, and crept out the back door into the woods, leaving my past life behind.

I spent the first few hours of my high-stakes runaway tramping through   4
the woods behind my house, vigorously putting distance between myself and the home of my enslavers. I knew it was only a matter of time before they would be after me. *As soon as the laundry is piled high and there are no*

more clean dishes, that's when they'll notice I'm gone, I told myself bitterly. With a renewed sense of determination I continued my journey.

Sweat began to trickle down my spine as I stopped for a break on a fallen tree, momentarily consumed by the image of the loving embrace my beautiful mother would wrap me in upon my arrival. I smiled to myself, thinking of the magnificent ball my father would hold in honor of my glorious return home. My daydreaming continued as I trekked through the undergrowth, and the bright ambiance of the forest began to fade into another hazy, orange, summer afternoon. It wasn't long after when my subconscious awoke me from my thoughts. I took a second glance to my left and wondered aloud to myself, *Was that the same tree I had rested on not long ago?* I reevaluated my surroundings. I had been traveling in circles. Exasperated, I contemplated heading back to my captors; that's when I heard the voices.

They were quiet at first—hardly audible. They sounded more like the high-pitched whine that wind tends to make when making its way through a crowded forest. However, I could swear the wind was calling my name. *This is it! My real family has finally found me!* I rushed toward the voices like a magnet to metal, heart beating out of my chest. Envisioning my mother's rosy pink cheeks and flowing blonde hair, I could practically already smell her sweet perfume as she wrapped me in a loving embrace. The voices were clearer now; I could see my regal father beaming at the sight of his long-lost daughter. "Lauren! Lauren!" the voices cried. "Where are you, Lauren!?"

"I'm here!" I cried. "I'm here!" Soon I would be united with my true family.

I rushed into the clearing, bewildered with excitement and joy. I took a look at the faces surrounding me; tired and exasperated faces gazed back at me. I stumbled back. Rubbing my eyes, I tried to make the faces reappear as the faces I desired. However, when I reopened my eyes I only found the concerned faces of my *former* family. *This can't be,* I thought to myself. *I can't go back to my old life. Not after I finally made it out.* Against my wishes and surrounded by a cloud of heartbreak and doom, I was begrudgingly led back to my cell.

Needless to say, I was watched with a careful eye. Long gone were the days of solitude and quiet. A babysitter was hired on the nights my parents worked late; I was even banned from reading my fairy tales. My parents acted out of concern for my ability to distinguish fact from fiction; however, I looked at it as an unforgivable punishment. The sole source of comfort I found in that household had been stripped away from me. Without my books to lose myself in, it became less of a "want" to escape this dungeon; it became a dire need.

The drama of my plight faded as my parents realized that I had a ten- 10 dency to return after each of my "wild escapades." After a few more attempts at escaping my captors, they stopped searching for me. It was commonly known that I would be back in a few hours when I became hungry or when it began to get dark outside. My efforts became something like a joke to the family, but they were not a joke to me. I was determined.

My time away from home was nothing special. I would wander 11 around the woods that circled my backyard. I would overturn rocks and practice my balancing skills on fallen trees. Sometimes I would play pretend, fencing stone walls and bushes with my stick-turned-sword. Every second was an adventure, but my parents were always right. When my knapsack was devoid of my regular apple, bread, and cheese, or when the shadows from the trees began to take on the persona of monsters and murderers, I would begin my shameful and begrudging trudge back home, determined to return next time and succeed in my task of beginning a new life.

It was one day such as this; I was at the top of my favorite tree scout- 12 ing for incoming pirates. As my twisted-leaf-telescope reported no results, I began my descent to the ground. I tentatively placed my weight upon a branch; it groaned under my seventy-five pounds of skin and bone, yet stayed true. Assured in its strength, I placed my full weight upon the tree, and in one swift movement the limb broke and sent me cascading toward the ground as it gave way to nothing. My feet, finding nothing beneath them, shot out in front of me; my desperate hands grappled for something, anything, to hold on to. Shocked and confused by the branch's betrayal, I hardly had time to scream as I received a cruel beating from the ground.

Often in times of extreme trauma or stress, people describe the events 13 occurring around them as though they happened in slow motion, as though their brains, motivated by survival, kicked into turbo mode. As I lay there, under that backstabbing tree, time did just that. For what seemed like hours, my crippled seven-year-old body writhed in agony, as I was unable to control my movement. I lay there, watching the shadows from the trees grow darker and angrier as the sun began to set. The forest began to change from the peaceful, safe haven of my daytime frolicking to a mysterious, unknown lair, home to demons and monsters my own imagination could hardly fathom.

Heart beating out of my chest, I kept hoping and wishing that my 14 "real" family would come and find me, that my beautiful fairy godmother or king father would recognize my distress and choose this time to rescue me from both my current dire situation and my lifetime of finitude and animosity. However, as the shadows grew deeper and the painful shooting from my leg intensified, I began to realize, for the first time, that perhaps they were never coming.

As the cold from the ground began to seep through my skin, the stark 15 reality of the situation began to creep into my heart. I didn't have a magical, enchanted family. I was average. The pain of the realization outshone the physical pain I was enduring. My worst fear had come true; I was nothing but a normal kid. Worse than that, I was a foolish normal child stuck in a very dangerous situation. For the very first time I realized that no amount of imagination or wishing was going to save me. I was all alone.

The wind began to whine in that pitiful way it did, serving only to 16 add to my misery. I listened to it whine as I began to accept my fate. My short seven years were going to end, right here, under this tree. I would never take the bus to school again. I would never see my friends. Even the thought of doing the dishes one more time made my heart ache with longing.

Slowly a realization dawned upon me: *that can't be the wind howling.* 17 I listened closer. *It almost sounds like voices.* It was distant at first, hardly audible over my pulsating heartbeat. I chalked it up to delusion from a loss of blood. But then I heard it again. Yes, it was definitely voices, and I might have been going crazy, but I could have sworn they were calling my name.

A sense of deranged, desperate hope washed over my entire being. 18 I mustered up every spare bit of energy I had left. "I'm over here!" I croaked, my throat raw and exhausted. I flashed back to the last time I had heard voices in the forest: I had so entirely hoped that those voices belonged to my fictitious family. This time all I could hope to see was the worn, familiar face of my *real* mother, or even the imperfect, often-infuriating countenance of my *real* older sister. "I'm here," I screamed desperately. "Help me! I'm here!"

The harsh beam of a flashlight glared against my dirty, tear-stained 19 face. I looked up to see the relieved faces of my *real* family. Not the family of my daydreams, but the family who worked full-time jobs to support me, the family who cared about me enough to worry when I was gone for too long. It was in that very moment I realized that no fantasy family, no matter how fantastic and alluring, would ever compare to my real family. I was giving up on the dream of being coated in jewels and whisked away on adventures on a daily basis, but in that moment it didn't matter. I had a family who loved me, and for an average seven-year-old girl, that is about as magical as it gets.

Meaning

1. Why did the seven-year-old Fulmore consider herself so mistreated that she felt compelled to run away on a regular basis?

2. Explain the **irony** of Fulmore's dream of finding her "real family" (paragraphs 3, 6, 14, 19).

3. Where in the essay does Fulmore state her thesis? Why do you suppose she chose to place it where she does?

4. If you are unsure of the meanings of any of the following words, try to guess them from the context of Fulmore's essay. Look the words up in a dictionary to test your guesses, and then use each word in a sentence of your own.

bindle (3)	regal (6)	finitude (14)
cordial (3)	devoid (11)	animosity (14)
ambiance (5)	persona (11)	mustered (18)
subconscious (5)	betrayal (12)	countenance (18)
exasperated (5, 8)	lair (13)	alluring (19)

Purpose and Audience

1. What do you believe is Fulmore's purpose in recording these episodes from her childhood: to understand her experience? to tell her peers about her childhood? to do something else?

2. What assumptions does Fulmore make about her readers and their familiarity with children's literature? Why are the stories and characters she **alludes** to significant to her experience? Can readers not acquainted with fairy tales understand Fulmore's narrative?

3. How does dialogue help re-create the fear and relief Fulmore felt in the woods?

Method and Structure

1. What features of narration make it an ideal method for describing childhood experiences like the ones documented by Fulmore?

2. Examine Fulmore's organization of events. What major sections does the essay consist of, and what happens in each? Why does she jump between time periods? How does the manipulation of narrative time serve the overall purpose of the essay?

3. How does Fulmore build suspense in the second half of her story?

4. **OTHER METHODS**   Fulmore makes extensive use of **description** (Chapter 6) in her essay, especially in portraying the woods surrounding her home. What do the descriptions contribute to her narrative? What **dominant impression** does Fulmore create?

Language

1. "Chasing Fairy Tales" is notable for the author's consistent use of strong verbs such as "smudged" (paragraph 3), "trekked" (5), "stumbled" (8), and "groaned" (12). Reread the essay, and pick out five or six additional examples. What weak verbs might Fulmore have used in their place? Why are the verbs she chose more effective? (If necessary, see p. 69 on strong versus weak verbs.)

2. Fulmore uses many figures of speech to enrich her prose, particularly when she recounts her emotional response to being injured and alone. List a few of the **metaphors**, **similes**, and **personifications** that you find especially effective. How do they contribute to the overall meaning of her essay?

3. Although she writes from the point of view of a seven-year-old girl, Fulmore uses relatively sophisticated vocabulary and sentence structures through most of her essay. How does the rhythm of her sentences reinforce her purpose?

Writing Topics

1. **JOURNAL TO ESSAY**   In your journal entry (p. 81), you described your childhood dreams for the future. Have your goals changed since then? Write an essay in which you describe your current ambitions. If they have changed, pinpoint the people or experiences that have caused you to modify your expectations. Do you believe that your plans will evolve in the future? Do you think that they could ever change completely?

2. "Chasing Fairy Tales" relies on narrative to recount an emotionally significant learning experience. Using the same method, write an essay in which you recapture one of the happiest or most exciting discoveries of your childhood: for example, finding a favorite hiding place, learning a skill such as skating or playing a musical instrument, making an unexpected friend, or receiving something you deeply desired. Use straightforward chronological time if that works best, or, like Fulmore, compress narrative time to emphasize the most significant moments.

3. In exploring the effects of children's books on Fulmore's imagination and her actions, "Chasing Fairy Tales" can be considered a literacy narrative,

a story about how a writer has learned (or is continuing to learn) to communicate through reading and writing. Try writing a literacy narrative of your own. You might consider how reading has influenced you, as a child or now. You might examine one or more of your experiences as a writer. Or you might reflect on some aspect of language that has challenged or inspired you. Whatever focus you choose, try to draw some conclusions about what written expression contributes to your life.

4. **CULTURAL CONSIDERATIONS**   In North America children are often tasked with household chores such as dusting, vacuuming, washing dishes, or doing laundry. Write about some task (or tasks) you have been responsible for. Was it something you did just because your parents forced you to, or did you enjoy any aspect of the experience? What lessons did you learn from your responsibility? Do you think it is a good idea for young people to help with housekeeping chores?

5. **CONNECTIONS**   Just as Fulmore explores how fairy tales made her unhappy as a child, Augusten Burroughs, in "Unhappily Ever After" (p. 282), suggests that wanting to be happy is itself a kind of fairy tale. In an essay, examine the function of fairy tales and folklore. Where do the stories come from? How do they influence children and adults alike? What purpose do they serve in modern cultures? How do they compare to other forms of mythology? Draw on the insights offered by Fulmore and Burroughs as you like, but feel free also to make your own observations and associations.

WRITING WITH THE METHOD

NARRATION

Select one of the following topics, or any other topic they suggest, for an essay developed by narration. Be sure to choose a topic you care about so that narration is a means of communicating an idea, not an end in itself.

Friends and Relations

1. An early infatuation
2. Another person's generosity or sacrifice
3. A wedding or funeral
4. An incident from family legend

The World around You

5. An interaction you witnessed on the street
6. A storm, a flood, an earthquake, or another natural event
7. The history of your neighborhood
8. A community event, such as a meeting, demonstration, or celebration
9. A time when a poem, story, film, song, or other work changed you

Lessons of Daily Life

10. An act of rebellion
11. A time when you had to deliver bad news
12. A moment of disappointment
13. Your biggest social blunder

Firsts

14. Your first day of school, as a child or more recently
15. The first time you met someone who became important to you
16. The first performance you gave
17. Your first job

Adventures

18. An especially satisfying sports experience, such as a run, tennis match, or bike ride
19. A surprising encounter with a wild animal
20. An episode of extrasensory perception
21. Solving a mystery
22. A trip to an unfamiliar place

WRITING ABOUT THE THEME

GROWING UP

1. The vulnerability of youth is a recurring theme in the essays and paragraphs in this chapter. Michael Ondaatje (p. 63), Jonathan Rauch (p. 64), Langston Hughes (p. 76), and Lauren Fulmore (p. 81) all write in some way about psychological pain. After considering each writer's situation individually, write an essay analyzing the differences among these situations. Based on these narratives, which writers seem to have the most in common? Which of their responses seem most relatable to you? Which are most likely to be outgrown?

2. While growing up inevitably involves fear, disappointment, and pain, most children experience security and happiness as well. Michael Ondaatje clearly finds comfort in his dead father's reappearance as a cobra, Annie Dillard relishes the joy of misbehaving (p. 70), and Lauren Fulmore believes that breaking her leg strengthened her relationship with her family. Write a narrative essay about a similarly mixed experience from your childhood, making sure to describe your feelings vividly so that your readers share them with you.

3. Childhood is full of epiphanies, or sudden moments of realization, insight, or understanding. Annie Dillard, Langston Hughes, and Lauren Fulmore all report such moments at the ends of their essays: Dillard recognizes that any experience of glorious happiness must end, Hughes loses faith in a Jesus who would not help him in church, and Fulmore discovers that her normal childhood is in fact "magical." Write a narrative essay in which you tell of events leading to an epiphany when you were growing up. Make sure both the events themselves and the nature of the epiphany are vividly clear.

6

DESCRIPTION

▶

EXPERIENCING NEW PLACES

Whenever you use words to depict or re-create a scene, an object, a person, or a feeling, you use **description**. A mainstay of conversation between people, description is likely to figure in almost any writing situation: a *Facebook* post may praise a friend's new spiky purple hair; a laboratory report may examine the colors and odors of chemicals; a business memo may distinguish the tastes of two competitors' gluten-free pizzas; an insurance claim may explain the condition of an apartment after a kitchen fire. Because the method builds detail and brings immediacy to a subject, description is an important part of most essay writing as well.

Reading Description

Description draws on perceptions of the five senses—sight, sound, smell, taste, and touch—to understand and communicate a particular experience of the world. The writer's purpose and involvement with the subject will largely determine how **objective** or **subjective** a description is.

- *Objective description* strives for precision, trying to convey the subject impersonally, without emotion. This is the kind of description required in scientific writing—for instance, a medical diagnosis or a report on an experiment in psychology—where cold facts and absence of feeling are essential for readers to judge the accuracy of procedures and results. It is also the method of news reports and of reference works such as encyclopedias.

- *Subjective description*, in contrast, draws on emotions, giving an impression of the subject filtered through firsthand experience. Instead of withdrawing to the background, the writer invests feelings in the subject and lets those feelings determine which details to describe and how best to describe them. State of mind—perhaps loneliness, anger, or joy—can be re-created by reference to sensory details such as numbness, heat, or sweetness.

In general, writers favor objective description when their purpose is explanation and subjective description when their purpose is self-expression or persuasion. But the categories are not exclusive, and most descriptive writing mixes the two. A news report on a tropical storm, for instance, might objectively describe bent and broken trees, fallen wires, and lashing rain, but the reporter's selection of details gives a subjective impression of the storm's fearsomeness.

Whether objective or subjective or a mixture of the two, effective description requires a **dominant impression**—a central theme or idea about the subject to which readers can relate all the details. The dominant impression may be something a writer sees in his or her subject, such as the purposefulness of city pedestrians or the expressiveness of an actor. Or it may derive from an emotional response to the subject, perhaps pleasure (or dismay) at the purposefulness of the pedestrians, perhaps admiration (or disdain) for the actor's technique. Whatever its source, the dominant impression serves as a unifying principle that guides both the writer's selection of details and the reader's understanding of the subject.

One aid in creating a dominant impression is a consistent **point of view**, the position from which a writer approaches a subject. Point of view in description has two main elements:

- A *physical* relation to the subject, real or imagined. A writer could view a mountain, for instance, from the bottom looking up, from fifteen miles away across a valley, or from an airplane passing overhead. The first two points of view are fixed because the writer remains in one position and scans the scene from there; the third is moving because the writer changes position.

- A *psychological* relation to the subject, conveyed partly by pronouns. In subjective description, where feelings are part of the message, writers might use *I* and *you* freely to narrow the distance between themselves and the subject and between themselves and the reader. But in the most objective, impersonal description, writers will use *one* ("One can see the summit") or avoid self-reference altogether in order to appear distant from and unbiased toward the subject.

Once a physical and psychological point of view has been established, readers come to depend on it. Thus a sudden and inexplicable shift from one view to another—zooming in from fifteen miles away to the foot of a mountain, abandoning *I* for the more removed *one*—can disorient readers and distract them from the dominant impression the writer intended to create.

Analyzing Description in Paragraphs

Rick Bragg, a prize-winning author and journalist, was born in 1959 in Possum Trot, Alabama, and raised amid the traditions and poverties of southern Appalachia. The following description of the Alabama highlands comes from *The Prince of Frogtown* (2008), a memoir that reflects on Bragg's efforts to raise a stepson whose background is much different from his own.

It was magic masquerading as nature. The round summits of the highlands seldom stood stark and clear, but were softened by hot, yellow haze in summer and gray, cool mist in winter. Even in their shrouds, they were beautiful. Poison ivy veined the trees, blistering even the lightest touch. Persimmons hung fat, yellow and inviting, but hexed your mouth into a whistling knot if you bit into them even a day too soon. Tornadoes tore through both springtime and the turning leaves, winter trees filled with a million keening blackbirds, and the summer ground lay red in wild strawberries. Water moccasins, fat as a rolled-up newspaper, rode rivers the color of English tea, bullfrogs beat the air like bass drums, and panthers, black as the inside of a box, watched from the branches of ancient trees.

Specific, concrete details (underlined once)

Figures of speech (underlined twice)

Point of view: moving; psychologically close

Dominant impression: magical dangers

Helene Cooper is a Pentagon correspondent for the *New York Times*. Born in 1966 to members of Liberia's ruling class, she enjoyed a privileged childhood until violent uprisings forced her family to seek asylum in the United States in 1980. This paragraph, from her memoir *The House at Sugar Beach* (2008), describes her first impressions upon returning to Africa as an adult.

Arriving on West African soil for the first time is unlike any other arrival in the world. The first thing that hits you is the smell: a combination of coal fires, dried fish, humid air, and the sea. After smell comes the feel of the air. It is heavy, even when the sun is shining and there is not a cloud in the sky. You can never escape the humidity of the West African coastline, and in the interior, even more so. It is air so heavy that it weighs on your tongue, as if you can open your mouth and take a sip. It is a soup, a big hot pot of soupy air, fetid under the equatorial sun.

Specific, concrete details (underlined once)

Figures of speech (underlined twice)

Point of view: fixed; psychologically somewhat distant

Dominant impression: oppressive humidity

Developing a Descriptive Essay

▶ Getting Started

The subject for a descriptive essay may be any object, place, person, animal, or state of mind that you have observed closely enough or experienced sharply enough to invest with special significance. A chair, a tree, a room, a shopping mall, a passerby on the street, an armadillo, a feeling of fear, a sense of achievement—anything you have a strong impression of can prompt effective description.

Observe your subject directly, if possible, or recall it as completely as you can. Jot down the details that seem to contribute most to the impression you're trying to convey. You needn't write the description of those details yet—that can wait for drafting—but you do want to capture the possibilities in your subject.

You should start to consider the needs and expectations of your readers early on. If the subject is something readers have never seen or felt before, you will need enough objective details to create a complete picture in their minds. A description of a friend, for example, might focus on his distinctive voice and laugh, but readers will also want to know something about his appearance. If the subject is essentially abstract, like an emotion, you will need plenty of details to make it concrete for readers. And if the subject is familiar, as a shopping mall or an old spruce tree on campus probably would be, you will want to skip obvious objective information in favor of fresh observations that will make readers see the subject anew.

▶ Forming a Thesis

When you have your subject, express in a sentence the dominant impression that you want to create for readers. The sentence will help keep you on track while you search for the sensory details that will make your description concrete and vivid. It should evoke a quality or an atmosphere or an effect, as these examples do:

> His fierce anger at the world shows in every word and gesture.
>
> The mall is a thoroughly unnatural place, like a space station in a science-fiction movie.

Such a sentence can serve as the thesis of your essay. You don't necessarily need to state it outright in your draft; sometimes you may prefer to let the details build to a conclusion. But the thesis should hover over the essay nonetheless, governing the selection of every detail and making itself as clear to readers as if it were stated.

▶ Organizing

Though the details of a subject may not occur to you in any particular order, you will need to arrange them so that readers are not confused by rapid shifts in focus. You can give readers a sense of the whole subject in the **introduction** to your essay: objective details of location or size or shape, the incident leading to a state of mind, or the reasons for describing a familiar object. In the introduction you may also want to state your thesis—the dominant impression you will create.

The organization of the body of the essay depends partly on point of view and partly on dominant impression. If you take a moving point of view—say, strolling down a city street—the details will probably arrange themselves naturally. But a fixed point of view, scanning a subject from one position, requires your intervention. When the subject is a landscape, a person, or an object, you'll probably want to use a **spatial organization**: near to far, top to bottom, left to right, or vice versa (see also pp. 36–37). Other subjects, such as a suburban shopping mall, might be better treated in groups of features: shoppers, main concourses, kiosks, insides of stores. Or a description of an emotional state might follow the **chronological sequence** of the event that aroused it (thus overlapping description and narration, the subject of the previous chapter). The specific order itself is not important, as long as there *is* an order that effectively channels readers' attention.

▶ Drafting

The challenge of drafting your description will be bringing the subject to life. Whether it is in front of you or in your mind, you may find it helpful to consider the subject one sense at a time—what you can see, hear, smell, touch, taste. Of course, not all senses are applicable to all subjects; a chair, for instance, may not have a noticeable odor, and you're unlikely to know its taste. But proceeding sense by sense can help you uncover details, such as the smell of a tree or the sound of a person's voice, that you might otherwise overlook.

Examining a subject one sense at a time is also one of the best ways to think of concrete words and figures of speech to represent sensations and feelings. For instance, does *acid* describe the taste of fear? Does an actor's appearance suggest the smell of soap? Does a shopping mall sound like crisp dollar bills? In creating distinct physical sensations for readers, such representations make meaning inescapably clear. (See pp. 53–54 and the Focus box on the next page for more on specific, concrete language and figures of speech.)

▶ Revising and Editing

When you are ready to revise and edit, use the questions below and the Focus box opposite as a guide.

- *Have you created the dominant impression you intended to create?* Check that you have plenty of specific details and that each one helps to pin down one crucial feature of your subject. Cut any irrelevant details that may have crept in. What counts is not the number of details but their quality and the strength of the impression they make.

- *Are your point of view and organization clear and consistent?* Watch for confusing shifts from one vantage point or organizational scheme to another. Watch also for confusing and unnecessary shifts in pronouns, such as from *I* to *one* or vice versa (see p. 47). Any shifts in point of view or organization should be clearly essential for your purpose and for the impression you want to create.

A Note on Thematic Connections

The writers represented in this chapter all set out to explore their reactions to the places they encountered on their travels. They probably didn't decide consciously to write a description, but turned to the method

FOCUS ON CONCRETE AND SPECIFIC LANGUAGE

For readers to imagine your subject, you'll need to use **concrete**, **specific** language that appeals to their experiences and senses. When editing your description, keep a sharp eye out for vague words such as *delicious*, *handsome*, *loud*, and *short* that force readers to create their own impressions or, worse, leave them with no impression at all. Using details that call on readers' sensory experiences, say why delicious or why handsome, how loud or how short. When stuck for a word, conjure up your subject and see it, hear it, touch it, smell it, taste it.

The first sentence below shows a writer's initial attempt to describe something she saw. The edited version that follows it is much more vivid.

VAGUE　　Beautiful, scented wildflowers were in the field.

CONCRETE AND SPECIFIC　　Backlighted by the sun and smelling faintly sweet, an acre of tiny lavender flowers spread away from me.

The writer might also have used **figures of speech** to show what she saw: for instance, describing the field as "a giant's bed covered in a quilt of lavender dots" (a metaphor) or describing the backlighted flowers as "glowing like tiny lavender lamps" (a simile).

Note that *concrete* and *specific* do not mean "fancy": good description does not demand five-dollar words when nickel equivalents are just as informative. The writer who uses *rubiginous* instead of *rusty red* actually says less because fewer readers will understand the less common word, and all readers will sense a writer showing off.

For more on concrete, specific language and figures of speech, see pages 53–54.

intuitively as they chose to record the perceptions of their senses. In a paragraph, Rick Bragg describes the otherworldly aspects of the Alabama highlands (p. 93). In another paragraph, Helene Cooper captures the dense unpleasantness of humidity in West Africa (p. 94). Marta K. Taylor's experience of a family trip through the American desert climaxes in the glory of a lightning storm (next page). William Least Heat-Moon's description of a bridge in Pennsylvania ponders the "beauty of plainness" (p. 102). And Ken Chen's essay about a visit to Hong Kong attempts to express what it is about that city that makes tourists feel dizzy (p. 109).

Memory is the diary that we all carry about with us.   —Oscar Wilde

I might have seen more of America when I was a child if I hadn't had to spend so much of my time protecting my half of the back seat from incursions by my sister.   —Calvin Trillin

Memory is a complicated thing, a relative to truth but not its twin.
                                             —Barbara Kingsolver

JOURNAL RESPONSE   Recall a childhood event such as a family outing, a long car ride, a visit to an unfamiliar place, or an incident in your neighborhood. Imagine yourself back in that earlier time and write down details of what you experienced and how you felt.

Marta K. Taylor

Marta K. Taylor was born in 1970 and raised in Los Angeles. She attended a "huge" public high school there before being accepted into Harvard University. She graduated from Harvard in 1992 with a degree in chemistry and from Harvard Medical School in 1998. She is now a physician in Philadelphia, where she specializes in ear, nose, and throat surgery.

Desert Dance
(Student Essay)

Taylor wrote this description of a nighttime ride when she was a freshman in college taking the required writing course. The essay was published in the 1988–89 edition of *Exposé*, a collection of student writing published by Harvard.

We didn't know there was a rodeo in Flagstaff. All the hotels were filled,   1
except the really expensive ones, so we decided to push on to Winslow that night. Dad must have thought we were all asleep, and so we should have been, too, as it was after one a.m. and we had been driving all day through the wicked California and Arizona desert on the first day of our August Family Trip. The back seat of our old station wagon was down, allowing two eleven-year-old kids to lie almost fully extended and still leaving room for the rusty green Coleman ice-chest which held the packages of pressed turkey breast, the white bread, and the pudding snack-pacs

that Mom had cleverly packed to save on lunch expenses and quiet the inevitable "Are we there yet?" and "How much farther?"

Jon was sprawled out on his back, one arm up and one arm down, reminding me of Gumby[1] or an outline chalked on the sidewalk in a murder mystery. His mouth was wide open and his regular breath rattled deeply in the back of his throat somewhere between his mouth and his nose. Beside the vibration of the wheels and the steady hum of the engine, no other sound disturbed the sacred silence of the desert night.

From where I lay, behind the driver's seat, next to my twin brother on the old green patchwork quilt that smelled like beaches and picnics — salty and a little mildewed — I could see my mother's curly brown head slumped against the side window, her neck bent awkwardly against the seat belt, which seemed the only thing holding her in her seat. Dad, of course, drove — a motionless, soundless, protective paragon of security and strength, making me feel totally safe. The back of his head had never seemed more perfectly framed than by the reflection of the dashboard lights on the windshield; the short, raven-colored wiry hairs that I loved so much caught and played with, like tinsel would, the greenish glow with red and orange accents. The desert sky was starless, clouded.

Every couple of minutes, a big rig would pass us going west. The lights would illuminate my mother's profile for a moment and then the roar of the truck would come and the sudden, the violent sucking rush of air and we would be plunged into darkness again. Time passed so slowly, unnoticeably, as if the whole concept of time were meaningless.

I was careful to make no sound, content to watch the rising and falling of my twin's chest in the dim light and to feel on my cheek the gentle heat of the engine rising up through the floorboards. I lay motionless for a long time before the low rumbling, a larger sound than any eighteen-wheeler, rolled across the open plain. I lifted my head, excited to catch a glimpse of the rain that I, as a child from Los Angeles, seldom saw. A few seconds later, the lightning sliced the night sky all the way across the northern horizon. Like a rapidly growing twig, at least three or four branches, it illuminated the twisted forms of Joshua trees and low-growing cacti. All in silhouette — and only for a flash, though the image stayed many moments before my mind's eye in the following black.

The lightning came again, this time only a formless flash, as if God were taking a photograph of the magnificent desert, and the long, straight road before us — empty and lonely — shone like a dagger. The trees looked

---

[1] An animated clay character that inspired a series of bendable toys in the 1980s. [Editors' note.]

like old men to me now, made motionless by the natural strobe, perhaps to resume their feeble hobble across the sands once the shield of night returned. The light show continued on the horizon though the expected rain never came. The fleeting, gnarled fingers grasped out and were gone; the fireworks flashed and frolicked and faded over and over—danced and jumped, acting out a drama in the quick, jerky movements of a marionette. Still in silence, still in darkness.

I watched the violent, gaudy display over the uninhabited, endless   7
expanse, knowing I was in a state of grace and not knowing if I was dreaming but pretty sure I was awake because of the cramp in my neck and the pain in my elbow from placing too much weight on it for too long.

Meaning

1. What does Taylor mean by "state of grace" in paragraph 7? What associations does this phrase have? To what extent does it capture the dominant impression of this essay?

2. If you do not know the meaning of any of the words below, try to guess it from its context in Taylor's essay. Test your guesses in a dictionary, and then try to use each word in a sentence or two of your own.

paragon (3)	gnarled (6)	marionette (6)
silhouette (5)	frolicked (6)	gaudy (7)
strobe (6)		

Purpose and Audience

1. Why does Taylor open with the sentence "We didn't know there was a rodeo in Flagstaff"? What purposes does the sentence serve?

2. Even readers familiar with the desert may not have had Taylor's experience of it in a nighttime lightning storm. Where does she seem especially careful about describing what she saw? What details surprised you?

Method and Structure

1. What impression or mood is Taylor trying to capture in this essay? How does the precise detail of the description help to convey that mood?

2. Taylor begins her description inside the car (paragraphs 1–5) and then moves out into the landscape (5–7), bringing us back into the car in her final thought. Why does she use such a sequence? Why do you think she devotes roughly equal space to each area?

3. Taylor's description is mainly subjective, invested with her emotions. Point to elements of the description that reveal emotion.

4. **OTHER METHODS** Taylor's description relies in part on **narration** (Chapter 5). How does the narrative strengthen the essay's dominant impression?

Language

1. How does Taylor's **tone** help convey the "state of grace" she feels inside the car? Point out three or four examples of language that establish that mood.

2. Why do you think Taylor titles her essay "Desert Dance"?

3. Notice the words Taylor uses to describe Joshua trees (paragraphs 5–6). If you're already familiar with the plant, how accurate do you find Taylor's description? If you've never seen a Joshua tree, what do you think it looks like, based on Taylor's description? (Look the plant up online or in an encyclopedia to test your impression.)

4. Taylor uses **similes** to make her description vivid and immediate. Find several examples, and comment on their effectiveness.

5. Taylor's last paragraph is one long sentence. Does this long sentence work with or against the content and mood of the paragraph? Why and how?

Writing Topics

1. **JOURNAL TO ESSAY** Using subjective description, expand your journal entry about a childhood event (p. 98) into an essay. Recalling details of sight, sound, touch, smell, and even taste, build a dominant impression for readers of what the experience was like for you.

2. Taylor's essay illustrates her feelings not only about the desert but also about her father, mother, and twin brother. Think of a situation when you were intensely aware of your feelings about another person (relative or friend). Describe the situation and the person in a way that conveys those feelings.

3. **CULTURAL CONSIDERATIONS** Though she had evidently seen the desert before, Taylor had not seen it the way she describes it in "Desert Dance." Write an essay in which you describe your first encounter with something new—for instance, a visit to the home of a friend from a different social or economic background, a visit to a big city or a farm, an unexpected view of your own backyard. Describe what you saw and your responses. How, if at all, did the experience change you?

4. **CONNECTIONS** Both Taylor and Brian Doyle, in "How to Read a Nature Essay" (p. 216), express awe at natural wonders. In a brief essay, analyze how these writers convey their sense of awe so that it is concrete, not vague. Focus on their words and especially on their figures of speech.

Beauty is in the eye of the beholder. —Margaret Wolfe Hungerford

And all the loveliest things there be / Come simply, so it seems to me.
—Edna St. Vincent Millay

The absence of flaw in beauty is itself a flaw. —Havelock Ellis

JOURNAL RESPONSE   Think of a building or public art installation that has been criticized for being ugly, plain, or otherwise ineffective. List some of the reasons critics give for disliking it. Next to each item in that list, explain why others might disagree.

William Least Heat-Moon

One of America's leading travel writers, William Least Heat-Moon consistently applies a journalist's eye for detail and a folksy, understated style to the physical and cultural landscape of rural America. He was born in 1939 in Kansas City, Missouri, to parents of Irish-English and Osage extraction, and in his extensive travels across the United States he has attended closely to the distinctive people and places he has encountered in small towns and little-known byways. After graduating from the University of Missouri at Columbia in 1961, Heat-Moon stayed on to earn a PhD in literature and a BA in photojournalism. He has contributed narratives of his journeys to many periodicals, including the *Atlantic, Esquire*, the *New Yorker*, and the *New York Times*. Heat-Moon is best known, however, for his meticulously researched travelogues: *Blue Highways* (1982), *PrairyErth* (1991), *This Land Is Your Land* (1997), *River-Horse* (1999), and most recently *Roads to Quoz* (2008). When he's not meandering about the country, Heat-Moon makes his home in Columbia, Missouri.

Starrucca Viaduct

In *Roads to Quoz,* Heat-Moon chronicles the sixteen-thousand-mile quest he and his wife, "Q," made in search of American "quoz," an archaic term for "anything strange, incongruous, or peculiar." They found one such instance in a nineteenth-century railroad trestle, lovingly described in this excerpt.

Where is the traveler who has never experienced arriving at a destination only to find anticipation surpassing reality? If the worth of the objective depends on expected awe, then one's disappointment may double. How many times have you heard "Is that it? Is that all of it? Isn't there more?" The gorge wasn't deep enough, the mountain high enough, the famed roller coaster frightful enough.

But for the Starrucca (star-RUCK-ah), the first time I came upon the 1848 masonry railroad bridge, it was unquestionably enough, and the longer I looked, it became more than enough, both at that moment and in recollection: its age, height, length, and solidity, its unembellished grace, its beauty of plainness—qualities residents living in its shadows almost take for granted. If they cherish it, to them it's still just "the stone bridge." 2

The Starrucca Viaduct at Lanesboro, Pennsylvania, circa 1897.

Q and I arrived beneath it one morning when the sun had about fin- 3 ished turning the eastern face of the viaduct into seventeen golden portals. Surrounded by interrupted woodlands, the tall arches of big blocks of bluestone appeared to be a rock wall of massive doorways opening into some country beyond America, a land that finds use and beauty in structures of yore. A few old two-story houses with backyards extending right up to the big stone piers introduced a dollop of reality and a sense of scale. Atop the sharp peaks of their steeply pitched roofs was space to set a seven-story building which would reach only to the level of the viaduct parapets edging the deck carrying the tracks that, when first laid, were a section of the longest railroad (at less than five-hundred miles) in the world.

By the time of completion of the span, thirteen years before com- 4 mencement of the Civil War, the surrounding hills had been heavily timbered off, and the bridge stood better revealed than today. It looked even longer and higher, much in the way a closely cropped head makes ears look bigger. Pieces of opened forest had returned to beautify the valley while somewhat minifying the span, although it could still call to mind a great, multiple-arched, classical Roman aqueduct, especially the one of the first century AD called the Claudian.[1]

A ten-story-high bridge a thousand-feet long is big enough to reach   5 across most American rivers, yet under it, a child could toss a pebble over Starrucca Creek and in many places wade to the opposite bank without wetting more than a shirttail. To say this another way, the span is about forty times longer and a hundred times higher than necessary to get over the stream. Because the Susquehanna River is less than a half-mile west, a visitor can be forgiven for thinking the contractor built the bridge above the wrong waterway. It was, of course, not the creek but its rather deep Appalachian valley that the old Erie Railroad—on a route from the Hudson River to Lake Erie—needed to cross. Even though Starrucca Creek is a fraction of the width of the Mississippi, its valley is deeper than anything the big river flows through in its two-thousand-mile descent.

America has other huge bridges. Only twenty-five miles southwest, to   6 name one, is the great Tunkhannock Creek Viaduct, a splendid 1915 monument of reinforced concrete. But, beyond that, since alterations to the rebuilt High (or Aqueduct) Bridge[2] over the Harlem River north of Manhattan, no longer is there a span anywhere in the country (and few in the world) of such size *and* age as the Starrucca. Designed to support fifty-ton engines of the mid-nineteenth century, its pure and scarcely modified masonry, 160 years later, carried two-hundred-ton locomotives with monstrous loads behind them, and until not long ago might bear two trains at once. The Starrucca Viaduct, in architecture and undeserved anonymity, stands supreme.

Meaning

1. Does Heat-Moon describe purely for the sake of describing, or does he have a thesis he wants to convey? If so, where does he most explicitly state this thesis?

2. What is the dominant impression Heat-Moon creates of the Starrucca Viaduct? Why, according to the author, might people living near the bridge not share his impression?

---

[1] Considered the grandest architectural example of the imperial Roman aqueducts, the Claudian was six miles long, featured arches as high as 109 feet, and carried more than 300 million gallons of water a day. [Editors' note.]

[2] Completed in 1848, the High (Aqueduct) Bridge transported water and pedestrians until the 1960s. The bridge is now under renovation and should be re-opened to foot traffic in 2015. [Editors' note.]

3. Explain what Heat-Moon means by the "beauty of plainness" (paragraph 2). Why would he characterize as *plain* a structure as massive and imposing as the Starrucca Viaduct?

4. Based on their context in the essay, try to guess the meanings of any of the following words that you don't know. Test your guesses in a dictionary, and then try out your knowledge of each word by using it in a sentence of your own.

viaduct (title, 3, 6)	portals (3)	parapets (3)
gorge (1)	yore (3)	timbered (4)
masonry (2)	piers (3)	aqueduct (4)
unembellished (2)	dollop (3)	shirttail (5)

Purpose and Audience

1. Why do you think Heat-Moon felt compelled to write about the Starrucca Viaduct? Consider whether he might have had a dual purpose.

2. What kind of audience is Heat-Moon writing for: architects? historians? tourists? people from Lanesboro, Pennsylvania? someone else? How do you know?

Method and Structure

1. What is the effect of the quotation Heat-Moon includes in the first paragraph?

2. Heat-Moon's description of the bridge relies almost entirely on sight. Why doesn't he involve more of the senses, such as smell or sound? Does their absence weaken or strengthen his description in any way? Why?

3. Why does Heat-Moon include a nineteenth-century illustration of the bridge? How does the photograph differ from and resemble Heat-Moon's description?

4. How does the author organize his description? What is the effect of this organization?

5. **OTHER METHODS** Paragraphs 4 and 6 **compare and contrast** (Chapter 11) the Starrucca Viaduct with other very large stone bridges. How do these comparisons help Heat-Moon make his point?

Language

1. Notice that Heat-Moon's first three paragraphs include several shifts in person, such as *one, you, I* (see p. 47 for an explanation of shifts). Trace these shifts, and consider their effect. Is Heat-Moon writing carelessly, or

does he shift person for a purpose? What do Heat-Moon's shifts contribute to, or take away from, his essay? Explain your answer.

2. What is the effect of the vivid **images** in paragraph 5? In what way does this imagery explain Heat-Moon's enjoyment of the bridge?

3. Heat-Moon uses several figures of speech, such as "It looked even longer and higher, much in the way a closely cropped head makes ears look bigger" (paragraph 4). Find two or three other figures of speech, and analyze how each contributes to Heat-Moon's meaning and helps convey his attitude toward the bridge.

Writing Topics

1. **JOURNAL TO ESSAY**   Using Heat-Moon's essay as a model, write a descriptive essay about something that you consider beautiful but others do not. Your subject could be a building or a work of art, such as the one you described in your journal entry (p. 102), or something else: a person, an animal, a natural phenomenon, an object you hold dear. You may use details from your own experience and observation, information culled from your reading and general knowledge, or, as Heat-Moon does, material from both sources.

2. Reread Heat-Moon's essay, paying particular attention to his use of concrete words and figures of speech that appeal to readers' fancy. Choose the details and language that you find most powerful or suggestive, and write a brief essay explaining how they contribute to Heat-Moon's dominant impression of the Starrucca Viaduct.

3. **RESEARCH**   In a travel magazine or the travel section of a newspaper, read a description of a place you are unfamiliar with. Then write a comparison of that piece and Heat-Moon's essay, explaining which you find more interesting, and why. To what extent do the authors' purposes and audiences account for the differences you perceive in the essays?

4. **CULTURAL CONSIDERATIONS**   In opening his essay with the disappointment of travelers who "arriv[e] at a destination only to find anticipation surpassing reality" (paragraph 1), Heat-Moon implies that people travel to be entertained. Is this a fair assumption? For what other reasons might someone go on a trip? In an essay, use **classification** (Chapter 9) to list as many reasons for traveling as you can think of, considering both the travelers' goals and the effects such journeys may have on them and on the places they visit.

5. **CONNECTIONS**   Both Heat-Moon and Marta Taylor, in "Desert Dance" (p. 98), create a fairy-tale sense of monsters in their essays. Compare the

way Taylor describes the Joshua trees as old men in paragraphs 5 and 6 of her essay to Heat-Moon's suggestions, in paragraphs 3–5 of "Starrucca Viaduct," that the Susquehanna valley is populated by giants. How does each writer combine striking images and original figures of speech to convey a strong sense of unreality? Do you think one author's imagery is more successful than the other's? Why?

Travel in all the four quarters of the earth, yet you will find nothing
anywhere. Whatever there is, is only here.   —Ramakrishna

Perhaps travel cannot prevent bigotry, but by demonstrating that all peoples
cry, laugh, eat, worry, and die, it can introduce the idea that if we try and
understand each other, we may even become friends.   —Maya Angelou

One's destination is never a place but rather a new way of looking at things.
    —Henry Miller

JOURNAL RESPONSE   You've probably ventured beyond your hometown at
least once in your life, perhaps on a family vacation, on a road trip with
friends, or to the town or city where your current school is located. Think
of one such trip and how the place you visited seemed strange to you.
Were you surprised by people's behavior or unfamiliar with local customs?
Could you understand the language or local dialect? Was the landscape
different? In your journal, describe any discomfort you felt. (If you've
never traveled, think of a place you'd like to go and imagine what it might
be like to be there.)

Ken Chen

A writer and a lawyer, Ken Chen has expressed a desire to "engage with people
who, whether they realize it or not, don't consider Asian Americans (or what they
write) as important." He was born in 1979 in San Diego, California, and grew up in
a blended family after his immigrant parents divorced. After graduating from the
University of California at Berkeley in 2001 and Yale University Law School in 2005,
Chen moved to New York City to begin a career in law. In 2008 he took on the role
of executive director for the Asian American Writers' Workshop, a nonprofit literary
organization. He is a regular contributor of articles and essays to a variety of publications, including *Palimpsest, Boston Review of Books*, and *Kyoto Journal*, and in 2009
he won the Yale Series of Younger Poets competition with his poetry collection
Juvenilia, published by Yale University Press in 2010.

City Out of Breath

In the following essay first published in the literary journal *Mānoa* in 2005 and later
selected for *Best American Essays*, Chen relates his dizzying impressions of the distinctly unusual island city of Hong Kong. A colonial outpost under British rule for a
century and a half, the region reverted to Chinese control in 1997, three years

before Chen visited. Hong Kong was then, and is now, governed by communist China under a principle known as "one country, two systems," which grants the city and its environs some autonomy but holds them to mainland standards overall. The quasi-democratic system has in recent years spurred civic unrest and public protests, particularly by university students seeking a more representative electoral process.

So all night, we walk in one direction: up. 1

This is really the only direction you can go in Hong Kong, a direction 2 hinted at by skyscrapers and aspired to by the Hong Kong Stock Exchange. By "we," I mean my father, myself, and our guide—my stepgrandmother-to-be—who somehow possesses both our combined age and our combined speed. Trudging up the stairs behind her, my father and I are already panting. We stop and laugh—really only an excuse to catch our breath—but by the top of the stairs we're bent and sagging, our hands on our knees. And there, at the end of the street, she's waving at us to hurry up, almost as if to fan away whatever remains of our quaint Californian version of walking. When we catch up with her, she says, in what seems like an especially Chinese blend of ridicule and public affection, that we walk too slowly.

If an American city at night is film noir,[1] then Hong Kong is just a 3 camera blur. The residents of Kowloon[2] speed around with the same look on their faces, as if they're irked at their bodies for not being cars. You feel that if you stood still, the city would just rotate past you, as if you have no other choice but motion. Hong Kong accelerates as though located on another, faster-spinning earth. Anyone who has been there knows that time and space can flick off their objectivity and instead pulse and jump, symphonic rather than metronomic. In Hong Kong the world stretches time until time—along with space and language—goes elastic. It's like a Chinese painting in which conflicting perspectives soak through the landscape like radiation. A McDonald's sits next to a vegetable cart tended by a woman who looks about five hundred years old. The all-Chinese police band plays bagpipes and marches in kilts for the St. Patrick's Day parade. Street markets are the opposite of flowers: opening up at night and closing at day. In Hong Kong, all times are contiguous. All times are simultaneous. This essay is an attempt to describe a city that is

---

[1] A style of detective movie characterized by dark shadows (*noir* is French for "black"), moodiness, and intrigue. [Editors' note.]

[2] A densely populated urban center across the harbor from Hong Kong center. [Editors' note.]

itself already a description—Hong Kong is a description of time. This essay is also an experiment in time travel—an artifact of memory from July 2000. Hong Kong is now the same city but a different place. Prosperity—once the city's one-word gloss—is slowly becoming synonymous with Shanghai.[3] "I hear everyone's real depressed over there," I say at dinner to the mother of a friend of mine from Hong Kong. "That they're jealous, with all the jobs heading over to the mainland and all." She chews on a piece of lettuce and says, "Yes, they are jealous. But they have a right to be."

Five years later, we spend the next half-hour taking elevators that   4
lead to stairs that lead to elevators. I don't have any idea where we're going and just follow my father, an immigrant from Taiwan whose Mandarin,[4] I realize, makes him only a third less lost than I am. He's following our guide, who, like Hong Kong itself, is all energy and no conversation. "We're headed for Victoria Peak today," my dad announced this morning. The touristy lookout could be the only spot where Hong Kong can be made comprehensible.

Suddenly our guide stops. Are we lost? This possibility is not sur-   5
prising. It feels like we've been going in spirals, victims of some kind of geographic hoax. Our guide decides to ask for directions in Cantonese.[5] She stops a man with a dark complexion who reminds me of the vendors at the Taipei night market. He has short, wiry hair that resembles a scouring pad and is wearing a security guard's uniform. Chinese—I think—obviously. Probably a migrant from the mainland. "Where is Victoria Peak?" she asks him in Cantonese. The security guard looks at her and says, "Do you speak English?"

Dad and I look at each other. He says, "This is a strange city," and I   6
start laughing, relieved that I'm not the only one who thinks so. We seem to be fumbling through different languages, shifting, testing, trying to find one we can all stand in. A bus rocking through the northern hills speaks to its passengers in Miltonic English: *Do not board or alight whilst bus is in motion.* (Lucifer alights. Buses throttle.[6]) And a week ago in Taiwan, my father had shed the most mundanely engrossing fear of any Chinese

---

[3] The largest city in mainland China. [Editors' note.]

[4] A dialect of Chinese, spoken in the northern and southwestern districts of China and the official language for government, education, and media. [Editors' note.]

[5] A dialect of Chinese, spoken in southern China and the official language (along with English) of Hong Kong. [Editors' note.]

[6] John Milton (1608–74) was an English poet. With "Lucifer," or Satan, Chen alludes to *Paradise Lost*, Milton's epic poem about the biblical Garden of Eden and humanity's fall from grace. [Editors' note.]

immigrant to America: his accent. He became a master of languages, all traces of self-consciousness suddenly gone from his voice. He chatted with taxi drivers and strangers about the drenching humidity or about which restaurants were good, casually code-switching to Taiwanese for jokes, Mandarin for information, and English for translation and one-word exclamations. When we showed up at the desk of the Taipei Hilton, the girls on staff spotted my dad and approached him in nervous English. He paused, got an odd look on his face—the fuzzy expression that Looney Tunes characters have when they're suspended in midair and about to fall—and said in Mandarin: "I'm Chinese!"

Back to searching for Victoria Peak, my father starts to ask the ques- 7 tion in English, but someone interrupts. A Hong Kong yuppie standing thirty feet away muffles his cell phone in his blazer lapel and tells us the answer in rushed Cantonese. Some men in black blazers walk by, and some teens with blond spiky hair walk by, and some middle-aged men with grimy white aprons walk by—mostly Chinese, but otherwise unidentifiable. Indian? Polynesian? British? Hong Kong is an intensely international city. Every street in Kowloon is an intersection, not only of wet-walled alleys and futuristic buildings of glass, but also of the more transparent rays of cultures.

Somehow you are supposed to teach yourself how to comprehend 8 Hong Kong's energy and flashy contradictions: Asian and Western; the encroaching Chinese mainland and the remnants of England; the greasy night markets of sticky-rice tamales and knockoff leather boots that slouch right across from Tiffany, Chanel, and Prada. The only things common to these are the offices sending air-conditioned blasts into the street, a kind of longing for money, and, most important, the sense of storytelling that the city seems to require as a visitor's pass. Hong Kong has a way of turning on your internal monologue. Walking becomes an act of silent storytelling, figuring people out. You feel like you are lost in some prelapsarian novel in which the plot has begun but the characters wait for you to name them. In some time, at some place, we step into an underground Cantonese restaurant and I see a gray-suited, red-tied man act like a parody of the States. American, I say, with an American accent: good-natured smiles, occasionally the slow English dispatched on foreigners and children, and a slightly uncomfortable look, as though he's worried he's outnumbered.

Finally we find Victoria Peak, by which I mean that we find the gon- 9 dola to get us there. We buy tickets and step in, waiting to be hoisted up into the humid nighttime atmosphere. The cab starts moving. At first, nothing in the windows but the ads on the sides of the tunnel, and then suddenly the city. Our gondola windows have become postcards. Hong Kong poses before us, bright, earnestly capitalist, electric, multiplying. A concrete wall blocks the view, and then the city is back again. Under us, a small red house sits on the cuff of the panorama. Light drops out of a pair of shutters, a door or window is open; someone is home. More stone, more wall. We hit the crest, reach our destination: Victoria Peak, the highest spot in Hong Kong and, for a tourist, the best. We have a God's-eye view of the skyline. The buildings shine yellow, white, orange, blue, all reflected in the dark bay waters; giant corporate logos shrink, skyscrapers huddle, and the city glows with a brilliant coolness. My eye seems too small to hold it all in.

We take the bus back. I sit on the top of a double-decker bus, on the left side, in a city where they drive on the left side of the road. As we shake downhill, making acute turns, I begin to regret my seating preference: the wobbly tourists' corner. The bus hits a few branches, careens over double yellow lines, winds downhill. Whipped by full-motion vertigo, I grope for the metal railing, squeezing it as if for juice, and then laugh at my own cowardice. I gasp, then yawn in a slow, measured sort of panic, a civilized form of suffocation. Hong Kong—a city out of breath.   10

After we've been back from Victoria Peak for a few hours, I go to the front desk of the hotel. A Hong Kong–Chinese woman in her mid-twenties looks up the Internet rates for me. She reads the per-minute charges off a small white card, and her voice compresses Mandarin, English, and Cantonese into a linguistic diamond: the Chinese-British accent. There's the Merchant-Ivory[7] sound, the lilt that movies tell us is cultured but that also seems austere and imperial, the way Chinese period films do. Yet the sound is also familiar, humble, and awkward: a Chinese voice wandering inside the English language. The sound of it reminds me of my parents. I can't get enough of it.   11

A few days later, we are ready to leave. Samuel Johnson[8] wrote that when one has tired of London, one has tired of life. But Hong Kong seems denser than any dream an American could have about London. We are suddenly sick of it. Everywhere is crowded: the restaurants at two on a Wednesday afternoon, the train platform every few minutes, the sidewalks wet with people. This is the opposite of loneliness. It is the abundance of people that alienates us.   12

---

[7] A film studio known for producing lavish movies on themes related to the English aristocracy. [Editors' note.]

[8] English poet, essayist, and linguist, 1709–84. [Editors' note.]

My father and I step into an underground Cantonese restaurant, the one with the red-tied American, and the other diners fly by us, blurred, the abstract expressionist's[9] version of people. A man sits across from us, the only person at his big round table. I'm guessing he's Indian. He has a sharp lawn mustache and a black satchel. A businessman from Britain? An engineer out for dinner? The other diners speed by us in streaks. I turn around and see the waiters coming by our table—or maybe just one waiter over and over—to set teacups upright, rip open chopsticks from their packaging, bring dishes, bring towels, even bring blankets when we say we are cold, bring the check. I hear another noise drift over the wheel of our table: the TV at the bar. The news is on: a fire yesterday in Tai O burns down homes in one of the few remaining fishing villages in Hong Kong, leaving seven hundred homeless. No, I'm getting it wrong. I'd read about it on the front page. There was no TV in that restaurant, not even a bar. Hong Kong quivers, not out of fear or sadness, but the way something quivers when our idea of it has changed. The waiters push out of the kitchen as if it's on fire, as if they're scrambling to escape it.   13

But the fire is Hong Kong.   14

Meaning

1. "City Out of Breath" does not include a thesis statement. Does the essay have a main point, and if so, what is it? How can you tell?

2. What is "code-switching" (paragraph 6)? What does the term—and the practice—have to do with Chen's main idea?

3. Identify the sources of Chen's **allusions** to literature, art, and popular culture. What do these references contribute to his meaning?

4. How might Chen's last sentence have multiple meanings?

5. If you're unsure of any of the following words, try to guess what they mean from the context of Chen's essay. Then look them up to see if you were right. Use each word in a sentence of your own.

symphonic (3)	prelapsarian (8)	linguistic (11)
metronomic (3)	parody (8)	austere (11)
contiguous (3)	panorama (9)	imperial (11)
prosperity (3)	acute (10)	alienates (12)
encroaching (8)	vertigo (10)	

---

[9] Abstract expressionism is a school of art characterized by bright colors, hurried brushstrokes, and a deliberate lack of recognizable forms. [Editors' note.]

Purpose and Audience

1. In paragraph 3, Chen writes, "This essay is an attempt to describe a city that is itself already a description—Hong Kong is a description of time." What does he mean?

2. How does Chen make his experience vivid and clear for readers who have never been to Hong Kong?

Method and Structure

1. What dominant impression of the city does Chen create?

2. What point of view does the author take toward his subject?

3. How many of the five senses does Chen appeal to in his description? Find words or phrases that seem especially precise in conveying sensory impressions.

4. **OTHER METHODS**   "City Out of Breath" uses **narration** (Chapter 5) almost as much as it uses description. While Chen relies on chronological order for most of the essay, in paragraphs 3 and 6 he flashes back to discussions and experiences in other places. What do these previous episodes contribute to his meaning and purpose?

Language

1. Note Chen's frequent use of the first person (*I* and *we*) and of the present tense. What does he achieve with this point of view?

2. A poet, Chen uses figures of speech to add depth to his descriptions. Locate two or three examples that you find especially striking, and explain their effect.

Writing Topics

1. **JOURNAL TO ESSAY**   Expanding on your journal entry (p. 108), write a descriptive essay about the discomfort you felt when you first visited a new place. Consider not only what made you uncomfortable but also why you reacted the way you did. You may, if you wish, use your essay as an opportunity to contemplate the broader significance of your experience.

2. Think of a place to which you feel a special connection. The place can be urban or suburban or rural, and it need not be far away. In an essay, describe the place for readers who are completely unfamiliar with it and who may be skeptical about your enthusiasm for it. Use concrete, specific details and, if appropriate, figures of speech to show clearly why you value the place.

3. **CULTURAL CONSIDERATIONS**   Through most of his essay, Chen sees the other people in Hong Kong as foreign, so different and strange that interacting with them makes him laugh nervously. But as an American visiting the Chinese city, Chen is the foreigner in this situation. Imagine any of the scenarios he describes from the point of view of one of the Hong Kong residents, businesspeople, or workers he encounters. How might they have perceived him?

4. **CONNECTIONS**   In "The Fake Trade" (p. 317), Dana Thomas also shares her impressions of Hong Kong, but she writes from the perspective of a reporter investigating the production and sale of counterfeit luxury goods such as those Chen briefly mentions in paragraph 8 of "City Out of Breath." Compare these two writers' portrayals of the same city. How are their descriptions similar? What perceptions seem unique to each? How might each writer's purpose for writing influence his or her emphasis and choice of details?

▶

DESCRIPTION

Select one of the following topics, or any other topic they suggest, for an essay developed by description. Be sure to choose a topic you care about so that description is a means of communicating an idea, not an end in itself.

People

1. An exceptionally neat or messy person
2. A person whose appearance and mannerisms are at odds with his or her real self
3. An annoying neighbor
4. A person you admire or respect
5. A person who intimidates you (teacher, salesperson, doctor, police officer, fellow student)

Places and Scenes

6. A department store, yard sale, or flea market
7. A frightening place
8. A prison cell, police station, or courtroom
9. Your home or workplace
10. A neighborhood devastated by foreclosures
11. A site of environmental destruction
12. The scene at a concert

Animals and Objects

13. Birds at a feeder
14. A work of art
15. An animal in a zoo, wildlife sanctuary, or rescue shelter
16. A prized possession

Sensations

17. The look and taste of a favorite or detested food
18. Waiting for important news
19. Being freed of some restraint
20. Sneezing
21. Writing
22. Skating, running, bodysurfing, skydiving, or some other activity
23. Extreme hunger, thirst, cold, heat, or fatigue

WRITING ABOUT THE THEME

EXPERIENCING NEW PLACES

1. Although we tend to think of travel as a form of entertainment or relaxation, some of the writers in this chapter recognize that unfamiliar places can be difficult to come to terms with. Ken Chen's description of Hong Kong (p. 109) and Helene Cooper's description of West African humidity (p. 94) are most notable in this respect, but even William Least Heat-Moon's examination of an oversized bridge (p. 102) emphasizes the unsettling effects of its weirdness, and Rick Bragg's experience of the Alabama highlands (p. 93) takes on a sense of unreality. Write a descriptive essay about a place that is special to you, emphasizing its strangeness rather than its beauty.

2. All of the writers in this chapter demonstrate strong feelings for the place, thing, or phenomenon they describe, but the writers vary considerably in the ways they express their feelings. For example, Ken Chen's own discomfort in Hong Kong colors all of his perceptions, whereas Marta Taylor's description of an electrical storm (p. 98) mixes serenity and awe. Write an essay analyzing the tone of these and the three other selections in this chapter: Helene Cooper's and Rick Bragg's paragraphs on the lands of their childhoods and William Least Heat-Moon's essay about the Starrucca Viaduct. Discuss which pieces you find most effective and why.

3. Each essay writer in this chapter vividly describes a specific place or thing that represents some larger, abstract concept: Marta Taylor's desert lightning represents the awesomeness of nature, Ken Chen's Hong Kong represents cultural dislocation, and William Least Heat-Moon's bridge represents the beauty of simplicity. Think of a specific, tangible place or thing in your life that represents some larger, abstract idea and write a descriptive essay exploring this relationship.

7

EXAMPLE

▶

USING LANGUAGE

An **example** represents a general group or an abstract concept or quality. Quentin Tarantino is an example from the group of movie directors. A friend's texting at two in the morning is an example of her inconsiderateness—or desperation. We habitually use examples to bring broad ideas down to specifics so that others will take an interest in them and understand them. You might use examples to entertain friends with the idea that you're accident prone, to persuade family members that a sibling is showing self-destructive behavior that requires intervention, to demonstrate to voters that your local fire department deserves a budget increase, or to convince your employer that competing companies' benefits packages are more generous. Examples are so central to human communication, in fact, that you will find them in nearly everything you read and use them in nearly everything you write.

Reading Examples

The chief purpose of examples is to make the general specific and the abstract concrete. Since these operations are among the most basic in writing, it is easy to see why illustration or exemplification (the use of example) is among the most common methods of writing. Examples appear frequently in essays developed by other methods. In fact, as diverse as they are, all the essays in this book employ examples for clarity, support, and liveliness. If the writers had not used examples, we might have only a vague sense of their meaning, or worse, we might supply mistaken meanings from our own experiences.

While nearly indispensable in any kind of writing, exemplification may also serve as the dominant method of developing an essay. When a writer's primary goal is to convince readers of the truth of a general statement—whether a personal observation or a controversial assertion—using examples is a natural choice. Any of the following **generalizations**, for instance, might form the central assertion of an essay developed by example:

- *Generalizations about trends:* "E-books are forcing the publishing industry to rethink the way it does business."
- *Generalizations about events:* "Some fans at the championship game were more competitive than the players."
- *Generalizations about institutions:* "A mental hospital is no place for the mentally ill."
- *Generalizations about behaviors:* "The personalities of parents are sometimes visited on their children."
- *Generalizations about rituals:* "A funeral benefits the deceased person's family and friends."

How many examples are necessary to support a generalization? That depends on a writer's subject, purpose, and intended audience. Two basic patterns are possible:

- *A single extended example* of several paragraphs or several pages fills in needed background and gives the reader a complete view of the subject from one angle. For instance, the purpose of a funeral might be made clear with a narrative and descriptive account of a particular funeral, the family and friends who attended it, and the benefits they derived from it.
- *Multiple examples*, from a few to dozens, illustrate the range covered by the generalization. The competitiveness of a team's fans might be captured with three or four examples. But supporting the generalization about mental hospitals might demand many examples of patients whose illnesses worsened in the hospital or (from a different angle) many examples of hospital practices that actually harmed patients.

Sometimes a generalization merits support from both an extended example and several briefer examples, a combination that provides depth along with range. For instance, half the essay on mental hospitals might be devoted to one patient's experiences, and the other half to brief summaries of other patients' experiences.

When you read essays developed by illustration and exemplification, pay attention to how writers use examples to develop a point. Rarely will a simple list do an idea justice. Effective writers, as you will see, not only provide examples but also explain how those examples support their ideas.

Analyzing Examples in Paragraphs

Deborah Tannen (born 1945), a respected scholar with a knack for popular writing, is widely known for her prolific work on how people communicate. The following paragraph is from the book *Talking from 9 to 5* (1994), Tannen's best-selling exploration of gender differences in workplace communication.

Women are often told they apologize too much. The reason they're told to stop doing it is that, to many men, apologizing seems synonymous with putting oneself down. <u>But there are many times when "I'm sorry" isn't self-deprecating, or even an apology; it's an automatic way of keeping both speakers on an equal footing.</u> For example, a well-known columnist once interviewed me and gave me her phone number in case I needed to call her back. I misplaced the number and had to go through the newspaper's main switchboard. When our conversation was winding down and we'd both made ending-type remarks, I added, "Oh, I almost forgot—I lost your direct number, can I get it again?" "Oh, I'm sorry," she came back instantly, even though she had done nothing wrong and *I* was the one who'd lost the number. But I understood she wasn't really apologizing; she was just automatically reassuring me she had no intention of denying me her number.

Generalization and topic sentence (underlined)

Single detailed example

William Lutz (born 1940) is an expert on doublespeak, which he defines as "language that conceals or manipulates thought. It makes the bad seem good, the negative appear positive, the unpleasant appear attractive or at least tolerable." In this paragraph from his book *Doublespeak* (1989), Lutz illustrates one use of this deceptive language.

Because it avoids or shifts responsibility, double-speak is particularly effective in explaining or at least glossing over accidents. An air force colonel in charge of safety wrote in a letter that rocket boosters weighing more than 300,000 pounds "have an explosive force upon surface impact that is sufficient to exceed the accepted overpressure threshold of physiological damage for exposed personnel." In English: if a 300,000-pound booster rocket falls on you, you probably won't survive. In 1985 three American soldiers were killed and sixteen were injured when the first stage of a Pershing II missile they were unloading suddenly ignited. There was no explosion, said Major Michael Griffen, but rather "an unplanned rapid ignition of solid fuel."

> Generalization and topic sentence (underlined)
>
> Two examples

Developing an Essay by Example

▶ Getting Started

You need examples whenever your experiences, observations, or reading lead you to make a general statement: the examples give readers evidence for the statement so that they see its truth. An appropriate subject for an example paper is likely to be a general idea you have formed about people, things, the media, or any other feature of your life. Say, for instance, that you have noticed while watching television that many scripted programs aimed at teenagers deal with sensitive topics such as drug abuse, domestic violence, or chronic illness. There is your subject: teen dramas that address controversial social issues.

After choosing a subject, you should make a list of all the pertinent examples that occur to you. This stage may take some thought and even some further reading or observation. When you're making this list, focus on identifying as many examples as you can, but keep your intended readers at the front of your mind: what do they already know about your subject, and what do they need to know in order to accept your view of it?

▶ Forming a Thesis

Having several examples of a subject is a good starting place, but you will also need a thesis that ties the examples together and gives them a point.

A clear thesis is crucial for an example paper because without it readers can only guess what your illustrations are intended to show.

To move from a general subject toward a workable thesis, try making a generalization based on what you know of individual examples:

> Some teen dramas do a surprisingly good job of explaining difficult social issues.
>
> Some teen dramas trivialize difficult social issues in their quest for ratings.

Either of these statements could serve as the thesis of an essay, the point you want readers to take away from your examples.

Avoid the temptation to start with a broad statement and then try to drum up a few examples to prove it. A thesis such as "Teenagers do poorly in school because they watch too much television" would require factual support gained from research. If your brother performs poorly in school and you blame his television habits, narrow your thesis so that it accurately reflects your evidence—perhaps "For my brother, the more time spent watching television the poorer the grades."

After arriving at your thesis, you should narrow your list of examples down to those that are most pertinent, adding new examples as necessary to persuade readers of your point. For instance, in illustrating the social value of teen dramas for readers who believe television is worthless or even harmful, you might concentrate on the programs or individual episodes that are most relevant to readers' lives, providing enough detail about each to make readers see the relevance.

▶ Organizing

Most example essays open with an **introduction** that engages readers' attention and gives them some context to relate to. You might begin the paper on teen dramas, for instance, by briefly narrating the plot of one episode. The opening should lead into your thesis sentence so that readers know what to expect from the rest of the essay.

Organizing the body of the essay may not be difficult if you use a single example, for the example itself may suggest a distinct method of development (such as narration) and thus an arrangement. But an essay using multiple examples usually requires close attention to arrangement so that readers experience not a list but a pattern. Consider these guidelines:

- *With a limited number of examples*—say, four or five—use a **climactic** organization, arranging the examples in order of increasing importance, interest, or complexity. Then the strongest and most detailed example provides a dramatic finish.

■ *With many examples*—ten or more—find some likenesses among them that will allow you to treat them in groups. For instance, instead of covering fourteen teen dramas in a shapeless list, you might group them by subject into shows dealing with family relations, those dealing with illness, and the like. (This is the method of **classification**, discussed in Chapter 9.) Covering each group in a separate paragraph or two avoids the awkward string of choppy paragraphs that might result from covering each example independently. And arranging the groups themselves in order of increasing interest or importance further structures your presentation.

To conclude your essay, you may want to summarize by elaborating on the generalization of your thesis now that you have supported it. But the essay may not require a **conclusion** at all if you believe your final example emphasizes your point and provides a strong finish.

▶ Drafting

While you draft your essay, remember that your examples must be plentiful and specific enough to support your generalization. If you use fifteen different examples, their range should allow you to treat each one briefly, in one or two sentences. But if you use only three examples, say, you will have to describe each one in sufficient detail to make up for their small number. And if you use only a single example, you must be as specific as possible so that readers see clearly how it illustrates your generalization.

▶ Revising and Editing

To be sure you've met the expectations that most readers hold for examples, revise and edit your draft by considering the following questions and the information in the Focus box on the next page.

■ *Is your generalization fully supported by your examples?* If not, you may need to narrow your thesis statement or add more evidence.

■ *Are all examples, or parts of a single example, obviously relevant to your generalization?* Be careful not to get sidetracked by interesting but unrelated information.

■ *Are the examples specific?* Examples bring a generalization down to earth only if they are well detailed. For an essay on the social value of teen dramas, for instance, simply naming programs and their subjects would not demonstrate their value. Each drama would need a plot or character summary that shows how the program illustrates the generalization.

■ *Do the examples, or the parts of a single example, cover all the territory mapped out by your generalization?* To support your generalization, you need to present a range of instances that fairly represents the whole. An essay would be misleading if it failed to acknowledge that not *all* teen dramas have social value. It would also be misleading if it presented several shows as representative examples of socially valuable teen programming when in fact they were the *only* instances.

FOCUS ON SENTENCE VARIETY

While accumulating examples and detailing them during drafting — both essential tasks for a successful essay — you may find yourself writing strings of similar sentences:

> UNVARIED   One example of a teen drama that deals with chronic illness is *Rockingham Place*. Another example is *The Beating Heart*. Another is *Tree of Life*. These three shows treat misunderstood or little-known diseases in a way that increases the viewer's sympathy and understanding. The characters in *Rockingham Place* include a little boy who suffers from cystic fibrosis. *The Beating Heart* features a mother of four who is weakening from multiple sclerosis. *Tree of Life* deals with brothers who are both struggling with muscular dystrophy. All these dramas show complex, struggling human beings caught blamelessly in desperate circumstances.

The writer of this paragraph was clearly pushing to add examples and to expand them, but the passage needs editing so that the writer's labor isn't so obvious and the sentences are more varied and interesting:

> VARIED   Three teen dramas dealing with chronic illness are *Rockingham Place*, *The Beating Heart*, and *Tree of Life*. In these shows people with little-known or misunderstood diseases become subjects for the viewer's sympathy and understanding. A little boy suffering from cystic fibrosis, a mother weakening from multiple sclerosis, a pair of brothers coping with muscular dystrophy — these complex, struggling human beings are caught blamelessly in desperate circumstances.

As you review your draft, be alert to repetitive sentence structures and look for opportunities to change them: try coordinating and subordinating, varying the beginnings and endings of sentences, shortening some and lengthening others. For more on sentence variety, turn to pages 51–52.

A Note on Thematic Connections

The authors represented in this chapter all have something to say about language—how we use it, abuse it, or change as a result of it. Their ideas probably came to them through examples as they read, talked, and listened, so naturally they use examples to demonstrate those ideas. In one paragraph, Deborah Tannen draws on a single example to show the layers of meaning a simple phrase can convey (p. 120). In the other, William Lutz uses two examples to illustrate how evasive doublespeak can be (p. 121). Kim Kessler's essay (next page) considers the emergence of the expression *blah blah blah* to end sentences. In another essay, David Sedaris uses humor to explore the difficulties of learning a second language (p. 131). And Perri Klass's essay grapples with why doctors use peculiar and often cruel jargon and contemplates how it affects them (p. 139).

Sometimes speech is no more than a device for saying nothing.

—Simone de Beauvoir

Continual eloquence is tedious.

—Blaise Pascal

One way of looking at speech is to say it is a constant stratagem to cover nakedness.

—Harold Pinter

JOURNAL RESPONSE   Pick a conversation filler that you have noticed, such as *you know* or *I mean*. Why do people use these fillers? Do you use them yourself? Write a journal entry reacting to these words and phrases.

Kim Kessler

Kimberly Anne Kessler was born in 1975 in New York City and grew up mostly in Greenwich, Connecticut. A political science major, she graduated from Brown University in 1997 and earned a law degree from New York University in 2003. Kessler worked as an attorney for several years and is now a director of the Resnick Program for Food Law and Policy at the UCLA School of Law.

Blah Blah Blah
(Student Essay)

Kessler published this essay in the *Brown Daily Herald* in 1996 after noticing, she says, that she and her friends "had basically stopped talking to each other in complete sentences." With ample examples and analysis, Kessler questions the uses of the title expression in place of words that the speaker, for some reason, doesn't want to utter.

"So he says to me, 'Well it just happened. I was this and that and blah blah blah.'"   1

That's an actual quote. That was the statement one of my oh-so-articulate friends made as an explanation of a certain situation. The thing about it is that I figured I knew exactly what he meant. The more important thing about it, the thing that makes this quote notable, is that I feel as though I've been hearing it all over the place these days. It has come to my attention in the last few weeks, maybe even in the last couple of months, that it is common for peers of mine to finish their sentences with "blah blah blah." Some people have their own less common versions of   2 the phrase—e.g., "yadda yadda" or "etc., etc."—but it all amounts to the same thing. Rather than completing a thought or detailing an explanation, sentences simply fade away into a symbol of generic rhetoric.

I'm not quite sure what I think about this recently noticed phenomenon quite yet. What does it mean that I can say "blah blah blah" to you and you consider it to be an acceptable statement? 3

I guess that there are a couple of good reasons for why this is going on. First, it's a commentary on just how trite so many of those conversations we spend our time having really are. Using the phrase is a simple acknowledgment of the fact that what is about to be said has been said so many times before that it is pretty much an exercise in redundancy to say it again. Some folks "blah blah blah" me (yeah, it's a verb) when they're using the phrase as a shortcut; they are eager to get to the part of their story that *does* distinguish it from all the other stories out there. Other times people "blah blah blah" me when they think that it is not worth their time or their energy to actually recount a story for my sake. In this case I feel dismissed, rejected. You can get "blah blahed" (past tense) in an inclusive way, too. In this scenario the "blah blah" construction is used to refer to something that both you and the speaker understand. This reflects a certain intimacy between the speaker and the listener, an intimacy that transcends the need for the English language that strangers would need in order to communicate. 4

I have discovered quite a different use for the phrase. I have found that because "blah blah" is an accepted part of our everyday discourse, and because people assume that with this phrase what you are referring to is indeed the same thing that they are thinking of, it is very easy to use this construction to lie. Well, maybe "lie" isn't the best word. It's usually more of a cover-up than a lie. I'll give an example to demonstrate my meaning here. 5

I'm walking across campus at some time on some Monday. I get accosted by some acquaintance and have the gratuitous "How was your weekend?" conversation. He's asking me about my Saturday night. I reply: "It was good, you know . . . went out to dinner then to a party, blah blah blah." The acquaintance smiles and nods and then goes merrily on his way, his head filled with thoughts of me and my normal Saturday night. What he will never know (as long as he's not reading this) is that I ended that night walking many, many blocks home alone in the rain without a coat, carrying on my back, of all things, a trombone. He also does not know about the mini-breakdown and moment of personal evaluation that my lonely, wet, trombone-carrying state caused me to have under a streetlight in the middle of one of those many blocks. He does not know 6 these things because he has constructed his own end to my night to fill in for my "blah blah blah." (I hope you can all handle that open display of vulnerability. It's not very often that I share like that.)

"Blah blah blah" implies the typical. I tend to use it in place of the atypical, usually the atypical of the most embarrassing sort. For me, it's a cop-out. The accepted use of the phrase has allowed me a refuge, a wall of meaningless words with which to protect myself. I'm definitely abusing the term. 7

Maybe there are a couple of you readers who would want to interject here and remind me that not everybody tells the *whole* truth *all* of the time. (I'd guess that there would even be a hint of sarcasm in your voice as you said this to me.) Well, I realize that. I just feel the slightest twinge of guilt because my withholding of the truth has a deceptive element to it. 8

But, hey, maybe I'm not the only one. Maybe everyone is manipulating the phrase "blah blah blah." What if none of us really knows what anyone else is talking about anymore? What are the repercussions of this fill-in-the-blank type of conversation? I feel myself slipping into that very annoying and much too often frequented realm of the overly analytical, so I'm going to stop myself. To those of you who are concerned about this "blah blah" thing I am going to offer the most reasonable solution that I know of—put on your Walkman[1] and avoid it all. The logic here is that the more time you spend with your Walkman on, the less time you spend having those aforementioned gratuitous conversations, and therefore the fewer "blah blahs" you'll have to deal with. 9

Meaning

1. How does Kessler's use of the phrase *blah blah blah* differ from the normal use, and why does her use bother her?

2. What is the "symbol of generic rhetoric" referred to in paragraph 2? What does Kessler mean by these words? (Consult a dictionary if you're not sure.) Does this sentence state Kessler's main idea? Why, or why not?

3. Try to guess the meanings of any of the following words you are unsure of, based on their context in Kessler's essay. Look the words up in a dictionary to test your guesses, and then use each word in a sentence of your own.

articulate (2)	transcends (4)	atypical (7)
phenomenon (3)	discourse (5)	interject (8)
trite (4)	accosted (6)	repercussions (9)
redundancy (4)	gratuitous (6)	

---

[1] Portable audiocassette player. [Editors' note.]

Purpose and Audience

1. What seems to be Kessler's purpose in this essay: to explain the various ways the phrase *blah blah blah* can be used? to argue against the overuse of the phrase? to do something else?

2. Whom did Kessler assume as her audience? (Look back at the note on the essay, p. 126, if you're not sure.) How do her subject, evidence, and tone reflect her assumptions?

Method and Structure

1. Why do you think Kessler chose to examine this linguistic phenomenon through examples? How do examples help her achieve her purpose in a way that another method might not? (Hint: What is lost when you skip from paragraph 5 to 7?)

2. What generalizations do the examples in paragraphs 4 and 6 support?

3. Which paragraphs fall into the introduction, body, and conclusion of Kessler's essay? What function does each part serve?

4. OTHER METHODS   Kessler's essay attempts to define the indefinable, an expression that would seem to have no meaning. What meanings does she find for *blah blah blah*? How does this use of **definition** (Chapter 12) help Kessler achieve her purpose?

Language

1. How would you characterize Kessler's tone: serious? light? a mix of both? How does this tone reflect her intended audience and her attitude toward her subject?

2. Point out instances of **irony** in the essay.

3. What does Kessler achieve by addressing the reader directly throughout the essay?

Writing Topics

1. JOURNAL TO ESSAY   Reread your journal entry (p. 126), and then listen carefully for the conversation filler you've selected in the speech of your friends, the talk you observe on campus or in online forums, and the dialogue in television shows and movies you watch. Form a generalization about the way the filler functions and the purpose or purposes it serves, and then, in an essay, support that generalization with plenty of examples.

2. Write an essay expressing your opinion of Kessler's piece. For instance, how did you react to her complaint that most of her conversations with her peers were "trite" or "gratuitous"? Do you think she is too critical of her peers? Agree or disagree with Kessler, supporting your opinion with your own examples.

3. **CULTURAL CONSIDERATIONS**   Although Kessler never explicitly says so, the phenomenon she writes about seems to apply mainly to people of her own generation. Think of an expression that you use when among a group to which you belong (family, ethnic group, others of your own gender, and so on) but feel uncomfortable using outside the group. Write an essay explaining and illustrating the uses of the expression in the group and the problems you experience using it elsewhere.

4. **CONNECTIONS**   To what extent, if at all, does *blah blah blah* resemble the jargon of the medical profession, as discussed by Perri Klass in "She's Your Basic LOL in NAD" (p. 139)? After reading Klass's essay, list the purposes she believes medical jargon serves. Does *blah blah blah* serve similar or different purposes for Kessler and her peers? Spell your answer out in an essay, drawing on Klass's and Kessler's essays as well as your own experience for evidence.

I always thought the saddest feeling in life is when you're dancing in a really joyful way, and then you hit your head on something.   —Lena Dunham

It is impossible to live without failing at something, unless you live so cautiously that you might as well not have lived at all.   —J. K. Rowling

That which does not kill us makes us stronger.   —Friedrich Nietzsche

JOURNAL RESPONSE   We've all suffered embarrassing moments. Think of a time when you felt humiliated or certain to fail. What happened? Is the embarrassment still as painful for you as it felt at the time? Reflect on the situation in your journal.

David Sedaris

David Sedaris's hilarious yet often touching autobiographical essays have earned him both popular and critical acclaim; in 2001 he received the Thurber Prize for American Humor and was named Humorist of the Year by *Time* magazine. Born in 1957, Sedaris grew up in North Carolina and attended the School of the Art Institute of Chicago, where he taught writing for several years before moving to New York City. Working odd jobs during the day and writing about them at night, Sedaris catapulted to near-overnight success in 1993 after reading on National Public Radio a piece about working as a department-store Christmas elf. Since then, he has been a frequent contributor to the *New Yorker*, *Esquire*, and public radio's *Morning Edition* and *This American Life*. In 1994 Sedaris published his first collection of essays, *Barrel Fever*, followed by *Naked* (1996), *Holidays on Ice* (1997), *Me Talk Pretty One Day* (2000), *Dress Your Family in Corduroy and Denim* (2004), *When You Are Engulfed in Flames* (2008), and *Let's Explore Diabetes with Owls* (2013). He is also the author of *Squirrel Seeks Chipmunk* (2010), a series of imaginative animal fables. Currently living in the English countryside, Sedaris has also resided in Paris and rural France.

Me Talk Pretty One Day

In this title essay from *Me Talk Pretty One Day*, Sedaris launches his trademark wit at a favorite target: the French language. Learning to speak a new language, he shows, involves a mixture of humiliations and triumphs.

At the age of forty-one, I am returning to school and have to think of   1
myself as what my French textbook calls "a true debutant." After paying

my tuition, I was issued a student ID, which allows me a discounted entry fee at movie theaters, puppet shows, and Festyland, a far-flung amusement park that advertises with billboards picturing a cartoon stegosaurus sitting in a canoe and eating what appears to be a ham sandwich.

I've moved to Paris with hopes of learning the language. My school is   2 an easy ten-minute walk from my apartment, and on the first day of class I arrived early, watching as the returning students greeted one another in the school lobby. Vacations were recounted, and questions were raised concerning mutual friends with names like Kang and Vlatnya. Regardless of their nationalities, everyone spoke in what sounded to me like excellent French. Some accents were better than others, but the students exhibited an ease and confidence I found intimidating. As an added discomfort, they were all young, attractive, and well dressed, causing me to feel not unlike Pa Kettle[1] trapped backstage after a fashion show.

The first day of class was nerve-racking because I knew I'd be expected   3 to perform. That's the way they do it here — it's everybody into the language pool, sink or swim. The teacher marched in, deeply tanned from a recent vacation, and proceeded to rattle off a series of administrative announcements. I've spent quite a few summers in Normandy, and I took a month-long French class before leaving New York. I'm not completely in the dark, yet I understood only half of what this woman was saying.

"If you have not *meimslsxp* or *lgpdmurct* by this time, then you should   4 not be in this room. Has everyone *apzkiubjxow*? Everyone? Good, we shall begin." She spread out her lesson plan and sighed, saying, "All right, then, who knows the alphabet?"

It was startling because (a) I hadn't been asked that question in a   5 while and (b) I realized, while laughing, that I myself did *not* know the alphabet. They're the same letters, but in France they're pronounced differently. I knew the shape of the alphabet but had no idea what it actually sounded like.

"Ahh." The teacher went to the board and sketched the letter *a*. "Do   6 we have anyone in the room whose first name commences with an *ahh*?"

Two Polish Annas raised their hands, and the teacher instructed them   7 to present themselves by stating their names, nationalities, occupations, and a brief list of things they liked and disliked in this world. The first Anna hailed from an industrial town outside of Warsaw and had front teeth the size of tombstones. She worked as a seamstress, enjoyed quiet times with friends, and hated the mosquito.

---

[1] A fictional hillbilly character featured in a series of books and movies in the 1940s and '50s. [Editors' note.]

"Oh, really," the teacher said. "How very interesting. I thought that 8 everyone loved the mosquito, but here, in front of all the world, you claim to detest him. How is it that we've been blessed with someone as unique and original as you? Tell us, please."

The seamstress did not understand what was being said but knew that 9 this was an occasion for shame. Her rabbity mouth huffed for breath, and she stared down at her lap as though the appropriate comeback were stitched somewhere alongside the zipper of her slacks.

The second Anna learned from the first and claimed to love sunshine 10 and detest lies. It sounded like a translation of one of those Playmate of the Month data sheets, the answers always written in the same loopy handwriting: "Turn-ons: Mom's famous five-alarm chili! Turnoffs: insecurity and guys who come on too strong!!!!"

The two Polish Annas surely had clear notions of what they loved 11 and hated, but like the rest of us, they were limited in terms of vocabulary, and this made them appear less than sophisticated. The teacher forged on, and we learned that Carlos, the Argentine bandonion[2] player, loved wine, music, and, in his words, "making sex with the womens of the world." Next came a beautiful young Yugoslav[3] who identified herself as an optimist, saying that she loved everything that life had to offer.

The teacher licked her lips, revealing a hint of the saucebox we would 12 later come to know. She crouched low for her attack, placed her hands on the young woman's desk, and leaned close, saying, "Oh yeah? And do you love your little war?"

While the optimist struggled to defend herself, I scrambled to think 13 of an answer to what had obviously become a trick question. How often is one asked what he loves in this world? More to the point, how often is one asked and then publicly ridiculed for his answer? I recalled my mother, flushed with wine, pounding the tabletop late one night, saying, "Love? I love a good steak cooked rare. I love my cat, and I love . . ." My sisters and I leaned forward, waiting to hear our names. "Tums," our mother said. "I love Tums."

The teacher killed some time accusing the Yugoslavian girl of master- 14 minding a program of genocide, and I jotted frantic notes in the margins of my pad. While I can honestly say that I love leafing through medical

---

[2] A South American musical instrument, similar to a small accordion. [Editors' note.]

[3] A native of Yugoslavia, a former communist country in Eastern Europe divided after several wars into Bosnia and Herzegovina, Croatia, Kosovo, Macedonia, Montenegro, Serbia, and Slovenia. [Editors' note.]

textbooks devoted to severe dermatological conditions, the hobby is beyond the reach of my French vocabulary, and acting it out would only have invited controversy.

When called upon, I delivered an effortless list of things that I detest: blood sausage, intestinal pâtés, brain pudding. I'd learned these words the hard way. Having given it some thought, I then declared my love for IBM typewriters, the French word for *bruise*, and my electric floor waxer. It was a short list, but still I managed to mispronounce *IBM* and assign the wrong gender to both the floor waxer and the typewriter.[4] The teacher's reaction led me to believe that these mistakes were capital crimes in the country of France. 15

"Were you always this *palicmkrexis*?" she asked. "Even a *fiuscrzsa tici-welmun* knows that a typewriter is feminine." 16

I absorbed as much of her abuse as I could understand, thinking— but not saying—that I find it ridiculous to assign a gender to an inani-mate object incapable of disrobing and making an occasional fool of itself. Why refer to Lady Crack Pipe or Good Sir Dishrag when these things could never live up to all that their sex implied? 17

The teacher proceeded to belittle everyone from German Eva, who hated laziness, to Japanese Yukari, who loved paintbrushes and soap. Italian, Thai, Dutch, Korean, and Chinese—we all left class foolishly believing that the worst was over. She'd shaken us up a little, but surely that was just an act designed to weed out the deadweight. We didn't know it then, but the com-ing months would teach us what it was like to spend time in the presence of a wild animal, something completely unpredictable. Her temperament was not based on a series of good and bad days but, rather, good and bad moments. We soon learned to dodge chalk and protect our heads and stom-achs whenever she approached us with a question. She hadn't yet punched anyone, but it seemed wise to protect ourselves against the inevitable. 18

Though we were forbidden to speak anything but French, the teacher would occasionally use us to practice any of her five fluent languages. 19

"I hate you," she said to me one afternoon. Her English was flawless. "I really, really hate you." Call me sensitive, but I couldn't help but take it personally. 20

After being singled out as a lazy *kfdtinvfm*, I took to spending four hours a night on my homework, putting in even more time whenever we 21

---

[4]In French, nouns are considered either male or female. Masculine nouns are preceded by the article *le*; feminine nouns are preceded by *la*. As is the case with English pronouns and antecedents, French nouns must agree in gender with the pronouns and adjectives used to describe them. [Editors' note.]

were assigned an essay. I suppose I could have gotten by with less, but I was determined to create some sort of identity for myself: David the hard worker, David the cut-up. We'd have one of those "complete this sentence" exercises, and I'd fool with the thing for hours, invariably settling on something like "A quick run around the lake? I'd love to! Just give me a moment while I strap on my wooden leg." The teacher, through word and action, conveyed the message that if this was my idea of an identity, she wanted nothing to do with it.

My fear and discomfort crept beyond the borders of the classroom   22 and accompanied me out onto the wide boulevards. Stopping for a coffee, asking directions, depositing money in my bank account: these things were out of the question, as they involved having to speak. Before beginning school, there'd been no shutting me up, but now I was convinced that everything I said was wrong. When the phone rang, I ignored it. If someone asked me a question, I pretended to be deaf. I knew my fear was getting the best of me when I started wondering why they don't sell cuts of meat in vending machines.

My only comfort was the knowledge that I was not alone. Huddled in   23 the hallways and making the most of our pathetic French, my fellow students and I engaged in the sort of conversation commonly overheard in refugee camps.

"Sometime me cry alone at night."   24

"That be common for I, also, but be more strong, you. Much work and   25 someday you talk pretty. People start love you soon. Maybe tomorrow, okay."

Unlike the French class I had taken in New York, here there was no   26 sense of competition. When the teacher poked a shy Korean in the eyelid with a freshly sharpened pencil, we took no comfort in the fact that, unlike Hyeyoon Cho, we all knew the irregular past tense of the verb *to defeat*. In all fairness, the teacher hadn't meant to stab the girl, but neither did she spend much time apologizing, saying only, "Well, you should have been *vkkdyo* more *kdeynfulh*."

Over time it became impossible to believe that any of us would ever   27 improve. Fall arrived and it rained every day, meaning we would now be scolded for the water dripping from our coats and umbrellas. It was mid-October when the teacher singled me out, saying, "Every day spent with you is like having a cesarean section." And it struck me that, for the first time since arriving in France, I could understand every word that someone was saying.

Understanding doesn't mean that you can suddenly speak the language.   28 Far from it. It's a small step, nothing more, yet its rewards are intoxicating and deceptive. The teacher continued her diatribe and I settled back, bathing in the subtle beauty of each new curse and insult.

"You exhaust me with your foolishness and reward my efforts with 29 nothing but pain, do you understand me?"

The world opened up, and it was with great joy that I responded, "I 30 know the thing that you speak exact now. Talk me more, you, plus, please, plus."

Meaning

1. Why do Sedaris and the other students have difficulty expressing their likes and dislikes in class?

2. Sedaris devotes the majority of his essay to enumerating the humiliations and frustrations he experienced as a student, but his feelings change markedly toward the end. What causes his shift in attitude?

3. In your own words, explain Sedaris's thesis. Where does he state it explicitly?

4. If you are uncertain of the meanings of any of the words listed below, try to guess them from the context of Sedaris's essay. Then look them up to see how close your definitions were to those in the dictionary. Test out the new words by using each of them in a sentence or two of your own.

debutant (1)	dermatological (14)	temperament (18)
saucebox (12)	inanimate (17)	diatribe (28)
genocide (14)		

Purpose and Audience

1. It can be painful to recall an embarrassing experience, yet Sedaris chooses to do so. What do you believe is his purpose in recording these episodes from his French class: to understand his experience? to mock his classmates? to express his frustrations? to argue a point about learning? to do something else?

2. What assumptions does Sedaris seem to make about his readers: their age, their nationality, their attitudes toward the French language, their experiences as students, and so on?

3. How does Sedaris characterize his classmates? his teacher? Does he mean for readers to take his examples literally? How can you tell?

4. What impression of himself does Sedaris create? How seriously does he expect readers to take him? What words and passages support your answer?

Method and Structure

1. How does Sedaris use examples for comic effect?

2. What generalizations do the examples in paragraphs 2–3 and 22 support?

3. What do Sedaris's examples reveal about his attitude toward his teacher and her methods? Does he feel anger? bitterness? shame? appreciation? amusement? Why do you think so?

4. **OTHER METHODS** "Me Talk Pretty One Day" relies on **narration** (Chapter 5) as much as it does example. How does Sedaris use **dialogue** to move his story forward?

Language

1. Analyze the structures and lengths of sentences in paragraph 2. What strategies does Sedaris use to achieve variety?

2. What is the effect of the nonsense words, such as *meimslsxp* and *lgpdmurct* (paragraph 4), that Sedaris sprinkles throughout his essay? Why doesn't he simply repeat the French words or their English translations instead?

Writing Topics

1. **JOURNAL TO ESSAY** Reread your journal entry and the quotations that precede Sedaris's essay (p. 131). Using specific examples, write an essay about the life lessons to be learned from failure.

2. If you are studying or have learned a second language, write an essay in which you explain the difficulty involved. Draw your examples not just from the new language's grammar and vocabulary but from its underlying logic and attitudes. For instance, does one speak to older people differently in the new language? make requests differently? describe love or art differently? What do you expect to gain—or lose—from acquiring a new language? If you like, try to achieve humor in your essay by imitating Sedaris's style.

3. **CULTURAL CONSIDERATIONS** As Sedaris points out, the French language assigns a gender to every noun, a convention that he finds bizarre and distracting but seems perfectly natural to native French speakers. Focusing on a single example, write an essay in which you contemplate the influence of language on culture, and vice versa. How might male and female forms for nouns, for instance, reflect social hierarchies? Why did feminists fight to eliminate the generic male pronoun from American

English (until the late twentieth century, it was standard practice to use *he*, *his*, and *man* to refer to both men and women)? Why does France have a government commission charged with banning English words like *weekend*, *volleyball*, and *surfer* from the French language? Other examples may come to mind; write about what interests you most.

4. **CONNECTIONS**   Like Sedaris, Ken Chen, in "City Out of Breath" (p. 109), relates an experience of discomfort with communicating in a different language. But while Sedaris focuses on his own trouble understanding French, Chen emphasizes the awkwardness of listening to his father speak Chinese. Write an essay analyzing what the two writers' examples have in common and any significant differences between them. How do their competing perspectives inform each other's experiences?

A passage is not plain English—still less is it good English—if we are obliged to read it twice to find out what it means.   —Dorothy Sayers

I'm bilingual. I speak English and I speak educationese.   —Shirley Hufstedler

You and I come by road or rail, but economists travel on infrastructure.
                                                        —Margaret Thatcher

JOURNAL RESPONSE   What words or expressions have you encountered in your college courses or in your college's rules and regulations that have confused, delighted, or irritated you? Write a brief journal entry describing the language and its effects on you.

Perri Klass

Perri Klass is a pediatrician, a writer, and a knitter. She was born in 1958 in Trinidad and grew up in New York City and New Jersey. Klass obtained a BA from Harvard University in 1979, finished Harvard Medical School in 1986, and teaches journalism and pediatrics at New York University. Her publications are extensive: short stories and articles in *Mademoiselle, Antioch Review*, the *New England Journal of Medicine*, and other periodicals; several novels, including *Other Women's Children* (1990) and *The Mercy Rule* (2009); five essay collections; a memoir, *Every Mother Is a Daughter* (2005); and the parenting guide *Quirky Kids* (2003). Klass is the president and medical director of Reach Out and Read, a nonprofit group that works with pediatricians to distribute books to disadvantaged children.

She's Your Basic LOL in NAD

Most of us have felt excluded, confused, or even frightened by the jargon of the medical profession—that is, by the special terminology and abbreviations for diseases and procedures. In this essay Klass uses examples of such language, some of it heartless, to illustrate the pluses and minuses of becoming a doctor. The essay first appeared in 1984 as a "Hers" column in the *New York Times*.

"Mrs. Tolstoy is your basic LOL in NAD, admitted for a soft rule-out MI,"   1
the intern announces. I scribble that on my patient list. In other words Mrs. Tolstoy is a Little Old Lady in No Apparent Distress who is in the hospital to make sure she hasn't had a heart attack (rule out a myocardial infarc-

tion). And we think it's unlikely that she has had a heart attack (a *soft* rule-out).

If I learned nothing else during my first three months of working in   2
the hospital as a medical student, I learned endless jargon and abbreviations. I started out in a state of primeval innocence, in which I didn't even know that "s̄ CP, SOB, N/V" meant "without chest pain, shortness of breath, or nausea and vomiting." By the end I took the abbreviations so for granted that I would complain to my mother the English professor, "And can you believe I had to put down *three* NG tubes last night?"

"You'll have to tell me what an NG tube is if you want me to sympa-   3
thize properly," my mother said. NG, nasogastric—isn't it obvious?

I picked up not only the specific expressions but also the patterns of   4
speech and the grammatical conventions; for example, you never say that a patient's blood pressure fell or that his cardiac enzymes rose. Instead, the patient is always the subject of the verb: "He dropped his pressure." "He bumped his enzymes." This sort of construction probably reflects that profound irritation of the intern when the nurses come in the middle of the night to say that Mr. Dickinson has disturbingly low blood pressure. "Oh, he's gonna hurt me bad tonight," the intern may say, inevitably angry at Mr. Dickinson for dropping his pressure and creating a problem.

When chemotherapy fails to cure Mrs. Bacon's cancer, what we say is,   5
"Mrs. Bacon failed chemotherapy."

"Well, we've already had one hit today, and we're up next, but at least   6
we've got mostly stable players on our team." This means that our team (group of doctors and medical students) has already gotten one new admission today, and it is our turn again, so we'll get whoever is next admitted in emergency, but at least most of the patients we already have are fairly stable, that is, unlikely to drop their pressures or in any other way get suddenly sicker and hurt us bad. Baseball metaphor is pervasive: a no-hitter is a night without any new admissions. A player is always a patient—a nitrate player is a patient on nitrates, a unit player is a patient in the intensive-care unit, and so on, until you reach the terminal player.

It is interesting to consider what it means to be winning, or doing   7
well, in this perennial baseball game. When the intern hangs up the phone and announces, "I got a hit," that is not cause for congratulations. The team is not scoring points; rather, it is getting hit, being bombarded with new patients. The object of the game from the point of view of the doctors, considering the players for whom they are already responsible, is to get as few new hits as possible.

These special languages contribute to a sense of closeness and profes-   8
sional spirit among people who are under a great deal of stress. As a medi-

cal student, it was exciting for me to discover that I'd finally cracked the code, that I could understand what doctors said and wrote and could use the same formulations myself. Some people seem to become enamored of the jargon for its own sake, perhaps because they are so deeply thrilled with the idea of medicine, with the idea of themselves as doctors.

I knew a medical student who was referred to by the interns on the team as Mr. Eponym because he was so infatuated with eponymous terminology,[1] the more obscure the better. He never said "capillary pulsation" if he could say "Quincke's pulses." He would lovingly tell over the multinamed syndromes — Wolff-Parkinson-White, Lown-Ganong-Levine, Henoch-Schonlein — until the temptation to suggest Schleswig-Holstein or Stevenson-Kefauver or Baskin-Robbins became irresistible to his less reverent colleagues.

And there is the jargon that you don't ever want to hear yourself using. You know that your training is changing you, but there are certain changes you think would be going a little too far.

The resident was describing a man with devastating terminal pancreatic cancer. "Basically he's CTD," the resident concluded. I reminded myself that I had resolved not to be shy about asking when I didn't understand things. "CTD?" I asked timidly.

The resident smirked at me. "Circling The Drain."

The images are vivid and terrible. "What happened to Mrs. Melville?"

"Oh, she boxed last night." To box is to die, of course.

Then there are the more pompous locutions that can make the beginning medical student nervous about the effects of medical training. A friend of mine was told by his resident, "A pregnant woman with sickle-cell represents a failure of genetic counseling."

Mr. Eponym, who tried hard to talk like the doctors, once explained to me, "An infant is basically a brainstem preparation." A brainstem preparation, as used in neurological research, is an animal whose higher brain functions have been destroyed so that only the most primitive reflexes remain, like the sucking reflex, the startle reflex, and the rooting reflex.

The more extreme forms aside, one most important function of medical jargon is to help doctors maintain some distance from their patients. By reformulating a patient's pain and problems into a language that the patient doesn't even speak, I suppose we are in some sense taking those

[margin numbers: 9, 10, 11, 12, 13, 14, 15, 16, 17]

---

[1] *Eponymous* means "named after" — in this case, medical terminology is named after researchers. [Editors' note.]

pains and problems under our jurisdiction and also reducing their emotional impact. This linguistic separation between doctors and patients allows conversations to go on at the bedside that are unintelligible to the patient. "Naturally, we're worried about adreno-CA," the intern can say to the medical student, and lung cancer need never be mentioned.

I learned a new language this past summer. At times it thrills me to   18
hear myself using it. It enables me to understand my colleagues, to communicate effectively in the hospital. Yet I am uncomfortably aware that I will never again notice the peculiarities and even atrocities of medical language as keenly as I did this summer. There may be specific expressions I manage to avoid, but even as I remark them, promising myself I will never use them, I find that this language is becoming my professional speech. It no longer sounds strange in my ears—or coming from my mouth. And I am afraid that as with any new language, to use it properly you must absorb not only the vocabulary but also the structure, the logic, the attitudes. At first you may notice these new alien assumptions every time you put together a sentence, but with time and increased fluency you stop being aware of them at all. And as you lose that awareness, for better or for worse, you move closer and closer to being a doctor instead of just talking like one.

Meaning

1. What point does Klass make about medical jargon in this essay? Where does she reveal her main point explicitly?

2. What useful purposes does medical jargon serve, according to Klass? Do the examples in paragraphs 9–16 serve these purposes? Why, or why not?

3. Try to guess the meanings of any of the following words that are unfamiliar. Check your guesses in a dictionary, and then use each word in a sentence or two of your own.

primeval (2)	syndromes (9)	locutions (15)
terminal (6)	reverent (9)	jurisdiction (17)
perennial (7)	pompous (15)	

Purpose and Audience

1. What does Klass imply when she states that she began her work in the hospital "in a state of primeval innocence" (paragraph 2)? What does this phrase suggest about her purpose in writing the essay?

2. From what perspective does Klass write this essay: that of a medical professional? someone outside the profession? a patient? someone else? To

what extent does she expect her readers to share her perspective? What evidence in the essay supports your answer?

3. Given that she is writing for a general audience, does Klass take adequate care to define medical terms? Support your answer with examples from the essay.

Method and Structure

1. Why does Klass begin the essay with an example rather than a statement of her main idea? What effect does this example produce? How does this effect support her purpose in writing the essay?

2. Although Klass uses many examples of medical jargon, she avoids the dull effect of a list by periodically stepping back to make a general statement about her experience or the jargon—for instance, "I picked up not only the specific expressions but also the patterns of speech and the grammatical conventions" (paragraph 4). Locate other places—not necessarily at the beginnings of paragraphs—where Klass breaks up her examples with more general statements.

3. **OTHER METHODS**   Klass uses several other methods besides example, among them **classification** (Chapter 9), **definition** (Chapter 12), and **cause-and-effect analysis** (Chapter 13). What effects—positive and negative—does medical jargon have on Klass, other students, and doctors who use it?

Language

1. What is the **tone** of this essay? Is Klass trying to be humorous or tongue-in-cheek about the jargon of the profession, or is she serious? Where in the essay is the author's attitude toward her subject the most obvious?

2. Klass refers to the users of medical jargon as both *we/us* (paragraphs 1, 5, 6, 17) and *they* (7), and sometimes she shifts from *I* to *you* within a paragraph (4, 18). Do you think these shifts are effective or distracting? Why? Do the shifts serve any function?

3. Klass obviously experienced both positive and negative feelings about mastering medical jargon. Which words and phrases in the last paragraph reflect positive feelings, and which negative?

Writing Topics

1. **JOURNAL TO ESSAY**   When she attended medical school, Perri Klass discovered a novel language to learn and with it some new attitudes. Working from your journal entry (p. 139), write an essay about the new languages

and attitudes you have encountered in college. Have you been confronted with different kinds of people (professors, other students) from the ones you knew before? Have you had difficulty understanding some words people use? Have you found yourself embracing ideas you never thought you would or speaking differently? Have others noticed a change in you that you may not have been aware of? Have you noticed changes in the friends you had before college? Focus on a particular kind of obstacle or change, using specific examples to convey this experience to readers.

2. Klass's essay explores the "separation between doctors and patients" (paragraph 17). Has this separation affected you as a patient or as a relative or friend of a patient? If so, write an essay about your experiences. Did the medical professionals rely heavily on jargon? Was their language comforting, frightening, irritating? Based on your experience and on Klass's essay, do you believe that the separation between doctors and patients is desirable? Why, or why not?

3. **CULTURAL CONSIDERATIONS**   Most groups focused on a common interest have their own jargon. If you belong to such a group—for example, runners, football fans, food servers, engineering students—spend a few days listening to yourself and others use this language and thinking about the purposes it serves. Which aspects of this language seem intended to make users feel like insiders? Which seem to serve some other purpose, and what is it? In an essay, explain what this jargon reveals about the group and its common interest, using as many specific examples as you can.

4. **CONNECTIONS**   Both Klass and David Sedaris, in "Me Talk Pretty One Day" (p. 131), suggest that the way we speak can create closeness to or distance from other people. Write an essay in which you examine the way members of a group—say, students, faculty members, relatives, politicians, or people from a particular region—use language to establish the nature of their relationships.

WRITING WITH THE METHOD

EXAMPLE

Select one of the following statements, or any other statement they suggest, and agree *or* disagree with it in an essay developed by example. The statement you choose should concern a topic you care about so that the example or examples are a means of communicating an idea, not an end in themselves.

Family

1. In happy families, talk is the main activity.
2. Sooner or later, children take on the personalities of their parents.
3. "Traditional" families are anything but traditional.

Behavior and Personality

4. Rudeness is on the rise.
5. Facial expressions often communicate what words cannot say.
6. New technologies are making us stupid and lazy.

Education

7. The best college courses are the difficult ones.
8. College is not for everybody.
9. Students at schools with enforced dress codes behave better than students at schools without such codes.
10. Social activities are essential to a well-rounded education.

Politics and Social Issues

11. Social media can influence government actions.
12. Drug or alcohol addiction is not restricted just to "bad" people.
13. Unemployment is hardest on those over fifty years old.
14. The best musicians treat social and political issues in their songs.

Rules for Living

15. Murphy's Law: If anything can go wrong, it will go wrong, and at the worst possible moment.
16. A good friend offers help and support without being asked.
17. Lying may be justified by the circumstances.

WRITING ABOUT THE THEME

USING LANGUAGE

1. Deborah Tannen (p. 120), William Lutz (p. 121), and Perri Klass (p. 139) discuss the power of language with a good deal of respect. Tannen refers to its social uses, Lutz to its effectiveness "in explaining . . . accidents," and Klass to its support as she became a doctor. Think of a time when you were in some way profoundly affected by language, and write an essay about this experience. Provide as many examples as necessary to illustrate both the language that affected you and how it made you feel.

2. Kim Kessler (p. 126), David Sedaris (p. 131), and Perri Klass all write about forms of language that do not obey traditional rules and are considered incorrect by some people. As you see it, what are the advantages and disadvantages of using nonstandard language when speaking and writing? How effective are these forms of language as ways to communicate? Write an essay that answers these questions, using examples from the selections and your own experience.

3. Perri Klass writes that medical jargon "contribute[s] to a sense of closeness and professional spirit among people who are under a great deal of stress" (paragraph 8) and that it helps doctors "maintain some distance from their patients" (17). Write an essay in which you analyze the function of "double-speak," as presented by William Lutz. Who, if anyone, is such language designed to help: accident victims? their families? someone else? Can a positive case be made for this language?

8

DIVISION OR ANALYSIS

▶
LOOKING AT POPULAR CULTURE

Division and **analysis** are interchangeable terms for the same method. *Division* comes from a Latin word meaning "to force asunder or separate." *Analysis* comes from a Greek word meaning "to undo." Using this method, we separate a whole into its elements, examine the relations of the elements to one another and to the whole, and reassemble the elements into a new whole informed by the examination.

At its simplest, analysis (as we will call it) looks closely at a subject for the knowledge to be gained and perhaps put to use. A more complex kind of analysis builds on this basic operation to become the foundation of **critical thinking**—the ability to see beneath the surface of things, images, events, and ideas; to uncover and test assumptions; to see the importance of context; and to draw and support independent conclusions.

The method, then, is essential to college learning, whether in discussing literature, reviewing a psychology experiment, or interpreting a business case. It is also fundamental in the workplace, from choosing a career to making sense of market research. Analysis even informs and enriches life outside of school or work, whether we ponder our relationships with others, decide whether a movie was worthwhile, evaluate a politician's campaign promises, or determine whether a new gaming system is worth buying.

We use analysis throughout this book when looking at paragraphs and essays. And it is the underlying task of at least four other methods discussed in other chapters: classification (Chapter 9), process analysis (Chapter 10), comparison and contrast (Chapter 11), and cause-and-effect analysis (Chapter 13).

Reading Division or Analysis

At its most helpful, division or analysis peers inside an object, institution, work of art, policy, or any other whole. It identifies the parts, examines how the parts relate, and leads to a conclusion about the meaning, significance, or value of the whole. The subject of any analysis is usually singular—a freestanding, coherent unit, such as a bicycle or a poem, with its own unique constitution of elements. (In contrast, classification, the subject of the next chapter, usually starts with a plural subject, such as bicycles or the poems of the Civil War, and groups them according to their shared features.) A writer chooses the subject and with it a **principle of analysis**, a framework that determines how the subject will be divided and thus what elements are relevant to the discussion.

Sometimes the principle of analysis is self-evident, especially when the subject is an object, such as a bicycle or a camera, that can be "undone" in only a limited number of ways. Most of the time, however, the principle depends on the writer's view of the whole. In academic disciplines, distinctive principles are part of what each field is about and are often the subject of debate within the field. In art, for instance, some critics see a painting primarily as a visual object and concentrate on its composition, color, line, and other formal qualities; other critics see a painting primarily as a social object and concentrate on its content and context (cultural, economic, political, and so on). Both groups use a principle of analysis that is a well-established way of looking at a painting, yet each group finds different elements and thus meaning in a work.

Writers have a great deal of flexibility in choosing a principle of analysis, but the principle also must meet certain requirements: it should be appropriate for the subject and the field or discipline, it should be significant, and it should be applied thoroughly and consistently. Analysis is done not for its own sake but for a larger goal of illuminating the subject, perhaps concluding something about it, perhaps evaluating it. But even when the method leads to evaluation—the writer's judgment of the subject's value—the analysis should represent the subject as it actually is, in all its fullness and complexity. In analyzing a movie, for instance, a writer may emphasize one element, such as setting, and even omit some elements, such as costumes; but the characterization of the whole must still apply to *all* the elements. If it does not, readers can be counted on to notice; so the writer must acknowledge any wayward elements and explain why their omission does not undermine the validity of the analysis and thus weaken the conclusion.

Analyzing Division or Analysis in Paragraphs

Jon Pareles (born 1953) is the chief critic of popular music for the *New York Times*. The following paragraph comes from "Gather No Moss, Take No Prisoners, but Be Cool," a review of a concert by the rock guitarist Keith Richards.

<u>Mr. Richards shows off by not showing off.</u> He uses rhythm chords as a goad, not a metronome, slipping them in just ahead of a beat or skipping them entirely. The distilled twang of his tone has been imitated all over rock, but far fewer guitarists have learned his guerrilla timing, his coiled silences. When he switches to lead guitar, Mr. Richards goes not for long lines, but for serrated riffing, zinging out three or four notes again and again in various permutations, wringing from them the essence of the blues. The phrasing is poised and suspenseful, but it also carries a salutary rock attitude: that less is more, especially when delivered with utter confidence.

Principle of analysis (topic sentence underlined): elements of "not showing off"

1. Chords as goad (or prod)

2. Timing

3. Silences

4. Riffing (or repeating variations of rhythms)

5. Confident, less-is-more attitude

Luci Tapahonso (born 1953) is a poet and teacher. This paragraph is from her essay "The Way It Is," which appears in *Sign Language,* a book of photographs (by Skeet McAuley) of life on the reservation for some Navajo and Apache Indians.

It is rare and, indeed, very exciting to see an Indian person in a commercial advertisement. Word travels fast when that happens. Nunzio's Pizza in Albuquerque, New Mexico, ran commercials featuring Jose Rey Toledo of Jemez Pueblo talking about his "native land—Italy" while wearing typical Pueblo attire—jewelry, moccasins, and hair tied in a chongo. Because of the ironic humor, because Indian grandfathers specialize in playing tricks and jokes on their grandchildren, and because Jose Rey Toledo is a respected and well-known elder in the Indian communities, word of this commercial spread fast among Indians in New Mexico. It was the cause of recognition and celebration of sorts on the reservations

Principle of analysis: elements of the commercial that appealed to Indians

1. Rarity of an Indian in a commercial

2. Indian dress

3. Indian humor

4. Indian tradition

5. Respected Indian spokesperson

and in the pueblos. His portrayal was not in the categories which the media usually associate with Indians but
as a typical sight in the Southwest. <u>It showed Indians as
we live today—enjoying pizza as one of our favorite
foods, including humor and fun as part of our daily lives,
and recognizing the importance of preserving traditional
knowledge.</u>

6. Realism

Topic sentence
(underlined)
summarizes
elements

Developing an Essay by Division or Analysis

▶ Getting Started

Analysis is one of the readiest methods of development: almost anything
whole can be separated into its elements, from a lemon to a play by
Shakespeare to an economic theory. In college and at work, many writing assignments will demand analysis with a verb such as *analyze*, *criticize*, *discuss*, *evaluate*, *interpret*, or *review*. If you need to develop your own
subject for analysis, think of something whose meaning or significance
puzzles or intrigues you and whose parts you can distinguish and relate
to the whole—for instance, an object such as a machine, an artwork such
as a poem, a media product such as a news broadcast, an institution such
as a hospital, a relationship such as stepparenting, or a social issue such as
homelessness.

Dissect your subject, looking at the actual physical thing if possible,
imagining it in your mind if necessary. Make detailed notes of all the elements you see, their distinguishing features, and how those features work
together. In analyzing someone's creation, tease out the creator's influences, assumptions, intentions, conclusions, and evidence. You may have
to go outside the work for some of this information—researching an
author's background, for instance, to uncover the biases that may underlie his or her opinions. Even if you do not use all this information in your
final draft, it will help you see the elements and help keep your analysis
true to the subject.

If you begin by seeking meaning or significance in a subject, you will
be more likely to find a workable principle of analysis and less likely to
waste time on a hollow exercise. Each question below suggests a distinct
approach to the subject's elements—a distinct principle of analysis—that
makes it easier to isolate the elements and see their connections:

To what extent is an enormously complex hospital a community in itself?

What is the function of the front-page headlines in the local tabloid newspaper?

Why did a certain movie have such a powerful effect on you and your friends?

▶ Forming a Thesis

A clear, informative thesis sentence (or sentences) is crucial in division or analysis because readers need to know the purpose and structure of your analysis in order to follow your points. If your exploratory question proves helpful as you gather ideas, you can also use it to draft a thesis sentence: answer it in such a way that you state your opinion about your subject and reveal your principle of analysis.

> QUESTION   To what extent is an enormously complex hospital a community in itself?
>
> THESIS SENTENCE   The hospital encompasses such a wide range of personnel and services that it resembles a good-sized town.
>
> QUESTION   What is the function of the front-page headlines in the local tabloid newspaper?
>
> THESIS SENTENCE   The newspaper's front page routinely appeals to readers' fear of crime, anger at criminals, and sympathy for victims.
>
> QUESTION   Why did a certain movie have such a powerful effect on you and your friends?
>
> THESIS SENTENCE   The film is a unique and important statement of the private terrors of adolescence.

Note that all three thesis statements imply an explanatory purpose—an effort to understand something and share that understanding with the reader. The third thesis sentence, however, suggests a persuasive purpose as well: the writer hopes that readers will accept her evaluation of the film.

A well-focused thesis sentence benefits not only your readers but also you as a writer, because it gives you a yardstick to judge the completeness, consistency, and supportiveness of your analysis. Don't be discouraged, though, if your thesis sentence doesn't come to you until *after* you've written a first draft and had a chance to focus your ideas. Writing about your subject may be the best way to find its meaning and significance.

▶ Organizing

In the **introduction** to your essay, let readers know why you are bothering to analyze your subject: Why is the subject significant? How might the essay relate to the experiences of readers or be useful to them? A subject unfamiliar to readers might be summarized or described, or some part of it (an anecdote or a quotation, say) might be used to grab readers' interest. A familiar subject might be introduced with a surprising fact or an unusual perspective. An evaluative analysis might open with reference to an opposing viewpoint.

In the body of the essay, you'll need to explain your principle of analysis according to the guidelines on page 148. The arrangement of elements and analysis should suit your subject and purpose: you can describe the elements and then offer your analysis, or you can introduce and analyze elements one by one. You can arrange the elements themselves from most to least important, least to most complex, most to least familiar, spatially, or chronologically. Devote as much space to each element as it demands: there is no requirement that all elements be given equal space and emphasis if their complexity or your framework dictates otherwise.

Most analysis essays need a **conclusion** that reassembles the elements, returning readers to a sense of the whole subject. The conclusion can restate the thesis, summarize what the essay has contributed, consider the influence of the subject or its place in a larger picture, or (especially in an evaluation) assess the effectiveness or worth of the subject.

▶ Drafting

If the subject or your view of it is complex, you may need at least two rough drafts of an analysis essay—one to work out what you think and one to clarify your principle, cover each element, and support your points with concrete details and vivid examples (including quotations if the subject is a written work). Plan on two drafts if you're uncertain of your thesis when you begin; you'll save time in the long run by attending to one goal at a time. Especially because an analysis essay says something about a subject by explaining its structure, you need to have a clear picture of the whole and how each part relates to it.

As you draft, be sure to consider your readers' needs as well as the needs of your subject and your own framework:

- *If the subject is unfamiliar to your readers*, you'll need to carefully explain your principle of analysis, define all specialized terms, distinguish the parts from one another, and provide ample illustrations.

- *If the subject is familiar to readers*, your principle of analysis may not require much justification (as long as it's clear), but your details and examples must be vivid and convincing.

- *If readers may dispute your way of looking at your subject*, be careful to justify as well as explain your principle of analysis.

Whether readers are familiar with your subject or not, always account for any evidence that may seem not to support your opinion—either by showing why, in fact, the evidence is supportive or by explaining why it is unimportant. (If contrary evidence refuses to be dispensed with, you may have to rethink your approach.)

▶ Revising and Editing

When you revise and edit your essay, use the following questions and the Focus box on the next page to uncover any remaining weaknesses.

- *Is your principle of analysis clear?* The significance of your analysis and your view of the subject should be apparent throughout your essay.

- *Is your analysis complete?* Have you identified all elements according to your principle of analysis and determined their relations to one another and to the whole? If you have omitted some elements from your discussion, will the reason for their omission be clear to readers?

- *Is your analysis consistent?* Have you applied your principle of analysis to the entire subject (including any elements you have omitted)? Do all elements reflect the same principle, and are they clearly separate rather than overlapping? You may find it helpful to check your draft against your list of elements or to outline the draft itself.

- *Is your analysis well supported?* Is the thesis supported by clear assertions about parts of the subject, and are the assertions supported by concrete, specific evidence (sensory details, facts, quotations, and so on)? Do not rely on your readers to prove your thesis.

- *Is your analysis true to the subject?* Is your thesis unforced, your analysis fair? Is your new whole (your reassembly of the elements) faithful to the original?

The most wasted of all days is one without laughter.   —e. e. cummings

There is a thin line that separates laughter and pain, comedy and tragedy, humor and hurt.   —Erma Bombeck

Analyzing humor is like dissecting a frog. Few people are interested and the frog dies of it.   —E. B. White

JOURNAL RESPONSE   Reflect for a moment on your favorite source of humor: a particular comedian, perhaps, or a television show, a Web site, a comic strip. Write a journal entry explaining what you like about this source of comedy, trying to pin down as many details as you can.

Scott Adams

Scott Adams (born 1957) is best known for his cubicle-bound comic strip, *Dilbert*, which dissects the painfully hilarious minutiae of office culture. Raised in upstate New York, Adams earned a BA in economics from Hartwick College and an MBA from the University of California at Berkeley. He started his career as a programmer for a bank and then a telephone company in the San Francisco area; the day jobs served as early inspirations for *Dilbert*, which Adams began publishing while still employed full time. He made the innovative decision in 1994 to provide his e-mail address in the panels, and the feedback from readers helped him to refine the strip into the acclaimed office staple it is today. Adams is the author of nearly four dozen books of comics, self-help, and business advice, most recently *How to Fail at Almost Everything and Still Win Big: Kind of the Story of My Life* (2013) and *Go Add Value Someplace Else* (2014). He is also the co-owner of a small restaurant in California and a certified hypnotist.

Funny Business

What makes a piece of writing funny? In this 2010 essay for the esteemed business newspaper the *Wall Street Journal*, Adams sets out to explain while he demonstrates.

Last weekend a French fry got lodged in my sinus cavity.   1

I suppose it all started when I was eleven years old. Two of my school   2
buddies and I were huddled on the schoolyard, whisper-sharing everything we knew about the mysteries of the human reproductive process. We patched together bits and pieces of what we had heard from our older

brothers. This was problematic, because two of our brothers were unreliable, and one was a practical joker. And to be fair, my friends and I were poor listeners.

As I later learned, we got a fairly important part of the reproductive 3 puzzle wrong. I can't be more specific about our faulty information, at least not in the *Wall Street Journal*, so instead I will tell you a story about golf. If you choose to draw any parallels, that's your own fault.

Okay, so this golfer hits a majestic drive, and follows it up with an 4 awesome chip and an improbable putt. The golfer pumps his fist and dances a little jig. He turns to his caddy for a high-five and gets no response. "Wasn't that some great golfing?" the golfer asks. The caddy says, "Yes . . . but it was the wrong hole."

Last weekend, I was visiting my tiny hometown of Windham, New 5 York, enjoying dinner out with my parents, my sister, and two eighty-ish widows who are longtime family friends. One of the ladies mentioned running into an old schoolmate of mine who was part of the misinformed schoolyard troika of way-back-then. When I heard my schoolmate's name, I flashed back to that day, vividly recalling the key bit of information we got wrong, and I wondered how long it took my buddies to correct their mistaken understandings. I took a bite of my French fry and listened to the rest of the story about how this fellow hadn't changed much since he was a kid. And then one of the widows added, sort of as an afterthought, "He never had any children."

Let me tell you that this was a bad time for me to have food in my 6 mouth. The situation demanded a spit-take, but this was a nice restaurant, and I was sitting directly across from the two innocent widows. I clamped my lips shut and hoped for the best. Something sneeze-like exploded inside me. It was an unholy combination of saliva, potato, laughter and compressed air. I squeezed my sphincter shut, closed my eyes, and well, I don't remember much after that. I think the French fry hit the top of my sinus cavity and caused some sort of concussion.

Anyway, the reason we're here today is so I can give you valuable 7 writing tips. My specialty is humor, so let's stick with that slice of the assignment.

The topic is the thing. Eighty percent of successful humor writing is 8 picking a topic that is funny by its very nature. My story above is true, up until the exaggeration about the French fry in the sinus cavity. You probably assumed it was true, and that knowledge made it funnier.

Humor likes danger. If you are cautious by nature, writing humor 9 probably isn't for you. Humor works best when you sense that the writer is putting himself in jeopardy. I picked the French-fry story specifically because it is too risqué for the *Wall Street Journal*. You can't read it without wondering if I had an awkward conversation with my editor. You might wonder if the people in my story will appreciate seeing my version of events in the *Wall Street Journal*. I wonder that too.

In the early days of my cartooning career, as the creator of *Dilbert*, 10 part of the strip's appeal was that I was holding a day job while mocking the very sort of company I worked for. If you knew my backstory, and many people did, you could sense my personal danger in every strip. (My manager eventually asked me to leave. He said it was a budget thing.)

Humor is about people. It's impossible to write humor about a con- 11 cept or an object. All humor involves how people think and act. Sometimes you can finesse that limitation by having your characters think and act in selfish, stupid or potentially harmful ways around the concept or object that you want your reader to focus on.

Exaggerate wisely. If you anchor your story in the familiar, your read- 12 ers will follow you on a humorous exaggeration, especially if you build up to it. My story was true and relatable until the French-fry exaggeration.

Let the reader do some work. Humor works best when the reader has 13 to connect some dots. Early in my story I made you connect the golf story to the playground story. The smarter your audience, the wider you can spread the dots. I used this method again when I said of my aborted spit-take, "I don't remember much after that." Your mind might have filled in a little scene in which, perhaps, my eyes bugged out, my cheeks went all chipmunk-like, and I fell out of my chair.

Animals are funny. It's a cheap trick, but animal analogies are gener- 14 ally funny. It was funnier that I said, "my cheeks went all chipmunk-like" than if I had said my cheeks puffed out.

Use funny words. I referred to my two schoolmates and myself as a 15 troika because the word itself is funny. With humor, you never say "pull" when you can say "yank." Some words are simply funnier than others, and you know the funny ones when you see them. (Pop Quiz: Which word is funnier, observe or stalk?)

Curiosity. Good writing makes you curious without being too heavy- 16 handed about it. My first sentence in this piece, about the French fry lodged in my sinus cavity, is designed to make you curious. It also sets the tone right away.

Endings. A simple and classic way to end humorous writing is with a 17 call-back. That means making a clever association to something especially humorous and notable from the body of your work. I would give you an example of that now, but I'm still having concentration issues from the French fry.

Meaning

1. What is the thesis of "Funny Business"? Does Adams state it explicitly? Try to summarize the central meaning of his analysis in a sentence or two of your own.

2. How does the *Dilbert* cartoon on the opposite page illustrate Adams's ideas about humor?

3. Why is the essay's last sentence particularly effective as a conclusion? Point to evidence from the text to support your answer.

4. If any of the following words are new to you, try to guess their meanings from the context of the essay. Test your guesses in a dictionary, and then use each new word in a sentence or two of your own.

parallels (3)	putt (4)	risqué (9)
majestic (4)	troika (5, 15)	finesse (11)
chip (4)	jeopardy (9)	analogies (14)

Purpose and Audience

1. What is Adams's purpose in writing this essay? How do you know?

2. What assumptions does Adams make about his audience? Where are those assumptions most clearly expressed?

Method and Structure

1. How does Adams use the method of analysis for comic effect? In what ways does analysis lend itself particularly well to a humorous subject such as this one?

2. What is Adams's principle of analysis, and into what elements does he divide his subject? Be specific, supporting your answer with examples from the text.

3. What do the first sentences of paragraphs 8, 9, and 11–17 have in common?

4. How does Adams organize his ideas?

5. **OTHER METHODS**   The first six paragraphs of the essay use **narration** (Chapter 5) to tell a joke. How is this **example** (Chapter 7) essential to Adams's analysis?

Language

1. Answer the "Pop Quiz" Adams poses in paragraph 15: "Which word is funnier, observe or stalk?" What other words in the essay strike you as inherently funny? Why does Adams repeat several of them?

2. What is Adams's **tone**? How seriously does he take his subject?

Writing Topics

1. **JOURNAL TO ESSAY**   In your journal entry (p. 156), you reflected on your favorite source of comedy. Now write a more formal essay in which you describe that source of comedy and explain what makes it so funny to you. You might cite Adams's elements of humor to explain your enjoyment, if you find them useful, or develop your own principle of analysis to assess just what it is that makes people laugh.

2. Adams claims that it is "impossible to write humor about a concept or an object" (paragraph 11). Is that true, in your experience? Drawing on the principles of humor that Adams outlines in his essay, try your hand at writing something funny. You might write about people or animals if you like, but feel free to choose as your topic a concept or an object that you find amusing on its own.

3. **CULTURAL CONSIDERATIONS**   Based on the examples Adams uses in this essay, what can you infer about his age, background, and economic status? Does Adams seem to assume his audience is similar to him? (Remember, this essay first appeared in the *Wall Street Journal*.) Are readers who don't match his assumptions (perhaps you yourself) likely to enjoy the essay as much as those who do match? Write an essay in which you analyze the writer's apparent assumptions, explaining how they strengthen the essay, weaken it, or don't affect it at all.

4. **CONNECTIONS**   Apply Adams's analysis to one or more of the other humorous essays in this book: David Sedaris's "Me Talk Pretty One Day" (p. 131), Brandon Griggs's "The Most Annoying Facebookers" (p. 186), and Jonathan R. Gould's "The People Next Door" (p. 191). Then write an essay that examines how these writers develop humor. Address as many of Adams's elements of humor as seem fitting, but consider especially what is gained from exaggeration and what qualities exaggeration often has. How does each writer make his readers laugh? Use quotations and paraphrases from "Funny Business" and the other essays as your support.

You can tell the ideals of a nation by its advertisements. —Norman Douglas

The art of publicity is a black art. —Learned Hand

Advertising may be described as the science of arresting the human intelligence long enough to get money from it. —Stephen Leacock

JOURNAL RESPONSE Think of a commercial or advertisement that you object to because it is offensive or annoying in some way. Write about why it bothers you so much.

Pat Mora

A poet, speaker, and literacy advocate, Pat Mora was born in 1942 in El Paso, Texas, and grew up in a bilingual family of Mexican heritage. She received a bachelor's degree from Texas Western College and a master's degree from the University of Texas, El Paso. Mora taught high school and college English for several years and worked as a college administrator and museum director at the University of New Mexico for nearly a decade before turning her focus to writing. "Like many Chicana writers," she says, she "was motivated to write because . . . our voices were absent from what is labeled American literature." In addition to voicing herself in two dozen books of poetry, Mora has written several illustrated books for children, the memoir *House of Houses* (1997), and a volume of literary and cultural criticism, *Nepantla: Essays from the Land in the Middle* (1993). She is also the founder of El día de los niños/El día de los libros (Children's Day/Book Day), a nationwide family literacy project. She lives in Santa Fe, New Mexico, and Cincinnati, Ohio.

Great Expectations

In this extract from *Nepantla* (the book's title is a Nahuatl, or Mexican Indian, word meaning "place in the middle"), Mora analyzes the overarching message sent to young Latinas by advertisers. When girls take such messages at face value, Mora worries, they help the advertisers but hurt themselves.

Latinas are labeled a *double minority*. The words are depressing. They don't   1
quite sound like "twice-blessed." Little wonder that most Latinas, whether in the Southwest or elsewhere in this country, don't dwell on this uncomfortable term. Anyway, who has time? We often are too busy playing the game of Great Expectations.

Most humans play some form of this game; most of us strive to fulfill   2
the dreams that our society, our family, and our self have for us. Latinas,
though, confront some unique challenges, and we often receive little support in fulfilling our potential.

In the eighties this country began to hear a Latin beat. Generations   3
of determined women and men had questioned discriminatory hiring
and promotion practices, immigration laws, inadequate health-care systems, biased arts council panels, and had endured meeting after meeting
requesting and ultimately demanding equal opportunities for our people.
Singers, writers, and artists had worked to capture the vigor of *lo meji-
cano*.[1] Their works are more and more visible. And demographics conspire
with us. These population shifts, combined with historic equity struggles,
mean we live in a society that finds it grudgingly necessary to notice our
community. We can't ignore even this lukewarm willingness to respond
to the needs of Latinos, whether by politicians, corporations, or federal or
state agencies, because we know the grim statistics on wages and education for US Latinos.

Ah, but our millions have billions to spend. Hundreds of millions are   4
targeted by advertisers, who now like us and suddenly care deeply about
our needs. Unlike those enmeshed in the political machinations of
English Only,[2] advertisers are happy to be bilingual. Well, their messages
are. They speak to us *en español*.[3] "*Ven es la hora de Miller.*"[4] Coors tells us,
"*Celebre! Cinco de mayo.*"[5] Canadian Club says, "*¡Qué pareja! Canadian
Club y tu!*"[6] Xerox tells us that its Hispana employees are "*especial.*"[7]

Advertisers track our values and thus our buying habits. Their analy-   5
ses confirm the conclusions of psychologists and sociologists: we are
loyal: to our families, the Spanish language, this country. Advertisers like
loyalty, which they hope translates to brand-name loyalty. For those to

---

[1] Spanish: *Mexicanness*. [Editors' note.]

[2] A movement to make English the official language of the United States, proposing that all official government documents and business be written and conducted
solely in English. [Editors' note.]

[3] Spanish: *in Spanish*. [Editors' note.]

[4] Spanish: "*It's Miller time.*" [Editors' note.]

[5] Spanish: "*Celebrate! The fifth of May.*" Cinco de Mayo, a commemoration of the
Mexican army's 1862 victory over the French in the Battle of Puebla during the
Franco-Mexican war (1862–67), is a minor holiday in Mexico. [Editors' note.]

[6] Spanish: "*What a pair!* Canadian Club *and you.*" Canadian Club is a brand of
whiskey. [Editors' note.]

[7] Spanish: "*special.*" [Editors' note.]

whom English is a new language, brand names probably do bring a sense of security and predictability in the cacophony of strange noises. I remember that when my grandmother, who never spoke or wanted to speak English though all three of her children were born here, had a headache, only Bayer would do. She trusted the symbol on that small, pain-easing white circle.

Politicians, of course, are busy courting our loyalty too, because we   6
are a young segment of an aging population. No more will candidates bite into a *tamal*[8] with corn husk in place. Media visibility, the occasional Latina actor, the occasional Latino family in a commercial, can in an odd way foster a sense of group identity, even though cultural symbols are usually being appropriated, used. Our growing population makes it less threatening to delve into our cultural past, for what we discover suddenly interests people—perhaps because it is trendy, but the information nourishes us.

Such targeted marketing doesn't change the reality that this coun-   7
try often views us as either fiery, and thus less rational, less than intellectual; or as docile, and thus less than effective, less than assertive. A woman named María might be considered as a candidate for a position as a domestic worker or secretary, but it is unlikely that she will seriously be considered as a candidate for senator. Yet. How easy is it, then, for a Latina to deal with a society that finds her dark eyes and hair attractive, but that is a bit surprised to see her aggressively pursuing a goal, striving to become an architect or veterinarian or literary critic? T'ain't easy.

And then there are our families. Intense emotional ties. Our parents,   8
siblings, and relatives are a source of indescribable strength. Perhaps because marriage traditionally has been so important in our culture, men and our families often equate an attractive physical appearance with true womanhood. Many a *tía* or *abuelita*[9] at home wants her niece to pursue a career, preferably in teaching or nursing, but *Tía* is secretly hoping—and probably praying—that we'll receive both a degree and a marriage proposal. She loves us and longs for some fine, respectful, hard-working man who will protect this vulnerable single woman from financial worries and the world's indifference.

Our parents also may do some frowning. How happy will they be at   9
the news that we're considering joining the space program or applying for graduate school in another state? Frowns may really multiply once we're

---

[8]Cornmeal dough stuffed with ground meat or sweet filling and steamed in a corn husk. [Editors' note.]

[9]*Tía* is Spanish for *aunt*. *Abuelita* means *grandmother*. [Editors' note.]

married with a family and announce that we need to begin traveling. Their frowns will say, "Neglect your children and husband? What kind of a woman are you?" Often their concern is genuine, and it is not easy to help them see that their desire to protect can be an unacknowledged desire to control.

Hard choices. We know women are socialized to please. How does a bright, talented Latina weather her family's displeasure when she works long hours rather than visiting regularly with sisters and cousins? *Tía's* frowns have a way of giving us tired blood. 10

And what about the woman who gazes back in the mirror? What Great Expectations does she have for us? Chances are she wants us to look energetic, to excel in our chosen work, to struggle against injustice, to be a loving and respectful daughter, niece. Chances are she will never be quite satisfied with our efforts. She will be pressuring us, often relentlessly, to try harder, to produce better work. She can be our harshest critic. Convincing her to wink back at us occasionally may be a lifelong challenge. 11

The Latina who completes her college education—a small percentage of us—may indeed now have more opportunities, whether for employment or for service on panels, committees, and boards, which is appropriate. As double minorities committed to societal change, though, we find ourselves working doubly hard, struggling to prove to others that women like us are not a risk. We often feel tired, alone. 12

Alone, yet enmeshed in family responsibilities, concerned about our parents and siblings, about our children. And we worry about our national family or community as we hear the statistics about our growing Latina population. If Latinas have families—and fewer of us are marrying—they tend to be larger than the average, and more and more we head these families alone, often in poverty. Although we have high participation in the work force, we tend to be clerical or service workers. Our median income remains below that of Anglos. How well prepared are we for these challenges? How are we assisting other women to plan for the future, to have realistic expectations? Too many of us don't finish high school, too many of us who complete community college programs don't transfer to four-year institutions, too many of us are denied the opportunity to attend colleges away from home, too many of us are not encouraged fully to develop our talents. 13

As we mother, teach, write, mentor the next generation of women, we need to examine the lives of women in this country, our lives, not as we might want them to be, but as they are. It's difficult to change what we don't understand. What do we know about ourselves and about the 14 women who will appear in our offices and classrooms? What do we know about our inside lives, the inside lives of the female middle class? Most women in the United States are not reading professional journals in their apartments or houses today. We ingest pollutants—toxic ideas and attitudes—while we watch movies and television or read steamy novels or relax with women's magazines. Women in this country continue to devour novels about women who find comfort in the image of being swept off tiny feet by determined, hard-muscled men.

We turn slick, musk-scented magazine pages that promise The Secrets   15
of Skin Polish, 9 Ways to Prevent Wrinkles, Beauty from Head to Toe. For the price of the magazine, we are lured to believe that we can transform our flabby egos and disappointing bodies into the confident creatures who gaze boldly, sirens who beckon us to become perfect, smiling decorations. Listen to the bait. We are promised that we can be glamorous, attractive, radiant, exhilarating, classic, breathtaking, dazzling, legendary, mysterious. Similar magazines from Mexico promise that we can be *sensual, increíble, sexy, elegante, bella, enigmática.*[10] We're taught the world over that it's our job to be pretty. Too often do we brood when we're five or eighty-five about our exteriors, peer in annoyance at our hips (too wide), noses (too long), lips (too thin). Some of us stop eating or eat until we're sick. We bare our unsatisfactory bodies so they can be reshaped, be made more loveable by surgeons who can mold us into beauty and happiness. How much time we spend looking the part, a part we didn't write.

In her documentary *A Famine Within*, Katherine Gilday skillfully   16
reveals our obsession with The Body, the difficulty we have accepting and loving ourselves, our imperfect selves. She shows how we are bombarded with images of women who seldom look like the women in our lives or in our mirror. Our shapes and the shapes of our mothers are steadily described as inferior, proof of our lack of self-control. We define others by their contours, equate thinness with morality. The young women Gilday interviews visibly struggle for words ugly enough to describe their reaction to being overweight. To be fat is to be "grotesque." Fashion models are often role models, says Gilday. Decorative, silent women.

Driving down the freeway, we see, "You've Come a Long Way, Baby."[11]   17
Baby? The woman smiling at us casually holding a cigarette is young, sleek, glamorous. Success is being defined for us as eternal youth, a carefree life, trendy clothes, and getting to do what men do—in this case,

---

[10] Spanish: *sensual, incredible, sexy, elegant, beautiful, mysterious.* [Editors' note.]

[11] An advertising slogan for Virginia Slims, a brand of cigarettes targeted at women. [Editors' note.]

savor a health hazard. We want to define ourselves in broader and richer terms than that, but how do we help young women, all young women, to perceive such manipulation and to wrench their lives free from images that bind?

Meaning

1. Why are Latinas "labeled a *double minority*" (paragraph 1)? What makes the label significant to Mora?

2. "We often are too busy playing the game of Great Expectations," Mora writes in her first paragraph. What does she mean? What does the "game" consist of, and what is its goal? Why is winning more difficult for Latinas?

3. What is wrong, in Mora's opinion, with media portrayals that depict Latinas as either "fiery" or "docile" (paragraph 7)?

4. Mora's essay does not contain a direct thesis statement, but her main idea is clear. Express the point of her analysis in your own words.

5. Try to guess the meanings of any of the following words that you are unsure of, based on their context in Mora's essay. Test your guesses in a dictionary, and then use each word in a sentence of your own.

vigor (3)	enmeshed (4)	delve (6)
demographics (3)	machinations (4)	docile (7)
conspire (3)	cacophony (5)	median (13)
equity (3)	appropriated (6)	sirens (15)

Purpose and Audience

1. For whom is Mora writing? How can you tell?

2. What kind of future does Mora envision for young Latinas? How does she propose they achieve such goals?

3. Mora concludes her essay with an unanswered question. Why does she ask it? What is the effect of ending this way?

Method and Structure

1. According to Mora, what have advertisers learned about Latino values? How does she use those values to organize her essay?

2. What elements of popular culture does Mora examine in her analysis? What principle of analysis does she use to reassemble those elements into a new whole?

3. In paragraph 16, Mora summarizes the content of a documentary film. What is the subject of the film? How does citing it contribute to or support Mora's analysis?

4. **OTHER METHODS**   Mora's essay relies on **cause-and-effect analysis** (Chapter 13) to examine the impact of popular culture on Latina women. If media messages promoting loyalty and beauty are the cause, what does Mora believe are the effects?

Language

1. A poet, Mora enlivens her prose with **metaphor** and **personification**. Find some examples and comment on their effectiveness.

2. Mora uses several Spanish words and phrases in this essay. Why doesn't she translate them for readers?

3. How would you characterize the **tone** of Mora's essay? Support your answer with examples from the essay.

Writing Topics

1. **JOURNAL TO ESSAY**   Expand your journal entry about a commercial or advertisement (p. 162) into a full essay analyzing its message. Describe the ad, and pinpoint why you find it offensive or annoying. Make sure your essay has a controlling thesis that draws together all the points of your analysis and asserts why the advertisement has the effect it does. Alternatively, you could choose a commercial you think is unusually entertaining, amusing, or moving, and explain why it works. Be sure to document your sources (see the Appendix).

2. Toward the end of her essay, Mora suggests that the images in fashion magazines make Latinas feel inadequate—a response that some say is the direct result of advertising practices that create insecurities for all types of people in order to exploit them. (Consider, for instance, automotive commercials suggesting that parents of adult children have boring lives or ads that push tooth-whitening products.) Choose an example of advertising that you think appeals to a real or invented insecurity to sell a product, and analyze its message in a brief essay or presentation. Are the advertiser's techniques effective? ethical? entertaining? Be sure to identify a principle of analysis for your response and to support your argument with details from the advertisement.

3. **CULTURAL CONSIDERATIONS**   This essay was written two decades ago. To what extent do Mora's concerns and criticisms still hold true? Select two or three of her statements, and think of some contemporary examples that

either support or undermine her claims. For instance, how visible are the works of Latino "[s]ingers, writers, and artists" (paragraph 3), today? Do you know of any Latina politicians or professionals (7)? Have fashion magazines changed in any way from what Mora describes (15)? Write an essay of your own responding to Mora's essay. Be sure to include examples to support your view.

4. **RESEARCH** Mora mentions demographics and the "grim statistics on wages and education for US Latinos" in paragraphs 3 and 13, but she doesn't specify the numbers. Go to the Web site of the Pew Research Center's Hispanic Trends Project (*pewhispanic.org*), and search the data sets and statistical portraits for recent information on these subjects. For instance, what percentage of the US population identifies as Latino? How many Latino men and women finish high school? How many finish college? How do their earnings compare with the national average? How many Latino families are headed by married couples? How many of them live in poverty? Report your findings.

5. **CONNECTIONS** Mora writes of familial disapproval of married Latina women who pursue educations and careers. How does this pressure relate to the marital roles that Judy Brady focuses on in her essay "I Want a Wife" (p. 277)? Write an essay analyzing these writers' attitudes toward tradition and feminism. How much do Mora and Brady seem to have in common? Use evidence from both essays to support your response.

Junk is the ideal product . . . the ultimate merchandise. No sales talk necessary. The client will crawl through a sewer and beg to buy.

—William S. Burroughs

Your responsibility as a parent is not as great as you might imagine. . . . If your child simply grows up to be someone who does not use the word *collectible* as a noun, you can consider yourself an unqualified success.

—Fran Lebowitz

Toys were lots of fun before they became capitalist tools.   —Beth Copeland Vargo

JOURNAL RESPONSE   Do you own, or did you ever own, merchandise tied to a movie or TV show, such as *Star Wars* drink glasses, a *Family Guy* T-shirt, or *Smurfs* bedding? Write about why you wanted a particular item or set of items and what, if anything, they still mean to you.

Andrew Warren III

Andrew Warren III was born in 1981 and grew up in Boston. He graduated from the Boston Latin School and worked as a computer technician for several years before completing a BA in English, with a minor in computer science, from the University of Massachusetts, Boston, in 2009. Now a quality-assurance engineer specializing in file transfer systems, Warren reports that his interests include "eating, cooking, watching movies, playing video games, and generally just being a nerd." He lives in Quincy, Massachusetts.

Throwing Darts at *The Simpsons*
(Student Essay)

In this entertaining analysis of the most enduring scripted prime-time show in the history of television (twenty-five years and counting), Warren offers detailed examples and information from a source to support a fresh take on *The Simpsons*. He wrote this essay for a composition class, and then at his instructor's suggestion submitted it to *Lux*, the literary magazine of the University of Massachusetts, Boston. Warren reports that he revised the finished essay twice before it was published, tightening the focus, dropping some of the deeper analysis, improving the style, and in the process trimming it to half its original length.

"C'mon dude . . . let's open it," my friend Sean begged. We were hanging   1
out in our apartment and, yet again, he wanted to play darts with my
Simpsons dartboard—a repeated episode throughout 2001. It was resting
on an end table in its unopened box, cellophane wrapper still intact. I had
purchased it earlier that year for $30 from a collectibles dealer on *eBay*, so
I had to protect it every few weeks from Sean or others who wanted to
actually play a game of darts. The board was, and still is, a snazzy decoration—a large, colorful square adorned with the images of Homer and Bart
Simpson, Moe the Bartender, Barney, and Krusty the Clown. I too have
occasionally thought about ripping open the plastic and chucking darts at
the board ("playing darts" gives me too much credit), badly scarring the
cork and surrounding walls. But I haven't had the heart.

I began watching *The Simpsons,* a satirical cartoon sitcom about a   2
nuclear small-town American family, every day starting in 1992 or 1993—
whenever the first episodes began running in syndication. Before then I
didn't really understand the show. I don't think I was old enough. But
starting in junior high school, the rest of my friends and I, including Sean,
used the show as a milestone for good taste. Those first years—up to
1998—are simply brilliant. (That is a fact, and I'll argue with anyone who
disagrees with me to the death.) Those who understood the show received
instant respect and inclusion (unless you were a jerk). Many conversations evolved out of strings of quotes from the show's characters, and
obscure references to various scenes became daily jokes. We developed a
sentimental attachment to *The Simpsons* that extended far beyond the
daily twenty-five-minute television commitment into the cores of our
lives, not only due to the resonant pleasure of the viewing experience, but
also due to the reinforced social connections my peers and I had crafted
among ourselves.

Amazingly, before I even started watching *The Simpsons,* it had already   3
reached its zenith in the public sphere. The show was the biggest pop
culture event of 1990 (Turner 25). Bart, the spiky-haired scion of the
Simpson clan, led the charge, as images of him and other members of the
family graced the covers of some of the most prominent media rags: "*Time*
and *Newsweek, Rolling Stone, TV Guide,* and *Mad Magazine,* even *Mother
Jones*" (Turner 25). In the wake of the advertising juggernaut came the
merchandise. This feverish love affair was dubbed "Bart-mania" by the
media, and most mainstream retailers had racks of clothing and shelves
of merchandise dedicated to *The Simpsons*—especially Bart. But unlike
most other pop culture phenomena, which tend to implode immediately
like an explosion starved for oxygen, *The Simpsons* did not die off; and

although the ratings slightly declined after the initial buzz dissipated, the show improved (this is a completely objective fact, I swear), revealing an ever deeper well of ironic and analytical satire of society and the media through carefully, hilariously employed humor.

One of the show's favorite, and funniest, satirical vehicles is Krusty   4 the Clown, Bart Simpson's childhood hero and a symbol of everything that is wrong with the entertainment industry. He is a morally destitute, corrupt, addicted, all-purpose wretch; he is also the most prominent icon in the lives of the Simpson family. The children watch his television show daily. Many episodes begin with the familiar scene of the children sitting in front of the tube after school, faces illuminated by the glow, watching the mindless string of gags that compose the Krusty the Clown Show. Sometimes Krusty is included in the absurd adventures in which the Simpsons are involved each week. Yet the most present he is to them is through the omnipresent, narcissistically personified branding in his merchandise, which constitutes the primary source of his fortunes. Bart's room is a virtual shrine to the entertainer, with many of his material goods bearing the visage and logo of Krusty and his media enterprise. Other examples of Krusty's products, sporting the Krusty Brand Seal of Approval (practically a guarantee that you *will* be injured; see the "Kamp Krusty" episode for explicit examples), are not even connected to toys and playthings. Some of the more blatant, hyperbolic examples are Krusty's Non-Narkotik Kough Syrup for Kids, Krusty's Sulfuric Acid, and the terrifying Krusty's Home Pregnancy Test (Warning: May Cause Birth Defects). So, although the TV experience ends at the same time every day, the relation to Krusty picks up again via his ever-present merchandise.

The writers of *The Simpsons* were well aware of a similar situation   5 developing between the show, its fans, and the Fox Broadcasting Company. Krusty was first introduced to lampoon the uncannily predictable seedy side behind most childhood icons, but later his omnipresence shifted into a satire of the entire enterprise of television and fandom. Like Bart and the rest of the citizens of Springfield, my sentiments have been reinforced through repeated viewing of syndicated broadcasts. Years ago, watching *The Simpsons* was a required activity—I needed my fix—and the Fox Broadcasting Company, well aware of this need since the initial Nielsen-reinforced popularity boom of 1990, produced tons of real-world merchandise spaces in order to occupy the space in between viewings of the show, expanding the potential to make more money. Several years later, I purchased my dartboard, a product with a vague association with the show at best (there has only been one scene, in Moe's Tavern, in which characters playing darts have been featured on *The Simpsons*), just as Bart's allegiance to Krusty is exemplified in an all-consuming collection of non-clown or even comedy-related merchandise from the show: dolls, bedding and bedroom furniture, decorative posters, and various other artifacts which round out and define his daily existence. They declare his love for his hero. Fans of *The Simpsons* do the same. I've seen countless posters, bottle openers, and other stuff like my dartboard present in my peers' living quarters since the madness began.

So, I recently rediscovered my once-treasured *Simpsons* dartboard in   6 my bedroom. It was up on top of a bookshelf, mostly hidden from view by a movie poster I stuck in front of it. I pulled it down, brushed off the dust, and examined its packaging—still mint. Its value on *eBay* has declined to around $8 (plus shipping), most likely due to a drop in interest in the show and the merchandising blitz following the less than mediocre movie release. I'm not surprised, as I rarely watch the reruns anymore (and never the Sunday episode premieres). My relationship with my dartboard is now relatively empty. I see it as nothing more than a toy, certainly not the symbol of something else I once loved. The show's creators have been reminding us all along that something like the dartboard is only worth as much as the public's interest in it. In the first episode in which we meet Krusty's character, his merchandise is burned by the citizens of Springfield when the public is tricked into believing that he robbed a convenience store at gunpoint. Our connections to merchandise are only as strong as the quality of the strongest memories of the events which give the products their value. I guess that leaves only one thing: does anyone want to play a game of darts?

Works Cited

"Kamp Krusty." *The Simpsons: The Complete Fourth Season.* 1992. 20th Cent. Fox, 2004. DVD. Disc 1.
Turner, Chris. *Planet Simpson.* Cambridge: Da Capo, 2004. Print.

Meaning

1. In your own words, explain Warren's thesis. Where does he state it explicitly?

2. Why, according to Warren, has he been reluctant to take his *Simpsons* dartboard out of its original packaging? What finally makes him decide to open it?

3. What does Warren mean in paragraph 6 when he refers to "the less than mediocre movie release"? What movie is he talking about? Did he like it or not?

4. If you are unfamiliar with any of the following words, try to guess their meanings from the context in which Warren uses them. Look up the words in a dictionary to check your guesses, and then use each one in a sentence of your own.

adorned (1)
satire/satirical (2, 3, 4)
syndication/
   syndicated (2, 5)
resonant (2)
zenith (3)
juggernaut (3)

phenomena (3)
implode (3)
dissipated (3)
destitute (4)
icon (4)
omnipresent/
   omnipresence (4, 5)

narcissistically (4)
visage (4)
hyperbolic (4)
lampoon (5)
uncannily (5)

Purpose and Audience

1. What do you think Warren's purpose was in writing this essay: to get more people to watch *The Simpsons*? to explain why his dartboard has lost its value? to convince merchandisers to change their ways? to do something else?

2. What assumptions does Warren seem to make about his readers—their gender or age, their attitudes toward *The Simpsons*, their attitudes toward advertising and merchandising, and so on?

3. In paragraph 3, Warren cites two pieces of information from a **source**. What does this information add to his analysis?

Method and Structure

1. Why do you think Warren chose the method of analysis to talk about the role of merchandising in the long-term success of *The Simpsons*? How does the method help Warren achieve his purpose?

2. What principle of analysis does Warren apply to his examination of *The Simpsons*? Why is that principle particularly well suited to his subject?

3. What does Warren accomplish in his first and last paragraphs?

4. **OTHER METHODS**   Warren's analysis essay is also a model of **comparison and contrast** (Chapter 11) because he examines the similarities between Krusty the Clown fans and *Simpsons* fans. Why do you think Warren devotes so much attention to Krusty? What makes the comparison significant?

Language

1. How would you describe Warren's **tone**? How seriously does he take his subject? Is the tone appropriate, given his purpose?

2. Notice the many sentences and phrases Warren encloses in parentheses, such as "That is a fact, and I'll argue with anyone who disagrees with me to the death" (paragraph 2). What is the function of these parenthetical remarks? What do they contribute to the writer's purpose?

Writing Topics

1. **JOURNAL TO ESSAY**   Expand your journal entry about pop culture merchandise (p. 170) into a full essay analyzing a single item. Describe the item and why you wanted it, considering your feelings about the characters it represents. Include a discussion of what the merchandise means to you now, explaining why it is or is not still part of your life. Make sure your essay has a controlling thesis that draws together all the points of your analysis. Document any sources you consult, as Warren does (see pp. 394–405).

2. How did you react to Warren's essay? Do you agree with his assessment of *The Simpsons* and his suggestion that merchandising both helped the show succeed and contributed to its decline? Or do you find his evaluation of the show's worth one-sided, his examples and opinions too personal to form the basis of an analysis? Write an essay that responds to Warren's conclusions. Be sure to include examples to support your view.

3. **CULTURAL CONSIDERATIONS**   In the Western world, we watch a lot of television: most of us watch it every day. Some people feel that TV can expand our vision of the world by showing us different people and places and exposing us to new ideas and issues. Others argue that TV narrows our views, inundating us with shallow content designed to please the crowd. What is your opinion about the effects of TV? Do you think that your viewing habits have an essentially positive or negative effect on you? Write an essay in which you explain how you think TV affects you.

4. **CONNECTIONS**   Like Warren, Antonio Ruiz-Camacho, in "Souvenirs" (p. 252), writes about the value he has attached to merchandise for a television show—in his case, a Kermit the Frog alarm clock. In an essay, compare and contrast how popular culture has affected these two writers. How do their respective points of view affect their experiences and attitudes? You might consider, for example, how each writer acquired the merchandise and why, or the meanings they see in their toys. Be sure to include examples from both essays to support your comparison.

WRITING WITH THE METHOD

DIVISION OR ANALYSIS

Select one of the following topics, or any other topic they suggest, for an essay developed by analysis. Be sure to choose a topic you care about so that analysis is a means of communicating an idea, not an end in itself.

People, Animals, and Objects

1. The personality of a friend or relative
2. The personality of a typical politician, teacher, or other professional
3. An animal such as a cat, dog, horse, cow, spider, or bat
4. A machine or an appliance such as a solar panel, hybrid engine, harvesting combine, smartphone, tablet, hair dryer, or toaster
5. A nonmotorized vehicle such as a skateboard, in-line skate, bicycle, or snowboard
6. A building such as a hospital, theater, or sports arena

Ideas

7. The perfect marriage
8. The perfect crime
9. A theory or concept in a field such as psychology, sociology, economics, biology, physics, engineering, or astronomy
10. The evidence in a political argument (written, spoken, or reported in the news)
11. A liberal arts education

Aspects of Culture

12. A stereotype
13. A style of dress or "look," such as that associated with the typical hipster, bodybuilder, or outdoors enthusiast
14. A typical hero or villain in children's movies, science fiction, or romance novels
15. A popular Web site or Internet meme
16. A literary work: short story, novel, poem, essay
17. A visual work: painting, sculpture, building
18. A musical work: song, concerto, symphony, opera
19. A performance: sports, acting, dance, music, speech
20. The slang of a particular group or occupation

WRITING ABOUT THE THEME

LOOKING AT POPULAR CULTURE

1. The essays by Scott Adams (p. 156), Pat Mora (p. 162), and Andrew Warren (p. 171) all include the theme that what you see — whether in entertainment, advertising, or consumer products — is not all you get. Think of something you have used, heard, seen, or otherwise experienced in popular culture that made you suspect a hidden message or agenda. Consider, for example, a childhood toy, a popular breakfast cereal, a political speech, a magazine, a textbook, a video game, a movie, or a visit to a theme park. Using the essays in this chapter as models, write an analysis of your subject, making sure to divide it into distinct elements and to conclude it by reassembling those elements into a new whole.

2. Pat Mora and Luci Tapahonso (p. 149) both analyze advertising aimed at minority groups. Mora calls for an awakening to negative "images that bind" Mexican American girls and young women. Tapahonso, in contrast, thinks that American Indians found cause for celebration in a positive commercial that "showed Indians as we live today." What do you think of niche advertising? Is Mora's concern justified, or are the ads she singles out unusual? How common are ads like the one Tapahonso analyzes? Consider ads you've seen, or pay close attention to the ads as you're watching television or surfing the Internet over a week or so. Then write an essay addressing whether advertisers seem to treat the differences among people fairly or to exploit those differences. Are there notable exceptions in either case?

3. Jon Pareles (p. 149), Luci Tapahonso, Pat Mora, and Andrew Warren all write seriously about popular culture, a subject that some people would consider trivial and unworthy of critical attention. How informative and useful are such analyses? Where does each selection tell us something significant about ourselves, or in contrast, where does it fail in trying to make the trivial seem important? Is popular culture — music, television, film, books, restaurant chains — best looked at critically, best ignored, or best simply enjoyed? Explain your answer in an essay, using plenty of examples to support your thesis.

9

CLASSIFICATION

▶

SORTING FRIENDS AND NEIGHBORS

We classify when we sort things into groups: kinds of cars, styles of writing, types of customers. Because it creates order, **classification** helps us make sense of our experiences and our surroundings. With it, we see the correspondences among like things and distinguish them from unlike things, similarities and distinctions that can be especially helpful when making a decision or encouraging others to see things from a new perspective. You use classification when you prioritize your bills, sort your laundry, or organize your music collection; you might also draw on the method to choose among types of data plans, to propose new pay scales at your workplace, or to argue at a town meeting that some types of community projects are more valuable than others. Because classification helps us name things, remember them, and discuss them with others, it is also a useful method for developing and sharing ideas in writing.

Reading Classification

Writers classify primarily to explain a pattern in a subject that might not have been noticed before: a sportswriter, for instance, might observe that great basketball defenders tend to fall into one of three groups based on their style of play: the shot blockers, the stealers, and the brawlers. Sometimes, writers also classify to persuade readers that one group is superior: the same sportswriter might argue that shot blockers are the most effective defenders because they not only create turnovers like the stealers do, but they also intimidate the opponent like the brawlers do.

Classification involves a three-step process:

1. Separate things into their elements, using the method of **division or analysis** (previous chapter).
2. Isolate the similarities among the elements.
3. Group or classify the things based on those similarities, matching like with like.

The following diagram illustrates a classification essay that appears later in this chapter, "The People Next Door" by Jonathan R. Gould, Jr. (p. 191). Gould's subject is neighbors, and he sees four distinct kinds:

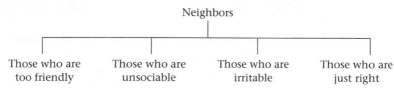

All the members of Gould's overall group share at least one characteristic: they have been Gould's neighbors. The members of each subgroup also share at least one characteristic: they are too friendly, for instance, or unsociable. The people in each subgroup are independent of one another, and none of them is essential to the existence of the subgroup: the kind of neighbor would continue to exist even if, at the moment, Gould didn't live next door to such a person.

The number of groups in a classification scheme depends entirely on the basis for establishing the classes in the first place. There are two systems:

■ In a *complex classification* like that used for neighbors, each individual fits firmly into one class because of at least one distinguishing feature shared with all members of that class but not with any members of any other classes. All the too-friendly neighbors are overly friendly, but none of the unsociable, irritable, or just-right neighbors shares this characteristic.

■ In a *binary or two-part classification*, two classes are in opposition to each other, such as constructive and destructive neighbors. Often, one group has a certain characteristic that the other group lacks. For instance, neighbors could be classified into those who respect your privacy and those who don't. A binary scheme is useful to emphasize the possession of a particular characteristic, but it is limited if it specifies nothing about the members of the "other" class except that they lack the trait. (An old joke claims that there are two kinds of people in the world—those who classify and all others.)

Sorting items demands a **principle of classification** that determines the groups by distinguishing them. For instance, Gould's principle in identifying four groups of neighbors is their behavior toward him and his family. Principles for sorting a year's movies might be genre (action-adventure, comedy, drama), place of origin (domestic, foreign), or cost of production (low-budget, medium-budget, high-budget). The choice of a principle depends on the writer's main interest in the subject.

Although a writer may emphasize one class over the others, the classification itself must be complete and consistent. A classification of movies by genre would be incomplete if it omitted comedies. It would be inconsistent if it included action-adventures, comedies, dramas, low-budget films, and foreign films: such a system mixes *three* principles (genre, cost, origin); it omits whole classes (what about high-budget domestic dramas?); and it overlaps other classes (a low-budget foreign action-adventure would fit in three different groups).

Analyzing Classification in Paragraphs

Dahlia Lithwick (born 1968) is a legal correspondent and a senior editor at *Slate*. This paragraph is adapted from "A Unified Theory of Muppet Types," a tongue-in-cheek article she wrote for that magazine in 2012. (Of the human examples she offers for each class, Zelda Fitzgerald was the free-spirited wife of *Great Gatsby* author F. Scott Fitzgerald; Stephen Breyer and John Roberts are Supreme Court justices.)

Every one of us is either a Chaos Muppet or an Order Muppet. Chaos Muppets are out-of-control, emotional, volatile. They tend toward the blue and fuzzy. They make their way through life in a swirling maelstrom of food crumbs, small flaming objects, and the letter C. Cookie Monster, Ernie, Grover, Gonzo, Dr. Bunsen Honeydew and—paradigmatically—Animal, are all Chaos Muppets. Zelda Fitzgerald was a Chaos Muppet. So, I must tell you, is Justice Stephen Breyer. Order Muppets—and I'm thinking about Bert, Scooter, Sam the Eagle, Kermit the Frog, and the blue guy who is perennially harassed by Grover at restaurants (the Order Muppet Everyman)—tend to be neurotic, highly regimented, averse to surprises and

Principle of classification (topic sentence underlined): Muppet types

1. Chaos Muppets

Characteristics of type

Muppet examples

Human examples

2. Order Muppets

Muppet examples

Characteristics of type

may sport monstrously large eyebrows. They sometimes resent the responsibility of the world weighing on their felt shoulders, but they secretly revel in the knowledge that they keep the show running. Your first-grade teacher was probably an Order Muppet. So is Chief Justice John Roberts. It's not that any one type of Muppet is inherently better than the other. It's simply the case that the key to a happy marriage, a well-functioning family, and a productive place of work lies in carefully calibrating the ratio of Chaos Muppets to Order Muppets within any closed system. That, and always letting the Chaos Muppets do the driving.

Human examples

Implications of classification

Luis Alberto Urrea (born 1955) is an award-winning poet, fiction writer, and journalist whose work often focuses on the lives of impoverished Mexicans. In the following passage from "Night Shift," a 2012 essay about his former job as a campground janitor, Urrea classifies temporary neighbors in a California RV park.

The better sections of the campground were reserved for the RVs and fifth wheels. They had nice fat pullouts with room for an extra car or pickup, a little grass so they could unfurl their awnings and set up their lawn chairs. Electric and sewer hookups. It was deluxe, as far as blacktop roughing it went. The smaller RVs, Class 1 and shorter, got tawdrier, smaller parking slots. Yellower grass in narrower strips. Fewer oleanders. Farther from the golf course. And the suckers who came with tents — who should have had the smarts to head up to the Cuyamaca Mountains and at least hear a blue jay — why, they were crammed over on the far side, near the beach, but also near the adjacent trailer park with its . . . nocturnal Bachman Turner Overdrive recitals. Stray cats from the trailer park cruised our property, but there wasn't any policy about them. They kept rodents under control and might have even dissuaded the skunks, which really enjoyed the French fries and Sno Balls scattered around the trailers.

Principle of classification: equipment ownership

1. Large RVs: given "deluxe" accommodations

2. Small RVs: provided with "tawdrier" spaces

3. Tents: pushed aside to an undesirable area

Developing an Essay by Classification

▶ Getting Started

Classification essays are often assigned in college: you might be asked to identify the major branches of government for a political science class, for instance, or to categorize difficult personality types for a business communication course. When you need to develop your own subject for a classification essay, think of one large class of things whose members you've noticed fall into subclasses, such as study habits, midnight shoppers, or charity fund-raising appeals. Be sure that your general subject forms a class in its own right—that all its members share at least one important quality. Then look for your principle of classification, the quality or qualities that distinguish some members from others, providing poles for the members to group themselves around. One such principle for charity fund-raising appeals might be the different methods of delivery, such as telephone calls, public gatherings, advertisements, and social media campaigns.

While generating ideas for your classification, keep track of them in a list, diagram, or outline to ensure that your principle is applied thoroughly (to all classes) and consistently (each class relating to the principle). Fill in the list, diagram, or outline with the distinguishing features of each class and with examples that will clarify your scheme.

▶ Forming a Thesis

You will want to state your principle of classification in a thesis sentence so that you know where you're going and your readers know where you're taking them. Be sure the sentence also conveys a *reason* for the classification so that the essay does not become a dull list of categories. The following tentative thesis sentence is mechanical; the revision below it is more interesting.

> TENTATIVE THESIS SENTENCE   Charity fund-raising requests are delivered in many ways.

> REVISED THESIS SENTENCE   Of the many ways to deliver charity fund-raising requests, the three that rely on personal contact are generally the most effective.

(Note that the revised thesis sentence implies a further classification based on whether the requests involve personal contact or not.)

▶ Organizing

The **introduction** to a classification essay should make clear why the classification is worthwhile: What situation prompted the essay? What do readers already know about the subject? What use might they make of the information you will provide? Unless your principle of classification is self-evident, you may want to explain it briefly—but save extensive explanation for the body of the essay.

In the body of the essay, the classes may be arranged in order of decreasing familiarity or increasing importance or size—whatever pattern provides the emphasis you want and clarifies your scheme for readers. You should at least mention each class, but some classes may demand considerable space and detail.

A classification essay often ends with a **conclusion** that restores the wholeness of the subject. Among other uses, the conclusion might summarize the classes, comment on the significance of one particular class in relation to the whole, or point out a new understanding of the whole subject gained from the classification.

▶ Drafting

For the first draft of your classification, your main goal will be to establish your scheme: spelling out the purpose and principle of classification and defining the groups so that they are complete and consistent, covering the subject without mixing principles or overlapping. The more you've been able to plan your scheme, the less difficult the draft will be. If you can also fill in the examples and other details needed to develop the groups, do so.

Be sure to consider your readers' needs as you draft. For a subject familiar to readers, such as study habits, you probably wouldn't need to justify your principle of classification, but you would need to enliven the classes themselves with vivid details. For an unfamiliar subject, in contrast, you might need to take considerable care in explaining the principle of classification as well as in detailing the classes.

▶ Revising and Editing

The following questions and the information in the Focus box on the next page can help you revise and edit your classification.

- *Will readers see the purpose of your classification?* Let readers know early on why you are troubling to classify your subject, and keep this purpose evident throughout the essay.

FOCUS ON PARAGRAPH DEVELOPMENT

A crucial aim of revising a classification is to make sure each group is clear: what's counted in, what's counted out, and why. It's not unusual to get so focused on identifying and sorting categories during the draft stage that you neglect the details. In that case, you'll need to go back and provide examples, comparisons, and other particulars to make the groups clear as you develop the paragraph(s) devoted to each group.

The following undeveloped paragraph gives just the outline of one group in a four-part classification of ex-smokers into zealots, evangelists, the elect, and the serene:

> The second group, evangelists, does not condemn smokers but encourages them to quit. Evangelists think quitting is easy, and they preach this message, often earning the resentment of potential converts.

Contrast this bare-bones adaptation with the actual paragraphs written by Franklin E. Zimring in his essay "Confessions of a Former Smoker":

> By contrast, the antismoking evangelist does not condemn smokers. Unlike the zealot, he regards smoking as an easily curable condition, as a social disease, and not a sin. The evangelist spends an enormous amount of time seeking and preaching to the unconverted. He argues that kicking the habit is not *that* difficult. After all, *he* did it; moreover, as he describes it, the benefits of quitting are beyond measure and the disadvantages are nil.
>
> The hallmark of the evangelist is his insistence that he never misses tobacco. Though he is less hostile to smokers than the zealot, he is resented more. Friends and loved ones who have been the targets of his preachments frequently greet the resumption of smoking by the evangelist as an occasion for unmitigated glee.

In the second sentence of both paragraphs, Zimring explicitly contrasts evangelists with zealots, the group he previously discussed. And he does more, as well: he provides specific examples of the evangelist's message (first paragraph) and of others' reactions to him (second paragraph). These details pin down the group, making it distinct from other groups and clear in itself.

For more advice on developing paragraphs through specifics, see pages 33–34.

- *Is your classification complete?* Your principle of classification should create categories that encompass every representative of the general subject. If some representatives will not fit the scheme, you may have to create a new category or revise the existing categories to include them.

- *Is your classification consistent?* Consistency is essential to save readers from confusion or irritation. Make sure all the classes reflect the same principle and do not overlap. Remedy flaws by adjusting the classes or creating new ones.

A Note on Thematic Connections

Writers classify people more than any other subject, perhaps because the method gives order and even humor to our relationships. The authors in this chapter explore the connections that give people a sense of where they fit in with friends and neighbors. In a paragraph, Dahlia Lithwick asserts that everyone we know can be classified as one of two distinct types of Muppet characters (p. 180). Also in a paragraph, Luis Alberto Urrea sorts campers at an RV park by their assigned parking spaces (p. 181). Then, in essays, Brandon Griggs identifies a dozen irritating behaviors among *Facebook* friends (next page), Jonathan R. Gould finds four kinds of next-door neighbors (p. 191), and David Brooks examines several characteristics of neighborhoods to argue that American society isn't as diverse as we like to think (p. 195).

Now the cliques are moving online.   —Kim Komando

Rather than bringing me closer to others, the time that I spend online isolates me from the most important people in my life: my family, my friends, my neighborhood, my community.   —Clifford Stoll

There are three kinds of death in this world. There's heart death, there's brain death, and there's being off the network.   —Guy Almes

JOURNAL RESPONSE   Do you have a *Facebook* page? a *Twitter* following? a *Tumblr* account? Write a short journal entry about how you connect with your friends online. How would your relationships suffer, or improve, if you didn't have access to a social-networking tool?

Brandon Griggs

Brandon Griggs (born 1960) is a journalist who writes about culture and technology. He went to high school in Washington, DC, graduated from Tufts University in 1982, and studied at Columbia University's Graduate School of Journalism under a fellowship with the National Arts Journalism Program. Griggs held a staff writing position as the "Culture Vulture" for the *Salt Lake Tribune* for fifteen years before taking his current position as a technology-section producer for *CNN.com*. He is the author of *Utah Curiosities: Quirky Characters, Roadside Oddities and Other Offbeat Stuff* (2008), a guide to the state's peculiar legends and unconventional tourist attractions.

The Most Annoying Facebookers

In this 2009 article for *CNN.com*, Griggs draws on his personal experience and his sense of humor to call attention to behaviors that are almost guaranteed to alienate anyone's network of friends.

Facebook, for better or worse, is like being at a big party with all your friends, 1
family, acquaintances, and coworkers. There are lots of fun, interesting
people you're happy to talk to when they stroll up. Then there are the
other people, the ones who make you cringe when you see them coming.
This article is about those people.

Sure, *Facebook* can be a great tool for keeping up with folks who are $\quad$ 2 important to you. Take the status update, the 160-character message that users post in response to the question, "What's on your mind?" An artful, witty, or newsy status update is a pleasure—a real-time, tiny window into a friend's life.

But far more posts read like navel-gazing diary entries, or worse, spam. $\quad$ 3 A recent study categorized 40% of *Twitter* tweets as "pointless babble," and it wouldn't be surprising if updates on *Facebook*, still a fast-growing social network, break down in a similar way.

Combine dull status updates with shameless self-promoters, "friend- $\quad$ 4 padders," and that friend of a friend who sends you quizzes every day, and *Facebook* becomes a daily reminder of why some people can get on your nerves.

Here are twelve of the most annoying types of *Facebook* users: $\quad$ 5

The Let-Me-Tell-You-Every-Detail-of-My-Day Bore. "I'm waking up." $\quad$ 6 "I had Wheaties for breakfast." "I'm bored at work." "I'm stuck in traffic." You're kidding! How fascinating! No moment is too mundane for some people to broadcast unsolicited to the world. Just because you have 432 *Facebook* friends doesn't mean we all want to know when you're waiting for the bus.

The Self-Promoter. OK, so we've probably all posted at least once $\quad$ 7 about some achievement. And sure, maybe your friends really do want to read the fascinating article you wrote about beet farming. But when almost EVERY update is a link to your blog, your poetry reading, your 10k results, or your art show, you sound like a bragger or a self-centered careerist.

The Friend-Padder. The average *Facebook* user has 120 friends on the $\quad$ 8 site. Schmoozers and social butterflies—you know, the ones who make lifelong pals on the subway—might reasonably have 300 or 400. But 1,000 "friends"? Unless you're George Clooney or just won the lottery, no one has that many. That's just showing off.

The Town Crier. "Michael Jackson is dead!!!" You heard it from me $\quad$ 9 first! Me, and the 213,000 other people who all saw it on TMZ. These Matt Drudge[1] wannabes are the reason many of us learn of breaking news not from TV or news sites but from online social networks. In their rush to trumpet the news, these people also spread rumors, half-truths, and innu-endo. No, Jeff Goldblum did not plunge to his death from a New Zealand cliff.

---

[1] Creator and editor of the *Drudge Report*, an online news and gossip site. [Editors' note.]

The TMIer. "Brad is heading to Walgreens to buy something for these   10
pesky hemorrhoids." Boundaries of privacy and decorum don't seem to
exist for these too-much-information updaters, who unabashedly offer up
details about their sex lives, marital troubles, and bodily functions. Thanks
for sharing.

The Bad Grammarian. "So sad about Fara Fauset but Im so gladd its   11
friday yippe." Yes, I know the punctuation rules are different in the digital
world. And, no, no one likes a spelling-Nazi schoolmarm. But you sound
like a moron.

The Sympathy-Baiter. "Barbara is feeling sad today." "Man, am I glad   12
that's over." "Jim could really use some good news about now." Like anglers
hunting for fish, these sad sacks cast out their hooks—baited with vague
tales of woe—in the hopes of landing concerned responses. Genuine bad
news is one thing, but these manipulative posts are just pleas for attention.

The Lurker. The Peeping Toms of *Facebook*, these voyeurs are too cau-   13
tious, or maybe too lazy, to update their status or write on your wall. But
once in a while, you'll be talking to them and they'll mention something
you posted, so you know they're on your page, hiding in the shadows. It's
just a little creepy.

The Crank. These curmudgeons, like the trolls who spew hate in blog   14
comments, never met something they couldn't complain about. "Carl isn't
really that impressed with idiots who don't realize how idiotic they are."
(Actual status update.) Keep spreading the love.

The Paparazzo. Ever visit your *Facebook* page and discover that some-   15
one's posted a photo of you from last weekend's party—a photo you didn't
authorize and haven't even seen? You'd really rather not have to explain
to your mom why you were leering like a drunken hyena and French-
kissing a bottle of Jägermeister.

The Obscurist. "If not now then when?" "You'll see . . ." "Grist for   16
the mill." "John is, small world." "Dave thought he was immune, but no.
No, he is not." (Actual status updates, all.) Sorry, but you're not being
mysterious—just nonsensical.

The Chronic Inviter. "Support my cause." "Sign my petition." "Play   17
Mafia Wars with me." "Which 'Star Trek' character are you?" "Here are the
'Top 5 cars I have personally owned.'" "Here are '25 Things about Me.'"
"Here's a drink." "What drink are you?" "We're related!" "I took the 'What
President Are You?' quiz and found out I'm Millard Fillmore! What presi-
dent are you?"

You probably mean well, but stop. Just stop. I don't care what presi-   18
dent I am—can't we simply be friends? Now excuse me while I go post
the link to this story on my *Facebook* page.

Meaning

1. Does Griggs have a thesis? Where in the essay does he make his point clear?

2. In which category or categories, if any, does Griggs place himself? How can you tell?

3. In paragraph 6, Griggs remarks of "every-detail-of-my-day" posts, "You're kidding! How fascinating!" Does he really mean to say that such information interests him? (Hint: look up *irony* in the Glossary.)

4. Try to guess the meanings of any of the following words that are unfamiliar to you. Test your guesses in a dictionary, and then come up with a sentence or two using each new word.

mundane (6)	unabashedly (10)	curmudgeons (14)
innuendo (9)	anglers (12)	paparazzo (15)
decorum (10)	voyeurs (13)	chronic (17)

Purpose and Audience

1. How can we tell that Griggs intends to entertain us with his essay? Do you detect any other purpose?

2. What assumptions does Griggs make about the readers of his essay? Are the assumptions correct in your case?

Method and Structure

1. How does Griggs use the method of classification for comic effect? In what ways does classification lend itself particularly well to a humorous subject such as this one?

2. What is the one quality that all members of Griggs's subject share, and what principle of classification does he use to sort them?

3. If Griggs's subject is *Facebook*, why does he mention a study of *Twitter* in his introduction (paragraph 3)? What do that study's findings have to do with his thesis?

4. **OTHER METHODS** In addition to classification, Griggs relies heavily on **example** (Chapter 7) to make his point. Why do you think he uses so many direct quotations from *Facebook* status updates? What would the essay lose if Griggs didn't provide these examples?

Language

1. Examine Griggs's **tone**. How would you characterize his attitude toward his subject? Is he angry, resigned, hopeful, something else? Does his overall tone strengthen his essay or weaken it? Why?

2. Find three places where Griggs uses **hyperbole**. What effect does this figure of speech have in this essay?

3. Consider the labels Griggs devises for each category. What **connotations** do these words and phrases have? How do they contribute to his overall point?

4. Notice that Griggs addresses his readers directly, as *you*. What is the effect of this choice? How does it contribute to his purpose?

Writing Topics

1. **JOURNAL TO ESSAY**   Building on your journal entry about your use of social-networking sites (p. 186), write a response to Griggs's essay. Does it amuse you? anger you? embarrass you? make you feel something else? Does it make you want to change your habits when writing status updates? Do you find Griggs's categories, examples, and conclusions fair? Why, or why not? Support your response with details from Griggs's essay and examples from your own experience.

2. Defend one of the groups of *Facebook* users that Griggs finds annoying. Write an essay explaining why someone might engage in a particular posting behavior, such as sharing minor moments or seeking sympathy, and consider what good might come of it, both for the poster and for his or her network of friends.

3. Using Griggs's essay as a model, write an essay that classifies a group of people (teachers, bosses, or salesclerks, for example) for the purpose of getting readers to examine their own behaviors. Sort your subject into classes according to a consistent principle, and provide plenty of details to clarify the classes you decide on. In your essay, be sure to explain to your readers why the classification should persuade them to change their ways.

4. **CULTURAL CONSIDERATIONS**   In questioning how anyone could have a thousand friends, Griggs reveals an assumption that online friendship is nothing more than a digital extension of real-world friendship. Do you agree, or is the definition of *friend* unique to each context? How do online communities function differently than face-to-face communities, and what distinct purposes are served by each? Write an essay answering these questions. As evidence for your response, you may want to discuss how, if at all, your own real-world and online friendships correlate with each other.

5. **CONNECTIONS**   Griggs and Jonathan R. Gould, Jr., in "The People Next Door" (next page), use similar means to achieve humorous effects. Write an essay in which you compare and contrast the tone, style, and use of language in each essay. How does each writer make his readers laugh? Is one more successful than the other, and why?

We make our friends; we make our enemies; but God makes our next-door neighbor.
— G. K. Chesterton

Good fences make good neighbors.
— Proverb

For what do we live, but to make sport for our neighbors, and laugh at them in our turn?
— Jane Austen

JOURNAL RESPONSE   Jot down a list of neighbors you have now and have had in the past. Then write a short journal entry about the different kinds of neighbors you have encountered.

Jonathan R. Gould, Jr.

Jonathan R. Gould, Jr., was born in 1968 in Little Falls, New York, and grew up on a dairy farm in nearby Fort Plain. After graduating from Little Falls Baptist Academy as valedictorian of his class, he served three years in the US Army, specializing in administration and computer programming. At the State University of New York (SUNY) at Oneonta, Gould was an honors student, received the Provost Award for academic distinction, and obtained a BS in mathematics education.

The People Next Door
(Student Essay)

From his experiences in many different settings, Gould identifies four types of neighbors, only one of which could be considered truly neighborly. Gould wrote this essay in 1994 for a writing course at SUNY.

I have moved more often than I care to remember. However, one thing   1
always stays the same no matter where I have been. There is always a
house next door, and that house contains neighbors. Over time, I have
begun putting my neighbors into one of four categories: too friendly,
unsociable, irritable, and just right.

Neighbors who are too friendly can be seen just about anywhere. I   2
mean that both ways. They exist in every neighborhood I have ever lived
in and seem to appear everywhere I go. For some strange reason these
people become extremely attached to my family and stop in as many as
eight to ten times a day. No matter how tired I appear to be, nothing short
of opening the door and suggesting they leave will make them go home

at night. (I once told an unusually friendly neighbor that his house was on fire, in an attempt to make him leave, and he still took ten minutes to say goodbye.) What is truly interesting about these people is their strong desire to cook for us even though they have developed no culinary skill whatsoever. (This has always proved particularly disconcerting since they stay to watch us eat every bite as they continually ask if the food "tastes good.")

The unsociable neighbor is a different story altogether. For reasons of   3 his own, he has decided to pretend that we do not exist. I have always found that one or two neighbors of this type are in my neighborhood. It is not easy to identify these people, because they seldom leave the shelter of their own house. To be honest, the only way I know that someone lives in their building is the presence of a name on the mailbox and the lights shining through the windows at night. My wife often tries to befriend these unique people, and I have to admire her courage. However, even her serenity is shaken when she offers our neighbors a fresh-baked apple pie only to have them look at her as if she intended to poison them.

Probably the most difficult neighbor to deal with is the irritable neigh-   4 bor. This individual probably has several problems, but he has reduced all those problems down to one cause—the proximity of my family to his residence. Fortunately, I have only encountered this type of neighbor in a handful of settings. (He is usually too busy with one group of "trouble-makers" to pick up a new set.) The times that I have encountered this rascal, however, have proved more than enough for my tastes. He is more than willing to talk to me. Unfortunately, all he wants to tell me is how miserable my family is making him. Ignoring this individual has not worked for me yet. (He just adds my "snobbishness" to his list of faults that my family displays.) Interestingly, this fellow will eat anything my wife (bless her soul) might make in an attempt to be sociable. Even though he never has anything good to say about the food, not a crumb will be left on the plate when he is finished (which leads me to wonder just how starved and impoverished he must be).

At the risk of sounding like Goldilocks, there is also a neighbor who   5 is "just right." One of the most wonderful things about this neighbor is that there has always been at least one everywhere I have gone. We meet often (though not too often), and our greetings are always sincere. Occasionally, our families will go out to eat or to shop, or just sit and talk. We tend to spend as much time at their house as they do at ours (two to three times a month), and everyone knows just when it is time to say goodnight. For some reason, this neighbor knows how to cook, and we frequently exchange baked goods as well as pleasantries. For obvious reasons, this type of neighbor is my favorite.

As I mentioned before, each type of neighbor I have encountered is a common sight in any neighborhood. I have always felt it was important to identify the type of neighbors that were around me. Then I am better able to maintain a clear perspective on our relationship and understand their needs. After all, people do not really change; we just learn how to live with both the good and the bad aspects of their behavior. 6

Meaning

1. Where does Gould state his thesis?
2. What is the difference between unsociable and irritable neighbors in Gould's classification?
3. From their context in Gould's essay, try to guess the meanings of any of the following words that are unfamiliar to you. Check your definitions against a dictionary's, and then write a sentence or two using each new word.

culinary (2) proximity (4) pleasantries (5)
disconcerting (2) impoverished (4)

Purpose and Audience

1. Why do you suppose Gould wrote this essay? Where does he give the clearest indication?
2. Does Gould make any assumptions about his audience? Does he seem to be writing for a certain type of reader?

Method and Structure

1. Why do you think Gould chose the method of classification to write about the subject of neighbors? How does the method help him achieve his purpose?
2. What is Gould's principle of classification? Do you think his classification is complete and consistent? How else might he have sorted neighbors?
3. Why do you think Gould stresses the fact that he has encountered most of these types of neighbors everywhere he has lived?
4. What does Gould accomplish in his conclusion?
5. OTHER METHODS Gould's categories lend themselves to **comparison and contrast** (Chapter 11). Based on his descriptions, what are the differences between the too-friendly neighbor and the just-right neighbor?

Language

1. What is Gould's tone? How seriously does he take the problem of difficult neighbors?

2. Point out several instances of **hyperbole** or overstatement in the essay. What effect do these have?

Writing Topics

1. **JOURNAL TO ESSAY** In your journal entry (p. 191) you began a process of classification by focusing on neighbors you have had. Now think of a group to which you belong—a religious organization, your family, a club or committee, even a writing class. Write a classification essay in which you sort the group's members into categories according to a clear principle of classification. Be sure to label and define each type for your readers, to provide examples, and to position yourself in one of the categories. What does your classification reveal about the group as a whole?

2. Most of us have had at least one colorful or bothersome neighbor at some time or another—a busybody, a recluse, a borrower. Write a descriptive essay (with some narration) about an interesting neighbor you have known or a narrative essay (with some description) about a memorable run-in with a neighbor.

3. **CULTURAL CONSIDERATIONS** "Good fences make good neighbors," says a character in Robert Frost's poem "Mending Wall," and many people in our live-and-let-live society would seem to agree. Is the best neighbor an invisible one? Or do we lose something when we ignore those who are literally closest to us? Write an essay giving a definition of what it means to be a good neighbor. Or, if you prefer, write an essay in which you compare and contrast neighboring habits in different types of communities you have lived in or know of.

4. **CONNECTIONS** Both Gould and David Brooks, in "People Like Us" (next page), classify communities: Gould distinguishes four categories of neighbors, while Brooks focuses on the kinds of neighborhoods people share. Write an essay in which you compare the two essays. How persuasive do you find each writer's groups? Which comes closest to your own experiences with neighborhoods? Why?

No two people are alike and both of them are glad of it.   —*Farmers' Almanac*

Growing up, I came up with this name: I'm a Cablinasian [Caucasian, black, Indian, and Asian].
—Tiger Woods

I think the expression "It's a small world" is really a euphemism for "I keep running into people I can't stand."
—Brock Cohen

JOURNAL RESPONSE   How does your religious, ethnic, or racial background influence your everyday life? Write a short journal entry to explore the answer to this question.

David Brooks

A distinguished journalist, political analyst, and moderate conservative, David Brooks has engaged readers across the political spectrum for three decades. He was born in 1961 in Toronto, Ontario, grew up in New York City and a Philadelphia suburb, and graduated from the University of Chicago in 1983. He began his journalism career as a police reporter for the Chicago City News Bureau, and in 1984 he moved to the *Washington Times*, writing editorials and movie reviews. Brooks has since worked as an international reporter and contributing editor for the *Wall Street Journal*, the *Weekly Standard*, *Newsweek*, and the *Atlantic*. In 2003 he launched a regular column for the *New York Times*, now appearing twice weekly on the op-ed page. He is the editor of the anthology *Backward and Upward: The New Conservative Writing* (1996) and the author of three books of what he calls "comic sociology": *Bobos in Paradise: The New Upper Class and How They Got There* (2000), *On Paradise Drive: How We Live Now (and Always Have) in the Future Tense* (2004), and *The Social Animal: The Hidden Sources of Love, Character, and Achievement* (2011). Brooks is a media personality as well, regularly appearing as a commentator on the NPR program *All Things Considered* and the PBS show *NewsHour*.

People Like Us

The United States is often described as a multicultural "melting pot," in which people with diverse backgrounds come together and form a shared American identity. Taking a close look at the populations of several US cities, towns, and universities, Brooks disputes this notion. "People Like Us" first appeared in the *Atlantic*.

Maybe it's time to admit the obvious. We don't really care about diversity   1
all that much in America, even though we talk about it a great deal. Maybe
somewhere in this country there is a truly diverse neighborhood in which
a black Pentecostal minister lives next to a white anti-globalization activist, who lives next to an Asian short-order cook, who lives next to a professional golfer, who lives next to a postmodern-literature professor and a
cardiovascular surgeon. But I have never been to or heard of that neighborhood. Instead, what I have seen all around the country is people making strenuous efforts to group themselves with people who are basically
like themselves.

Human beings are capable of drawing amazingly subtle social distinc-   2
tions and then shaping their lives around them. In the Washington, DC,
area Democratic lawyers tend to live in suburban Maryland, and Republican lawyers tend to live in suburban Virginia. If you asked a Democratic
lawyer to move from her $750,000 house in Bethesda, Maryland, to a
$750,000 house in Great Falls, Virginia, she'd look at you as if you had
just asked her to buy a pickup truck with a gun rack and to shove chewing
tobacco in her kid's mouth. In Manhattan the owner of a $3 million SoHo
loft would feel out of place moving into a $3 million Fifth Avenue apart-
ment. A West Hollywood interior decorator would feel dislocated if you
asked him to move to Orange County. In Georgia a barista from Athens
would probably not fit in serving coffee in Americus.

It is a common complaint that every place is starting to look the   3
same. But in the information age, the late writer James Chapin[1] once told
me, every place becomes more like itself. People are less often tied down
to factories and mills, and they can search for places to live on the basis
of cultural affinity. Once they find a town in which people share their
values, they flock there, and reinforce whatever was distinctive about the
town in the first place. Once Boulder, Colorado, became known as congenial to politically progressive mountain bikers, half the politically progressive mountain bikers in the country (it seems) moved there; they made
the place so culturally pure that it has become practically a parody of
itself.

But people love it. Make no mistake—we are increasing our happi-   4
ness by segmenting off so rigorously. We are finding places where we are
comfortable and where we feel we can flourish. But the choices we make
toward that end lead to the very opposite of diversity. The United States

---

[1] A progressive Democrat, Professor Chapin (1942–2002) was a political analyst, a
writer for United Press International, and an author of history textbooks. [Editors'
note.]

might be a diverse nation when considered as a whole, but block by block and institution by institution it is a relatively homogeneous nation.

When we use the word "diversity" today we usually mean racial integration. But even here our good intentions seem to have run into the brick wall of human nature. Over the past generation reformers have tried heroically, and in many cases successfully, to end housing discrimination. But recent patterns aren't encouraging: according to an analysis of the 2000 census data, the 1990s saw only a slight increase in the racial integration of neighborhoods in the United States. The number of middle-class and upper-middle-class African American families is rising, but for whatever reasons—racism, psychological comfort—these families tend to congregate in predominantly black neighborhoods.

In fact, evidence suggests that some neighborhoods become more segregated over time. New suburbs in Arizona and Nevada, for example, start out reasonably well integrated. These neighborhoods don't yet have reputations, so people choose their houses for other, mostly economic reasons. But as neighborhoods age, they develop personalities (that's where the Asians live, and that's where the Hispanics live), and segmentation occurs. It could be that in a few years the new suburbs in the Southwest will be nearly as segregated as the established ones in the Northeast and the Midwest.

Even though race and ethnicity run deep in American society, we should in theory be able to find areas that are at least culturally diverse. But here, too, people show few signs of being truly interested in building diverse communities. If you run a retail company and you're thinking of opening new stores, you can choose among dozens of consulting firms that are quite effective at locating your potential customers. They can do this because people with similar tastes and preferences tend to congregate by ZIP code.

The most famous of these precision marketing firms is Claritas, which breaks down the US population into sixty-two psycho-demographic clusters, based on such factors as how much money people make, what they like to read and watch, and what products they have bought in the past. For example, the "suburban sprawl" cluster is composed of young families making about $41,000 a year and living in fast-growing places such as Burnsville, Minnesota, and Bensalem, Pennsylvania. These people are almost twice as likely as other Americans to have three-way calling. They are two and a half times as likely to buy Light n' Lively Kid Yogurt. Members of the "towns & gowns" cluster are recent college graduates in places such as Berkeley, California, and Gainesville, Florida. They are big consumers of DoveBars and *Saturday Night Live*. They tend to drive small foreign cars and to read *Rolling Stone* and *Scientific American*.

Looking through the market research, one can sometimes be amazed 9
by how efficiently people cluster—and by how predictable we all are.
If you wanted to sell imported wine, obviously you would have to find
places where rich people live. But did you know that the sixteen counties with the greatest proportion of imported-wine drinkers are all in the
same three metropolitan areas (New York, San Francisco, and Washington, DC)? If you tried to open a motor-home dealership in Montgomery County, Pennsylvania, you'd probably go broke, because people in
this ring of the Philadelphia suburbs think RVs are kind of uncool. But
if you traveled just a short way north, to Monroe County, Pennsylvania,
you would find yourself in the fifth motor-home-friendliest county in
America.

Geography is not the only way we find ourselves divided from people 10
unlike us. Some of us watch Fox News, while others listen to NPR. Some
like David Letterman, and others—typically in less urban neighborhoods—
like Jay Leno. Some go to charismatic churches; some go to mainstream
churches. Americans tend more and more often to marry people with education levels similar to their own, and to befriend people with backgrounds
similar to their own.

My favorite illustration of this latter pattern comes from the first, 11
noncontroversial chapter of *The Bell Curve*.[2] Think of your twelve closest
friends, Richard J. Herrnstein and Charles Murray write. If you had chosen them randomly from the American population, the odds that half of
your twelve closest friends would be college graduates would be six in a
thousand. The odds that half of the twelve would have advanced degrees
would be less than one in a million. Have any of your twelve closest friends
graduated from Harvard, Stanford, Yale, Princeton, Caltech, MIT, Duke,
Dartmouth, Cornell, Columbia, Chicago, or Brown? If you chose your
friends randomly from the American population, the odds against your
having four or more friends from those schools would be more than a billion to one.

Many of us live in absurdly unlikely groupings, because we have or- 12
ganized our lives that way.

It's striking that the institutions that talk the most about diversity 13
often practice it the least. For example, no group of people sings the diversity anthem more frequently and fervently than administrators at just

---

[2] Published in 1994, the book uses statistical analysis to argue that IQ is inherited
and to warn that the American population will become less intelligent (and less
affluent) if college graduates continue having fewer children than less educated
people do—both controversial claims that upset many readers. [Editors' note.]

Cartoon by Steve Brodner, 2003

such elite universities. But elite universities are amazingly undiverse in their values, politics, and mores. Professors in particular are drawn from a rather narrow segment of the population. If faculties reflected the general population, 32% of professors would be registered Democrats and 31% would be registered Republicans. Forty percent would be evangelical Christians. But a recent study of several universities by the conservative Center for the Study of Popular Culture and the American Enterprise Institute found that roughly 90% of those professors in the arts and sciences who had registered with a political party had registered Democratic. Fifty-seven professors at Brown were found on the voter-registration rolls. Of those, fifty-four were Democrats. Of the forty-two professors in the English, history, sociology, and political-science departments, all were Democrats. The results at Harvard, Penn State, Maryland, and the University of California at Santa Barbara were similar to the results at Brown.

What we are looking at here is human nature. People want to be around others who are roughly like themselves. That's called community. It probably would be psychologically difficult for most Brown professors to share an office with someone who was pro-life, a member of the National Rifle Association, or an evangelical Christian. It's likely that hiring committees would subtly—even unconsciously—screen out any such people they encountered. Republicans and evangelical Christians have sensed that they are not welcome at places like Brown, so they don't

14

even consider working there. In fact, any registered Republican who contemplates a career in academia these days is both a hero and a fool. So, in a semi-self-selective pattern, brainy people with generally liberal social mores flow to academia, and brainy people with generally conservative mores flow elsewhere.

The dream of diversity is like the dream of equality. Both are based   15
on ideals we celebrate even as we undermine them daily. (How many times have you seen someone renounce a high-paying job or pull his child from an elite college on the grounds that these things are bad for equality?) On the one hand, the situation is appalling. It is appalling that Americans know so little about one another. It is appalling that many of us are so narrow-minded that we can't tolerate a few people with ideas significantly different from our own. It's appalling that evangelical Christians are practically absent from entire professions, such as academia, the media, and filmmaking. It's appalling that people should be content to cut themselves off from everyone unlike themselves.

The segmentation of society means that often we don't even have   16
arguments across the political divide. Within their little validating communities, liberals and conservatives circulate half-truths about the supposed awfulness of the other side. These distortions are believed because it feels good to believe them.

On the other hand, there are limits to how diverse any community   17
can or should be. I've come to think that it is not useful to try to hammer diversity into every neighborhood and institution in the United States. Sure, Augusta National[3] should probably admit women, and university sociology departments should probably hire a conservative or two. It would be nice if all neighborhoods had a good mixture of ethnicities. But human nature being what it is, most places and institutions are going to remain culturally homogeneous.

It's probably better to think about diverse lives, not diverse insti-   18
tutions. Human beings, if they are to live well, will have to move through a series of institutions and environments, which may be individually homogeneous but, taken together, will offer diverse experiences. It might also be a good idea to make national service a rite of passage for young people in this country: it would take them out of their narrow neighborhood segment and thrust them in with people unlike themselves. Finally,

---

[3] Located in Georgia, the private Augusta National Golf Club hosts the prestigious annual Masters tournament; until August 2012, it excluded women from membership. [Editors' note.]

it's probably important for adults to get out of their own familiar circles. If you live in a coastal, socially liberal neighborhood, maybe you should take out a subscription to *The Door*, the evangelical humor magazine; or maybe you should visit Branson, Missouri.[4] Maybe you should stop in at a megachurch. Sure, it would be superficial familiarity, but it beats the iron curtains that now separate the nation's various cultural zones.

Look around at your daily life. Are you really in touch with the broad   19 diversity of American life? Do you care?

Meaning

1. Can you find a statement of Brooks's thesis anywhere in his essay? Try to express the author's main idea in your own words.

2. What are "psycho-demographic clusters" (paragraph 8)? What do they have to do with Brooks's thesis?

3. What useful purposes are served by segregation, according to Brooks? What are the negative consequences of people choosing to live in areas where the neighbors are similar?

4. If you do not know the meanings of the following words, try to guess them from the context of Brooks's essay. Test your guesses in a dictionary, and then use each word in a sentence of your own.

globalization (1)	congenial (3)	charismatic (10)
postmodern (1)	segmenting (4)	mores (13)
strenuous (1)	homogeneous (4, 17, 18)	evangelical (13, 18)
dislocated (2)	demographic (8)	renounce (15)

Purpose and Audience

1. Does Brooks make any assumptions about his audience? Where does he give the clearest indication of the type of person he imagines reading his essay?

2. What seems to be Brooks's purpose for writing "People Like Us"? Does he want to inform, persuade, or entertain his readers? How can you tell?

3. How does the cartoon by Steve Brodner (p. 199) relate to Brooks's essay? Why do you suppose the *Atlantic* included it with the article?

---

[4] A tourist destination that features amusement parks, wax museums and similar attractions, and more than fifty theaters and music venues showcasing country-and-western acts and pop stars from the 1950s, '60s, and '70s. [Editors' note.]

Method and Structure

1. What principle of classification does Brooks use to examine American society?

2. What kinds of diversity does Brooks consider in his classification? Diagram or outline his categories. Do any of them overlap?

3. Examine the examples and details Brooks uses to develop his classification. Where did this information come from? What **sources** does Brooks cite, and what evidence does he draw from them? How does he use the evidence he cites?

4. **OTHER METHODS**   At several points in his essay, Brooks uses **comparison and contrast** (Chapter 11) to shape his ideas. Locate two or three uses of this method, and explain what they contribute to the author's point.

Language

1. How would you characterize Brooks's **tone**? Why is the tone crucial in helping him achieve his purpose for writing?

2. Point out several **metaphors** in the essay. What effect do they have?

Writing Topics

1. **JOURNAL TO ESSAY**   In your journal entry (p. 195), you considered the effect of your cultural heritage on your everyday experiences. Now develop your ideas into an essay in which you evaluate the importance you assign to any outward symbols of your inheritance: food, music, holidays, customs, religious services, clothing, and the like. For example, do such signs serve to strengthen your cultural identity? If you don't have such signs, how important is their absence?

2. How accurately do Brooks's classifications represent your experience? Are all the people in your neighborhood alike—economically, racially, academically, and so forth? Write an essay that responds to Brooks, answering the two questions he poses in his final paragraph: "Are you really in touch with the broad diversity of American life? Do you care?"

3. Brooks encourages readers to seek out diversity in their experiences by interacting with people who are not like them—to find a way to connect with strangers. What, in your view, is the appropriate way to interact (or not interact) with a stranger? In answering, ignore situations that might be risky, such as deserted nighttime streets or strangers who appear clearly threatening. Think instead of a safe situation, such as a long line at the grocery store or coffee shop or the waiting room of a doctor's office.

What are your "rules" for initiating conversation and for responding to a stranger's overtures? What informs your rules: experience? personality? upbringing? How can readers apply your rules to make diverse acquaintances in their own lives?

4. **RESEARCH**   Brooks notes in paragraph 5 that "according to an analysis of the 2000 census data, the 1990s saw only a slight increase in the racial integration of neighborhoods in the United States." Visit the Web site of the US Census Bureau (*census.gov*), and find more recent information on racial integration in your local area. How has the shape of your community changed? Is it more diverse, or less, than it was a decade ago—or a generation ago? Write an essay analyzing the state of diversity in your community, considering how recent changes have affected the ways people relate to one another.

5. **CONNECTIONS**   Like "People Like Us," "Funny Business" by Scott Adams (p. 156) uses a cartoon to help illustrate the author's point. Both cartoons might be considered offensive to some readers. Why include them, then? Examine the visual elements of these two essays, and, in an essay of your own, assess the risks and rewards of using cartoons as evidence. Consider each author's purpose for writing and the overall tone of his essay, as well as the effectiveness (or lack thereof) of the visual presented. Do both writers mean to amuse, for instance, or do the cartoons serve other purposes?

WRITING WITH THE METHOD

CLASSIFICATION

Select one of the following topics, or any other topic they suggest, for an essay developed by classification. Be sure to choose a topic you care about so that classification is a means of communicating an idea, not an end in itself.

People

1. Boring people
2. Laundromat users
3. Politicians
4. Passengers on public transportation

Psychology and Behavior

5. Punishments
6. Obsessions
7. Medical patients
8. Dreams

Things

9. Buildings on campus
10. Junk foods
11. Games
12. Mobile devices

Sports and Leisure

13. Gym members
14. Campers
15. Styles of baseball pitching, tennis serving, or another sports skill
16. Styles of dance, guitar playing, acting, or another performance art

Communications Media

17. Talk-show hosts
18. Blogs
19. Sports announcers
20. Advertisements

WRITING ABOUT THE THEME

SORTING FRIENDS AND NEIGHBORS

1. Write a brief essay in which you classify students at your college or university or at a competing school. You may devise your own classification system, if you wish, or you might try adapting the categories of one of the other writers in this chapter to this subject. Are some students "Chaos Muppets" and some "Order Muppets," of the sort described by Dahlia Lithwick (p. 180)? Do they exhibit, in person, any of the characteristics that Brandon Griggs complains about in "The Most Annoying Facebookers" (p. 186)? Are they, like Jonathan Gould's neighbors, "too friendly, unsociable, irritable, and just right" (p. 191)? Do they, like the subjects of David Brooks's "People Like Us" (p. 195), fit into a particular "psycho-demographic cluster"?

2. Dahlia Lithwick, Brandon Griggs, and Jonathan Gould all classify and label people with some intention to amuse readers. However, as David Brooks suggests, not all labels used to classify people are harmless. Consider, for example, labels based on gender or race or sexual orientation. Write an essay in which you discuss both the benefits and the costs of assigning labels to people — for those using the labels, for those being labeled, and for society as a whole. Give plenty of specific examples.

3. Groups of friends and neighbors often form distinct communities, such as the neighborhoods David Brooks examines, Brandon Griggs's *Facebook* friends, Jonathan Gould's mutually supportive neighbors, or the campers at Luis Alberto Urrea's RV park (p. 181). Write an essay in which you offer your definition of *community*. Consider not only what constitutes a group identity but also why people might seek (or reject) a connection with others. What do communities offer their members, and what do they demand of individuals in return?

10

PROCESS ANALYSIS

CONSIDERING THE NATURAL ENVIRONMENT

Game rules, repair manuals, cookbooks, science textbooks—these and many other familiar works are essentially process analyses. They explain how to do something (play Monopoly, patch a hole in the wall), how to make something (an omelet), or how something happens (how hormones affect behavior, how a computer stores and retrieves data). That is, they explain a sequence of actions with a specified result (the **process**) by dividing it into its component steps (the **analysis**). You might use process analysis to explain how a hybrid engine saves gas or how a student organization can influence cafeteria menus. You also use process analysis when you want to teach someone how to do something, such as create a fundraising Web page or follow a new office procedure.

Process analysis overlaps several other writing methods discussed in this book. The analysis component is the method examined in Chapter 8—dividing a thing or concept into its elements. And we analyze a process much as we analyze causes and effects (Chapter 13), except that cause-and-effect analysis asks *why* something happens or *why* it has certain results, whereas process analysis asks *how*. Process analysis also overlaps narration (Chapter 5), for the steps involved are almost always presented in chronological sequence. But narration recounts a unique sequence of events with a unique result, whereas process analysis explains a series of steps with the same predictable result. You might narrate a particularly exciting lacrosse game, for instance, but you would analyze the process—the rules—of lacrosse as a sport.

Reading Process Analysis

Almost always, the purpose of process analysis is to explain, but sometimes a parallel purpose is to prove something about a process or to evaluate it: a writer may want to show how easy it is to change a tire, for instance, or urge aspiring marathon runners to follow a training regimen on the grounds of its safety and effectiveness.

Processes occur in several varieties, including mechanical (a car engine), natural (cell division), psychological (acquisition of sex roles), and political (the electoral college). Process analyses generally fall into one of two types:

- A *directive* process analysis tells how to do or make something: bake a cake, tune a guitar, negotiate a deal, write a process analysis. It outlines the steps in the process completely so that the reader who follows them can achieve the specified result. Generally, a directive process analysis addresses the reader directly, using the second-person *you* ("You should think of negotiation as collaboration rather than competition") or the imperative (commanding) mood of verbs ("Add one egg yolk and stir vigorously").

- An *explanatory* process analysis provides the information necessary for readers to understand the process, but more to satisfy their curiosity than to teach them how to perform it. It may address the reader directly, but the third-person *he, she, it,* and *they* are more common.

Whether directive or explanatory, process analyses usually follow a **chronological order.** Most processes can be divided into phases or stages, and these in turn can be divided into steps. The stages of changing a tire, for instance, may be jacking up the car, removing the flat, putting on the spare, and lowering the car. The steps within, say, jacking up the car may be setting the emergency brake, blocking the other wheels, loosening the lug nuts, positioning the jack, and raising the car. Following a chronological order, a writer covers the stages in sequence and, within each stage, covers the steps in sequence.

To ensure that the reader can duplicate the process or understand how it unfolds, a process analysis must fully detail each step and specify the reasons for it. In addition, the writer must ensure that the reader grasps the sequence of steps, their duration, and where they occur. To this end, **transitions** that signal time and place—such as *after five minutes, meanwhile, to the left,* and *below*—can be invaluable.

Though a chronological sequence is usual for process analysis, the sequence may be interrupted or modified to suit the material. A writer may need to pause in a sequence to provide definitions of specialized terms or to explain why a step is necessary or how it relates to the preceding and following steps. Instructions on how to change a tire, for instance, might stop briefly to explain that the lug nuts should be loosened slightly *before* the car is jacked up in order to prevent the wheel from spinning once the weight is off the tire.

Analyzing Processes in Paragraphs

Miranda Smith (1944–2011), the author of several best-selling gardening books, was a master horticulturalist and an organic farmer. The following instructions are from her comprehensive guide to vegetables, flowers, and private landscapes, *Complete Home Gardening* (2006).

Planting depth is important. You want the plant to grow at the same depth that it did at the nursery. To accomplish this, position the plant so that the former soil mark is an inch or so above the ground when you finish planting. This allows for the inevitable sinking of roots into the soil during the first year or so, without having the plant drop so low that the crown will be suffocated. Add or remove soil as necessary to adjust the level. Now lower the roots or root ball into the hole, and gently backfill the hole with soil. Pack the soil firmly throughout the process to eliminate air pockets. When the hole is half full, water well to make the soil settle. Finish filling the hole with soil, and water again. With fall planting, when the ground is drier, dig the hole a day before, and fill it with water before planting. In the spring, when the ground is already wet, you can skip this step.

Side notes:
Directive process analysis: tells how to plant a tree

Process divided into steps

Reason for step

Reason for step

Reason for step

Reason for step

Transitions (underlined) signal time and place

Sequence altered to offer optional step

Ted Genoways (born 1972) has contributed to several publications, including *Mother Jones*, *onEarth*, and *Best American Travel Writing*. The paragraph below comes from "The High Cost of Oil," a 2014 investigative report for *Outside*. The article explores the impacts on Canada's First Nations people of mining the Alberta tar sands region for bitumen, a controversial form of crude oil.

Seemingly unchecked by regulations, the mines expanded into giant black caverns, where massive shovel loaders <u>now scoop</u> the coal-like rock, <u>seventy tons at a time</u>, into dump trucks three stories tall. Heavy haulers deliver mined material into a double-roll crusher, <u>then</u> a conveyor system carries the ground-up rock into a cyclofeeder. <u>In sprawling</u> coking and refining facilities, hot water melts the tar sands into a slurry, sending clouds of thick smoke and steam across the landscape. <u>What remains</u> is chemically separated to produce a thin top layer of bitumen froth, <u>but everything else</u>—the heavy sand, the toxic wastewater, and the leftover chemicals—is by-product, and it's emptied into tailings ponds the size of enormous lakes.

> Explanatory process analysis: tells how oil is extracted from tar sands
>
> Process examined in chronological sequence
>
> Transitions (underlined) signal steps
>
> Result of the process

Developing an Essay by Process Analysis

▶ Getting Started

You'll find yourself writing process analyses for your courses in school (for instance, explaining how a drug alters brain chemistry), in memos at work (recommending a new procedure for approving cost estimates), or in life outside work (sharing a recipe for vegan curry). To find a subject when an assignment doesn't specify one, examine your interests or hobbies or think of something whose workings you'd like to research in order to understand them better. Explore the subject by listing chronologically all the necessary stages and steps.

Remember your readers while you are generating ideas. Consider how much background information they need, where specialized terms must be defined, and where examples must be given. Especially if you are providing instructions, consider what special equipment readers will need, what hitches they may encounter, and what the interim results should be. To build a table, for instance, what tools would readers need? What should they do if the table wobbles even after the corners are braced? What should the table feel like after the first sanding or the first varnishing?

▶ Forming a Thesis

While you are exploring your subject, decide on the point of your analysis and express it in a thesis sentence that will guide your writing and tell your readers what to expect. The simplest thesis states what the process is and outlines its basic stages. For instance:

> Building a table is a three-stage process of cutting, assembling, and finishing.

You can increase your readers' interest in the process by also conveying your reason for writing about it. You might assert that a seemingly difficult process is actually quite simple, or vice versa:

> Changing a tire does not require a mechanic's skill or strength; on the contrary, a ten-year-old child can do it.
>
> Windsurfing may look easy, but it demands the knowledge of an experienced sailor and the balance of an acrobat.

You might show how the process demonstrates a more general principle:

> The process of getting a bill through Congress illustrates majority rule at work.

Or you might assert that a process is inefficient or unfair:

> The state's outdated licensing procedure forces new drivers to waste hours standing in line.

Regardless of how you structure your thesis sentence, try to make it clear that your process analysis has a point. Usually you will want to include a direct statement of your thesis in your introduction so that readers know what you're writing about and why the process should matter to them.

▶ Organizing

Many successful process analyses begin with an overview of the process to which readers can relate each step. In such an **introduction** you can lead up to your thesis sentence by specifying when or where the process occurs, why it is useful or interesting or controversial, what its result is, and the like. Especially if you are providing instructions, you can also use the introduction (perhaps a separate paragraph) to provide essential background information, such as the materials readers will need.

After the introduction, you should present the stages distinctly, perhaps one or two paragraphs for each, and usually in chronological order. Within each stage, you then cover the necessary steps, also chronologically. This chronological sequence helps readers see how a process unfolds or how to perform it themselves. Try not to deviate from it unless you have good reason to—perhaps because your process requires you to group simultaneous steps or your readers need definitions of terms, reasons for steps, connections between separated steps, and other explanations.

A process essay may end simply with the result. But you might **conclude** with a summary of the major stages, with a comment on the significance or usefulness of the process, or with a recommendation for changing a process you have criticized. For a directive process essay, you might state the standards by which readers can measure their success or give an idea of how much practice may be necessary to master the process.

▶ Drafting

While drafting your process analysis, concentrate on getting in as many details as you can: every step, how each relates to the one before and after, how each contributes to the result. In revising you can always delete unnecessary details and connective tissues if they seem cumbersome, but in the first draft it's better to overexplain than underexplain.

Drafting a process analysis is a good occasion to practice a straightforward, concise writing style, for clarity is more important than originality of expression. Stick to plain language and uncomplicated sentences. If you want to dress up your style a bit, you can always do so after you have made yourself clear.

▶ Revising and Editing

When you've finished your draft, ask a friend to read it. If you have explained a process, he or she should be able to understand it. If you have given instructions, he or she should be able to follow them, or imagine following them. Then examine the draft yourself against the following questions and Focus box.

■ *Have you adhered to a chronological sequence?* Unless there is a compelling and clear reason to use some other arrangement, the stages and steps of your analysis should proceed in chronological order. If you had to depart from that order—to define or explain or to sort out simultaneous steps—the reasons should be clear to your readers.

FOCUS ON CONSISTENCY

While drafting a process analysis, you may start off with subjects or verbs in one form and then shift to another form because the original choice feels awkward.

■ In *directive* analyses that tell readers how to do something, shifts occur most often with the subjects *one* or *a person*:

> INCONSISTENT   To keep the car from rolling while changing the tire, <u>one</u> should first set the car's emergency brake. Then <u>you</u> should block the other three tires with objects like rocks or chunks of wood.

To repair the inconsistency here, you could stick with *one* for the subject (*one should block*), but that usually sounds stiff. It's better to revise the earlier subject to be *you*:

> CONSISTENT   To keep the car from rolling while changing the tire, <u>you</u> should first set the car's emergency brake. Then <u>you</u> should block the other three tires with objects like rocks or chunks of wood.

Sometimes, writers try to avoid *one* or *a person* or even *you* by shifting to passive verbs that don't require actors:

> INCONSISTENT   To keep the car from rolling while changing the tire, <u>you</u> should first set the car's emergency brake. . . . Before the car <u>is raised</u>, the lug nuts of the wheel <u>should be loosened</u>. . . .

But the passive voice is wordy and potentially confusing, especially when directions should be making it clear who does what. (See p. 48 for more on passive verbs.)

The easiest solution to the problem of inconsistent subjects and voices is to use the imperative, or commanding, form of verbs, in which *you* is understood as the subject:

> CONSISTENT   To keep the car from rolling while changing the tire, first <u>set</u> the car's emergency brake. Then <u>block</u> the other three tires with objects like rocks or chunks of wood.

■ In *informative* analyses that explain how something happens, passive verbs may be necessary if you don't know who the actor is or want to emphasize the action over the actor. But identifying the actor is generally clearer and more concise:

CONSISTENT   A mechanic always loosens the lug nuts of the wheel before raising the car.

Imperative and active verbs should be consistent, too. Don't shift back and forth between *block* and *you should block* or between *is raised* and *loosens.*

See page 47 for more on shifts and how to avoid them.

- *Have you included all necessary steps and omitted any unnecessary digressions?* The explanation should be as complete as possible but not cluttered with information, however interesting, that contributes nothing to the readers' understanding of the process.

- *Have you accurately gauged your readers' need for information?* You don't want to bore readers with explanations and details they don't need. But erring in the other direction is even worse, for your essay will achieve little if readers cannot understand it.

- *Have you shown readers how each step fits into the whole process and relates to the other steps?* If your analysis seems to break down into a multitude of isolated steps, you may need to organize them more clearly into stages.

- *Have you used plenty of informative transitions?* Transitions such as *at the same time* and *on the other side of the machine* indicate when steps start and stop, how long they last, and where they occur. (A list of such expressions appears in the Glossary under *transitions.*) The expressions should be as informative as possible; signals such as *first . . . second . . . third . . . fourteenth* and *next . . . next* do not help indicate movement in space or lapses in time, and they quickly grow tiresome.

A Note on Thematic Connections

The authors represented in this chapter set out to examine the steps involved in maintaining a healthy relationship with the natural environment, and for that purpose process analysis is the logical choice of method. In paragraphs, Miranda Smith provides detailed instructions for planting a tree (p. 208), while Ted Genoways explains how mining operations extract oil from sand (p. 209). Brian Doyle, in an essay, recommends a way for readers to engage with nature writing—and for writers to make a difference (opposite). Marina Keegan contemplates the damages inflicted by natural forces (p. 220). And in a dramatic depiction of the annual spring melts in the Pacific Northwest, Rick Bass makes a poetic plea for conservation (p. 227).

If you only read [what] everyone else is reading, you can only think what everyone else is thinking.
—Haruki Murakami

If there's a book you really want to read, but it hasn't been written yet, then you must write it.
—Toni Morrison

Until I feared I would lose it, I never loved to read. One does not love breathing.
—Harper Lee

JOURNAL RESPONSE   What do you read for pleasure, and how do you tend to read it? That is, do you read in any particular way? In your journal, identify the kinds of writing that most appeal to you (true crime, mysteries, poetry, biography, celebrity magazines, and so forth), and list the steps in the reading process you usually undertake. If you don't read for pleasure, list the steps you take to avoid reading.

Brian Doyle

A writer and an editor, Brian Doyle is known for his breathtaking reflections on faith, human connection, and the natural world. He was born in 1956 in New York City and graduated from the University of Notre Dame in 1978. He is currently the editor of *Portland* magazine and a regular contributor to *Atlantic Monthly*, *Harper's*, *Orion*, and *The Sun*, among others. A person deeply affected by matters of family, Doyle wrote his first book, *Two Voices* (1996), in collaboration with his father and his second, *The Wet Engine* (2005), in exploration of his infant son's heart condition. He has also published two novels and several critically acclaimed collections of essays, fiction, and poetry, including *Leaping: Revelations and Epiphanies* (2003), *Epiphanies and Elegies: Very Short Stories* (2006), *Grace Notes* (2011), and *Children and Other Wild Animals* (2014). Doyle is the recipient of three Pushcart Prizes, six *Best American Essays* designations, and a John Burroughs Award for nature writing. In his spare time he enjoys playing basketball.

How to Read a Nature Essay

"The best writers," Doyle has said, "are the best listeners." In this unusual take on how-to, he explores his idea of what goes into good environmental writing while at the same time explaining how readers should let themselves be affected by someone else's work. Doyle's "greatest nature essay *ever*" first appeared in *Orion* in 2008.

The greatest nature essay *ever* would begin with an image so startling and lovely and wondrous that you would stop riffling through the rest of the mail, take your jacket off, sit down at the table, adjust your spectacles, tell the dog to lie *down*, tell the kids to make their *own* sandwiches for heavenssake, that's why God gave you *hands*, and read straight through the piece, marveling that you had indeed seen or smelled or heard *exactly* that, but never quite articulated it that way, or seen or heard it articulated that way, and you think, *Man, this is why I read nature essays, to be startled and moved like that, wow.*

The next two paragraphs would smoothly and gently move you into a story, seemingly a small story, a light tale, easily accessed, something personal but not self-indulgent or self-absorbed on the writer's part, just sort of a cheerful nutty everyday story maybe starring an elk or a mink or a child, but then there would suddenly be a sharp sentence where the dagger enters your heart and the essay spins on a dime like a skater, and you are plunged into waaay deeper water, you didn't see it coming at *all*, and you actually shiver, your whole body shimmers, and much later, maybe when you are in bed with someone you love and you are trying to evade his or her icy feet, you think, *My God, stories do have roaring power, stories are the most crucial and necessary food, how come we never hardly say that out loud?*

The next three paragraphs then walk inexorably toward a line of explosive Conclusions on the horizon like inky alps. Probably the sentences get shorter, more staccato. Terser. Blunter. Shards of sentences. But there's no opinion or commentary, just one line fitting into another, each one making plain inarguable sense, a goat or even a senator could easily understand the sentences and their implications, and there's no shouting, no persuasion, no eloquent pirouetting, no pronouncements and accusations, no sermons or homilies, just calm clean clear statements one after another, fitting together like people holding hands.

Then an odd paragraph, this is a most unusual and peculiar essay, for right here where you would normally expect those alpine Conclusions, some Advice, some Stern Instructions & Directions, there's only the quiet murmur of the writer tiptoeing back to the story he or she was telling you in the second and third paragraphs. The story slips back into view gently, a little shy, holding its hat, nothing melodramatic, in fact it offers a few gnomic questions without answers, and then it gently slides away off the page and off the stage, it almost evanesces or dissolves, and it's only later after you have read the essay three times with mounting amazement that you see quite how the writer managed the stagecraft there, but that's the stuff of another essay for another time.

And finally the last paragraph. It turns out that the perfect nature essay is quite short, it's a lean taut thing, an arrow and not a cannon, and here at the end there's a flash of humor, and a hint or tone or subtext of sadness, a touch of rue, you can't quite put your finger on it but it's there, a dark thread in the fabric, and there's also a shot of espresso hope, hope against all odds and sense, but rivetingly there's no call to arms, no clarion brassy trumpet blast, no Web site to which you are directed, no hint that you, yes you, should be ashamed of how much water you use or the car you drive or the fact that you just turned the thermostat up to seventy, or that you actually have not voted in the past two elections despite what you told the kids and the goat. Nor is there a rimshot ending, a bang, a last twist of the dagger. Oddly, sweetly, the essay just ends with a feeling eerily like a warm hand brushed against your cheek, and you sit there, near tears, smiling, and then you stand up. Changed.

Meaning

1. Does Doyle mean for readers to accept this particular essay as the "greatest nature essay *ever*" (paragraph 1)? Why do you think so? Examine the essay closely before you answer. (Hint: start by comparing the number of paragraphs in Doyle's essay with the number of paragraphs in the essay he describes.)

2. What is the main point of Doyle's process analysis? Can you find a direct statement of his thesis?

3. Of the sentences in a perfect nature essay, Doyle says that "a goat or even a senator could easily understand" (paragraph 3). Where in Doyle's essay does this **image** reappear? Why a goat?

4. If you are not familiar with any of the following words, try to guess their meanings based on their context in Doyle's essay. Check your guesses in a dictionary, and then use each new word in a sentence.

articulated (1)	homilies (3)	taut (5)
inexorably (3)	alpine (4)	clarion (5)
staccato (3)	gnomic (4)	
pirouetting (3)	evanesces (4)	

Purpose and Audience

1. What, according to Doyle, is the purpose of reading? of writing?

2. This piece was originally written for *Orion*, a literary magazine focused on nature, environment, and politics. What, then, could Doyle assume about his audience? What else does he seem to assume about his readers? How are those assumptions reflected in his essay? (You might want to look at the magazine's mission statement, available at *orionmagazine.org*, for more clues.)

Method and Structure

1. Doyle identifies five main stages in reading an effective nature essay. What are these stages, and do they necessarily occur in a sequence? Support your answer with evidence from the essay.

2. How does Doyle organize his process analysis? Point to the transitional phrases that lend his essay **coherence**.

3. Doyle's first paragraph is one long sentence, and his essay contains many **comma splices** and **sentence fragments**. Identify at least two examples of each. Is this sloppy writing, or does Doyle break the rules of sentence grammar for a reason? What do Doyle's sentence faults contribute to (or take away from) his essay? Explain your answer.

4. **OTHER METHODS**   Doyle's process analysis depends on **division or analysis** (Chapter 8) of "the perfect nature essay" (paragraph 5). What, according to Doyle, are the elements of an effective essay? What does a good essay *not* do?

Language

1. Doyle frequently switches point of view between third person (*it*) and second person (*you*). Why? Are these shifts purposeful? distracting? Why do you think so?

2. Doyle uses several figures of speech in his essay—for example, "a sharp sentence where the dagger enters your heart" (paragraph 2), a **metaphor**. Find other examples of metaphor, as well as **simile** and **personification**. What do these nonliteral expressions contribute to the essay? Do any strike you as particularly inventive or effective?

3. In paragraphs 3 and 4 Doyle capitalizes words that do not normally require capitals: "Conclusions, . . . Advice, . . . Stern Instructions & Directions." Why? What point is he making by employing this device?

4. Doyle uses many **colloquial** expressions, such as "tell the dog to lie *down*" (paragraph 1). Identify a few other expressions common to everyday speaking. Why are they appropriate (or not), given Doyle's purpose for writing?

Writing Topics

1. **JOURNAL TO ESSAY**   You may have a particular method of reading, writing, or studying that works or doesn't work for you. In your journal you listed the steps you normally take when reading or when avoiding reading

(p. 215). Now, take that list, or another like it, and transform it into a how-to or how-not-to guide for other students. Be sure your essay clearly outlines the materials your readers will need, outlines the steps they will need to take to successfully follow your instructions, and specifies the result they can expect to achieve.

2. Write a directive process analysis explaining how to do something that is important to you but that others may not know about. For instance, you might tell readers how to thwart identity thieves, how to build a birdhouse, or how to reduce their carbon footprints. Be sure to explain why your subject is meaningful and to identify all the steps involved.

3. Doyle says that "it's only later after you have read [an] essay three times with mounting amazement that you see quite how the writer managed the stagecraft there, but that's the stuff of another essay for another time" (paragraph 4). Write that essay at this time. Reread "How to Read a Nature Essay" at least twice, and then analyze Doyle's "stagecraft." How do the parts of his essay work individually and together to move readers?

4. RESEARCH   Doyle is critical of writers who lecture people busy with family responsibilities about changing their habits for the sake of the environment, but his references to behaviors such as washing a car, raising the thermostat, and neglecting to vote deliberately invoke many people's concerns that American lifestyles have significant environmental consequences. Locate and read a few essays, articles, or books that argue for reducing personal consumption. (*Orion* magazine would be a useful starting point.) Then write a serious argumentative essay that addresses some aspect of limited natural resources, such as water or fossil fuels. Do Americans take more than their fair share of such resources? How does American consumption compare to that in other countries, such as Sweden or China? Under what circumstances, if any, should personal choice be limited in the name of global responsibility? Be sure to include examples to support your opinions, and be careful to cite your sources (see the Appendix).

5. CONNECTIONS   Like Doyle, Scott Adams offers tips for writers who seek to have an emotional impact on their readers. Read "Funny Business" (p. 156) if you haven't already, and then compare Adams's purpose, structure, and advice with Doyle's. What assumptions do the two writers share, and where do their perspectives diverge? How do they use similar methods to achieve their goals? What might humorists learn from naturalists, and vice versa? Do you find one essay more useful than the other? Why, or why not?

It's the great gift of human beings that we have this power of empathy. . . .
We can all sense a mysterious connection with each other.   —Meryl Streep

This is a wonderful planet, and it is being completely destroyed by people
who have too much money and power and no empathy.   —Alice Walker

The quality of mercy is not strain'd, / It droppeth as the gentle rain from
heaven / Upon the place beneath.   —William Shakespeare

JOURNAL RESPONSE   Have you ever been confronted with the problem of a
sick or injured animal—an ailing family pet, perhaps, a bird fallen from a
nest, or an unexpected deer on a back road? What happened, and what
did you do? How did the incident make you feel? Write about the experience in your journal.

Marina Keegan

While still a college student, Marina Keegan gained national attention as a promising—and devastatingly insightful—writer. She worked as a staff writer for the
Yale Daily News, interned at the *Paris Review*, blogged for the *New Yorker*, published a stinging critique of Wall Street in the *New York Times*, and staged a reading of one of her plays at a major drama festival. Born in Wayland, Massachusetts,
in 1989, Keegan spent her summers on the beaches of Cape Cod and sailed com-
petitively throughout her youth. She completed her bachelor's degree at Yale
University in 2012 and had an entry-level job with the *New Yorker* lined up, but
she was killed in a car accident five days after graduation. *The Opposite of Loneliness* (2014), an anthology of Keegan's best short stories and essays, was published
posthumously.

Why We Care about Whales
(Student Essay)

The following selection from *The Opposite of Loneliness* traces a heartbreaking proc-
ess to explore the cruelties of nature and the inadequacies of human response.
Keegan wrote this essay when she was a sophomore; it was first published in the
Yale Daily News in 2009.

When the moon gets bored, it kills whales. Blue whales and fin whales and   1
humpback, sperm, and orca whales; centrifugal forces don't discriminate.

With a hushed retreat, the moon pulls waters out from under fins and   2
flippers, oscillating them backward and forward before they slip outward.
At nighttime, the moon watches its work. Silver light traces the strips of
lingering water, the jittery crabs, the lumps of tangled seaweed.

Slowly, awkwardly, the whales find their footing. They try to fight the   3
waves, but they can't fight the moon. They can't fight the world's rotation
or the bathymetry of oceans or the inevitability that sometimes things
just don't work out.

More than two thousand cetaceans die from beaching every year.   4
Occasionally they trap themselves in solitude, but whales are often beached
in groups, huddled together in clusters and rows. Whales feel cohesion, a
sense of community, of loyalty. The distress call of a lone whale is enough
to prompt its entire pod to rush to its side—a gesture that lands them nose
to nose in the same sand. It's a fatal symphony of echolocation; a siren[1]
call to the sympathetic.

The death is slow. As mammals of the Cetacea order, whales are con-   5
scious breathers. Inhalation is a choice, an occasional rise to the ocean's
surface. Although their ancestors lived on land, constant oxygen exposure overwhelms today's creatures.

Beached whales become frantic, captives to their hyperventilation.   6
Most die from dehydration. The salty air shrinks their oily pores, capturing their moisture. Deprived of the buoyancy water provides, whales can
literally crush themselves to death. Some collapse before they dry out—
their lungs suffocating under their massive bodies—or drown when high
tides cover their blowholes, filling them slowly while they're too weak to
move. The average whale can't last more than twenty-four hours on land.

In their final moments, they begin belching and erupting in violent   7
thrashing. Finally, their jaws open slightly—not all the way, but just
enough that the characteristic illusion of a perpetual smile disappears.
This means it's over. I know this because I watched as twenty-three whale
mouths unhinged. As twenty-three pairs of whale eyes glazed over.

I had woken up that morning to a triage center outside my win-   8
dow. Fifty or so pilot whales were lying along the stretch of beach in front
of my house on Cape Cod, surrounded by frenzied neighbors and animal
activists. The Coast Guard had arrived while I was still sleeping, and
guardsmen were already using boats with giant nets in an attempt to pull
the massive bodies back into the water. Volunteers hurried about in groups,
digging trenches around the whales' heads to cool them off, placing wet

---

[1] In Greek mythology, sirens are sea nymphs whose irresistible singing lures sail-
ors to their deaths against a rocky shoreline. [Editors' note.]

towels on their skin, and forming assembly lines to pour buckets of water on them. The energy was nervous, confused, and palpably urgent.

Pilot whales are among the most populous of the marine mammals in   9 the cetacean order. Fully grown males can measure up to twenty feet and weigh three tons, while females usually reach sixteen feet and 1.5 tons.

Their enormity was their problem. Unlike the three dolphins that   10 had managed to strand themselves near our house the previous summer, fifty pilot whales were nearly impossible to maneuver. If unfavorable tidal currents and topography unite, the larger species may be trapped. Sandbars sneak up on them, and the tides tie them back.

People are strange about animals. Especially large ones. Daily, on the   11 docks of Wellfleet Harbor, thousands of fish are scaled, gutted, and seasoned with thyme and lemon. No one strokes their sides with water. No one cries when their jaws slip open.

Pilot whales are not an endangered species, yet people spend tens of   12 thousands of dollars in rescue efforts, trucking the wounded to aquariums and in some places even airlifting them off of beaches. Perhaps the whales' sheer immensity fosters sympathy. Perhaps the stories of Jonah or Moby Dick[2] do the same. Or maybe it's that article we read last week about that whale in Australia understanding hand signals. Intelligence matters, doesn't it? Brain size is important, right? Those whales knew they were dying. They have some sort of language, some sort of emotion. They give birth, for God's sake! There aren't any pregnant fish in the Wellfleet nets. No communal understanding of their imminent fatality.

I worry sometimes that humans are afraid of helping humans. There's   13 less risk associated with animals, less fear of failure, fear of getting too involved. In war movies, a thousand soldiers can die gruesomely, but when the horse is shot, the audience is heartbroken. It's the *My Dog Skip*[3] effect. The *Homeward Bound*[4] syndrome.

When we hear that the lady on the next street over has cancer, we   14 don't see the entire town flock to her house. We push and shove and wet

---

[2] In the Old Testament of the Bible, the prophet Jonah is swallowed by a whale as punishment for disobeying God; he spends three days in the creature's belly before it spits him out and he repents. Moby Dick is the great white whale obsessively hunted by Captain Ahab in Herman Melville's 1851 novel of the same name. [Editors' note.]

[3] A sentimental 2000 movie, based on Willie Morris's 1995 memoir, about a boy's relationship with his dog. [Editors' note.]

[4] A 1993 remake of a 1963 movie that follows two dogs and a cat as they travel across the United States to reunite with their human family. [Editors' note.]

whales all day, then walk home through town past homeless men curled up on benches—washed up like whales on the curbsides. Pulled outside by the moon and struggling for air among the sewers. They're suffocating too, but there's no town assembly line of food. No palpable urgency, no airlifting plane.

Fifty stranded whales are a tangible crisis with a visible solution. There's   15 camaraderie in the process, a *Free Willy*[5] fantasy, an image of Flipper[6] in everyone's mind. There's nothing romantic about waking up a man on a park bench and making him walk to a shelter. Little self-righteous fulfillment comes from sending a check to Oxfam International.

Would there be such a commotion if a man washed up on the beach?   16 Yes. But stranded humans don't roll in with the tide—they hide in the corners and the concrete houses and the plains of exotic countries we've never heard of, dying of diseases we can't pronounce.

In theory I can say that our resources should be concentrated on   17 saving human lives, that our "Save the Whales" T-shirts should read "Save the Starving Ethiopians."[7] Logically, it's an easy argument to make. Why do we spend so much time caring about animals? Yes, their welfare is important, but surely that of humans is more so.

Last year a nonprofit spent $10,000 transporting a whale to an aquar-   18 ium in Florida, where it died only three days after arriving. That same $10,000 could have purchased hundreds of thousands of food rations. In theory, this is easy to say.

But when I was looking in the eye of a dying pilot whale at four in   19 the morning, my thoughts were not so philosophical. Four hours until high tide. Keep his skin moist. Just three hours now. There wasn't time for logic. My rationality had slipped away with the ebbing dance of the waves.

I had helped all day. We had managed to save twenty-seven of the   20 fifty whales, but twenty-three others were deemed too far up shore, too old, or already too close to death. That night, after most of the volunteers had gone home, I went back outside my bedroom to check on the whales.

---

[5] A 1993 family movie about a troubled boy's efforts to release a performing whale from captivity. [Editors' note.]

[6] *Flipper* was a popular television program in the sixties about a dolphin who could communicate with its park-ranger friend. [Editors' note.]

[7] Ethiopia, an independent but impoverished country in northeast Africa, has long been plagued by drought and famine. [Editors' note.]

It was mid-tide, and the up-shore seaweed still crunched under my bare feet. The water was rising. The moonlight drifted down on the salt-caked battlefield, reflected in the tiny pools of water and half-shell oysters.   21

It was easy to spot the living whales. Their bodies, still moist, shined in the moonlight. I weaved between carcasses, kneeling down beside an old whale that was breathing deeply and far too rapidly for a healthy pilot.   22

I put my hands on his nose and placed my face in front of his visible eye. I knew he was going to die, and he knew he was going to die, and we both understood that there was nothing either of us could do about it.   23

Beached whales die on their sides, one eye pressed into the sand, the other facing up and forced to look at the moon, at the orb that pulled the water out from under its fins.   24

There's no echolocation on land. I imagined dying slowly next to my mother or a lover, helplessly unable to relay my parting message. I remember trying to convince myself that everything would be fine. But he wouldn't be fine. Just like the homeless man and the Ethiopian aren't fine.   25

Perhaps I should have been comforting one of them, placing my hands on one of their shoulders. Spending my time and my money and my life saving those who walked on two legs and spoke without echoes.   26

The moon pulled the waters forward and backward, then inward and around my ankles. Before I could find an answer, the whale's jaw unclenched, opening slightly around the edges.   27

Meaning

1. Summarize the gist of the process Keegan analyzes. How do whales end up on shore? How do they die?

2. Why, according to Keegan, are whales "often beached in groups" (paragraph 4)? What point is she making here?

3. What would you say is Keegan's thesis? Why *do* we care about whales, in her estimation?

4. If you do not know the meanings of the following words, try to guess them from their context in Keegan's essay. Then look them up in a dictionary, and use each one in a sentence of your own.

centrifugal (1)	buoyancy (6)	camaraderie (15)
oscillating (2)	triage (8)	romantic (15)
bathymetry (3)	palpable (8, 14)	exotic (16)
cetaceans (4, 9)	topography (10)	ebbing (19)
echolocation (4, 25)	tangible (15)	

Purpose and Audience

1. Why do you think Keegan chose this topic for her essay? Does she have a reason for writing beyond explaining whale rescue? How does her process analysis help to accomplish this purpose?

2. Keegan poses two questions in paragraph 12 but doesn't answer them. What is the purpose of these questions? What do they reveal about how Keegan imagines her audience?

Method and Structure

1. Keegan's process analysis does not follow a strictly chronological order. Trace the organization of her essay. Where does the process analysis begin and end? Why does Keegan deviate from the process analysis when she does? What is the effect of her deviations?

2. Point out transitional words, phrases, and sentences that Keegan uses as guideposts in her process analysis.

3. Weigh the evidence that Keegan gives to support her ideas. Which evidence is personal, and which is not? Are both the personal and the nonpersonal equally effective? Why, or why not?

4. OTHER METHODS   Where and how does Keegan use **comparison and contrast** (Chapter 11) to establish the significance of her subject?

Language

1. What effect does Keegan achieve with her opening sentence? How does the moon function as a **symbol** throughout the essay?

2. How would you describe Keegan's **tone**? How can you tell that the author is personally invested in the process she is explaining?

Writing Topics

1. JOURNAL TO ESSAY   Our attitudes toward the natural world are often influenced by the family, community, or larger culture in which we grew up. Building on your journal entry (p. 220), write an essay in which you examine the feelings that you have had about a particular sick or injured animal. To what extent were your reactions to the animal's plight at least partly due to other people? Describe the animal and your emotions, and explain the origins of your feelings as best you can. If you wish, you may incorporate information about the animal gleaned from your reading, as Keegan does in her essay.

2. Reread Keegan's essay for instances of **personification** in her descriptions of the moon and of the whales. Starting with your response to the first question on language, write an essay analyzing Keegan's use of personification, concentrating on how that figure of speech in particular contributes to the overall effect of her essay.

3. **CULTURAL CONSIDERATIONS**   Look again at the quotations preceding Keegan's essay. Does our culture encourage empathy, or does it reward selfishness? What do communities do for people, and what do people owe their communities in return? How much can one person do? In an essay, examine the relationship between the community and the individual in American society, drawing a conclusion about the importance, relevance, or practicality of volunteering one's time, money, or talents.

4. **CONNECTIONS**   Keegan means to teach her readers about whales and whale rescue, certainly, but she also attempts to persuade readers to examine their assumptions about homelessness as an overwhelming problem without "a visible solution" (paragraph 15). In "The Box Man" (p. 258), Barbara Lazear Ascher also writes about homelessness, but she comes at the problem from a very different perspective. Consider your own experiences and observations as well as the ideas in Keegan's and Ascher's essays, and then write an essay in which you examine your stereotypes about homeless people. Describe both personal encounters and media images, and discuss how these experiences led to your beliefs.

We abuse land because we regard it as a commodity belonging to us. When we see land as a community to which we belong, we may begin to use it with love and respect.

—Aldo Leopold

I am I plus my surroundings, and if I do not preserve the latter, I do not preserve myself.

—José Ortega y Gasset

If we had no winter, the spring would not be so pleasant; if we did not sometimes taste of adversity, prosperity would not be so welcome.

—Anne Bradstreet

JOURNAL RESPONSE Write a journal entry about a natural phenomenon that affected you, such as a lightning storm, a hurricane, or a blizzard. How did the event make you act and feel?

Rick Bass

Born in Texas in 1958, Rick Bass is a fiction writer, a naturalist, and a teacher. For almost a decade he worked as a petroleum geologist, figuring out where to drill for oil and natural gas. He was educated at Utah State University and earned a BS in geology and wildlife management in 1979. Bass's stories and essays have appeared in the *Paris Review, Esquire, Outside, Tricycle: The Buddhist Review, The Best American Short Stories, Prize Stories: The O. Henry Awards, The Pushcart Prizes, The Watch* (1989), *The Lives of Rocks* (2006), and many other periodicals and anthologies. His novels include *Nashville Chrome* (2010), *All the Land to Hold Us* (2013), and *Where the Sea Used to Be* (2014). Bass has also written several award-winning books about the natural environment, among them *The Deer Pasture* (1985), *Oil Notes* (1989), *Why I Came West* (2009), and *The Black Rhinos of Namibia: Searching for Survivors in the African Desert* (2013). He lives on a ranch in northern Montana, where he works to protect his adopted home from logging.

Gardens of Ice and Stone

First published in the *Southern Review* in 2009, "Gardens of Ice and Stone" portrays a gloriously violent natural event in action. In the process, Bass tries to explain why it's important to defend what's left of the wilderness from human activity.

The last bridges and cornices of ice cave in alongside the river, floating   1
downstream like rafts or leisure boats, stacking up at the bend or against

a logjam, piling high into a hastily constructed but impressive piece of jumbled architecture, forcing the little rushing river to build and build and then at last overflow the ice, swelling and rising and broadening out across the floodplain until, over the course of a few magical days, the little river appears to be as wide and brown and ambitious as the great Missouri or the Mississippi: a giant that sprawls through and across our valley.

And in those shallow, spreading floodwaters, a shimmering glitter of   2
silt and all kinds of other organic matter—bear dung and rotting log mulch and deer pellets and dead trout and winter-killed elk and everything else within the river's hungry reach—sparkles suspended, and is distributed far and wide, into the forest and across the brown and sullen floodplain.

The river will keep rising, choosing at first the myriad paths of least   3
resistance, carrying the richness of its casually spreading breadth into all the places that are so hungry for that distribution of wealth.

But beneath the easygoing demeanor, beneath the gentle, sleepy, wan-   4
dering flood, a desire is quivering, and an anxiousness. This river is run-ning late now. Its destined path runs to the great curve of the Kootenai, which receives the straight-running river, notched with its feathery side tributaries, as the arc of a bow cradles a drawn arrow. The Kootenai then sends these waters into the greatest American river of the Pacific North-west, the Columbia, which follows its mandate to the ocean, and to the salmon, and the sturgeon, and the cedars. . . .

The old saw about a sculptor looking at a piece of wood or a chunk of   5
marble and somehow seeing the buried shape within is a hackneyed artis-tic cliché, an oversimplification of the mysteries of the creative process. And yet so often, particularly when measured against the scale of history or landscape, an observer of that process can see the emergence of repeat-ing patterns, some simple and others complex, which in the cumulative, laid out on the table like cards dealt—hearts, clubs, diamonds, spades—one through ten, and jack, queen, king, ace—reveal but a slight recasting of the same story, more or less familiar with each passing shuffling and playing, assembly and disassembly and reassembly.

The specifics change, or against a tiny human scale they *seem* to   6
change—a three is played instead of a four, a two instead of a five—but the game itself is always intimately familiar, and so very much the same, if rarely quite predictable; and in this manner of a story that must get told, a story that cannot help but be told, the strength of the river backed up behind and underlying the ice jam must always be released: sometimes sooner, other times later, but always.

For a while, then, before that release, the jammed river meanders,   7
spreading nutrients and richness to the most unlikely places. It reaches

into distant nooks and crevices, a digressive storytelling that ignores the pressure continuing to build and strain against the thickened bridge of milk-colored ice.

The story must be told, however, must and will be completed.   8

One day the ice begins to tremble. Not noticeably, at first, but faintly.   9
Trembling, then stilling itself, trembling, then stilling. It might only be one's imagination. Perhaps nothing of consequence is occurring.

A few days later, however, the trembling is more pronounced, and   10
noticeable—a visible shuddering. And at night, as the day's surge of high-mountain meltwater finally makes its way down to the ice bridge on the valley floor below, all the way down from the tops of the mountains that had been bathed in May sun twelve hours earlier—at night, then, the first melodies of cracking or straining ice can be heard, sounding at first like a perfunctory stroke of a fiddler's bow drawn once or twice across the quivering, taut strings of the instrument: the warming up, the preparation.

Beyond that first draw of the bowstring, it will sometimes take a full   11
week before all the sound is engaged: before the gates of ice crash open, and the river is born or resurrected again, and goes hurtling, singing, calling down its old waiting stone canyons, leaping and shouting and carrying along in its roar the xylophonic arrangement of a winter's worth of driftwood, entire forests bobbing and surging along in wild and clattering arrhythmia.

Every year, that story gets told. And every year, the sun returns and   12
dries out the coat of mud slime that was deposited on the floodplain, leaving rich gardens of river dirt that speak in a mosaic to where the ice bridges were.

In subsequent years, rich willow and verdant meadows will encroach   13
upon the new soil; and in late May, and on into the calm of summer, moose and deer and elk will wander out into those wild and seemingly random gardens to graze upon the fruits that are the flood's bounty, and the same story will be told over and over again, up and down the length of the wild river, the locations of the new gardens shifting only slightly, like waves. . . .

In this valley, we have but fifteen of these wild gardens—officially called   14
"roadless areas"—left. They require a minimum size of one thousand acres to be classified as such, and in order to qualify, they must never have been invaded by any roads.

Such has been the frenzy of extraction in this forest, the subsidized   15
liquidation of the biggest and best of the timber—well over a million loaded logging trucks have rolled out of this forest, out of this valley, and

out of this impoverished county—Where did all the money go? Was there ever any money, or was it all simply given or traded away?—that in the million or so acres lying between the Canadian border and the curve of the Kootenai River, spanning east of Idaho to west of Lake Koocanusa, virtually none remain.

Heroically, this gasping strand of wild archipelago provides refuge   16 not only to the last of many threatened and endangered species, such as wolves and grizzlies and caribou and wolverines, but also to reservoirs of spirit. Fifteen: and worse yet, not a single one of them has any form of permanent legal protection whatsoever. Despite the living, pulsing, breath-taking wildness of this landscape—a biological wildness, rather than a recreational wildness—perhaps the wildest valley in the lower forty-eight, in that regard—there's still not a single acre—*not one acre*—of protected public land.

It's a big injustice.   17

I didn't mean to get back into any of this. All I wanted to do with   18 this essay was to paint; and since it's May, to paint with the color green, the forms and swirls of motion that emerge so dramatically in this sea-son. Too, I know that my yowling about environmental justice can be counterproductive; that it jars the composition, that it makes a part of me awaken from what can be—what *is*—otherwise a splendid, even phenomenal, dream.

And far more effective here might be a simple presentation of beauty,   19 so that you, gentle reader, would come on your own initiative, unsum-moned, to love this landscape.

I should remind you, however, that this valley isn't a tourist destina-   20 tion filled with glamorous lakes and majestic spines of rock and ice. It's not really a place to come to. It's a place to dream of. It's a biological wil-derness, full of frog-roar and swamp-muck and tangled blowdown[1] and mosquitoes and deeply angry, suspicious people, none of whom would be pleased to see your shining, happy-vacationing face.

This is a place of mud and mire, a celebration of the rank and the   21 fecund, the cold and the uncomfortable, the frayed and the wild. This is a place whose last wild gardens should be protected for their own sake, not yours or mine.

And they are gardens. In May, while much of the world is puttering   22 about in the warming black earth, coaxing carrot seeds and lettuce sprouts

---

[1] Trees and branches knocked to the ground by wind. [Editors' note.]

into the bright new world, the gardens I am most interested in have been planted by no hand of man or woman but are instead bulging, swelling, shifting, on the verge of delivering spotted elk calves from their mothers and delivering bears back into the world, bears ascending once more to the surface from their earthen burrows like astronauts returning from the strangest of journeys.

More gardening: the mountains delivering torrents of rushing water, 23 recharging the buried aquifers between immense slabs of tilted stone; the fossils of ancient sea creatures tumbling with the season's new talus down into the bed of bright glacier lilies below: trilobites, fenestellids, cephalo-pods, and ostracods[2] on the prowl once more, and the earth itself stretch-ing and yawning like a wildcat, supple and hungry, awakened, youthful, vibrant.

Swirling bouquets of dragonflies rising from the waving marsh fronds 24 like sun-lit jewels summoned by no gardener we will ever meet in this life, though perhaps the next. . . .

Meaning

1. What do you make of the title of this essay? What are the gardens to which Bass refers? How are they created, and why are they important?

2. Examine the author's depiction of a game of cards in paragraphs 5–6. What point is Bass making with this **analogy**?

3. What does Bass mean by "a tiny human scale" in paragraph 6? What attitude toward human beings and their activities does he go on to con-vey in paragraphs 20–22?

4. Does Bass have a thesis? What does he suggest the annual spring melt in Montana can teach us about the threat of climate change in general?

5. Some of the following words may be new to you. Before looking them up in a dictionary, try to guess their meanings from their context in Bass's essay. Then use each new word in a sentence.

cornices (1)	xylophonic (11)	fecund (21)
silt (2)	arrhythmia (11)	ascending (22)
tributaries (4)	verdant (13)	torrents (23)
hackneyed (5)	encroach (13)	aquifers (23)
perfunctory (10)	archipelago (16)	talus (23)

---

[2] Bass lists here four common types of fossils that might be found among the talus, or a pile of fallen rocks at the bottom of a cliff. [Editors' note.]

Purpose and Audience

1. What seems to be Bass's main purpose in writing this essay? What does he want for the Kootenai River watershed? What passages support your interpretation?

2. What assumptions does Bass make about his audience? Does he assume his readers will agree with his ideas, or is he also writing for people who might disagree? How can you tell?

Method and Structure

1. Why do you think Bass chose to write a process analysis instead of simply narrating one of his experiences of the spring melt or arguing his point directly? In other words, what does he gain by emphasizing the yearly repetition and the stages of the process?

2. Bass's essay is divided into two sections: paragraphs 1–13 and 14–24. Consider the different focus of each section. How does this structure serve Bass's purpose?

3. **OTHER METHODS**   Bass's essay is full of rich, telling **description** (Chapter 6). How many senses does he appeal to? (Give examples.) How do these sensory details play an important part in the essay, given the subject matter?

Language

1. Bass uses several figures of speech, such as the **simile** of chunks of ice "floating downstream like rafts or leisure boats" (paragraph 1). Find two or three other figures of speech—such as **metaphor**, **personification**, **hyperbole**, or **paradox**—and analyze how each one contributes to Bass's meaning and helps convey his attitude toward his subject.

2. Each of the first three paragraphs of this essay consists of one long sentence. What effect does Bass create by writing this way?

3. Three times in the essay Bass ends the last sentence of a paragraph with an ellipsis mark ("...") instead of a period, question mark, or exclamation mark. Why? What could be the purpose of trailing off the way he does?

Writing Topics

1. **JOURNAL TO ESSAY**   Using Bass's essay as a model, write a contemplative process analysis of something that fascinates you, frightens you, or upsets you. Your subject could be a natural phenomenon or an instance of envi-

ronmental injustice, such as those Bass portrays, or something else: visiting a health-care clinic, meeting a deadline for an important project, obtaining a permit through a government agency. You may use examples from your own experience and observation, from experiences you have read or heard about, or from both sources.

2. Think of a time when you felt that you experienced in nature "a story that must get told" (paragraphs 6, 8, 12, 13)—perhaps on a hike or a camping trip, on a vacation, or even on your street. Write an essay trying to re-create this experience, using concrete language and figures of speech to make your readers feel, hear, see, taste, or smell what you did.

3. Do you agree with Bass that human activities damage the wilderness but nature will regenerate itself? Or do you think he overlooks positive contributions that humans have made to the earth? Write an essay in which you agree or disagree with Bass's assumptions, citing specific examples to support your opinion. How does your response to Bass lead you to answer his claim of "injustice" in paragraph 17?

4. **CULTURAL CONSIDERATIONS**   Despite his obvious affection for it, Bass portrays the Kootenai River valley as "a biological wilderness, full of frog-roar and swamp-muck and tangled blowdown and mosquitoes and deeply angry, suspicious people, none of whom would be pleased to see your shining, happy-vacationing face" (paragraph 20). Why would he discourage tourists? Consider a place you know well and describe how some aspect of the climate or weather affects the culture, not only during a particular event or season but throughout the year. Why should, or shouldn't, people who don't already live there treat it as a destination?

5. **CONNECTIONS**   Both Bass and Marta Taylor, in "Desert Dance" (p. 98), depict dramatic natural phenomena that occur in the American West. Compare the way Taylor describes a desert lightning storm in paragraphs 5 and 6 of her essay to Bass's description of a mountain river melt in paragraphs 1–4 and 9–11 of his essay. How does each writer combine striking images and original figures of speech to convey a strong sense of mood and a feeling in the reader that he or she is there? Do you think one author's description is more successful than the other's? Why?

WRITING WITH THE METHOD

PROCESS ANALYSIS

Select one of the following topics, or any other topic they suggest, for an essay developed by process analysis. Be sure to choose a topic you care about so that process analysis is a means of communicating an idea, not an end in itself.

Technology

1. How an engine or other machine works
2. How to guard privacy online
3. How to get through an automated voice-recognition system
4. How to recover lost or damaged computer files
5. How wind can be converted into electricity

Education and Career

6. Training an animal such as a dog, a horse, or a flea
7. Learning a foreign language
8. Interviewing for a job
9. Succeeding in biology, history, computer science, or another course
10. Coping with a difficult boss

Entertainment and Hobbies

11. Performing a magic trick
12. Throwing a really *bad* party
13. Playing a sport or a musical instrument
14. Making great chili or some other dish

Health and Appearance

15. Getting physically fit
16. Climbing a mountain
17. Falling down gracefully
18. Treating a sprained ankle or wrist

Family and Friends

19. Offering constructive criticism
20. Driving your parents, brother, sister, friend, or roommate crazy
21. Assigning chores fairly
22. Making new friends in a new place

WRITING ABOUT THE THEME

▶

CONSIDERING THE NATURAL ENVIRONMENT

1. All of the writers in this chapter are concerned in some way with how humans affect the earth, whether positively or negatively. Miranda Smith (p. 208) encourages gardeners to plant trees, while Ted Genoways (p. 209) investigates how fossil fuels are pulled from the ground. Brian Doyle (p. 215) worries about the impact of daily activities like raising the thermostat, Marina Keegan (p. 220) wonders why some people put more effort into helping animals than each other, and Rick Bass (p. 227) rails against the logging industry. Write an essay of your own about harming or protecting some aspect of the environment. Do you regard climate change, pollution, or extinction as critical problems, for instance? Do you believe the government is taking adequate steps to protect the planet? Do you believe that the actions of individuals can make a difference? Your essay may but need not be an argument: that is, you could explain your answer to any of these questions, or you could argue a specific point. Either way, use examples and details to support your ideas.

2. Although we tend to think of nature as unspoiled wilderness, some of the authors in this chapter recognize that the natural world can be both beautiful and harsh. Marina Keegan's portrayal of the moon as a killer and Rick Bass's celebration of the violence of the Montana spring melt are most notable in this respect, but even Brian Doyle's examination of nature writing praises "a subtext of sadness," while Miranda Smith acknowledges that plantings can suffocate and Ted Genoways portrays ponds filled with toxic runoff. Write a process analysis about a natural phenomenon that is important to you, emphasizing its blemishes rather than its beauty.

3. Apply Brian Doyle's ideas about the "greatest nature essay *ever*" to the other two essays in this chapter. How well do Marina Keegan's "Why We Care about Whales" and Rick Bass's "Gardens of Ice and Stone" adhere to Doyle's standards? Does either qualify as a "perfect nature essay"? Why, or why not? Write an essay using Doyle's principles to analyze one or both of these selections. Quote Doyle's analysis and passages from the other writers as appropriate, being sure to use proper citation format (see pp. 394–405) to acknowledge your sources.

11

COMPARISON AND CONTRAST

▶ EXAMINING STEREOTYPES

An insomniac watching late-night television faces a choice between two vampire movies broadcasting at the same time. To make up her mind, she uses the dual method of **comparison and contrast**.

- *Comparison* shows the similarities between two or more subjects: the similar broadcast times and topics of the two movies force the insomniac to choose between them.

- *Contrast* shows the differences between subjects: the different actors, locations, and reputations of the two movies make it possible for the insomniac to choose one.

As this example suggests, comparison and contrast usually work together because any subjects that warrant side-by-side examination usually resemble each other in some respects and differ in others. (Since comparison and contrast are so closely related, the terms *comparison* and *compare* will be used from now on to designate both.)

You use the method instinctively whenever you need to choose among options—for instance, two political candidates, four tiers of health coverage, or several pairs of running shoes. You might also use comparison to make sense of competing proposals for calming traffic in a congested neighborhood, to explain how nursing has changed in the past decade, or to determine whether you should be more concerned about the sun's harmful rays or the chemicals in sunscreen.

Writers, too, often draw on the method, especially when a comparison can explain something that may be unfamiliar to their readers.

Reading Comparison and Contrast

Writers generally use comparison for one of two purposes:

- To *explain* the similarities and differences between subjects so as to make either or both of them clear.
- To *evaluate* subjects so as to establish their advantages and disadvantages, strengths and weaknesses.

The explanatory comparison does not take a position on the relative merits of the subjects; the evaluative comparison does, and it usually concludes with a preference or a suggested course of action. An explanatory comparison in a consumer magazine, for example, might show the similarities and differences between two music download services; an evaluative comparison on the same subject might argue that one service is better than the other.

Whether explanatory or evaluative, comparisons treat two or more subjects in the same general class or group: tax laws, religions, attitudes toward marriage, diseases, advertising strategies, diets, contact sports, friends. A writer may define the class to suit his or her interest—for instance, a television critic might focus on crime dramas, on cable news programs, or on classic situation comedies. The class likeness ensures that the subjects share enough features to make comparison worthwhile. With subjects from different classes, such as an insect and a tree, the similarities are so few and differences so numerous—and both are so obvious—that explaining them would be pointless.

In putting together a comparison, a writer selects subjects from the same class and then, using division or analysis, identifies the features shared by the subjects. These **points of comparison** are the characteristics of the class and thus of the subjects within the class. For instance, the points of comparison for music download services may be music selection, price per song, and device compatibility; for air pollutants they may be sources and dangers to plants, animals, and humans. These points help to arrange similarities and differences between subjects, and, more important, they ensure direct comparison rather than a random listing of unrelated characteristics.

In an effective comparison, a thesis or controlling idea governs the choice of class, points of comparison, and specific similarities and differences, while also making the comparison worthwhile for the reader. Clearly, comparison requires a firm organizational hand. Writers have two options for arranging a comparison:

- *Subject-by-subject*, in which the points of comparison are grouped under each subject so that the *subjects* are covered one at a time.

- *Point-by-point*, in which the subjects are grouped under each point of comparison so that the *points* are covered one at a time.

The brief outlines that follow illustrate the different arrangements as they might be applied to music download services:

Subject-by-subject	*Point-by-point*
Tunelet	Music selection
Music selection	Tunelet
Price per song	Spindle
Device compatibility	Price per song
Spindle	Tunelet
Music selection	Spindle
Price per song	Device compatibility
Device compatibility	Tunelet
	Spindle

Since the subject-by-subject arrangement presents each subject as a coherent unit, it is particularly useful for comparing impressions of subjects: the dissimilar characters of two people, for instance. However, covering the subjects one at a time can break an essay into discrete pieces and strain readers' memories, so this arrangement is usually confined to essays that are short or that compare several subjects briefly. For longer comparisons requiring precise treatment of the individual points—say, an evaluation of two proposals for a new student-aid policy—the point-by-point arrangement is more useful. Its chief disadvantage is that the reader can get lost in the details and fail to see any subject as a whole. Because each arrangement has its strengths and weaknesses, writers sometimes combine the two in a single work, using the divided arrangement to introduce or summarize overall impressions of the subjects and using the alternating arrangement to deal specifically with the points of comparison.

Analyzing Comparison and Contrast in Paragraphs

Firoozeh Dumas (born 1966), a California-based writer who emigrated from Iran with her family at the age of seven, hopes to dispel Americans' fears of Iranians by revealing their "shared humanity." The following paragraph is adapted from her essay collection *Laughing without an Accent* (2008).

Good old Iranian or American qualities such as aiming high and striving despite difficulties have been replaced with everyone receiving a <u>trophy</u> for participating, but that's not the only obstacle. <u>In Iran</u>, we celebrated the <u>math geniuses</u>, the <u>ones with neat handwriting</u>, the <u>ones who tried to excel in school</u>, the <u>ones who spent a lot of time on their homework</u>. They received <u>prizes</u>. Their names were in the newspaper. We applauded them and wished our children could be like them. <u>Here</u>, those kids are called <u>nerds</u> and <u>geeks</u> and <u>dorks</u>. This may be the only country where people make fun of the <u>smart kids</u>. Now *that's* stupid. I only hope that the engineer who built the bridge that I drive across or the nurse who administers our vaccines or the teacher who teaches my kids was a <u>total nerd</u>.

(Margin annotations)
- Subject-by-subject organization
- 1. Iranian students
- 2. American students
- Comparison clarified by transitions (underlined once) and repetition (underlined twice)

Sherman Alexie (born 1966) is a celebrated poet, fiction writer, and filmmaker who, as a member of the Spokane/Coeur d'Alene tribe, explores American Indian issues and experiences, especially as they apply to reservation life. The following paragraph comes from "Superman and Me," an essay first published in the *Los Angeles Times* in 1998.

A smart Indian is a dangerous person, widely feared and ridiculed by Indians and non-Indians alike. I fought with my classmates on a daily basis. They wanted me to stay quiet when the non-Indian teacher asked for answers, for volunteers, for help. We were Indian children who were expected to be stupid. <u>Most lived up to those expectations inside the classroom but subverted them on the outside.</u> They struggled with basic <u>reading</u> in school <u>but could remember</u> how to sing a few dozen powwow songs. They <u>were monosyllabic</u> in front of their non-Indian teachers <u>but could tell</u> complicated stories and jokes at the dinner table. They <u>submissively ducked</u> their heads when confronted by a non-Indian adult <u>but would slug</u> it out with the Indian bully who was ten years older. As Indian children, we were expected to fail

(Margin annotations)
- Point-by-point organization
- Comparison clarified by topic sentence (underlined once) and parallel structure (underlined twice)
- 1. Reading
- 2. Speaking
- 3. Fighting

in the non-Indian world. Those who failed were <u>ceremo-</u>
<u>niously accepted</u> by other Indians and <u>appropriately pit-</u>
<u>ied</u> by non-Indians.

Developing an Essay by Comparison and Contrast

▶ Getting Started

Whenever you observe similarities or differences between two or more members of the same general class—activities, people, ideas, things, places—you have a possible subject for comparison and contrast. Just be sure that the subjects are worth comparing and that you can do the job in the space and time allowed. For instance, if you have a week to complete a three-page paper, don't try to show all the similarities and differences between country music and rhythm and blues. The effort can only frustrate you and irritate your readers. Instead, limit the subjects to a manageable size—for instance, the lyrics of a representative song in each type of music— so that you can develop the comparisons completely and specifically.

To generate ideas for a comparison, explore each subject separately to pick out its characteristics, and then explore the subjects together to see what characteristics one suggests for the other. Look for points of comparison. Early on, you can use **division or analysis** (Chapter 8) to identify points of comparison by breaking the subjects' general class into its elements. A song lyric, for instance, could be divided into story line or plot, basic emotion, and special language such as dialect or slang. After you have explored your subjects fully, you can use **classification** (Chapter 9) to group your characteristics under the points of comparison. For instance, you might classify characteristics of two proposals for a new student-aid policy into qualifications for eligibility, minimum and maximum amounts to be made available, and repayment terms.

As you gain increasing control over your material, consider also the needs of your readers:

- Do they know your subjects well, or will you need to take special care to explain one or both of them?
- Will your readers be equally interested in similarities and differences, or will they find one more enlightening than the other?

▶ Forming a Thesis

While you are shaping your ideas, you should also begin formulating your controlling idea, your thesis. The first thing you should do is look over your points of comparison and determine whether they suggest an evaluative or explanatory approach.

The thesis of an evaluative comparison will generally emerge naturally because it coincides with your purpose of supporting a preference for one subject over another:

> THESIS SENTENCE (EVALUATION)   Both download services offer a wide range of music, but Spindle is less expensive and more flexible than Tunelet.

In an explanatory comparison, however, your thesis will need to do more than merely reflect your general purpose in explaining. It should go beyond the obvious and begin to identify the points of comparison. For example:

> TENTATIVE THESIS SENTENCE (EXPLANATION)   Rugby and American football are the same in some respects and different in others.

> REVISED THESIS SENTENCE (EXPLANATION)   Though rugby requires less strength and more stamina than American football, the two games are very much alike in their rules and strategies.

These examples suggest other decisions you must make when formulating a thesis:

- Will you emphasize both subjects equally or stress one over the other?
- Will you emphasize differences, similarities, or both?

Keeping your readers in mind as you make these decisions will make it easier to use your thesis to shape the body of your essay. For instance, if you decide to write an evaluative comparison and your readers are likely to be biased against your preference or recommendation, you will need to support your case with plenty of specific reasons. If the subjects are equally familiar or important to your readers (as the music download services are in the previous examples), you'll want to give them equal emphasis, but if one subject is unfamiliar (as rugby is in the United States), you will probably need to stress it over the other.

Knowing your audience will also help you decide whether to focus on similarities, differences, or both. Generally, you'll stress the differences between subjects your readers consider similar (such as music download services) and the similarities between subjects they are likely to consider different (such as rugby and American football).

▶ Organizing

Your readers' needs and expectations can also help you plan your essay's organization. An effective **introduction** to a comparison essay often provides some context for readers—the situation that prompts the comparison, for instance, or the reason you see a need for the comparison. Placing your thesis sentence in the introduction also informs readers of your purpose and point, and it may help keep you focused while you write.

For the body of the essay, choose the arrangement that will present your material most clearly and effectively. Remember that the subject-by-subject arrangement suits brief essays comparing dominant impressions of the subjects, whereas the point-by-point arrangement suits longer essays requiring emphasis on the individual points of comparison. If you are torn between the two—wanting both to sum up each subject and to show the two side by side—then a combined arrangement may be your wisest choice.

A rough outline like the models on page 238 can help you plan the basic arrangement of your essay and also the order of the subjects and points of comparison. If your subjects are equally familiar to your readers and equally important to you, then it may not matter which subject you treat first, even in a subject-by-subject arrangement. But if one subject is less familiar or if you favor one, then that one should probably come second. You can also arrange the points themselves to reflect their importance and your readers' knowledge: from least to most significant or complex, from most to least familiar. Be sure to use the same order for both subjects.

Most readers know intuitively how comparison and contrast works, so they will expect you to balance your comparison feature for feature as well. In other words, all the features mentioned for the first subject should be mentioned as well for the second, and any features not mentioned for the first subject should not suddenly materialize for the second.

The **conclusion** to a comparison essay can help readers see the whole picture: the chief similarities and differences between two subjects compared in a divided arrangement, or the chief characteristics of subjects compared in an alternating arrangement. In addition, you may want to comment on the significance of your comparison, advise readers on how they can use the information you have provided, or recommend a specific

course of action for them to follow. As with all other methods of development, the choice of conclusion should reflect the impression you want to
leave with readers.

▶ Drafting

Drafting your essay gives you the chance to spell out your comparison so
that it supports your thesis or, if your thesis is still tentative, to discover
what you think by writing about your subject. You can use **paragraphs** to
help manage the comparison as it unfolds:

- In a *subject-by-subject* arrangement, if you devote two paragraphs to
  the first subject, try to do the same for the second subject. For both
  subjects, try to cover the points of comparison in the same order and
  group the same ones in paragraphs.

- In a *point-by-point* arrangement, balance the paragraphs as you move
  back and forth between subjects. If you treat several points of comparison for the first subject in one paragraph, do the same for the
  second subject. If you apply a single point of comparison to both
  subjects in one paragraph, do the same for the next point of
  comparison.

This way of drafting will help you achieve balance in your comparison and see where you may need more information to flesh out your
subjects and your points. If the finished draft seems too rigid in its pattern, you can always loosen things up when revising.

▶ Revising and Editing

When you are revising and editing your draft, use the following questions
and the information in the Focus box on the next page to be certain that
your essay meets the principal requirements of the comparative method.

- *Are your subjects drawn from the same class?* The subjects must have
  notable differences *and* notable similarities to make comparison
  worthwhile—though, of course, you may stress one group over the
  other.

- *Does your essay have a clear purpose and say something significant about
  the subject?* Your purpose of explaining or evaluating and the point
  you are making should be evident in your thesis *and* throughout the
  essay. A vague, pointless comparison will quickly bore readers.

■ *Do you apply all points of comparison to both subjects?* Even if you emphasize one subject, the two subjects must match feature for feature. An unmatched comparison may leave readers with unanswered questions or weaken their confidence in your authority.

■ *Does the pattern of comparison suit readers' needs and the complexity of the material?* Although readers will appreciate a clear organization and roughly equal treatment of your subjects and points of comparison, they will also appreciate some variety in the way you move back and forth. You needn't devote a sentence to each point, first for one subject and then for the other, or alternate subjects sentence by sentence through several paragraphs. Instead, you might write a single sentence on one point or subject but four sentences on the other — if that's what your information requires.

FOCUS ON PARALLELISM

With several points of comparison and alternating subjects, a comparison will be easier to follow if you emphasize likenesses and differences in your wording. Take advantage of the technique of parallelism to help readers keep your subjects straight. **Parallelism** — the use of similar grammatical structures for elements of similar importance — balances a comparison and clarifies the relationship between elements. At the same time, lack of parallelism can distract or confuse readers.

As you edit, look for groups of related ideas. To make the elements of a comparison parallel, repeat the forms of related words, phrases, and sentences:

NONPARALLEL   Both music services allow subscribers to download songs to their <u>computers</u>, <u>MP3 players</u>, or <u>a smartphone</u>.

PARALLEL   Both music services allow subscribers to download songs to their computers, MP3 players, or <u>smartphones</u>.

NONPARALLEL   <u>Tunelet sells</u> songs individually, but <u>Spindle users can get</u> unlimited downloads for a monthly subscription fee.

PARALLEL   Tunelet sells songs individually, but <u>Spindle allows</u> unlimited downloads for a monthly subscription fee.

For more on parallelism, see pages 50–51.

A Note on Thematic Connections

Each writer represented in this chapter uses comparison and contrast to understand or challenge stereotypes that have been applied to a culture or group of people. A paragraph by Firoozeh Dumas contrasts Iranian admiration for serious students with the ridicule heaped on their American counterparts (p. 239). Another paragraph, by Sherman Alexie, examines how low expectations for American Indian students compare to their behavior inside the classroom and out (p. 239). Alaina Wong explains how playing with dolls helped a young girl come to terms with her Chinese features (next page). Antonio Ruiz-Camacho finds surprising parallels in his youthful visions of the United States and his American sons' impressions of his home country of Mexico (p. 252). And Barbara Lazear Ascher contrasts assumptions about homeless people with the dignity she observes in one man's behavior (p. 258).

If Barbie is so popular, why do you have to buy her friends? —Steven Wright

I think they should have a Barbie with a buzz cut. —Ellen DeGeneres

Barbie is just a doll. —Mary Schmich

JOURNAL RESPONSE Think of a toy you wanted desperately when you were a child. Write a brief journal entry that explains why you wanted it. What was so special about it? If you did receive the toy, did it live up to your expectations? If you didn't get it, how did you react to your disappointment?

Alaina Wong

Alaina Wong was born in 1981 and grew up in New Jersey. As a communications major at the University of Pennsylvania, she served as managing editor of *Mosaic*, a magazine for Asian American students. Wong graduated in 2002 and for a decade marketed children's titles for the publishing companies Simon & Schuster and Penguin Books. She is currently a marketing manager for HIT Entertainment, a division of Fisher-Price/Mattel.

China Doll
(Student Essay)

Wong wrote "China Doll" when she was a college junior as a submission for the teen anthology *YELL-Oh Girls! Emerging Voices Explore Culture, Identity, and Growing Up Asian American* (2001). The essay, Wong explains, "provides a whimsical glimpse into the mind of a child, detailing the ways girls may come to terms with their Asian features, which so often contrast with the media-defined ideal of beauty."

I wanted Princess Barbie, with long blond hair that you could brush and a 1 beautiful shiny gown. She even came with a shimmery white tiara, which, in my eight-year-old mind, crowned her at the top of her Barbie world. My parents looked at me expectantly as I tore through the wrapping paper in childlike excitement. As the pile of shredded paper around me grew larger, so did my anticipation.

But instead of a beautiful princess with golden tresses, what I found 2 was an unfamiliar black-haired "friend" of Barbie, who wore a floral wrap skirt over a pink bathing suit.

Disappointment passed over my eyes as I examined the doll more   3
closely. With her dark hair and slanted eyes, she was a dull comparison to
her blond friend. My other dolls were all alike and beautiful with their
clouds of blond (or light-brown) hair, broad, toothy smiles, and wide-open
eyes. Even Ken had a perfectly painted-on coif of blond hair and flashed
a winning grin. I didn't think this new doll would go riding in Barbie's
convertible with Ken. Why would he pick her when he already had so
many blond friends to choose from? Besides, instead of a wide movie-star
grin, her lips were curved into a more secretive, sly smile. I wondered
what secrets she was hiding. Maybe she had crooked teeth.

I announced that I loved my new doll. I didn't want my mom and   4
dad to feel bad. Maybe the store didn't have any more Princess Barbie
dolls, so they had to buy me the leftovers, or the ones that no one wanted.
I looked at the name of this new black-haired addition to my perfect Barbie family. Kira. Kira didn't even have shoes, though her feet were still
arched up, as if they were waiting expectantly for their missing shoes. She
seemed incomplete. She was probably missing lots of things besides her
shoes. My other Barbies all had colorful plastic high heels to complement
their fashionable dresses. Their outfits were perfect.

"Alaina," my mom said, "get your things ready so I can drive you   5
over to Sarah's house!" I threw the dark-haired doll into my backpack
with the other Barbies I was bringing; Sarah and I always shared the latest
additions to our Barbie collections. Everyone always said that Sarah would
grow up to look like Goldie Hawn, some famous movie star. I didn't think
I would grow up to look like anybody important, not unless I was like
Cinderella, and a fairy godmother went Zap! so I could be transformed,
like magic. Sarah's hair fell in soft waves down her back, while my own
black hair was slippery and straight, like uncooked spaghetti. I bet Sarah
had gotten the Princess Barbie for Christmas.

I liked going over to Sarah's house. Her mom didn't care if we ate   6
raspberries from the backyard without washing them. The last time I went
there, I saw my best friend pluck a juicy purple berry right off the bush
and into her mouth. I was amazed that she didn't care about dirt. Sarah's
mom let us taste cookie dough from the batter when she baked cookies. I
guess only Chinese people cared about germs. My mother never baked
cookies anyway. Baking cookies is what white mothers do all the time—
they like to make things from "scratch" that turn out soft and chewy,
while Chinese mothers buy cookies from the supermarket that are dry and
go crunch, unless you dip them in milk. Sarah's mother made the best
macaroni and cheese too. Obviously she made it from "scratch." I hoped
I was eating lunch there today.

After we pulled into Sarah's driveway, I jumped out of the car and said   7
good-bye to my mom. Inside, Sarah and I ran up the stairs so I could look
at her new dollhouse. On the way, we passed piles of laundry warm from
the dryer, toys spread out on the floor in front of the TV, and newspapers
scattered on the kitchen table. I was jealous. Sarah's mother probably
didn't make them clean up every time someone came over.

Upstairs, I dumped my Barbies out of my backpack so we could com-   8
pare our collections. Before I could even look at her dolls, Sarah turned
to me.

"Look what I got!" she said proudly.   9

I knew it. Sarah had gotten the Princess Barbie.   10

And what did I have to show her? A plain Barbie friend with a funny   11
name, Kira, in an ordinary bathing suit and a skirt that was just a piece
of cloth that needed to be tied; it didn't even slip on like real clothes.
My doll had straight black hair, no shoes, and worst of all, she didn't even
know how to smile right.

"Well . . . she has pretty flowers on her skirt," Sarah said helpfully.   12
"And she looks kind of like you!"

She did? But I didn't want to look like this strange new "friend"   13
of Barbie. Everyone knew that the Barbies with the blond hair were the
best. They were the original ones. And they always got to wear the pretti-
est dresses. I noticed something, but I didn't want to say it out loud. The
best dolls, the most glamorous ones, were always the ones that seemed to
look like Sarah.

"Sarah, honey," her mom called. "Why don't you help me bring up   14
some cookies for you and Alaina?"

My best friend turned to me. "I'll be right back!" she chirped. "If   15
you want to, your dolls can try on Princess Barbie's clothes," she offered
generously.

Sarah skipped out of the room, her blond pigtails swinging around   16
her head. I turned to my Kira doll, regarding her simple outfit. I highly
doubted that Princess Barbie's costume would look right on her. Whoever
heard of a black-haired doll with slanted eyes wearing a crown? Maybe it
wouldn't even fit right. Hesitatingly, I picked up Sarah's Princess Barbie.
She really was beautiful. Slowly, I slipped off her gown and dressed her in
one of the extra doll outfits, a shiny purple top and silver pants. Princess
Barbie continued smiling blankly at me. I was glad she didn't mind that I
had changed her clothes.

Carefully, I buttoned my Kira doll into the glittery princess gown.   17
No Velcro closures here; this dress was glamorous, like what a princess
would wear in real life. The sunlight through Sarah's bedroom window

made the dress sparkle, as if my plain dark-haired Kira doll was actually a princess. The doll's secretive smile began to comfort me, as if we shared a secret together. We both knew this wasn't her real gown, but maybe she could be princess for a day. Just maybe. I stared at her. Finally I placed Barbie's iridescent tiara on top of Kira's jet-black hair. And what do you know? It fit perfectly.

Meaning

1. In her opening paragraphs Wong compares her new Kira doll with the other Barbie dolls in her collection. How were they different?

2. In paragraph 4, an eight-year-old Wong wonders why her parents didn't get her the doll she wanted, contemplating that "[m]aybe the store didn't have any more Princess Barbie dolls, so they had to buy me the leftovers, or the ones that no one wanted." By the end of the essay, however, Wong seems to realize that her parents may have had a different reason. Why do you think they chose the Kira doll for their daughter?

3. Wong's essay compares both her Kira doll with Princess Barbie and herself with her best friend, Sarah. In what ways do the dolls function as **symbols** for the girls?

4. Based on their context in Wong's essay, try to guess the meanings of any of the following words that you don't already know. Test your guesses in a dictionary, and then use each new word in a sentence or two of your own.

tresses (2)	complement (4)	chirped (15)
coif (3)	scratch (6)	regarding (16)
sly (3)	glamorous (13)	iridescent (17)

Purpose and Audience

1. What do you think might have prompted Wong to write about a doll she received as a child? What evidence from the text can you use to support your opinion?

2. Although this essay speaks from the perspective of an eight-year-old Chinese American and was written specifically for a collection aimed at young Asian girls, to what extent can other readers—adults, males, or Caucasians, for example—sympathize with Wong's experience? How does she try to make sure that they can do so? Find examples from the essay that show she is addressing people who might not share her experience, as well as girls who may have had similar feelings growing up.

Method and Structure

1. Why is comparison and contrast particularly well suited to Wong's subject and purpose?

2. Where in the essay does Wong focus on similarities between herself and her best friend? Where does she focus on differences? Why do you think she might have chosen to organize her essay as she does?

3. **OTHER METHODS**   **Description** (Chapter 6) features prominently in Wong's essay. She also uses **narration** (Chapter 5) to explain her experience. What dimensions do these other methods add to the piece?

Language

1. What is the overall **tone** of the essay?

2. Throughout "China Doll" Wong uses **metaphors** and **similes** to make her comparisons vivid and immediate. Find two or three examples, and comment on their effectiveness.

Writing Topics

1. **JOURNAL TO ESSAY**   In your journal entry (p. 246), you wrote about a toy that you wanted as a child. Now think about that toy more critically. Did it carry meanings besides pure entertainment? Make a list of messages that the makers of the toy might intentionally or unintentionally have been sending to children. Using Wong's essay as a model, write an analysis of what the toy represented to you. Your essay may be serious or humorous, but it should include plenty of description so that readers unfamiliar with the toy can picture it in their minds.

2. Although Wong's essay is written with greater skill and range of vocabulary than an eight-year-old would be capable of, it reveals the many facets of a young girl's emotional life. Write an essay in which you analyze the girlish concerns evident in "China Doll," demonstrating how Wong's writing captures a girl's frame of mind. Consider, for example, the way she compares Chinese and white people's attitudes toward food (paragraph 6), or her certainty that "Sarah had gotten the Princess Barbie for Christmas" (5). How does the author use diction and point of view to evoke the childish outlook she no longer has?

3. **CULTURAL CONSIDERATIONS**   In her essay Wong explores the complex reasons behind her initial dislike for a doll with Asian features, commenting that "[t]he best dolls, the most glamorous ones, were always the ones that seemed to look like Sarah" (paragraph 13). In other words, the most

popular dolls were unmistakably white. Write an essay in which you consider the implications of Wong's observation. To what extent do contemporary fashion dolls (or some other aspect of popular entertainment) reflect, reinforce, or reject racial stereotypes? How might their popularity affect children's self-esteem? You may draw on Wong's essay or your own experience for examples, or, if none come to mind, consider doing some research on the topic. (See the Appendix for tips on writing from sources.)

4. **CONNECTIONS**   Like Wong, Antonio Ruiz-Camacho, in "Souvenirs" (next page), explores the cultural significance of objects marketed to children. What characteristics of Wong's doll and Ruiz-Camacho's alarm clock strike you as especially American? How might such toys be different if they were designed intentionally for children in or from other countries? Why do you think so? The characteristics you identify may come from the authors' comparisons or your own experience, but be sure to explain why you think they are distinctly American.

There's no place like home. There's no place like home. There's no place like home.
—Dorothy Gale

Where we love is home—home that our feet may leave, but not our hearts.
—Oliver Wendell Holmes, Sr.

You can keep my things; they've come to take me home.
—Peter Gabriel

JOURNAL RESPONSE Many people derive comfort from a childhood object throughout life: they may no longer sleep with a teddy bear, but the sight of it on the shelf provides security and a connection with the past. Think of such an object that exists for you—a doll, a model ship or car, a pillow, a ball, something one of your parents gave you. Describe the object as specifically as you can.

Antonio Ruiz-Camacho

Storyteller Antonio Ruiz-Camacho was born in 1973 in Toluca, Mexico, and graduated from Universidad Iberoamericana, in Mexico City, in 1996. He worked as a journalist in Mexico City and in Madrid, Spain, for several years before settling in Texas with his family. He earned a master's degree in fine arts from the University of Texas at Austin, where he now teaches creative writing; he has also run an online news service for Univision and occasionally teaches bilingual writing workshops for elementary schoolchildren. Ruiz-Camacho's reporting and fiction have appeared in both English and Spanish in the *New York Times*, *Kirkus Reviews*, *Poets and Writers*, *Etiqueta Negra*, and other publications. His first compilation of short stories, *Barefoot Dogs*, was published in 2015.

Souvenirs

In this 2014 essay for the *New York Times*'s "Private Lives" series, Ruiz-Camacho contrasts his own childhood vacations in the United States with his sons' recent vacations in Mexico. The keepsakes each child chose to remember his visit strikes the author with a nostalgia for home, wherever that may be.

It was the summer of 1980, and I was seven years old, when I traveled to 1 America for the first time. I came to Los Angeles with my mom. The trip, which included visits to Disneyland and Sea World and Knott's Berry

Farm,[1] was the reward my parents gave me for finishing first grade with honors. The Mexican middle class has always been as pampering in its affections as aspirational in its customs, and my family was no exception.

We came to California from another galaxy. We lived in a town called Toluca. It was only forty miles from Mexico City, but felt light years away from any form of civilization. Five channels on TV, only one of them for kids, which I'd watch from the moment I came back from school until I had to go to bed. (I know; my kids now hear this and gasp.) El Pájaro Loco and Don Gato[2] would air early in the afternoon, while Los Picapiedra and Los Supersónicos—the Flintstones and Jetsons[3]—the absolute prime timers, would come on later. In between cartoons, American ads dubbed in Spanish would sell otherworldly toys local stores hardly ever carried—the Elastic Man, the Duncan yo-yo, the Millennium Falcon Spaceship from Star Wars. My seven-year-old self firmly believed that life Up North was better, more advanced and irresistibly alluring.

Upon landing in Los Angeles I was a bit disappointed that cars didn't glide along the streets as I'd imagined, but everything else seemed to confirm my theories about America. The control tower at LAX[4] looked exactly like a house from Los Supersónicos, the milk I had for breakfast at the hotel—served in half-pint cartons, as if in a Hollywood movie!—tasted so delicious and real-milk-like, and the avenues were decorated with palm trees, something back home I had seen only in Acapulco.

I came back from California with my first wristwatch. The strap was white and the dial black, decorated with Mickey Mouse as Tony Manero[5]—Mickey's hands, Saturday Night Fever -style, pointed to the minutes and the hours.

After that first trip, we traveled to America every year. We went to Orlando and Miami, then to New York City and Niagara Falls. It was during that trip to the Northeast that I got my most treasured memento from those early expeditions to the Better North. It's an apple-green plastic

---

[1] Three popular theme parks in Southern California. [Editors' note.]

[2] Woody Woodpecker and Top Cat. [Editors' note.]

[3] Both Hanna-Barbera cartoons with similar story lines and with multiple voice actors in common, The Flintstones centers on a Stone Age family, and The Jetsons takes place one hundred years in the future. [Editors' note.]

[4] Los Angeles International Airport. [Editors' note.]

[5] Played by John Travolta, Tony Manero is the hero of the 1977 disco movie Saturday Night Fever. The still image of Travolta poised in a dance move—one arm pointing up, the other down—is iconic. [Editors' note.]

alarm clock that features Kermit the Frog[6] as a film director, sitting on his director's chair, holding a megaphone.

I lost that groovy watch long ago, but the apple-green alarm clock stayed with me, tagging along as I left my hometown and ultimately my home country, moving from Toluca to Mexico City, then to Madrid, then to Austin. Last year, the alarm system on the clock started to get faulty, and I, with a heavy heart, had to start using a different device to wake up in the mornings. But Kermit and his megaphone still sit on my bedside table, like a keepsake from the time I dreamed of going to more intriguing and far-off lands.

My kids were nine and twelve when they visited Mexico for the first time. I wanted to do that trip before, but it wasn't possible for many reasons, including time, money, green-card procedures and the wave of violence that struck my home country soon after I left.

But last summer we went to the Yucatán Peninsula, one of the safest regions in the country, among the least impacted by the drug and extortion and kidnapping wars of recent years. We spent the first couple of days in Tulum, then paid visits to the archaeological zones of Chichén Itzá, Uxmal and Coba.

Before the trip, I was jittery. Despite the reassurances of friends and relatives from Mexico, I was concerned about our safety. But it wasn't only that. I was secretly afraid my kids wouldn't connect with the place I came from. I was afraid they'd compare Mexico and America the same way I had as a kid.

And they did. The Yucatán Peninsula blew their minds just as California did mine thirty-three years before. At a small restaurant by the beach in Tulum called Zamas, they had the best chicken tacos of their lives. At a supermarket outside Merida, they had the most delicious *pan dulce*[7] ever. Above absolutely everything else, they fell in love with the Maya pyramids.

We were on our way back to Austin when my older son, Emiliano, asked why we live where we live. Why can't we live in Mexico?

In December, my family and I went back, and spent Christmas in Toluca, my hometown, for the first time. It was a more sobering experience for my kids, as Central Mexico showed them a side of the country Yucatán hadn't—the wild gap between rich and poor, slums alongside skyscrapers, kids their own age begging at the stoplights.

---

[6] A popular Muppet character, Kermit was the on-screen director of *The Muppet Show* (1976–81). See also Dahlia Lithwick's classification of Muppet personalities on page 180. [Editors' note.]

[7] "Sweet bread," or pastry. [Editors' note.]

During that trip, they implored that we pay a visit to Teotihuacán,   13
about an hour and a half away. We were atop the Pyramid of the Sun,
along with dozens of other visitors, when it started to pour heavily, in
typical Mexico City fashion. The people around us were less preoccupied
with keeping themselves from the rain, though, than they were with
waiting their turn to touch the very center point of the pyramid, marked
by a minute metallic knob, for a chance to absorb the pyramid's mythic
energy. We were no exception.

Back on the ground, my younger son, Guillermo, spent part of his trip   14
allowance on two ocarinas—traditional wind instruments—made out of
clay by local craftsmen. One, bright brown and white, has the shape of an
eagle; the other, more colorful and with a rougher finish, resembles the
head of a jaguar warrior from Aztec mythology. If you blow through them
at the right angle, they are supposed to reproduce these symbolic figures'
calls.

Those were the kinds of souvenirs the Mexican middle-class kid that   15
I was, fascinated by all things Up North, infused with prejudices about my
own country, would dismiss as too rustic, too dull, too low-class.

But there they are, those clay ocarinas, handmade and otherworldly,   16
alongside Guillermo's Kindle, sitting every night on his bedside table.

Meaning

1. Ruiz-Camacho explores differences between American and Mexican cultures. What is his main idea? Try to express his implied thesis in your
   own words.

2. Why do you suppose Ruiz-Camacho translates the titles of *Los Picapiedra*
   and *Los Supersónicos* but not *El Pájaro Loco* or *Don Gato* (paragraph 2)?
   What makes the Flintstones and the Jetsons particularly significant to his
   comparison?

3. Why was Ruiz-Camacho worried that his sons would "compare Mexico
   and America the same way [he] had as a kid" (paragraph 9)? What impression did Mexico actually make on them?

4. If any of the following words are new to you, try to guess their meanings
   from their context in Ruiz-Camacho's essay. Check your guesses against
   a dictionary's definitions, and then use each word in a sentence or two of
   your own.

   aspirational (1)   memento (5)   archaeological (8)
   alluring (2)   expeditions (5)   rustic (15)

Purpose and Audience

1. Is Ruiz-Camacho's comparison explanatory or evaluative? Does he conclude that one country is better than the other? Draw evidence from the essay to support your answer.

2. The author refers at several points to violence and poverty in Mexico, but he doesn't elaborate. Does it seem, then, that he is writing primarily to an American audience, to a Mexican audience, or to any reader, regardless of country of origin?

Method and Structure

1. Is "Souvenirs" arranged point-by-point or subject-by-subject? What are the main points of comparison?

2. Does the author focus on similarities or differences in his comparison? Why do you think he chose one emphasis over the other?

3. **OTHER METHODS** Ruiz-Camacho uses **narration** (Chapter 5) and **examples** (Chapter 7) to develop his comparison. Locate specific uses of these methods, and explain what they contribute to the essay.

Language

1. "We came to California from another galaxy," Ruiz-Camacho writes in paragraph 2. Locate other words and phrases that invoke outer space or a futuristic world. What does this use of **metaphor** and **hyperbole** contribute to the author's meaning?

2. Why does Ruiz-Camacho capitalize "Up North" in paragraph 2? Where else does he use capital letters in unconventional ways? What is the effect?

3. What key terms does Ruiz-Camacho repeat or restate to help give his essay **coherence**? Identify those that seem most significant.

Writing Topics

1. **JOURNAL TO ESSAY** In your journal entry (p. 252), you described an object of attachment from your childhood. Expand that description into an essay that explores its significance for you. How did you acquire it? Why is it special? What does it mean to you? Consider both the positive and negative associations the object holds for you.

2. Recall a time when you accompanied a parent or other adult (aunt, uncle, grandparent, and so on) to a place he or she knew well but you were seeing for the first time. It could be a place where the person grew up, went

to school, lived for a time, or vacationed. Write an essay in which you compare your reactions to the place with what you remember of the adult's reactions or what, with hindsight, you think the adult's reactions might have been.

3. Ruiz-Camacho feels a powerful connection to the place where he grew up, yet he chose, as most children do eventually, to leave home. If you have left home and experience similar feelings of ambivalence when you return to visit, use Ruiz-Camacho's essay as a model for writing about this conflict. Attempt your own definition of *home*, making sure to use plenty of examples and description to show your readers what the word means to you.

4. **RESEARCH**   Ruiz-Camacho refers to the Yucatán Peninsula as a region of Mexico "among the least impacted by the drug and extortion and kidnapping wars of recent years" (paragraph 8). What is he talking about? Research the current situation of violent unrest in Mexico, considering especially the impact of the drug trade on politics and daily life. Then write an essay in which you present your findings.

5. **CONNECTIONS**   In "Great Expectations" (p. 162), Pat Mora also examines the influence American popular culture has on Mexican Americans. Read or reread her essay, and compare and contrast her examination of advertising with Ruiz-Camacho's assessment of entertainment. Whose concept of cultural influence strikes you as more realistic or insightful? Why? Explain your answer in an essay, using plenty of details from both readings to support your thesis.

You are where you live.
　　　　　　　　　　　　　　　　　　　　　　　　　　　—Anna Quindlen

People who are homeless are not social inadequates. They are people
without homes.
　　　　　　　　　　　　　　　　　　　　　　　　　—Sheila McKechnie

How does it feel/To be without a home/Like a complete unknown/
Like a rolling stone?
　　　　　　　　　　　　　　　　　　　　　　　　　　　　　—Bob Dylan

JOURNAL RESPONSE In your journal write briefly about how you typically
feel when you encounter a person who appears to be homeless. Are you
sympathetic? disgusted? something in between?

Barbara Lazear Ascher

Born in 1946, American writer Barbara Lazear Ascher is known for her insightful,
inspiring essays. She obtained a BA from Bennington College in 1968 and a JD from
Cardozo School of Law in 1979. After practicing law for two years, Ascher turned to
writing full time. Her work has appeared in a diverse assortment of periodicals,
including the *New York Times*, *Vogue*, the *Yale Review*, *Redbook*, and *National Geographic Traveler*. Ascher has also published a memoir of her brother, who died of
AIDS, titled *Landscape without Gravity: A Memoir of Grief* (1993), and several collections of essays: *Playing after Dark* (1986), *The Habit of Loving* (1989), and *Dancing in
the Dark: Romance, Yearning, and the Search for the Sublime* (1999). She lives in New
York City.

The Box Man

In this classic essay from *Playing after Dark*, the evening ritual of a homeless man
prompts Ascher's reflection on the nature of solitude. By comparing the Box Man
with two other solitary people, Ascher distinguishes between chosen and unchosen loneliness.

The Box Man was at it again. It was his lucky night. 　　　　　　　1

　　The first stroke of good fortune occurred as darkness fell and the 　2
night watchman at 220 East Forty-fifth Street neglected to close the door
as he slipped out for a cup of coffee. I saw them before the Box Man did.
Just inside the entrance, cardboard cartons, clean and with their top flaps
intact. With the silent fervor of a mute at a horse race, I willed him toward
them.

It was slow going. His collar was pulled so high that he appeared 3
headless as he shuffled across the street like a man who must feel Earth
with his toes to know that he walks there.

Standing unselfconsciously in the white glare of an overhead light, 4
he began to sort through the boxes, picking them up, one by one, inspect-
ing tops, insides, flaps. Three were tossed aside. They looked perfectly good
to me, but then, who knows what the Box Man knows? When he found
the one that suited his purpose, he dragged it up the block and dropped it
in a doorway.

Then, as if dogged by luck, he set out again and discovered, behind 5
the sign at the parking garage, a plastic Dellwood box, strong and clean,
once used to deliver milk. Back in the doorway the grand design was
revealed as he pushed the Dellwood box against the door and set its cardboard cousin two feet in front—the usual distance between coffee table
and couch. Six full shopping bags were distributed evenly on either side.

He eased himself with slow care onto the stronger box, reached into 6
one of the bags, pulled out a *Daily News*, and snapped it open against his
cardboard table. All done with the ease of IRT Express passengers whose
white-tipped, fair-haired fingers reach into attaché cases as if radar-
directed to the *Wall Street Journal*. They know how to fold it. They know
how to stare at the print, not at the girl who stares at them.

That's just what the Box Man did, except that he touched his tongue 7
to his fingers before turning each page, something grandmothers do.

One could live like this. Gathering boxes to organize a life. Wander- 8
ing through the night collecting comforts to fill a doorway.

When I was a child, my favorite book was *The Boxcar Children*. If I 9
remember correctly, the young protagonists were orphaned, and rather
than live with cruel relatives, they ran away to the woods to live life on
their own terms. An abandoned boxcar was turned into a home, a bubbling
brook became an icebox. Wild berries provided abundant desserts and
days were spent in the happy, adultless pursuit of joy. The children never
worried where the next meal would come from or what February's chill
might bring. They had unquestioning faith that berries would ripen and
streams run cold and clear. And unlike Thoreau,[1] whose deliberate living
was self-conscious and purposeful, theirs had the ease of children at play.

Even now, when life seems complicated and reason slips, I long to live 10
like a Boxcar Child, to have enough open space and freedom of movement

---

[1] Henry David Thoreau (1817–62) was an American essayist and poet who for two
years lived a solitary and simple life in the woods. He wrote of his experiences in
Walden (1854). [Editors' note.]

to arrange my surroundings according to what I find. To turn streams into iceboxes. To be ingenious with simple things. To let the imagination hold sway.

Who is to say that the Box Man does not feel as Thoreau did in his   11
doorway, not "crowded or confined in the least," with "pasture enough for . . . imagination." Who is to say that his dawns don't bring back heroic ages? That he doesn't imagine a goddess trailing her garments across his blistered legs?

His is a life of the mind, such as it is, and voices only he can hear.   12
Although it would appear to be a life of misery, judging from the bandages and chill of night, it is of his choosing. He will ignore you if you offer an alternative. Last winter, Mayor Koch[2] tried, coaxing him with promises and the persuasive tones reserved for rabid dogs. The Box Man backed away, keeping a car and paranoia between them.

He is not to be confused with the lonely ones. You'll find them every-   13
where. The lady who comes into our local coffee shop each evening at five-thirty, orders a bowl of soup and extra Saltines. She drags it out as long as possible, breaking the crackers into smaller and smaller pieces, first in halves and then halves of halves and so on until the last pieces burst into salty splinters and fall from dry fingers onto the soup's shimmering surface. By 6 p.m., it's all over. What will she do with the rest of the night?

You can tell by the vacancy of expression that no memories linger   14
there. She does not wear a gold charm bracelet with silhouettes of boys and girls bearing grandchildren's birthdates and a chip of the appropriate birthstone. When she opens her black purse to pay, there is only a crumpled Kleenex and a wallet inside, no photographs spill onto her lap. Her children, if there are any, live far away and prefer not to visit. If she worked as a secretary for forty years in a downtown office, she was given a retirement party, a cake, a reproduction of an antique perfume atomizer and sent on her way. Old colleagues—those who traded knitting patterns and brownie recipes over the water cooler, who discussed the weather, health, and office scandal while applying lipstick and blush before the ladies' room mirror—they are lost to time and the new young employees who take their places in the typing pool.[3]

---

[2] Edward Koch was the mayor of New York City from 1978 through 1989. [Editors' note.]

[3] Before personal computers became commonplace, many businesses hired people—usually women—to type the handwritten letters, memos, and other documents prepared by higher-level employees. The group of secretaries was known as a typing pool. [Editors' note.]

Each year she gets a Christmas card from her ex-boss. The envelope is   15
canceled in the office mailroom and addressed by memory typewriter.[4]
Within is a family in black and white against a wooded Connecticut landscape. The boss, his wife, who wears her hair in a gray page boy, the three
blond daughters, two with tall husbands and an occasional additional
grandchild. All assembled before a worn stone wall.

Does she watch game shows? Talk to a parakeet, feed him cuttlebone,   16
and call him Pete? When she rides the buses on her Senior Citizen pass,
does she go anywhere or wait for something to happen? Does she have a
niece like the one in Cynthia Ozick's story "Rosa," who sends enough
money to keep her aunt at a distance?

There's a lady across the way whose lights and television stay on all   17
night. A crystal chandelier in the dining room and matching Chinese
lamps on Regency end tables in the living room. She has six cats, some
Siamese, others Angora and Abyssinian. She pets them and waters her
plethora of plants—African violets, a ficus tree, a palm, and geraniums in
season. Not necessarily a lonely life except that 3 a.m. lights and television seem to proclaim it so.

The Box Man welcomes the night, opens to it like a lover. He moves   18
in darkness and prefers it that way. He's not waiting for the phone to ring
or an engraved invitation to arrive in the mail. Not for him a PO number.
Not for him the overcrowded jollity of office parties, the hot anticipation
of a singles' bar. Not even for him a holiday handout. People have tried
and he shuffled away.

The Box Man knows that loneliness chosen loses its sting and claims   19
no victims. He declares what we all know in the secret passages of our
own nights, that although we long for perfect harmony, communion, and
blending with another soul, this is a solo voyage.

The first half of our lives is spent stubbornly denying it. As children   20
we acquire language to make ourselves understood and soon learn from
the blank stares in response to our babblings that even these, our saviors,
our parents, are strangers. In adolescence when we replay earlier dramas
with peers in the place of parents, we begin the quest for the best friend,
that person who will receive all thoughts as if they were her own. Later we
assert that true love will find the way. True love finds many ways, but no
escape from exile. The shores are littered with us, Annas and Ophelias,
Emmas and Juliets,[5] all outcasts from the dream of perfect understanding.

---

[4] An early word processor. [Editors' note.]

[5] These are all doomed heroines of literature. Anna is the title character of Leo
Tolstoy's novel *Anna Karenina* (1878). Emma is the title character of Gustave Flau-
bert's novel *Madame Bovary* (1856). Ophelia and Juliet are in Shakespeare's plays—
the romantic partners, respectively, of Hamlet and Romeo. [Editors' note.]

We might as well draw the night around us and find solace there and a friend in our own voice.

   One could do worse than be a collector of boxes.   21

Meaning

1. What is the **subject** of "The Box Man"? Is Ascher writing primarily about homelessness or something else?

2. What is the main idea of Ascher's essay—the chief point the writer makes about her subject, to which all the other ideas and details in the essay relate?

3. What are the subordinate ideas that contribute to Ascher's main idea? That is, how does Ascher support her thesis?

4. Ascher mentions several works of literature in this essay. Make a list of these **allusions**. What do they contribute to Ascher's meaning? Is familiarity with these works essential to understanding her point?

5. If any of the following words are new to you, try to guess their meanings from their context in Ascher's essay. Check your guesses against a dictionary's definitions, and then use each word in a sentence of your own.

fervor (2)	coaxing (12)	cuttlebone (16)
dogged (5)	vacancy (14)	plethora (17)
attaché (6)	silhouettes (14)	jollity (18)
ingenious (10)	atomizer (14)	solace (20)

Purpose and Audience

1. What seems to be Ascher's reason for writing this piece? Does she simply want to express her admiration for a homeless person she encountered, or is she trying to do something else here? What does she seem to hope readers will gain from her essay?

2. What does Ascher assume about the characteristics, knowledge, and interests of her readers? How are these assumptions reflected in her essay?

Method and Structure

1. Ascher compares a solitary homeless man with two solitary women. What are her points of comparison? How do these points lead up to her evaluation of chosen versus unchosen loneliness?

2. Sketch an informal outline of "The Box Man." How does Ascher organize the ideas in her comparison? How does the organization serve her subject and purpose?

3. **OTHER METHODS**   In developing her comparison, Ascher draws on several methods, including **narration** (Chapter 5), **description** (Chapter 6), **example** (Chapter 7), and **division or analysis** (Chapter 8). Locate instances of each of these methods, and comment on their effectiveness.

Language

1. Examine closely the words Ascher uses in her depictions of the Box Man and the two women. What does her language reveal about her attitudes toward these people?

2. Ascher occasionally uses incomplete sentences, such as "To turn streams into iceboxes" (paragraph 10). Identify some of the other **sentence fragments** in her essay. What effect does Ascher achieve with them?

3. Where and how does Ascher use parallelism to emphasize ideas of equal importance?

Writing Topics

1. **JOURNAL TO ESSAY**   In your journal you recorded your thoughts on how you typically respond to the sight of a homeless person (p. 258). Now that you've read Ascher's thoughts after seeing one homeless man, respond to her essay, particularly her assumptions. Does anyone really *choose* homelessness, as Ascher suggests in paragraph 12? What is a home, in her estimation? How might a person end up living on the street? Can a homeless person really be as content as she says? Why do you think so?

2. With Ascher's essay as a model, write an essay of your own that uses examples and comparison to explain why you admire another person. You might write about a stranger, as Ascher does, or about anyone who has had a positive influence on your outlook on life.

3. **RESEARCH**   If you live in or have visited an urban area, you have probably seen people sleeping in doorways or scavenging for food. And you have almost certainly seen homelessness and extreme poverty discussed in the news and depicted in the media. Research the problem of homelessness and any solutions that have been proposed or attempted, whether locally or on a national level. Then, considering the information you find, your own experiences, and the observations in Ascher's essay, write an essay proposing a solution to the problem.

4. **CONNECTIONS**   Barbara Ehrenreich, in a paragraph from *Nickel and Dimed* (p. 298), examines how competition for housing leaves poor people with inadequate shelter. And like Ascher, Ehrenreich seems to question the foundation of the American dream, which holds that a person from even

the most humble circumstances can achieve prosperity through determination and hard work. How realistic, or not, do you think the American dream is today? Write an essay answering this question. As evidence for your argument, you may want to discuss how, if at all, the American dream applies to you, given your social and economic background.

WRITING WITH THE METHOD

COMPARISON AND CONTRAST

Select one of the following topics, or any other topic they suggest, for an essay developed by comparison and contrast. Be sure to choose a topic you care about so that the comparison and contrast is a means of communicating an idea, not an end in itself.

Experience

1. Two jobs you have held or are considering
2. High school and college
3. Your own version of an event you witnessed or participated in and someone else's view of the same event (perhaps a friend's or a reporter's)

People

4. A vegetarian and an omnivore
5. Gender roles
6. Two or more candidates for public office
7. The homes of two friends

Places and Things

8. City and country
9. Public and private transportation
10. Contact lenses and Lasik surgery
11. Print and electronic books

Art and Entertainment

12. The work of two artists, or two works by the same artist
13. Broadcast television and streaming media
14. A college sports game and a professional game in the same sport
15. Vampires and zombies

Education and Ideas

16. Talent and skill
17. Learning and teaching
18. Poverty and wealth
19. Your study method and that of a classmate

WRITING ABOUT THE THEME

▶
EXAMINING STEREOTYPES

1. All of the authors in this chapter suggest that stereotypes play a significant part in our perceptions of others and ourselves. Firoozeh Dumas (p. 239) refers to American disdain for "nerds and geeks and dorks," Sherman Alexie (p. 239) to expectations that American Indians are destined to fail, Alaina Wong (p. 246) to her misguided preference for blond Barbie dolls, Antonio Ruiz-Camacho (p. 252) to his lingering "prejudices" about his home country of Mexico, and Barbara Lazear Ascher (p. 258) to assumptions that homeless people lack dignity. To what extent, if at all, are such stereotypes the result of media hype or distortion, whether in advertising, news stories, television programming, movies, or elsewhere? What else might contribute to popular assumptions in each case? Write an essay explaining how stereotypes arise in the first place. You could use the misconceptions identified by the authors in this chapter for your examples, or you could supply examples of your own.

2. Firoozeh Dumas, Sherman Alexie, Antonio Ruiz-Camacho, and Barbara Lazear Ascher refer to misperceptions of a minority group on the part of the dominant society. Think of a minority group to which you belong. It could be based on race, ethnicity, language, sexual orientation, religion, physical disability, or any other characteristic. How is your minority perceived in the dominant culture, and how does this perception resemble or differ from the reality as you know it? Write an essay comparing the perception of and the reality of your group.

3. Most of the writers in this chapter wrestle with questions of identity, addressing issues as diverse as the emotional impact of racial stereotypes (Dumas, Alexie, Wong), cultural attitudes toward intelligence and education (Dumas, Alexie, Ruiz-Camacho), the role of peers and family in the development of an individual's self-esteem (Dumas, Alexie, Wong, Ruiz-Camacho, Ascher), and the importance of a sense of home (Ruiz-Camacho, Ascher). All five authors rely on comparison and contrast, but otherwise they go about their tasks very differently. Most notably, perhaps, their **tones** vary widely, from irony to vulnerability to anger. Choose the two works that seem most different in this respect, and analyze how the tone of each helps the author achieve his or her purpose. Give specific examples to support your ideas. Does your analysis lead you to conclude that one tone is likely to be more effective than another in addressing stereotypes?

12

DEFINITION

▶

PURSUING HAPPINESS

Definition sets the boundaries of a thing, a concept, an emotion, or a value. In answering "What is it?" and also "What is it *not*?" definition specifies the main qualities of a subject and its essential nature. Since words are only symbols, pinning down their precise meanings is essential for us to understand ourselves and one another. Thus we use definition constantly, whether we are explaining a new word like *clickbait* to someone who has never heard it, specifying what we're after when we say we want to do something *fun*, or clarifying the diagnosis of a child as *hyperactive*.

We often use brief definitions to clarify the meanings of words—for instance, taking a few sentences to explain a technical term in an engineering study. But we may also need to define concepts at length, especially when they are abstract, complicated, or controversial. Drawing on other methods of development, such as example, analysis, or comparison and contrast, entire essays might be devoted to debated phrases (such as *family values*), to the current uses of a word (*monopoly* in business), or to the meanings of a term in a particular context (like *personality* in psychological theory). Definition is, in other words, essential whenever we want to be certain that we are understood.

Reading Definition

There are several kinds of definition, each with different uses. One is the **formal definition**, usually a statement of the general class of things to which the word belongs, followed by the distinction(s) between it and other members of the class. For example:

	General class	*Distinction(s)*
A submarine is	a seagoing vessel	that operates underwater.
A parable is	a brief, simple story	that illustrates a moral or religious principle.
Pressure is	the force	applied to a given surface.
Insanity is	a mental condition	in which a defendant does not know right from wrong.

A formal definition usually gives a standard dictionary meaning of the word (as in the first two examples) or a specialized meaning agreed to by the members of a profession or discipline (as in the last two examples, from physics and criminal law, respectively). Writers use formal definition to explain the basic meaning of a term so that readers can understand the rest of a discussion. Occasionally, a formal definition can serve as a springboard to a more elaborate, detailed exploration of a word. For instance, an essay might define *pride* simply as "a sense of self-respect" before probing the varied meanings of the word as people actually understand it and then settling on a fuller and more precise meaning of the author's own devising.

This more detailed definition of *pride* could fall into one of two other types of definition: stipulative and extended. A **stipulative definition** clarifies the particular way a writer is using a word: it stipulates, or specifies, a meaning to suit a larger purpose; the definition is part of a larger whole. For example, to show how pride can destroy personal relationships, a writer might first stipulate a meaning of *pride* that ties in with that purpose. Though a stipulative definition may sometimes take the form of a brief formal definition, most require several sentences or even paragraphs. In a physics textbook, for instance, the physicist's definition of *pressure* quoted above probably would not suffice to give readers a good sense of the term and eliminate all the other possible meanings they may have in mind.

Whereas a writer may use a formal or stipulative definition for some larger purpose, he or she would use an **extended definition** for the sake of defining—that is, for the purpose of exploring a thing, quality, or idea in its full complexity and drawing boundaries around it until its meaning is complete and precise. Extended definitions usually treat subjects so complex, vague, or laden with emotions or values that people misunderstand or disagree over their meanings. The subject may be an abstract concept like *patriotism*, a controversial phrase like *beginnings of life*, a colloquial or slang expression like *hype*, a thing like *nanobot*, a scientific idea like *neural plasticity*, even an everyday expression like *nagging*. Besides defining, the purpose may be to persuade readers to accept a definition (for instance, that life begins at conception, or at birth), to explain (what is neural plasticity?), or to amuse (nagging as exemplified by great nags).

As the variety of possible subjects and purposes may suggest, an extended definition may draw on whatever methods will best accomplish the goal of specifying what the subject encompasses and distinguishing it from similar things, qualities, or concepts. Several strategies are unique to definition:

- **Synonyms**, or words of similar meaning, can convey the range of the word's meanings. For example, a writer could equate *misery* with *wretchedness* and *distress*.

- **Negation**, or saying what a word does not mean, can limit the meaning, particularly when a writer wants to focus on only one sense of an abstract term, such as *love*, that is open to diverse interpretations.

- The **etymology** of a word—its history—may illuminate its meaning, perhaps by showing the direction and extent of its change (*pride*, for instance, comes from a Latin word meaning "to be beneficial or useful") or by uncovering buried origins that remain implicit in the modern meaning (*patriotism* comes from the Greek word for "father"; *happy* comes from the Old Norse word for "good luck").

These strategies of definition may be used alone or together, and they may occupy whole paragraphs in an essay-length definition; but they rarely provide enough range to surround the subject completely. That's why most definition essays draw on at least some of the other methods discussed in this book. One or two methods may predominate: an essay on nagging, for instance, might be developed with brief **narratives**. Or several methods may be combined: a definition of *patriotism* might **compare** it with *nationalism*, analyze its **effects** (such as the actions people take on its behalf), and give **examples** of patriotic individuals. By drawing on the appropriate methods, a writer defines and clarifies a specific perspective on the subject so that the reader understands the meaning exactly.

Analyzing Definition in Paragraphs

Carlin Flora (born 1975) is a science journalist and the author of *Friendfluence: The Surprising Ways Friends Make Us Who We Are* (2013). The following paragraph is from "The Pursuit of Happiness," an article she wrote for the magazine *Psychology Today*.

What *is* happiness? The most useful definition—and it's one agreed upon by neuroscientists, psychiatrists, behavioral economists, positive psychologists, and Buddhist monks—is more like satisfied or content than "happy" in its strict bursting-with-glee sense. It has depth and deliberation to it. It encompasses living a meaningful life, utilizing your gifts and your time, living with thought and purpose. It's maximized when you also feel part of a community. And when you confront annoyances and crises with grace. It involves a willingness to learn and stretch and grow, which sometimes involves discomfort. It requires acting on life, not merely taking it in. It's not joy, a temporary exhilaration, or even pleasure, that sensual rush—though a steady supply of those feelings course through those who seize each day.

Question introduces concept to be defined

Synonyms

Factors that contribute to happiness:
meaningful life
community
positive attitude
activity

Concluding sentence states what happiness is not

Dagoberto Gilb (born 1950) is a fiction writer and an essayist. Raised in Southern California by Mexican and German American parents, Gilb often celebrates the lives of working-class Latinos in his work. This paragraph is from his essay "Pride," first published in the *Texas Observer*.

Pride hears gritty dirt blowing against an agave whose stiff fertile stalk, so tall, will not bend—the love of land, rugged like the people who live on it. Pride sees the sunlight on the Franklin Mountains in the first light of morning and listens to a neighbor's gallo—the love of culture and history. Pride smells a sweet, musky drizzle of rain and eats huevos con chile in corn tortillas heated on a cast iron pan—the love of heritage. Pride is the fearless reaction to disrespect and disregard. It is knowing the future will prove that wrong.

Definition by description:
Sound and touch

Sight and sound (a gallo is a rooster)

Smell and taste (huevos are eggs)

Explanations (underlined once) and topic sentence (underlined twice) clarify meaning

Developing an Essay by Definition

▶ Getting Started

You'll sometimes be asked to write definition essays, as when a psychology exam asks for a discussion of *schizophrenia* or a political science assignment calls for an explanation of the term *totalitarianism*. To come up with a subject on your own, consider words that have complex meanings and are either unfamiliar to readers or open to varied interpretations. The subject should be something you know and care enough about to explore in great detail. An idea for a subject may come from an overheard conversation (for instance, a reference to someone as "too patriotic"), a personal experience (an accomplishment that filled you with pride), or something you've seen or read (another writer's definition of *jazz*).

Begin exploring your subject by examining and listing its conventional meanings (consulting an unabridged dictionary may help here, and the dictionary will also give you synonyms and etymology). Also examine the differences of opinion about the word's meanings—the different ways, wrong or right, that you have heard or seen it used. Run through the other methods to see what fresh approaches to the subject they open up:

- How can the subject be described?
- What are some examples?
- Can the subject be divided into qualities or characteristics?
- Can its processes help define it?
- Will comparing and contrasting it with something else help sharpen its meaning?
- Do its causes or effects help clarify its sense?

Some of the questions may turn up nothing, but others may open your eyes to meanings you had not seen.

▶ Forming a Thesis

When you have generated a good list of ideas about your subject, settle on the purpose of your definition. Do you mostly want to explain a word that is unfamiliar to readers? Do you want to express your own view so that readers see a familiar subject from a new angle? Do you want to argue in favor of a particular definition or perhaps persuade readers to look more critically at themselves or their surroundings? Try to work your purpose into a thesis sentence that summarizes your definition and—just as important—asserts something about the subject. For example:

> TENTATIVE THESIS STATEMENT   The prevailing concept of *patriotism* is dangerously wrong.

> REVISED THESIS STATEMENT   Though generally considered entirely positive in meaning, *patriotism* in fact reflects selfish, childish emotions that have no place in a global society.

(Note that the revised thesis statement not only summarizes the writer's definition and makes an assertion about the subject, but it also identifies the prevailing definition she intends to counter in her essay.)

With a thesis sentence formulated, reevaluate your ideas in light of it and pause to consider the needs of your readers:

- *What do readers already know about your subject*, and what do they need to be told in order to understand it as you do?

- *Are your readers likely to be biased for or against your subject?* If you were defining *patriotism*, for example, you might assume that your readers see the word as representing a constructive, even essential value that contributes to the strength of a country. If your purpose were to contest this view, as implied by the revised thesis statement, you would have to build your case carefully to win readers to your side.

▶ Organizing

The **introduction** to a definition essay should provide a base from which to expand and at the same time explain to readers why the forthcoming definition is useful, significant, or necessary. You may want to report the incident that prompted you to define, say why the subject itself is important, or specify the common understandings, or misunderstandings, about its meaning. Several devices can serve as effective beginnings: the etymology of the word; a quotation from another writer supporting or contradicting your definition; or an explanation of what the word does *not* mean (negation). (Try to avoid the overused opening that cites a dictionary: "According to *Webster's Dictionary*, _____ means. . . ." Your readers have probably seen this opening many times before.) If it is not implied in the rest of your introduction, you may want to state your thesis so that readers know precisely what your purpose and point are.

The body of the essay should then proceed, paragraph by paragraph, to refine the characteristics or qualities of the subject, using the arrangement and methods that will distinguish it from anything similar and provide your perspective. For instance, you might try any of the following approaches:

- *Draw increasingly tight boundaries around the subject*, moving from broader, more familiar meanings to the one you have in mind.
- *Arrange your points in order of increasing drama.*
- *Begin with your own experience of the subject* and then show how you see it operating in your surroundings.

The **conclusion** to a definition essay is equally a matter of choice. You might summarize your definition, indicate its superiority to other definitions of the same subject, quote another writer whose view supports your own, or recommend that readers make some use of the information you have provided. The choice depends—as it does in any kind of essay—on your purpose and the impression you want to leave with readers.

▶ Drafting

While drafting your extended definition, keep your subject vividly in mind. Say too much rather than too little about it to ensure that you capture its essence; you can always cut when you revise. And be sure to provide plenty of details and examples to support your view. Such evidence is particularly important when, as in the earlier example of patriotism, you wish to change readers' perceptions of your subject.

In definition the words you use are especially important. Abstractions and generalities cannot draw precise boundaries around a subject, so your words must be as **concrete** and **specific** as you can make them. You'll have chances during revising and editing to work on your words, but try during drafting to pin down your meanings. Use words and phrases that appeal directly to the senses and experiences of readers. When appropriate, use **figures of speech** to make meaning inescapably clear; instead of "Patriotism is childish," for example, write "The blindly patriotic person is like a small child who sees his or her parents as gods, all-knowing, always right." The **connotations** of words—the associations called up in readers' minds by words like *home*, *ambitious*, and *generous*—can contribute to your definition as well. But be sure that connotative words trigger associations suited to your purpose. And when you are trying to explain something precisely, rely most heavily on words with generally neutral meanings.

FOCUS ON UNITY

When drafting a definition, you may find yourself being pulled away from your subject by the descriptions, examples, comparisons, and other methods you use to specify meaning. Let yourself explore byways of your subject — doing so will help you discover what you think. But in revising you'll need to direct all paragraphs to your thesis, and within paragraphs you'll need to direct all sentences to the paragraph topic, generally expressed in a **topic sentence**. In other words, you'll need to ensure that your essay and its paragraphs have **unity**.

One way to achieve unity is to focus each paragraph on some part of your definition and then to focus each sentence within the paragraph on that part. Judy Brady's "I Want a Wife" (p. 276) proceeds in just such a pattern, as the following outline shows. The first two paragraphs conclude with Brady's thesis. Then the sentences from paragraphs 3–9 specify the paragraph topics. A look at Brady's essay will show you that each of her paragraphs elaborates on its topic.

THESIS (PARAGRAPH 2)   I . . . would like to have a wife.

PARAGRAPH 3   I want a wife who will work and send me to school. And . . . I want a wife to take care of my children.

PARAGRAPH 4   I want a wife who will take care of *my* physical needs.

PARAGRAPH 5   I want a wife who will not bother me with rambling complaints. . . . But I want a wife who will listen to me.

PARAGRAPH 6   I want a wife who will take care of the details of my social life.

PARAGRAPH 7   I want a wife who is sensitive to my sexual needs.

PARAGRAPH 8   I want the liberty to replace my present wife with another one.

PARAGRAPH 9   When I am through with school and have a job, I want my wife to quit working and remain at home.

If some part of your definition requires more than a single paragraph, by all means expand it. But keep the group of paragraphs focused on a single idea.

For more on unity in essays and paragraphs, see pages 34–35.

▶ Revising and Editing

When you are satisfied that your draft is complete, revise and edit it against the following questions and the information in the Focus box on the previous page.

- *Have you defined your subject completely and tightly?* Your definition should not leave gaps, nor should the boundaries be so broadly drawn that the subject overlaps something else. For instance, a definition of *hype* that focuses on exaggerated and deliberately misleading claims should include all such claims (some political speeches, say, as well as some advertisements), and it should exclude appeals that do not fit the basic definition (some public-service advertising, for instance).

- *Does your definition reflect the conventional meanings of the word?* Even if you are providing a fresh slant on your subject, you can't change its meaning entirely, or you will confuse your readers and undermine your own credibility. *Patriotism*, for example, could not be defined from the first as "hatred of foreigners," for that definition strays into an entirely different realm. The conventional meaning of "love of country" would have to serve as the starting point, though your essay might interpret the meaning in an original way.

A Note on Thematic Connections

Happiness is the core topic of this chapter. The authors represented here all offer their own perspectives on the meanings of an abstract concept that many of us take for granted. In paragraphs, Carlin Flora presents the meaning of happiness as most psychologists understand it (p. 270), and Dagoberto Gilb outlines the sources of pride for one Latino community (p. 270). Judy Brady examines the traditional gender roles that made her miserable (next page), while Augusten Burroughs writes about the satisfaction to be found in accepting unhappiness as a natural state (p. 281). And Jessica Sayuri Boissy finds pleasure in adhering to the Zen principle of living in the moment (p. 287).

Happiness in marriage is entirely a matter of chance.   —Jane Austen

Our nation must defend the sanctity of marriage.   —George W. Bush

What is fascinating about marriage is why anyone wants to get married.
                                                              —Alain de Botton

JOURNAL RESPONSE   Contemporary society exerts great pressure on single adults to form lasting romantic partnerships. Many unattached people, however, insist that they are perfectly happy to be alone, and many couples are content to live together without a formal commitment. Is marriage a prerequisite for happiness, or is it overrated? Reflect for a moment on what marriage means to you, and write a journal entry that explains your feelings on the subject.

Judy Brady

Judy Brady was born in 1937 in San Francisco. She attended the University of Iowa and graduated with a bachelor's degree in painting in 1962. Married in 1960, she was raising two daughters within a few years. She began working in the women's movement in 1969 and through it developed an ongoing concern with political and social issues, especially women's rights, cancer, and the environment. She believes that "as long as women continue to tolerate a society which places profits above the needs of people, we will continue to be exploited as workers and as wives." Besides the essay reprinted here, Brady has written articles for various magazines and edited *One in Three: Women with Cancer Confront an Epidemic* (1991), motivated by her own struggle with the disease. She is also a founding member of the Toxic Links Coalition and an honorary board member of Greenaction for Health and Environmental Justice, both organizations concerned with the environment and human health.

I Want a Wife

Writing after eleven years of marriage, and before divorcing her husband, Brady here pins down the meaning of the word *wife* from the perspective of someone profoundly unhappy with the role. This essay was first delivered as a speech at a San Francisco women's rally in 1970 and was then published in the premier issue of *Ms.* magazine in December 1971. It has since been reprinted widely. Is Brady's harsh portrayal of gender roles still relevant today?

I belong to that classification of people known as wives. I am A Wife. And,   1
not altogether incidentally, I am a mother.

Not too long ago a male friend of mine appeared on the scene fresh   2
from a recent divorce. He had one child, who is, of course, with his ex-
wife. He is looking for another wife. As I thought about him while I was
ironing one evening, it suddenly occurred to me that I, too, would like to
have a wife. Why do I want a wife?

I would like to go back to school so that I can become economically   3
independent, support myself, and, if need be, support those dependent
upon me. I want a wife who will work and send me to school. And while I
am going to school I want a wife to take care of my children. I want a wife
to keep track of the children's doctor and dentist appointments. And to
keep track of mine, too. I want a wife to make sure my children eat properly
and are kept clean. I want a wife who will wash the children's clothes and
keep them mended. I want a wife who is a good nurturant attendant to my
children, who arranges for their schooling, makes sure that they have an
adequate social life with their peers, takes them to the park, the zoo, etc. I
want a wife who takes care of the children when they are sick, a wife who
arranges to be around when the children need special care, because, of
course, I cannot miss classes at school. My wife must arrange to lose time
at work and not lose the job. It may mean a small cut in my wife's income
from time to time, but I guess I can tolerate that. Needless to say, my wife
will arrange and pay for the care of the children while my wife is working.

I want a wife who will take care of *my* physical needs. I want a wife   4
who will keep my house clean. A wife who will pick up after my children,
a wife who will pick up after me. I want a wife who will keep my clothes
clean, ironed, mended, replaced when need be, and who will see to it that
my personal things are kept in their proper place so that I can find what I
need the minute I need it. I want a wife who cooks the meals, a wife who
is a *good* cook. I want a wife who will plan the menus, do the necessary
grocery shopping, prepare the meals, serve them pleasantly, and then do
the cleaning up while I do my studying. I want a wife who will care for me
when I am sick and sympathize with my pain and loss of time from
school. I want a wife to go along when our family takes a vacation so that
someone can continue to care for me and my children when I need a rest
and change of scene.

I want a wife who will not bother me with rambling complaints   5
about a wife's duties. But I want a wife who will listen to me when I feel
the need to explain a rather difficult point I have come across in my
course of studies. And I want a wife who will type my papers for me when
I have written them.

I want a wife who will take care of the details of my social life. 6
When my wife and I are invited out by friends, I want a wife who will take
care of the babysitting arrangements. When I meet people at school that
I like and want to entertain, I want a wife who will have the house clean,
will prepare a special meal, serve it to me and my friends, and not inter-
rupt when I talk about things that interest me and my friends. I want a
wife who will have arranged that the children are fed and ready for bed
before my guests arrive so that the children do not bother us. I want a wife
who takes care of the needs of my guests so that they feel comfortable,
who makes sure that they have an ashtray, that they are passed the hors
d'oeuvres, that they are offered a second helping of the food, that their
wine glasses are replenished when necessary, that their coffee is served to
them as they like it. And I want a wife who knows that sometimes I need
a night out by myself.

I want a wife who is sensitive to my sexual needs, a wife who makes 7
love passionately and eagerly when I feel like it, a wife who makes sure
that I am satisfied. And, of course, I want a wife who will not demand sexual attention when I am not in the mood for it. I want a wife who assumes
the complete responsibility for birth control, because I do not want more
children. I want a wife who will remain sexually faithful to me so that I
do not have to clutter up my intellectual life with jealousies. And I want
a wife who understands that *my* sexual needs may entail more than strict
adherence to monogamy. I must, after all, be able to relate to people as
fully as possible.

If, by chance, I find another person more suitable as a wife than the 8
wife I already have, I want the liberty to replace my present wife with
another one. Naturally, I will expect a fresh, new life; my wife will take the
children and be solely responsible for them so that I am left free.

When I am through with school and have a job, I want my wife to 9
quit working and remain at home so that my wife can more fully and
completely take care of a wife's duties.

My God, who *wouldn't* want a wife? 10

Meaning

1. In one or two sentences, summarize Brady's definition of a wife. Consider not only the functions she mentions but also the relationship she
portrays.

2. Brady provides many instances of a double standard of behavior and
responsibility for the wife and the wife's spouse. What are the wife's chief
responsibilities and expected behaviors? What are the spouse's?

3. If any of the following words are unfamiliar, try to guess what they mean from the context of Brady's essay. Look up the words in a dictionary to check your guesses, and then use each one in a sentence or two of your own.

nurturant (3)   replenished (6)   monogamy (7)
hors d'oeuvres (6)   adherence (7)

Purpose and Audience

1. Why do you think Brady wrote this essay? Was her purpose to explain a wife's duties, to complain about her own situation, to poke fun at men, to attack men, to attack society's attitudes toward women, or something else? Was she trying to provide a realistic and fair definition of *wife*? What passages in the essay support your answers?

2. What does Brady seem to assume about her readers' gender (male or female) and their attitudes toward women's roles in society, relations between the sexes, and work inside and outside the home? Does she seem to write from the perspective of a particular age group or social and economic background? In answering these questions, cite specific passages from the essay.

3. Brady clearly intended to provoke a reaction from readers. What is *your* reaction to this essay: do you think it is realistic or exaggerated, fair or unfair to men, relevant or irrelevant to the present time? Why?

Method and Structure

1. Why would anybody need to write an essay defining a term like *wife*? Don't we know what a wife is already? How does Brady use definition in an original way to achieve her purpose?

2. Analyze Brady's essay as a piece of definition, considering its thoroughness, its specificity, and its effectiveness in distinguishing the subject from anything similar.

3. Analyze the introduction to Brady's essay. What function does paragraph 1 serve? In what way does paragraph 2 confirm Brady's definition? How does the question at the end of the introduction relate to the question at the end of the essay?

4. **OTHER METHODS** Brady develops her definition primarily by **classification** (Chapter 9). What does she classify, and what categories does she form? What determines her arrangement of these categories? What does the classification contribute to the essay?

Language

1. How would you characterize Brady's **tone**: whining, angry, contemptuous, or something else? What phrases in the essay support your answer?

2. Why does Brady repeat "I want a wife" in almost every sentence, often at the beginning of the sentence? What does this stylistic device convey about the person who wants a wife? How does it fit in with Brady's main idea and purpose?

3. Why does Brady never substitute the personal pronoun "she" for "my wife"? Does the effect gained by repeating "my wife" justify the occasionally awkward sentences, such as the last one in paragraph 3?

4. What effect does Brady achieve with the expressions "of course" (paragraphs 3 and 7), "Needless to say" (3), "after all" (7), and "Naturally" (8)?

Writing Topics

1. **JOURNAL TO ESSAY** In your journal entry (p. 276), you explained what marriage means to you. Now expand your thoughts into an essay-length definition of *marriage*. Does your definition correspond to traditional assumptions about marriage, or is it unconventional? What characteristics does your definition *not* include?

2. Using your own observations and ideas generated by reading Brady's essay, analyze a role that is defined by gender, such as that of a wife or husband, mother or father, sister or brother, daughter or son. First write down the responsibilities, activities, and relationships that define that role, and then elaborate your ideas into an essay defining this role as you see it. You could, if appropriate, follow Brady's model by showing how the role is influenced by the expectations of another person or people.

3. **RESEARCH** Brady's essay was written in the specific cultural context of the early 1970s. Undoubtedly, many cultural changes have taken place since then, particularly changes in gender roles. However, one could also argue that much remains the same. Write an essay in which you compare the stereotypical role of a wife now with the role Brady defines. In addition to your own observations and experiences, consider images of wives presented by the media—for instance, in advertising or sitcoms—then and now.

4. **CONNECTIONS** Like Brady's "I Want a Wife," Roberto Rodríguez's "The Border on Our Backs" (p. 374) is also notable for a strong, uncompromising tone. Write an analysis of the language Brady and Rodríguez use to define an oppressed group's position in society. How are their attitudes similar or different? Use specific examples from both works.

We are happy when we have family, we are happy when we have friends, and almost all the other things we think make us happy are just ways of getting more family and friends.
—Daniel Gilbert

You cannot protect yourself from sadness without protecting yourself from happiness.
—Jonathan Safran Foer

I do not think we have a "right" to happiness. If happiness happens, say thanks.
—Marlene Dietrich

JOURNAL RESPONSE   Have you ever said, "I just want to be happy"? Most of us have at some point, whether out loud to a friend or family member or silently to ourselves. Take a few moments to write in your journal about what happiness means to you. What do you want out of life? How do you plan to get it?

Augusten Burroughs

Augusten Burroughs was born Christopher Robinson in 1965 and legally changed his name when he turned eighteen, an effort to distance himself from a traumatic youth. He has held a variety of positions, including advertising copywriter, dog trainer, and commentator for National Public Radio, but Burroughs is best known for a series of painfully open memoirs about his struggles with abuse and addiction: *Running with Scissors* (2002), an examination of parental abandonment and an unwelcome relationship with a pedophile; *Dry* (2003), a personal study of alcoholism; and *A Wolf at the Table* (2008), an indictment of the author's father. Burroughs has also written a novel and several collections of essays and stories, and in 2012 he published *This Is How: Proven Aid in Overcoming Shyness, Molestation, Fatness, Spinsterhood, Grief, Disease, Lushery, Decrepitude and More*, a self-help book he says he "was born to write." Recently the recipient of a Lambda Literary Award as well as an honorary doctorate of letters from the Savannah College of Art and Design, Burroughs lives with his husband in Manhattan.

Unhappily Ever After

In this self-contained chapter from *This Is How*, Burroughs draws on personal experience and a dark sense of humor to advise readers on the perils of pursuing happiness. Wanting to be happy, he cautions, is a sure-fire way to make yourself miserable.

"I just want to be happy."   1

    I can't think of another phrase capable of causing more misery and   2
permanent unhappiness. With the possible exception of, "Honey, I'm in
love with your youngest sister and she's agreed to marry me so I'd like a
divorce."

    Yet at first glance, it seems so guileless. Children just want to be happy.   3
So do puppies and some middle-aged custodians.

    Happy seems like a healthy, normal desire. Like wanting to breathe   4
fresh air or shop only at Whole Foods.

    But "I just want to be happy" is a hole cut out of the floor and covered   5
with a rug.

    Here's the problem: when you say to yourself or somebody else, "I   6
just want to be happy," the implication is that you're not.

    So what you want is something you don't have.   7

    That's a mole behind your ear. Maybe it's just a mole and that's all it   8
is. Wanting health insurance when you don't have it, wanting your kids
to get a good education—nothing troubling about that.

    But maybe that mole is something worse that's going to spread. And   9
you become a person who moves frantically through life grabbing things
off the shelf—the dark-haired boyfriend with the great parents since the
blond musicians haven't worked out so well, the breast implants because
then you'll like your body, the law degree that will make your father so
proud of you and maybe you'll learn to like the law—but never managing
to find the right thing, the one thing that will finally make you feel you
aren't missing something essential, such as the point.

    The "I just want to be happy" bear trap is that until you define pre-   10
cisely, just exactly what "happy" is, you will never feel it.

    By defining what "happy" means to you in absolutely concrete terms   11
you can then see what actions you need to take—or subtractions you
need to make—to be able to say, "Yup, okay. This is the happy I was looking for. I've got it now. It's safe to get the breast implants."

    If you're not a bespoke sort of person, you could use the standard,   12
off-the-shelf definition.

    Happiness is "a state of well-being characterized by emotions ranging   13
from contentment to intense joy."

    It's probably far-fetched to think you could be in a state of intense joy   14
for most of the day. But maybe you could be mostly content.

    Whatever being happy means to you, it needs to be specific and also   15
possible. Maybe if you didn't have to go to work every day at a job you
only tolerate but instead started your own online jewelry business. Maybe
this would make you happy because you love jewelry; you find it interesting, you like to make it, you like the people who like it.

When you have a blueprint for what happiness is, lay it over your life   16
and see what you need to change so the images are more aligned.

This recipe of defining what happiness means to you and then fid-   17
dling with your life to make the changes needed to make yourself happy
will work for some people. But not for others.

I am one of the others.   18

I am not a happy person.   19

There are things that do make me experience joy. But joy is a fleeting   20
emotion, like a very long sneeze.

I feel contentment rarely, but I do feel it.   21

A lot of the time what I feel is interested. Or I feel melancholy. And I   22
also frequently feel tenderness, annoyance, confusion, fear, hopelessness,
friskiness.

It doesn't all add up to anything I would call happiness.   23

What I'm thinking is, is that so terrible?   24

I used to say "I just want to be happy" all the time. I said it so fre-   25
quently and without care that I forgot to refill the phrase with meaning,
so it was just a shell of words.

When I said these words, I had only a vague sense of what happiness   26
even meant to me.

I can see it in others. I even know one person who is happy 95% of the   27
time, seriously. He's not stupid. As a matter of fact, he's right here beside
me as I write, his own computer on his own lap organizing his playlist.
And he makes me happy more often than I have ever been happy. But I
will never be as happy as he is. And I don't mind this because I might not
appreciate his happiness so much if I had it, too.

Also, I know a physicist who loves his work. People mistake his con-   28
stant focus and thought with unhappiness. But he's not unhappy. He's
busy. I bet when he dies, there will be a book on his chest.

Happiness is a wonderful goal for those who are inclined on a genetic   29
level toward that emotional end of the spectrum.

Happiness is a treadmill of a goal for people who are not happy by   30
nature.

Being an unhappy person does not mean you must be sad or dark.   31
You can be interested instead of happy. You can be fascinated instead of
happy.

Meaning

1. What is wrong, in Burroughs's estimation, with saying "I just want to be
   happy" (paragraph 1)? What's the harm in expressing a universal human
   desire?

2. In your own words, **paraphrase** Burroughs's understanding of the "standard, off-the-shelf definition" of happiness (paragraph 13). How would he like to see happiness defined instead?

3. The title of this essay is an **allusion**, a reference to something else that Burroughs assumes his readers know of. What does the title refer to? How does the allusion reinforce his meaning?

4. Based on their context in Burroughs's essay, try to guess the meanings of any of the following words that you don't already know. Test your guesses in a dictionary, and then use each new word in a sentence or two of your own.

guileless (3)	contentment (13, 21)	friskiness (22)
bespoke (12)	melancholy (22)	spectrum (29)

Purpose and Audience

1. Burroughs identifies two kinds of people: those who are happy and those who are not. Which of these groups (if either) do you think Burroughs is addressing, and why?

2. What assumptions does Burroughs make about his audience? How do those assumptions influence his purpose? Support your response with evidence from the essay.

3. What is your attitude toward happiness? Did Burroughs's essay change your way of thinking? If so, how? If not, why not? Use specific examples from the essay to support your answer.

Method and Structure

1. "Unhappily Ever After" identifies several potential synonyms for *happiness*. Make a list of those synonyms, both the "standard" ones (paragraph 13) and Burroughs's own. Which ones come closest to your own understanding of what happiness is? What other synonyms would you propose?

2. Consider how Burroughs uses negation to develop his definition. Why does he focus on unhappiness to the extent that he does?

3. This essay contains many short paragraphs. Do you find the short paragraphs more or less readable than the longer paragraphs used by most of the other writers in this book? As an exercise in revision, link Burroughs's short paragraphs into longer paragraphs wherever such links seem sensible. What specific reasons can you give for each of your changes?

4. **OTHER METHODS** As writers often do, Burroughs employs several methods to develop his definition, including **division or analysis** (Chapter 8), **cause-and-effect analysis** (Chapter 13), **process analysis** (Chapter 10), **comparison and contrast** (Chapter 11), **classification** (Chapter 9), and **example** (Chapter 7). What do the examples of happy people he cites in paragraphs 27–28 have in common?

Language

1. In several places throughout his essay, Burroughs uses **metaphors** to add depth to his definition. Locate two examples that you find especially striking, and explain their meaning and their effect.

2. Burroughs generally uses the second-person *you* or the first-person *I*. Do you think the essay would have been more or less effective if he had stuck with less intimate alternatives, such as *he, she, they,* or *the unhappy person* throughout? Why?

3. "Unhappily Ever After" contains many vague pronoun references, **comma splices**, and, most notably, **sentence fragments**. Identify at least three instances. (Refer to pp. 42–47 if you need help.) Is this sloppy writing, or does Burroughs break the rules of grammar and punctuation for a purpose? What do the sentence errors contribute to (or take away from) his essay? Explain your answer.

Writing Topics

1. **JOURNAL TO ESSAY** Burroughs claims that "until you define precisely, just exactly what 'happy' is, you will never feel it" (paragraph 10). In your journal entry (p. 281), you pondered what happiness means to you. Now, build on that entry to write an extended definition of *happiness*. As Burroughs does, present a wide range of examples to suggest various aspects of your subject, and be careful that your personal definition is "specific and also possible," as Burroughs advises (15). Does your definition correspond to traditional assumptions about happiness, or is it more like Burroughs's definition? What characteristics does your definition *not* include?

2. Think of a person you know or know of whose life is unhappy by contemporary standards but satisfying by Burroughs's standards. Write an essay describing this person's personality, interests, and accomplishments in detail, showing how his or her personal values and goals ensured contentment despite pressure from society to be externally happy. Be sure to include plenty of concrete details and examples.

3. **RESEARCH**   Burroughs insists that some people are simply unhappy by nature. Do some library research on the psychological problem of depression. (A periodicals database or the *Diagnostic and Statistical Manual of Mental Disorders* can give you a start, and many books have been written on the subject.) Write a brief essay outlining the contemporary definition of depression and some of its treatments, including therapy and medication.

4. **CONNECTIONS**   While Judy Brady (p. 276) suggests that having a "wife" of her own would make her happy, Burroughs cautions that saying "I want" is a mental trap destined to make a person miserable. In what ways could "Unhappily Ever After" be read as a response to "I Want a Wife"? Consider, for instance, the functions Brady and Burroughs assign to marriage, each writer's assumptions about personal responsibility for happiness, and the constraints of gender roles as they appear to factor in each essay. What advice might Burroughs offer Brady? How might she respond?

We're all so busy chasing the extraordinary that we forget to stop and be grateful for the ordinary.
—Brené Brown

What I regret most in life are failures of kindness.
—George Saunders

We are cups, constantly and quietly being filled. The trick is knowing how to tip ourselves over and let the beautiful stuff out.
—Ray Bradbury

JOURNAL RESPONSE How do you cope with the stress of college? of life in general? In your journal, make a list of the activities and mental strategies you use to keep yourself calm and centered. Do some efforts work better than others? Why do you think that is?

Jessica Sayuri Boissy

Jessica Sayuri Boissy was born in 1988 and raised in a bilingual household in San Francisco. The product of a cross-cultural marriage in a highly diverse city, she often found herself effortlessly switching between English and Japanese in order to communicate with her American-born father and her Japanese-born mother. Boissy graduated in 2010 from the University of California, Davis. Two years later she achieved her "childhood dream" of living in Japan, where she currently teaches English, studies written Japanese (which Boissy describes as "a complex but beautiful writing system"), and practices Bikram yoga. She spends her free time exploring the museums of modern Tokyo and the shrines and temples of ancient Kyoto.

One Cup at a Time
(Student Essay)

Boissy wrote "One Cup at a Time" for her first-year writing class in response to a prompt asking students to examine a language barrier they had experienced with a single word or phrase. Of *ichigo ichie*, the Japanese proverb the assignment inspired her to translate, Boissy says it reminds us "to cherish even the most seemingly mundane days, for these days will only occur once, never to happen again." Her essay was first published in *Prized Writing*, an anthology of the best student work to come out of the writing program at the University of California, Davis.

Ichigo ichie conveys a Japanese aesthetic ideal relating to transience that, when translated into English, literally signifies "one encounter, one chance." The philosophy behind it is that one should always do one's best 1

287

when meeting someone, treasuring each encounter as a once-in-a-lifetime event, even if it is a friend whom one sees often. For me, this phrase has brought awareness of the value of living each day, hour, minute, and second to the fullest and seizing each chance encounter that life unexpectedly brings. Though the ritual of meeting people follows a regular routine, this phrase stresses that each moment is a unique meeting to be lived intently, never to be repeated, as if today were the last time you might meet—in other words, this phrase teaches one to live his or her whole life now—the fullest in the moment.

Unlike the English alphabet, the Japanese writing system is composed of *kanji*, characters that embody the meanings in graphic forms. Although *ichigo ichie* can be written with the English alphabet, in Japanese, the phrase is written as 一期一会, giving a more visual representation of the meaning. The first part of the word, *ichigo* or 一期, symbolizes one period, in the terms of *ichigo ichie*, one lifetime. The second part, *ichie* or 一会, symbolizes one meeting. Thus, when put together the phrase *ichigo ichie* is formed, a phrase that easily rolls out of my mouth. Each character has three syllables, and the *ichi*, signifying the number one, at the beginning of each character gives a particular ring to the phrase, a consistency if not an echo—stressing the importance of only "*one* meeting" in our "*one* lifetime."

2

3

Jessica Sayuri Boissy

Also, because the meaning of *ichigo ichie* can be comprehended visually, nothing impinges on one's understanding. It is as though no interpretation is needed because the visual representation of the characters gives the reader the feeling of the word through the characters. Thus, the reader can be the sole interpreter of what *ichigo ichie* means to him or her.

However, the simplicity of meaning shatters when translated into English. Instead, the English language suggests a blizzard of wordy interpretations, such as "with every departure there is an encounter" or "one chance in a lifetime" or "treasure every meeting, for it will never reoccur"—phrases that sound nice but still cannot communicate the simplicity and wholeness of the original phrase.

Phrases and words can be translated into many different languages, but the culture still plays a significant role in understanding not just the

4

5

literal meaning but also the roots of words. The English equivalents lack the Zen spirit that permeates this phrase. Much like the Zen teachings, *ichigo ichie* teaches the importance of living in the present moment.

In fact, this Zen thinking lies at the heart of *chado*, the Japanese tea   6
ceremony. By concentrating on making tea inside a quiet tearoom, participants in the Japanese tea ceremony can reach a calm state of mind and reflect on themselves, cultivating a serene and mindful attitude towards each ceremony and towards life outside the tearoom. This attitude demands the awareness that although the steps of the ritual have not changed over the centuries, every time people come together over a bowl of tea, they create an original experience. In this context *ichigo ichie* retains the meaning of "one encounter, one chance," but also acquires another meaning — "one cup, one moment." In this context, *ichie* maintains the meaning of "one encounter" but *ichigo* becomes "one bowl of tea."

It wasn't until I attended my first tea ceremony in my first year of   7
middle school that I actually experienced *ichigo ichie* in its fullest sensory delight. I can remember slowly sliding the door to the tearoom and being showered by an abundance of sensations . . .

> . . . *from the fragrance of the sandalwood incense set into the charcoal beneath the hot water kettle to the aroma of freshly whisked green tea* . . .
>
> . . . *from the sound of water coming to a boil to the sound of soft cotton socks gliding over tatami* . . .
>
> . . . *from the handling of the* yakimono, *pottery streaked with ash glaze, to the small wooden lacquer-ware plates* . . .
>
> . . . *from the visual beauty of the calligraphy hanging beside the flower arrangement and, ultimately, from the taste of sweet bean cakes to the flavor of bitter green tea* . . .

In that moment, this mixing of sensory impressions—whereas in   8
everyday life one at a time will do—helps to create the feeling of *ichigo ichie*. Although incense smoke always rises and the water in the kettle eventually boils, the combination of sounds, tastes, smells, textures, and visual pleasures of the day's tea ceremony will never be reproduced exactly that way again. This reflection brings to mind another aspect of the physical nature of the tea ceremony—the interrelationship of three basic elements: *monosuki, furumai,* and *chashitsu,* or things, behavior, and setting. The tea ceremony that I experienced on that day when I was twelve will never be relived in a tea ceremony when I am eighteen. And the same philosophy can be applied to each day we experience in a lifetime—one

should always do one's best, whether it is making tea for another or simply meeting up with a friend, treasuring each encounter as a once-in-a-lifetime event.

Even before you knew the phrase *ichigo ichie*, you were living this   9
word in your life, because life is about the coming and going—about the changes. These changes can take on many forms: our first tea ceremony, high school graduation, twenty-first birthday, or receiving our PhD. And even if we meet each other in class every Tuesday and Thursday, I am not the same student and you are not the same teacher, because we are all participants in this inevitable change. But it is through these changes that *ichigo ichie* stresses the importance of treating each encounter as a once-in-a-lifetime event and focusing on the details of each occasion, the particular people and things involved daily. In other words, living fully in the present—*ichigo ichie*—drinking life, and tea, to its fullest—one cup at a time.

Meaning

1. What is the "cup" to which the title of this essay refers? What is Boissy's main idea?

2. What is the meaning of *Zen* as Boissy uses it in paragraphs 5 and 6? (If necessary, look up the word in an encyclopedia or unabridged dictionary.) How do Zen teachings relate to Boissy's thesis?

3. If any of the following words are unfamiliar, try to guess what they mean from the context of Boissy's essay. Look up the words in a dictionary to check your guesses, and then use each one in a sentence or two of your own.

aesthetic (1)	permeates (5)	tatami (7)
transience (1)	serene (6)	lacquer (7)
impinges (3)		

Purpose and Audience

1. What is Boissy's purpose or purposes in writing this essay: to express herself? to explain something? to persuade readers of something? Support your answer by referring to passages from the essay.

2. How can you tell that Boissy wrote this essay for her teacher and classmates at the University of California, Davis? How do you think her original readers may have responded to her ideas? How do *you* respond? Why?

Method and Structure

1. Why is definition particularly well suited to Boissy's subject and purpose? In what ways is the literal translation of *ichigo ichie* inadequate to explain its meaning?

2. What is the function of the hand-painted Japanese characters Boissy includes with her essay? What additional meanings does the calligraphy impart?

3. Why do you suppose Boissy uses italics and ellipses so extensively in paragraph 7? What is their effect?

4. **OTHER METHODS**   Explain the tea ceremony Boissy depicts in paragraphs 6–8. How does this use of **process analysis** (Chapter 10) and **description** (Chapter 6) help to develop her definition?

Language

1. In addition to *ichigo ichie*, Boissy uses several other Japanese words in her essay. How does she ensure that readers understand their meaning? What do they contribute to her main idea?

2. How would you characterize the overall **tone** of the essay? How does Boissy achieve it?

Writing Topics

1. **JOURNAL TO ESSAY**   In your journal entry (p. 287), you listed some of your strategies for managing stress. How do you react to Boissy's essay? Do you agree with her that life is an endless series of changes and so we must take care to live in the moment? Or do you find her philosophy impractical, her suggestions overly idealistic? Write an essay of your own responding to Boissy's ideas and advice. Be sure to include examples to support your view.

2. Boissy writes that the ritual of a traditional Japanese tea ceremony teaches a lesson that "can be applied to each day we experience in a lifetime—one should always do one's best, whether it is making tea for another or simply meeting up with a friend, treasuring each encounter as a once-in-a-lifetime event" (paragraph 8). Think of some rituals that are important to you and your friends or your family—for instance, a holiday celebration, a vacation activity, a way of decompressing after a difficult week. Choose one such ritual and, in a brief essay, explain it to outsiders. Focus on the details and steps of the ritual as well as on the significance it has for you and other members of your group.

3. **CULTURAL CONSIDERATIONS**   As noted on page 287, Boissy wrote her essay in response to a prompt asking her to examine a language barrier she had experienced with a single word or phrase. Try your hand at a similar essay of your own. Start by recalling a language barrier you have encountered. It may have involved a language other than English, a regional dialect, a slang term, workplace or academic jargon, or perhaps a generation gap. Focusing on a single word or phrase, examine the misunderstandings you have experienced. You might choose to define the term, as Boissy did, or you could narrate a representative incident involving it or compare and contrast your understanding with other people's comprehension. Whatever approach you choose, be sure to use concrete and specific words as well as vivid descriptions and plenty of detail to ensure that readers understand your meaning.

4. **CONNECTIONS**   While Boissy writes about the pleasures to be found in even the most mundane personal interactions, Barbara Lazear Ascher, in "The Box Man" (p. 258), asserts that we should learn to appreciate our own company, to find "a friend in our own voice." In an essay, compare these two writers' assumptions about relationships, and then draw your own conclusions about the value of friends and family. Consider, for instance, in what ways Ascher's "Box Man" and two lonely women might be said to have embraced or rejected Boissy's notion of *ichigo ichie*, as well as what we stand to gain—or lose—by treasuring each encounter with another person, as Boissy advises. What role do other people play in building and maintaining a happy life?

WRITING WITH THE METHOD

▶
DEFINITION

Select one of the following topics, or any other topic they suggest, for an essay developed by definition. Be sure to choose a topic you care about so that definition is a means of communicating an idea, not an end in itself.

Personal Qualities

1. Intelligence
2. Introversion or extroversion
3. Empathy
4. Responsibility
5. Hypocrisy

Experiences and Feelings

6. A nightmare
7. Love
8. Parenthood
9. An emotion such as fear, excitement, or shame

Social Concerns

10. Charity
11. Homelessness
12. Domestic violence
13. Addiction
14. Racism

Art and Entertainment

15. Dubstep or some other kind of music
16. Steampunk
17. Abstract expressionism or some other art movement

Ideas

18. Freedom
19. Respect
20. Feminism
21. Success or failure
22. A key concept in a course you're taking

WRITING ABOUT THE THEME

▶
PURSUING HAPPINESS

1. The authors in this chapter approach the subject of happiness from very different angles, and each offers a unique definition as a result. Carlin Flora (p. 270) offers a clinical explanation of a psychological state. Dagoberto Gilb (p. 270) considers the emotional benefits of a tight-knit community. Judy Brady (p. 276) examines her dissatisfaction from a feminist angle, while Augusten Burroughs (p. 281) reflects on the sources of unhappiness. And Jessica Sayuri Boissy (p. 287) draws on personal experience and cultural tradition to find pleasure in each moment. How do these writers' perspectives influence their ideas? What do their definitions have in common, and where do they disagree? How do *you* define happiness? Answer in an essay, citing as examples the paragraphs and essays in this chapter and your own experiences and desires.

2. Many of the writers in this chapter identify education as a prerequisite to a happy life. Carlin Flora cites the importance of "a willingness to learn and stretch and grow." Judy Brady wants to go back to school, Augusten Burroughs notes that the happiest people he knows are also the smartest, and Jessica Sayuri Boissy treasures the twice-weekly meetings of her college English class. What, in your mind, constitutes a good education? Has school been a positive or a negative experience for you? How can you get the most out of your time as a student? Write an essay analyzing the role you think education will play in your potential for success and happiness in the future.

3. In an epigraph on page 281, psychologist Daniel Gilbert asserts, "We are happy when we have family, we are happy when we have friends, and almost all the other things we think make us happy are just ways of getting more family and friends." Most of the writers in this chapter would seem to agree. Dagoberto Gilb, Judy Brady, Augusten Burroughs, and Jessica Sayuri Boissy all write of the impact that loved ones have on a person's satisfaction with life, and even Carlin Flora stresses that happiness is enhanced "when you also feel part of a community." How important is family (immediate or extended) in shaping our sense of who we are and what we want? To what extent does the larger community — friends, teachers, neighbors — also play a significant role in forming a person's identity? Answer in an essay, citing as examples the selections in this chapter and observations of your own.

13

CAUSE-AND-EFFECT ANALYSIS

▶

INVESTIGATING THE WORKING WORLD

Why did free agency become so important in professional baseball, and how has it affected the sport? What caused the recent warming of the Pacific Ocean, and how did the warming affect the earth's weather? We answer questions like these with **cause-and-effect analysis**, the method of dividing occurrences into their elements to find relationships among them. Cause-and-effect analysis is a specific kind of analysis, the method discussed in Chapter 8.

When we analyze *causes*, we try to discover which of the events preceding a specified outcome actually made it happen:

What caused Adolf Hitler's rise in Germany?

Why have herbal medicines become so popular?

When we analyze *effects*, we try to discover which of the events following a specified occurrence actually resulted from it:

What do we do for (or to) drug addicts when we imprison them?

What happens to our foreign policy when the president's advisers disagree over its conduct?

These are existing effects of past or current situations, but effects are often predicted for the future:

How would a cure for cancer affect the average life expectancy of men and women?

How might your decision to take family leave affect your future job prospects?

Causes and effects can also be analyzed together, as the questions opening this chapter illustrate.

Like everyone else, you probably consider causes and effects many times a day: Why is the traffic so heavy? What will happen if I major in art rather than business? In writing you'll also draw often on cause-and-effect analysis, perhaps explaining why the school's basketball team has been so successful this year, what made a bridge collapse, or how a new stoplight has worsened rush-hour traffic. You'll use the method for persuasion, too, as in arguing that families, not mass media, bear responsibility for children's violence (focusing on causes) or that adult illiteracy threatens American democracy (focusing on possible effects). Because cause-and-effect analysis attempts to answer *why* and *what if*—two of the most basic questions of human experience—you'll find the method often in your reading as well.

Reading Cause-and-Effect Analysis

Cause-and-effect analysis is found in just about every discipline and occupation, including history, social science, natural science, engineering, medicine, law, business, and sports. In any of these fields, as well as in writing done for college courses, the purpose in analyzing may be to explain or to persuade. In explaining why something happened or what its outcome was or will be, writers try to order experience and pin down connections. In arguing with cause-and-effect analysis, they try to demonstrate why one explanation of causes is more accurate than another or how a proposed action will produce desirable or undesirable consequences.

The possibility of arguing about causes and effects points to the main challenge of this method. Related events sometimes overlap, sometimes follow one another immediately, and sometimes connect over gaps in time. They vary in their duration and complexity. They vary in their importance. Analyzing causes and effects thus requires not only identifying them but also discerning their relationships accurately and weighing their significance fairly.

Causes and effects often do occur in a sequence, each contributing to the next in what is called a *causal chain*. For instance, an unlucky man named Jones ends up in prison, and the causal chain leading to his imprisonment can be outlined as follows: Jones's neighbor, Smith, dumped trash on Jones's lawn. In reprisal, Jones set a small brush fire in Smith's yard. A spark from the fire accidentally ignited Smith's house. Jones was prosecuted for the fire and sent to jail. In this chain each event is the cause of an effect, which in turn is the cause of another effect, and so on to the unhappy conclusion.

Identifying a causal chain partly involves sorting out events in time:

- *Immediate* causes or effects occur nearest an event. For instance, the immediate cause of a town's high unemployment rate may be the closing of a large manufacturing plant where many townspeople work.

- *Remote* causes or effects occur further away in time. The remote cause of the town's unemployment rate may be a drastic decline in the company's sales or (more remote) a weak regional or national economy.

Analyzing causes also requires distinguishing their relative importance in the sequence:

- *Major* causes are directly and primarily responsible for the outcome. For instance, if a weak economy is responsible for low sales, it is a major cause of the manufacturing plant's closing.

- *Minor* causes (also called *contributory* causes) merely contribute to the outcome. The manufacturing plant may have closed for the additional reason that the owners could not afford to repair its machines.

As these examples illustrate, time and significance can overlap in cause-and-effect analysis: a weak economy, for instance, is both a remote and a major cause; the lack of funds for repairs is both an immediate and a minor cause.

Since most cause-and-effect relationships are complex, several pitfalls can weaken an analysis or its presentation. One is a confusion of coincidence and cause —that is, an assumption that because one event preceded another, it must have caused the other. This error is nicknamed **post hoc**, from the Latin *post hoc, ergo propter hoc*, meaning "after this, therefore because of this." Superstitions often illustrate post hoc: a basketball player believes that a charm once ended her shooting slump, so she now wears the charm whenever she plays. But post hoc also occurs in more serious matters. For instance, the office of a school administrator is vandalized, and he blames the incident on a recent speech by the student-government president criticizing the administration. But the administrator has no grounds for his accusation unless he can prove that the speech incited the vandals. In the absence of proof, the administrator commits the error of post hoc by asserting that the speech caused the vandalism simply because the speech preceded the vandalism.

Another potential problem to watch for in cause-and-effect writing is **oversimplification**. An effective analysis must consider not just the causes and effects that seem obvious or important but all the possibilities: remote as well as immediate, minor as well as major. One form of oversimplification confuses a necessary cause with a sufficient cause:

- A *necessary* cause, as the term implies, is one that must happen in order for an effect to come about; an effect can have more than one necessary cause. For example, if emissions from a factory cause a high rate of illness in a neighborhood, the emissions are a necessary cause.

- A *sufficient* cause, in contrast, is one that brings about the effect *by itself.* The emissions are not a sufficient cause of the illness rate unless all other possible causes—such as water pollution or infection—can be eliminated.

Oversimplification can also occur if opinions or emotions are allowed to cloud the interpretation of evidence. Suppose that a writer is examining the reasons a gun-control bill she opposed was passed by the state legislature. Some of the evidence strongly suggests that a member of the legislature, a vocal supporter of the bill, was unduly influenced by lobbyists. But if the writer attributed the passage of the bill solely to this legislator, she would be exaggerating the significance of a single legislator and ignoring the opinions of the many others who also voted for the bill. To achieve a balanced analysis, she would have to put aside her personal feelings and consider all possible causes for the bill's passage.

Analyzing Causes and Effects in Paragraphs

Barbara Ehrenreich (born 1941) is an investigative journalist with a PhD in biology. A contributing writer for a wide range of periodicals, she is probably best known for her books about contemporary class struggles in the United States, especially *Nickel and Dimed: On (Not) Getting By in America* (2001), the book in which the following paragraph appears.

The problem of rents is easy for a noneconomist, even a sparsely educated low-wage worker, to grasp. . . . When the rich and the poor compete for housing on

Cause (topic sentence underlined): competition for housing

<u>the open market, the poor don't stand a chance.</u> The rich can always outbid them, buy up their tenements or trailer parks, and replace them with condos, McMansions, golf courses, or whatever they like. Since the rich have become more numerous, thanks largely to rising stock prices and executive salaries, the poor have necessarily been forced into housing that is more expensive, more dilapidated, or more distant from their places of work. . . . Insofar as the poor have to work near the dwellings of the rich—as in the case of so many service and retail jobs— they are stuck with lengthy commutes or dauntingly expensive housing.

Effects:

Rich buy inexpensive properties for themselves

Poor are forced to pay more, accept less, or move

Malcolm Gladwell was born in 1963 to an English father and a Jamaican mother and immigrated with his parents to Canada when a child. Now a staff writer at the *New Yorker*, he is known for his highly readable articles and books that synthesize complex research in the sciences and social sciences. This paragraph is from *Outliers* (2008), an exploration of why some people are more successful in their work than others.

<u>Personal explanations of success don't work.</u> People don't rise from nothing. We do owe something to parentage and patronage. The people who stand before kings may look like they did it all by themselves. But in fact they are invariably the beneficiaries of hidden advantages and extraordinary opportunities and cultural legacies that allow them to learn and work hard and make sense of the world in ways others cannot. It makes a difference where and when we grew up. The culture we belong to and the legacies passed down by our forebears shape the patterns of our achievements in ways we cannot begin to imagine. It's not enough to ask what successful people are like, in other words. It is only by asking where they are *from* that we can unravel the logic behind who succeeds and who doesn't.

Effect (topic sentence underlined): success

Causes:

Background

Opportunities

Influences

Developing an Essay by Cause-and-Effect Analysis

▶ Getting Started

Assignments in almost any course or line of work ask for cause-and-effect analysis: What caused the Vietnam War? In the theory of sociobiology, what are the effects of altruism on the survival of the group? Why did costs exceed the budget last month? You can find your own subject for cause-and-effect analysis from your experiences, from observation of others, from your course work, or from your reading outside school. Anytime you find yourself wondering what happened or why or what if, you may be onto an appropriate subject.

Remember that your treatment of causes or effects or both must be thorough; thus your subject must be manageable within the constraints of time and space imposed on you. Broad subjects like those in the following examples must be narrowed to something whose complexities you can cover adequately.

BROAD SUBJECT   Causes of the decrease in American industrial productivity

NARROWER SUBJECT   Causes of decreasing productivity on one assembly line

BROAD SUBJECT   Effects of cigarette smoke

NARROWER SUBJECT   Effects of parents' secondhand smoke on small children

Whether your subject suggests a focus on causes or effects or both, list as many of them as you can from memory or from further reading. If the subject does not suggest a focus, then ask yourself questions to begin exploring it:

- Why did it happen?
- What contributed to it?
- What were or are its results?
- What might its consequences be?

One or more of these questions should lead you to a focus and, as you explore further, to a more complete list of ideas.

But you cannot stop with a simple list, for you must arrange the causes or effects in sequence and weigh their relative importance: Do the events break down into a causal chain? Besides the immediate causes and effects, are there also less obvious, more remote ones? Besides the major causes or effects, are there also minor ones? At this stage, you may find that diagraming relationships helps you see them more clearly. The following diagram illustrates the earlier example of the plant closing (see p. 297):

Though uncomplicated, the diagram does sort out the causes and effects and shows their relationships and sequence.

While you are developing a clear picture of your subject, you should also be anticipating the expectations and needs of your readers. As with the other methods of essay development, consider especially what your readers already know about your subject and what they need to be told:

- Do readers require background information?
- Are they likely to be familiar with some of the causes or effects you are analyzing, or should you explain every one completely?
- Which causes or effects might readers already accept?
- Which ones might they disagree with?

If, for instance, the plant closing affected many of your readers—putting them or their relatives out of work—they might blame the company's owners rather than economic forces beyond the owners' control. You would have to address these preconceptions and provide plenty of evidence for your own interpretation.

▶ Forming a Thesis

To help manage your ideas and information, try to develop a working thesis sentence that states your subject, your perspective on it, and your purpose. For instance:

EXPLANATORY THESIS SENTENCE Unemployment has affected not only my family's finances but also our relationships.

PERSUASIVE THESIS SENTENCE   Contrary to local opinion, the many people put out of work by the closing of Windsor Manufacturing were victims not of the owners' incompetence but of the nation's weak economy.

Notice that these thesis sentences reflect clear judgments about the relative significance of possible causes or effects. Such judgments can be difficult to reach and may not be apparent when you start writing. Often you will need to complete a draft of your analysis before you are confident about the relationship between cause and effect. And even if you start with an idea of how cause and effect are connected, you may change your mind after you've mapped out the relationship in a draft. That's fine: just remember to revise your thesis sentence accordingly.

▶ Organizing

The **introduction** to a cause-and-effect essay can pull readers in by describing the situation whose causes or effects you plan to analyze, such as the passage of a bill in the legislature or a town's high unemployment rate. The introduction may also provide background, such as a brief narrative of a family quarrel; or it may summarize the analysis of causes or effects that the essay disputes, such as townspeople blaming owners for a plant's closing. If your thesis is not already apparent in the introduction, stating it explicitly can tell readers exactly what your purpose is and which causes or effects or both you plan to highlight. But if you anticipate that readers will oppose your thesis, you may want to delay stating it until the end of the essay, after you have provided the evidence to support it.

The arrangement of the body of the essay depends primarily on your material and your emphasis. If events unfold in a causal chain with each effect becoming the cause of another effect, and if stressing these links coincides with your purpose, then a simple chronological sequence will probably be clearest. But if events overlap and vary in significance, their organization will require more planning. Probably the most effective way to arrange either causes or effects is in order of increasing importance. Such an arrangement helps readers see which causes or effects you consider minor and which major, while it also reserves your most significant (and probably most detailed) point for last. The groups of minor or major events may then fit into a chronological framework.

To avoid being preoccupied with organization while you are drafting your essay, prepare some sort of outline before you start writing (see p. 27). The outline need not be detailed so long as you have written the details elsewhere or can retrieve them easily from your mind. But it should show all the causes or effects you want to discuss and the order in which you will cover them.

In the **conclusion** to your essay, you may want to restate your thesis—or state it, if you deliberately withheld it for the end—so that readers are left with the point of your analysis. If your analysis is complex, readers may also benefit from a summary of the relationships you have identified. And depending on your purpose, you may want to specify why your analysis is significant, what use your readers can make of it, or what action you hope they will take.

▶ Drafting

While drafting your essay, strive primarily for clarity—sharp details, strong examples, concrete explanations. To make readers see not only *what* you see but also *why* you see it, you can draw on just about any method of writing discussed in this book. For instance, you might **narrate** the effect of a situation on one person, analyze a **process**, or **compare and contrast** two interpretations of cause. Particularly if your thesis is debatable (like the earlier example asserting the owners' blamelessness for the plant's closing), you will need accurate, representative facts to back up your interpretation, and you may also need quotations from experts such as witnesses and scholars. If you do not support your assertions specifically, your readers will have no reason to believe them. (For more on evidence in persuasive writing, see pp. 330 and 336–37. For more on finding and documenting sources, see the Appendix.)

▶ Revising and Editing

While revising and editing your draft, consider the following questions and the Focus box on the next page to be sure your analysis is sound and clear.

- *Have you explained causes or effects clearly and specifically?* Readers will need to see the pattern of causes or effects—their sequence and relative importance. And readers will need facts, examples, and other evidence to understand and accept your analysis.

- *Have you demonstrated that causes are not merely coincidences?* Avoid the error of post hoc, of assuming that one event caused another just because it preceded the other. To be convincing, a claim that one event caused another must be supported with ample evidence.

FOCUS ON CONCISENESS

While drafting a cause-and-effect analysis, you may need to grope a bit to discover just what you think about the sequence and relative importance of reasons and consequences. As a result, your sentences may grope a bit, too, reflecting your need to circle around your ideas in order to find them. The following draft passage reveals such difficulties:

> WORDY   Employees often worry about negative comments from others. The employee may not only worry but feel the need to discuss the situation with coworkers. One thing that is an effect of harassment, especially verbal harassment, in the workplace is that productivity is lost. Plans also need to be made to figure out how to deal with future comments. Engaging in these activities is sure to take time and concentration from work.

Drafting this passage, the writer seems to have built up to the idea about lost productivity (third sentence) after providing support for it in the first two sentences. The fourth sentence then adds more support. And sentences 2–4 all show a writer working out ideas: sentence subjects and verbs do not focus on the main actors and actions of the sentences, words repeat unnecessarily, and word groups run longer than needed for clarity.

These problems disappear from the edited version below, which moves the main ideas up front, uses subjects and verbs to state what the sentences are about, and cuts unneeded words.

> CONCISE   Verbal harassment in the workplace causes loss of productivity. Worrying about negative comments, discussing those comments with coworkers, planning how to deal with future comments — all these activities take a harassed employee's time and concentration away from work.

For more on editing for conciseness, see pages 48–49.

■ *Have you considered all the possible causes or effects?* Your analysis should go beyond what is most immediate or obvious so that you do not oversimplify the cause-and-effect relationships. Your readers will expect you to present the relationships in all their complexity.

■ *Have you represented the cause-and-effect relationships honestly?* Don't deliberately ignore or exaggerate causes or effects in a misguided effort to strengthen your essay. If a cause fails to support your thesis but still does not invalidate it, mention the cause and explain why you believe it to be unimportant. If a change you are proposing will have bad effects as well as good, mention the bad effects and explain how they are outweighed by the good. As long as your reasoning and evidence are sound, such admissions will not weaken your essay; on the contrary, readers will appreciate your fairness.

■ *Have you used transitions to signal the sequence and relative importance of events?* **Transitions** between sentences can help you pinpoint causes or effects (*for this reason, as a result*), show the steps in a sequence (*first, second, third*), link events in time (*in the same month*), specify duration (*a year later*), and indicate the weights you assign events (*equally important, even more crucial*).

A Note on Thematic Connections

Analyzing the workplace often prompts writers to ask what leads to success or failure or what may result from a business decision. The authors in this chapter all attempt to pinpoint a cause-and-effect relationship between business practices and their consequences for workers. In a paragraph, Barbara Ehrenreich considers how the real estate market makes it difficult for low-wage workers to find housing (p. 298). In another paragraph, Malcolm Gladwell asserts that our chances for success are determined by hidden opportunities (p. 299). In essays, Ellen Goodman examines the results of overwork (next page), while student writers Stephanie Alaimo and Mark Koester (p. 311) and journalist Dana Thomas (p. 316) investigate the impacts our shopping choices have on workers around the globe.

The Bustle in a House / The Morning after Death / Is solemnest of
industries / Enacted upon Earth.   —Emily Dickinson

Any man's death diminishes me, because I am involved in mankind.
                                                                —John Donne

No one on his deathbed has ever said, "I wish I'd spent more time at the
office."   —Paul Tsongas

JOURNAL RESPONSE   In your journal, reflect on the purpose of living. What
do you hope to accomplish in your lifetime, and where do your priorities
lie? Is career most important? family? community? country? service?
faith? something else? Why?

Ellen Goodman

Social commentator Ellen Goodman has had a distinguished career as a journalist
and speaker. She was born in 1941, grew up in Boston, Massachusetts, and earned
a degree from Radcliffe College (a part of Harvard University) in 1963. Goodman
researched for *Newsweek* and reported for the *Detroit Free Press* and the *Boston
Globe* before becoming a full-time syndicated columnist in 1974. Her observations
on life and politics have been published in more than four hundred newspapers
nationwide and collected in six volumes: *Close to Home* (1979), *At Large* (1981),
Keeping in Touch (1985), *Making Sense* (1989), *Value Judgments* (1993), and *Paper
Trail: Common Sense in Uncommon Times* (2004). One of the first American women
to make a career as a columnist, Goodman won the Pulitzer Prize for distinguished
commentary in 1980 and a lifetime achievement award from the National Society
of Newspaper Columnists in 2008. She lives in Boston and spends summers with
her family on the coast of Maine.

The Company Man

Goodman is known for her evenhanded thoughtfulness on contentious subjects
ranging from the women's movement to bioethics. In this essay from *Close to Home*,
she relates a story about one man's career to show how competitive office culture
can damage lives.

He worked himself to death, finally and precisely, at 3:00 a.m. Sunday   1
morning.

The obituary didn't say that, of course. It said that he died of a coro- 2
nary thrombosis—I think that was it—but everyone among his friends
and acquaintances knew it instantly. He was a perfect Type A, a workaholic, a classic, they said to each other and shook their heads—and
thought for five or ten minutes about the way they lived.

This man who worked himself to death finally and precisely at 3:00 3
a.m. Sunday morning—on his day off—was fifty-one years old and a vice-
president. He was, however, one of six vice-presidents, and one of three
who might conceivably—if the president died or retired soon enough—
have moved to the top spot. Phil knew that.

He worked six days a week, five of them until eight or nine at night, 4
during a time when his own company had begun the four-day week for
everyone but the executives. He worked like the Important People. He had
no outside "extracurricular interests," unless, of course, you think about a
monthly golf game that way. To Phil, it was work. He always ate egg salad
sandwiches at his desk. He was, of course, overweight, by twenty or twenty-
five pounds. He thought it was okay, though, because he didn't smoke.

On Saturdays, Phil wore a sports jacket to the office instead of a suit, 5
because it was the weekend.

He had a lot of people working for him, maybe sixty, and most of 6
them liked him most of the time. Three of them will be seriously considered for his job. The obituary didn't mention that.

But it did list his "survivors" quite accurately. He is survived by his 7
wife, Helen, forty-eight years old, a good woman of no particular market-
able skills, who worked in an office before marrying and mothering. She
had, according to her daughter, given up trying to compete with his work
years ago, when the children were small. A company friend said, "I know
how much you will miss him." And she answered, "I already have."

"Missing him all those years," she must have given up part of herself 8
which had cared too much for the man. She would be "well taken care of."

His "dearly beloved" eldest of the "dearly beloved" children is a hard- 9
working executive in a manufacturing firm down South. In the day and a
half before the funeral, he went around the neighborhood researching his
father, asking the neighbors what he was like. They were embarrassed.

His second child is a girl, who is twenty-four and newly married. She 10
lives near her mother and they are close, but whenever she was alone with
her father, in a car driving somewhere, they had nothing to say to each
other.

The youngest is twenty, a boy, a high school graduate who has spent 11
the last couple of years, like a lot of his friends, doing enough odd jobs
to stay in grass and food. He was the one who tried to grab at his father,

and tried to mean enough to him to keep the man at home. He was his father's favorite. Over the last two years, Phil stayed up nights worrying about the boy.

The boy once said, "My father and I only board here."   12

At the funeral, the sixty-year-old company president told the forty-   13
eight-year-old widow that the fifty-one-year-old deceased had meant much to the company and would be missed and would be hard to replace. The widow didn't look him in the eye. She was afraid he would read her bitterness and, after all, she would need him to straighten out her finances—the stock options and all that.

Phil was overweight and nervous and worked too hard. If he wasn't   14
at the office, he was worried about it. Phil was a Type A, a heart-attack natural. You could have picked him out in a minute from a lineup.

So when he finally worked himself to death, at precisely 3:00 a.m.   15
Sunday morning, no one was really surprised.

By 5:00 p.m. the afternoon of the funeral, the company president   16
had begun, discreetly of course, with care and taste, to make inquiries about his replacement. One of three men. He asked around: "Who's been working the hardest?"

Meaning

1. What killed Phil, according to his obituary? according to Goodman?

2. "The Company Man" does not include a thesis statement. What is Goodman's point? Express the author's main idea in your own words.

3. Notice Goodman's frequent use of numbers: "five or ten minutes" (paragraph 2), "fifty-one years old" (3), "six vice-presidents" (3), and so on. What other numbers does she cite in this essay? What does the focus on such details contribute to her point?

4. If you do not know the following words, try to determine their meanings from the context of Goodman's essay. Test your guesses in a dictionary, and then use each word in a sentence or two of your own.

   coronary (2)   board (12)   discreetly (16)
   thrombosis (2)

Purpose and Audience

1. For whom is Goodman writing: Phil's family? his employer? the men in line for his job? someone else? Why do you think so?

2. Describing the reaction to Phil's death among his friends, Goodman says they "shook their heads—and thought for five or ten minutes about the

way they lived" (paragraph 2). What does this comment reveal about her purpose for writing?

Method and Structure

1. What cause does Goodman examine? What effects does she identify?

2. "He worked himself to death, finally and precisely, at 3:00 a.m. Sunday morning," Goodman says in paragraph 1, then again (with some variation) in paragraphs 3 and 15. Why does she stress these details? What other details does she repeat? What is the effect of her repetitions?

3. Goodman gives no indication of what Phil's job was. Why not? What does leaving out this detail contribute to her meaning? What other details does she omit?

4. **OTHER METHODS** "The Company Man" is also a model of **definition** (Chapter 12). What does "Type A" (paragraphs 2 and 14) mean? What other details in the essay give you a clue to Phil's personality?

Language

1. How would you characterize Goodman's **tone**? Support your answer with specific details, sentence structures, and phrases from the essay.

2. At several points in the essay Goodman quotes Phil's obituary as well as comments made by his family and coworkers. How do these quotations reinforce the main idea of her essay?

3. Explain the **irony** of Goodman's conclusion.

Writing Topics

1. **JOURNAL TO ESSAY** Most of us have to work to support ourselves and our families, but as Goodman suggests, the demands of some jobs can overshadow, or even destroy, the rest of a person's life. Look again at the quotations preceding her essay and at your journal notes (p. 306), and then compose an essay on the subject of work/life balance. What role does work play in a person's happiness? What role do personal relationships play? How can a person successfully juggle the demands and rewards of both?

2. Goodman writes that Phil's two sons took very different approaches to their independence as adults: the elder followed in his father's footsteps and became a "hard-working executive" (paragraph 9), while the younger chose to drift through odd jobs after finishing high school (11). How would you define *independence* for young adults? What freedoms does

independence entail? What responsibilities? What problems can occur for the newly independent person?

3. **CULTURAL CONSIDERATIONS**   Contemporary American society places great importance on work, encouraging people to find and devote themselves to jobs that entail responsibility and opportunity for advancement, to put in long hours when required, and to be available and productive at all times. In contrast, many other cultures emphasize leisure (in some European countries, for instance, businesses shut down for a few hours every afternoon; in others, workers are entitled to eight weeks of paid vacation a year). Write an essay in which you consider the benefits and drawbacks of the American work ethic. What do we gain through hard work and determination? What do we lose?

4. **RESEARCH**   Phil's oldest son "went around the neighborhood researching his father, asking the neighbors what he was like," Goodman writes in paragraph 9. How well do you know your parents? Even if you're close, you may not be fully aware of what they do with their time or how they get along with others. Pick a parent to research, and interview several people—coworkers, for example, siblings, neighbors, or friends—to learn how others perceive him or her. In an essay, write a profile of your parent, focusing on how he or she interacts with the larger community.

5. **CONNECTIONS**   While Goodman writes with compassion about the consequences of pressures put on business executives, Stephanie Alaimo and Mark Koester, in "The Backdraft of Technology" (opposite), blame those executives for putting low-wage employees out of work. In an essay of your own, consider some aspect of competition and fairness in a capitalist economy. Are executive salaries too high, for instance? Should all workers be guaranteed a living wage? What role should the government play in ensuring citizens' economic well-being? Why do you think so?

There is no reason that the universe should be designed for our convenience.

—John D. Barrow

All of the biggest technological inventions created by man—the airplane, the automobile, the computer—say little about his intelligence, but speak volumes about his laziness.

—Mark Kennedy

Besides black art [such as voodoo and witchcraft], there is only automation and mechanization.

—Federico García Lorca

JOURNAL RESPONSE   Write a short journal entry about a modern convenience that you dislike. (Examples might include online banking, cruise control, or automated call centers.) Why don't you care for it? In what ways is this technology harmful or just more trouble than it's worth?

Stephanie Alaimo and Mark Koester

Stephanie Alaimo (born 1984) and Mark Koester (born 1983) both studied at DePaul University of Chicago and the Université de Strasbourg in France. Alaimo, a Spanish major while at DePaul, volunteered as a tutor of English as a second language and as an intern with the Interfaith Committee for Worker Justice. She is currently a graduate student at the University of California, San Diego, where she is studying the sociology of migration and development. Koester, a native of Omaha, Nebraska, majored in philosophy and taught English in Hangzhou, China, after graduation. Now an entrepreneur, he still lives in China and is working on multiple startups that aim to merge Web technology, business, and sustainable development.

The Backdraft of Technology
(Student Essay)

How important is it to save a few minutes in the supermarket? Would you stand in line to save someone else's job? Alaimo and Koester think you should—and they explain why by analyzing the causes and effects of self-service checkout machines. They collaborated on this op-ed piece for the *DePaulia*, a student newspaper, in 2006.

You have picked up the bread and the milk and the day's miscellaneous   1
foodstuffs at your local grocery store. The lines at the traditional, human-operated checkouts are a shocking two customers deep. Who wants to

311

wait? Who would wait when we have society's newest upgrade in not having to wait: the self-checkout?

Welcome to the automated grocery store. "Please scan your next   2
item," a repetitively chilling, mechanical voice orders you.

If you have yet to see it at your nearest grocer, a new technological   3
advance has been reached. Instead of waiting for some minimally waged, minimally educated, and, most likely, immigrant cashier to scan and bag your groceries for you, you can now do it yourself. In a consumer-driven, hyperactive, "I want" world, an increase in speed is easily accepted thoughtlessly. We're too busy. But, in gaining efficiency and ease, a number of jobs have been lost, particularly at the entry level, and a moment of personal, human engagement with actual people has vanished.

It seems easy enough to forget about the consequences when you are   4
rushed and your belly is grumbling. The previously utilized checkout lanes at local grocery stores and super, mega, we-have-everything stores are now routinely left unattended during the peak hours. In these moments, your options are using the self-checkout or waiting for a real human being. Often in a hurried moment we choose the easiest, fastest, and least mentally involved option without much consideration.

We forget to consider that with the aid of the self-checkout at least   5
two jobs have been lost. As a result, a human cashier and grocery bagger are now waiting in the unemployment line. Furthermore, self-checkout machines are probably not manufactured in the United States, thus shipping more jobs overseas. And sadly, the job openings are now shrinking by putting consumers to work. The wages from these jobs are stockpiled by those least in need — corporations and those who own them.

The mechanization of the service industry has been occurring through-   6
out our lifetimes. Gas stations were once full-service. Human bank tellers handled simple cash withdrawals, instead of ATMs. Even video stores are being marginalized from people ordering online from companies like Netflix. And did you know that you can now order a pizza for delivery online without even talking to a person?

Sure, these new robots and computers reduce work, which could   7
potentially be a really good thing. But these mechanizations have only increased profit margins for large corporations and have reduced the need to hire employees. Jobs are lost along with means of providing for one's self and family.

For those who find the loss of grocery store labor to be meaningless   8
and, quite frankly, beyond impacting their future lives as accountants or lawyers, it does not seem to be entirely implausible that almost any job or task could become entirely technologically mechanized and your elitist job market nuked.

We are a society trapped in a precarious fork in the road. We can   9
either eliminate the time and toil of the human workload and still allow
people to have jobs and maintain the same standard of living, though
working less, or, in a darker scenario, we can eliminate human work in
terms of actual human jobs and make the situation of the lower classes
more tenuous. Is it our goal to reduce the overall time that individuals
spend laboring? Or is it our goal to increase corporate profits at the loss of
many livelihoods?

At present, corporations and their executives put consumers to work,   10
cut the cost of labor through the use of technology such as self-checkouts
and ATMs, and profit tremendously. But a host of workers are now scrambling to find a way to subsist. To choose the self-checkout simply as a
convenience cannot be morally justified unless these jobs remain.

The choices we make on a daily basis affect the whole of our society.   11
Choosing convenience often translates to eliminating actual jobs that
provide livelihoods and opportunities to many. Think before you simply
follow the next technological innovation. Maybe it could be you in their
soon-to-be-jobless shoes. Say "No!" to self-checkout.

Meaning

1. What do you make of the title of this essay? What is a backdraft, and
   what does it have to do with technology?

2. In paragraph 4, Alaimo and Koester write, "Often in a hurried moment
   we choose the easiest, fastest, and least mentally involved option without much consideration." Do they condemn this tendency?

3. Try to guess the meanings of the following words, based on their context
   in Alaimo and Koester's essay. Test your guesses in a dictionary, and then
   try to use each word in a sentence or two of your own.

stockpiled (5)	implausible (8)	tenuous (9)
marginalized (6)	precarious (9)	subsist (10)

Purpose and Audience

1. Do you believe that Alaimo and Koester are writing mainly to express
   their viewpoint or to persuade readers to do something? Make specific
   references to the text to support your opinion.

2. Who is the "you" being addressed in the two opening paragraphs? What
   do these paragraphs and the rest of the essay tell you about the authors'
   conception of their audience?

Method and Structure

1. Why do you think Alaimo and Koester rely on cause-and-effect analysis to develop their ideas? What are some causes of long checkout lines, in their opinion? What is the effect of the option to serve ourselves rather than wait for a cashier?

2. The authors open and close their essay by having their readers imagine waiting in line at the supermarket. What is the effect of this scenario?

3. In your opinion, is the cause-and-effect analysis in this essay sufficiently thorough and convincing? Why, or why not?

4. **OTHER METHODS**   In addition to cause-and-effect analysis, Alaimo and Koester rely on **example** (Chapter 7) and **argument and persuasion** (Chapter 14). What does each of these other methods contribute to the essay?

Language

1. How would you describe the authors' **tone**? Are they angry? optimistic? passionate? earnest? hesitant? friendly?

2. Alaimo and Koester begin paragraph 7 with the interjection "Sure." They also use phrases such as "miscellaneous foodstuffs" (1), "super, mega, we-have-everything stores" (4), "nuked" (8), and "fork in the road" (9). How would you characterize this language? What does it add to (or take away from) the essay?

Writing Topics

1. **JOURNAL TO ESSAY**   On the basis of your journal entry and your reaction to the quotations preceding this essay (p. 311), expand your ideas about the drawbacks of a modern convenience. Do you agree with Alaimo and Koester that "[t]he choices we make on a daily basis affect the whole of our society" (paragraph 11)? When do technological conveniences help us? At what point does convenience for ourselves become harmful and destructive for others? Write to persuade your readers to change their behavior, as Alaimo and Koester do, or from a narrower personal perspective. If you choose the latter course, however, be sure to make your experience meaningful to others and offer plenty of details and examples.

2. Alaimo and Koester challenge their readers to reject self-service opportunities because they believe mechanization deprives unskilled workers of desperately needed jobs. But are such menial, low-paying jobs really worth saving? Write an essay that offers an alternative solution to the

employment issue Alaimo and Koester describe. Define the problem as you interpret it, and explain its causes. In your proposal, outline the changes you would like to see take place, identify who would have to make them, and predict how your changes would improve things.

3. **CULTURAL CONSIDERATIONS**   In paragraph 3, Alaimo and Koester say that many cashiers are immigrants; later they express concern that American jobs are being shipped to other countries (paragraph 5). What is your response to these remarks? Write an essay that considers the impact of foreign labor on the US job market. What are some sources of friction? What are some advantages? To what extent should the United States encourage immigration and globalization, and to what extent should the country restrict them? Why? Use examples from your own experience, observations, and reading.

4. **CONNECTIONS**   Like Alaimo and Koester, Brandon Griggs, in "The Most Annoying Facebookers" (p. 186), questions the need for a modern technology while understanding why people use it anyway. But whereas Alaimo and Koester take their subject quite seriously, Griggs draws on humor to make his point. Compare and contrast these writers' strategies in an effort to determine when humor is appropriate and when it detracts from a writer's purpose. How, for example, would "The Backdraft of Technology" have worked if the authors had taken a more lighthearted approach? What would be lost in Griggs's essay if he hadn't tried to make his readers laugh?

A bargain is in its very essence a hostile transaction. Do not all men try to abate the price of all they buy? I contend that a bargain even between brethren is a declaration of war.
—Lord Byron

Every time you see the Wal-Mart smiley face, whistling and knocking down the prices, somewhere there's a factory worker being kicked in the stomach.
—Sherrie Ford

Real happiness is cheap enough, yet how dearly we pay for its counterfeit.
—Hosea Ballou

JOURNAL RESPONSE Are name brands and designer logos important to you? Have you ever knowingly purchased something that pretended to be a luxury product but obviously wasn't, such as fake Versace sunglasses or an imitation Coach wallet? Do you have any reservations about making such purchases? Why, or why not? In your journal, write a few paragraphs exploring your thoughts about counterfeit goods.

Dana Thomas

Fashion journalist Dana Thomas (born 1964) grew up in an upscale neighborhood of Philadelphia, attended the American University in Washington, DC, and taught journalism at the American University in Paris. A contributing editor for the *Wall Street Journal*'s monthly magazine *WSJ*, she was a style reporter for *Newsweek* and has contributed articles to the *New York Times Magazine*, the *New Yorker*, *Harper's Bazaar*, and *Vogue*, as well as several international newspapers. Noticing in the 1990s that high-end fashion brands such as Louis Vuitton, Gucci, and Prada had begun marketing low-end versions of their products, Thomas was inspired to research and write *Deluxe: How Luxury Lost Its Luster* (2007), an exposé of diminishing standards in the luxury industry that quickly became an international bestseller. She lives in Paris with her husband and daughter.

The Fake Trade

Thomas has been praised for offering an unexpected look at luxury merchandise and its impact on the people who make, sell, and buy it. In this article from *Harper's Bazaar Australia*, she relates a story about a little girl and a fake Louis Vuitton purse to explain why trading in counterfeit goods is not the victimless crime many shoppers assume it to be.

On a cool August evening, my family and I visited the preppy town of 1
Mill Valley, California, outside San Francisco. In the town square was an
all-American sight: a couple of kids behind a card table selling homemade
lemonade. My six-year-old wanted some, so I gave her a quarter and sent
her over to the booth. After a few minutes, I joined the kids and noticed
that one, a cute eight- or nine-year-old girl with a blonde blunt cut, had a
little Murakami[1] pouch slung over her shoulder.

"Nice handbag," I said to her.   2

"It's Louis Vuitton," she responded proudly.   3

"No," I thought to myself as I gave it a good look-over. "It's a coun- 4
terfeit Louis Vuitton. And it was probably made by a Chinese kid the same
age as you in a slum halfway around the world."

Though the fashion business has muscled up its fight against coun- 5
terfeiting, with many brands investing millions of dollars each year, the
battle is ongoing. Since 1982, the global trade in counterfeit and pirated
goods has grown from an estimated $5.5 billion to approximately $600
billion annually. Experts believe that counterfeiting costs American businesses $200 billion to $250 billion annually and is directly responsible for
the loss of more than 750,000 jobs in the United States.

What's counterfeited? Everything. A couple of years ago, a counterfeit 6
investigator discovered a workshop in the Thai countryside that produced
fake versions of the classic Ferrari P4. Ferrari itself originally made only
three P4s back in 1967. The Food and Drug Administration has said that
counterfeit medicine could account for upwards of 10% of all drugs world-
wide. Unknowingly taking a fake version of your medicine could have
horrific effects on your health. European Union officials have seen a dramatic rise in the seizure of counterfeit personal-care items such as creams,
toothpastes, and razor blades. The television series *Law & Order: Criminal
Intent* recently highlighted this problem in an episode in which several
children died after ingesting counterfeit mouthwash that had been made
with a poisonous chemical found in antifreeze. "There have been counterfeit perfumes tested by laboratories that have found that a major component was feline urine," says Heather McDonald, a partner at the law firm
Baker Hostetler in New York who specializes in anticounterfeiting litiga-
tion. Counterfeit automotive brakes made with compressed grass and
wood have been found in US stores.

One of the primary reasons counterfeiting keeps flourishing is that, as 7
the little girl in Mill Valley proved, people keep happily buying fakes.

---

[1]Japanese artist Takashi Murakami designed a line of Louis Vuitton handbags
featuring whimsical, colorful patterns. [Editors' note.]

According to a study published last year by the British law firm Davenport Lyons, almost two-thirds of UK consumers are "proud to tell their family and friends that they bought fake luxury [fashion items]." And according to a 2003 survey carried out by Market & Opinion Research International in Great Britain, around a third of those questioned would consider buying counterfeits. Why? Because we still think of counterfeiting as a "victimless crime." Buying a counterfeit Vuitton bag surely doesn't affect the company, we reason. The parents of that Mill Valley girl probably wouldn't have invested in a real Vuitton Murakami for her, so it wasn't a loss of sales for the company.

But the reality is that we're all victims of counterfeiting, whether   8 from the loss of jobs or of tax revenue that could fund our schools and our roads, or because by buying counterfeit goods, we are financing international crime syndicates that deal in money laundering, human trafficking, and child labor. Each time I read the horrid tales about counterfeiting from my book, *Deluxe: How Luxury Lost Its Luster*—like the raid I went on in a clandestine factory in the industrial city of Guangzhou, China, where we found children making fake Dunhill and Versace handbags—audience members or radio listeners tell me they had no idea it was such a dark and dangerous world and that by purchasing these goods they were contributing personally to it. Then they invariably swear that they will never knowingly buy another fake good.

Brands as well as law enforcement have cracked down on the coun-   9 terfeit business severely in the past few years, here in the US and abroad. I saw a difference in Hong Kong, for example: a decade ago, you could buy a fake Vuitton handbag or Burberry knapsack for a couple of bucks from a vendor in the subway; today you can't even find them on the street. There are still dealers, but now they lurk in doorways, whispering, "Rolex? Chanel?" and you hurry down dark streets to armored hideaways to close the deal. To say it's scary is an understatement. "If you can keep the stuff out of the public eye, you are halfway to winning the battle," McDonald says. "The brands that are doing aggressive enforcement are hidden in back alleys and not on the street corners."

As long as there is a demand, however, there will be a supply. Tradi-   10 tionally, the supply chain worked like this: an order of ten thousand handbags would be divided into ten groups of one thousand to be made— often by children—in hidden workshops in Guangzhou. Once completed, the items would be wrapped up and deposited in a neutral place, like the courtyard of a local school, where they were picked up by a local transporter, often simply a guy on a bike with a cart. The transporter delivered the package to the wholesaler, who would take it to another neutral place to be picked up by the international shipping agent and put in a shipping container. The goods were often packed in shipments of foodstuffs or legitimately manufactured clothing to escape detection by receiving customs officials. Each time the goods changed hands, the prices doubled. All transactions were done in cash.

But as fashion companies grew wise to the process and went after the 11 sources in China, leading to raids on workshops and busts at ports, the counterfeit-crime rings came up with new routes to supply fake goods: produce them, or at least finish them, in the destination country. Law enforcement witnessed this firsthand during a big bust this past October. The New York Police Department raided a commercial building in Queens, arrested thirteen, and seized around $4 million in counterfeit apparel that carried the logos of major brands including Polo, Lacoste, Rocawear, the North Face, and 7 for All Mankind. Officers also found a stash of fake labels and buttons for Tommy Hilfiger, Nike, and Adidas as well as embroidery machines. Investigators believe that the site was a finishing facility. Workers took generic items that may have been imported legally and sewed on fake logos and labels, turning the items into counterfeit branded goods.

Another trick is to import counterfeit items that are hiding under a 12 legitimate face. "Some of the counterfeiters put a whole separate coating on the bag, and you peel it off like contact paper to see the logo fabric underneath," McDonald tells me. "We seized a load of Lacoste men's dress shirts, and on the left breast pocket, where the alligator should be, there was a little generic label that read, 'Metro.' When you pulled out the threads and removed the Metro label, you found the alligator."

There's another method that is catching on rapidly: counterfeiters 13 who will take a legitimate logo, tinker with it slightly, apply for a trademark for the new design, then import those items under a false pretense of legality, showing the official application paperwork as their defense. For example, a company takes the Ralph Lauren polo-horse-and-rider logo and puts the polo mallet down instead of up in the air. The counterfeiter files a trademark application with the US Patent and Trademark Office and gets a document that states the application is pending. "It's a legitimate document fraudulently secured, and the application will probably be rejected in six months," the intellectual-property counsel for a luxury brand explains to me. "But between now and then, the customs agents will approve the importation of the items—believing, incorrectly, that the pending application proves the importer must have a legitimate right to the trademark."

By the time the brand realizes what's going on, the lawyer says, thou- 14 sands of items will have been imported and the counterfeiter will have "made millions" and fled. Luxury companies discovered one operation using this technique about two years ago, and now several more have popped up. "We must be doing a good job, since counterfeiters are looking for such complicated ways to get in," the lawyer says.

People often ask me, "How do you know it's fake?"   15

Well, if it's being sold at a fold-up table on a sidewalk corner or on   16
the back of a peddler on the beach, chances are it's fake. Or if it's at a flea market. Or a church fundraiser. Or in Wal-Mart or Sam's Club or other discount mass retailers. In June 2006, Fendi filed suit in a US district court against Wal-Mart Stores, Inc., asserting that the world's largest retailer was selling counterfeit Fendi handbags and wallets in its Sam's Club stores. For example, one bag was offered for $295; the legitimate Fendi handbag of the same design normally retailed for $925. In the suit, Fendi stated that Wal-Mart has never purchased Fendi products and never checked with Fendi to see if the items were real. The case was settled out of court last summer after Sam's Club agreed to pay Fendi an undisclosed sum.

If you want to guarantee that your luxury-brand purchases are legiti-   17
mate, don't shop in wholesale markets like those in Chinatown in Manhattan or Santee Alley in Los Angeles. "We'll go on raids on Chinatown wholesalers, and we'll find five or six suburban women standing there — customers," New York security expert Andrew Oberfeldt has told me. "We'll say to these women, 'The dealers take you down dark corridors, through locked doors. The police say, "Open up!" The lights are turned out and everyone is told to be quiet. At what point did you realize that something was amiss here?'"

If you find an item for sale on the Internet for a price so low that it   18
seems too good to be true, it probably is too good to be true. Last fall, the UK-based Authentics Foundation, an international nonprofit organization devoted to raising public awareness about counterfeiting, launched *myauthentics.com*, a Web site that helps Internet shoppers determine if the products they are eyeing on the Web are real. It includes blogs and forums, news, myths, and tips on how to spot fakes; *eBay* now has links to the site. *EBay* also works with brands in its VeRO (Verified Rights Owner) program to find out if the items for offer on the site are genuine. If the brand deems a particular item to be counterfeit, the sale will be shut down. However, not all online sales sites have such verification processes in place. Besides, counterfeiters are known to post photos of genuine items to sell fakes. So as the old saying goes, buyer beware.

Of course, the best way to know if you are buying a genuine product   19
is to buy it from the brand, either in directly operated boutiques or in a company's shop in a department store. If you are curious about the

authenticity of a used Vuitton item you purchased at a vintage shop or online, you can always contact one of the brand's boutiques.

Most important, we need to spread the word on the devastating 20
effects counterfeiting has on society today. I didn't tell the girl in Mill Valley that her bag was fake. It wasn't her fault her family had given it to her. But if I had met her parents, I would have said something. Awareness is key. Counterfeiting will never go away—it's been around since the dawn of time—but we can surely cut it down to size if we just stop buying the stuff. Without the demand, the supply will shrink. It's up to us.

Meaning

1. Throughout her essay, Thomas repeats the words *counterfeit* and *legitimate*. How does she define these terms? Why is the distinction between the two important?

2. In paragraph 7, Thomas says that consumers believe counterfeiting is a "victimless crime." What does that mean? Does she believe it herself? Why does she bring it up?

3. Although Thomas stresses the importance of raising awareness of counterfeiting, she does not say anything to the girl with the fake designer handbag. Why not? Do you think she was right to keep quiet?

4. If any of the following words are new to you, try to guess their meanings from their context in Thomas's essay. Look up the words in a dictionary to check your guesses, and then use each word in a sentence of your own.

pirated (5)	flourishing (7)	pretense (13)
ingesting (6)	syndicates (8)	fraudulently (13)
feline (6)	clandestine (8)	counsel (13)
litigation (6)	invariably (8)	devastating (20)

Purpose and Audience

1. What seems to be Thomas's primary purpose in this piece? Does she want to express her opinion about counterfeit goods? persuade consumers not to buy them? educate her readers? How can you tell?

2. To whom does Thomas seem to be writing here? Why do you think so?

Method and Structure

1. How well does cause-and-effect analysis suit Thomas's subject? How does this method provide Thomas with an effective means of achieving her purpose?

2. "The Fake Trade" explores both causes and effects of counterfeiting. What, according to Thomas, are the main reasons for the practice? What are the most significant consequences?

3. Analyze the organization of Thomas's essay by creating an outline of her major points. What is the effect of this structure?

4. A journalist, Thomas supports her ideas with information from published studies and quotations from interviews with experts. Locate at least two examples of each. How effective do you find this evidence? Is it more, or less, persuasive than the examples she takes from her own experience? Why do you think so?

5. OTHER METHODS   Thomas provides many **examples** (Chapter 7) of counterfeit goods, and she uses **process analysis** (Chapter 10) to describe how such goods are manufactured, distributed, and sold. What does she accomplish by using these methods?

Language

1. How does Thomas use transitions to guide readers through her cause-and-effect analysis?

2. How would you characterize Thomas's **tone**? Is it appropriate, given her purpose and her audience?

Writing Topics

1. JOURNAL TO ESSAY   In your journal entry (p. 316), you wrote about your attitude toward counterfeit goods. Now that you've read "The Fake Trade," has your attitude changed in any way? Has Thomas persuaded you that counterfeiting has "devastating effects," or are you unmoved by her analysis? Why? Drawing on your own experience with fake goods and on what Thomas has to say, write an essay that argues for or against buying counterfeits. (If you share Thomas's concerns, be careful not just to repeat her points; look for additional examples of counterfeit products, and add your own reasons for rejecting them.)

2. Thomas focuses on luxury goods, but in paragraph 6 she mentions that medicine is frequently counterfeited as well, compromising the health and threatening the lives of people who inadvertently buy ineffective or tainted drugs. Many supporters of health-care reform have raised the same point to argue that drugmakers charge excessive prices for medications and that such costs should be controlled through government action. Write an essay that explores your thoughts on this issue. Should

everyone have access to safe and effective medications, regardless of cost? Who should pay? Should some drugs be made available to all while other drugs are available only to those who can afford them? Do pharmaceutical companies have an obligation to make drugs affordable, or do they have a right to profit from the fruits of their research and development efforts? What, if anything, can be done to strike a fair balance between patients' and corporations' needs?

3. **CULTURAL CONSIDERATIONS**   Thomas suggests that American culture promotes a desire for luxury, or at least an approximation of it. Many cultures, however, actively discourage indulgence, prizing thrift and generosity over personal acquisition. Write an essay that defends or argues against consumption for its own sake, making a point of explaining what, in your mind, constitutes a necessity and a luxury. Do we have a right—even an obligation—to spend money on things we don't truly need? Why, or why not?

4. **CONNECTIONS**   In "The Fake Trade," Thomas shows how efforts to get a bargain can impose high costs on people in less affluent countries. Conversely, Stephanie Alaimo and Mark Koester, in "The Backdraft of Technology" (p. 311), assert that self-checkout machines and similar labor-saving technologies ship jobs overseas. Write an essay that compares these authors' beliefs about the benefits and drawbacks of a global economy. What assumptions, if any, do both essays share? Where do their perspectives diverge? How do their attitudes reinforce or conflict with your own views?

WRITING WITH THE METHOD

▶ CAUSE-AND-EFFECT ANALYSIS

Select one of the following questions, or any question they suggest, and answer it in an essay developed by analyzing causes or effects. The question you choose should concern a topic you care about so that your cause-and-effect analysis is a means of communicating an idea, not an end in itself.

People and Their Behavior

1. What makes a soldier, police officer, or firefighter a hero?
2. What does a sound body contribute to a sound mind?
3. Why do people root for the underdog?
4. How does a person's alcohol or drug dependency affect others?

Gender and Sexuality

5. Why would a man or woman enter a field that has traditionally been filled by the opposite sex, such as nursing or engineering?
6. What effect has the legalization of gay marriage in several states had on you and your friends?
7. At what age should a person be allowed to seek gender-reassignment surgery, and why?
8. How has feminism changed men's lives, for better or for worse?

Art and Entertainment

9. Why did hip-hop music become so popular both in the United States and abroad?
10. How has the Internet changed the music industry?
11. What makes some professional sports teams succeed year after year while others consistently fail?
12. What impact has a particular television show or movie had on American culture?

Contemporary Issues

13. Why does the United States spend so much money on health care?
14. How will global climate change influence the nature and frequency of extreme weather events?
15. Is a college education worth the expense?
16. Why have political debates become so heated and angry?

WRITING ABOUT THE THEME

INVESTIGATING THE WORKING WORLD

1. The writers in this chapter seem to take a dim view of the working world. Barbara Ehrenreich (p. 298) and Stephanie Alaimo and Mark Koester (p. 311) portray service workers as victims. Malcolm Gladwell (p. 299) suggests that success in the workplace is determined by forces beyond our control. Dana Thomas (p. 316) describes the "horrid" reality of child labor in China and the dangers counterfeit workers face as they do their jobs. And Ellen Goodman (p. 306) equates work with death. But for many people, working is a source of happiness, even joy. Some define themselves by the work they do; some take deep satisfaction in their efforts; others enjoy the benefits of employment even if they don't particularly like their jobs. What does work mean to you? Is it merely a means to a paycheck, or do you expect to get something more out of a job or career? Write an essay explaining how you perceive work, making sure to provide plenty of examples to support your claims. To get started, you might want to think about a job you particularly enjoyed or hated, or what kind of career you want to start when you finish college.

2. Many of the writers in this chapter examine the unintended consequences of actions taken by businesses and consumers. Stephanie Alaimo and Mark Koester's warning against self-service checkout and Dana Thomas's exposé on counterfeiting are most notable in this respect, but even Barbara Ehrenreich's analysis of high rents suggests wealthier people's real estate purchases can affect lower-income strangers. Think of a contemporary product or service that you believe holds the potential to do unexpected harm — or that could bring unanticipated benefits — and write an essay predicting its consequences. (Be sure to review the cause-and-effect guidelines on pp. 296–98 and 300–305 before beginning your analysis.)

3. Although the writers represented in this chapter all touch on questions of success or failure, their tones vary widely, from urgent to ironic to moralistic. Choose the two selections that seem most different in tone, and analyze how their tones help clarify the authors' points. Is one piece's tone more effective than the other's? If so, why?

14

ARGUMENT AND PERSUASION

DISCUSSING SOCIAL ISSUES

Since we argue all the time—with relatives, with friends, with the auto mechanic or a sales associate—a chapter devoted to argument and persuasion may at first seem unnecessary. But arguing with a sales associate over the cost of an extended warranty is quite a different process from arguing with readers over a complex issue. In both cases we are trying to find common ground with our audience, perhaps to change others' views or even to compel them to act as we wish. But the salesperson is in front of us; we can shift our tactics in response to his or her gestures, expressions, and words. The reader, in contrast, is "out there"; we have to anticipate those gestures, expressions, and words in the way we structure the argument, the kinds of evidence we use to support it, even the way we conceive of the subject.

A great many assertions that are worth making are debatable at some level—whether over the facts on which the assertions are based or over the values they imply. Two witnesses to an accident cannot agree on what they saw; two economists cannot agree on what measures will reduce unemployment; two doctors cannot agree on what constitutes life or death. We see such disagreements play out in writing all the time, whether we're reading an accident report, a magazine article claiming the benefits of unemployment rates, or an editorial responding to a Supreme Court decision.

Reading Argument and Persuasion

Technically, **argument and persuasion** are two different processes:

- *Argument* appeals mainly to an audience's sense of reason in order to negotiate a common understanding or to win agreement with a claim. It is the method of a columnist who defends a president's foreign policy on the grounds of economics and defense strategy.

- *Persuasion* appeals mainly to an audience's feelings and values in order to compel some action, or at least to win support for an action. It is the method of a mayoral candidate who urges voters to support her because she is sensitive to the poor.

But argument and persuasion so often mingle that we will use the one term *argument* to mean a deliberate appeal to an audience's reason and emotions in order to create compromise, win agreement, or compel action. Making an effective case for an opinion requires upholding certain responsibilities and attending to several established techniques of argumentation, most of them dating back to ancient Greece.

▶ The Elements of Argument

All arguments share certain elements:

- *The core of any argument is a debatable claim about the subject.* Generally, this **assertion** or **proposition** is expressed as a thesis statement. It may defend or attack a position, suggest a solution to a problem, recommend a change in policy, or challenge a value or belief. Here are a few examples:

  > The college should give first priority for on-campus jobs to students who need financial aid.

  > School prayer has been rightly declared unconstitutional and should not be reinstituted in any form.

  > Smokers who wish to poison themselves should be allowed to do so, but not in any place where their smoke will poison others.

- *The central assertion is broken down into subclaims*, each one supported by evidence.

- *Significant opposing arguments are raised and dispensed with*, again with the support of evidence.

- *The parts of the argument are organized into a clear, logical structure* that pushes steadily toward the conclusion.

A writer may draw on classification, comparison, or any other rhetorical method to develop the entire argument or to introduce evidence or strengthen the conclusion. For instance, in a proposal arguing for raising a college's standards of admission, a dean might contrast the existing standards with the proposed standards, analyze a process for raising the standards over a period of years, and predict the effects of the new standards on future students' preparedness for college work.

▶ Appeals to Readers

Effective arguments appeal to readers: they ask others to listen to what someone has to say, judge the words fairly, and, as much as possible, agree with the writer. Most arguments combine three kinds of appeals to readers: ethical, emotional, and rational. These appeals are sometimes referred to as *ethos*, *pathos*, and *logos*.

Ethical Appeal

Known to classical rhetoricians as *ethos* (the Greek word for "character"), the **ethical appeal** is often not explicit in an argument, yet it pervades the whole. It is the sense a writer conveys of his or her expertise and character, projected by the reasonableness of the argument, by the use of evidence, and by tone. A rational argument shows readers that the writer is thinking logically and fairly (see pp. 330–32). Strong evidence establishes credibility (see pp. 336–38). And a sincere, reasonable tone demonstrates balance and goodwill (see pp. 340–41).

Emotional Appeal

An **emotional appeal** (*pathos* in Greek) aims directly for readers' hearts— for the beliefs, values, and feelings deeply embedded in all of us. We are just as often motivated by these ingrained ideas and emotions as by our intellects. Even scientists, who stress the rational interpretation of facts above all else, are sometimes influenced in their interpretations by emotions deriving from, say, competition with other scientists. And the willingness of a nation's citizens to go to war may result more from their patriotism and pride than from their reasoned considerations of risks and gains. An emotional appeal in an argument attempts to tap such feelings for any of several reasons:

- To heighten the responsiveness of readers
- To inspire readers to new beliefs
- To compel readers to act
- To assure readers that their values remain unchallenged

A writer's use of *pathos* may be explicit, as when an argument against capital punishment appeals to readers' religious values by citing the Bible's Sixth Commandment, "Thou shalt not kill." But an emotional appeal may also be less obvious, because individual words may have **connotations** that elicit emotional responses from readers. For instance, one writer may characterize an environmental group as "a well-organized team representing diverse interests," while another may call the same group "a hodge-podge of nature lovers and profit-seeking businesspeople." The first appeals to readers' preference for order and balance, the second to readers' fear of extremism and disdain for greed.

The use of *pathos* requires care:

- *An emotional appeal must be directed at the audience's actual beliefs and feelings.*
- *An emotional appeal must be presented calmly* enough that readers have no reason to doubt the fairness in the rest of the argument.
- *An emotional appeal must be appropriate to the subject and to the argument.* For instance, in arguing against a pay raise for city councilors, a legislator might be tempted to appeal to voters' resentment of wealthy people by pointing out that two of the councilors are rich enough to work for nothing. But such an appeal would divert attention from the issue of whether the pay raise is justified for all councilors on the basis of the work they do and the city's ability to pay the extra cost.

Carefully used, *pathos* has great force, particularly when it contributes to an argument based largely on sound reasoning and evidence. The appropriate mix of emotion and reason in a given essay is entirely dependent on the subject, the writer's purpose, and the audience. Emotions are out of place in most arguments in the natural sciences, for instance, where rational interpretations of factual evidence are all that will convince readers of the truth of an assertion. But emotional appeals may be essential to persuade an audience to support or take an action, for emotion is frequently a stronger motivator than reason.

Rational Appeal

A **rational appeal** is one that, as the name implies, addresses the rational faculties of readers—their capacity to reason logically about a problem. It establishes the truth of a proposition or claim by moving through a series of related subclaims, each supported by evidence. In doing so, rational appeals—*logos* to the ancient Greeks—follow processes of reasoning that are natural to all of us. These processes are induction and deduction.

INDUCTION   **Inductive reasoning** moves from the particular to the general, from evidence to a generalization or conclusion about the evidence. It is a process we begin learning in infancy and use daily throughout our lives: a child burns herself the first two times she touches a stove, so she concludes that stoves burn; a moviegoer has liked four movies directed by Guillermo del Toro, so he forms the generalization that Guillermo del Toro makes good movies. Inductive reasoning is also very common in argument: a nurse administrator might offer data to show that two hundred past patients in the psychiatric ward received drugs but no therapy and then conclude that the hospital relies exclusively on drugs to treat mental illness.

The movement from particular to general is called an *inductive leap* because we must make something of a jump to conclude that what is true of some instances (the patients whose records were examined) is also true of all other instances in the class (the rest of the patients). In an ideal world we could perhaps avoid the inductive leap by pinning down every conceivable instance, but in the real world such thoroughness is usually impractical and often impossible. Instead, we gather enough evidence to make our generalizations probable. The evidence for induction may be of several kinds:

- *Facts*: statistics or other hard data that are verifiable or, failing that, attested to by reliable sources (for instance, the types of drugs prescribed, derived from hospital records).

- *The opinions of recognized experts on the subject*, opinions that are themselves conclusions based on research and observation (for instance, the testimony of an experienced hospital doctor).

- *Examples* illustrating the evidence (for instance, the treatment history of one patient).

DEDUCTION   A sound inductive generalization can form the basis for the second reasoning process, **deductive reasoning**. Working from the general to the particular, we start with such a generalization and apply it to a new situation in order to draw a conclusion about that situation. Like induction, deduction is a process we use constantly to order our experience. The child who learns from two experiences that all stoves burn then sees a new stove and concludes that this stove also will burn. The child's thought process can be written in the form of a **syllogism**, a three-step outline of deductive reasoning:

All stoves burn me.
This is a stove.
Therefore, this stove will burn me.

The first statement, the generalization derived from induction, is called the *major premise*. The second statement, a more specific assertion about some element of the major premise, is called the *minor premise*. And the third statement, an assertion of the logical connection between the premises, is called the *conclusion*. The following syllogism takes the earlier example about a psychiatric ward one step further:

MAJOR PREMISE   The hospital relies exclusively on drugs to treat psychiatric patients.

MINOR PREMISE   Drugs do not cure mental illness.

CONCLUSION   Therefore, the hospital does not cure psychiatric patients.

Unlike an inductive conclusion, which requires a leap, the deductive conclusion derives necessarily from the premises: as long as the reasoning process is valid and the premises are accepted as true, then the conclusion must also be true. To be valid, the reasoning must conform to the process outlined earlier. The following syllogism is *not* valid, even though the premises are true:

All radicals want to change the system.
Georgia Allport wants to change the system.
Therefore, Georgia Allport is a radical.

The flaw in this syllogism is that not *only* radicals want to change the system, so Allport does not *necessarily* fall within the class of radicals just because she wants to change the system. The conclusion, then, is invalid.

A syllogism can be valid without being true if either of the premises is untrue. For example:

All people who want political change are radicals.
Georgia Allport wants political change.
Therefore, Georgia Allport is a radical.

The conclusion here is valid because Allport falls within the class of people who want political change. But the conclusion is untrue because the major premise is untrue. As commonly defined, a radical seeks extreme change, often by revolutionary means. But other forms and means of change are also possible. Allport, for instance, may be interested in improving the delivery of services to the poor and in achieving passage of tougher environmental-protection laws—both political changes, to be sure, but neither radical.

In arguments, syllogisms are rarely spelled out as neatly as in these examples. Sometimes the order of the statements is reversed, as in this sentence paraphrasing a Supreme Court decision:

> The state may not imprison a man just because he is too poor to pay a fine; the only justification for imprisonment is a certain danger to society, and poverty does not constitute certain danger.

The buried syllogism can be stated thus:

MAJOR PREMISE   The state may imprison only those who are a certain danger to society.

MINOR PREMISE   A man who is too poor to pay a fine is not a certain danger to society.

CONCLUSION   Therefore, the state cannot imprison a man just because he is too poor to pay a fine.

Often, one of a syllogism's premises or even its conclusion is implied but not expressed. Each of the following sentences omits one part of the same syllogism:

> All five students cheated, so they should be expelled. [Implied major premise: cheaters should be expelled.]
>
> Cheaters should be punished by expulsion, so all five students should be expelled. [Implied minor premise: all five students cheated.]
>
> Cheaters should be punished by expulsion, and all five students cheated. [Implied conclusion: all five students should be expelled.]

▶ Fallacies

Inappropriate emotional appeals and flaws in reasoning—called logical **fallacies**—can trap writers as they construct arguments. Watch out for the following errors:

- *Hasty generalization*: an inductive conclusion that leaps to include *all* instances when at best only *some* instances provide any evidence. Hasty generalizations form some of our worst stereotypes:

  > Physically challenged people are mentally challenged, too.
  >
  > African Americans are good athletes.
  >
  > Italians are volatile.

- *Oversimplification*: an inductive conclusion that ignores complexities in the evidence that, if heeded, would weaken the conclusion or suggest an entirely different one. For example:

  > The newspaper folded because it couldn't compete with the Internet.

  Although the Internet may have taken some business from the newspaper, other newspapers continue to thrive; thus the Internet could not be the only cause of the newspaper's failure.

- *Begging the question*: assuming a conclusion in the statement of a premise, and thus begging readers to accept the conclusion—the question—before it is proved. For example:

  > We can trust the president not to neglect the needy because he is a compassionate man.

  This sentence asserts in a circular fashion that the president is not uncompassionate because he is compassionate. He may indeed be compassionate, but the question that needs addressing is what will he do for the needy.

- *Ignoring the question*: introducing an issue or consideration that shifts the argument away from the real issue. Offering an emotional appeal as a premise in a logical argument is a form of ignoring the question. The following sentence, for instance, appeals to pity, not to logic:

  > The mayor was badly used by people he loved and trusted, so we should not blame him for the corruption in his administration.

- *Ad hominem* (Latin for "to the man"): a form of ignoring the question by attacking the opponent instead of the opponent's arguments. For example:

  > O'Brien is married to a convict, so her proposals for prison reform should not be taken seriously.

■ *Either-or*: requiring that readers choose between two interpretations or actions when in fact the choices are more numerous.

> Either we imprison all drug users, or we will become their prisoners.

The factors contributing to drug addiction, and the choices for dealing with it, are obviously more complex than this statement suggests. Not all either-or arguments are invalid, for sometimes the alternatives encompass all the possibilities. But when they do not, the argument is false.

■ *Non sequitur* (Latin for "it does not follow"): a conclusion derived illogically or erroneously from stated or implied premises. For instance:

> Children are too immature to engage in sex, so they should not be taught about it.

This sentence implies one of two meanings, both of them questionable: only the sexually active can learn anything about sex, or teaching children about sex will cause them to engage in it.

■ *Post hoc* (from the Latin *post hoc, ergo propter hoc,* "after this, therefore because of this"): assuming that because one thing preceded another, it must have caused the other. For example:

> After the town banned smoking in public places, the incidence of vandalism went up.

Many things may have caused the rise in vandalism, including warmer weather and a climbing unemployment rate. It does not follow that the ban on smoking, and that alone, caused the rise.

Analyzing Argument and Persuasion in Paragraphs

Jenny Price (born 1960) is a public scholar whose research interests include history and environment. The following paragraph is from "Gun Violence at UC Irvine," a 2009 op-ed article she wrote for the *Los Angeles Times* in response to readers' shock that a woman was shot and killed in a college neighborhood generally considered safe. The paragraph offers an inductive argument.

Twelve thousand people are shot to death in the United States every year—accounting for more than two out of every three killings. That's an average of 33 people daily. An additional 240 people get shot and injured every day, and more than 65 million Americans own a total of 283 million firearms. Where, exactly, do we expect the 12,000 homicides to happen? Do we really think that the places with gangs and high crime rates are the only places where people are going to use their guns? The widespread numbness to the especially high murder rates in our poor inner-city neighborhoods is egregious enough. But that's matched by the widespread denial that the epidemic of gun violence is playing out every day in every kind of neighborhood across America.

> Evidence:
> Number of gun-related homicides
> Number of non-fatal shootings
> Extent of gun ownership

> The generalization (underlined): shootings can happen anywhere

Martin Luther King, Jr. (1929–68), was a revered and powerful leader of the civil rights movement during the 1950s and 1960s. When leading sit-ins, boycotts, and marches, he always insisted on nonviolent resistance. In this paragraph from "Letter from Birmingham Jail" (1963), King uses deduction to argue in favor of civil disobedience.

You express a great deal of anxiety over our willingness to break laws. This is certainly a legitimate concern. Since we so diligently urge people to obey the Supreme Court's decision of 1954 outlawing segregation in the public schools, at first glance it may seem rather paradoxical for us consciously to break laws. One may well ask: "How can you advocate breaking some laws and obeying others?" The answer lies in the fact that there are two types of laws: just and unjust. I would be the first to advocate obeying just laws. One has not only a legal but a moral responsibility to obey just laws. Conversely, one has a moral responsibility to disobey unjust laws. I would agree with St. Augustine that "an unjust law is no law at all."

> Major premise: laws should be obeyed

> Minor premise: some laws are unjust and therefore are not laws

> Conclusion: unjust laws should not be obeyed

Developing an Argumentative and Persuasive Essay

▶ Getting Started

You will have many chances to write arguments, from defending or opposing a policy such as progressive taxation in an economics course to justifying a new procedure at work to persuading a company to refund your money for a bad product. To choose a subject for an argumentative essay, consider a behavior or policy that irks you, an opinion you want to defend, a change you would like to see implemented, or a way to solve a problem. The subject you pick should meet certain criteria:

- *It should be something you have some knowledge of*—from your own experience or observations, from class discussions, or from reading, although you may need to do further research as well.

- *It should be limited to a topic you can treat thoroughly in the space and time available to you*—for instance, the quality of computer instruction at your school rather than in the whole nation.

- *It should be something that you feel strongly about* so that you can make a convincing case. (However, it's best to avoid subjects that you cannot view with some objectivity, seeing the opposite side as well as your own; otherwise, you may not be open to flaws in your argument, and you may not be able to represent the opposition fairly.)

Once you have selected a subject, do some preliminary research to make sure that you will have enough evidence to support your opinion. This step is especially important with issues that we all tend to have opinions about whether we know the facts or not, such as welfare cheating or tax advantages for the wealthy. Where to seek evidence depends on the nature of your argument.

- *For an argument derived from your own experiences and observations*, such as a recommendation that all students work part-time for the education if not for the money, gathering evidence will be primarily a matter of searching your own thoughts and also uncovering opposing views, perhaps by consulting others.

- *For some arguments derived from personal experience*, you can strengthen your evidence with judicious use of facts and opinions from other sources. An essay arguing in favor of vegetarianism, for instance, could mix the benefits you have felt with those demonstrated by scientific data.

- *For an argument on a nonpersonal or a controversial subject*, you will have to gather the evidence of other sources. Though you might strongly favor or oppose a massive federal investment in solar-energy research, your opinions would count little if they were not supported with facts and the opinions of experts.

For advice on conducting research and using the evidence you find, see the Appendix.

In addition to evidence, knowledge of readers' needs and expectations is absolutely crucial in planning an argument. In explanatory writing, detail and clarity alone may accomplish your purpose, but you cannot hope to move readers in a certain direction unless you have some idea of where they stand. You need a sense of their background in your subject, of course. But even more, you need a good idea of their values and beliefs, their attitudes toward your subject—in short, their willingness to be convinced. In a composition class, your readers will probably be your instructor and your classmates, a small but diverse group. A good target when you are addressing a diverse audience is the reader who is neutral or mildly biased one way or the other toward your subject. This person you can hope to influence as long as your argument is reasonable, your evidence is thorough and convincing, your treatment of opposing views is fair, and your appeals to readers' emotions are appropriate to your purpose, your subject, and especially your readers' values and feelings.

▶ Forming a Thesis

With your subject and some evidence in hand, you should develop a tentative thesis. But don't feel you have to prove your thesis at this early stage; fixing it too firmly may make you unwilling to reshape it if further evidence, your audience, or the structure of your argument so demands.

Stating your thesis in a preliminary thesis sentence can help you form your idea. Make this sentence as clear and specific as possible. Don't resort to a vague generality or a nondebatable statement of fact. Instead, state the precise opinion you want readers to accept or the precise action you want them to take or support. For instance:

VAGUE   Computer instruction is important.

NONDEBATABLE   The school's investment in computer instruction is less than the average investment of the nation's colleges and universities.

PRECISE Money designated for new dormitories and athletic facilities should be diverted to constructing computer facilities and hiring first-rate computer faculty.

VAGUE Cloning research is promising.

NONDEBATABLE Scientists have been experimenting with cloning procedures for many years.

PRECISE Those who oppose cloning research should consider the potentially valuable medical applications.

Since an argumentative thesis is essentially an opinion reached by examining evidence, you will probably need to do some additional reading to ensure that you have a broad range of facts and ideas supporting not only your view of a subject but also any opposing views. Though it may be tempting to ignore your opposition in the hope that readers know nothing of it, it is dishonest and probably futile to do so. Acknowledging and, whenever possible, refuting significant opposing views will enhance your credibility with readers. If you find that some counterarguments damage your own argument too greatly, then you will have to rethink your thesis.

▶ Organizing

Once you have formulated your thesis and evaluated your reasons and evidence against the needs and expectations of your audience, begin planning how you will arrange your argument.

The **introduction** to your essay should draw readers into your framework, making them see how the subject affects them and predisposing them to consider your argument. Sometimes a forthright approach works best, but an eye-opening anecdote or quotation can also be effective. Your thesis sentence may end your introduction. However, if you think readers will not even entertain your thesis until they have seen some or all of your evidence, withhold your thesis for later.

The body of the essay consists of your reasons and your evidence for them. The evidence you generated or collected should suggest the reasons that will support the claim of your thesis—essentially the minor arguments that bolster the main argument. In an essay favoring federal investment in solar-energy research, for instance, the minor arguments might include the need for sustainable resources, the feasibility of widespread use of solar energy, and its cost and safety compared with other energy sources. It is in developing these minor arguments that you are most likely to use induction and deduction consciously—generalizing from specifics or applying generalizations to new information. Thus the minor arguments provide the entry points for your evidence, and together they should encompass all the relevant evidence.

Unless the minor arguments form a chain, with each link growing out of the one before, their order should be determined by their potential effects on readers. In general, it is most effective to arrange the reasons in order of increasing importance or strength so as to finish powerfully. But to engage readers in the argument from the start, try to begin with a reason that they will find compelling or that they already know and accept; that way, the weaker reasons will be sandwiched between a strong beginning and an even stronger ending.

The views opposing yours can be raised and refuted wherever it seems most appropriate to do so. If a counterargument pertains to just one of your minor arguments, then dispose of it at that point. But if the counterarguments are more basic, pertaining to your whole thesis, you should dispose of them either after the introduction or shortly before the conclusion. Bring up counterarguments early if the opposition is particularly strong and you fear that readers will be disinclined to listen unless you address their concerns first. Hold counterarguments for the end when they are generally weak or easily dispensed with once you've presented your case.

In the **conclusion** to your essay, you may summarize the main point of your argument and restate your thesis from your introduction, or state it for the first time if you have saved it for the end. An effective quotation, an appropriate emotional appeal, or a call for support or action can often provide a strong finish to an argument.

▶ Drafting

While you are drafting the essay, work to make your reasoning clear by showing how each bit of evidence relates to the reason or minor argument being discussed and how each minor argument relates to the main argument contained in the thesis. In working through the reasons and evidence, you may find it helpful to state each reason as the first sentence in a paragraph and then support it in the following sentences. If this scheme seems too rigid or creates overlong paragraphs, you can always make changes after you have written your draft. Draw on a range of methods to clarify your points. For instance, define specialized terms or those you use in a special sense, compare and contrast one policy or piece of evidence with another, or carefully analyze causes or effects.

▶ Revising and Editing

When your draft is complete, use the following questions and the Focus box to guide your revision and editing.

- *Is your thesis debatable, precise, and clear?* Readers must know what you are trying to convince them of, at least by the end of the essay if not up front.

- *Is your argument unified?* Does each minor claim support the thesis? Do all opinions, facts, and examples provide evidence for a minor claim? On behalf of your readers, question every sentence you have written to be sure it contributes to the point you are making and to the argument as a whole.

- *Is the structure of your argument clear and compelling?* Readers should be able to follow easily, seeing when and why you move from one idea to the next.

- *Is the evidence specific, representative, and adequate?* Facts, examples, and expert opinions should be well detailed, should fairly represent the available information, and should be sufficient to support your claim.

- *Have you slipped into any logical fallacies?* Detecting fallacies in your own work can be difficult, but your readers will find them if you don't. Look for the fallacies discussed earlier (pp. 332–34): hasty generalization, oversimplification, begging the question, ignoring the question, ad hominem, either-or, non sequitur, and post hoc. (All of these are also listed in the Glossary under *fallacies*.)

FOCUS ON TONE

Readers are most likely to be persuaded by an argument when they sense a strong *ethos*, meaning that the writer comes across as reasonable, trustworthy, and sincere. A rational appeal, strong evidence, and acknowledgment of opposing views do much to convey these attributes, but so does **tone**, the attitude implied by word choices and sentence structures.

Generally, you should try for a tone of moderation in your view of your subject and a tone of respectfulness and goodwill toward readers and opponents.

■ State opinions and facts calmly:

OVEREXCITED   One clueless administrator was quoted in the newspaper as saying she thought many students who claim learning disabilities are faking their difficulties to obtain special treatment! Has she never heard of dyslexia, attention deficit disorder, and other well-established disabilities?

CALM   Particularly worrisome was one administrator's statement, quoted in the newspaper, that many students who claim learning disabilities may be "faking" their difficulties to obtain special treatment.

■ Replace arrogance with deference:

ARROGANT   I happen to know that many students would rather party or just bury their heads in the sand than get involved in a serious, worthy campaign against the school's unjust learning-disabled policies.

DEFERENTIAL   Time pressures and lack of information about the issues may prevent students from joining the campaign against the school's unjust learning-disabled policies.

■ Replace sarcasm with plain speaking:

SARCASTIC   Of course, the administration knows even without meeting students what is best for every one of them.

PLAIN SPEAKING   The administration should agree to meet with each learning-disabled student to understand his or her needs.

■ Choose words whose connotations convey reasonableness rather than anger, hostility, or another negative emotion:

HOSTILE   The administration coerced some students into dropping their lawsuits. [*Coerced* implies the use of threats.]

REASONABLE   The administration convinced some students to drop their lawsuits. [*Convinced* implies the use of reason.]

See pages 37–38 for more on tone and pages 52–53 for more on connotation.

A Note on Thematic Connections

Argument and persuasion is the ideal method for presenting an opinion or a proposal on a controversial topic, making it a natural choice for the writers in this chapter, all of whom wanted to make a case about a social or political concern. In paragraphs, Jenny Price argues that we should expect gun violence rather than be shocked by it (p. 335), while Martin Luther King, Jr., urges readers to condone civil disobedience (p. 335). Anna Quindlen asserts that changing our attitude toward mental illness may help to prevent school shootings (opposite). In an essay based on careful research and his own experience as an inmate, Charlie Spence explains why he believes that trying juveniles as adults is morally wrong (p. 349). Sherry Turkle draws on her work as a social psychologist to warn that giving up privacy online damages the foundations of our democracy (p. 356). And the final three essays all touch on issues of immigration: George F. Will (p. 363) and Marie Myung-Ok Lee (p. 368) square off on the question of whether children born in America to illegal immigrants should be granted citizenship, while Roberto Rodríguez (p. 374) insists that calls for immigration reform are both racist at heart and beside the point.

I am not insane. I am angry. . . . I killed because people like me are
mistreated every day.

—Luke Woodham

He just seemed strange. . . . He didn't seem dangerous in any way.

—Karan Grewal

The reality is that schools are very safe environments for our kids.   —Jim Mercy

JOURNAL RESPONSE   School shootings seem to have become an epidemic in
the United States. Most notoriously, in 1999 two students at Columbine
High School in Colorado killed thirteen people, in 2007 a student at Virginia Tech killed thirty-two people, and in 2012 a former student forced
his way into an elementary school in Newtown, Connecticut, killing
twenty children and six adults. Because of such tragedies, many students
now must pass through locked doors and metal detectors on their way to
class, and several school districts have initiated zero-tolerance policies that
call for the removal of children who show any potential to do harm. How
do you feel about the violence and its consequences? In a journal entry,
comment on the problem of student violence. How extensive is it? What
causes it? What should be done about it?

Anna Quindlen

Winner of the Pulitzer Prize for commentary in 1992, Anna Quindlen writes sharp,
candid columns on subjects ranging from family life to social issues to international politics. She was born in 1953 in Philadelphia, where she grew up, as she
puts it, "an antsy kid with a fresh mouth." After graduating from Barnard College,
Quindlen began writing for the *New York Post* and then joined the *New York Times,*
where she worked her way up from a city hall reporter to a columnist. From 1999
to 2009 she wrote a regular column for *Newsweek*. Her columns have been collected in *Living Out Loud* (1988), *Thinking Out Loud* (1993), and *Loud and Clear*
(2004). Quindlen is also the author of the nonfiction books *How Reading Changed
My Life* (1998), *A Short Guide to a Happy Life* (2000), and *Being Perfect* (2005); the
memoirs *Good Dog. Stay.* (2007) and *Lots of Candles, Plenty of Cake* (2012); and the
novels *Object Lessons* (1991), *One True Thing* (1994), *Black and Blue* (1998), *Blessings*
(2002), *Rise and Shine* (2006), *Every Last One* (2010), and *Still Life with Bread Crumbs*
(2014).

The C Word in the Hallways

Quindlen wrote this selection in November 1999, a few months after the massacre at Columbine High School. Similar events since then have made her message as urgent as ever.

The saddest phrase I've read in a long time is this one: psychological 1
autopsy. That's what the doctors call it when a kid kills himself, and they go back over the plowed ground of his short life, and discover all the hidden markers that led to the rope, the blade, the gun.

There's a plague on all our houses, and since it doesn't announce 2
itself with lumps or spots or protest marches, it has gone unremarked in the quiet suburbs and busy cities where it has been laying waste. The number of suicides and homicides committed by teenagers, most often young men, has exploded in the last three decades, until it has become routine to have black-bordered photographs in yearbooks and murder suspects with acne problems. And everyone searches for reasons, and scapegoats, and solutions, most often punitive. Yet one solution continues to elude us, and that is ending the ignorance about mental health, and moving it from the margins of care and into the mainstream where it belongs. As surely as any vaccine, this would save lives.

So many have already been lost. This month Kip Kinkel was sen- 3
tenced to life in prison in Oregon for the murders of his parents and a shooting rampage at his high school that killed two students. A psychiatrist who specializes in the care of adolescents testified that Kinkel, now seventeen, had been hearing voices since he was twelve. Sam Manzie is also seventeen. He is serving a seventy-year sentence for luring an eleven-year-old boy named Eddie Werner into his New Jersey home and strangling him with the cord to an alarm clock because his Sega Genesis was out of reach. Manzie had his first psychological evaluation in the first grade.

Excuses, excuses. That's what so many think of the underlying pathol- 4
ogy in such hideous crimes. In the 1956 movie *The Bad Seed*, little Patty McCormack played what was then called a "homicidal maniac" and the film censors demanded a ludicrous mock curtain call in which the child actress was taken over the knee of her screen father and spanked. There are still some representatives of the "good spanking" school out there, although today the spanking may wind up being life in prison. And there's still plenty of that useless adult "what in the world does a sixteen-year-old have to be depressed about" mind-set to keep depressed sixteen-year-olds from getting help.

It's true that both the Kinkel and the Manzie boys had already been 5 introduced to the mental health system before their crimes. Concerned by her son's fascination with weapons, Faith Kinkel took him for nine sessions with a psychologist in the year before the shootings. Because of his rages and his continuing relationship with a pedophile, Sam's parents had tried to have him admitted to a residential facility just days before their son invited Eddie in.

But they were threading their way through a mental health system 6 that is marginalized by shame, ignorance, custom, the courts, even by business practice. Kip Kinkel's father made no secret of his disapproval of therapy. During its course he bought his son the Glock that Kip would later use on his killing spree, which speaks sad volumes about our peculiar standards of masculinity. Sam's father, on the other hand, spent days trying to figure out how much of the cost of a home for troubled kids his insurance would cover. In the meantime, a psychiatrist who examined his son for less time than it takes to eat a Happy Meal concluded that he was no danger to himself or others, and a judge lectured Sam from the bench: "You know the difference between right and wrong, don't you?"

The federal Center for Mental Health Services estimates that at least 7 six million children in this country have some serious emotional disturbance and, for some of them, right and wrong take second seat to the voices in their heads. Fifty years ago their parents might have surrendered them to life in an institution, or a doctor flying blind with an ice pick might have performed a lobotomy, leaving them to loll away their days. Now lots of them wind up in jail. Warm fuzzies aside, consider this from a utilitarian point of view: psychological intervention is cheaper than incarceration.

The most optimistic estimate is that two-thirds of these emotion- 8 ally disturbed children are not getting any treatment. Imagine how we would respond if two-thirds of America's babies were not being immunized. Many health insurance plans do not provide coverage for necessary treatment, or financially penalize those who need a psychiatrist instead of an oncologist. Teachers are not trained to recognize mental illness, and some dismiss it, "Bad Seed" fashion, as bad behavior. Parents are afraid, and ashamed, creating a home environment, and national atmosphere, too, that tells teenagers their demons are a disgrace.

And then there are the teenagers themselves, slouching toward adult- 9 hood in a world that loves conformity. Add to the horror of creeping depression or delusions that of peer derision, the sound of the C word in the hallways: crazy, man, he's crazy, haven't you seen him, didn't you hear? Boys, especially, still suspect that talk therapy, or even heartfelt talk, is somehow sissified, weak. Sometimes even their own fathers think so, at least until they have to identify the body.

Another sad little phrase is "If only," and there are always plenty of   10
them littering the valleys of tragedy. If only there had been long-term intervention and medication, Kip Kinkel might be out of jail, off the tax-payers' tab, and perhaps leading a productive life. If only Sam Manzie had been treated aggressively earlier, new psychotropic drugs might have slowed or stilled his downward slide. And if only those things had happened, Faith Kinkel, William Kinkel, Mikael Nickolauson, Ben Walker, and Eddie Werner might all be alive today. Mental health care is health care, too, and mental illness is an illness, not a character flaw. Insurance providers should act like it. Hospitals and schools should act like it. Above all, we parents should act like it. Then maybe the kids will believe it.

Meaning

1. What is Quindlen's main idea, and where do you find it in the essay?

2. What examples of teen violence does Quindlen give? What reason does she provide to explain these students' behavior?

3. Why is Quindlen so alarmed about our attitudes toward mental illness? Whom does she blame for the problems experienced by troubled teenagers?

4. In paragraph 6, Quindlen writes that William Kinkel's purchase of a gun for his son "speaks sad volumes about our peculiar standards of mascu-linity." What does she mean?

5. If you are unsure of any of the following words used by Quindlen, try to determine their meanings from their context in the essay. Check their meanings in a dictionary to test your guesses. Then use each word in a sentence or two of your own.

scapegoats (2)	loll (7)	oncologist (8)
pathology (4)	utilitarian (7)	derision (9)
marginalized (6)	incarceration (7)	psychotropic (10)

Purpose and Audience

1. What seems to be Quindlen's purpose in writing this essay? Is she writ-ing mainly to express a concern, offer a solution to a problem, influence government decisions, change individuals' attitudes, or do something else? What evidence from the text supports your answer?

2. Who do you think is the author's target audience? How does Quindlen engage these readers' support?

3. Although this essay was written only a few months after the tragedy at Columbine (which at the time was the deadliest school shooting in American history), Quindlen makes no mention of the shooters in that attack, Eric Harris and Dylan Klebold. Why do you suppose she leaves them out of her discussion?

Method and Structure

1. Is Quindlen's appeal mostly emotional or mostly rational? Explain your answer with examples from the essay.

2. Where in the essay does Quindlen address opposing viewpoints? How fair is her depiction of people with conflicting opinions?

3. Quindlen makes two literary references in this essay: "a plague on all our houses" (paragraph 2) is an **allusion** to Shakespeare's play *Romeo and Juliet*, and "slouching toward adulthood" (9) is an allusion to William Butler Yeats's poem "The Second Coming." What is the effect of these references?

4. **OTHER METHODS**   Quindlen supports her argument with other methods, such as **example** (Chapter 7), **comparison and contrast** (Chapter 11), and **cause-and-effect analysis** (Chapter 13). Locate one instance of each method. What does each contribute to the essay?

Language

1. What is the "*C* word" to which Quindlen refers in her title? Why do you suppose she waits until the end of the essay to use the word itself?

2. How does Quindlen use **parallel** sentence structure in her conclusion to drive home her point?

3. How would you describe Quindlen's tone? Is it consistent throughout? Is it appropriate for her subject?

Writing Topics

1. **JOURNAL TO ESSAY**   Take off from the comments you made in your journal entry (p. 343) to write an essay that agrees or disagrees with Quindlen. Has the incidence of teenage suicide and homicide really "exploded" (paragraph 2) to the degree that Quindlen describes? Are teenage killers victims of inadequate mental health care? Is better psychological treatment the answer to the problem? Are there other solutions we should consider? Your essay may but need not be an argument: that is, you could explain your answer to any of these questions or argue a specific point. Either way, use examples and details to support your ideas.

2. **CULTURAL CONSIDERATIONS**   At several points in her essay, Quindlen suggests that American codes of masculinity are at least partly to blame for teenage boys' tendency toward violence. Write an essay that explores what our culture expects of boys and men, and how those expectations might translate into inappropriate behavior. How does American culture define manhood? Do we, in fact, pressure boys to keep silent about their emotions? To what extent is masculine aggression encouraged or rewarded? How does society respond to boys—and men—who don't conform to expectations? And to what extent are individuals responsible for their own behavior? In formulating your analysis, consider also how a person from another culture might respond—a resident of, say, Mexico or Japan or France.

3. **RESEARCH**   Although Quindlen's essay demonstrates a large degree of compassion for troubled teenagers, some scholars and psychologists would caution that the cause-and-effect relationship it draws between mental illness and violence is misinformed. Using the library or the Internet, research articles or studies concerning media stigmatization of the mentally ill. In an essay, discuss whether you think Quindlen's analysis of teen violence reflects negative stereotypes. If you find that it does, consider whether such stereotypes affect the persuasiveness of her argument. (For advice on finding and using research sources, see the Appendix.)

4. **CONNECTIONS**   Both Quindlen and Marie Myung-Ok Lee, in "I Was an Anchor Baby" (p. 368), write with emotion about a social issue—mental illness in Quindlen's case, illegal immigration in Lee's. In an essay, explore how the concept of personal shame, or social taboo, informs each writer's approach. How effective is each writer's strategy of tackling a controversial issue from an emotional perspective? What would these essays have lost (or gained) if they had been written from a more psychologically distant point of view?

Prison continues, on those who are entrusted to it, a work begun elsewhere, which the whole of society pursues on each individual through innumerable mechanisms of discipline.

—Michel Foucault

Man is not made better by being degraded; he is seldom restrained from crime by harsh measures, except the principle of fear predominates in his character; and then he is never made radically better for its influence.

—Dorothea Dix

Of the three official objects of our prison system—vengeance, deterrence, and reformation of the criminal—only one is achieved; and that is the one which is nakedly abominable.

—George Bernard Shaw

JOURNAL RESPONSE   What is the purpose of prison in a civilized society? Do we jail people to punish them, to rehabilitate them, or to protect others from them? Are there other ways to respond to crime? In your journal, write a few paragraphs exploring your thoughts on these questions.

Charlie Spence

Charlie Spence was born in 1980 and grew up in Sacramento, California, with two brothers and a single mother "who always tried her best." At the age of sixteen, Spence was sentenced to a prison term of twenty-six years to life; he is serving his time at San Quentin and has been working with at-risk youth since 2005. He completed an associate of arts degree from Patten University through the Prison University Project in 2013 and plans to continue studying social psychology, with the goal of eventually becoming licensed as a marriage and family therapist. Spence reports that he "strongly desires to be not only free, but a leading voice for change in America's juvenile justice practices." Beyond sentencing reform, his interests include reading and sports.

Sixteen
(Student Essay)

Spence first wrote "Sixteen" for a Prison University Project composition course in 2009 and revised it for the *Compact Reader* in 2010. Not surprisingly, Spence is opposed to sentencing juveniles as adults. Although we might have reason to suspect his objectivity, he overcomes the problem by presenting his case rationally and by backing up his claims with ample evidence from reliable sources. In accordance with MLA style, Spence names his sources in the text and lists them at the end. (See the Appendix for information on using and citing sources.)

They seemed larger than me that day, the rain drops, as they fell from an   1
endless gray sky. They illuminated the headlights of oncoming traffic in
an iridescent and blurred shine. The display of colors seemed only to
intensify the fear and magnify the pain I felt inside about yet another
tragedy taking place in my life. I sat there dressed in an orange jumpsuit,
feet shackled together and a waist chain tightly secured around my mid-
section to restrict my arms firmly to my sides. The sheriff's van traveled at
what felt like the speed of light, never allowing me to collect my thoughts
before arriving at my next destination: life in an adult institution at the
age of sixteen. The words compassionately spoken by the sheriff that
day have never left the confines of my soul: "I didn't even start to get it
together until I was twenty-five," he said. The sheriff will never understand the extent to which his words thrashed about my heart. Had I been
tried and convicted as a juvenile, I would have been given a better chance
at rehabilitation and a second chance in society at the age of twenty-five.
I feel even more strongly now than I did back then that trying juvenile
offenders as adults and sentencing them to life in prison is immoral.

   In the year 2000, the people of California voted and passed Proposi-   2
tion 21. This allowed for juveniles as young as fourteen who are accused
of a serious crime to be tried as adults at the discretion of the district
attorney trying the case. Prior to Proposition 21, juveniles accused of such
crimes were given what is called a "707(b) hearing" in front of a judge, to
determine if they met the criteria to be tried as an adult. Before Proposition 21 was introduced, only in rare and extreme cases of violence were
juveniles tried as adults.

   It is easy for me to understand the feelings of one who is opposed to   3
my position. Juveniles do commit crimes that are serious and are considered to be "adult crimes." The juveniles who receive life sentences are
certainly not receiving them for petty crimes; it is not as if the fourteen-
year-old shoplifter is locked up and the key is then thrown away. I would
agree, too, that most juveniles have a sense of right and wrong from an
early age. Surely children know that they are not supposed to take cookies out of the cookie jar unless given permission by their parents. On a
greater scale most adolescents know it is wrong to smoke, use drugs,
cheat, or steal and, therefore, know it is wrong to commit crime, period.
But it seems only fair that if we are going to take into account the social
development of morality within these children, then by that same token

we should also consider their mental development and take into account the neuroscience and the high likelihood of rehabilitating these same children.

According to a newspaper article published in the *Los Angeles Times*   4 and a study conducted for the University of San Francisco's Center for Law and Global Justice, 2,387 juvenile offenders have been given life sentences here in the United States (Weinstein; Leighton and de la Vega 2). To understand this prodigious number, and to contemplate the depraved nature of this practice, consider that Israel, the *only other* country in the world to hand out such sentences, is a far and distant second with seven. According to the study, Israel has not handed out such sentences since 2004 (Leighton and de la Vega iii). While the populations in these two countries widely differ, these statistics seem to suggest that Israel uses such sentences in extreme cases only. It should be noted that of the juveniles sentenced to life without parole here in the United States, half of those sentences were issued to first-time offenders (Leighton and de la Vega 14). It is alarming that we are willing to sentence, at a staggering number, our youth offenders to life with or without parole considering that juveniles stand the greatest chance to be rehabilitated.

Senator Leland Yee of San Francisco–San Mateo, whose background   5 is in child psychology, states, "Children have the highest capacity for rehabilitation. The neuroscience is clear; brain maturation continues well through adolescence and thus impulse control, planning, and critical-thinking skills are not fully developed" (qtd. in Weinstein). Other studies support this same finding: the San Francisco Center for Law and Global Justice study asserts, "Psychologically and neurologically, children cannot be expected to have achieved the same level of mental development as an adult, even when they become teenagers" (Leighton and de la Vega i). A perfect example of an immature brain is a fourteen-year-old child, with whom I became acquainted in juvenile hall, who had been asked by a peer to beat up a homeless man for twenty-five cents. This child, having never been accepted by a peer group before, proceeded to beat up the homeless man. The subsequent and tragic outcome of the situation was the homeless man died from his injuries and the child was given life in prison, all because he acted on an impulse to be accepted by friends and lacked the critical thinking skills of a fully developed mind. Had this been a mature adult who had been asked to beat up a homeless man for twenty-five cents, I find it hard to believe that he would have done it.

Juvenile offenders should be punished for serious crimes they commit, but as juveniles in juvenile facilities, where a "life" sentence ends at   6 age twenty-five. The oldest that children can be tried as minors is seventeen, an age that allows for eight years of time in which they can serve their punishment and in which we have an opportunity to rehabilitate them. Age sixteen allows for nine years and so on. By placing our youth in adult facilities with life sentences, we are giving up on them. According to the Center on Juvenile and Criminal Justice, fifteen- to twenty-one-year-olds make up 13% of our prison population and together they make up 22% of all suicide deaths in our institutions. Juveniles are 7.7 times more likely to commit suicide in adult facilities than in juvenile facilities. Whereas only 1% of juveniles reported rape in the juvenile system, that actual number is nine times higher in the adult system. It is not just about these numbers, though. At what point do we brand a person for life for the worst thing he or she did as a child?

The lack of mental maturity and development within the minds of 7
juveniles is what sets the stage for a 2005 US Supreme Court ruling in which the Court determined that it is unconstitutional to execute a person under the age of eighteen. In their majority opinion, the Court cited research saying that the mental capacity of juveniles was not the same as that of adults (*Roper v. Simmons*). Here, the highest court in the United States is acknowledging that juveniles lack careful and exact evaluation and judgment, as well as the ability to control sudden spontaneous inclinations or urges because of their undeveloped minds. Perhaps this is the reason why juveniles are not allowed to choose for themselves whether or not they can go watch an R-rated movie until the age of seventeen. They cannot vote until age eighteen, buy a pack of cigarettes until age eighteen, or buy alcohol until the age of twenty-one. The contrast here is drastic: by one means we are suggesting that seventeen-year-old teenagers are only entering a mature enough mental state to choose whether they wish to watch an R-rated movie, yet by another we are suggesting that they are mature enough to understand the full consequences of a crime they may commit.

Obviously, we as a society recognize the difference between the men- 8
tal capacity of juveniles and adults too, or we would not have constructed laws based on the age of an individual as a determining factor for conduct. It seems unfair that we only want to recognize the difference in mental development between adult and child up to the point when the child exercises bad judgment. I hate to think that we are so cruel as a society and a country that we would rather place our children in prison because of poor decision making with an immature brain, for a crime they are convicted of, than try to rehabilitate them while their mental capacity for reform is at its pinnacle.

Works Cited

Center on Juvenile and Criminal Justice. *Center on Juvenile and Criminal Justice.* CJCJ, n.d. Web. 2 Feb. 2010.

Leighton, Michelle, and Connie de la Vega. *Sentencing Our Children to Die in Prison: Global Law and Practice.* San Francisco: U of San Francisco School of Law, 2007. Print.

Roper v. Simmons 543 US 551. Supreme Court of the US. 2005. *Supreme Court Collection.* Legal Information Inst., Cornell U Law School, n.d. Web. 10 Feb. 2010.

Weinstein, Henry. "Focus on Youth Sentences." *Los Angeles Times.* Los Angeles Times, 19 Nov. 2007. Web. 2 Feb. 2010.

Meaning

1. According to Spence, what is the purpose of sending people to prison? What *should* be the purpose, as he sees it? Where in the text does he state the central assumption that grounds his argument?

2. Why does Spence believe that sentencing juveniles to life is immoral? Summarize his supporting arguments in your own words.

3. Spence tells readers that he is serving a life sentence, but he doesn't say what crime he committed. Does it matter? Why, or why not?

4. Some of the following words may be new to you. Try to guess their meanings from the context of Spence's essay. Test your guesses in a dictionary, and then use each new word in a sentence of your own.

iridescent (1)	prodigious (4)	spontaneous (7)
confines (1)	depraved (4)	inclinations (7)
discretion (2)	capacity (5, 8)	pinnacle (8)
neuroscience (3, 5)	subsequent (5)	

Purpose and Audience

1. What is the purpose of the personal story with which Spence opens his essay? How did it affect you?

2. Who would Spence's ideal readers be: politicians? prisoners? average citizens? Why do you think so?

Method and Structure

1. Examine how Spence uses information and ideas from sources to develop and support his main idea. What might his argument have lost without this material?

2. How would you rate Spence's *ethos*, or ethical appeal? What strategies does he use to overcome readers' potential doubts about his objectivity?

3. How does Spence handle opposing viewpoints? What is the effect of acknowledging that juveniles do commit serious crimes and that life sentences for juvenile offenders are not handed down lightly?

4. **OTHER METHODS**   In paragraph 4, Spence uses **comparison and contrast** (Chapter 11) to examine the sentencing practices in the United States and Israel. What are the differences? How does this comparison further Spence's argument that trying juveniles as adults is wrong?

Language

1. How would you describe Spence's attitude toward his subject? What is the overall tone of his argument?

2. Why does Spence take such pains to refer to juvenile offenders as "children" throughout his essay? How does he use **repetition** of key words to reinforce his main point?

Writing Topics

1. **JOURNAL TO ESSAY**   The United States imprisons more of its citizens than almost any other country. Why is this the case? Look again at the quotations you read and the journal entry you wrote before reading Spence's essay (p. 349). Develop your ideas into an essay that explains and supports your thoughts on the uses of imprisonment in America. Do we, as Spence suggests, jail people to punish them for their crimes, or do other motives come into play? Are such motives reasonable? Is imprisonment effective at accomplishing the purposes assigned to it? Is the institution abused or misused in any way? Whatever your position, be sure to support it with plenty of details and examples and to consider how others might disagree with you.

2. Prison is a perennially popular subject in fiction. Pick a novel, film, or television show that takes prison, or something related to prison (such as involuntary commitment to a mental hospital), as its subject. (For novels, you might consider Charles Dickens's *Little Dorrit*, Malcolm Braly's *On the Yard*, or Kurt Vonnegut's *Hocus Pocus*. Films touching on this subject include *Cool Hand Luke*, *Escape from Alcatraz*, *Bad Boys*, *The Green Mile*, and *The Shawshank Redemption*, the last two based on stories by Stephen King. Popular television programs include *The Wire* and *Orange Is the New Black*.) Write an essay comparing and contrasting the novel's, film's, or show's attitudes toward prison with Spence's views. Are the criticisms the same? Where do they differ?

3. **CULTURAL CONSIDERATIONS**   As the quotation from Michel Foucault (p. 349) suggests, laws reflect and reinforce basic social values: What behaviors are acceptable? What transgressions are punishable? How far should we go to enforce social norms? Although incarceration practices might seem reasonable in a contemporary cultural context, viewed from an outsider's perspective they can often be quite surprising. For much of American history, for instance, whole families—including dependent infants—were routinely placed in debtors' prisons for a father's failure to provide for them. And in the early twentieth century, unmarried women could be jailed for pregnancy. Think of a past or current law that strikes you as absurd or extreme, and look for the underlying social value that it's meant to enforce. Then write an essay that explains the law to somebody from another culture or another time who might have trouble understanding it. You may be ironic or satiric, if you wish, or you may prefer a more straightforward informative approach.

4. **CONNECTIONS**   Spence and Anna Quindlen, in "The C Word in the Hallways" (p. 343), both write about violent crimes committed by teenagers, and both use psychology to suggest that juvenile offenders aren't fully responsible for their actions. While Spence refrains from detailing such crimes, Quindlen indicates that the subjects of her essay are serving life sentences for brutal, premeditated murders. How, if at all, do Quindlen's examples affect the persuasiveness of Spence's argument? Are some crimes so terrible that the perpetrators should be locked away forever, regardless of circumstance? Why do you think so? Write an essay that explains your answers to these questions, drawing for evidence on Spence's and Quindlen's arguments as well as your own opinions.

I don't want to live in a world where everything that I say, everything I do, everyone I talk to, every expression of creativity or love or friendship, is recorded.   —Edward Snowden

We increasingly know things about each other (or think we do) that we should not know, have no right to know, and have a right, actually, not to know.   —Peggy Noonan

I love solitude, but I prize it most when company is available.   —Saul Bellow

JOURNAL RESPONSE   Think of a moment when you either did something embarrassing or witnessed someone else's embarrassment online. In your journal, write about the incident as you remember it.

Sherry Turkle

Sherry Turkle was born in New York City in 1948, completed her PhD at Harvard University in 1976, and has taught at the Massachusetts Institute of Technology ever since. She is regarded as the leading expert in the psychology and sociology of electronic media, a subject she has explored in her best-selling books *Life on the Screen: Identity in the Age of the Internet* (1995), *The Second Self: Computers and the Human Spirit* (2005), and *Alone Together: Why We Expect More from Technology and Less from Each Other* (2011). A frequent guest on television and radio programs, Turkle is a licensed clinical psychologist and the founding director of MIT's Initiative on Technology and Self, a group of scholars who study the interactions between people and machines from a social perspective. She lives in Boston.

Privacy Has a Politics

Turkle's *Alone Together* draws on laboratory research and hundreds of interviews with users of technology to assess the impact that robotics, artificial intelligence, and digital connectivity have had on human interaction. In this self-contained section from the book, Turkle argues that despite the many opportunities and advantages inherent in social networking, the Internet also poses a potential threat to democracy.

It has become commonplace to talk about all the good the Web has done   1
for politics. We have new sources of information, such as news of political events from all over the world that comes to us via photographs and videos taken by the cameras on cell phones. There is organizing and fund-raising; ever since the 2004 primary run of Howard Dean, online

connections have been used as a first step in bringing people together physically. The Barack Obama campaign transformed the Dean-era idea of the "meet up" into a tool for bringing supporters out of the virtual and into each other's homes or onto the streets.[1] We diminish none of these very positive developments if we attend to the troubling realities of the Internet when it comes to questions of privacy. Beyond passivity and resignation, there is a chilling effect on political speech.

When they talk about the Internet, young people make a disturbing distinction between embarrassing behavior that will be forgiven and political behavior that might get you into trouble. For high school and college students, stalking and anything else they do to each other fall into the first category. Code such antics as embarrassing. They believe that you can apologize for embarrassing behavior and then move on. Celebrity culture, after all, is all about transgression and rehabilitation. (These young people's comfort with "bullying" their peers is part of this pattern— something for which they believe they will be forgiven.) But you can't "take back" political behavior, like signing a petition or being at a demonstration. One eighteen-year-old puts it this way: "It [the Internet] definitely makes you think about going to a protest or something. There would be so many cameras. You can't tell where the pictures could show up."   2

Privacy has a politics. For many, the idea "we're all being observed all the time anyway, so who needs privacy?" has become a commonplace. But this state of mind has a cost. At a Webby Awards ceremony, an event to recognize the best and most influential websites, I was reminded of just how costly it is. The year I attended the Webbies, the ceremonies took place just as a government wiretapping scandal dominated the press. When the question of illegal eavesdropping arose, a common reaction among the gathered "Weberati" was to turn the issue into a nonissue. There was much talk about "all information being good information," "information wanting to be free," and "if you have nothing to hide, you have nothing to fear." At a pre-awards cocktail party, one Web luminary spoke to me with animation about the wiretapping controversy. To my surprise, he cited Michel Foucault on the panopticon[2] to explain why he was not worried about privacy on the Internet.   3

---

[1] Early in the 2004 campaign, Howard Dean used *Meetup.com*, an early social-networking site built around message boards, to reach out to voters and collect donations. Four years later, Barack Obama's team tapped the interactive and streaming abilities of Web 2.0 to organize and galvanize supporters on a scale that most observers described as revolutionary. [Editors' note.]

[2] Michel Foucault (1926–84) was a French philosopher. He discusses his theory of the panopticon in *Discipline and Punish: The Birth of the Prison* (1979). [Editors' note.]

For Foucault, the task of the modern state is to reduce its need for   4
actual surveillance by creating a citizenry that will watch itself. A disci-
plined citizen minds the rules. Foucault wrote about Jeremy Bentham's
design for a panopticon because it captured how such a citizenry is
shaped. In the panopticon, a wheel-like structure with an observer at its
hub, one develops the sense of always being watched, whether or not the
observer is actually present. If the structure is a prison, inmates know
that a guard can potentially always see them. In the end, the architecture
encourages self-surveillance.

The panopticon serves as a metaphor for how, in the modern state,   5
every citizen becomes his or her own policeman. Force becomes unnecessary because the state creates its own obedient citizenry. Always available
for scrutiny, all turn their eyes on themselves. By analogy, said my Webby
conversation partner, on the Internet, someone might always be watching, so it doesn't matter if, from time to time, someone actually is. As long
as you are not doing anything wrong, you are safe. Foucault's critical take
on disciplinary society had, in the hands of this technology guru, become
a justification for the US government to use the Internet to spy on its citizens. All around us at the cocktail party, there were nods of assent. We
have seen that variants of this way of thinking, very common in the technology community, are gaining popularity among high school and college students.

If you relinquish your privacy on *MySpace* or *Facebook* about every-   6
thing from your musical preferences to your sexual hang-ups, you are less
likely to be troubled by an anonymous government agency knowing
whom you call or what websites you frequent. Some are even gratified by
a certain public exposure; it feels like validation, not violation. Being seen
means that they are not insignificant or alone. For all the talk of a generation empowered by the Net, any discussion of online privacy generates
claims of resignation and impotence. When I talk to teenagers about the
certainty that their privacy will be invaded, I think of my very different
experience growing up in Brooklyn in the 1950s.

As the McCarthy era swirled about them, my grandparents were   7
frightened.[3] From Eastern European backgrounds, they saw the McCarthy

---

[3] Spurred by fears of Soviet expansion, Senator Joseph McCarthy, the FBI, and the
House Un-American Activities Committee led a campaign through the 1950s
accusing government employees, actors, teachers, union members, and others of
engaging in communist activities or being sympathetic to communist ideals. Thousands of Americans who fell under suspicion lost their jobs or their reputations;
others were sent to jail. [Editors' note.]

hearings not as a defense of patriotism but as an attack on people's rights. Joseph McCarthy was spying on Americans, and having the government spy on its citizens was familiar from the old world. There, you assumed that the government read your mail, which never led to good. In America, things were different. I lived with my grandparents as a young child in a large apartment building. Every morning, my grandmother took me downstairs to the mailboxes. Looking at the gleaming brass doors, on which, she noted, "people were not afraid to have their names listed, for all to see," my grandmother would tell me, as if it had never come up before, "In America, no one can look at your mail. It's a federal offense. That's the beauty of this country." From the earliest age, my civics lessons at the mailbox linked privacy and civil liberties. I think of how different things are today for children who learn to live with the idea that their e-mail and messages are shareable and unprotected. And I think of the Internet guru at the Webby awards who, citing Foucault with no apparent irony, accepted the idea that the Internet has fulfilled the dream of the panopticon and summed up his political position about the Net as follows: "The way to deal is to just be good."

But sometimes a citizenry should not simply "be good." You have to   8
leave space for dissent, real dissent. There needs to be technical space (a sacrosanct mailbox) and mental space. The two are intertwined. We make our technologies, and they, in turn, make and shape us. My grandmother made me an American citizen, a civil libertarian, a defender of individual rights in an apartment lobby in Brooklyn. I am not sure where to take my eighteen-year-old daughter, who still thinks that *Loopt* (the application that uses the GPS capability of the iPhone to show her where her friends are) seems "creepy" but notes that it would be hard to keep it off her phone if all her friends had it. "They would think I had something to hide."

In democracy, perhaps we all need to begin with the assumption that   9
everyone has something to hide, a zone of private action and reflection, one that must be protected no matter what our techno-enthusiasms. I am haunted by the sixteen-year-old boy who told me that when he needs to make a private call, he uses a pay phone that takes coins and complains how hard it is to find one in Boston. And I am haunted by the girl who summed up her reaction to losing online privacy by asking, "Who would care about me and my little life?"

I learned to be a citizen at the Brooklyn mailboxes. To me, opening   10
up a conversation about technology, privacy, and civil society is not romantically nostalgic, not Luddite in the least. It seems like part of democracy defining its sacred spaces.

Meaning

1. How does Turkle account for young people's willingness to reveal personal information on the Web? What reasons does she give to discourage such behavior?

2. Where does Turkle place the blame for the average American's reluctance to participate in political activities?

3. By what means does the author bring her argument around to the subject of civil liberties?

4. Try to guess the meanings of the following words, based on their context in Turkle's essay. Test your guesses in a dictionary, and then use each word in a sentence of your own.

transgression (2)	assent (5)	impotence (6)
rehabilitation (2)	relinquish (6)	dissent (8)
wiretapping (3)	gratified (6)	libertarian (8)
luminary (3)	validation (6)	

Purpose and Audience

1. What thesis does Turkle attempt to support? What is her purpose?

2. Judging from the **allusions** made in this essay, would you say that Turkle is writing for a highly specialized audience or an educated but non-specialized general audience?

Method and Structure

1. What does the author accomplish by opening with examples of the political good that has been done by the Internet?

2. As a whole, is this essay an example of appeal to emotion or reasoned argument or both? Give evidence for your answer.

3. OTHER METHODS   Turkle includes as evidence two **narratives** (Chapter 5) of her personal experiences. What is the point of the narrative about her grandmother (paragraph 7)?

Language

1. What is a "panopticon" (paragraphs 3–5)? Why does the **metaphor** trouble Turkle?

2. What does Turkle mean when she insists that her position is "not Luddite in the least" (paragraph 10)?

3. Examine Turkle's tone. How would you characterize her attitude toward young people in particular? As a student, how do you respond to that attitude?

Writing Topics

1. JOURNAL TO ESSAY   In your journal entry (p. 356) you recalled an embarrassing moment that you experienced or witnessed on the Internet. Now expand your notes into an essay that explains why you believe that a personal Web presence is risky—or beneficial. Narrate the incident to set the scene, but consider also the concerns that Turkle explores in her essay. For instance, what motivated the embarrassing behavior, and what were the consequences? Was the mistake, in fact, forgiven? What lessons might readers take from the incident as you understand it?

2. Write a paper in which you analyze and evaluate any one of the subclaims Turkle uses to support her argument. For instance: Do the people you know distinguish between personal and political activities online (paragraph 2)? Are we as resigned to lack of privacy as Turkle says (6)? Do we really need privacy in the first place (8)? Support your view with evidence from your experience, observations, or reading.

3. CULTURAL CONSIDERATIONS   "We make our technologies, and they, in turn, make and shape us," writes Turkle (paragraph 8). What does she mean? And do you agree? In an essay of your own, develop one example of a technology—such as television, streaming media, smartphones, or GPS navigation—that, in your opinion, has (or has not) affected society or culture in a meaningful way. As you write, consider the original purposes for the technology, the ways it came to be used, and its intended and unintended effects on individual behavior.

4. CONNECTIONS   While Turkle is concerned with protecting the foundations of democracy, George F. Will, in "Subject to Interpretation" (next page), argues for reinterpreting the US Constitution to deny some residents the protections of citizenship. In an essay, compare these two writers' perspectives on American civil liberties. What rights, privileges, and responsibilities does US citizenship confer on individuals, in Turkle's mind and in Will's? What are the primary functions of a democracy, as each author sees it? What are the primary threats to it? What assumptions, if any, do their arguments have in common? How might their differences be resolved?

ON DEMOCRACY

Common sense is not so common. — Voltaire

It's in the democratic citizen's nature to be like a leaf that doesn't believe in the tree it's part of. — David Foster Wallace

What is a moderate interpretation [of the US Constitution]? Halfway between what it really means and what you'd like it to mean? — Antonin Scalia

JOURNAL RESPONSE What does American citizenship mean to you? Is it something you take for granted, a source of pride (or shame), or is it something you hope to achieve someday? Why? In your journal, reflect on the privileges and responsibilities that come with being a citizen of the United States.

George F. Will

George F. Will, born in 1941 in Champaign, Illinois, is a nationally known political columnist and television commentator. He was educated at Trinity College, Oxford University, and Princeton University (PhD, 1967). He taught politics at Michigan State University and the University of Toronto, served as an aide to a US senator, and in 1972 became Washington editor of the *National Review*. Since the mid-1970s he has been the author of a syndicated newspaper column that received a Pulitzer Prize for commentary in 1977 and now appears in more than 450 papers across the country. After providing more than three decades of columns for *Newsweek* and on-air commentary for ABC News, Will joined the Fox News Channel in 2013. His essays — notable for their wit, eloquence, and lasting influence on conservative politics — have been collected in multiple volumes, including *The Pursuit of Happiness and Other Sobering Thoughts* (1978), *The Pursuit of Virtue and Other Tory Notions* (1982), and *With a Happy Eye, But . . . : America and the World, 1997–2002* (2003). Will has also written several books on politics and baseball, the latest being *A Nice Little Place on the North Side: Wrigley Field at One Hundred* (2014). He lives outside Washington, DC.

Subject to Interpretation

With the exception of American Indians, every person who lives in the United States can trace his or her ancestry back to relatives who moved here from another country. Recent years, however, have seen a renewed push for various reforms of immigration policy, from calls for tighter border controls to demands that those in the country without proper documentation be found and deported. One area of especially contentious debate has been the legal tenet of birthright citizenship. Some scholars and politicians have proposed repealing the Fourteenth Amendment of the US Constitution — which traditionally confers citizenship to anybody born in the United States — on the grounds such a birthright incentivizes illegal immigration and places excess pressure on already overburdened institutions and social benefit programs. Will proposes an alternate solution to this problem of so-called "anchor babies" in the essay reprinted here. "Subject to Interpretation" (editors' title) first appeared in the *Washington Post* in 2010.

A simple reform would drain some scalding steam from immigration arguments that may soon again be at a roiling boil. It would bring the interpretation of the Fourteenth Amendment into conformity with what the authors of its text intended, and with common sense, thereby removing an incentive for illegal immigration. 1

To end the practice of "birthright citizenship," all that is required is to correct the misinterpretation of that amendment's first sentence: "All persons born or naturalized in the United States, and subject to the jurisdiction thereof, are citizens of the United States and of the state wherein they reside." From these words has flowed the practice of conferring citizenship on children born here to illegal immigrants. 2

A parent from a poor country, writes professor Lino Graglia of the University of Texas law school, "can hardly do more for a child than make him or her an American citizen, entitled to all the advantages of the American welfare state." Therefore, "It is difficult to imagine a more irrational and self-defeating legal system than one which makes unauthorized entry into this country a criminal offense and simultaneously provides perhaps the greatest possible inducement to illegal entry." 3

Writing in the *Texas Review of Law and Politics*, Graglia says this irrationality is rooted in a misunderstanding of the phrase "subject to the jurisdiction thereof." What was this intended or understood to mean by those who wrote it in 1866 and ratified it in 1868? The authors and ratifiers could not have intended birthright citizenship for illegal immigrants because in 1868 *there were and never had been any illegal immigrants* because *no law ever had restricted immigration*. 4

If those who wrote and ratified the Fourteenth Amendment *had* imagined laws restricting immigration — and had anticipated huge waves of illegal immigration — is it reasonable to presume they would have wanted to provide the reward of citizenship to the children of the violators of those laws? Surely not. 5

The Civil Rights Act of 1866 begins with language from which the   6
Fourteenth Amendment's citizenship clause is derived: "All persons born
in the United States, *and not subject to any foreign power*, excluding Indians
not taxed, are hereby declared to be citizens of the United States." (Emphasis added.) The explicit exclusion of Indians from birthright citizenship
was not repeated in the Fourteenth Amendment because it was considered unnecessary. Although Indians were at least partially subject to US
jurisdiction, they owed allegiance to their tribes, not the United States.
This reasoning—divided allegiance—applies equally to exclude the children of resident aliens, legal as well as illegal, from birthright citizenship.
Indeed, today's regulations issued by the departments of Homeland Security and Justice stipulate:

"A person born in the United States to a foreign diplomatic officer   7
accredited to the United States, as a matter of international law, is not
subject to the jurisdiction of the United States. That person is not a United
States citizen under the Fourteenth Amendment."

Senator Lyman Trumbull of Illinois was, Graglia writes, one of two   8
"principal authors of the citizenship clauses in [the] 1866 act and the
Fourteenth Amendment." He said that "subject to the jurisdiction of the
United States" meant subject to its "complete" jurisdiction, meaning "not
owing allegiance to anybody else." Hence children whose Indian parents
had tribal allegiances were excluded from birthright citizenship.

Appropriately, in 1884 the Supreme Court held that children born to   9
Indian parents were not born "subject to" US jurisdiction because, among
other reasons, the person so born could not change his status by his "own
will without the action or assent of the United States." And "no one can
become a citizen of a nation without its consent." Graglia says this decision "seemed to establish" that US citizenship is "a consensual relation,
requiring the consent of the United States." So: "This would clearly settle
the question of birthright citizenship for children of illegal aliens. There
cannot be a more total or forceful denial of consent to a person's citizenship than to make the source of that person's presence in the nation
illegal."

Congress has heard testimony estimating that more than two-thirds   10
of all births in Los Angeles public hospitals, and more than half of all
births in that city, and nearly 10% of all births in the nation in recent
years, have been to mothers who are here illegally. Graglia seems to establish that there is no constitutional impediment to Congress ending the
granting of birthright citizenship to those whose presence here is "not
only without the government's consent but in violation of its law."

Meaning

1. Where does Will identify the intertwined problems he intends to address? What solution does he propose? Where does he state his thesis?

2. What does Will mean by "birthright citizenship"? How does he say the practice originated?

3. Why do you suppose Will emphasizes the citizenship status of American Indians in paragraphs 6–9? What does this have to do with immigration policy?

4. Some of the following words may be new to you. Try to guess their meanings from the context of Will's essay. Test your guesses in a dictionary, and then use each new word in a sentence of your own.

roiling (1)	inducement (3)	stipulate (6)
naturalized (2)	ratified (4, 5)	accredited (7)
jurisdiction (2, 6, 8, 9)	derived (6)	assent (9)
conferring (2)	allegiance (6, 8)	impediment (10)

Purpose and Audience

1. Will makes his purpose quite clear in the last paragraph: he wants Congress to put an end to the practice of granting automatic citizenship to the children of illegal immigrants. Can an essay like this one, published in a newspaper with a circulation in the millions, have an effect on national legislation? What would the intermediary steps have to be?

2. Who would Will's ideal readers be: immigrants? lawyers? members of Congress? average Americans? Why do you think so?

3. Whether you are a legal American citizen or not, you probably have some strong responses to this essay. What *are* your responses? Why? Do you think Will intended for at least some readers to respond the way you do? What in the essay supports your answer?

Method and Structure

1. Will's argument is primarily deductive. Express his reasoning in the form of a syllogism (see pp. 331–32). Do you detect any flaws in his logic? If so, what are they?

2. What kinds of evidence does the author provide? Where does it come from, and is it reliable and convincing? Why, or why not? (See pp. 387–88 for information on evaluating sources.)

3. Can you find any reference to opposing viewpoints in Will's essay? How, if at all, does his treatment of alternative perspectives on the issue affect the persuasiveness of his argument?

4. **OTHER METHODS** Will's argument is based on **division or analysis** (Chapter 8) of the wording of the Fourteenth Amendment. What does he interpret the text to mean?

Language

1. Explain the **metaphor** Will uses to introduce his argument. How does it help him express his reason for writing?

2. This essay includes several difficult words, many of which appear in the vocabulary list on the previous page. How does Will's **repetition** of legal terms relate to his subject, purpose, and audience?

3. What connotations do the words *illegal* and *welfare* have for you as a reader? Why do you suppose Will uses them?

4. What is the overall tone of Will's argument? Is it mainly impassioned or mainly reasoned?

Writing Topics

1. **JOURNAL TO ESSAY** In your journal entry (p. 362) you reflected on what American citizenship means to you. Now that you've read Will's argument against automatic citizenship for children of immigrants, write a response to his essay. You may find it helpful to do some **freewriting** first to work out what you think about the issue and why. And you may find it helpful to consider one or more of these questions: Do you see any weaknesses in Will's argument? Do you find that he backs up his claims with convincing and sufficient evidence? Does he overstate his case anywhere or neglect to address important points? Do you agree with certain parts of his argument but not others? Or are you in complete agreement with him? Support your response with details from Will's essay and examples from your own experience.

2. Examine Will's use of argumentative appeals—*ethos*, *pathos*, and *logos*—and write a rhetorical analysis of his essay. Which elements are most effective, and why?

3. Choose a political, social, or other kind of problem you care about—it could be the difficulty of obtaining health insurance, overcrowding in public schools, violence in the media, child neglect, or anything else.

Describe the problem as you understand it, particularly how it affects people. Then discuss your solution to the problem or some part of it. Be sure to at least acknowledge opposing views.

4. **CULTURAL CONSIDERATIONS**   The United States is noteworthy among nations for the rights and protections it affords citizens and others suspected of breaking laws. In some other countries, for instance, law-enforcement officers may use almost any means deemed necessary to obtain evidence against a suspected wrongdoer, whereas in the United States not only the Constitution but also federal, state, and local laws protect the rights of individuals and ensure that these protections are enforced equally. Do you think the US system achieves an appropriate balance between fairness to individuals and effectiveness in deterring or stopping illegal activity, or does it lean too far one way or the other? Write an essay stating your opinion and supporting it with examples from your experience, observations, and reading. If you are familiar with individual rights and law-enforcement procedures in another country, you may want to use **comparison and contrast** (Chapter 11) to help make your point.

5. **CONNECTIONS**   Unlike Will, Marie Myung-Ok Lee, the author of the next essay ("I Was an Anchor Baby"), is strongly in favor of birthright citizenship. On what major points do the authors agree and disagree? How do the tones of the two essays compare? Does either writer seem more convinced of being in the right? Which essay do you find more convincing, and why?

ON FAMILY

All happy families are alike; each unhappy family is unhappy in its own way.
—Leo Tolstoy

You don't choose your family. They are God's gift to you, as you are to them.
—Desmond Tutu

We all grow up with the weight of history on us. Our ancestors dwell in the attics of our brains as they do in the spiraling chains of knowledge hidden in every cell of our bodies.
—Shirley Abbott

JOURNAL RESPONSE Everybody has a history. What is yours? In your journal, write some notes on your family's backstory based on what you know about your parents, your grandparents, or other relatives who have had an influence on you. Where do they come from, and where are they now? What obstacles have they overcome, and what have they achieved? What aspects of your past would you like to know more about?

Marie Myung-Ok Lee

Fiction writer Marie Myung-Ok Lee (born 1964) grew up the daughter of Korean refugees in the nearly all-white town of Hibbing, Minnesota. Best known for her novels for teenagers — *Finding My Voice* (1992), *Saying Goodbye* (1994), *Necessary Roughness* (1996), and *Somebody's Daughter* (2005) — Lee has explained that she endured bullying and racial taunts in school and writes "coming-of-age stories of people who, for some reason, feel different than those around them." She has also written fiction for middle-school readers and regularly contributes short stories and essays to a wide range of publications, from *Slate* and the *New York Times* to the *Kenyon Review* and *TriQuarterly*. Lee is the winner of several literary prizes, including an O. Henry Award honorable mention for a story about Korean birth mothers of adopted children, adapted from a chapter in *Somebody's Daughter*. A graduate of Brown University (BA, 1986), a former fiction judge for the National Book Awards, and a founder of the Asian American Writer's Workshop, she currently teaches creative writing at Columbia University.

I Was an Anchor Baby

In the following essay published in the *Los Angeles Times* in 2010, Lee combines her family's story with a brief lesson in American history to counter arguments, like those made by George F. Will in "Subject to Interpretation" (p. 362), that American children of illegal immigrants should not be granted citizenship at birth.

I was an "anchor baby." According to family lore, the day I was born at   1
Hibbing Memorial Hospital in Minnesota in the early 1960s was also the
day my parents received their deportation papers. They had come to America from war-torn Korea on student visas that had run out. Laws at the
time prohibited most Asians from immigrating, so they were told to leave,
even with three American children.

The Fourteenth Amendment, with its guarantee that anyone born   2
here is an American, protected my siblings and me from being countryless. Today, in the growing clamor over illegal immigration, there have
been calls to repeal this amendment, with the pejorative "anchor baby"
invoked as a call to arms. The words suggest that having a child in America confers some kind of legal protection on illegal parents, that it gives
them a foothold here.

But in reality, merely having a baby on American soil doesn't change   3
the parents' status. As a so-called anchor baby, my existence did nothing
to resolve my parents' situation; if anything, it only added to their stress.

In Korea, my father was a talented physician who also happened to   4
speak fluent English. These skills led to his appointment as a medical liaison officer with a MASH[1] unit during the Korean War. The assignment
brought him to the attention of some American officers who, after the
war ended, arranged for him and my mother to come to the US so my
father could continue his education. He ended up training with Dr. C.
Walton Lillehei, a pioneer of heart surgery; my father was one of the first
anesthesiologists in the world capable of administering anesthesia during
open-heart surgery.

Other wartime contacts led to his job as an anesthesiologist in Hib-   5
bing, a northern Minnesota town that, because of its isolation and bitter winters, had trouble attracting doctors. My father was the sole anesthesiologist for miles, which meant that he spent long hours at the hospital,
where he met with each patient the night before their surgeries and
wouldn't leave until he'd answered all their questions. At home, a phone
call during dinner—announcing springtime chain-saw accidents, appendectomies, emergency C-sections—often sent him rushing back to the
hospital.

It wasn't until years later, when he made friends with another anes-   6
thesiologist who could cover for him—a German immigrant in Duluth,

---

[1] Mobile Army Surgical Hospital. [Editors' note.]

seventy miles away—that we could finally take a family vacation; until then, my father even had to be careful about drinking a beer at a cookout in case the hospital should call with another emergency.

It was peculiar laws rather than criminal intent that made my par-   7
ents outlaws at the time of my birth. For most of American history, our country has had an open-door policy on immigration, restricting only people employed in certain kinds of occupations (such as prostitution) and those with communicable diseases. Then, in 1882, Congress passed the Chinese Exclusion Act out of fear that Chinese immigrants would take American jobs.

In 1924, the Immigration and Naturalization Act established quotas   8
that heavily favored "desirable" Western Europeans while banning immigration from Japan, Korea and other Asian countries. Had my father been from Germany—like his anesthesiologist friend in Duluth, also toiling away at a job American doctors eschewed—citizenship would have happened easily. The same if my father had been from Mexico, as the act placed no quota restrictions on immigration from countries in the Western Hemisphere.

Instead, my parents went through an awful period of uncertainty,   9
instability and stress, which included being swindled by a number of "immigration lawyers." In the end, self-interest won out. Not my parents' self-interest (although they did want to stay in the US) but the interest of a town that needed its anesthesiologist.

Another friend of mine, also Korean American—an academic who   10
has written groundbreaking books and nurtured a generation of scholars—mentioned to me that when her parents died, she opened a special box she'd always thought held secret, glittery treasures, only to find it stuffed with deportation warnings from the INS.[2] Many of my immigrant and second-generation friends share this secret shame festering underneath the foil seals on our college and graduate degrees and our taxpaying lives. Studies show that immigrants, legal and not, are more law-abiding than the rest of the populace, and possibly more patriotic.

As a writer, I receive letters from readers who tell me how my work   11
has touched, even changed, their lives; as a child, I often heard my father's patients expressing similar sentiments of gratitude. Even the most anti-immigrant citizens have probably been touched by an illegal alien and/or an anchor baby in ways they probably cannot fully fathom.

Our Minnesota town, where people prided themselves on following   12
the law to the letter, did not rush to bring in the INS and run our illegal

---

[2] Immigration and Naturalization Service. [Editors' note.]

family out on a rail. People were instead so fearful of losing my father and his skills that the entire town signed a petition to protest the deportation order. This petition was brought to Congress by our local representative and eventually signed into a law to "provide relief" for my mother and father—but only them.

And although they were legal, they still weren't entitled to become citizens. This satisfied the townspeople, who were happy we were anchor babies—that we anchored my father to this place where his skills were so needed. But my parents, even as "permanent alien residents" with three (later four) American-born children, were still left in legal limbo, inhabiting an America that allowed them to stay, work, pay taxes, but not vote. 13

As an alien, my father worked at a job that other Americans did not want to do, and others like him have, too, harvesting crops, performing surgery, nurturing children, working in factories, making scientific discoveries, mopping floors. 14

In 1965, at the foot of the Statue of Liberty, President Lyndon Johnson signed a new immigration act to correct "a cruel and enduring wrong in the conduct of the American nation." It meant my parents were no longer "aliens ineligible for citizenship." They passed their citizenship tests with flying colors and received passports with blue covers and gilt eagles that matched their children's. My father went on to work at Hibbing Memorial Hospital for three more decades. And finally, we were an American family. 15

Meaning

1. Where, if at all, does Lee state her thesis? What claim does she want readers to accept, and what does she want them to do or believe as a result of reading her essay?

2. What does an anesthesiologist do? Why, according to Lee, did most American doctors not want her father's job?

3. Why did Lee's parents immigrate to the United States? Why didn't they become citizens until after she was born?

4. If you do not know any of the following words, try to determine their meanings from the context of Lee's essay. Test your guesses in a dictionary, and then use each word in a sentence of your own.

visas (1)	liaison (4)	alien (13)
clamor (2)	eschewed (8)	gilt (15)
invoked (2)	fathom (11)	
confers (2)	entitled (13)	

Purpose and Audience

1. To whom does Lee seem to be writing? What assumptions does Lee make about her readers' values?

2. Why do you believe Lee wrote this essay? To share a painful personal experience? To express her indignation? To argue for or against something? (If so, what?) For some other purpose? What evidence from the text supports your answer?

Method and Structure

1. What subclaims does Lee make to support her defense of birthright citizenship? Do you find her reasons convincing? Why, or why not?

2. Consider how Lee supports her argument. What kinds of evidence does she provide? How reliable is it, in your opinion?

3. How does Lee present and handle opposing arguments? Does she seem fair? Why, or why not?

4. **OTHER METHODS**   Lee combines **narration** (Chapter 5) and **example** (Chapter 7) to develop her argument. Where in the essay does she tell her family's story? Where does she explain the "peculiar laws" that affected their immigration status? How does she overlap personal history with American history to make her point?

Language

1. What does "anchor baby" mean? If the term is "pejorative," or insulting, as Lee claims in paragraph 2, why does she use it?

2. How would you describe Lee's tone? How does she appeal to readers?

Writing Topics

1. **JOURNAL TO ESSAY**   Starting with the notes you drafted in your journal entry (p. 368), and using Marie Myung-Ok Lee's essay as a model, write a brief history of your family. You may need to conduct some research to expand your knowledge and provide necessary information—perhaps by interviewing a few older family members, by digging through family documents and photographs, or by looking into the historical context, as Lee does. How does your family history align with events in American history? How have your relatives' experiences affected you and your sense of who you are?

2. How do you react to Lee's essay? Do you agree with her assessment of immigration laws and their impact on families? Or do you find her evalu-

ation of the issue one-sided, her examples and opinions too personal to form the basis of an argument? Write an essay that analyzes Lee's strategies and responds to her conclusions. Be sure to cite examples from her essay to support your analysis.

3. **CULTURAL CONSIDERATIONS**   The United States is a country of immigrants, and each group has made an indelible mark on American identity. For example, consider just foods: salsa outsells ketchup, tacos are offered everywhere, and cappuccino and sushi are everyday indulgences for many Americans who have no Italian or Japanese heritage. Write an essay about the effects of immigration on your daily life: the food you consume, the music you listen to, the clothing you prefer, and so forth. Include personal examples and historical information to bring your ideas to life, as Lee does.

4. **CONNECTIONS**   Does the Fourteenth Amendment to the US Constitution really "guarantee that anyone born here is an American," as Lee claims in paragraph 2? George F. Will doesn't think so. Read or reread "Subject to Interpretation" (p. 362), and then locate the full text of the amendment as well as one or two competing interpretations of its meaning. In a short essay, paraphrase the first section of the amendment itself and summarize the controversy surrounding it. Based on the conflicting opinions and your own analyses, what do you interpret the amendment to mean?

ON RACISM

Racism and class hatred are a learned activity, and as a kid I found myself in a society that was all too ready to teach it.　　　　—Henry A. Giroux

Sometimes, I feel discriminated against, but it does not make me angry. It merely astonishes me. How can any deny themselves the pleasure of my company?　　　　—Zora Neale Hurston

I have a dream that my four little children will one day live in a nation where they will not be judged by the color of their skin but by the content of their character.　　　　—Martin Luther King, Jr.

JOURNAL RESPONSE　Prejudice is so pervasive in our society that it can be difficult to avoid. Think of a time when somebody made an assumption about you because of your membership in a group (as a racial, ethnic, religious, or sexual minority; as a science or humanities major; as a club member; as a woman or man; as a "jock," "nerd," or "townie," and so on). Write a journal entry about the incident and how it made you feel.

Roberto Rodríguez

Born in Aguascalientes, Mexico, in 1954 and raised in Los Angeles, California, Roberto Cintli Rodríguez balances journalism with a professorship in the Department of Mexican American Studies at the University of Arizona. He began his career in 1972, writing for the student newsmagazine *La Gente* at the University of California, Los Angeles. His columns have since been syndicated in the *Los Angeles Times*, *USA Today*, the *Washington Post*, and a hundred other newspapers nationwide; Rodríguez has also written for the *Guardian*, *truth-out.org*, *Black Issues in Higher Education*, *La Opinion*, and several other publications in English and Spanish. He earned a PhD in mass communications from the University of Wisconsin at Madison in 2008; his current areas of research include the role of corn in traditional Mexican cultures, migrations, and oral narratives. Rodríguez has coproduced a documentary film and published several books, among them *Justice: A Question of Race* (1997) and *Our Sacred Maíz Is Our Mother: Indigeneity and Belonging in the Americas* (2014). In 2013, he received the Baker-Clarke Human Rights Award from the American Educational Research Association for his defense of ethnic studies in the college classroom.

The Border on Our Backs

For sixteen years, Rodríguez's syndicated *Column of the Americas* focused on issues of indigenous cultures and politics, human rights, and what he calls "anti-immigrant hysteria." In this column, he lashes out at attitudes and policies that treat a large segment of the population as somehow less than human. At the time he wrote, Congress was debating the Comprehensive Immigration Reform Act of 2006, which proposed, among other things, increased border security, a path to legal status for some long-term immigrants, and special visas for guest workers. (The bill did not pass.)

Look up the word *Mexican* or *Central American* in any US political diction- 1
ary and you will find these definitions:

> 1) people who are illegal, or are treated as such, no matter how long they've been living in this country; 2) the nation's number one threat to homeland security; 3) people who do the jobs no Americans want and who threaten the American Way of Life; 4) as a result of extremist politicians, the nation's favorite scapegoats; and 5) people, who due to vicious anti-immigrant hysteria, are prone to become Democrats.

By next year, there may be two new entries: 6) peoples who carry the border on their backs, and 7) peoples not afraid to stand up for their rights.

Who could have predicted that millions of peoples would be taking 2
to the streets nationwide to protest draconian immigration bills that call for the building of Berlin-style walls, more migra,[1] massive repatriations, the criminalization of human beings and the creation of a new anti-family apartheid-style Bracero[2] or Guest Worker program? Beyond the bills, the protests are actually about asserting the right—virtually a cry—to be treated as full human beings.

How long was this community supposed to remain in silence? 3
Perhaps it is racial/cultural fatigue. 4
Let's not pretend that this hysteria is not about race, color and dehu- 5
manization. It's not even anti-immigrant or even anti-Latino/Hispanic bigotry. It's the exploitation of a deep-seated fear and loathing of Mexicans and Central Americans by shameless politicians. Why? Because of

---

[1] Mexican shorthand for *policía de inmigración*, meaning "immigration police," or border patrol. [Editors' note.]

[2] Spanish, meaning "farmer" or "migrant laborer." [Editors' note.]

what our color represents. Otherwise, how and why do government agents single us out at lines, borders and internal checkpoints? Otherwise, why do dragnet immigrant raids always target brown peoples? Why is all the hate and vilification directed at brown peoples and the southern border? Otherwise, why are these politicians also not bothered by the millions of Canadians, Europeans or Russians who overstay their visas? (No one should hate them either.)

Just what does brown represent in this country? Shall we delude our-   6
selves like the Census Bureau and pretend that we're actually White?

Or should we simply stop speaking our languages, stop eating our   7
own foods . . . and stop identifying with our home countries of Mexico, El Salvador, Guatemala, Peru, Colombia, et cetera? In other words, we're OK if we stop being who we are—if we culturally deport ourselves and conduct auto–ethnic cleansing campaigns (we're also OK if we fight their illegal permanent wars).

And yet, there's that small matter of our red-brown skin. Just what could   8
it possibly represent? A reminder? Memory? Might it be our thousands-of-years-old indigenous cultures—the ones that were supposedly obliter-ated—the ones we were supposed to reject?

We deny the nopal[3] no longer. We know full well we're not on foreign   9
soil, but on Indian lands. (Were we supposed to forget that too?) So there's no going back. If anything, we are back. The whole continent, the whole earth—which our ancestors have traversed for thousands of years—is our mother. Meanwhile, we watch Congress and the president do a dance about not pardoning or not granting amnesty to those who've been remanded to live in shadows. Sinverguenzas![4] Just who precisely needs to be pardoned? Those who are exploited and who've been here forever? Or those who've been complicit in our dehumanization?

Through all this, we've been baited into fighting with African Ameri-   10
cans, American Indians, Asians, Mexican Americans, and poor and white middle-class workers—because Mexicans supposedly steal their jobs and are ruining the quality of life.

The truth is, American Indians, African Americans and Asians should   11
be at the head of our protests—for it is they and their struggles against

---

[3] Literally a prickly pear cactus, a *nopal* is a symbol of traditional Mexican culture as well as Mexican slang for someone who rejects that culture. The word is short-hand for the saying "tienes un nopal en la frente," or "you have a cactus on your forehead"—a metaphoric observation that a person is clearly of Mexican heritage. [Editors' note.]

[4] Spanish, meaning "Scoundrels!" [Editors' note.]

dehumanization that we draw inspiration from. But in the end, it is those who allow extremists to speak in their name, who must also step forward and tell their representatives that a society divided into legal and illegal human beings is no longer acceptable.

Every cell in our bodies tells us this. And the unprecedented protests have created the consciousness that a two-tiered society—the definition of apartheid—is intolerable.   12

A flawed bill will pass—many bills will pass—yet some sectors of the population will continue to view and treat Mexicans/Central Americans as illegal, unwanted and subhuman.   13

But enough. Ya Basta! IKUALI![5] As is said at the rallies: Nosotros no somos ilegales ni inmigrantes. Somos de este continente.[6] We are neither illegal nor even immigrants. Tojuan Titehuaxkalo Panin Pacha Mama.[7]   14

Meaning

1. What does Rodríguez mean by "the border on our backs" (title)? To what is he **alluding** with this phrase?

2. Does this essay have a thesis? Where does Rodríguez stand on the issue of immigration reform? For instance, does he insist on amnesty for illegal immigrants, demand tighter borders, seek protections for migrant workers, or plead for equal rights for all? Where does he make his position clear?

3. Why does the author bring up the Berlin Wall in paragraph 2? Where else in the essay does he mention political divides in other parts of the world? What does he seem to be suggesting with these examples?

4. "We know full well we're not on foreign soil, but on Indian lands," Rodríguez writes in paragraph 9. What does he mean? What point is he making?

5. What groups does Rodríguez look to as models for immigrants from Mexico and Central America? Why? What does he think "brown peoples" (paragraph 5) can learn from these groups?

---

[5] Spanish and Nahuatl (Aztec), respectively, both meaning "Enough!" [Editors' note.]

[6] Spanish: "We are neither illegal nor even immigrants. We are from this continent." [Editors' note.]

[7] Nahuatl (Aztec) proverbial expression, meaning roughly "We are of this earth." [Editors' note.]

6. Some of the following words may be new to you. Try to guess their meanings from the context of the essay. Test your guesses in a dictionary, and then use each new word in a sentence of your own.

scapegoats (1)	exploitation (5)	amnesty (9)
prone (1)	vilification (5)	remanded (9)
draconian (2)	indigenous (8)	complicit (9)
repatriations (2)	obliterated (8)	
apartheid (2)	traversed (9)	

Purpose and Audience

1. What do you think inspired Rodríguez to write this essay for his nationally syndicated newspaper column? Is he simply expressing his frustration? What else might he be trying to accomplish? What evidence from the text supports your opinion?

2. What effect does Rodríguez achieve with the frequent use of *we, us,* and *our,* as in "we're OK if we stop being who we are—if we culturally deport ourselves" (paragraph 7)? What does this **point of view** suggest about his vision of his readers?

3. Rodríguez poses several questions in this essay, such as "How long was this community supposed to remain in silence?" (paragraph 3) and "Just what does brown represent in this country?" (6). What is the purpose of such questions?

Method and Structure

1. Does Rodríguez rely mainly on emotional appeal or logical reasoning? Does he offer sufficient evidence for his claims, in your view?

2. Against whom or what is Rodríguez arguing in this essay? How does he characterize his opponents? Do the characterizations seem fair?

3. Rodríguez suggests that objections to immigration are based on faulty reasoning. What logical fallacies does he implicitly or explicitly identify? Does Rodríguez lapse into any fallacies himself? If so, where?

4. **OTHER METHODS** Rodríguez opens the essay with seven **definitions** (Chapter 12) of *Mexican* and *Central American.* What purpose do these definitions serve? Does he intend for readers to take them literally? How can you tell?

Language

1. How would you characterize the tone of this essay? How does it affect you as a reader?

2. Rodríguez uses some strong words, such as *dehumanization* (paragraphs 5, 9, 11), *criminalization* (2), and *exploitation* (5) to make his argument. What similar words capture your notice? What is the effect of such language?

3. Since he writes in English, Rodríguez is presumably addressing English-speaking readers. Why, then, does he occasionally use Spanish and Nahuatl words and phrases (such as *migra*, paragraph 2, and *ikuali*, 14) without translating them? What do these languages contribute to the essay?

Writing Topics

1. JOURNAL TO ESSAY   Rodríguez writes about racial prejudices that frustrate him, and in your journal entry (p. 374) you recorded a personal experience of being prejudged for your membership in a group. Now write an essay in which you recount this experience in more detail. How were you perceived, and by whom? What about this perception was accurate? What was unfair? How did the experience affect you? Write for a reader who is not a member of the group in question, being sure to include enough detail to bring the experience to life.

2. Think of an issue you feel strongly about, with no hesitation about your point of view being the right one. Write an essay, based largely on emotional appeal, in which you argue your point of view on that issue and state as your thesis the action you think should be taken. Remember that *emotional* does not mean *irrational*: your reasoning must be sound even when you rely on readers' feelings and beliefs, and your appeal must be appropriate to the subject and to the argument (see pp. 328–29).

3. CULTURAL CONSIDERATIONS   In paragraph 7, Rodríguez asks if Mexicans and Central Americans in the United States should "simply stop speaking our languages, stop eating our own foods . . . and stop identifying with our home countries." What do you think is his answer? Write an essay that identifies and analyzes Rodríguez's position on the issue of cultural assimilation of immigrants to the United States, paying close attention to each of his examples and explaining how he reaches his conclusions.

4. CONNECTIONS   Rodríguez, like Marie Myung-Ok Lee in "I Was an Anchor Baby" (p. 368), argues in favor of immigration and against those who would restrict it. Both Rodríguez and Lee take the issue personally, but where Lee calmly notes the "peculiar intent" of immigration laws and the impact they had on her Korean family, Rodríguez angrily emphasizes the "racial/cultural fatigue" and hostility toward Latinos implicit in such laws. George F. Will, in contrast, takes a distinctly academic, theoretical perspective to the issue in "Subject to Interpretation" (p. 362),

hoping to "drain some scalding steam" from a very heated debate. Which writer's approach to argument in general do you find most effective, and why? Drawing on the three essays in this casebook for examples, write an essay that evaluates the respective roles of *ethos*, *logos*, and *pathos* in argument.

WRITING WITH THE METHOD

▶

ARGUMENT AND PERSUASION

Choose one of the following statements, or any other statement they suggest, and support or refute it in an argumentative essay. The statement you decide on should concern a topic you care about so that argument is a means of convincing readers to accept an idea, not an end in itself.

Popular Culture

1. Reality television has a negative influence on society.
2. Targeted online advertising benefits individual consumers.
3. Web sites encouraging anorexia or similar pathologies should be shut down.
4. Football should be banned.
5. The inhumane treatment of circus animals must be stopped.

Health and Technology

6. American health care should be reformed to a single-payer system like that in Canada or Europe.
7. Terminally ill people should have the right to choose when to die.
8. Private automobiles should be restricted in cities.
9. Texting while driving should be illegal in every state.

Education

10. Students caught in any form of academic cheating should be expelled.
11. Public universities should offer free tuition for in-state students.
12. Like high school textbooks, college textbooks should be purchased by the school and loaned to students for the duration of a course.
13. College is not for everyone.

Social and Political Issues

14. Corporate executives are overpaid.
15. Feminism is dead.
16. Police officers who harm civilians should be held accountable for their actions.
17. Public libraries should provide free, unlimited access to the Internet.
18. Women in the military should be allowed to fight on the front lines.
19. When adopted children turn eighteen, they should have free access to information about their birth parents.

WRITING ABOUT THE THEME

▶

DISCUSSING SOCIAL ISSUES

1. Several of the essays in this chapter discuss issues concerning young adults, yet the authors write from very different perspectives and with widely varied purposes. Jenny Price (p. 335), for instance, reminds readers that college neighborhoods are not immune to gun violence. Anna Quindlen (p. 343) takes an earnest tone in urging authority figures to do more to protect teenagers from harm, while teen offender Charlie Spence (p. 349) asks, "At what point do we brand a person for life for the worst thing he or she did as a child?" And Sherry Turkle (p. 356) expresses concern that young people expose too much of themselves online while neglecting their civic responsibilities. Think of a risky or illegal behavior typical of teenagers or young adults, and write an essay that argues your position on how authorities should respond to it. For instance, you might write about tagging, reckless driving, binge drinking, or pirating media. How harshly should such behavior be punished, if at all? In your essay, be sure to consider the potential consequences of both the behavior and the response and to support your opinion with plenty of evidence.

2. Many of the authors in this chapter disagree on the success and failure of incarceration in American society. Martin Luther King, Jr. (p. 335), advocating civil disobedience from his prison cell, suggests that incarceration is often unjust. Charlie Spence argues that lifelong prison terms for juvenile offenders are unreasonable, and Sherry Turkle likens Web users monitoring their own behaviors online to inmates keeping themselves in check under the watch of a prison guard. Write an essay in which you defend or propose a reform to the American penal system. Choose a prison program or policy that doesn't work, and explain what should change, how that change should be effected, and what the outcome might be if your reform were put into effect. (If you don't see a need for reform, write an essay explaining why reform advocates such as Spence and King are wrong to seek a change.)

3. The last three essays in this chapter tackle issues surrounding immigration. George F. Will (p. 362) argues that children born to immigrants do not have an inherent right to American citizenship, Marie Myung-Ok Lee (p. 368) asserts that merely having a child born in the United States does nothing to benefit immigrant parents' legal status, and Roberto Rodríguez (p. 374) denounces efforts at restricting immigration as morally wrong. Write an essay in which you establish your own position on the debate over immigra-

tion reform. Do you agree with Rodríguez that attempts to control American borders are racist and imperial, for instance, or do you take George F. Will's view that restricting immigration is necessary and right? Or does your opinion, like Marie Myung-Ok Lee's, fall somewhere between the two extremes? You may want to think broadly about the issue to start, but bring your essay down to earth by focusing on a specific aspect of immigration reform — quotas, amnesty, birthright citizenship, work visas, border security, and so forth — and be careful to support your argument with ample evidence and clear reasoning to explain the rationale for your position.

APPENDIX
WORKING WITH SOURCES

▶

Writing is a means of communicating, a conversation between writers and readers—and between writers and other writers. Finding out what others have said about a subject, or looking for information to support and develop your thesis, is a natural part of the composing process.

A **source** is any work that you draw on for ideas or evidence in the course of writing an essay or research paper. Whether you are analyzing or responding to an essay in this book or using research to support your interpretation of a subject, the guidelines in this appendix will help you to use the work of others effectively in your own writing.

Writing about Readings

Many of the assignments that follow the readings in this book ask you to respond directly to an essay or to write about it in relation to one or more other essays—to analyze two writers' approaches, to compare several writers' ideas about a subject, or to use the ideas in one reading to investigate the meanings of another. The same will be true of much writing you do throughout college, whether you are examining literary works, psychological theories, business case studies, historical documents, or lesson plans.

In some academic writing, you'll be able to use an idea in a selection as a springboard for an essay about your own opinions or experiences, as Nicole Lang does in "Foundations" (p. 56), her response to Edward P. Jones's "Shacks" (p. 9). However, when academic writing requires you to write *about* one or more readings, you will analyze the material (see Chapter 1) and synthesize, or recombine, the elements of that analysis to form an original idea of your own (see pp. 389–92). Your goal is to think critically about what other writers have said and to reach your own conclusions.

When writing about reading, refer to the writer's ideas directly and cite evidence from the text to support your conclusions; the questions that follow each selection in this book can help to guide your analysis. Use summary, paraphrase, and quotation (see pp. 389–91) to give readers a sense of the work, a clear picture of the elements that you are responding to, and a measured understanding of how those elements contribute to your thesis.

Using Research to Support a Thesis

Often, when you draft an essay, you'll discover that you need more information to clarify part of your subject or to develop a few of your points more fully—when you need several examples to develop your draft, when you are troubled by conflicting assertions in essays you're comparing, or when you want expert opinion or facts to support your argument, perhaps. A little outside material can contribute compelling and informative support for an essay.

Sometimes, however, you'll need to do more extensive research. Some of the writing suggestions in this book, for instance, ask you to conduct focused, short-term research in service of exploring ideas for a brief essay. Other times, you may need to look up information to guide your analysis of a work or gather supporting evidence for an argument. And sometimes, you will be assigned a full-scale research paper that involves finding and using multiple sources to develop and support an original thesis.

No matter the scale of a writing project, research takes time and requires careful thought. This section explains the basics of researching sources and using what you find responsibly and correctly.

▶ Asking Questions

Researching a topic provides an opportunity for you to build knowledge and to think critically about what you learn. The effort will be more productive if you start your search with a specific question (or questions) in mind. Such questions might be provided for you—as is the case with the research questions that follow many of the readings in this book—or you may need to ask them on your own. In that case, think about what interests or puzzles you about a subject. What do you know about it? What don't you know? What bothers you, confuses you, or intrigues you? Do you sense a problem in need of a solution, a source of disagreement among some writers, a desire for more information?

The techniques for generating ideas and for narrowing a topic discussed on pages 18–24 and 29–30 can help you develop fruitful research questions. Whatever questions occur to you, focus on those you care about most, because you will spend significant time and effort exploring them.

▶ Finding Sources

Once you have a question in mind, you have two basic options for locating material that can help you answer it: the library and the Internet. Although both can be good sources of information, usually you will find that printed sources and information located through a library's electronic research portals (such as subject directories and databases) are more trustworthy. Library resources are more likely to have gone through an editorial review process to ensure the information is accurate, reliable, and accepted by experts in the field.

When you're looking for sources, never be shy about asking librarians for help, but make a point of familiarizing yourself with the most useful research tools.

- *Library catalogs* offer a comprehensive listing of the printed materials (books, magazines, newspapers, reference works, and the like) housed in a library. Most catalogs are computerized, which means you can plug in a search term—subject keyword, author, or title, for instance—and pull up a list of what the library has. Many colleges also let you search the holdings of related libraries and arrange for interlibrary loans (allow plenty of time to arrange for transfers).

- *Periodical indexes* provide listings of the articles in thousands of magazines, scholarly journals, and newspapers. Electronic subscription services, such as EBSCO and ProQuest, often provide full-text copies of some of the articles located in a search; other times, you will need to use the information listed in the citation to track down the relevant issue on the library shelves.

- *Subject directories* organize material on the Web into categories. Although the open Internet can be less reliable than the library, a good directory is a helpful starting point because it can show the broad dimensions of a subject and lead to questions worth asking. The best are those compiled by librarians, particularly *ipl2.org* and directories created for individual colleges (check your library's home page).

- *Online search engines*, such as *Google* and *Bing*, can help to locate information unavailable anywhere else—some government reports, for instance, many Web-only publications, current data from research groups. Navigating the Internet effectively, however, takes effort. A single word plugged into a search box can easily bring up millions of results, with no indication of which ones are worthy of your time. To get the most out of a Web search, experiment with multiple keywords and use advanced search features to focus your hunt, narrowing results by kind of document (images, news, and so on), by type of site (government, educational, or commercial, for instance), by date, and by other parameters offered by the search engine. The more detailed the search terms, the more productive the results.

- *Wikis*, such as *Wikipedia* and *SourceWatch*, are collaborative documents hosted online; generally they are written by anonymous users and can be edited by anyone with an Internet connection and an opinion. You should never use a wiki as a source for a research paper: a post can look very different from day to day, and even hour to hour, making the information unpredictable and unreliable. All the same, *Wikipedia* can be a useful tool. Frequently it is a good place to start if you are generating ideas and looking for topics to explore. *Wikipedia* articles also tend to list sources at the bottom; those links are generally reliable (although you should judge for yourself) and could serve as valuable starting points for more involved research.

▶ Evaluating Sources

When you read a written work for an assignment, you read it critically, considering the author's intentions and analyzing the use of evidence (see Chapter 1). The same is true when you use sources to build and support your ideas. Drawing on reliable information and balancing varied opinions strengthens your essay.

Critical thinking becomes especially important when you are doing research. A quick search online, for instance, might bring up useful articles from quality publications, but it might also bring up personal blogs filled with unproven opinions, political arguments using fabricated statistics, stealth marketing sites that skew information to promote a product, and many other types of misinformation. Being able to determine what is credible or trustworthy thus becomes much more difficult and much more important.

You need not read everything you find closely. Instead, scan potential sources to see how well each one satisfies the following criteria:

- *Is the source relevant?* Keep your question in mind as you research, and use it to help you focus on sources that are directly related to your subject. If you are writing about the treatment of animals in the circus, for instance, your readers are not going to find information from an article on zoos convincing. With so many sources available, you can afford to be selective.

- *Are you looking at a primary or a secondary source?* A primary source is an original document written by a creator or an eyewitness — for instance, a personal essay, a short story, a lab report, a speech delivered at an event. A secondary source is a writer's interpretation of a primary source or sources — a movie review, a summary of recent scientific discoveries, a historian's explanation of an event. While secondary sources can be very helpful in obtaining factual data and general overviews of a subject, primary sources usually provide more valuable evidence for analysis.

- *How current is the information?* In most cases, the more recently your source was published or updated, the better. Know when a document was created, and consider how its age affects its usefulness for your purposes.

- *What is the author's purpose?* Consider, for instance, whether a source is meant to provide information, argue a point, support a political view, or sell a product. In books, the preface and table of contents will often provide clues to the author's intentions. When you're looking at a periodical or a Web site, scanning the titles of nearby articles or checking the "About" page can give you a sense of the purpose of the material.

- *Is the author reliable?* Determine not only who wrote the material but also the writer's qualifications for writing on the subject, and look for any potential biases — especially in the case of online sources. Be wary of writers who use inflammatory or sensationalist language, and notice how the author uses evidence: reliable writers provide detailed support for their ideas, distinguish between facts and opinions, acknowledge opposing viewpoints, and cite their sources.

Once you've determined that a source is worth using, the checklist for critical reading on page 8 can help you to examine it more closely.

Synthesizing Source Material

When you bring information and ideas from outside sources into your writing, your goal is to develop and support an argument of your own making, not to report on what others have written. Always strive to maintain your voice. It can be tempting to string together facts and quotations from your sources and to think that they speak for themselves—or for you—but your own argument should always be the main event. Aim instead for **synthesis**, weaving the elements into a new whole: gather related information and ideas from your sources, and summarize, paraphrase, and quote them to support your thesis.

▶ Summarizing

A **summary** is a condensed statement, *in your own words*, of the main meaning of a work. Summaries omit supporting details and examples to focus on the original author's thesis. You can find short summaries of essays throughout this book in the sections "A Note on Thematic Connections," which appear in Chapters 5–14. For example:

> Langston Hughes pinpoints the moment during a church revival when he lost his faith (76–78).

> Perri Klass's essay grapples with why doctors use peculiar and often cruel jargon and contemplates how it affects them (139–42).

Notice that each summary names the author of the work being summarized and provides page numbers; it also refrains from using any of the original authors' language.

Summarizing is one of the most effective ways to bring the ideas of others into your writing without losing your voice or bogging down your essay with unnecessary details. Depending on the length of the original work and your reasons for using it, your summary might be a single sentence or a paragraph; keep it as short as possible—generally no longer than 10% of the original. If you're responding to a short essay, for example, a handful of sentences will usually be enough to express its meaning.

▶ Paraphrasing

A **paraphrase** is a restatement, again *in your own words*, of a short passage from another writer's work. While summarizing makes it possible to explain someone else's main idea without repeating specifics, paraphrasing lets you incorporate important details that support your own main idea.

A paraphrase is about the same length as the original, but it does not use any of the other writer's unique words, phrasings, or sentence structures. Simply replacing a few words with synonyms won't suffice; in fact, that shortcut counts as plagiarism (see pp. 393–94). If you cannot avoid using some of the writer's language, put it in quotation marks:

> ORIGINAL PASSAGE   "Poverty is defined, in my system, by people not being able to cover the basic necessities in their lives. Indispensable medical care, nutrition, a place to live: all these essentials, for poor people, are often and classically beyond reach. If a poor person needs $10 a day to make ends meet, often he or she only makes eight and a half."
>
> —Walter Mosley, "Show Me the Money," p. 6.

> PARAPHRASE   As Walter Mosley sees it, poverty is a matter of inadequate resources. The poor have difficulty obtaining adequate health care, food, and shelter—things most of us take for granted—not because they have no income at all, but because the money they earn is not enough to cover these basic expenses (6).

> ORIGINAL PASSAGE   "Wealth, in my definition, is when money is no longer an issue or a question. Wealthy people don't know how much money they have or how much they make. Their worth is gauged in property, natural resources, and power, in doors they can go through and the way the law works."
>
> —Walter Mosley, "Show Me the Money," p. 6.

> PARAPHRASE   Wealth, in contrast, is defined by freedom. The rich don't have to worry about finances; indeed, their "property, natural resources, and power" confer social and legal privileges far more significant than freely available cash (Mosley 6).

Notice here, too, that a paraphrase identifies the original source and provides a page number. Even if the words are your own, the ideas are someone else's, and so they must be credited.

▶ Quoting

Sometimes a writer's or speaker's exact words will be so well phrased or so important to your own meaning that you will want to quote them. When you are responding to or analyzing passages in a written work, such as an essay or a novel, direct **quotations** will be essential evidence as you develop your points. Even when you are borrowing ideas from other writers, however, quoting can be useful if the author's original wording makes a strong impression that you want to share with your readers.

Be sparing in your use of quotations. Limit yourself to those lines you're analyzing or responding to directly and perhaps a handful of choice passages that would lose their punch or meaning if you paraphrased them. Quoting others too often will make you vanish as a writer, leaving your readers wondering what *you* have to say and why they should care.

When you do use a quotation, be careful to copy the original words and punctuation exactly and to identify clearly the boundaries and source of the quotation:

- *Put quotation marks around all quoted material shorter than four typed lines.*

- *Use block quotations for quoted passages longer than four typed lines.* Introduce the quotation with a complete sentence followed by a colon, start the quotation on a new line, and indent the whole passage ten spaces or one inch. Don't use quotation marks; the indention shows that the material is quoted.

- *Cite the source of the quotation, giving a page number as well as the author's name* (see pp. 395–98). For short quotations, place a parenthetical citation after the final quotation mark and before the period. For block quotations, place a parenthetical citation after the final period.

You can make changes in quotations so that they fit the flow of your own sentences—say, by deleting a word or sentence that is not relevant to your purpose or by inserting a word or punctuation mark to clarify meaning. However, such changes must be obvious.

- Use an *ellipsis mark*, or three spaced periods (. . .), to show a deletion:

  > Stewart and Elizabeth Ewen have suggested that "for hardworking, ill-housed immigrants, . . . clothing offered one of the few avenues by which people could assume a sense of belonging" (156).

- Use *brackets* ([ ]) around any change or addition you make:

  > Most fashion historians echo Thorstein Veblen's assertion that "members of each [social] stratum accept as their ideal of decency the scheme of life in vogue in the next higher stratum" (84).

For examples of the use and formatting of quotations, see the sample research paper by Jarrod Ballo (p. 407).

▶ Integrating

When you incorporate material from outside sources, make a point to introduce every summary, paraphrase, or quotation and to specify why it's relevant to your thesis. At the same time, make it clear where your thoughts end and someone else's thoughts begin. Three techniques are especially helpful in giving your readers the necessary guidance.

■ *Use signal phrases to introduce summaries, paraphrases, and quotations.* A signal phrase names the author of the borrowed material and thus provides a transition between your idea and someone else's. If the information is relevant, you might also explain why the author is an authoritative source or name the article or book you're referring to. Here are some examples of signal phrases:

> As neurologist Oliver Sacks points out in his book *The Mind's Eye*, . . .
>
> US Census Bureau data reveal . . .
>
> Not everyone agrees. Pat Mora, for example, insists that . . .
>
> In his trial summation, Darrow argued that nobody has control over his or her fate: . . .

Note that a signal phrase followed by a colon must be a complete sentence (see p. 43). Be careful, as well, to craft each signal phrase to reflect your reasons for including a source. Using the same phrase over and over (such as "According to _____") will frustrate your readers.

■ *Generally, mark the end of borrowed material with a parenthetical citation identifying at least the page number of your source* (see pp. 395–98). In most cases, the citation is required—an exception would be a source lacking page or other reference numbers—and it makes clear that you've finished with the source and are returning to your own argument.

■ *Follow up with a brief explanation of how the material supports your point.* To show that the borrowed material backs up your ideas, comment afterward on what it contributes to your essay. You might, for example, comment on the meaning of the borrowed material, dispute it, or summarize it in the context of a new idea. Such follow-ups are especially necessary after block quotations.

For examples of effective integration of source materials, see Jarrod Ballo's sample researched essay (p. 407).

Avoiding Plagiarism

Claiming credit for writing that you didn't compose yourself is considered **plagiarism**, a form of academic dishonesty that can carry serious consequences. Buying an essay online and submitting it as your own, copying a friend's essay and submitting it as your own, or copying just a sentence from a source and including it as your own—these are the most obvious forms of plagiarism. But plagiarism is often unintentional, caused not by deliberate cheating but by misunderstanding or sloppiness. Be aware of the rules and responsibilities that come with using the work of others in your writing.

- *Take careful notes.* No matter what your system for researching—formal note cards, dedicated notebooks, photocopies, electronic files—thorough and accurate records are essential. It's all too easy to forget, when you return to your notes, which words are your own and which ones are borrowed. If you copy down the exact words of a source, enclose them in quotation marks and make note of the source. If you paraphrase or summarize, make a note that the language is your own, and double-check that you haven't picked up any of the original phrasing. Always record full source information for any material you find, using the models on pages 398–405.

- *Use electronic sources with care.* Just because something appears on the Internet doesn't mean you're free to use it however you wish. Any language or idea you find, regardless of where you find it, must be credited to its source. Resist the urge to cut and paste snippets from online sources directly into your working draft: later on you won't be able to distinguish the borrowed text from your own words. Print electronic documents for your records, or save them as clearly labeled individual files.

- *Know the definition of* common knowledge. *Common knowledge* is information that is so widely known or broadly accepted that it can't be traced to a particular writer. Facts that you can find in multiple sources—the date of a historic event, the population of a major city—do not need to be credited as long as you state them in your own words. In contrast, original material that can be traced to a particular person—the lyrics to a song, an article on the Web—must be cited even if it has been distributed widely. Note that even if a piece of information is common knowledge, the wording of that information is not: put it in your own words.

■ *Never include someone else's ideas in your writing without identifying the borrowed material and acknowledging its source.* Whether you quote directly or rephrase information in your own words, you must make it clear to readers when ideas are not your own. If you use another writer's exact words, enclose them in quotation marks and identify the source. If you summarize or paraphrase, clearly distinguish your ideas from the source author's with a signal phrase and a source citation. Then, at the end of your paper, list all your sources in a works-cited list. (See the next section, "Documenting Sources in MLA Style.")

When in doubt, err on the side of caution. It's better to have too much documentation in your essay than not enough.

Documenting Sources in MLA Style

The purpose of citing your sources is twofold: you acknowledge the sources that helped you, and you enable curious readers to verify your information by looking it up themselves.

In English classes, and in some other humanities as well, you will be expected to document your sources with the system outlined by the Modern Language Association in *MLA Handbook for Writers of Research Papers* (7th ed., 2009). MLA style calls for a parenthetical citation for each use of a source within the body of the essay combined with a comprehensive list of works cited at the end. The two elements work together: the citation in the text identifies the source as briefly and unobtrusively as possible, referring readers to the works-cited entry for complete publication information.

PARENTHETICAL TEXT CITATION

In the essay "The Box Man," Barbara Lazear Ascher says that a homeless man who has chosen solitude can show the rest of us how to "find . . . a friend in our own voice" (262).

ENTRY IN LIST OF WORKS CITED

Ascher, Barbara Lazear. "The Box Man." *The Compact Reader: Short Essays by Method and Theme*. Ed. Jane E. Aaron and Ellen Kuhl Repetto. 10th ed. Boston: Bedford, 2016. 258-62. Print.

▶ In-Text Citations

Citations within the body of your essay include just enough information for readers to recognize the boundaries of borrowed material and to locate the full citation in the list of works cited. Generally, they name the author of a source and the page number on which you found the information or idea cited.

Keep in-text citations unobtrusive by making them as brief as possible without sacrificing necessary information. The best way to do this is to name the author of the source in a signal phrase, limiting the parenthetical information to the page number. Otherwise, include the author's name in the parenthetical citation.

AUTHOR NAMED IN THE TEXT

Historian Thomas French notes that Mount Auburn Cemetery was a popular leisure destination for city residents (37).

AUTHOR NOT NAMED IN THE TEXT

Mount Auburn Cemetery was a popular leisure destination for city residents (French 37).

A work by multiple authors

If a source has two or three authors, list all of their names.

Some of the most successful organized tours in New York bring visitors on guided walks or bus rides to locations featured in television shows (Espinosa and Herbst 228).

In the case of four or more authors, you may list all of the names or shorten the reference by naming the first author and following with et al. (short for *et alii*, Latin for "and others"). Whichever option you choose, use the same format for your works-cited list. (See p. 399.)

As early as 1988, scholars cautioned against educators' dependence on computers, warning that technology is "accompanied by rapid change, instability, and general feelings of insecurity and isolation" (Ferrante, Hayman, Carlson, and Phillips 1).

As early as 1988, scholars cautioned against educators' dependence on computers, warning that technology is "accompanied by rapid change, instability, and general feelings of insecurity and isolation" (Ferrante et al. 1).

A work by a corporate or government author

For works written in the name of an organization, company, or government that doesn't list individual authors, treat the name of the group as the author.

> Progressive neurological disorders damage the body in repeated but unpredictable intervals, forcing patients to adapt to new losses several times over (National Multiple Sclerosis Society 2).

Two or more works by the same author(s)

If your essay cites more than one work by the same author(s), include the title of the specific source within each citation. In the following examples, both works are by Maura Fredey, who is named in the text.

> Maura Fredey notes that most of the nurses at the Boston Home have been on staff for more than five years, and at least seven boast a quarter century or more of service ("21st Century" 26).

> The home's high level of care includes not only medical, dental, and vision treatments, says Fredey, but also round-the-clock nursing attention and extensive social and rehabilitative services ("Bridges" 13).

If the title is long, you may shorten it. (The complete titles for the articles cited above are "The 21st Century Home: How Technology Is Helping to Improve the Lives of Patients at the Boston Home" and "Bridges to Care: The Boston Home Reaches Out").

An anonymous work

If no author is named, include the title within the parentheses. You may shorten the title if it is long.

> The population of Pass Christian, Mississippi, is less than a third of what it was before Hurricane Katrina ("A New Town Crier" 22).

An indirect source

Use the abbreviation qtd. in (for "quoted in") to indicate that you did not consult the source directly but found it quoted in another source.

> As psychologist Robert Sternberg has pointed out, a high IQ does not guarantee success. Just as important is "knowing what to say to whom,

knowing when to say it, and knowing how to say it for maximum effect"
(qtd. in Gladwell 101).

A literary work

For a novel, list the part or chapter cited in addition to the page number; this helps readers locate the quotation in an edition different from the one you consulted.

> The newspaper reporters investigating the death of Mary Dalton in Richard Wright's *Native Son* are quick to recognize the similarities between her murder and that of Bobby Franks fifteen years earlier: "This is better than Loeb and Leopold," one of them remarks enthusiastically (214; bk. 2).

If a verse play (such as a work by William Shakespeare) is divided into parts, cite any part, act, scene, and line numbers, leaving out page numbers. For a prose play (such as Henrik Ibsen's *A Doll's House*), include the page number or numbers and a semicolon before the rest of the citation.

> In Shakespeare's *The Tragedy of Macbeth*, a trio of witches famously chants, "Double, double toil and trouble; / Fire burn, and caldron bubble" (4.1.12-13).

> A fight over money in the opening scene of Ibsen's *A Doll's House* reveals immediately that Nora and Torvald Helmer struggle for power in their marriage (7-12; act 1).

Cite the line numbers of a poem instead of pages. Include the word line or lines in the first citation; omit it in later references.

> Robert Frost's "Design" contrasts the deadliness of "a dimpled spider, fat and white" (line 1) with the curative powers of a "flower like froth" (7).

An electronic source

Treat most electronic sources as you would any other source—cite the author's name if it is available, or cite the title if no author is named. For electronic sources that number paragraphs instead of pages, insert a comma between the author's name and the abbreviation par. (for "paragraph"). If neither pages nor paragraphs are numbered, include the author's name only.

> At the time *Dr. Strangelove* was released, filmmakers had begun to believe that fictional portrayals of nuclear war were actually "contributing to the nuclear threat" by instilling fear in American audiences (Abbot, par. 35).

One teacher who successfully brought computers into his classroom argues that to use new technologies effectively, teachers need to become "side-by-side learners" with their students (Rogers).

▶ List of Works Cited

The works-cited list provides complete publication information for every source you refer to within your essay. Format the list as follows:

- Start the list on a new page following the conclusion to your essay.
- Center the title Works Cited at the top of the page.
- Double-space everything in the list.
- Alphabetize the entries by authors' last names. If a work doesn't have a listed author, alphabetize by title, ignoring the initial words *A*, *An*, and *The*.
- For each entry, align the first line with the left margin and indent subsequent lines five spaces or one-half inch.

The elements of individual entries will vary somewhat, as shown in the models in this section. The basic content and formatting rules, however, can be summarized in a few general guidelines:

- Start with the author's last name, followed by a comma and the author's first name. (For more than one author, list the names as they appear in the work, reversing only the first author's name.)
- Provide the full title of the work, with all major words capitalized. Italicize the titles of books, periodicals, whole Web sites, and longer creative works such as plays or television series; put quotation marks around the titles of book chapters, periodical articles, pages on Web sites, and short creative works such as stories, poems, and song titles.
- Include complete publication information. At a minimum this includes city of publication, publisher, and date (for books); date and inclusive page numbers (for periodicals); sponsor, date of publication, and access date (for Web sites); and medium of publication (Print, Web, Television, Radio, DVD, CD, Lecture, and so on).
- Separate the elements of an entry (author, title, publication information) with periods.

MLA does not require URLs for Web sources, but your instructor might. If so, place the URL at the end of the entry, enclosed in angle brackets and followed by a period (see p. 403 for an example). If you must break a long URL to fit, break it only after a slash, and do not add a hyphen.

Print Books

A book by one author

Treuer, David. *Rez Life: An Indian's Journey through Reservation Life*. New York: Atlantic, 2012. Print.

A book by multiple authors

List all of the authors, or, if there are more than three, you may provide the first author's name followed by et al. (Latin abbreviation for *et alii*, "and others"). Whichever option you choose, use the same format for your in-text citations (see p. 395).

Cooper, Martha, and Joseph Sciorra. *R.I.P.: Memorial Wall Art*. London: Thames, 1994. Print.

Ferrante, Reynolds, John Hayman, Mary Susan Carlson, and Harry Phillips. *Planning for Microcomputers in Higher Education: Strategies for the Next Generation*. Washington: Assn. for Study of Higher Educ., 1988. Print.

Ferrante, Reynolds, et al. *Planning for Microcomputers in Higher Education: Strategies for the Next Generation*. Washington: Assn. for Study of Higher Educ., 1988. Print.

A book with an author and an editor

Cather, Willa. *My Antonia*. Ed. Guy Reynolds. Boston: Bedford, 2013. Print.

A book with a translator

Ovid. *Metamorphoses*. Trans. Z. Philip Ambrose. Newburyport: Focus, 2004. Print.

A book by a corporate or government author

For books written in the name of an organization, company, or government that doesn't list individual authors, treat the name of the group as the author.

United States. Dept. of Commerce. *Statistical Abstract of the United States: The National Data Book*. Blue Ridge Summit: Bernan, 2013. Print.

More than one work by the same author(s)

Roach, Mary. *Bonk: The Curious Coupling of Science and Sex*. New York: Norton, 2008.
    Print.

---. *Gulp: Adventures on the Alimentary Canal*. New York: Norton, 2013. Print.

Edition other than the first

Gonzales, Manuel G. *Mexicanos: A History of Mexicans in the United States*. 2nd ed.
    Bloomington: Indiana UP, 2009. Print.

An illustrated book or graphic narrative

For a book that contains both text and illustrations, begin the entry with
the name of the contributor whose work you are emphasizing (author,
editor, or illustrator), using the abbreviations illus. for illustrator and ed.
for editor. Treat a graphic narrative written and illustrated by the same
person as you would a book with one author.

Moser, Barry, illus. *Mark Twain's Book of Animals*. Ed. Shelley Fisher Fishkin. Berkeley:
    U of California P, 2010. Print.

Weaver, Lila Quintero. *Darkroom: A Memoir in Black and White*. Tuscaloosa: U of
    Alabama P, 2012. Print.

An anthology

Cite an entire anthology only when you are referring to the editor's
materials or cross-referencing multiple selections that appear within it.

Burns, Catherine, ed. *The Moth: Fifty True Stories*. New York: Hyperion, 2013. Print.

The next model shows how to combine a citation for an entire anthology
with cross-references.

A selection from an anthology

List the work under the selection author's name. Include the page numbers for the entire selection after the publication date.

Lee, Marie Myung-Ok. "I Was an Anchor Baby." *The Compact Reader: Short Essays by
    Method and Theme*. Ed. Jane E. Aaron and Ellen Kuhl Repetto. 10th ed. Boston:
    Bedford, 2016. 368-71. Print.

If you are citing two or more selections from the same anthology, you can
avoid unnecessary repetition by listing the anthology in its own entry

and cross-referencing it in the selection entries. Put each entry in its proper alphabetical place in the list of works cited, and include the medium of publication only in the anthology entry.

Aaron, Jane E., and Ellen Kuhl Repetto, eds. *The Compact Reader: Short Essays by Method and Theme*. 10th ed. Boston: Bedford, 2016. Print.

Chen, Ken. "City Out of Breath." Aaron and Repetto 108-13.

Thomas, Dana. "The Fake Trade." Aaron and Repetto 316-21.

A section of a book

When referring to only part of a book (such as an introduction, a fore-word, or a specific chapter), name the author and indicate the part of the book you are citing, with page numbers.

Kaling, Mindy. "Karaoke Etiquette." *Is Everyone Hanging Out without Me? (And Other Concerns)*. New York: Crown, 2011. 64-65. Print.

Schlosser, Eric. Foreword. *The Jungle*. By Upton Sinclair. New York: Penguin, 2006. vii-xv. Print.

A reference work

"Social Security." *The Encyclopedia Americana*. 2006 ed. Print.

Print or Online Journals, Magazines, and Newspapers

The formats for articles in journals, magazines, and newspapers are similar whether the publication appears only in print, appears in print with additional online content, or appears only online. The key differences are (1) the inclusive page numbers for print articles and some online journal articles; (2) the sponsor or publisher of the site for online magazine and newspaper content; and (3) the date you consulted any online source.

An article in a scholarly journal

Include the author's name, the article title, the volume and any issue number (separated by a period), the year, and the page numbers. If an online journal does not number pages, use n. pag. instead.

Mizzi, Shannon. "*Star Trek*'s Underappreciated Feminist History." *Wilson Quarterly* 38.1 (2014): n. pag. Web. 12 Dec. 2014.

Sewald, Ronda L. "Forced Listening: The Contested Use of Loudspeakers for Commercial and Political Messages in the Public Soundscape." *American Quarterly* 63.3 (2011): 761-80. Print.

An article in a magazine

If you consult an online magazine or newspaper, including one that also has a print version, provide the publisher's or sponsor's name between the periodical title and the publication date. Use N.p. if no publisher or sponsor is named.

Finnegan, William. "Dignity: Fast-Food Workers and a New Labor Movement." *New Yorker* 15 Sept. 2014: 70-79. Print.

Fuller, Alexandra. "In the Shadow of Wounded Knee." *National Geographic*. Natl. Geographic Soc., Aug. 2012. Web. 18 Sept. 2015.

Lamott, Anne. "A Slow Walk into the Amazing Now." *Salon*. Salon Media Group, 11 Nov. 2014. Web. 3 Feb. 2015.

Percy, Jen. "Love Crimes." *Harper's Magazine* Jan. 2015: 51-66. Print.

An article in a newspaper

Many print newspapers appear in more than one edition, so you need to specify which edition you used (late ed. in the model below). Give the section label as part of the page number when the newspaper does the same (A1 in the model). Otherwise, give the section after the edition (for example, natl. ed., sec. 3: 7). Cite an article that runs on nonconsecutive pages with the starting page number followed by a plus sign (+). For an article in an online newspaper, omit page numbers and add the site's sponsor or publisher and the date you accessed it.

Alvarez, Lizette. "Law Favoring Cuban Arrivals Is Challenged." *New York Times* 2 Feb. 2015, late ed.: A1+. Print.

Daum, Meghan. "I 'Like' Me, I Really 'Like' Me." *Los Angeles Times*. Los Angeles Times, 3 Jan. 2013. Web. 5 Feb. 2015.

A letter to the editor

Wing, Joseph. Letter. *Washington Post*, 13 Feb. 2012: A16. Print.

An unsigned article or editorial

"It's Simple: Break the Law, Pay the Price." Editorial. *Eagle-Tribune* 5 Feb. 2012: 8. Print.

"Teenagers' Argot: Purists May Disapprove, but Multi-Ethnic Dialects Are Spreading." *Economist.com*. Economist, 11 Feb. 2012. Web. 19 Oct. 2012.

An article in an online database

Cite a full-text source that you obtain through a database in much the same way as a print article, but instead of ending with Print as the medium, add the database name, the medium Web, and your access date.

Porco, Carolyn. "Adventures in Wonderland." *New Statesman* 19 Dec. 2011: 34-37.
    Academic Search Premier. Web. 17 Apr. 2015.

Other Online Sources

An entire Web site

Start with the author(s) or editor(s) of the site, followed by the site title in italics, the name of the sponsoring organization or publisher, the date of publication or most recent update, the medium, and the date you visited the site. If any of this information is unavailable, include as much as you can find. (Use N.p. if there is no publisher or sponsor and n.d. If there is no date.)

Carson, Clayborne, ed. *The King Papers Project*. The Martin Luther King, Jr., Research
    and Educ. Inst., Stanford U., n.d. Web. 19 Jan. 2015.
Songwriter's Resource Network. N.p., 2015. Web. 4 Apr. 2015.

A short work from a Web site

Include as much information from the entire Web site as you can find (see above), as well as a title for the work. If your instructor requires a URL, or if the page would be difficult to find without one, include it at the end of the entry, enclosed in angle brackets.

Dryden-Edwards, Roxanne. "Obsessive-Compulsive Disorder." *MedicineNet*. WebMD,
    21 Oct. 2014. Web. 4 May 2015.
Mikkelson, Barbara. "Organ Nicked: Vegetable." *Urban Legends Reference Pages*.
    Barbara and David P. Mikkelson, 30 June 2011. Web. 4 Nov. 2014. <http://
    www.snopes.com/horrors/robbery/kidney2.asp>.

A blog entry

Follow the preceding guidelines for a short work from a Web site. If an entry is not titled, use Online posting.

Hoke, Casey. "I'm a Transgendered Teen and Which Restroom I Use Is None of Your
    Business." *Huffington Post*. Huffington Post Media Group, 29 Jan. 2015. Web.
    2 Feb. 2015.

Rumpel Stiltskin. Online posting. *Huffington Post*. Huffington Post Media Group,
    29 Jan. 2015. Web. 2 Feb. 2015.

Audio and Visual Sources

A television or radio program

Provide as much of the following as available: episode or segment title,
program or series title, network, local station, broadcast date, and medium.
Include the name of the director (Dir.), performers (Perf.), narrator (Narr.),
or host (Host) if such information is significant.

"Call for Help." *This American Life*. Host Ira Glass. Natl. Public Radio. WBUR, Boston,
    9 May 2014. Radio.
How Sherlock Changed the World. Love Productions. PBS. 1 June 2014. Television.

A sound recording

Lorde. "Royals." *Pure Heroine*. Universal, 2013. MP3 file.
Zappa, Frank. *Ship Arriving Too Late to Save a Drowning Witch*. Barking Pumpkin,
    1982. LP.

A film, video, or DVD

Cain, Susan. "The Power of Introverts." *TED: Ideas Worth Spreading*. TED Conf., Feb.
    2012. Web. 19 Apr. 2015.
Donnie Darko. Dir. Richard Kelly. Perf. Jake Gyllenhaal, Jena Malone, Drew Barrymore,
    Noah Wyle, Patrick Swayze, and Mary McDonnell. 2001. 20th Cent. Fox, 2004.
    DVD.
International Forum on Globalization. "Greensumption." *YouTube*. YouTube, 24 May
    2007. Web. 18 Jan. 2015.

A photograph or other work of art

For original works viewed in person, provide the artistic medium and the
museum's or collection's name and location. For reproductions, omit the
artistic medium, indicate where the original is located, and provide complete publication information for the source, including a page number if
available.

Kandinsky, Wassily. *Improvisation No. 30 (Cannons)*. 1913. Oil on canvas. Art Inst. of
    Chicago.

Magritte, René. *The Human Condition II*. 1935. Coll. Madame E. Happé-Lorge, Brussels. *Surrealists and Surrealism*. Ed. Gaëtan Picon. New York: Rizzoli, 1983. 145. Print.

Riis, Jacob. *Nine Boys Waist Deep in Country Stream*. N.d. Prints and Photographs Div., Lib. of Cong. *Jacob A. Riis Papers*. Web. 25 May 2015.

An advertisement

Budweiser. Advertisement. NBC. WNKY, Bowling Green, 1 Feb. 2015. Television.

Spiriva. Advertisement. *Reader's Digest* Mar. 2012: 32-35. Print.

Other Sources

E-mail

Jones, Liza. "Re: Question about Group Homes." Message to the author. 9 May 2015. E-mail.

A personal interview

Conti, Regina. Personal interview. 3 Mar. 2015.

Sample Research Paper

The research paper presented here was written by Jarrod Ballo, a part-time student at Northern Essex Community College in Haverhill, Massachusetts. After reading Barbara Lazear Ascher's "The Box Man" (p. 258), he considered the writing topic labeled "Research" that follows it:

> If you live in or have visited an urban area, you have probably seen people sleeping in doorways or scavenging for food. And you have almost certainly seen homelessness and extreme poverty discussed in the news and depicted in the media. Research the problem of homelessness and any solutions that have been proposed or attempted, whether locally or on a national level. Then, considering the information you find, your own experiences, and the observations in Ascher's essay, write an essay proposing a solution to the problem.

On reflection, Ballo found himself thinking about a New Hampshire friend who had been forced to sleep in a car for a few weeks. His initial research question was a practical one: "Where can a newly homeless person turn for help?" In the course of looking for answers, he discovered a fact that not only surprised him but made him angry. The resulting research paper, which took Ballo six weeks to complete, outlines the problem he found and proposes a solution.

As you read, notice that Ballo goes beyond reporting facts and uses what he learned to develop an argument of his own. Notice also how he synthesizes information and ideas from his sources to develop his thesis without relying on those sources to speak for him. His essay isn't perfect, but Ballo does an exemplary job of combining reasoning and evidence to support an argument while also addressing opposing points of view convincingly and fairly.

Jarrod Ballo

5 December 2014

Women and Children First

When most people think of homelessness, they imagine someone like the character Barbara Lazear Ascher describes in "The Box Man"—an unemployed, mentally ill man who has been living on the streets for years. That old stereotype, however, is no longer true. In fact, working families now make up the largest segment of the homeless population in America, and their numbers are rising. Given the shift in the nature of homelessness, it is time to shift focus in looking for solutions. Public service agencies should concentrate on preventing family homelessness by helping people get back on their feet if they fall on hard times.

When Ascher wrote her essay, most people without a place to live were "chronically" homeless, defined by the United States government as adult "individuals with disabilities who have been continually homeless for a year or more" (5). Only a tiny fraction of homeless people were in families (Rosenberg N1). Today, however, the National Center on Family Homelessness (NCFH) reports that families represent 37% of the homeless overall, more than double the number of those categorized as chronic (9). Families also represent the fastest-growing portion of the homeless population: while individual homelessness has dropped by approximately 10% over the last decade (United States 1), family homelessness has increased by a similar ratio (NCFH 14). Typically, a homeless family consists of a single mother with two children in tow, and many of those children are younger than six (NCFH 9). Innocent kids, it turns out, are the real face of homelessness.

A lot of people assume that when children wind up homeless it must be the parents' fault—they were too irresponsible to hold down a job, or too lazy to look for one in the first place. Most homeless parents, however, do have jobs, sometimes two or three, but their incomes still fall below the poverty line (NCFH 74-75). Others believe that the parents are alcoholics or

Surprising fact grabs readers' attention and clearly introduces topic

Thesis statement makes an arguable claim

Analysis of trends in homelessness

Quotation, paraphrase, and summary integrate evidence from three sources

Follow-up comment explains significance of data

Causes of family homelessness

Two opposing claims acknowledged and disputed

drug addicts, but homeless mothers rarely show signs of substance abuse (Culhane and Metraux 117). The real cause of
homelessness for families comes down to financial emergencies:
unexpected layoffs, uninsured medical expenses, missed rent
payments, disasters such as fires (Kozol 5-11). Usually such
emergencies are temporary, but poor families have few resources
for dealing with them.

Besides bunking with relatives or friends or staying on the
street, what can a homeless family do? Traditionally, a patchwork
assistance system has provided three basic options: emergency
shelters, transitional housing units, and hotel vouchers. Each
comes with limitations and obstacles, especially for families with
children.

The first place a homeless family normally goes is an emergency shelter. As one homeless mother describes them, shelters
provide meals and a place to sleep, but that's about it. Residents
must leave during the day and return in time to check in for the
next night—impossible for those who work late shifts—and they
have to put up with "having no right[s] whatsoever" (Felix).
Another advocate, Jonathan Kozol, points out that emergency
shelters can also be dangerous for women and children: shared
sleeping areas and bathrooms leave them vulnerable to theft and
assault, and expose them to prostitution and drugs. At the same
time, residents are deliberately treated poorly, on the theory that
making shelters unpleasant will stop people from staying long
(69, 111-12).

Transitional housing programs are slightly better. They offer
private rooms, let people stay for up to two years, and usually
provide social services to help families regroup (Culhane and
Metraux 112). They have one big drawback, though: men and
teenage boys are almost always excluded, so families may be
forced to split up (Kozol 58-59). Transitional housing also
involves interventions, such as job training and mental counseling, that are not only disruptive but also unnecessary for
most residents (Culhane and Metraux 117). Families get hassled
and treated like losers, when all they need is a place to stay.

Citations for
summaries identify
all pages
summarized

Classification of
shelter options

Brackets indicate
change in direct
quotation; no page
numbers in citation
because online
article doesn't
have them

Concrete details
support example

Summaries of two
sections separated
by comma

Authors not named
in signal phrases
listed in parentheti-
cal citations

Summaries and
paraphrases
integrate evidence
from two sources

Some cities provide hotel vouchers, paying market rates for families to stay in double rooms. While it might sound glamorous, hotel life is tough. As *Boston Globe* reporter Steven Rosenberg reveals, participating hotels tend to be located in suburbs, forcing long commutes to work and to school. They offer no space for children to play, no room for privacy, and no kitchens; homeless "guests" are forced to live on fast food and cold cuts (N1). Families may find themselves stuck in these conditions for months, even years, before they manage to find a better place to live (N9). And the instability of temporary housing makes it difficult for them to transition out of homelessness, creating a vicious cycle that adds to public expense while solving nothing.

Solutions do exist, though. In 2009 Congress passed the Homeless Emergency Assistance and Rapid Transition to Housing, or HEARTH, act, which put a new emphasis on "permanent supportive housing" (NCFH 11). As Malcolm Gladwell explains in an influential essay, chronically homeless people consume the majority of assistance funds even though they represent the smallest portion of the homeless population; the idea behind HEARTH is to put them in stable homes *before* addressing issues such as addiction, improving the chances for recovery and saving millions of dollars in the long run (183-86). Although it may seem absurd to give "mentally ill substance abusers the keys to a new place" (Surowiecki 42), studies show that permanent supportive housing *works*. Most states have seen promising results, with chronic homelessness dropping by 30% nationwide (United States 58)—and public expenses dropping along with it.

As successful as HEARTH has been for individuals, it has left families in the cold. Permanent supportive housing, limited to people with disabilities, now accounts for more beds than any other shelter option (United States 66-67). If homeless families do manage to find a spot in a shelter, many will find themselves stuck for a year or more, simply because they can't find afford-able housing or scrape together the costs of moving (Felix). Yet public service agencies spend close to $45,000 annually for each person housed in a shelter (Surowiecki 42)—more than enough

Signal phrase names author and gives credentials

Summary of newspaper article

Page numbers only because author (Rosenberg) is named in signal phrase

Example of solution for chronically homeless people

Definition outlines solution

Paraphrase integrates direct quotation

Effects of chronic solution for families

to cover the rent for a decent apartment or a down payment on a modest house.

Rather than waste so much money on temporary shelter, agencies should apply the logic behind permanent supportive housing to families: get them into real homes first. In arguing this solution, sociologists Dennis Culhane and Stephen Metraux make an important point:

> Most homeless households need temporary, low-cost assistance with resolving a recent housing loss or other displacement, or with transitioning out of an institutional living environment. They do not necessarily need a shelter stay or a shelter stay of long duration. (112)

Block format for long quotation

The HEARTH act allows for this kind of help, providing rental subsidies and moving costs, but eligibility is very restricted and few families qualify (NCFH 75). Harsh limitations put parents in a difficult situation, mostly because opponents worry that offering handouts "encourages them to behave irresponsibly" (Gladwell 190). Such concerns, however, have been proven false. Most recipients of cash assistance need help for less than three months, and almost all of them find independent housing and self-sufficiency within a year (United States 66).

Opposing claim acknowledged and disputed

Treating women and children in need as potential frauds only makes it more difficult for families to get their lives in order. Because most family homelessness is caused by short-term financial emergencies, most homeless families would be better off with short-term cash assistance. Shelters create obstacles to recovery, and they cost much more than putting people into stable homes. The success of permanent supportive housing for chronically homeless individuals has reduced costs and opened up more resources for homeless families, and that's where the money should go. By increasing access to rental assistance, we might even help families avoid homelessness in the first place.

Conclusion summarizes reasons, restates thesis, and offers solution

Works Cited

Ascher, Barbara Lazear. "The Box Man." *The Compact Reader: Short Essays by Method and Theme*. Ed. Jane E. Aaron and Ellen Kuhl Repetto. 10th ed. Boston: Bedford, 2016. 258-62. Print.

Culhane, Dennis P., and Stephen Metraux. "Rearranging the Deck Chairs or Reallocating the Lifeboats? Homelessness Assistance and Its Alternatives." *Journal of the American Planning Association* 74.1 (2008): 111-21. *Academic Search Premier*. Web. 6 Nov. 2014.

Felix, Mary. "Grateful for a Shelter, but Life Still Isn't Easy." *Spare Change News*. Homeless Empowerment Project, 13 Jan. 2012. Web. 3 Dec. 2014.

Gladwell, Malcolm. "Million-Dollar Murray: Why Problems Like Homelessness May Be Easier to Solve than to Manage." *What the Dog Saw: And Other Adventures*. New York: Little, 2009. 177-98. Print.

Kozol, Jonathan. *Rachel and Her Children: Homeless Families in America*. Rev. ed. New York: Three Rivers, 2006. Print.

National Center on Family Homelessness. *America's Youngest Outcasts: A Report Card on Child Homelessness*. Waltham: Amer. Inst. for Research, Nov. 2014. Web. 11 Nov. 2014.

Rosenberg, Steven A. "No Home to Call Their Own." *Boston Sunday Globe* 16 Nov. 2014, Metro North ed.: N1+. Print.

Surowiecki, James. "Home Free?" *New Yorker*. Condé Nast, 22 Sept. 2014: 42. Web. 6 Nov. 2014.

United States. Dept. of Housing and Urban Development. Office of Community Planning and Development. *The 2014 Annual Homeless Assessment Report to Congress*. Dept. of Housing and Urban Development, Oct. 2014. Print.

List of works cited starts on a new page

Selection from an anthology

Scholarly article in an online database

Article in an online newspaper

Section of a book

Book edition other than the first

Online book by a corporate author

Article in a print newspaper

Article in a weekly magazine archived online

Book by a government author

GLOSSARY

▶

abstract and **concrete words**   An **abstract** word refers to an idea, quality, attitude, or state that we cannot perceive with our senses: *democracy, generosity, love, grief.* It conveys a general concept or an impression. A **concrete** word, in contrast, refers to an object, person, place, or state that we can perceive with our senses: *lawnmower, teacher, Chicago, moaning.* Concrete words make writing specific and vivid. See also pp. 53 and 97; *general and specific words.*

active reading   Direct interaction with a work to discover its meaning, the author's intentions, and your own responses. Active reading involves taking notes and annotating passages to reach a deeper understanding. See also pp. 6–7; *critical thinking and reading.*

ad hominem argument   See *fallacies.*

allusion   A brief reference to a real or fictitious person, place, object, or event. An allusion can convey considerable meaning with few words, as when a writer describes a movie as "potentially this decade's *Star Wars*" to imply both that the movie is a space adventure and that it may be a blockbuster. But to be effective, the allusion must refer to something readers know well.

analogy   Closely related to metaphor, a comparison of two essentially unlike subjects that uses some similarities as the basis for establishing other similarities. A medical writer, for instance, might explain the workings of neurons in the human brain by comparing them to a computer network. A favorite technique of natural and social scientists and of philosophers who wish to clarify a subject that is unobservable, complex, or abstract, an analogy may have an explanatory or persuasive purpose. See also *comparison and contrast; metaphor.*

analysis (also called **division**)   The method of development in which a subject is separated into its elements or parts and then reassembled into a new whole. See Chapter 8 on division or analysis, p. 147.

anecdote   A brief narrative that recounts an episode from a person's experience. See, for instance, Adams, paragraphs 1–4, pp. 156–57. See also Chapter 5 on narration, p. 61.

antecedent The noun to which a pronoun refers: *Six days after Martin Luther King, Jr., picked up the Nobel Peace Prize in Norway, he was jailed in Alabama.* Antecedents should be clearly identified, and they should match their related pronouns in number and gender. See also p. 45.

argument The form of writing that appeals to readers' reason and emotions in order to win agreement with a claim or to compel some action. This definition encompasses both argument in a narrower sense — the appeal to reason to win agreement — and **persuasion** — the appeal to emotion to compel action. See Chapter 14 on argument and persuasion, p. 326.

assertion A debatable claim about a subject; the central idea of an argument.

audience A writer's audience is the group of readers for whom a particular work is intended. To communicate effectively, the writer should estimate readers' knowledge of the subject, their interest in it, and their biases toward it and should then consider these needs and expectations in choosing what to say and how to say it. For further discussion of audience, see pp. 4, 12, and 18.

begging the question See *fallacies.*

binary classification See *classification.*

body The part of an essay that develops the main idea. See also pp. 27 and 33–36.

brainstorming A method for generating ideas that involves listing thoughts without judgment. See pp. 21–22.

cause-and-effect analysis The method of development in which occurrences are divided into their elements to find what made an event happen (its causes) and what the consequences were (its effects). See Chapter 13 on cause-and-effect analysis, p. 295.

chronological order A pattern of organization in which events are arranged as they occurred over time, earliest to latest. Narratives usually follow a chronological order; see Chapter 5 on narration, p. 61.

classification The method of development in which the members of a group are sorted into classes or subgroups according to shared characteristics. In a **binary** classification, two classes are examined in opposition to each other, typically when one group has a certain characteristic that the other group lacks. In a **complex** classification, each individual fits into one class because of at least one distinguishing feature shared with all members of that class but not with members of any other classes. See Chapter 9 on classification, p. 178.

cliché An expression that has become tired from overuse and that therefore deadens rather than enlivens writing. Examples: *in over their heads, turn over a new leaf, march to a different drummer, as heavy as lead, as clear as a bell.* See also p. 54.

climactic order   A pattern of organization in which elements—words, sentences, examples, ideas—are arranged in order of increasing importance or drama. See also p. 37.

coherence   The quality of effective writing that comes from clear, logical connections among all the parts, so that the reader can follow the writer's thought process without difficulty. See also pp. 35–36 and 154.

colloquial language   The language of conversation, including contractions (*don't, can't*) and informal words and expressions (*hot* for new or popular, *boss* for employer, *ad* for advertisement, *get away with it, flunk the exam*). Most dictionaries label such words and expressions *colloquial* or *informal*. Colloquial language is inappropriate when the writing situation demands precision and formality, as a college term paper or a business report usually does. But in other situations it can be used selectively to relax a piece of writing and reduce the distance between writer and reader (see, for instance, Hughes, p. 76). See also *diction*.

comma splice   A sentence error in which two or more independent clauses run together with only a comma between them. See p. 44.

comparison and contrast   The method of development in which the similarities and differences between subjects are examined. Comparison examines similarities and contrast examines differences, but the two are generally used together. See Chapter 11 on comparison and contrast, p. 236.

conclusions   The endings of written works—the sentences that bring the writing to a close. A conclusion provides readers with a sense of completion, with a sense that the writer has finished. Sometimes the final point in the body of an essay may accomplish this purpose, especially if it is very important or dramatic (for instance, see Doyle, p. 215). But usually a separate conclusion is needed to achieve completion. It may be a single sentence or several paragraphs, depending on the length and complexity of the piece of writing. And it may include one of the following, or a combination, depending on your subject and purpose:

- A summary of the main points of the essay (see Heat-Moon, p. 102; Burroughs, p. 281; and Ballo, p. 407)

- A statement of the main idea of the essay, if it has not been stated before (see Jones, p. 9; Klass, p. 139), or a restatement of the main idea incorporating information from the body of the essay (see Lang, p. 56; Spence, p. 349)

- A comment on the significance or implications of the subject (see Dillard, p. 70; Fulmore, p. 81; Boissy, p. 287; and Lee, p. 368)

- A call for reflection, support, or action (see Mora, p. 162; Griggs, p. 186; and Alaimo and Koester, p. 311)

■ A prediction for the future (see Thomas, p. 316; Quindlen, p. 343; and Rodríguez, p. 374)

■ An example, anecdote, question, or quotation that reinforces the point of the essay (see Chen, p. 108; Sedaris, p. 131; Adams, p. 156; Warren, p. 170; Brooks, p. 195; Brady, p. 276; Goodman, p. 306; and Will, p. 362)

Excluded from this list are several endings that should be avoided because they tend to weaken the overall effect of an essay: (1) an example, fact, or quotation that pertains to only part of the essay; (2) an apology for your ideas, for the quality of the writing, or for omissions; (3) an attempt to enhance the significance of the essay by overgeneralizing from its ideas and evidence; (4) a new idea that requires the support of an entirely different essay.

concrete words See *abstract and concrete words.*

connotation and denotation A word's **denotation** is its literal meaning: *famous* denotes the quality of being well known. A word's **connotations** are the associations or suggestions that go beyond its literal meaning: *notorious* denotes fame but also connotes sensational, even unfavorable, recognition. See also pp. 52–53.

contrast See *comparison and contrast.*

critical thinking and reading The practice of examining the meanings and implications of things, images, events, ideas, and written works; uncovering and testing assumptions; seeing the importance of context; and drawing and supporting independent conclusions. Critical reading applies critical thinking to look beneath the surface of a work, seeking to uncover both its substance and the writer's interpretation of the substance. See Chapter 1 on reading, especially pp. 5–8.

deductive reasoning The method of reasoning that moves from the general to the specific. See Chapter 14 on argument and persuasion, especially pp. 330–32. See also *syllogism.*

definition An explanation of the meaning of a word. A **formal**, or dictionary, definition identifies the class of things to which the word belongs and then distinguishes it from other members of the class; a **stipulative** definition clarifies how a word or phrase is being used in a particular context; an **extended** definition may serve as the primary method of developing an essay. See Chapter 12 on definition, p. 267.

denotation See *connotation and denotation.*

description The form of writing that conveys the perceptions of the senses—sight, hearing, smell, taste, touch—to make a person, place, object, or state of mind vivid and concrete. See Chapter 6 on description, p. 91.

development The accumulation of details, examples, facts, opinions, and other evidence to support a writer's ideas. Development begins in sentences, with concrete and specific words to explain meaning. At the level of the paragraph, the sentences develop the paragraph's topic. Then, at the level of the whole essay, the paragraphs develop the governing thesis. See pp. 26–27 and 33–34.

dialogue   A narrative technique that quotes the speech of participants in the story. See pp. 67–68.

diction   The choice of words you make to achieve a purpose and make meaning clear. Effective diction conveys your meaning exactly, emphatically, and concisely, and it is appropriate to your intentions and audience. **Standard English**, the language of formal written expression, is expected in all writing for college, business and the professions, and publication. The vocabulary of standard English is large and varied, encompassing, for instance, both *comestibles* and *food* for edible things, both *paroxysm* and *fit* for a sudden seizure. In some writing situations, standard English may also include words and expressions typical of conversation (see *colloquial language*). But it excludes other levels of diction that only certain groups understand or find acceptable. Most dictionaries label expressions at these levels as follows:

- **Nonstandard**: words spoken among particular social groups, such as *ain't*, *them guys*, *hisself*, and *nowheres*

- **Obsolete**: words that have passed out of use, such as *cleam* for smear

- **Regional** or **dialect**: words spoken in a particular region but not in the country as a whole, such as *poke* for a sack or bag, *holler* for a hollow or small valley, *wicked* for excellent

- **Slang**: words that are usually short-lived and that may not be understood by all readers, such as *tanked* for drunk, *bling* for jewelry, and *honcho* for one in charge

See also *connotation and denotation* and *style*.

division or analysis   See *analysis*.

documentation   A system of identifying your sources so that readers know which ideas are borrowed and can locate the original material themselves. Papers written for English and other humanities courses typically follow the MLA (Modern Language Association) documentation system, which requires brief parenthetical citations within the body of the essay and a comprehensive list of works cited at the end. See the Appendix, especially pp. 394–405.

dominant impression   The central idea or feeling conveyed by a description of a person, place, object, or state of mind. See Chapter 6 on description, especially p. 92.

drafting   The stage of the writing process in which ideas are tentatively written out in sentences and paragraphs. Drafts may be messy, incomplete, disorganized, and filled with misspellings and grammatical errors; such problems can be repaired during *revision* and *editing*. See pp. 28–29.

editing   The final stage of the writing process, in which sentences and words are polished and corrected for accuracy, clarity, and effectiveness. See Chapter 4 on editing, p. 42.

effect   See *cause-and-effect analysis*.

either-or   See *fallacies*.

emotional appeal (also called *pathos*)   In argumentative and persuasive writing, the appeal to readers' values, beliefs, or feelings in order to win agreement or compel action. See pp. 328–29.

essay   A prose composition on a single nonfictional topic or idea. An essay usually reflects the personal experiences and opinions of the writer.

ethical appeal (also called *ethos*)   In argumentative and persuasive writing, the sense of the writer's expertise and character projected by the reasonableness of the argument, the use and quality of evidence, and the tone. See p. 328.

etymology   The history of a word, from its origins and uses to changes in its meaning over time. See p. 269.

evidence   The details, examples, facts, statistics, or expert opinions that support any general statement or claim. See pp. 327–34 and 336–41 on the use of evidence in argumentative writing, pp. 385–88 on finding evidence in sources, and pp. 394–405 on documenting researched evidence.

example   An instance or representative of a general group or an abstract concept or quality. One or more examples may serve as the primary method of developing an essay. See Chapter 7 on example, p. 118.

exposition   The form of writing that explains or informs. Most of the essays in this book are primarily expository, and some essays whose primary purpose is self-expression or persuasion employ exposition to clarify ideas.

extended definition   See *definition*.

fallacies   Flaws in reasoning that weaken or invalidate an argument. Some of the most common fallacies follow (the page numbers refer to further discussion in the text).

- **Ad hominem** ("to the man") argument, attacking an opponent instead of the opponent's argument: *She is just a student, so we need not listen to her criticisms of foreign policy* (p. 333).

- **Begging the question**, assuming the truth of a conclusion that has not been proved: *Acid rain does not do serious damage, so it is not a serious problem* (p. 333).

- **Either-or**, presenting only two alternatives when the choices are more numerous: *If you want to do well in college, you have to cheat a little* (p. 334).

- **Hasty generalization**, leaping to a conclusion on the basis of inadequate or unrepresentative evidence: *Every one of the twelve students polled supports the change in the grading system, so the administration should implement it* (p. 333).

- **Ignoring the question**, shifting the argument away from the real issue: *A fine, churchgoing man like Charles Harold would make an excellent mayor* (p. 333).

- **Non sequitur** ("It does not follow"), deriving a wrong or illogical conclusion from stated premises: *Because students are actually in school, they should be the ones to determine our educational policies* (p. 334).

- **Oversimplification**, overlooking or ignoring inconsistencies or complexities in evidence: *If the United States banned immigration, our unemployment problems would be solved* (pp. 298, 333).

- **Post hoc** (from *post hoc, ergo propter hoc*, "after this, therefore because of this"), assuming that one thing caused another simply because it preceded the other: *Two students left school in the week after the new policies were announced, proving that the policies will eventually cause a reduction in enrollments* (pp. 297–98, 334).

figures of speech   Expressions that imply meanings beyond or different from their literal meanings in order to achieve vividness or force. Common figures of speech include *hyperbole, metaphor, paradox, personification*, and *simile*. See p. 54 for discussion and examples of specific figures.

flashback   In narration, an interruption of chronological sequence that shifts backward in time to recall or explore the significance of an earlier event. See p. 62.

formal definition   See *definition*.

formal style   See *style*.

freewriting   A technique for discovering ideas for writing that involves writing for a fixed amount of time without stopping to reread or edit. See p. 21.

general and specific words   A **general** word refers to a group or class: *car, mood, book*. A **specific** word refers to a particular member of a group or class: *Toyota, irritation, dictionary*. Usually, the more specific a word is, the more interesting and informative it will be for readers. See also pp. 53 and 97; *abstract and concrete words*.

generalization   A statement about a group or a class derived from knowledge of some or all of its members: for instance, *Dolphins can be trained to count* or *Television news rarely penetrates beneath the headlines*. The more examples the generalization is based on, the more accurate it is likely to be. A generalization is the result of *inductive reasoning*. See also pp. 118–20 and 330.

hasty generalization   See *fallacies*.

hyperbole   Deliberate overstatement or exaggeration: *The desk provided an acre of work surface.* See also p. 54. (The opposite of hyperbole is understatement, discussed under *irony*.)

ignoring the question   See *fallacies.*

image   A verbal representation of sensory experience—that is, of something seen, heard, felt, tasted, or smelled. Images may be literal: *Snow stuck to her eyelashes; The red car sped past us.* Or they may be figures of speech: *Her eyelashes were snowy feathers; The car rocketed past us like a red missile* (see p. 54). Through images, a writer touches the readers' experiences, thus sharpening meaning and adding immediacy. See also *abstract and concrete words.*

independent clause   A word group that contains a subject and a verb and expresses a complete thought. A single independent clause can be punctuated as a sentence; two independent clauses in a row need a clear separation: a period, a semicolon, or a comma along with *and, but, or, nor, for, so,* or *yet.* See p. 44.

inductive reasoning   The method of reasoning that moves from the particular to the general. See Chapter 14 on argument and persuasion, especially p. 330.

informal style   See *style.*

introductions   The openings of written works, the sentences that set the stage for what follows. An introduction to an essay identifies and restricts the subject while establishing the writer's attitude toward it. Accomplishing these purposes may require anything from a single sentence to several paragraphs, depending on the writer's purpose and how much readers need to know before they can begin to grasp the ideas in the essay. The introduction often includes a *thesis sentence* stating the main idea of the essay (see pp. 24–26). To set up the thesis sentence, or as a substitute for it, any of the following openings, or a combination, may be effective:

- An anecdote or other reference to the writer's experience that forecasts or illustrates the main idea or that explains what prompted the essay (see Dillard, p. 70; Adams, p. 156; Warren, p. 170; Brady, p. 276; and Spence, p. 349)

- Background on the subject that establishes a time or place or that provides essential information (see Jones, p. 9; Fulmore, p. 81; Chen, p. 108; Sedaris, p. 131; and Gould, p. 191)

- An example, quotation, or question that reinforces the main idea (see Heat-Moon, p. 102; Kessler, p. 126; Klass, p. 139; and Burroughs, p. 281)

- An explanation of the significance of the subject (see Mora, p. 162; Boissy, p. 287; Alaimo and Koester, p. 311; and Quindlen, p. 343)

- An outline of the situation or problem that the essay will address, perhaps using interesting facts or statistics (see Griggs, p. 186; Will, p. 362; and Ballo, p. 407)

- A statement or quotation of an opinion that the writer will modify or disagree with (see Lang, p. 56; Brooks, p. 195; Lee, p. 368; and Rodríguez, p. 374)

A good introduction does not mislead readers by exaggerating the significance of the subject or the essay, and it does not bore readers by saying more than is necessary. In addition, a good introduction avoids three openings that are always clumsy: (1) beginning with *The purpose of this essay is . . .* or something similar; (2) referring to the title of the essay in the first sentence, as in _____ *is not as hard as it looks* or . . . *This is a serious problem* or . . . *We've all asked that question*; and (3) starting too broadly or vaguely, as in *Ever since humans walked upright . . .* or *In today's world . . .*

irony In writing, irony is the use of words to suggest a meaning different from their literal meaning. An ironic statement might rely on reversal: saying the opposite of what the writer really means. But irony can also derive from understatement (saying less than is meant) or hyperbole (exaggeration). Irony can be witty, teasing, biting, or cruel. At its most humorless and heavily contemptuous, it becomes **sarcasm**: *Thanks a lot for telling Dad we stayed out all night; that was really bright of you.*

journal A tool for discovering ideas for writing: an informal record of ideas, observations, questions, and thoughts kept in a notebook or electronic file for the writer's personal use. See pp. 19–21.

logos See *rational appeal.*

metaphor A figure of speech that compares two unlike things by saying that one is the other: *Bright circles of ebony, her eyes smiled back at me.* See also p. 54.

modifier A word, phrase, or clause that describes another word (or words) in a sentence. Modifiers can add emphasis and variety to sentences, but they must be placed carefully to avoid confusing readers. See pp. 46–47.

narration The form of writing that tells a story, relating a sequence of events. See Chapter 5 on narration, p. 61.

negation A technique for clarifying the definition of a word or phrase by explaining what it does *not* mean. See p. 269.

non sequitur See *fallacies.*

nonstandard English See *diction.*

objective writing Writing that focuses on the subject itself and strives to be direct and impartial, without dwelling on the writer's perspective or feelings. Newspaper accounts, scientific reports, process analyses, and rational arguments are typical examples. See also pp. 91–92; *subjective writing*.

organization   The arrangement of ideas and supporting points in a piece of writing. See pp. 26–28 and 36–37; *chronological order; climactic order; spatial organization*.

oversimplification   See *fallacies*.

paradox   A seemingly self-contradictory statement that, on reflection, makes sense: *Children are the poor person's wealth* (wealth can be monetary, or it can be spiritual). *Paradox* may also refer to a situation that is inexplicable or contradictory, such as the restriction of one group's rights to secure the rights of another group.

paragraph   A group of related sentences, set off by an initial indentation, that develops an idea. By breaking continuous text into units, paragraphing helps the writer manage ideas and helps the reader follow those ideas. Each paragraph makes a distinct contribution to the main idea governing the entire piece of writing. The idea of the paragraph itself is often stated in a *topic sentence*, and it is supported with sentences containing specific details, examples, and reasons. Like the larger piece of writing to which it contributes, the paragraph should be unified, coherent, and well developed. For examples of successful paragraphs, see the paragraph analyses in the introduction to each method of development (Chapters 5–14). See also pp. 34–35 and 274 (unity), pp. 35–36 and 154 (coherence), and pp. 27, 33–34, and 184 (development).

parallelism   The use of similar grammatical forms for ideas of equal importance. Parallelism occurs within sentences: *The doctor recommends swimming, bicycling, or walking*. It also occurs among sentences: *Strumming her guitar, she made listeners feel her anger. Singing lines, she made listeners believe her pain*. See also pp. 50–51 and 244.

paraphrase   A restatement—in your own words—of another writer's ideas. A paraphrase is about the same length as the original passage, but it does not repeat words, phrases, or sentence patterns. See also pp. 389–90.

pathos   See *emotional appeal*.

personification   A figure of speech that gives human qualities to things or abstractions: *The bright day smirked at my bad mood*. See also p. 54.

persuasion   See *argument*.

plagiarism   The failure to identify and acknowledge the sources of words, information, or ideas that are not your own. Whether intentional or accidental, plagiarism is a serious offense and should always be avoided. See pp. 393–94.

point of view   The position of the writer in relation to the subject. In *narration*, point of view depends on the writer's place in the story and on his or her relation to it in time (see pp. 62–63). In *description*, point of view depends on the writer's physical and psychological relation to the subject (see pp. 92–93). Grammatically, point of view refers to a writer's choice of *pronouns*: first person (*I, we, our*), second person (*you, yours*), or third person (*he and she, it, they, theirs*). More broadly, point of view can also mean the writer's particular mental stance or attitude. For instance, an employee and an employer might have different points of view toward the employee's absenteeism or the employer's sick-leave policies.

points of comparison   The set of attributes used to distinguish and organize the elements of two or more subjects being compared to each other. See Chapter 11 on comparison and contrast, especially pp. 237–38.

post hoc   See *fallacies*.

premise   The generalization or assumption on which an argument is based. See also *syllogism*.

principle of analysis   The interpretive framework or set of guidelines used to divide a subject into components. The choice of a principle depends on the writer's interest and will determine the focus and outcome of an analysis. One writer analyzing a contemporary television show set in the 1960s, for instance, might focus on historical context and implications, while another might emphasize production values, and yet another might focus on literary qualities such as plot and character. See Chapter 8 on division or analysis, especially p. 148.

principle of classification   The distinctive characteristics used to sort things into categories or general classes. A writer's focus determines the principle, which in turn shapes and limits the contours of a classification. An essay about apartment dwellers, for example, might group them by noise (too loud, too quiet, just right), by income (poor, working class, middle class, wealthy), or by relationship status (bachelors, couples, widows); it should not, however, mix them into unrelated categories (too loud, middle class, widows). See Chapter 9 on classification, especially pp. 178–80.

process analysis   The method of development in which a sequence of actions with a specified result is divided into its component steps. Process analysis may be **directive**, telling how to do or make something; or **explanatory**, providing the necessary information for readers to understand how something happens. See Chapter 10 on process analysis, p. 206.

pronoun   A word that refers to a noun or other pronoun: *Six days after King, Jr., picked up his Nobel Peace Prize in Norway, he was jailed in Alabama.* The most common personal pronouns are *I, you, he, she, it, we,* and *they*. See also pp. 45 and 47; *point of view*.

proposition   A debatable claim about a subject; the central idea of an argument.

purpose The reason for writing, the goal the writer wants to achieve. The purpose may be primarily to explain the subject so that readers understand it or see it in a new light; to convince readers to accept or reject an opinion or to take a certain action; to entertain readers with a humorous or exciting story; or to express the thoughts and emotions triggered by a revealing or instructive experience. The writer's purpose overlaps the main idea—the particular point being made about the subject. In effective writing, the two together direct and control every choice the writer makes. See also pp. 12, 17–18, and 32–33; *thesis*; *unity*.

quotation The exact words of another writer or speaker, copied word for word, clearly identified, and attributed to their source. Short quotations are enclosed in quotation marks; longer quotations are set off from the text by indenting. See pp. 390–91.

rational appeal (also called *logos*) In argumentative and persuasive writing, the appeal to readers' rational faculties—to their ability to reason logically—in order to win agreement or compel action. See pp. 330–32.

repetition and restatement The careful use of the same words or close parallels to clarify meaning and tie sentences together. See also pp. 35–36 and 154.

revision The stage of the writing process devoted to "re-seeing" a draft, divided into fundamental changes in content and structure (revision) and more superficial changes in grammar, word choice, and the like (editing). See Chapter 3 on revising, p. 31; Chapter 4 on editing, p. 42.

rhetoric The art of using words effectively to communicate with an audience, or the study of that art. To the ancient Greeks, rhetoric was the art of the *rhetor*—orator, or public speaker—and included the art of persuasion. Later the word shifted to mean elegant language, and a version of that meaning persists in today's occasional use of *rhetoric* to mean pretentious or hollow language, as in *Their argument was mere rhetoric*.

run-on sentence A sentence error in which two or more independent clauses run together without punctuation between them. See p. 44.

sarcasm See *irony*.

satire The combination of wit and criticism to mock or condemn human foolishness or evil. The intent of satire is to arouse readers to contempt or action, and thus it differs from comedy, which seeks simply to amuse. Much satire relies on irony—saying one thing but meaning another (see *irony*).

sentence See *independent clause*.

sentence fragment A word group that is punctuated like a sentence but is not a complete sentence because it lacks a subject, lacks a verb, or is just part of a thought. See p. 43.

simile   A figure of speech that equates two unlike things using *like* or *as*: *The crowd was restless, like bees in a hive.* See also p. 54.

slang   See *diction*.

source   Any outside or researched material that helps to develop a writer's ideas. A source may be the subject of an essay, such as when you are writing about a reading in this book, or it may provide evidence to support a particular point. However a source is used, it must always be documented. See the Appendix on working with sources, p. 384.

spatial organization   A pattern of organization that views an object, scene, or person by paralleling the way we normally scan things—for instance, top to bottom or near to far. See also pp. 37 and 95.

specific words   See *general and specific words*.

standard English   See *diction*.

stipulative definition   See *definition*.

style   The *way* something is said, as opposed to *what* is said. Style results primarily from a writer's characteristic word choices and sentence structures. A person's writing style, like his or her voice or manner of speaking, is distinctive. Style can also be viewed more broadly as ranging from formal to informal. A very **formal style** adheres strictly to the conventions of standard English (see *diction*); tends toward long sentences with sophisticated structures; and relies on learned words, such as *malodorous* and *psychopathic*. A very **informal style**, in contrast, is more conversational (see *colloquial language*); tends toward short, uncomplicated sentences; and relies on words typical of casual speech, such as *smelly* or *crazy*. Among the writers represented in this book, Ascher (p. 258) writes quite formally, Burroughs (p. 281) quite informally. The formality of style may often be modified to suit a particular audience or occasion: a college term paper, for instance, demands a more formal style than an essay narrating a personal experience. See also *tone* and Chapter 3 on revising, especially pp. 37–38.

subject   What a piece of writing is about. The subject of an essay is its general topic, such as college (Jones, p. 9; Lang, p. 56), childhood (Ondaatje, p. 63; Rauch, p. 63; Dillard, p. 70; Hughes, p. 76; Fulmore, p. 81), or language (Tannen, p. 120; Lutz, p. 120; Kessler, p. 126; Sedaris, p. 131; Klass, p. 139). Because writers narrow a subject until they have a specific point to make about it, multiple essays on the same subject will typically be very different from one another. See also pp. 17–18; *purpose*; *thesis*.

subjective writing   Writing that focuses on the writer's own perspective, feelings, and opinions. Memoirs, personal reflections, and emotional arguments, for example, tend to be subjective. See also pp. 91–92; *objective writing*.

summary   A condensed version—in your own words—of the main idea of a longer work. A summary is much shorter than the original and leaves out most of the supporting details. See also p. 389.

syllogism   The basic form of deductive reasoning, in which a conclusion derives necessarily from proven or accepted premises. For example: *The roof always leaks when it rains* (the major premise). *It is raining* (the minor premise). *Therefore, the roof will leak* (the conclusion). See Chapter 14 on argument and persuasion, especially pp. 330–32.

symbol   A person, place, or thing that represents an abstract quality or concept. A red heart symbolizes love; the Golden Gate Bridge symbolizes San Francisco's dramatic beauty; a cross symbolizes Christianity.

synonym   A word that has nearly but not exactly the same meaning as another word. For example: *angry* and *furious*, *happy* and *ecstatic*, *skinny* and *thin*.

synthesis   The practice of combining elements into a new whole. In writing, synthesis usually involves connecting related ideas from multiple sources to form an original idea of your own. See pp. 389–92.

thesis   The main idea of a piece of writing to which all other ideas and details relate. The main idea is often stated in a **thesis sentence** (or sentences), which asserts something about the subject and conveys the writer's purpose. The thesis sentence is often included near the beginning of an essay. Even when the writer does not state the main idea and purpose, however, they govern all the ideas and details in the essay. See also pp. 23–26 and 32–33; *unity.*

tone   The attitude toward the subject, and sometimes toward the audience and the writer's own self, expressed in choice of words and sentence structures as well as in what is said. Tone in writing is similar to tone of voice in speaking, from warm to serious, amused to angry, joyful to sorrowful, sympathetic to contemptuous. For examples of strong tone in writing, see Adams (p. 156), Griggs (p. 186), Doyle, (p. 215), Keegan (p. 220), Brady (p. 276), Burroughs (p. 281), and Rodríguez (p. 374). See also pp. 37–38 and 340–41.

topic sentence   A statement of the main idea of a paragraph, to which all other sentences in the paragraph relate. See pp. 34–35.

transitions   Links between sentences and paragraphs that relate ideas and thus contribute to clarity and smoothness. Transitions may be sentences beginning paragraphs or brief paragraphs that shift the focus or introduce new ideas. They may also be words and phrases that signal and specify relationships. Some of these words and phrases—but by no means all—are listed here:

- **Addition or repetition**: again, also, finally, furthermore, in addition, moreover, next, that is

- **Cause or effect**: as a result, consequently, equally important, hence, then, therefore, thus

- **Comparison**: also, in the same way, likewise, similarly

- **Contrast**: but, even so, however, in contrast, on the contrary, still, yet

- **Illustration**: for example, for instance, specifically, that is
- **Intensification**: indeed, in fact, of course, truly
- **Space**: above, below, beyond, farther away, here, nearby, opposite, there, to the right
- **Summary or conclusion**: all in all, in brief, in conclusion, in short, in summary, therefore, thus
- **Time**: afterward, at last, earlier, later, meanwhile, simultaneously, soon, then

understatement   See *irony*.

unity   The quality of effective writing that occurs when all the parts relate to the main idea and contribute to the writer's purpose. See also pp. 34–35 and 274.

writing process   The series of activities involved in creating a finished piece of writing. Rather than produce a polished essay in one sitting, most writers work back and forth in a series of overlapping stages: analyzing the writing situation, discovering ideas, forming a thesis, organizing, drafting, revising, and editing. See pp. 16–17.

Acknowledgments (continued from page iv)

Scott Adams. "Funny Business," adapted from "How to Write Like a Cartoonist." From *The Wall Street Journal*, October 9, 2010. Copyright © 2010 by The Dow Jones Company. Used by permission.

Stephanie Alaimo and Mark Koester. "The Backdraft of Technology" from *The DePaulia*, 2006. Reprinted by permission of the authors.

Barbara Lazear Ascher. "The Box Man," from *Playing After Dark*. Copyright © 1982 by Barbara Lazear Ascher. Used by permission of the Emma Sweeney Agency, LLC.

Rick Bass. "Gardens of Ice and Stone." From *The Southern Review*, Spring 2009. Used by permission of the author.

Jessica Sayuri Boissy. "One Cup at a Time." Courtesy of Jessica Sayuri Boissy.

Judy Brady. "I Want a Wife." Originally published in *Ms.* Magazine, December 31, 1971. Copyright © 1970 by Judy Brady. Used by permission of the author.

David Brooks. "People Like Us." *The Atlantic Monthly*, September 2003. Reprinted by permission of the author.

Augusten Burroughs. "How to Live Unhappily Ever After" from *This Is How*. Copyright © 2012 Augusten, Inc. Published by permission of Augusten Burroughs c/o Selectric Artists LLC.

Ken Chen. "City Out of Breath." First published in *Mānoa*, Summer 2005. Copyright © 2005 by Ken Chen. Reprinted by permission of the author.

Annie Dillard. From *An American Childhood*. Copyright © 1987 by Annie Dillard. Reprinted by permission of HarperCollins Publishers, Inc.

Brian Doyle. "How to Read a Nature Essay." Adapted from "The Greatest Nature Essay *Ever*." First published in the November/December 2008 issue of *Orion Magazine*. Copyright © by Brian Doyle. Used by permission of the author.

Lauren Fulmore. "Chasing Fairy Tales." Courtesy of Lauren Fulmore and UNH.

Ellen Goodman. "The Company Man." *The Boston Globe*, January 1, 1976. Copyright © 1976 The Boston Globe. All rights reserved. Used by permission and protected by the Copyright Laws of the United States. The printing, copying, redistribution, or retransmission of this Content without express written permission is prohibited.

Jonathan R. Gould, Jr. "The People Next Door." Copyright © Bedford/St. Martin's. Reprinted by permission of Bedford/St. Martin's.

Brandon Griggs. "The Most Annoying Facebookers." CNN.com/Technology, August 25, 2009. Courtesy CNN.

William Least Heat-Moon. "Starrucca Viaduct" from *Roads to Quoz*. Copyright © 2008 by William Least Heat-Moon. Reprinted by permission of Little, Brown and Company. All rights reserved.

Langston Hughes. "Salvation," from *The Big Sea*. Copyright © 1940 by Langston Hughes. Copyright renewed © 1968 by Arna Bontemps and George Houston Bass. Reprinted by permission of Hill and Wang, a division of Farrar, Straus, and Giroux LLC.

Edward P. Jones. "Shacks," from *The New Yorker*, June 13 and 20, 2011. Used by permission of William Morris Endeavor Entertainment, LLC.

INDEX OF AUTHORS AND TITLES

Guide to the Elements of Writing

The Compact Reader offers advice on writing from the general, such as organizing and revising, to the particular, such as tightening sentences and choosing words. Consult the page numbers here for help with your writing. To find the meaning of a particular term or concept, consult the Glossary on pages 412–26.

Resources for Teaching

The Compact Reader

SHORT ESSAYS BY METHOD AND THEME

Tenth Edition

Jane E. Aaron

Ellen Kuhl Repetto

Manufactured in the United States of America.

0   9   8   7   6   5

f   e   d   c   b   a

For information, write: Bedford/St. Martin's, 75 Arlington Street, Boston, MA 02116   (617-399-4000)

ISBN-10: 1-4576-3297-7

ISBN-13: 978-1-4576-3297-6

Cover photo: © Getty Images/chrupka

PREFACE

This manual has four parts, all intended to help you take maximum advantage of *The Compact Reader* as a classroom text. Part I discusses the content and possible classroom uses of the four introductory chapters, each element of the editorial apparatus in the reading chapters, and the research appendix. Part II presents two sample syllabi to show how *The Compact Reader* might be used in writing courses taking rhetorical or thematic approaches. Part III discusses additional course materials with which *The Compact Reader* may be combined. And Part IV offers teaching suggestions, a content quiz, and a vocabulary quiz for each essay in the book, as well as possible answers to the critical reading questions following each essay.

CONTENTS

Contents

Contents

I
USING *THE COMPACT READER*

The Compact Reader's structure is uncomplicated: four introductory chapters coach students on reading, writing, revising, and editing; ten thematically organized chapters explain and illustrate ten rhetorical methods of development; an appendix offers guidelines for using and documenting sources in writing; and a glossary defines key writing terms.

Four Introductory Chapters on Reading and Writing

You may wish to discuss these chapters explicitly in class, adapting all or parts of them to your syllabus, or you may find the chapters self-explanatory enough simply to ask students to read them on their own. Either way, these chapters lay useful groundwork for a reading and writing course. They explain and illustrate how critical reading is linked to good writing, how to read a text critically, how to work productively through the initial stages of writing, and how to revise and edit one's own drafts.

Reading (Chapter 1)

The introduction to reading addresses the key skills needed to read nonfiction texts, both written and visual, actively and critically.

A highlight of the chapter is the discussion of Edward P. Jones's essay "Shacks," showing how a critical reader might approach an essay and what conclusions might result. (Barbara Lazear Ascher's "The Box Man," long a favorite with instructors and students, has been relocated to Chapter 11.) This discussion is organized around generalized versions of the questions that appear after each essay in Chapters 5–14. These questions—divided into the four categories of Meaning, Purpose and Audience, Method and Structure, and Language—invite students to consider the elements an author calls upon in constructing an essay. By observing how a critical reader might answer these questions for Jones's essay, students have an opportunity to see what kinds of answers they might provide to the questions following the other essays in the book—and, more significant, to begin honing their own skills as critical readers.

Jones's essay combines many of the methods of development (description, example, and so on), thus providing an overview of the methods treated separately in the subsequent chapters. At the same time, the discussion of Jones's essay introduces a point assumed throughout *The Compact Reader*: writers rarely use a single method alone, but rather gain shape, texture, and clarity for their writing by applying whatever method is best suited to a particular point or purpose.

To engage students actively in writing during the first or second class period, you might ask them to do some prewriting as preparation for reading the Jones essay. Here are some possible questions: What about the first months of college make you feel lonely or overwhelmed? How do you stay connected with family and friends from home? How do you cope with stress? Or, to move in another direction, you might ask these questions: What special talent(s) do you have? How do you feel about your abilities as a writer? Do you think you can improve with practice? After reading Jones's essay, students could compare their responses with his and with one another's. They may see Jones's literacy narrative as more complete and insightful than their own, noting that he presents his experience and feelings vividly; but that may prompt some students to recall similar lessons from their own college experience so far and help them see how revelations such as Jones's might enrich their own writing. This comparison would provide a useful springboard to a discussion of the writer's task—and to Chapter 2.

A brief discussion of reading visuals helps students understand how to apply critical reading skills to the images they might come across in their reading or daily life, such as photographs, paintings, or drawings. A sample photograph, with annotations, continues Part I's college success theme and shows students how a critical reading of an image might work. Because students tend to respond well to visuals, and to discover in the process that they already possess some critical reading facilities that can be applied to written texts, the tenth edition also includes a few essays with visual components: William Least Heat-Moon's "Starrucca Viaduct" (Chapter 6) is illustrated with an archival photograph, Scott Adams's "Funny Business" (Chapter 8) and David Brooks's "People Like Us" (Chapter 9) both include cartoons, and Jessica Sayuri Boissy's "One Cup at a Time" (Chapter 12) presents hand-painted Japanese calligraphy to support the author's analysis.

Developing an Essay (Chapter 2)

This chapter provides an overview and illustrations of the discovery and drafting process, detailing the basic concepts, terms, and stages that are used in the introductions to the rhetorical methods.

The introduction to the writing process emphasizes the importance of writing with a thesis and focuses on the work in progress of a student, Nicole Lang, as she develops a critical response to Jones's "Shacks." Chapter 2 includes Lang's journal writing (p. 19) and freewriting (p. 21), along with her complete first draft (p. 29). If your class does peer review, you might ask students to comment on the draft as a beginning exercise. In discussing their own and their classmates' comments, they will come to see what kinds of responses are appropriate and how best to phrase them.

Revising (Chapter 3)

Continuing the introduction to the writing process, this chapter covers the crucial stages of revision, aiming to help students with questions they may have about revising and continuing to follow student writer Nicole Lang's work in progress. Concise text and specific examples explain each element of writing, and a boxed checklist guides students through rethinking their own work.

Later, in the introduction to each rhetorical method, a more specific revision checklist appears to help students assess their drafts.

Editing (Chapter 4)

A separate chapter on editing expands on the ninth edition's overview, with new discussions of grammatical errors and stylistic choices, each illustrated with clearly marked examples.

The chapter focuses on the most common writing problems that students are likely to encounter, such as sentence fragments, comma splices, and word choice. The content is not, of course, comparable to a handbook in scope or detail, but it should provide just enough to help students who struggle to recognize or address sentence-level issues; it also suggests realistic techniques for student writers to polish their style, such as using parallel structure and streamlining sentences for clarity and emphasis. The chapter concludes with student writer Nicole Lang's final draft of "Foundations," annotated to highlight the elements of an effective essay.

To further aid students in recognizing potential problems and opportunities, a "Focus" box in the introduction to each rhetorical chapter calls out an element of revision or editing especially relevant to the method—for instance, verbs in narration, paragraph development in classification, and consistency in process analysis. All discussions of the elements—in Chapters 2, 3, and 4 and in the method introductions—are indexed inside the book's back cover so that students know just where to go for help.

Ten Thematic Chapters on the Methods of Development

Chapter Introductions

Though brief, *The Compact Reader* anticipates many student questions about the uses of the methods of development; hence you can ask students to read the chapter introductions independently, reserving class time to discuss the chapter's theme or the application of the writing principles.

The introductions to Chapters 5–14 all proceed in the same way. The opening section, "Reading _____," discusses the purposes for which the method is suited and provides essential concepts and definitions while showing students what elements to look for when reading paragraphs and essays that use the method. The next section, "Analyzing _____ in Paragraphs," annotates two paragraphs to illustrate the method in a manageable form. As noted above, a "Focus" box in each chapter emphasizes a particular element that students should be aware of when revising or editing, whether it is concrete and specific language in Description or parallelism in Comparison and Contrast. Finally, "A Note on Thematic Connections" highlights the common topic of the chapter's reading selections.

The two annotated paragraphs in each introduction allow students to study the method in brief, uncomplicated examples before moving on to complete essays. If you discuss the methods of development in class, the annotated paragraphs can serve as concrete illustrations of each method's special concerns. In addition, the paragraphs can serve as models for students to follow in writing paragraphs of their own (perhaps drawing on the list of topics at the end of each chapter) before they move on to more complex, essay-length applications of the method.

Chapter 14, "Argument and Persuasion: Discussing Social Issues," is slightly different from the chapters before it. Because argumentation is so central to academic writing, this chapter introduction is more extensive than the others, with detailed discussions of the elements of argument; ethical, emotional, and rational appeals (or *ethos*, *pathos*, and *logos*); and common logical fallacies. The chapter also offers three extra essays that argue multiple viewpoints on a single issue (immigration reform).

The Essays

The thirty-three essays in Part Two of *The Compact Reader* satisfy several criteria. Most important, they are interesting, and they plainly illustrate the rhetorical methods. The essays are also short, averaging two to four pages, so students will find them imitable; yet they are substantial enough for sharpening reading skills and encouraging lively discussion. A few longer essays provide a transition to more challenging academic work. Significantly, more than a third of the readings in *The Compact Reader*—one in each chapter—were written by students, demonstrating what is possible while reassuring your students that they, too, can write essays that others will want to read.

Though organized as a rhetorical reader, *The Compact Reader* offers a parallel thematic approach: the paragraphs and essays in each chapter relate in subject as well as form. Thus, for example, Chapter 5's narrative selections all deal with the subject of growing up, and Chapter 12's definition essays all address what happiness means. You might have students read two or three of a chapter's essays and then discuss in class their theme as an entry to a discussion of the rhetorical approach. Or you could focus discussion on just the theme. As noted on the following page, a "Connections" writing topic for each essay and a set of thematic topics for each chapter help students perceive and write about the thematic links both within and among chapters.

Prereading Activities

Provocative quotations from a wide variety of sources—pop culture to literature to social theory—precede each essay and focus on the essay's core theme. Journal prompts after these quotations emphasize writing *before* reading to encourage students to read more actively and critically.

Biographical and Essay Headnotes

The preface to each essay establishes a context for the essay, offering background on the writer's interests and expertise in his or her subject and providing information about his or her intended audience. Students are often inclined to skip such sections, so it may be worthwhile to point out how helpful the brief headnotes can be for analyzing the essays along with the discussion questions.

Critical Reading Questions

The questions following each essay help students analyze and evaluate the essay, either on their own or in class discussions. The questions are organized in four groups—Meaning, Purpose and Audience, Method and Structure, and Language—that lead students to examine the essay with an increasingly sharp focus. As mentioned earlier, the four groups of questions correspond to those following Jones's essay in the chapter on reading (Chapter 1). Possible answers to the questions are provided in this manual (see Part IV).

Writing Topics

At least four writing topics follow each essay. Some relate to the essay's content; some suggest a subject compatible with the method introduced in the chapter; several ask students to do research on a subject raised by the essay. "Journal to Essay" topics offer guidance on developing prereading journal entries into works for readers. Topics labeled "Cultural Considerations" lead students to examine the differences and likenesses between cultures and subcultures. "Research" prompts suggest focused library or Web investigations of topics suggested by the essays. And a final topic, labeled "Connections," encourages students to tease out thematic or rhetorical links between an essay and either a sample paragraph or another essay in the book.

In addition to the topics following each essay, every chapter ends with two sets of supplementary writing suggestions. The first set, "Writing with the Method," includes many possibilities for applying the chapter's method of development. The second set, "Writing about the Theme," includes three detailed ideas for drawing on the chapter's resources to explore its topic.

Appendix on Working with Sources

A brief overview of research and documentation gives students guidance on incorporating material from their reading into essays of their own. The appendix covers the most important elements of source-based writing.

The overarching assumption of this appendix is that students will be drawing on the readings in *The Compact Reader* and ideas gathered from minor research to support their own ideas in short essays, rather than developing formal research or term papers. Accordingly, the emphasis is on synthesizing outside materials to develop an original argument, with a focus on summarizing, paraphrasing, quoting, integrating sources, and avoiding plagiarism. The appendix also offers a few pointers on finding and evaluating sources in the library and on the Web, along with several MLA documentation models—for in-text citations and for works cited—for the types of sources students are most likely to use.

The appendix culminates in an annotated sample student essay that both demonstrates how research can help students discover ideas and illustrates the most important mechanical aspects of documented writing. Written in response to the "Research" prompt following Barbara Lazear Ascher's "The Box Man" (Chapter 11), "Women and Children First" is a brief essay, drawing on nine sources and effectively showing how research can inform a thesis without overwhelming a writer's voice.

Taking advantage of this coverage, many of the essays in *The Compact Reader* include a suggested writing topic, labeled "Research," that asks students to investigate a subject, in the library or online, as they respond to reading and develop their ideas.

Glossary

Newly integrated with the body of the book, this section provides definitions of key terms used in *The Compact Reader* and highlighted in bold in the text. Because most entries include page references to longer text discussions, the glossary can serve as an index as well as a freestanding quick reference. In some cases, the glossary offers specific aids — such as strategies for writing effective introductions and conclusions, with cross-references to the book's essays — that could serve as the basis of class discussion.

II
SAMPLE SYLLABI

The Compact Reader is designed to be flexible while offering enough material to support a composition class taking either a rhetorical or a thematic approach, as illustrated by the two possible syllabi offered here. Instructors can tailor reading selections and assignments to suit their own students' abilities and interests, incorporating additional texts or instruction as desired.

Rhetorical Approach

10-week term; 3 classes per week

Week	Activities

1   **Introductions**

Reading: Chapter 1
> Discuss Edward P. Jones, "Shacks"

Developing an Essay: Chapter 2
> Draft paragraph in response to Edward P. Jones, "Shacks"

Revising: Chapter 3

Editing: Chapter 4 (skim)

In-Class Peer-Review Workshop
> Revise and edit "Shacks" response

2   **Narration: Chapter 5**

Introduction to Narration, pp. 61–69
Annie Dillard, from *An American Childhood*
Lauren Fulmore, "Chasing Fairy Tales"
> Quiz

Description: Chapter 6

Introduction to Description, pp. 91–97
Marta K. Taylor, "Desert Dance"
> Journal Response

Description: Chapter 6
Ken Chen, "City Out of Breath"
William Least Heat-Moon, "Starrucca Viaduct"
    Turn in draft of first paper

3   **Example: Chapter 7**
Introduction to Example, pp. 118–25
Kim Kessler, "Blah Blah Blah"
    Journal Response

Example: Chapter 7
David Sedaris, "Me Talk Pretty One Day"
    Quiz

Example: Chapter 7
Perri Klass, "She's Your Basic LOL in NAD"
    Turn in revised draft of first paper

4   **Division or Analysis: Chapter 8**
Introduction to Division or Analysis, pp. 147–55
Scott Adams, "Funny Business"
    Journal Response

Division or Analysis: Chapter 8
Pat Mora, "Great Expectations"
    In-Class Peer-Review Workshop

Division or Analysis: Chapter 8
Andrew Warren III, "Throwing Darts at *The Simpsons*"
    Turn in edited, final draft of first paper

5   **Classification: Chapter 9**
Introduction to Classification, pp. 178–85
Brandon Griggs, "The Most Annoying Facebookers"
    Journal Response

Classification: Chapter 9
Jonathan R. Gould, "The People Next Door"
    Quiz

Classification: Chapter 9
David Brooks, "People Like Us"
    Turn in rough draft of second paper

6   **Process Analysis: Chapter 10**
     Introduction to Process Analysis, pp. 206–14
     Brian Doyle, "How to Read a Nature Essay"
        Journal Response

     Process Analysis: Chapter 10
     Marina Keegan, "Why We Care about Whales"
        Quiz

     Process Analysis: Chapter 10
     Rick Bass, "Gardens of Ice and Stone"
        Turn in revised draft of second paper

7   **Comparison and Contrast: Chapter 11**
     Introduction to Comparison and Contrast, pp. 236–45
     Alaina Wong, "China Doll"
        Journal Response

     Comparison and Contrast: Chapter 11
     Antonio Ruiz-Camacho, "Souvenirs"
        In-Class Peer-Review Workshop

     Comparison and Contrast: Chapter 11
     Barbara Lazear Ascher, "The Box Man"
        Turn in edited, final draft of second paper

8   **Definition: Chapter 12**
     Introduction to Definition, pp. 267–75
     Judy Brady, "I Want a Wife"
        Journal Response

     Definition: Chapter 12
     Augusten Burroughs, "Unhappily Ever After"
        Quiz

     Definition: Chapter 12
     Jessica Sayuri Boissy, "One Cup at a Time"
        Turn in rough draft of final paper

9   **Cause-and-Effect Analysis: Chapter 13**
     Introduction to Cause-and-Effect Analysis, pp. 295–305
     Ellen Goodman, "The Company Man"
        Journal Response

Cause-and-Effect Analysis: Chapter 13
Stephanie Alaimo and Mark Koester, "The Backdraft of Technology"
    Quiz

Cause-and-Effect Analysis: Chapter 13
Dana Thomas, "The Fake Trade"
    Turn in revised draft of final paper

10   **Argument and Persuasion: Chapter 14**
Introduction to Argument and Persuasion, pp. 326–42
Charlie Spence, "Sixteen"
    Journal Response

Argument and Persuasion: Chapter 14
George F. Will, "Subject to Interpretation"
    In-Class Peer-Review Workshop

Argument and Persuasion: Chapter 14
Marie Myung-Ok Lee, "I Was an Anchor Baby"
Roberto Rodríguez, "The Border on Our Backs"
    Turn in edited, final draft of final paper

Thematic Approach

14-week term; 3 classes per week

Week   *Activities*

1   **Introductions**

Reading: Chapter 1
    Discuss Edward P. Jones, "Shacks"

Developing an Essay: Chapter 2
    Draft paragraph in response to Edward P. Jones, "Shacks"

Revising: Chapter 3

Editing: Chapter 4 (skim)
In-Class Peer-Review Workshop
    Revise and edit "Shacks" response

2   **Experiencing New Places: Chapter 6**
Paragraphs: Rick Bragg and Helene Cooper
Marta K. Taylor, "Desert Dance"
    Critical Reading Questions

Experiencing New Places: Chapter 6
Ken Chen, "City Out of Breath"
William Least Heat-Moon, "Starrucca Viaduct"
    Journal Response

Writing Workshop: Thesis Statements and Outlines
    Turn in rough draft of first paper

3   **Sorting Friends and Neighbors: Chapter 9**
    Paragraphs: Dahlia Lithwick and Luis Alberto Urrea
    Brandon Griggs, "The Most Annoying Facebookers"
        Critical Reading Questions

    Sorting Friends and Neighbors: Chapter 9
    Jonathan R. Gould, "The People Next Door"
        Journal Response

    Sorting Friends and Neighbors: Chapter 9
    David Brooks, "People Like Us"
        Turn in revised draft of first paper

4   **Looking at Popular Culture: Chapter 8**
    Paragraphs: Jon Pareles and Luci Tapahonso
    Scott Adams, "Funny Business"
        Critical Reading Questions
    In-Class Peer-Review Workshop

    Looking at Popular Culture: Chapter 8
    Pat Mora, "Great Expectations"
        Journal Response

    Looking at Popular Culture: Chapter 8
    Andrew Warren III, "Throwing Darts at *The Simpsons*"
        Turn in edited, final draft of first paper

5   **Examining Stereotypes: Chapter 11**
    Paragraphs: Firoozeh Dumas and Sherman Alexie
    Alaina Wong, "China Doll"
        Critical Reading Questions

    Examining Stereotypes: Chapter 11
    Antonio Ruiz-Camacho, "Souvenirs"
        Journal Response

Examining Stereotypes: Chapter 11
Barbara Lazear Ascher, "The Box Man"
 Begin extended midterm paper

6   **Working with Sources: Appendix**
Jarrod Ballo, "Women and Children First"

Discussing Social Issues: Chapter 14
Paragraphs: Jenny Price and Martin Luther King, Jr.
Charlie Spence, "Sixteen"
 Journal Response

Discussing Social Issues: Chapter 14
Anna Quindlen, "The C Word in the Hallways"
 Turn in first draft of extended midterm paper

7   **Focus on Revision and Editing: Revisiting Chapters 3 and 4**
In-Class Peer-Review Workshop

8   **Midterm papers due/Midterm examinations**
 Turn in revised and edited midterm paper

9   **Discussing Social Issues (Immigration): Chapter 14**
George F. Will, "Subject to Interpretation"
 Outline brief argument essay

Discussing Social Issues (Immigration): Chapter 14
Marie Myung-Ok Lee, "I Was an Anchor Baby"
 Draft brief argument essay

Discussing Social Issues (Immigration): Chapter 14
Roberto Rodríguez, "The Border on Our Backs"
 Turn in brief argument essay

10   **Using Language: Chapter 7**
Paragraphs: Deborah Tannen and William Lutz
Kim Kessler, "Blah Blah Blah"
 Journal Response

Using Language: Chapter 7
David Sedaris, "Me Talk Pretty One Day"
 Journal Response

Using Language: Chapter 7
Perri Klass, "She's Your Basic LOL in NAD"
 Outline final paper

11 **Growing Up: Chapter 5**
Paragraphs: Michael Ondaatje and Jonathan Rauch
Annie Dillard, from *An American Childhood*
 Journal Response

Growing Up: Chapter 5
Langston Hughes, "Salvation"
 Critical Reading Questions

Growing Up: Chapter 5
Lauren Fulmore, "Chasing Fairy Tales"
 Turn in first draft of final paper

12 **Investigating the Working World: Chapter 13**
Paragraphs: Barbara Ehrenreich and Malcolm Gladwell
Ellen Goodman, "The Company Man"
 Journal Response

Investigating the Working World: Chapter 13
Stephanie Alaimo and Mark Koester, "The Backdraft of Technology"
 In-Class Peer-Review Workshop

Investigating the Working World: Chapter 13
Dana Thomas, "The Fake Trade"
 Turn in revised draft of final paper

13 **Considering the Natural Environment: Chapter 10**
Paragraphs: Miranda Smith and Ted Genoways
Brian Doyle, "How to Read a Nature Essay"
 Journal Response

Considering the Natural Environment: Chapter 10
Marina Keegan, "Why We Care about Whales"
 Critical Reading Questions

Considering the Natural Environment: Chapter 10
Rick Bass, "Gardens of Ice and Stone"
 Turn in edited final draft of final paper

14   **Pursuing Happiness: Chapter 12**
Paragraphs: Carlin Flora and Dagoberto Gilb
Judy Brady, "I Want a Wife"
   Journal Response

Pursuing Happiness: Chapter 12
Augusten Burroughs, "Unhappily Ever After"
   Writing reflection for journal

Pursuing Happiness: Chapter 12
Jessica Sayuri Boissy, "One Cup at a Time"
   Reflect on happiness and enjoy the end of the term

III
COMBINING *THE COMPACT READER* WITH OTHER MATERIALS

Because of its thematic focus and brevity, *The Compact Reader* can easily be combined with other classroom materials and approaches. Teachers using previous editions report that they have successfully integrated the reader with literary works, grammar textbooks, library research, current media, and the writing of their own students.

Literature

You may want to pair *The Compact Reader* with individual works of literature or with an anthology, using the chapter introductions and the essay models to guide students as they construct their own essays in response to literature.

The discussions of description (Chapter 6) and narration (Chapter 5) may help students analyze the descriptive and narrative passages they encounter in short stories or novels; and you may want to discuss the similarities and differences between fictional and nonfictional description and narration. Using these methods, students could experiment with either fiction or nonfiction (or both, contrasting in a class discussion the challenges they encountered with each). You can also emphasize that much writing about literature relies heavily on example (Chapter 7), comparison and contrast (Chapter 11), cause-and-effect analysis (Chapter 13), and argument and persuasion (Chapter 14); and you can tailor assignments in which students use these methods to explain, analyze, or evaluate the readings in the literature anthology.

Grammar Textbooks

Given its coverage of the writing process, *The Compact Reader* can complement a handbook or a workbook. The reader can inspire writing assignments and guide students through the stages of drafting, revising, and editing. For more detailed discussion of their specific challenges—such as paragraph coherence, sentence structure, or word choice—and for practice editing for grammar and punctuation, students can consult the other textbook. A class that meets three days a week could spend one day discussing an essay from the reader, one day discussing and planning the students' own essays, and one day covering sentence-level issues.

Research Tools

You may wish to help prepare students for academic writing by asking them to use outside sources in at least some of their work. Many of the essays and themes in *The Compact Reader* invite further investigation. Frequent suggestions for research writing ask students to consult a dictionary, an encyclopedia, or a book or article found through the library catalog or the Internet. When possible, specific sources are suggested in the entries in this manual. The assignments are limited so that students can quickly find and read the other sources, using most of their time to construct their essays.

If you incorporate research into the course, you may wish to spend a class period or two introducing students to the library and its basic reference tools. You may also teach formats for documentation of sources, such as the MLA system discussed in the Appendix.

Multimedia from Current Sources

One advantage of a brief collection like *The Compact Reader* is that you can supplement the paragraphs and essays with audiovisual and popular media on the book's themes or examples of the methods of development, or both. Op-ed pieces, *YouTube* videos, TED talks, artwork, infographics, essays in *Time* and *Newsweek*, articles in the school paper, letters to the editor—all of these are good sources. Students are often surprised to see how the "textbook" methods abound in current media, and at the same time they often respond well to the immediacy of last week's or yesterday's news items. In small groups or with the class as a whole, students can analyze the structure of these samples using questions like those first presented in Chapter 1 on reading. Outside readings can also serve as the basis for in-class writing topics. For instance, Brandon Griggs's "The Most Annoying Facebookers" might be compared with a blog post on or a critical analysis of the virtues and defects of social networking.

You can also encourage students to look for thematic connections or applications of the methods and bring them to class. For instance, students may watch for ways they use the methods in their own lives: comparing and contrasting in order to buy a new tablet; analyzing causes and effects in order to uncover the reasons for an unexpectedly high or low grade. Or students may examine their favorite podcasts, television programs, films, magazines, and other sources for ideas to support the readings' or the class's approach to a chapter topic such as work or the environment. And, of course, students can watch for the methods in the readings, lectures, and exams of their other courses: the descriptive lab report in chemistry, the cause-and-effect analysis in history, and so on.

Student Writing

Like many instructors, you may rely on students' own writing to provide the substance of some class discussion. Given drafts of student papers to read, students may work in small groups or in pairs, using the method of careful reading and analysis recommended in Chapter 1. Then, using the information and checklists in Chapters 2–4, students can evaluate their peers' writing, making specific recommendations for improving each draft. When the paper employs a particular method of development, students may tailor their recommendations by referring to the chapter introduction to that method. To instruct students in this kind of peer-editing procedure—or instead of small-group work—you may want to go over Nicole Lang's early drafts with the whole class and encourage them to practice the elements of peer review on her work, freed from worries of insulting or demoralizing their own classmates.

In addition to responding to the essays in the reader, students may respond, in writing, to one another's essays. Especially for topics in argument and persuasion (Chapter 14), you can circulate one or two provocative student essays and ask the class to write arguments countering (or reinforcing) the arguments in those essays. Or students can exchange their own argumentative essays blindly, and then write an essay in response to the one they receive. Knowing that someone will be responding to their essays invites students to formulate their arguments specifically and persuasively—perhaps more so than if they were writing just for you.

Chapter 5

Narration

Growing Up

Annie Dillard

from *An American Childhood* (p. 70)

Students should enjoy Dillard's dramatic rendering of a childhood thrill, which is likely to inspire them to write their own tales of glories past. Dillard is at her narrative and descriptive best here, capturing the feeling of childhood and the rhythm of the chase. Vivid, convincing detail is, of course, the key to making a story compelling, and only through careful word choice will students be able to re-create their excitement as effectively as Dillard does hers. The narrative provides rich opportunity to discuss how such description operates: see question 4 under "Method and Structure" and question 3 under "Language."

Content Quiz

1. How old was Dillard when the snowball event took place?
    [Seven years old.]

2. What kind of car did Dillard and her friends throw snowballs at?
    [A black Buick.]

3. Who got chased by the driver?
    [Dillard and Mikey Fahey.]

4. What did the driver say when he finally caught them?
    ["You stupid kids."]

5. How would Dillard have reacted if the driver "cut off [their] heads"?
    [She would have "died happy."]

Vocabulary Quiz

1. *Translucent* (paragraph 6) is closest in meaning to
   a. clear   b. frozen   c. solid
   [a. clear]

2. *Impelled* (14) is closest in meaning to
   a. chased   b. drove   c. knocked
   [b. drove]

3. *Compelled* (14) is closest in meaning to
   a. forced   b. teased   c. chased
   [a. forced]

4. *Obscure* (16) is closest in meaning to
   a. mountainous   b. hidden   c. empty
   [b. hidden]

5. *Exalting* (20) is closest in meaning to
   a. furious   b. close   c. glorious
   [c. glorious]

Answers

Meaning

1. "[T]hat you have to fling yourself at what you're doing, you have to point yourself, forget yourself, aim, dive" (paragraph 13); that the unbridled, unfettered enthusiasm of childhood comes from wholehearted concentration on whatever you're doing; that the courage to do it is simultaneously the catalyst for and reward of childhood enthusiasms, enthusiasms most adults (though not the driver of the Buick) abandon.

2. Getting in trouble is not per se a means to happiness—total concentration and courage and commitment, to the point of forgetting yourself, is. Being open to this kind of abandon may well get you into trouble, but it's the *abandon* rather than the trouble that leads to happiness.

Purpose and Audience

1. To recapture the glories of childhood, to re-create its adrenaline rush, and possibly to remind adults what they are missing—getting the most out of life.

2. Dillard's shift to *you* moves the spotlight from herself, the narrator, to the reader. The reader becomes an active participant in the football plays described, thus increasing the immediacy and intensity of the scene Dillard is trying to create.

Method and Structure

1. Dillard could have chosen to illustrate the enthusiasm of youth and its loss in adulthood through example, which would have brought concreteness to a general observation (much as the narration, a kind of extended example, does here), or comparison and contrast, which would have placed the change at the center of the essay. But the vivid narration brings with it an immediacy and a memorableness that might be hard to achieve through these other methods.

2. The elaborate detail in paragraph 12—including specific homes, a wood-pile, and an intersection—gives a feel for the intricacy and length of the chase. But to go on in this way, mentioning every feature of the landscape, would probably try readers' patience. Thus, in succeeding paragraphs, Dillard summarizes: the chase runs "block after block" (13, 14).

3. This sentence entices readers to read on and also lets readers know that whatever "trouble" Dillard got into was not serious. Hence, readers can relax, become fully engaged in the story, and vicariously enjoy the chase.

4. Description contributes specific concrete details that bring the scene to life. Some are "up to our boot tops in snow" (paragraph 3), "tire chains come clanking from afar" (7), "a smashed star with a hump in the middle" (8), "every breath tore my throat" (14), "there was a prow of snow beneath [the man's cuffs] on his shoes and socks" (16).

Language

1. Dillard seamlessly interweaves the straightforward, declarative language and limited experience of a child ("Some boys taught me to play football" [paragraph 1]; "we all popped it one" [5]; "this time, the only time in all of life" [9]) with the greater powers of observation and more sophisticated perspective of an adult ("complex trail of beige chunks like crenellated castle walls" [5]; "we reverted to the natural solitude of children" [5]).

2. Dillard feels admiration and approval because the man throws himself into the chase with the same verve she and her friends do. Some evidence: "a man got out of it [the car], running. He didn't even close the car door" (paragraph 9); "incredibly, he was still after us" (10); "Any normal adult would have quit. . . . He was a thin man, all action. All of a sudden, we were running for our lives" (10); all of paragraph 13; "He impelled us forward" (14); "he would never give up, this man" (14); "The point was that he had chased us passionately without giving up, and so he had caught us" (19).

3. Both images suggest presents, gifts, magic, enchantment, a childhood fantasy world.

Langston Hughes
Salvation (p. 76)

Students usually understand and identify with Hughes's childhood emotions, for nearly everyone can recall an early experience of disappointed expectations. That point of connection can provide a starting place for discussion of the essay.

Though Hughes does provide informative details on the revival, students who are unfamiliar with the ideas of sin, salvation, and the like may participate in discussion more actively if they are given some brief background information. In contrast, students whose own religious experiences parallel those of Hughes's aunt, rather than of Hughes himself, may bring to the essay their own strong convictions and may therefore have difficulty understanding (and accepting, even as a different opinion) Hughes's point.

Content Quiz

1. What is Hughes "not really" saved from?
    [Sin.]

2. Where is "Salvation" mainly set?
    [In Hughes's Auntie Reed's church.]

3. What is the "mourner's bench"?
    [The place in church for those who had not yet been "saved."]

4. Who is Westley?
    [The last boy to be saved besides Hughes.]

5. What did Hughes do the night of the day he was saved?
    [Cried in bed.]

Vocabulary Quiz

1. *Dire* (paragraph 3) is closest in meaning to
    a. dreadful   b. angry   c. sacrilegious
    [a. dreadful]

2. *Fold* (3) is closest in meaning to
    a. class   b. bevy   c. flock
    [c. flock]

3. *Rounder* (6) is closest in meaning to
    a. minister   b. watchman   c. mortician
    [b. watchman]

4. *Deacons* (6) is closest in meaning to
    a. fathers   b. minister's assistants   c. singers
    [b. minister's assistants]

5. *Rejoicing* (13) is closest in meaning to
   a. singing   b. praying   c. expressing joy
   [c. expressing joy]

Answers

Meaning

1. Hughes's point seems to be that his faith was shattered because he was not saved and because his lie passed for salvation. Whereas at first he is naively faithful, in the end he feels shameful and betrayed.

2. Hughes decides to get up because of the pressure he feels and because Westley has lied without suffering for it. Afterward, however, he feels betrayed that Jesus did not save him from the pressure or from lying.

3. Hughes plays on the word *salvation*. In saying that he "was saved from sin. . . . But not really saved" (first two sentences), he means that he performed the ritual convincingly yet felt no spiritual change. He pretended to be saved and in doing so lost his faith. For Hughes, at least, salvation seems a sham. (It is also possible that the adult Hughes felt that he *had* in a sense been saved—from hypocrisy.)

Purpose and Audience

1. Clearly, the experience was a significant one for Hughes (paragraph 15), and that fact alone could explain his including the essay in his autobiography. He does not seem critical of his aunt and the other adults in the congregation; as an adult he seems to understand that they would "see" Jesus in other than the literal way he expected to "see" (15). But this play on *see* itself may point out another purpose of the essay: to underscore the literal-mindedness of children, their inability to comprehend the abstractions by which adults live. Hughes may also have wanted to illustrate the point at which a child learns to rely on himself or herself, not on others, for truth.

2. Hughes does not assume that his readers are familiar with the kind of service he describes. Particularly in paragraphs 1, 3, 4, 11, 13, and 14, he provides details that clarify the procedure, such as the purpose and activity of a revival (1), the appeals made to the children (3, 4), and the blessing of the children (14).

3. The dialogue, lines from hymns, and descriptions of the noise level in the church (e.g., paragraphs 3, 7) re-create the pressure Hughes felt in a way that simple assertions such as "Everyone was after me to get up" could not possibly do. Besides sound, the details contributing to the sense of pressure include heat (6), loneliness (6, 11), time (6, 11), the aunt's presence (7), and Westley's proud grin (11).

Method and Structure

1. The autobiographical narrative form makes this more personal, and probably more memorable, than an argumentative essay would be. A title of an argumentative essay on the same subject might be "Hypocrisy in Organized Religion." Such an essay would probably also be more objective, presenting both sides of the subject, and possibly more objectionable to those who disagreed with the author's opinion.

2. Examples of explanation in Hughes's narrative: what he expects salvation to be like (paragraph 2); who Westley is (6). Examples of compression of time: several weeks of the revival retold in just a few sentences (1); the procession of children to the altar (6). Examples of omitted events: the gap between the end of the meeting (14) and Hughes in bed that night (15). Example of expanded time: the moments before Hughes decides to be saved (7–12).

   By condensing or omitting some events, Hughes keeps the narrative moving and emphasizes the crucial moments of pressure leading to his decision. These moments are drawn out in a way that makes us sympathize with Hughes's predicament, understand his reason for lying, and share his sense of shame and betrayal.

3. Examples of transitions: "then" (paragraph 3); "still" (5); "finally," "now" (6); "then," "while" (7); "now" (11); "suddenly" (13); "when," "then" (14); "that night," "now," "anymore" (15).

4. The process analysis is important because many readers will not have been to a revival meeting or will not understand how one works. It also puts us inside the process, allowing us to see it through Hughes's eyes.

Language

1. Hughes as an adult seems both amused and sorrowful. His use of "young sinners" (paragraph 1) is ironic, and a similar wryness runs through his descriptions of Westley (6, 11) and even of his own predicament (7, 11). But there is no amusement in the last paragraph, where Hughes conveys his pain and a sense of loss. Here the juxtaposition of Hughes's wish not to cry (because it is childish and he does not want his aunt to hear) with his inability to keep from crying (some form of *cry* appears four times) intensifies the sense of sorrow.

2. Hughes achieves the breathless pattern of a child reporting an overwhelming experience, thus leading us to see the experience from a child's point of view rather than an adult's.

3. The young Hughes seems to expect a literal physical experience (paragraphs 5, 7, 15); he will "see" something that "comes to" him from the outside. Hughes's aunt, in contrast, believes that one can "see" Jesus in one's soul (2); the seeing is not literal but spiritual. Hughes's understanding of *see* makes his disappointment and sense of betrayal inevitable.

Lauren Fulmore

Chasing Fairy Tales (p. 81)

In this cleverly told account of a lesson learned in childhood, a student writer draws on the structures and themes of fairy tales to share her discovery of an important truth. Fulmore's essay is an excellent example of a first-person narrative shaped by a strong thesis. Indeed, she told *The Compact Reader* that she chose her subject because the "specific moment of clarity" she recounts was one of the first times she understood herself and her place in the world: "I wrote this essay as a new freshman at a big college, a time of true self-discovery and uncertainty, so it was important . . . to reflect upon the self-assurance and security I felt that day, through this piece. I still look at it from time to time," she says, "when I need a reminder."

Fulmore relates her story, then, not merely for the sake of telling it but also to make a point about how literacies can both fuel imagination and affect one's understanding of self. Her details are clear and engaging, her verbs are strong and compelling, and her manipulation of narrative time is deliberate and logical. You might want to spend some time with your students analyzing the way Fulmore structures her narrative as two distinct, and contrasting, episodes that foreshadow and echo each other while making the significance of her experience clear.

Content Quiz

1. How old was Fulmore when she started running away from home?
   [Seven years old.]

2. Where did Fulmore always go when she tried to escape her family?
   [The woods behind their house.]

3. What did she usually pack to bring on her escapades?
   [A bindle—or cloth tied to a stick—filled with "a chunk of bread, a few slices of cheese, and an apple."]

4. What kind of parents did Fulmore wish she had?
   [Fairy-tale royalty. She imagined a "beautiful mother" and "regal father" who would throw a *Cinderella*-type ball to celebrate her return, as well as a "fairy godmother and king father."]

5. What kind of parents did she actually have?
   [Loving, hard-working, and "magical."]

Vocabulary Quiz

1. *Bindle* (paragraph 3) is closest in meaning to
   a. candle   b. sword   c. knapsack
   [c. knapsack]

2. *Ambiance* (5) is closest in meaning to
   a. atmosphere   b. uncertainty   c. emergency vehicle
   [a. atmosphere]

3. *Exasperated* (5, 8) is closest in meaning to
   a. breathless   b. worsened   c. irritated
   [c. irritated]

4. *Devoid* (11) is closest in meaning to
   a. lacking   b. annoyed   c. evil
   [a. lacking]

5. *Lair* (13) is closest in meaning to
   a. swamp   b. hiding place   c. fear
   [b. hiding place]

Answers
Meaning

1. Fulmore explains that her imagination was influenced by the fairy tales and similar children's stories she read or otherwise consumed. Although she was a normal girl with a normal family, she came to think of herself as a kind of "Cinderella" character forced to do chores by an "evil" family that had stolen her from her birth parents (paragraph 1). Prone to drama, she took to exploring the woods around her home while she fantasized about finding her "real" family.

2. As readers know from the start, Fulmore was with her "real family" all along; she just hadn't appreciated them until they came to her rescue.

3. Fulmore's thesis appears at the very end of her essay: "I had a family who loved me, and for an average seven-year-old girl, that is about as magical as it gets" (paragraph 19). She expresses this epiphany at the end because she has built up to it, both in her experience as a child and in the structure of her essay.

Purpose and Audience

1. Fulmore's purpose, it seems, is to re-create a significant experience from her childhood and to express the understanding it brought to her. In telling her story in the detached form of a fairy tale, she effectively relates the influence such stories had on her.

2. She reasonably assumes basic familiarity with the stories that affected her, but even if readers haven't been exposed to *Cinderella*, *Gone with the Wind*, or any Western fairy tales that tell of enchanted forests and abducted royalty, Fulmore makes it clear from her descriptions what those stories tend to entail.

3.   Fulmore uses internal dialogue (italicized) and spoken utterances (in quotation marks) to express her own feelings and to re-create the voices she both imagined and heard. The repetition of "I'm here!" in paragraphs 7 and 18 in particular foreshadows the climax of her story and circles back to her first adventure in a satisfying way.

Method and Structure

1.   Narration is all about telling a story, and that's what Fulmore does here. She makes full use of summary, descriptive details, dialogue, and narrative time to share her experience and what she learned from it.

2.   Besides the introduction, the body of Fulmore's essay has three major sections: paragraphs 2–8 narrate the first time she roamed the woods in search of her imagined family, paragraphs 9–11 condense several additional adventures as a transition between the two framing episodes, and paragraphs 12–19 relate the episode when she got hurt and was rescued by her family. By emphasizing the two contrasting experiences and minimizing several uneventful outings, Fulmore effectively focuses her readers on the point of her narrative while keeping them engaged.

3.   Fulmore builds suspense by relating her story in the form of a fairy tale, bringing readers along with her from the point of view of an injured, frightened child.

4.   The dominant impression is of an ominously enchanted forest populated with monsters. The details make the story vivid for readers and help them to imagine the woods as Fulmore experienced them.

Language

1.   Additional examples of strong verbs include "devised" (paragraph 2); "planted," "donned," "crept" (3); "tramping" (4); "trickle" (5); "beaming" (6); "rushed," "gazed," "stumbled" (8); "stripped" (9); "wander," "fencing" (11); "scouting," "cascading," "grappled" (12); "kicked," "writhed," "frolicking," "fathom" (13); "shooting" (14); "seep," "creep" (15); "whine," "ache" (16); "dawned," "howling," "pulsating," "chalked" (17); "washed," "mustered," "croaked," "flashed," "screamed" (18); "glared," "whisked" (19). Fulmore could have used forms of *make* or *be*, for instance, or less vivid verbs in general, but the verbs she chose are more colorful and meaningful, and they make the story far more vivid and compelling for readers.

2.   Fulmore demonstrates skill in crafting and using figures of speech that echo fairy-tale tropes. Most effective is her deliberate personification of the "backstabbing tree" from which she fell as a monster with intent to harm (paragraphs 12–13), as well as her personification of the wind (6, 16–17). Additional figures of speech include similes and metaphors of slavery

(1, 4), the simile of "like a magnet to metal" (6), the metaphorical "cloud of heartbreak and doom" (8), images of cells and dungeons (1, 8, 9), and more. Students will point to their own favorites.

3. Fulmore tells her story with a certain amount of detached irony, appropriate because as an adult she now understands the implications of her experience and the lesson it taught her.

Chapter 6

Description
Experiencing New Places

Marta K. Taylor
Desert Dance (p. 98)

Taylor's piece provides an excellent example of description and, as a student essay, is most inspiring. Her images are strong and fresh, relying on figures of speech throughout, so you might focus discussion on how Taylor's use of figures contributes to the emotion of her description. (See question 4 under "Language.") As noted in question 2 under "Method and Structure," the essay builds to a climax and effectively juxtaposes the two components of her piece: safety and violence.

Taylor's essay may remind students of significant places from their childhood, and the prereading journal prompt and "Journal to Essay" writing topic have them explore their memories in a subjective description. You might have students do some freewriting to help them recall as much detail as possible from their memories, exploring each of their senses in relation to the place.

Content Quiz

1. Why does Taylor's family drive through the night?
   [The hotels are filled because of the rodeo.]

2. Where did Taylor grow up?
   [Los Angeles.]

3. What phenomenon was seldom seen in Taylor's childhood?
   [Rain.]

4. What looks like old men to Taylor?
   [The twisted forms of the Joshua trees.]

5. What tells Taylor that she is not dreaming?
   [The cramp in her neck and the pain in her elbow.]

Vocabulary Quiz

1. *Paragon* (paragraph 3) is closest in meaning to
   a. tower   b. model   c. protection
   [b. model]

2. *Silhouette* (5) is closest in meaning to
    a. figure   b. outline   c. frame
    [b. outline]

3. *Gnarled* (6) is closest in meaning to
    a. contorted   b. mangled   c. extended
    [a. contorted]

4. *Frolicked* (6) is closest in meaning to
    a. played   b. zigzagged   c. lit
    [a. played]

5. *Gaudy* (7) is closest in meaning to
    a. magnificent   b. costly   c. showy
    [c. showy]

Answers

Meaning

1. "State of grace" (paragraph 7) does seem to capture Taylor's dominant impression. For her, this state consists of feeling safe (e.g., "motionless, soundless, protective paragon" [3]) while witnessing a violent, God-created lightning storm (5, 6). Taylor's trip through the desert resembles a religious experience: besides "state of grace," she refers to "sacred silence" (2), draws an image of her father's haloed head (3), notes the timelessness of the experience (4), and alludes to God (6).

Purpose and Audience

1. Taylor's opening sentence explains why she and her family are traveling at night and at the same time pulls the reader quickly into the story. By using the pronoun *we* without any initial explanation of who "we" is, she captures her reader's interest.

2. Students' answers will vary, perhaps depending on whether they're familiar with the desert. Some especially vivid images: the Joshua trees like old men, God taking a photograph, the flashing fireworks of the lightning (all paragraph 6).

Method and Structure

1. Taylor is trying to convey a contrast between the interior peace of the car and the exterior chaos of the storm. The "violent, gaudy display" (paragraph 7) going on outside makes her feel even safer and more cocooned in the car, where her father, the "protective paragon of security and strength" (3) is in control, there is no noise, her sleeping brother's chest rises and falls, and the "gentle heat of the engine" (5) keeps her warm.

2. The structure builds to a climax and evenly juxtaposes safety and violence, the components of Taylor's "state of grace" (paragraph 7).

3.   Taylor's emotions appear, for example, in "wicked" and "cleverly" (paragraph 1), "sacred silence" (2), "protective paragon" (3), "violent sucking rush of air" (4), "gentle heat of the engine" (5), the "empty and lonely" road (6).

4.   Since the narrative framework builds to a climax at Taylor's "state of grace" (paragraph 7), it rivets attention on that impression.

Language

1.   Taylor's language creates an atmosphere of peace, stillness, and protection: "sacred silence" (paragraph 2); "protective paragon of security and strength" (3); "gentle heat of the engine" (3); "still in silence, still in darkness" (6).

2.   The title refers to the "dance" of the lightning, and several phrases in paragraphs 6 and 7 support the notion of movement: the "natural strobe" of the lightning, the "hobble" of the trees, the fireworks that "frolicked," the "movements of a marionette," the "gaudy display."

3.   The Joshua trees are "twisted" and look like "old men" with a "feeble hobble" (paragraph 6). This is a vivid if economical description of the trees, which are thought to have been named after Joshua, the biblical leader of Israel, because their limbs angle upward like arms. In the desert, they stand taller than their surroundings and do resemble gnarled humans.

4.   Similes: hair playing with light "like tinsel" (paragraph 3), the lightning "like a rapidly growing twig" (5), a flash "as if God were taking a photograph" (6), the road that "shone like a dagger" (6), the trees that "looked like old men" (6).

5.   The final long sentence intensifies the sense that Taylor is coming out of the spell of the storm. The rush of words parallels the rush of feeling in her neck and elbow.

William Least Heat-Moon
Starrucca Viaduct (p. 102)

Heat-Moon's portrait of an old railroad bridge offers the most objective description in this chapter and is an excellent example of a writer's use of description for its own sake. If the relative lack of emotion leads some students to complain that the essay is dull, point them to the ways in which the author's sense of awe colors even the most mundane details of his subject. Heat-Moon wishes to share his impressions without trying to infuse them with a larger meaning, and sometimes, that's enough.

The author is also a trained photojournalist, which is suggested by the rich visual details in this piece. Students could compare and contrast the power of a photograph and the power of language to capture a scene. Class discussion would also be enriched by asking students to share images of unusual structures in their hometowns or from their travels.

Content Quiz

1.   What is the Starrucca viaduct?
     [A nineteenth-century masonry bridge for trains.]

2.   Where is the viaduct located?
     [Lanesboro, Pennsylvania.]

3.   When was the viaduct built?
     [In the mid-nineteenth century. Construction was completed in 1848.]

4.   Describe the landscape in the immediate vicinity of the Starrucca viaduct.
     [The bridge spans a deep, wide valley that has a small creek running through it; the surrounding hills are heavily wooded.]

5.   Are there other structures in the United States comparable to the Starrucca viaduct?
     [Heat-Moon identifies two similar bridges, but they're not as grand or as old.]

Vocabulary Quiz

1.   *Gorge* (paragraph 1) is closest in meaning to
     a. overindulge   b. bridge   c. valley
     [c. valley]

2.   *Unembellished* (2) is closest in meaning to
     a. true   b. plain   c. clear
     [b. plain]

3.   *Yore* (3) is closest in meaning to
     a. possession   b. past   c. distant
     [b. past]

4.   *Dollop* (3) is closest in meaning to
     a. dose   b. run   c. cookie
     [a. dose]

5.   *Aqueduct* (4) is closest in meaning to
     a. blue   b. journey   c. pipeline
     [c. pipeline]

Answers

Meaning

1. Although "Starrucca Viaduct" is primarily an exercise in pure description, Heat-Moon does have a point: that the Starrucca viaduct is wonderful. He frames his essay with two statements of this main idea, starting with "it was unquestionably enough, and the longer I looked, it became more than enough" (paragraph 2) and concluding with "The Starrucca Viaduct, in architecture and undeserved anonymity, stands supreme" (6).

2. Heat-Moon's dominant impression is awe, something local residents may no longer feel because people who see the bridge every day "almost take [it] for granted" (2).

3. By "plainness" the author is referring to the solidness of the stone structure and its lack of architectural embellishments (such as curlicues or gargoyles, one supposes). He finds beauty in its simplicity and functionality.

Purpose and Audience

1. The writer's primary purpose is to explain the beauty of a site that he feels local people fail to appreciate. He seems to be responding to the problem he states in paragraph 2: "If they cherish it, to them it's still just 'the stone bridge.'" At the same time, there is a personal element to the essay: Heat-Moon delights in incongruity and absurdity—two traits epitomized by the bridge as he describes it—and he wants readers to find pleasure in the strangeness around them.

2. Heat-Moon is writing for a general audience, one that he nonetheless assumes is educated and has a broad set of interests, ranging from folklore to architecture to history. Notice, for instance, how he uses architectural terms (such as *portals*, *piers*, and *parapets* in paragraph 3) and historic references (most notably in paragraph 4, but also in 5 and 6) without feeling a need to explain them. Although it's possible that residents of Lanesboro would read the essay, Heat-Moon introduces it with a reference to travelers, suggesting that such people are the kind of readers he has in mind.

Method and Structure

1. By vocalizing other travelers' disappointments with their destinations, Heat-Moon sets up the contrast with his own experience: the Starrucca viaduct was everything he anticipated, and more.

2. The author dwells on sight because the bridge's visual appearance is the whole point of the essay. Invoking smell or taste would detract from the dominant impression Heat-Moon is trying to create. There is some element of touch in his description, however: notice the references to solidity (paragraph 2), sharpness (3), and wetness (5). And the absence of sound is a particularly elegant touch, invoking the silence of the place and suggesting that the bridge has fallen out of use.

3. Students may not notice at first that the picture illustrates the bridge as it was, not as it is. Although the architecture and scale remain unchanged, visually showing the houses at the foot of the bridge emphasizes Heat-Moon's point about its overwhelming size. As he describes the site today, the surrounding area is more forested, which makes the structure seem somewhat smaller to contemporary visitors than it would have looked originally. The contrast contributes to Heat-Moon's admiration for his subject by underscoring both the bridge's longevity and its adaptability to change.

4. Heat-Moon uses a spatial organization, starting at the view from beneath the bridge and moving to the top, shifting in distance from near to far. The effect is something akin to stepping back from an impressionist or pointillist painting, clarifying the image by distancing it.

5. The comparisons situate the Starrucca viaduct in architectural history and allow Heat-Moon to back up his assertion that the underappreciated structure is just as impressive as anything that came before it and even more impressive than what may have been built or rebuilt in later years.

Language

1. Heat-Moon shifts from third person ("one's disappointment" [paragraph 1]) to second person ("have you heard" [1]) to first person ("the first time I came upon" [2]) back to third person ("If they cherish it" [2]) and again to first person ("Q and I arrived" [3]) before settling into the third-person point of view he prefers for the description itself. Students may reasonably object that such shifts are unnecessary and distracting, but Heat-Moon manages them skillfully enough. In switching back and forth (and back again) in the introduction, he establishes what he considers a universal truth, appeals directly to readers' experiences, and invokes his personal involvement with the subject of his description before assuming a relatively objective point of view.

2. The colorful imagery (the enormous span juxtaposed with the pebble-throwing child and narrow creek beneath, the thought that a builder made a mistake) makes the bridge more real for readers and underscores the absurdity of its scale.

3. The description in "Starrucca Viaduct" is mostly objective, but Heat-Moon's figures of speech allow him to convey the love he feels for his subject without making explicit reference to his emotions. Especially striking figures include the fanciful idea that the bridge is "a rock wall of massive doorways opening into some country beyond America" (paragraph 3) and trains with "monstrous loads behind them" (6), which, combined with the giant's head suggested in the imagery of paragraph 4, helps to create a fairy-tale landscape in readers' minds.

Ken Chen
City Out of Breath (p. 108)

Chen's essay is the most challenging of the readings in this chapter, subtly using description of a family visit to a crowded city to explore issues of otherness, imperialism, and cultural dislocation without directly naming any as his subject. But even if students miss Chen's deeper points, "City Out of Breath" offers promising topics for writing: getting lost and adjusting to unfamiliar surroundings. Chen's experience is highly personal, and in using description both impressionistic and precise, he succeeds in creating a sense of gleeful confusion that his readers can easily appreciate.

Content Quiz

1. With whom did the author visit Hong Kong?
   [His father and "stepgrandmother-to-be"—either his father's fiancée's mother or his grandfather's fiancée.]

2. When are the street markets in Hong Kong open?
   [At night.]

3. What is Victoria Peak?
   [A "touristy lookout"; the highest point in Hong Kong.]

4. What three languages are most often heard in the city?
   [Mandarin, Cantonese, and English]

5. To what event did seven hundred people in Tai O, a fishing village, lose their homes while Chen was in Hong Kong?
   [A fire.]

Vocabulary Quiz

1. *Symphonic* (paragraph 3) is closest in meaning to
   a. loud   b. crashing   c. harmonious
   [c. harmonious]

2. *Contiguous* (3) is closest in meaning to
   a. catching   b. simultaneous   c. constant
   [b. simultaneous]

3. *Encroaching* (8) is closest in meaning to
   a. misleading   b. invasive   c. awkward
   [b. invasive]

4. *Vertigo* (10) is closest in meaning to
   a. dizziness   b. height   c. truth
   [a. dizziness]

5. *Austere* (11) is closest in meaning to
    a. stingy   b. lovely   c. stern
    [c. stern]

Answers
Meaning

1. Because Chen's essay is so poetic and impressionistic, his main idea can be difficult to pinpoint. Essentially, his point seems to be that Hong Kong is a place of dizzying contradictions imposed by a mix of international cultures converging in one place—that it is, in his father's words, "a strange city" (paragraph 6). Students may well have different interpretations; encourage them to explain their conclusions.

2. As Chen suggests, code-switching is the practice of adjusting language, dialect, or diction to the circumstance—so that, for instance, college students might speak formal academic English in class but revert to slang or regionalisms when conversing with friends or family. The concept is central to Chen's idea that "Hong Kong is an intensely international city" (paragraph 7), where everyone shifts among languages and cultures as needs dictate.

3. Most of Chen's allusions—to Milton's *Paradise Lost* (paragraphs 6 and 8), to Merchant Ivory (11), to Samuel Johnson (12)—are products of the England that colonized Hong Kong. But the author also throws in references to American film noir (3) and cartoons (6) and to Chinese paintings (3), postcards (9), and films (11) to emphasize the extent of the cultural intermixing evident in the city.

4. Chen's final sentence is deliberately ambiguous, its multiple possible meanings reinforcing his idea that the very meaning of Hong Kong is impossible to pin down. The "fire" is a metaphor—a mixed sense of energy, destruction and rebirth, oxygen consumption, and spectacle that perfectly captures Chen's impression of the city. At the same time, it offers a literal reference back to Chen's misremembering of the news of the fire that displaced seven hundred residents of the fishing village in Tai O (paragraph 13), as well as an impressionistic reference back to Chen's description of the restaurant waiters scurrying as though the kitchen were on fire (13).

Purpose and Audience

1. The sentence is a statement of the author's purpose in writing this essay. It also expresses a paradox, much as Hong Kong itself is a paradox for Chen.

2. Chen provides extensive detail and uses concrete language and fresh figures of speech to bring his experiences to life for readers, who he rightly assumes may not be familiar with Hong Kong or its history. Note, for instance, the way he describes his impression of the crowded streets of Kowloon in paragraph 3, his depiction of the man with "short, wiry hair

that resembles a scouring pad" whom the guide asks for directions (5), and the care he takes in depicting the view from the gondola to Victoria Peak (9). In combining subjective and objective description, Chen ensures that readers will recognize the sensations and confusion he felt even if the city of Hong Kong itself remains remote and unknowable for readers.

Method and Structure

1. The dominant impression is one of breathlessness brought on by vertigo.

2. Chen's point of view is moving (upward, especially) and psychologically close.

3. Chen appeals to all five senses, often multiple ones in the same paragraph or sentence: sight ("If an American city at night is film noir, then Hong Kong is just a camera blur" [paragraph 3]); touch ("drenching humidity" [6], "wet-walled alleys" [7], "greasy night markets" [8]); implied smell ("panting" [2]; "a city out of breath" [10]; Chanel perfume [8]); sound ("The all-Chinese police band plays bagpipes" [3], "the slow English dispatched on foreigners and children" [8]); and taste ("She chews on a piece of lettuce" [3], "A McDonald's sits next to a vegetable cart" [3], "sticky-rice tamales" [8]).

4. The flashbacks help to establish context, but even more so, they contribute to Chen's "experiment in time travel" (paragraph 3)—his idea that Hong Kong is a place where time and space disorient by shifting constantly.

Language

1. "City Out of Breath" offers an example of highly subjective description. The use of first person makes the essay more personal and intimate, helping us feel the sensations Chen describes as though we were breathlessly climbing our way through Hong Kong with him. The present tense gives a sense of immediacy to the essay, creating the impression that Chen is spontaneously recording his thoughts—even though he chose to describe the city five years after he had been there.

2. Just a few examples of Chen's abundant figures of speech include metaphors such as "Street markets are the opposite of flowers: opening up at night and closing at day"; similes such as "It's like a Chinese painting in which conflicting perspectives soak through the landscape like radiation"; personifications such as "time and space can flick off their objectivity and instead pulse and jump, symphonic rather than metronomic"; and hyperboles such as "a woman who looks about five hundred years old"—all in paragraph 3 alone. Students will find similarly inventive figures of speech throughout the essay.

Chapter 7

Example

Using Language

Kim Kessler
Blah Blah Blah (p. 126)

Kessler wrote this essay as a student to comment on a seemingly meaningless phrase common among her peers. Using examples, she shows that the phrase "blah blah blah" does have meaning—"generic rhetoric" (paragraph 2), "an intimacy that transcends . . . language" (4), and finally a "cover-up" (5). For this last meaning, Kessler provides a narrative example whose concrete, specific details are particularly effective.

One way to initiate class discussion may be to ask students who Kessler's audience is. Building on this question, have students discuss the various audiences they write to when they create compositions. Their instructors? Their friends? The free world? How do their examples change according to their audience?

Content Quiz

1. What are two other versions of "blah blah blah" used by Kessler's friends?
   ["yadda yadda" and "etc., etc."]

2. What are some of the "good reasons" that people use "blah blah blah"?
   [What one is about to say is so trite that it's not worth repeating; one wants to cut to the chase; the speakers are intimates who understand each other without words.]

3. Whom does Kessler bump into while walking across campus?
   [An acquaintance.]

4. What caused Kessler to have a mini-breakdown?
   [She was caught in the rain, lonely, wet, and carrying a heavy trombone.]

5. What solution does Kessler offer to "this 'blah blah' thing"?
   ["Put on your Walkman and avoid it all."]

Vocabulary Quiz

1. *Articulate* (paragraph 2) is closest in meaning to
   a. intelligent   b. well-spoken   c. interesting
   [b. well-spoken]

2. *Transcends* (4) is closest in meaning to
   a. rises above   b. eliminates   c. climbs
   [a. rises above]

3. *Accosted* (6) is closest in meaning to
   a. molested   b. priced   c. approached
   [c. approached]

4. *Gratuitous* (6) is closest in meaning to
   a. pointless   b. typical   c. tedious
   [a. pointless]

5. *Repercussions* (9) is closest in meaning to
   a. reasons   b. consequences   c. drumbeats
   [b. consequences]

Answers
Meaning

1. Kessler feels that she's being deceptive by using the phrase to avoid a subject she doesn't want to talk about. She uses it "in place of the atypical" rather than to "impl[y] the typical" (paragraph 7).

2. The "symbol of generic rhetoric" (paragraph 2) is "blah blah blah." The phrase is symbolic in that it takes the place of something else—it has no meaning of its own. It's generic because it can mean anything. This captures Kessler's main idea: that the phrase is deceptive because it is open to almost any interpretation the listener chooses to assign to it. The speaker can use this ambiguity to avoid speaking the truth without actually lying.

Purpose and Audience

1. Both: although Kessler says she is on the fence about "blah blah blah," most of her examples imply criticism of the phrase. She disparagingly refers to her "oh-so-articulate friends" (paragraph 2) who use it, and she feels dismissed and rejected when its use implies that "it is not worth their time or their energy to actually recount a story for my sake" (4). Equally, she feels guilty when she finds herself using the phrase to cover up something she doesn't want to talk about. Kessler may also be trying to amuse, as is indicated by her ironic tone: "oh-so-articulate friends" (2), "yeah, it's a verb" (4), "It's not very often that I share like that" (6).

2. Kessler is writing for an audience of her fellow college students. The subject is current slang among young adults, her peers; the evidence consists

of anecdotes from campus life; and the tone is ironic and informal (see question 1 under "Language").

Method and Structure

1. It's hard to talk about language in the abstract; it's a subject that calls for examples. The long example in paragraph 6 shows us exactly how Kessler uses "blah blah blah" to avoid subjects she doesn't want to talk about. Without it we'd have no idea what she means.

2. In paragraph 4, the examples illustrate the "couple of good reasons" for the prevalence of the phrase: many conversations are trite, and intimates do not always require language. The extended example in paragraph 6 shows that for the author the expression is "a refuge, a wall of meaningless words with which to protect myself" (7).

3. The introduction consists of paragraphs 1–3: these provide the background of the phenomenon and Kessler's main idea. In the body of the essay (4–8), Kessler gives examples that illustrate her main idea, showing how the phrase is used and misused. Paragraph 9 serves as the conclusion, offering a "solution" to the problem.

4. Kessler not only shows how "blah blah blah" is used but also explains what it may mean in these uses. "Blah blah blah" can be a shortcut for something trite or obvious; it can suggest that the person speaking doesn't want to waste his or her time; it can indicate intimacy between the speakers; and it can mean that the speaker doesn't wish to tell the whole truth. This use of definition helps Kessler demonstrate her thesis from paragraph 2.

Language

1. Kessler's tone is partly serious, partly ironic. Her style is at times very informal, almost like spoken language: "The thing about it is" (paragraph 2); "Well, maybe 'lie' isn't the best word" (5); "But, hey" (9); and all of her parenthetical remarks. This informality is appropriate for an audience of college peers: she writes as if she were talking to a group of friends. At other times she takes on a mock-serious tone, imitating an earnest academic analysis: "It has come to my attention," "symbol of generic rhetoric" (2); "recently noticed phenomenon" (3); and much of paragraph 4. Kessler means everything she says (until the last paragraph), but she seems to realize that there are more important problems than this one.

2. "[O]h-so-articulate friends" (paragraph 2); "I hope you can all handle that open display of vulnerability. It's not very often that I share like that" (6); the "reasonable solution" at the end of paragraph 9.

3. Kessler gives the piece an informal, chatty feel and makes it clear that she is writing for her peers.

David Sedaris
Me Talk Pretty One Day (p. 131)

In this direct, personal essay, humorist David Sedaris uses exaggerated examples to explore the frustrations of learning a new language by fits and starts. The essay provides a likely occasion for class discussion of the value of education and the reasons for persevering through failure. It is also almost guaranteed to get a laugh from students, many of whom have likely struggled through similar difficulties and feelings of inadequacy in their own foreign language classes.

Sedaris's reading of *Me Talk Pretty One Day*, from which this essay comes, is available on CD or mp3. Students may enjoy his distinctive delivery, familiar to anyone who has heard him on National Public Radio.

Content Quiz

1. Why did Sedaris move to Paris?
   [To learn French.]

2. What was the subject of the first lesson in the author's French class?
   [The alphabet.]

3. What do *vkkdyo*, *kdeynfulh*, *meimslsxp*, and *kfdtinvfm* represent to Sedaris?
   [French words he does not understand.]

4. What were the students asked to list about themselves by way of introduction to their classmates?
   [Name, nationality, occupation, and likes and dislikes.]

5. At the end of the essay, what does the author discover he has accomplished?
   [He can understand what his teacher is saying.]

Vocabulary Quiz

1. *Genocide* (paragraph 14) is closest in meaning to
   a. punishment   b. jail   c. murder
   [c. murder]

2. *Dermatological* (14) is closest in meaning to
   a. skin   b. beautiful   c. external
   [a. skin]

3. *Inanimate* (17) is closest in meaning to
   a. physical   b. nonliving   c. expensive
   [b. nonliving]

4. *Temperament* (18) is closest in meaning to
   a. weather   b. behavior   c. appearance
   [b. behavior]

5. *Diatribe* (28) is closest in meaning to
   a. lecture   b. pairing   c. question
   [a. lecture]

Answers
Meaning

1. Sedaris gives two reasons for the students' difficulties. To begin with, "they were limited in terms of vocabulary" (paragraph 11). And the teacher's hostile, sarcastic responses to their answers intimidated them from speaking freely.

2. About halfway through the term, Sedaris discovers that he's learned enough French to "understand every word" of one of his teacher's insults (paragraph 27). Able after months of hard work and perceived failure, he has a renewed sense of possibility, even though his final sentence makes it clear that his speaking abilities are still a work in progress.

3. Sedaris's thesis would seem to be that learning is difficult but worthwhile. He states this most clearly in his conclusion: "Understanding . . . [is] a small step, nothing more, yet its rewards are intoxicating and deceptive" (paragraph 28).

Purpose and Audience

1. Sedaris's purpose is to entertain, as evidenced by his humor throughout.

2. Sedaris is writing for an audience of his peers: adult Americans with an appreciation for ironic humor. He assumes a familiarity with the frustrations of trying to learn a language, a basic understanding of how French grammar works (gender assignment in paragraphs 15–17 and tense in 26), some awareness of European geography and history, and perhaps a begrudging admiration of French culture.

3. Sedaris describes his classmates as a motley group of immigrants from a wide range of countries who are "all young, attractive, and well dressed" and speak French better than he does (paragraph 2). He portrays the teacher as an angry, abusive villain bent on humiliating her students. Although he quotes her and the students frequently, he freely admits that he "understood only half of what this woman was saying" (3) and reveals through quotations that his classmates' French is not as good as he first imagined; furthermore, his examples are so over the top and clearly exaggerated for comic effect (especially the stabbing in paragraph 26) that readers know not to take them at face value.

4. As he does in most of his writing, Sedaris portrays himself as an oddball character who shouldn't be taken too seriously. Raised by a mother who purportedly prefers antacids to her children (paragraph 13), he enjoys "leafing through medical textbooks devoted to severe dermatological conditions" (14), expresses a fondness for "IBM typewriters, the French word for *bruise*, and [his] electric floor waxer" (15). Considering himself a "hard worker" and a "cut-up" (21), he nonetheless reveals a somewhat twisted imagination and determined irreverence in completing his homework (21).

Method and Structure

1. Sedaris piles on examples of awkward speaking and ridiculous insults, each more absurd and exaggerated than the last. He also offers examples of his own likes and dislikes to portray himself as irreverent and odd. The net effect is humor at the author's expense. Readers can share in Sedaris's pain even as they laugh at it.

2. The examples in paragraphs 2–3 illustrate Sedaris's initial fear of speaking French in class; those in paragraph 22 demonstrate his newfound fear of speaking French in public.

3. Sedaris's feelings appear to be mixed. It's clear throughout that he doesn't like the teacher and that he felt humiliated by her at every turn, and yet he seems to find her approach amusing for its bizarreness; he also reveals an admiration for the "subtle beauty" (paragraph 28) of her cruelties. Ultimately, her unorthodox teaching method worked for him, which gave him "great joy" (30) and an eagerness to continue learning from her.

4. By quoting his classmates, Sedaris chronicles their struggles to speak French. But by quoting his teacher's insults, he shows his own progression as a student. Riddled with nonsense words (see "Language" question 2) at first, her statements grow increasingly abusive—and yet more fully understood—over time.

Language

1. The sentences in paragraph 2 range in length from ten to thirty-three words. Some begin with the subject ("I've moved . . . ," "My school is . . ."); others begin with transitional and modifying phrases ("Regardless of their nationalities . . . ," "Some accents were better than others . . . ," "As an added discomfort . . ."). One sentence ("Vacations were recounted . . .") is in the passive voice to emphasize the author's own sense of nonparticipation. The second sentence coordinates three separate ideas, and the last two sentences use subordinate clauses.

2. The words are completely foreign and unpronounceable for both Sedaris and his readers. In using them, he re-creates the incomprehension he experienced. He can't repeat or translate the French words because he didn't recognize them or understand their meaning.

Perri Klass
She's Your Basic LOL in NAD (p. 139)

Klass's subject is inherently interesting to students: even if they don't hope or plan to go to medical school, they are at least intrigued by doctors. This essay addresses the issue of how language establishes the boundaries of groups. As such, it could initiate a discussion of special languages—in particular, technical terminology, jargon, and slang. Before or after reading the essay, students could discuss (in class or in writing) the purposes and effects of special language—is it alienating? mysterious? authoritative? Other sources of jargon worth examining include a sports broadcast, a conversation between computer specialists, or the writing class itself (for example, what effects do expressions such as *comma splice* and *relative clause* have on students?). The goal of any of these discussions is to arrive at an understanding of when jargon is useful, necessary, and effective, and when it is superfluous, distracting, or downright harmful.

Klass's essay beautifully surmounts a central difficulty in essays developed by example: how to weave together many examples without sounding monotonous. She avoids tedium through sentence variety (see the Focus box on p. 124 in the text) and also by varying the way she presents her examples: she explains some medical terms in parenthetical comments, others by anecdote; she treats some briefly, lingers over others; she groups those having to do with baseball into a separate class. Students often overlook the importance of variety—or, if they are aware that their writing lacks it, don't quite know how to remedy the problem. Klass's essay provides a useful model. (Question 2 under "Method and Structure" focuses their attention on this point.)

Content Quiz

1. What does the abbreviation "LOL" stand for in this essay?
    [Little Old Lady.]

2. In medical jargon, what is a "no-hitter"?
    [A night without any new admissions.]

3. In medical jargon, what is the accepted abbreviation for "nasogastric"?
    [NG.]

4. What nickname did the interns give the medical student who liked to cite syndromes named after researchers?
    [Mr. Eponym.]

5. In neurological research, what is a "brainstem preparation"?
    ["An animal whose higher brain functions have been destroyed."]

Vocabulary Quiz

1. *Primeval* (paragraph 2) is closest in meaning to
    a. mean   b. blissful   c. earliest
    [c. earliest]

2. *Terminal* (6) is closest in meaning to
    a. dead   b. final   c. calloused
    [b. final]

3. *Pompous* (15) is closest in meaning to
    a. pretentious   b. important   c. principled
    [a. pretentious]

4. *Locutions* (15) is closest in meaning to
    a. phrases   b. exclamations   c. jokes
    [a. phrases]

5. *Jurisdiction* (17) is closest in meaning to
    a. government   b. authority   c. guidance
    [b. authority]

Answers

Meaning

1. Klass's point: learning medical jargon marks a rite of passage into doctor-hood, a passage mitigated by her realization that the "new alien assumptions" (paragraph 18) of the language are not wholly positive or for the better. She reveals her full point in the final paragraph.

2. To Klass, medical jargon serves two useful purposes: the language builds "closeness and professional spirit" (paragraph 8), and it creates distance between doctors and patients (17). Given Klass's evident distaste for the disrespectful and even inhumane jargon illustrated in paragraphs 10–16, those particular expressions seem unlikely to build her professional spirit. They certainly do create distance between doctor and patient.

Purpose and Audience

1. Klass implies that she lost something by becoming a doctor; that there was something idyllic about the lack of knowledge she had before and something corrupted about her now complex life. The phrase suggests that she wants to explain a process that medical students must go through and also *why* they must go through it — in part, why the corrupted state is necessary for doctors.

2. Klass is halfway between a nondoctor and a doctor; she's looking ahead, gaining knowledge, but still clearly remembers that state of "primeval innocence" (paragraph 2). She expects her readers not to know about the doctor side, which she is at pains to explain to them in paragraphs 1, 2, 4, and many others, but she expects readers to identify with the nondoctor side: see, for example, "endless jargon and abbreviations" (2), terms that go "a little too far" (10), "I had resolved not to be shy" (11), jargon that makes "the beginning medical student nervous about the effects of medical training" (15).

3. Answers will vary. Klass does not define every term (for example, "naso-gastric" [paragraph 3]; "cardiac enzymes" [4]; "sickle-cell" [15]). But in most if not all cases, her meaning is clear without definitions: we don't need to know exactly what's wrong with the patient to see the point being made about jargon.

Method and Structure

1. Klass begins with an example for the sake of interest—and to create a sense of mystery: What are these terms? Will they be defined? She immediately makes her audience feel befuddled, thus putting them in the position she was in when she started working in the hospital—and in the position of a patient. The opening example in effect gives readers a capsule version of Klass's experience, which is what she wants to explain.

2. Other examples: "This sort of construction probably reflects . . . profound irritation" (paragraph 4); "Baseball metaphor is pervasive" (6); "Some people seem to become enamored of the jargon for its own sake" (8); "Then there are the more pompous locutions" (15).

3. Effects: camaraderie (paragraph 8), excitement (8, 18), arrogance and pomposity (8–15), discomfort (15, 18), distance (17).

Language

1. Klass is deeply concerned about the desensitizing effects that medical jargon has had on her and her colleagues. This seriousness toward her subject is most evident in the last paragraph: the tone becomes graver as Klass makes her concerns explicit. The essay's black humor is cautionary, serving to expose a troubling phenomenon.

2. Answers will vary. The shifts between *we/us* and *they/them* may be seen as emphasizing that Klass's own role is shifting: she doesn't identify fully with the doctors. The shifts between *I* and *you* are more difficult to justify thematically, though Klass evidently uses *you*—especially in paragraph 18—to extend her conclusions beyond herself.

3. Positive: "thrills," "communicate effectively," "professional speech," "closer and closer to being a doctor." Negative: "uncomfortably," "peculiarities and even atrocities," "avoid," "strange," "afraid," "alien."

Chapter 8

Division or Analysis
Looking at Popular Culture

Scott Adams
Funny Business (p. 156)

This brief, engaging essay by *Dilbert* cartoonist Scott Adams is not only amusing and entertaining in its own right; it's the rare division or analysis essay that analyzes itself. Opening with an admittedly "risqué" (paragraph 9) extended joke involving childish misunderstandings of human reproduction, golf, and an ill-fated French fry, Adams proceeds to explain to readers, piece by piece, why the joke is funny — while keeping them laughing through his lesson.

Spend some time with students examining the ways the author takes apart his own story to illustrate the elements of humor as he sees them. They should come to appreciate the skill with which Adams applies his principle of analysis, element by element, to his introductory story and, at the same time, keeps coming back to the joke — ensuring that the essay is neither dull nor an empty exercise, but a self-contained little gem.

Content Quiz

1. What did Adams accidentally inhale while at a dinner with his family and friends?
   [A French fry.]

2. According to Adams, what element is responsible for "[e]ighty percent of successful humor writing"?
   [The topic.]

3. Where did Adams work when he started creating the comic strip *Dilbert*?
   [In exactly the kind of office he mocked with the strip.]

4. Why does Adams refer to himself and his two schoolmates as a *troika*?
   [Because the word, which technically refers to a trio of horses, is inherently funny.]

5. In humor writing, what is a call-back?
   [The technique of "making a clever association to something especially humorous and notable from the body of your work," or circling back to an earlier joke.]

Vocabulary Quiz

1. *Troika* (paragraphs 5, 15) is closest in meaning to
   a. Russian   b. threesome   c. trick
   [b. threesome]

2. *Jeopardy* (9) is closest in meaning to
   a. game   b. danger   c. animal
   [b. danger]

3. *Risqué* (9) is closest in meaning to
   a. improper   b. playful   c. French
   [a. improper]

4. *Finesse* (11) is closest in meaning to
   a. fancy   b. reject   c. refine
   [c. refine]

5. *Analogies* (14) is closest in meaning to
   a. jokes   b. comparisons   c. chipmunks
   [b. comparisons]

Answers

Meaning

1. Adams does not state his thesis, but the main point of the essay is his answer to an implied question: "what makes writing funny?" (see "Forming a Thesis" on p. 151 of the text and the introductory remarks for "Funny Business" on p. 156).

2. The classic daily strip from 1994, an example of the *Dilbert* cartoons published in the days Adams was still working in an office (paragraph 10), illustrates every one of the principles of humor outlined in his essay: the topic (8) of evolution is itself dangerous (9), as is Adams's implication (13) that office workers are less evolved than monkeys; the strip features an animal (14); it pokes fun at people acting stupidly (11); it invites curiosity (16) and exaggerates (12) with the monkey's suggestion that people will be "kept in cages as pets"; it uses the funny word (15) "cubicle"; and the ironic ending (17) circles back to the first panel.

3. The last sentence is a "call-back," the essay's final element of humor (paragraph 17). Despite Adams's claim that he can't "give . . . an example of that now," it *is* an example, and in harking back to the first sentence with the image of an inhaled French fry as well as to the conclusion of the funny story (6), it makes readers chuckle while giving the essay a satisfying coherence.

Purpose and Audience

1. Adams certainly means to entertain, as is evident throughout; but he also intends to offer advice for writers, a purpose he states explicitly in paragraph 7.

2. Adams assumes an intelligent audience of *Wall Street Journal* readers (paragraph 9) who can "connect some dots" (13) in a story and make use of his "writing tips" (7). Because the essay was written for the *Wall Street Journal*, and because Adams is best known for a comic strip about office workers, he likely also assumes that his readers are businesspeople with at least a passing familiarity with golf (4) and an adult sense of humor.

Method and Structure

1. Despite E. B. White's assertion that analyzing humor kills it (see the quotation preceding the essay on p. 156), Adams injects humor throughout his analysis by using an extended joke as his subject. In first telling the story and then referring back to it again and again, he not only illustrates each point about humor with humor but makes those points unmistakably clear (and enjoyable) for readers.

2. Adams's subject is writing; his principle of analysis is the elements of humor that make a story funny. Those elements are the topic (paragraph 8), danger (9), human behavior (11), exaggeration (12), implication (13), animals (14), language (15), curiosity (16), and endings (17).

3. They are all topic sentences (even the one-word fragments); each identifies one of the elements of humor as Adams sees it.

4. After telling his joke in paragraphs 1–6, Adams explains the elements of humor from most to least important.

5. The story draws readers in, of course, but it also anchors Adams's analysis of humor writing. As both an example of a funny story and the source for examples for each of Adams's elements of humor, the joke makes his analysis concrete and his concepts relatable.

Language

1. Adams would expect readers to answer that *stalk* is funnier than *observe*, presumably because the latter is formal and academic while the former is more colloquial, carries a little "danger" (paragraph 9) with its connotations, and, like *troika* (5, 15), has more of an ineffable punch. True to his style, Adams uses several words in this essay that readers could consider inherently funny, because of either juvenile associations or the kick of consonants. A few examples: *French fry* (1, 5, 6, 8, 9, 12, 16, 17), *lodged* (1, 16), *sinus cavity* (1, 6, 8, 16), *puzzle* (3), *jig* (4), *spit-take* (6, 13), *sneeze-like* (6), *sphincter* (6), *risqué* (9), *awkward* (9), *dots* (13), *bugged out* (13). Students may well pick others, and at least some should point out that in repeating and restating several such words, Adams adds coherence to his essay.

2. Adams's tone is decidedly humorous, even juvenile, yet he takes the subject of humor writing seriously enough to analyze it carefully. It is, after all, his stock in trade.

Pat Mora
Great Expectations (p. 162)

Pat Mora is best known for her young-adult poetry and children's books, but she is also an astute literary and cultural critic with a sincere concern for the well-being of her primary readers, as this essay shows.

Mora's feminist analysis of advertising and media messages aimed at young women of Mexican American heritage is rich, intriguing, and complex. If students have difficulty following her line of thought, you might want to spend some time in class analyzing the essay's organization, a task suggested in the second "Method and Structure" question. Class discussion would also be enriched by asking students to find and share examples of Spanish-language advertising in current media, attempting to apply Mora's principle of analysis to what they bring to class.

Another fruitful avenue for class discussion could be the lingering relevance of Mora's examples, particularly her concerns that Latinos are marginalized in popular culture and politics (see Writing Topic 3). Students' assessments will, of course, vary. Some may be quick to name Latino musicians and athletes, for instance, and Mexican Americans have become better represented on television and film since 1993, if not nearly to the degree that Mora might hope for. Politically aware students may point out not only that several Latinas serve in government positions, but also that some, like Sonia Sotomayor and Amanda Renteria, hold or have held positions of great power. And yet fashion magazines have changed little, despite the occasional effort to promote more realistic body images—and debates over Mexican immigration have become increasingly hostile and heated. Encourage students to explore their ideas, but remind them to keep the discussion civil and fair-minded.

Content Quiz

1. What two groups of people, according to the author, appeal to the loyalty of Latinas?
   [Advertisers and politicians.]

2. Why are Latinas deemed "double minorities"?
   [They are women, and they are Hispanic.]

3. According to the author, what two conflicting adjectives do Americans often use to describe Latinas?
   [*Fiery* and *docile*.]

4. Name at least three of the six "Great Expectations" held for Latinas in America.
    [Loyalty, family values, marriage, ambition, education, and employment.]

5. What is a *tía*?
    [An aunt.]

Vocabulary Quiz

1. *Vigor* (paragraph 3) is closest in meaning to
    a. energy   b. lethargy   c. essence
    [a. energy]

2. *Machinations* (4) is closest in meaning to
    a. industries   b. logistics   c. conspiracies
    [c. conspiracies]

3. *Cacophony* (5) is closest in meaning to
    a. unpleasantness   b. combination   c. harmony
    [a. unpleasantness]

4. *Docile* (7) is closest in meaning to
    a. intelligent   b. submissive   c. strong
    [b. submissive]

5. *Median* (13) is closest in meaning to
    a. minimum   b. average   c. televised
    [b. average]

Answers

Meaning

1. Latinas are neither white nor male, so their minority status—and thus their disadvantages in American society—is compounded. Mora finds that "depressing" (paragraph 1), both because Latinas tend not to think about their position and because it forces them to "confront some unique challenges, [with] little support in fulfilling [their] potential" (2). At the same time, "double minorities committed to societal change . . . find [themselves] working doubly hard, struggling to prove to others that women like [them] are not a risk" (12). Such efforts, Mora says, are exhausting and alienating.

2. The "game" is, essentially, a process of overcoming obstacles in pursuit of success. What defines success, however, and how likely a person is to achieve it, are both shaped by the influences of family and society. Mora argues that achieving success is more of a challenge for Latinas because expectations have been set low and obstacles are more numerous. Discouraged from pursuing educations or professional careers, they are pressured by relatives to focus on family, limited by employment opportunities "to

be clerical or service workers" (paragraph 13), and "taught the world over that it's [their] job to be pretty" (15). Mora wants better for them. (Students who have read Dickens's *Great Expectations* may catch the implied comparison with the orphaned Pip, who starts out disadvantaged but rises to success because a mysterious benefactor both expects him to and provides the means to do so.)

3. Such portrayals are inaccurate stereotypes. Both limit opportunities for a Latina woman: If she's "fiery," she's not taken seriously; if she's "docile," she's taken advantage of. Overcoming either assumption, as Mora puts it, "T'aint easy" (paragraph 7).

4. Mora's thesis is that media messages emphasizing traditional values such as loyalty, femininity, and beauty limit Latinas' potential to become successful, productive members of society. She wants educators in particular to teach girls to recognize and reject such messages so that they can "wrench their lives free from images that bind" (paragraph 17).

Purpose and Audience

1. Mora's intended audience consists of her peers: Latinas in general and educators in particular. The use of *we*, *our*, and *us* throughout, along with the untranslated Spanish, reveals Mora's assumption that her readers are Spanish-speaking women. And she appeals directly to educators in paragraph 14: "As we mother, teach, write, mentor the next generation of women, we need to examine the lives of women in this country. . . . What do we know about ourselves and about the women who will appear in our offices and classrooms?"

2. Mora looks to a day when Latinas can "fulfill the dreams that our society, our family, and our self have for us" (paragraph 2), the twist being that she'd like those dreams to aim higher and include college educations and personally satisfying professional careers. To that end, she wants adult women to set the bar higher, to teach girls and young women to recognize the obstacles placed before them, to offer them encouragement, and to help them resist the "manipulation" (17) exacted by limiting media messages.

3. Mora's pleading question involves readers in the problem she has analyzed and encourages them to find solutions. Although some readers might take her question as an expression of hopelessness, it is in fact a call to action.

Method and Structure

1. After establishing her subject and providing background information about Latino demographics in her introduction (paragraphs 1–4), Mora identifies the most important value in paragraph 5: "we are loyal: to our families, the Spanish language, this country." She then traces several forms of that loyalty in the body of her essay: "brand-name loyalty" (5), cultural

loyalty that leads to "a sense of group identity" to which politicians appeal (6), and family loyalty that pressures women to marry and raise children rather than pursue their own dreams (8–13). Her analysis then shifts to focus on how media manipulations of such loyalties affect Latinas (14–16) before invoking an implied loyalty to children and concluding with a call for change.

2. Mora looks at advertising (paragraphs 4–6, 15), traditions (8–13), movies and television and novels (14), and women's magazines (14–15). Her principle of analysis centers on the messages sent to Latinas in particular, which allows her to conclude that such cultural elements, if consumed uncritically, conspire to keep such women from realizing their potential.

3. Although Mora doesn't say so explicitly, Gilday's documentary would appear to be about eating disorders among girls. She cites the film partly to show that she is not alone in her concerns, but more so because in documenting the negative physical and psychological effects of images of women in advertising, the film provides evidence for Mora's claim that images used in advertising hurt women.

4. Such messages set low expectations for Latina women, damage their self-esteem, lead many into poverty, lead others to eating disorders, and discourage all from achieving their full potential as human beings.

Language

1. Metaphors: "the game of Great Expectations" (paragraph 1), "In the eighties this country began to hear a Latin beat" (3), "cacophony of strange noises" (5), "the information nourishes us" (6), "We ingest pollutants" (14), "devour novels" (14), "sirens who beckon us" (15), "smiling decorations" (15), "How much time we spend looking the part, a part we didn't write" (15). Personifications: "demographics conspire with us" (3), "the woman who gazes back in the mirror" (11), "magazine pages that promise" (15), "flabby egos" (15), "images that bind" (17).

2. Mora is writing for an audience of educated Latinas, most of whom presumably need no translations (see question 1 under "Purpose and Audience"). Even for those who speak little or no Spanish, however, the meanings of the words she uses are easy enough to figure out from the cognates and the context of the essay. At the same time, using the occasional Spanish phrase helps Mora to show that she is a part of Latina culture even as she criticizes the messages aimed at Latinas.

3. Mora's tone is motherly and caring, bordering on mournful. She expresses sincere concern for a younger generation of Latinas and a deep desire to help them have better, happier lives than those afforded to most Latinas her own age.

Andrew Warren III

Throwing Darts at *The Simpsons* (p. 170)

This student essay provides a thought-provoking critique of a beloved television program and a good example of division or analysis. With a thesis that the success of *The Simpsons* is closely tied to its merchandising, the analysis may surprise students who do not view animation—or toys—critically. Warren examines various elements that have contributed to the show's popularity and then reassembles those elements to draw his conclusion that, although *The Simpsons* may not be what it once was, it can still entertain fans, if perhaps in unintended ways.

Warren's piece could open up class discussion about the commodification of entertainment. As an assignment, have students bring in their own samples of television or movie merchandise to demonstrate just how common and sales oriented such things are. Students should feel free to explore other areas of American culture where commercialization plays a role, such as sports and music.

Content Quiz

1. How did Warren acquire his *Simpsons* dartboard?
   [He got it on *eBay* for $30.]

2. What is "Bart-mania"?
   [The phenomenon of *The Simpsons*'s remarkable success in its first years, epitomized in the "marketing juggernaut" that accompanied it.]

3. According to Warren, what is "one of the show's favorite, and funniest, satirical vehicles"?
   [Krusty the Clown.]

4. What, for Warren, was "a milestone for good taste" when he was in junior high school?
   [Whether or not a person watched and appreciated *The Simpsons*.]

5. Does Warren watch *The Simpsons* anymore?
   ["[R]arely . . . and never the Sunday episode premieres."]

Vocabulary Quiz

1. *Adorned* (paragraph 1) is closest in meaning to
   a. loved   b. complicated   c. decorated
   [c. decorated]

2. *Zenith* (3) is closest in meaning to
   a. television   b. peak   c. low
   [b. peak]

3. *Implode* (3) is closest in meaning to
   a. fire   b. collapse   c. hint
   [b. collapse]

4. *Destitute* (4) is closest in meaning to
   a. poor   b. desperate   c. cruel
   [a. poor]

5. *Lampoon* (5) is closest in meaning to
   a. Harvard   b. fishing   c. mock
   [c. mock]

Answers
Meaning

1. Warren's thesis is that the value of pop-culture merchandise is determined by consumers' personal involvement with the show it represents. He states this most clearly in his conclusion.

2. He purchased the dartboard as a collectible. To remove it from its packaging would transform it from an investment to a toy, and he doesn't want to do that. After many years of holding it sacred, however, his attachment to the show has waned, and the monetary value of the board has dropped. He's ready to let go.

3. After years of stalled efforts, *The Simpsons Movie* hit theaters in 2007. Expectations were high, and some fans and critics exulted over it while others disparaged the movie as a disappointing attempt to revive interest in a show that has lost its relevance. Warren's phrase "less than mediocre" perfectly captures his ambivalence toward the movie: he didn't love it, but he didn't think it was necessarily weak, either.

Purpose and Audience

1. Warren's primary purpose seems to be to evaluate the cultural value of the television show itself, as reflected in the monetary value of *Simpsons*-themed merchandise; he also attempts to explain the connection between the two. At the same time, he clearly wants to entertain his readers.

2. Warren is writing for an audience of his peers: educated young men and women in their twenties with an appreciation for popular culture. More than anything, he assumes a familiarity with *The Simpsons* show and its merchandise. Warren's expectation of readers' familiarity is most striking in his casual reference to the "Kamp Krusty" episode in paragraph 4—he gives no indication of the episode's content, yet it's a fairly safe bet that his intended readers can summon a memory of it. (For those who cannot, the episode features the horrors Bart and Lisa face over a summer at the clown's sleep-away camp: rickety bridges, collapsing cabins, tire fires, starvation, and slave labor among them.)

3. The facts from Chris Turner's history of the show provide background information that Warren and younger readers may not have known from their own experience. You may want to point out to students that the quotation in this paragraph is problematic: the information itself could be considered common knowledge, and because Turner's words are hardly distinctive, Warren should have paraphrased. But because he did pick up the wording from Turner, Warren had no choice but to enclose it in quotation marks.

Method and Structure

1. He is trying to fashion a fresh interpretation of the show's meanings and cultural implications. Division is a natural choice: it allows Warren to apply an unexpected (but wholly appropriate) principle of analysis to his subject and to reassemble the elements into a new whole.

2. Warren uses the show's merchandising to direct his analysis. It's an excellent choice, not only because *Simpsons* memorabilia is so ubiquitous and closely connected with the program's long-running success, but also because the show satirizes such merchandise mercilessly.

3. The example of his *Simpsons* dartboard gives Warren an effective framing device. By starting with a memorable conflict over a physical object, Warren grabs readers' attentions and uses a concrete image to set up the subject of what might otherwise be an abstract analysis. He then circles back to his introduction in the end, neatly resolving the conflict while summarizing his evaluation.

4. Krusty the Clown is the perfect embodiment of Warren's point about *The Simpsons* and is key to his interpretation. The character, along with his show's ridiculous tie-ins, both exemplifies the function of merchandising in a popular program and satirizes it. The meaningful irony of the examples is somewhat complex, so Warren needs to take proportionally more space explaining it.

Language

1. Warren's tone is both authoritative and friendly—a difficult feat accomplished through a combination of academic and colloquial language. The tone is particularly appropriate for his lighthearted but serious evaluation of a popular comedy program.

2. The parenthetical remarks are a clever touch. Each one functions as a comical aside, allowing the author to inject some wry humor into an otherwise academic analysis and make a personal connection with his readers.

Chapter 9

Classification
Sorting Friends and Neighbors

Brandon Griggs
The Most Annoying Facebookers (p. 186)

With the continuing popularity of social networking, Griggs's essay should be compelling to students, most of whom will undoubtedly recognize themselves (and their friends) in at least one of the groups he identifies. Indeed, it's likely that many of your students spend time on *Facebook*; if some don't, consider starting a class discussion about why some people are resistant to the platform, or what other sites they prefer. What are the advantages and disadvantages of social networking? Why do some people embrace it so wholeheartedly, while others find it pointless—or even dangerous?

Content Quiz

1. To what social activity does the author compare *Facebook*?
   [It's "like being at a big party with all your friends, family, acquaintances, and coworkers."]

2. How did a recent study describe a significant percentage of *Twitter* posts?
   ["As pointless babble."]

3. How many *Facebook* friends does the average user have?
   [120.]

4. Did Jeff Goldblum "plunge to his death from a New Zealand cliff"?
   [No.]

5. Which category of *Facebook* users does Griggs describe as "just a little creepy"?
   [The Lurker.]

Vocabulary Quiz

1. *Mundane* (paragraph 6) is closest in meaning to
   a. weekly   b. unimportant   c. incorrect
   [b. unimportant]

2. *Innuendo* (9) is closest in meaning to
    a. suggestion   b. perfection   c. opposite
    [a. suggestion]

3. *Unabashedly* (10) is closest in meaning to
    a. argumentatively   b. harmlessly   c. shamelessly
    [c. shamelessly]

4. *Anglers* (12) is closest in meaning to
    a. fishers   b. mathematicians   c. liars
    [a. fishers]

5. *Chronic* (17) is closest in meaning to
    a. marijuana   b. constant   c. coughing
    [b. constant]

Answers
Meaning

1. Griggs's thesis is simple and can be found in paragraphs 4 and 5: ". . . *Face-book* becomes a daily reminder of why some people can get on your nerves" and "Here are twelve of the most annoying types of *Facebook* users."

2. The author seems to hold himself above the behaviors he criticizes, imply-ing but not stating outright that his own status updates are of the type he describes in paragraph 2: "artful, witty, or newsy . . . a real-time, tiny win-dow into a friend's life." His concluding sentence, however, suggests that Griggs may sometimes be a "Self-Promoter."

3. Griggs does not find such posts interesting; on the contrary, he finds them "mundane" and unnecessary. He is being sarcastic, a tone that surfaces throughout the essay. Other instances include "Thanks for sharing" (para-graph 10) and "Keep spreading the love" (14).

Purpose and Audience

1. The entire essay is tongue-in-cheek. Griggs's humor grows above all out of hyperbole (see question 2 under "Language"), with examples of posts that are so outrageous he sometimes feels a need to emphasize that he's not making them up. To achieve comic effect, he also uses a consistently dead-pan style, as well as sarcasm (see question 3 under "Meaning"). As funny as his examples can be, however, Griggs clearly has another purpose for sharing them. He wants readers to find themselves in at least one of the categories, and he wants them to change: "You probably mean well, but stop. Just stop" (paragraph 19).

2. Griggs assumes, probably rightly, that all or most CNN.com readers will have firsthand experience with *Facebook* and that most have been guilty (at one time or another) of the behaviors he criticizes. Even if some readers are blameless in that regard, however, they've probably seen posts of the type

he describes and shared in his annoyance and frustration. For readers who are not personally familiar with *Facebook*, Griggs offers enough examples to give a flavor of the kinds of things people share with their online friends.

Method and Structure

1. Griggs uses classification in order to exaggerate: the idea that all of any one person's posts fall neatly into one of his categories is absurd. The humor also depends on recognition: Griggs's categories are funny because, as overstated as they are, most *Facebook* users have been frustrated enough with posts of these types to believe him.

2. Griggs identifies his group, their shared characteristic, and his principle of classification in paragraph 2: "Sure, *Facebook* can be a great tool for keeping up with folks who are important to you. Take the status update. . . ."

3. The study of *Twitter* tweets, supposedly an academic source, found that 40% of them are "pointless babble." He mentions this because *Twitter* and *Facebook* have similar functions and because the findings help him establish, in a relatively objective way, the truth of his complaint that too many *Facebook* updates are also pointless.

4. The examples make it clear how Griggs forms his classes, provide a sense of recognition, help prove his point, and contribute to the essay's humor. Without them, his essay would be nothing more than a list of insulting labels, and his categories would make no sense.

Language

1. Griggs's tone is one of barely contained annoyance mixed with condescension toward the perpetrators he describes. Given the title of his essay, it's certainly appropriate, although some readers may take umbrage if they recognize themselves in any of the types.

2. Nearly every one of Griggs's quotations can be read as hyperbole, particularly the ones that he insists are real examples. (Students might rightfully object that they've seen the exact same or very similar posts from their own *Facebook* friends; the hyperbole lies in the accumulation of examples.) The exaggerations establish Griggs's comic tone of exasperation.

3. Griggs's labels for his categories all carry negative connotations as undesirable personality traits. By attaching harsh judgment to every category of status update he lists, Griggs makes clear to readers that they should not be indulging in such behaviors if they want to keep their friends.

4. By writing in the second person, Griggs includes readers in his categories of *Facebook* users and accuses them of behaving as badly as everyone else does. By confronting them with their own behaviors even as he makes them laugh at other *Facebook* users' foibles, Griggs stands a better chance of convincing readers of their complicity and persuading them to change.

Jonathan R. Gould, Jr.
The People Next Door (p. 191)

Writing for a composition course, Gould puts classification to good use in rendering his experiences with neighbors. Students may be inspired to write their own classifications of the types of neighbors they've encountered. Gould's style is sometimes simple, sometimes humorous, but always direct and engaging—as reflected in his classification system. You might ask students what kind of neighbor Gould himself seems to be, based on his narratives, portrayals of his wife, and references to his family: too friendly, unsociable, irritable, or just right? You may then want to ask students what kind of neighbors they are: what category would their neighbors place them in?

Another way to prompt discussion is suggested by the first writing topic. Ask students to classify the members of a group they belong to, such as one centering on family background, ethnic group, musical interest, or political belief. Gould's distinct classes and clear examples can provide a model for such a discussion.

Content Quiz

1. How often has Gould moved?
   [More often than he "care[s] to remember."]

2. How does Gould get rid of neighbors who are too friendly?
   [He opens the door and suggests they leave, or tells them their house is on fire.]

3. What is the rarest type of neighbor?
   [The irritable neighbor. ("Fortunately, I have only encountered this type of neighbor in a handful of settings.")]

4. Which neighbors like to cook?
   [Too-friendly neighbors and just-right neighbors. But too-friendly neighbors cook poorly.]

5. Can a neighbor change from one type to another?
   [Not according to Gould: "people do not really change."]

Vocabulary Quiz

1. *Culinary* (paragraph 2) is closest in meaning to
   a. social   b. tasteful   c. cooking related
   [c. cooking related]

2. *Disconcerting* (2) is closest in meaning to
   a. deceitful   b. ironic   c. disturbing
   [c. disturbing]

3. *Proximity* (4) is closest in meaning to
   a. approximateness   b. nearness   c. togetherness
   [b. nearness]

4. *Impoverished* (4) is closest in meaning to
   a. hungry   b. poor   c. dirty
   [b. poor]

5. *Pleasantries* (5) is closest in meaning to
   a. small talk   b. advice   c. niceties
   [a. small talk]

Answers
Meaning

1. "Over time, I have begun putting my neighbors into one of four categories: too friendly, unsociable, irritable, and just right" (paragraph 1).

2. Unsociable neighbors pretend that Gould and his family don't exist, while irritable neighbors blame the Goulds for everything wrong in their lives.

Purpose and Audience

1. Gould's conclusion makes his purpose clear: identifying neighbors by type, he (and by extension his readers) will be better able to understand and deal with them. Gould wants to share his system so that others might use it, and at the same time, it seems, he wants to entertain readers with types they'll recognize.

2. Not really; his essay could register with anyone who has a neighbor.

Method and Structure

1. Classification helps Gould arrange neighbors—an otherwise unmanageably diverse group—into recognizable and amusing categories.

2. His classification is based on levels of friendliness or hostility toward his family. The classification seems complete and consistent on its own terms. He could have chosen to classify neighbors by how well they kept up appearances, their level of activity, their wealth, or any number of other criteria.

3. Gould wants to show that his categories are universal, not just based on his own limited or unrepresentative experience.

4. He restores the wholeness of the subject and suggests one reason for writing the essay: the ability to recognize the four types of neighbors makes for better relations with them.

5. The too-friendly neighbor doesn't seem to recognize boundaries (actual or psychological) between himself and Gould. The just-right neighbor has good instincts about Gould's need for privacy and sociability.

Language

1. Gould's tone is deadpan: "For some strange reason these people become extremely attached to my family" (paragraph 2); "Interestingly, this fellow will eat anything my wife (bless her soul) might make in an attempt to be sociable" (4). In the final paragraph, he shows that his true attitude toward bad neighbors is one of good-humored resignation: he sees them as unavoidable nuisances to be taken in stride.

2. A few examples: "[S]top in as many as eight to ten times a day" (paragraph 2); Gould's pretending his neighbor's house is on fire (2); "the only way I know that someone lives in their building is the presence of a name on the mailbox and the lights shining through the windows at night" (3); "have them look at her as if she intended to poison them" (4); "not a crumb" (4); "starved and impoverished" (4). Students may make a case for other examples. The effect is to create humor by exaggerating the faults of bad neighbors.

David Brooks
People Like Us (p. 195)

In many ways an essay about the drawbacks of classifying, "People Like Us" uses classification to argue some controversial points: that multiculturalism is a flawed concept, and that elite liberals are out of touch with the majority of the American population. Depending on their backgrounds, students may find Brooks's essay enlightening, or they may cite their own communities to dispute his claims — a good starting point for discussion, suggested by the first writing topic.

Charles Murray, one of the authors of *The Bell Curve* (which Brooks cites in paragraph 11), expands on Brooks's concerns about liberal isolation in his 2012 book *Coming Apart: The State of White America, 1960–2010*. After discussing his thesis during an interview on *PBS Newshour*, Murray created an interactive, annotated quiz — "How Thick Is Your Bubble?" — to measure elites' awareness of mainstream culture (*pbs.org/newshour/rundown/2012/03/white-educated-and -wealthy-congratulations-you-live-in-a-bubble.html*). Having students take the quiz and discuss their results would be an interesting and entertaining way to examine some of the assumptions that underlie both his and Brooks's arguments.

Content Quiz

1. What does Brooks blame for the segmentation of America?
   [Human nature.]

2. Name three factors the market research firm Claritas uses to classify the US population into "psycho-demographic clusters."
   [Income, interests, and consumer habits.]

3. According to Brooks, do American college professors tend to be politically liberal or politically conservative?
   [Liberal.]

4. At the time Brooks wrote this essay, what percentage of Americans were evangelical Christians?
   [40.]

5. How does the author recommend that Americans make their lives more diverse?
   [Experience a range of different institutions and environments, encourage young people to do national service, and encourage adults to venture outside of familiar circles.]

Vocabulary Quiz

1. *Strenuous* (paragraph 1) is closest in meaning to
   a. strong   b. defiant   c. ironic
   [a. strong]

2. *Congenial* (3) is closest in meaning to
   a. sticky   b. friendly   c. hostile
   [b. friendly]

3. *Homogeneous* (4) is closest in meaning to
   a. segregated   b. similar   c. eclectic
   [b. similar]

4. *Mores* (13) is closest in meaning to
   a. additional   b. restrictions   c. customs
   [c. customs]

5. *Renounce* (15) is closest in meaning to
   a. quit   b. speak   c. balance
   [a. quit]

Answers

Meaning

1. Brooks withholds his thesis for the conclusion: "It's probably better to think about diverse lives, not diverse institutions. Human beings, if they

are to live well, will have to move through a series of institutions and environments, which may be individually homogeneous but, taken together, will offer diverse experiences" (paragraph 18). His point is that while diversity is a noble goal, it cannot—nor should it—be achieved in geographical clusters such as neighborhoods and workplaces. Instead, he'd like to see people seek out diversity through their experiences, reaching out to interact with and understand people who are different from themselves.

2. As Brooks suggests elsewhere in the essay, psycho-demographics is a marketing tool used to identify groups of "people with similar tastes and preferences" (paragraph 7). He invokes the concept to make his point that diversity can be measured in a seemingly infinite number of ways—not just by "race and ethnicity" (7). He then supports this point with multiple examples of varying tastes and preferences, from the "suburban sprawl" and "towns & gowns" clusters identified by the marketing firm Claritas (8), to "imported-wine drinkers" and motor-home aficionados (9), pop culture consumers (10), ivy-league graduates (11–13), and Republicans and evangelical Christians (13–14).

3. Brooks points out that self-segregation enables people to build communities of like-minded people (paragraph 3), which makes them happy and enables them to "flourish" (4). But the resulting insularity limits employment opportunities (14), promotes inequality (15), and fosters divisiveness (16).

Purpose and Audience

1. As paragraphs 11–13 in particular make clear, Brooks addresses his argument to highly educated, affluent, liberal readers. He assumes that they, or their friends, have attended elite universities. He also assumes that they "live in a coastal, socially liberal neighborhood" (18), and that they value diversity even as they fail to be "in touch with the broad diversity of American life" (19).

2. The purpose is clearly persuasive. Brooks opens with a controversial assertion, devotes the essay to proving its validity, and ends with a call to action.

3. The cartoon illustrates the comparison Brooks makes in paragraph 14. Some students may object to the negative stereotypes it presents, but they're the point of both Brooks's words and Brodner's drawing: each image captures the assumptions that elite liberals and regular conservatives make about each other.

Method and Structure

1. Diversity.

2. Brooks's classification scheme is complex. He considers racial diversity (paragraphs 5–6), cultural diversity (7–14), intellectual diversity (11–13),

and political and religious diversity (13–14, 16). Although his categories do overlap, seemingly breaking the rules of effective classification, the overlapping categories are part of his point that diversity is a fluid concept subject to interpretation.

3. "People Like Us" is a model of synthesis. Citing ideas and statistics from a personal interview (paragraph 3), the US Census (5), the marketing firm Claritas (8–9), the book *The Bell Curve* (11), and a study conducted by the Center for the Study of Popular Culture and the American Enterprise Institute (13), Brooks avoids direct quotation completely, instead using summary, paraphrase, and follow-up comments to build a new idea of his own. (If students question why the essay has no works-cited list, you may want to explain that like most magazine writers, Brooks does not follow MLA style. He is careful, all the same, to identify ideas and information that are drawn from sources, even if readers would have a hard time tracking down those sources for themselves.)

4. Brooks compares and contrasts people in different regions of Washington, DC, Manhattan, California, and Georgia (paragraph 2); "suburban sprawl" and "towns & gowns" psycho-demographic clusters (8); motor-home popularity in two Pennsylvania counties (9); news, entertainment, and worship preferences (10); the distribution of Democrats, Republicans, and evangelical Christians in the general population and in elite universities (13), university professors and conservatives (14 and the cartoon). In each case, the comparison and contrast helps to clarify the distinctions between different types of people.

Language

1. Brooks's metaphors include "people . . . tied down to factories and mills" (paragraph 3), "the brick wall of human nature" (5), "building diverse communities" (7), "sings the diversity anthem" (13), "to hammer diversity into every neighborhood . . ." (17), and "the iron curtains that now separate the nation's various cultural zones" (18)—the last a reference to the Cold War between the US and the Soviet Union that students are likely to miss. The most effective metaphors emphasize construction and barriers of some sort, reinforcing Brooks's point that Americans deliberately separate themselves from others.

2. The tone is calm, civil, and even-handed. As a conservative addressing liberals whose thought and attitudes he hopes to change, Brooks has to take a reasonable tone to avoid alienating readers.

Chapter 10

Process Analysis
Considering the Natural Environment

Brian Doyle
How to Read a Nature Essay (p. 215)

Students should find that Doyle's short piece is spectacular and moving. In five ecstatic paragraphs the author outlines his idea of what good environmental writing should do to a reader and, just as important, what it should *not* do. A writer known for his focus on the spiritual, Doyle nonetheless emphasizes that good nature essays are not sermons, not homilies, not exercises in guilt or recrimination. Rather, they are a way for writers and readers to connect, and for both to change in elemental ways.

Many students will, on a first read, assume that Doyle is arrogantly suggesting that his own essay is "the greatest essay *ever*" (first line, and the author's original title for *Orion*). You may want to spend some time in class constructing an outline of the essay he depicts and comparing it to an outline of "How to Read a Nature Essay" (see question 1 under "Meaning" and question 4 under "Method and Structure"). Although Doyle's poetic, moving essay shares many of the features he discusses as ideal, it does not match all of them. Ask students why they think that is. What is he trying to accomplish, then?

Content Quiz

1. Why, according to Doyle, did God give children hands?
   ["[T]o make their *own* sandwiches for heavenssake."]

2. What is the purpose of reading nature essays, in Doyle's view?
   ["[T]o be startled and moved"—that is, to have one's perspective affected and changed.]

3. What elements of writing does Doyle think are *"the most crucial and necessary food"*?
   [Stories.]

4. Should writers of effective nature essays offer advice, lecture, or argue?
   [No.]

5. How long is the "perfect nature essay," as Doyle sees it?
   [It is "quite short."]

Vocabulary Quiz

1. *Articulated* (paragraph 1) is closest in meaning to
    a. touched   b. spoken   c. painted
    [b. spoken]

2. *Pirouetting* (3) is closest in meaning to
    a. dancing   b. explaining   c. stealing
    [a. dancing]

3. *Homilies* (3) is closest in meaning to
    a. treats   b. comparisons   c. sermons
    [c. sermons]

4. *Evanesces* (4) is closest in meaning to
    a. evaporates   b. sparkles   c. straightens
    [a. evaporates]

5. *Taut* (5) is closest in meaning to
    a. learned   b. tight   c. small
    [b. tight]

Answers

Meaning

1. Yes and no. Although Doyle certainly structures the essay so that it illus-
    trates many of his ideas, he's not outlining his own essay, which does not
    follow the same structure of "The greatest nature essay *ever*" (paragraph 1),
    at least not exactly. To begin with, Doyle's essay is five paragraphs long;
    the essay he imagines contains at least eight paragraphs. Also, the "perfect
    nature essay" (5), while "quite short" like Doyle's, opens with an "image . . .
    startling and lovely" (1) followed by a "small story, a light tale" (2); "How
    to Read a Nature Essay" does not. And yet Doyle's essay does arrest the
    reader's attention and encourage that he or she "read straight through the
    piece, marveling" (1); it avoids "explosive Conclusions" (3); it is indeed a
    model of "one line fitting into another, each one making plain inarguable
    sense" (3); and it certainly will make many readers "actually shiver" (2)
    with emotion.

2. Doyle states his thesis at the end of paragraph 2: "*My God, stories do have
    roaring power, stories are the most crucial and necessary food, how come we never
    hardly say that out loud?*" His point, reminiscent of Joan Didion's famous
    quip "We tell ourselves stories in order to live" (see p. 9 of *The Compact
    Reader*) is that storytelling is essential to human (and planetary) survival.

3. Doyle's image of a goat serves several functions. For one, goats are part of
    nature. As animals they aren't particularly intelligent, of course (nor, Doyle
    implies, are senators), and they're known for being ravenous, indiscrimi-
    nating eaters—a fact that invokes Doyle's depiction of stories as "*the most
    crucial and necessary food*" (paragraph 2). The idea of a goat reading brings

in the "flash of humor" (5) Doyle says is part of an effective essay; in repeating the image toward the end of paragraph 5 with ". . . despite what you told the kids and the goat" (notice that "kids" is the term for young goats as well as for human children), Doyle is also "tiptoeing back to [a] story" (4) from earlier in the essay.

Purpose and Audience

1. Doyle expresses his idea of the purpose of reading at the end of his first paragraph, italicized for emphasis: *"Man, this is why I read nature essays, to be startled and moved like that, wow."* The purpose of writing, accordingly, is to startle and move readers, or as Doyle suggests with his final, one-word line, to leave them "Changed."

2. Doyle's primary assumption is that his audience not only enjoys reading nature essays but also is accustomed to (and perhaps a little tired of) pieces that lecture readers about their personal responsibility to the environment. His essay is meant as an antidote to such pieces, a plea for nature writing that readers can enjoy without guilt. Additional assumptions, evident in Doyle's essay, include that his readers are married or in committed relationships; have children, pets, and responsibilities; and believe in God.

Method and Structure

1. The stages of reading, as Doyle presents them, are as follows. Stage one: stop what you're doing and focus on reading (paragraph 1). Stage two: let the essay affect you (1–5). Stage three: reflect on what you've read (2, 5). Stage four: reread (4). Stage five: stand up and be changed (5). Although there's a general sequence, the stages overlap in a reader's experience, as they do in the structure of Doyle's essay.

2. Doyle organizes his process analysis not chronologically but following the progression of paragraphs in the ideal nature essay. The transitional line starting each of his own paragraphs after the introduction reveals this order and helps readers to follow Doyle's analysis: "The next two paragraphs . . ." (2); "The next three paragraphs . . ." (3); "Then an odd paragraph . . ." (4); "And finally the last paragraph."

3. Some comma splices: *"Man, this is why I read nature essays, to be startled and moved like that, wow"* (paragraph 1); the entire second paragraph; the last sentence of paragraph 3; the first sentence of paragraph 4; and so on. Some fragments: "Terser. Blunter" (3); "And finally the last paragraph" (5). As Doyle suggests with the sentence fragment "Shards of sentences" (3) in describing the "shorter, more staccato" sentences of a good nature essay (3), his sentence faults are deliberate and used for effect. The long, comma-splice-infused first sentence/paragraph, for instance, has the effect of the kind of breathlessness he hopes to inspire in readers; similarly, the fragments echo the terse, blunt shards Doyle suggests will arrest readers' attention. Some students may reasonably argue that the sentence faults are distracting or confusing: if they do, you might suggest they try editing the

essay to correct the errors, and then compare the effectiveness of the edited sentences against Doyle's originals.

4. An effective nature essay, as Doyle imagines it, grabs readers' attention and doesn't let go. Ideally short and "lean" (paragraph 5), it opens with "an image [that is] startling and lovely" (1) and centers on a simple, personal story (2). It surprises readers with vivid metaphors (2), but its sentences each make "plain inarguable sense" (3). It includes "a flash of humor" (5) along with "a hint or tone or subtext of sadness" (5), and it ends simply (5). A good essay does *not*, according to Doyle, include "sermons" (3) or "Stern Instructions & Directions" (4) or "accusations" (3, 5), and it does not overdramatize (4).

Language

1. The shifts are purposeful. Doyle uses the second person when analyzing the reading process and the third person when analyzing the elements of a good nature essay.

2. Nearly the whole of Doyle's essay is one inventive figure of speech after another; they hold readers' interest with surprises, and they convey meaning vividly and economically by calling on associations. Some examples: "paragraphs then walk" (paragraph 3), personification; "one line fitting into another" (3), a metaphor; "no shouting" (3), personification; "no elegant pirouetting" (3), more metaphor; "fitting together like people holding hands" (3), simile and personification combined; "the story slips back into view gently, a little shy, holding its hat" (4), more personification; "it evanesces or dissolves" (4), metaphor again; "a feeling eerily like a warm hand brushed against your cheek" (5), simile and personification combined. The personifications, in particular, create the impression that an essay is a living, breathing, human thing that readers can connect with. We see only one cliché: "spins on a dime" (2), but even that is part of an elaborate extended metaphor—involving figure skating, breaking through the ice, and shivering—that nonetheless works.

3. Capitalization creates emphasis and elevates the terms to the status of big, important concepts, as if they were laws engraved in stone. Doyle is being ironic: he does not believe that nature essays should emphasize conclusions, advice, or instructions at all.

4. Additional colloquialisms include but are not limited to "tell the kids to make their *own* sandwiches for heavenssake"; "*Man*"; "*wow*" (paragraph 1); "just sort of a cheerful nutty everyday story maybe starring an elk or a mink or a child" (2); "you are plunged into waaay deeper water, you didn't see it coming at *all*" (2); "that's the stuff of another essay" (4); "you can't quite put your finger on it" (5). Doyle insists that writers should connect with their readers, so a conversational style achieved with casual, everyday language is an effective choice.

Marina Keegan
Why We Care about Whales (p. 220)

Student writer Marina Keegan became something of a viral sensation when her graduation column for the *Yale Daily News*, a celebration of youth and possibility, appeared almost simultaneously with the news of her untimely death. In her introduction to *The Opposite of Loneliness*, however, Keegan's teacher Anne Fadiman makes an important point about the tragedy: "Marina wouldn't want to be remembered because she's dead. She would want to be remembered because she's *good*." And so she is. As this stunning essay attests, Keegan's prose was unusually sophisticated—not just for a college student, but for any writer. Taking as her ostensible subject the processes of whale beaching and rescue (based on an episode she experienced as a girl), Keegan slyly forces herself and her readers to think about human empathy and the practical limits of compassion—and breaks our hearts in doing it.

Class discussion might focus on Keegan's comparison of the human response to whales in distress to our treatment of people in distress (see questions 1 and 4 under "Method and Structure"). "Why We Care about Whales" is an excellent example of process analysis undertaken for a larger purpose. Why is it emotionally easier to rescue one group than the other? What kinds of solutions are feasible when problems seem insurmountable?

Content Quiz

1. What, according to Keegan, does the moon do when it "gets bored"?
["[I]t kills whales."]

2. How many whales get beached and die in an average year?
[More than two thousand.]

3. What telltale sign indicates that a beached whale is on the verge of death?
[Its jaw unhinges.]

4. Are pilot whales an endangered species?
[No.]

5. Whose welfare does Keegan consider more important: animals or human beings?
[Keegan acknowledges that humans are more important, but she believes it's emotionally easier to help animals.]

Vocabulary Quiz

1. *Oscillating* (paragraph 2) is closest in meaning to
a. throwing   b. alternating   c. crying
[b. alternating]

2. *Buoyancy* (6) is closest in meaning to
   a. floatability   b. heaviness   c. cheer
   [a. floatability]

3. *Triage* (8) is closest in meaning to
   a. threesome   b. volunteer   c. prioritizing
   [c. prioritizing]

4. *Palpable* (8, 14) is closest in meaning to
   a. physical   b. visible   c. emotional
   [a. physical]

5. *Camaraderie* (15) is closest in meaning to
   a. strict organization   b. friendly cooperation   c. fair judgment
   [b. friendly cooperation]

Answers
Meaning

1. Keegan blames the moon for beaching whales. Specifically, its gravitational pull causes tides to move in and out, churning waves and currents that spin whales around, disorienting them and pushing them close to shore, where they get stranded in low water; when the tide moves out, they're trapped on land (paragraphs 2–4). Once beached, the whales hyperventilate and become dehydrated; their own weight crushes their organs, particularly their lungs; and they either suffocate or drown (5–6, 23–24). In the end, "their jaws open slightly," their eyes become "glazed over," they stop breathing, and they die (7, 24, 27). Although teams of volunteers attempt to keep the beached whales cool and hydrated until high tide returns, and sometimes try to move them back into deeper water or truck or airlift them to medical treatment, they cannot save every whale (8, 12, 18–22, 25).

2. Distressed whales call to each other. The animals are highly empathetic by nature and will rush to the side of a peer in trouble; the urge to help basically gets them in trouble. Keegan's point seems to be that rushing to help someone in crisis, however well intentioned, can have negative consequences for the community while at the same time failing to solve the problem.

3. Keegan suggests that we care about whales because they're very much like people in their intelligence and their sense of community, and because they present a "tangible crisis with a visible solution" (paragraph 15)—unlike overwhelming human problems such as homelessness, cancer, or famine.

Purpose and Audience

1. Keegan makes it fairly clear that she was personally traumatized by the events she recounts in her essay, especially by her sense of helplessness as the one whale died while she tried to comfort it. Her purpose in writing

may have been to process her feelings but also to contemplate the impulse to help animals when limited resources might go instead to helping other humans—and to persuade readers to examine their own assumptions about charity.

2. The questions are rhetorical: "Intelligence matters, doesn't it? Brain size is important, right?" In asking these questions, Keegan reveals that she assumes an audience of young, idealistic, and intelligent college students—exactly what she might expect of readers of the *Yale Daily News*.

Method and Structure

1. The process analysis takes place in paragraphs 1–7 (beaching), 11–12 (rescue), and 19–27 (rescue; dying). Paragraphs 8–10 (as well as 19–27) narrate Keegan's personal experience with beached whales; and paragraphs 13–18 compare and contrast beached whales with humans in crisis (see question 4 under "Method and Structure"). Keegan deviates from the process analysis proper to examine the larger implications of the process, which is her purpose for writing. The combination of process, narration, and comparison gives her essay personal and social significance.

2. Examples of transitions include "Slowly, awkwardly" (paragraph 3); "Occasionally" (4); "In their final moments," "Finally," "I know this because I watched as twenty-three whale mouths unhinged" (7); "Unlike the three dolphins that had managed to strand themselves near our house the previous summer" (10); "Daily" (11); "I worry sometimes" (13); "When we hear" (14); "In theory" (17, 18); "But when I was looking in the eye of a dying pilot whale at four in the morning" (19); and "Before I could find an answer" (27).

3. Keegan's experience with the fifty beached whales outside her summer home both prompts the essay and supports it. But Keegan also strengthens her observations with more objective evidence such as the number of whales that die each year (paragraph 4), scientific information about whale behavior and biology (4–6, 9), allusions to popular culture and literature (12, 13, 15), and an example of another whale rescue in which she was not involved (18). Students may find the mixture of personal and objective evidence more convincing than either alone.

4. Keegan explicitly compares beached whales with dying, homeless, and starving people in paragraphs 13–18 and returns to that comparison in her conclusion (25–26). The comparison *is* the significance of her subject, her reason for considering how people respond to whales in distress. The essay, it turns out, isn't only about whales but about human compassion and the practical limits of empathy.

Language

1. In personifying the moon as a bored killer, Keegan uses it as a symbol for the cruelty and indifference of nature. She returns to the image in her

conclusion, as the moonlit ocean water tugs at her ankles (implicitly threatening to kill her) and the whale dies, staring helplessly at the cause of its death.

2. Keegan's tone is pained and earnest; she takes the whales' deaths personally and is clearly troubled that she and others don't attempt to tackle human suffering with the same levels of conviction and determination that volunteers bring to whale rescue.

Rick Bass
Gardens of Ice and Stone (p. 227)

Poet Rick Bass's beautifully written essay on natural destruction and regeneration may be difficult for some students to comprehend or appreciate. It is, however, a wonderful example of nature writing. Bringing readers into the depths of a changing season in the Pacific Northwest, Bass captures the visceral glories of natural violence while at the same time contemplating the implications of climate change and making a passionate plea for government protections of public wildernesses.

Bass also shows students that process analysis need not be a dull series of directions and demonstrates how the method can be used to explain and support a strongly held belief. It may be worth pointing out to your students that only the first half of the essay demonstrates process analysis per se (see question 2 under "Method and Structure"). Bass uses the method to establish the relevance of his subject and to educate readers about a basic geological fact, and then builds on the implications of his process analysis in the remaining paragraphs to make an impassioned argument for political protections and cultural change.

Since Bass is concerned primarily with the fragile soil system in the wilderness and the threats posed to it by the logging industry, students may want to discuss other ways in which humans are said to be destroying the environment, such as the mining for petroleum in which Bass once participated (see Genoways, p. 208), carbon emissions, air and water pollution, waste production, monocultures, the clearcutting of rain forests, and so forth. The writing topics following the other essays in this chapter, as well as those listed under "Writing about the Theme" (p. 235), offer some starting points for discussion.

Content Quiz

1. What is the Kootenai?
   [The river into which the waters of the spring melt flow.]

2. In what month does the spring melt that Bass describes typically occur?
   [May.]

3. How large does a "wild garden," or "roadless area," have to be to qualify for preservation status?
   [At least a thousand acres. But "not one acre" of land is technically protected.]

4. What industry's activities threaten the wilderness, as Bass sees it?
   [Commercial logging.]

5. Does Bass encourage readers to come to Montana and witness the spring melt themselves?
   [No. He says that local residents would not be happy to see a tourist's "shining, happy-vacationing face."]

Vocabulary Quiz

1. *Silt* (paragraph 2) is closest in meaning to
   a. window   b. mud   c. smooth
   [b. mud]

2. *Hackneyed* (5) is closest in meaning to
   a. overused   b. driven   c. creative
   [a. overused]

3. *Perfunctory* (10) is closest in meaning to
   a. perfect   b. tentative   c. half-hearted
   [c. half-hearted]

4. *Archipelago* (16) is closest in meaning to
   a. group of islands   b. band of musicians   c. pack of wolves
   [a. group of islands]

5. *Fecund* (21) is closest in meaning to
   a. smelly   b. fertile   c. waste
   [b. fertile]

Answers
Meaning

1. The "gardens" are large deposits of rich soil left behind by the annual process of river melting and flooding: the rush of water captures and carries organic debris—scattered plant material, dead animals, fecal matter—then drops it together in one place, where the fresh soil supports new growth that feeds new life. The gardens show natural regeneration at work and provide the resources for plants and wildlife to flourish, but they're not protected and the few that remain are at risk from the incursion of logging in the area. Savvy students might notice, as well, that the "ice" and "stone" in the title refer not just to elements involved in the melt but also to prehistoric geological eras: the Ice Age and the Stone Age.

2. In likening geological processes to a game of cards, Bass implies that we're gambling with the environment—and that the house always wins.

3. Bass suggests that human beings have existed for a minuscule fraction of the earth's life but in that time have managed to destroy much of it by treating the wilderness as a resource. The natural world—or at least his corner of it—exists for its own sake, he says, not for human consumption or recreation.

4. Bass's thesis seems to be that massive natural change—exemplified by the annual spring melt—is normal and inevitable. And while it might seem catastrophic and inconvenient for people, it's necessary, even beneficial, for the wilderness. The natural world will be "resurrected" (paragraph 11) or, in other words, it will go on without us—and despite of us.

Purpose and Audience

1. Although he says he started the essay intending merely "to paint" a portrait of "the forms and swirls of motion that emerge so dramatically" during the spring melt (paragraph 18), Bass admits his purpose shifted in the process of writing. He wants justice for the river valley, particularly in the form of "permanent legal protection" (16) for the "officially called 'roadless areas'" (14)—the gardens of ice and stone—that he portrays in his essay.

2. Bass is writing for an audience of like-minded, "artistic" (paragraph 5) types who appreciate natural beauty, are concerned about environmental destruction, and are already committed to conservation ideals. His assumptions are most apparent when he acknowledges that his "yowling about environmental justice can be counterproductive" (18), and when he expresses hope that in reading his writing "you, gentle reader, would come on your own initiative, unsummoned, to love this landscape" (19). Bass is preaching to the choir, so to speak, and he knows it.

Method and Structure

1. Process analysis emphasizes the cyclical, predictable nature of environmental destruction and regeneration. In focusing on a process rather than an individual event or threat, Bass is best able to make his point that the natural world has never been static.

2. Bass follows the process analysis proper (the first half of the essay) with a contemplation of its implications (the second half), allowing him to extend his analysis and give it a broader significance as he argues for government protection of public lands.

3. Bass appeals to each of the five senses, often simultaneously and several times over. We list just a few examples here. Sight: "shimmering glitter of silt" (paragraph 2), "milk-colored ice" (7), "a visible shuddering" (10); sound: "the first melodies of cracking or straining ice can be heard ..." (10), "xylophonic arrangement of a winter's worth of driftwood" (11),

"frog-roar" (20); taste: "the river's hungry reach" (2), "hungry for that distribution of wealth" (3), "to graze upon the fruits" (13); touch: "a desire is quivering" (4), "as the arc of a bow cradles a drawn arrow" (4), "the pressure continuing to build and strain" (7), "quivering, taut strings of the instrument" (10), "swamp-muck" (20); smell: "bear dung and rotting log mulch and deer pellets . . ." (2), "a celebration of the rank and the fecund" (21). The overall effect is visceral, as though readers were experiencing the spring melt right with the author. In creating that effect, Bass emphasizes that we're all part of nature, not separate from it, and certainly not in control of it.

Language

1. Almost all of the first half of the essay, and much of the second, is steeped in deeply poetic figurative language—perhaps to be expected from a naturalist who is also a poet. Students should have no trouble picking out multiple examples of simile, metaphor, personification, hyperbole, and paradox: it would be more difficult to isolate a sentence that is not figurative. The effect is a sense of awesome beauty in creation.

2. The breathless, cascading, one-sentence paragraphs re-create the rush and pileup of ice that Bass is describing. Note that Bass returns to this device when he returns to the description of the melt in paragraphs 10 and 11 and again in paragraph 23. It's very deliberate, and quite effective.

3. Bass means to impart the sense that he's simply musing on the subject and that his thoughts, like the process he analyzes, are unfinished. This is most notable in his conclusion, where he trails off with a suggestion, but no promise, of a future life.

Chapter 11

Comparison and Contrast

Examining Stereotypes

Alaina Wong
China Doll (p. 246)

Wong skillfully interweaves a number of complex comparisons into this account of learning to embrace her Chinese American identity when she was a girl. Students will be intrigued by the differences between Wong and her best friend, the girls' families, the Barbie and Kira dolls, and Wong's initial and revised views of herself.

Our families' and friends' influence on our self-perceptions are, of course, topics of enduring interest and could lead to a discussion of the question we are all asked at one point or another: Who is your role model?

Content Quiz

1. What did Wong want for Christmas?
   [A Princess Barbie doll.]

2. What, to Wong's mind, made the Princess Barbie special?
   [Besides its general glamour and beauty, it came with a tiara.]

3. What did Sarah's hair look like?
   [She had long blond hair that "fell in soft waves down her back."]

4. What did Wong's hair look like?
   [Her "black hair was slippery and straight, like uncooked spaghetti."]

5. Why did Wong like to eat at her friend's house?
   [Because Sarah's mother let them eat things (such as raspberries off the bush and raw cookie dough) that Wong's mother would have forbidden because of germs, she cooked from "scratch," and she "made the best macaroni and cheese."]

Vocabulary Quiz

1. *Tresses* (paragraph 2) is closest in meaning to
   a. clothing   b. hair   c. skin
   [b. hair]

2. *Sly* (3) is closest in meaning to
   a. evil b. tight c. mischievous
   [c. mischievous]

3. *Complement* (4) is closest in meaning to
   a. praise b. wear c. match
   [c. match]

4. *Glamorous* (13, 17) is closest in meaning to
   a. beautiful b. famous c. expensive
   [a. beautiful]

5. *Iridescent* (17) is closest in meaning to
   a. heavy b. borrowed c. shiny
   [c. shiny]

Answers

Meaning

1. Wong's doll collection is populated by "real," brand-name Barbies. They are "all alike and beautiful with their clouds of blond (or light-brown) hair, broad toothy smiles, and wide-open eyes" (paragraph 3), and they all have "colorful plastic high heels to complement their fashionable dresses" and "perfect" outfits (4). The Kira doll, on the other hand, is not a Barbie but a "'friend' of Barbie" (2), features "dark hair and slanted eyes" (3), has "lips . . . curved into a more secretive, sly smile" (3), wears a "floral wrap skirt" (2) that is "just a piece of cloth that need[s] to be tied" (11), and came without shoes. As far as Wong is concerned, Kira is clearly inferior to Barbie.

2. We can't be sure, of course, but Wong's parents almost certainly selected the Kira doll for their daughter precisely because it has vaguely Asian features rather than Barbie's overtly Caucasian ones. Like many parents of ethnic girls, they probably wanted her to have a doll that she could identify with, and they probably meant for it to make young Alaina feel good about herself. Wong fails to appreciate that the doll "looks kind of like" (paragraph 12) her until her friend Sarah points it out to her, but she slowly comes to see herself in it and in the process to find promise in her own appearance.

3. The "dark-haired" Kira and the blond Princess Barbie stand for Wong's sense of herself and her friend Sarah. The parallels are rather obvious, although Wong does reinforce them by stressing that Kira is Barbie's "friend" (paragraph 2). What may not be so obvious to students is the way Wong projects her feelings about her own appearance onto the dolls. At first she rejects the Kira doll, who to her mind is neither as pretty nor as glamorous as the Barbies, and she wonders how Kira could possibly be attractive to men (in the form of Ken), who "already had so many blond friends to choose from" (3). She assumes that the Asian-looking doll has

defects even beneath her unsatisfactory appearance—"crooked teeth," for example (3), and "probably missing lots of things" (4)—an assumption that suggests the state of Wong's own lack of self-esteem as a Chinese American girl growing up in a predominantly white community. When Wong dresses her doll in Princess Barbie's clothes with her friend Sarah's encouragement, she feels as if she's doing something slightly wrong, although she's not sure why she feels that way. The borrowed clothes symbolize, perhaps, Wong's ambivalence about assimilating into white culture—although her discovery that Barbie's tiara "fit perfectly" suggests the beginning of Wong's comfort with her own identity.

Purpose and Audience

1. In comments she wrote for the introduction to "China Doll" in *YELL-Oh Girls!* Wong explained that her "experiences growing up and slowly becoming race conscious inspired [her] to write this story." She continued, "I hope to evoke a sense of familiarity and understanding from people who may have also experienced these feelings."

2. Wong justifiably assumed that the young Asian girls for whom *YELL-Oh Girls!* was published would recognize themselves in at least some aspects of her story. At the same time, Wong was aware that her feelings might be unfamiliar to readers beyond the *YELL-Oh Girls!* audience, so she took care to emphasize whatever universal experiences she could find. For example, her disappointment with a gift (paragraphs 1–3) and the guilt that accompanied that feeling (4) are emotions that most readers felt at some point in their childhoods or have witnessed in their own or other children.

Method and Structure

1. The method works for Wong's story because she is trying to understand the source of her disappointment in the Kira doll. By comparing the doll she received with the one she wanted, she can explore the positive and negative aspects of each and determine whether one is indeed better than the other. And because the dolls symbolize the writer and her best friend, the method of comparison and contrast lets her recognize not only how they are different but also how they are alike.

2. In paragraphs 2–4, Wong emphasizes the differences between her Kira doll and her Barbie dolls (and, by extension, herself and Sarah); in paragraphs 5–7, she outlines her reasons for liking Sarah's family better than her own; and in paragraphs 8–15, she emphasizes (again with the dolls serving as stand-ins) her perception of her friend's superiority. It is only in the last two paragraphs (16, 17) that Wong begins to see the possibility that they are more alike than they are different, and even then her assessment is tentative. This organization reflects her own emotional journey, from rejection to a hesitant acceptance of her Chinese American identity.

3. Because Wong's self-image in this essay is based on her appearance, the descriptions of the dolls' features are essential in conveying her meaning.

Without them, the essay would be based on abstractions and would lack immediacy for readers, especially for those not acquainted with girls' fashion dolls. The narration, however, puts Wong's comparison in a familiar context that most readers will understand. It not only personalizes her experience but encourages readers to connect it with their own childhoods.

Language

1. Wong manages to write the essay with a voice that combines a girl's naïveté and insecurity with an adult's perspective of her youthful feelings. Her tone is innocent, measured, and imbued with a sense of childlike wonder.

2. Examples include Wong's assertion that Princess Barbie's tiara "crowned her at the top of her Barbie world" (paragraph 1), her description of her dolls' "clouds of blond (or light-brown) hair" (3), and her disparaging assessment of her own hair as being "like uncooked spaghetti" (5). Wong's metaphors and similes catch readers' attention without distracting them from her message, and they bring color and wit to her writing.

Antonio Ruiz-Camacho
Souvenirs (p. 252)

Ruiz-Camacho's comparison of two distinct cultures, Mexican and American, is also a comparison of past and future. In contrasting his childhood dreams of a space-age America with his children's fascination with Mexico's mythic history, he uses specific examples to examine the assumptions we make about cultures different from our own.

It might interest students to know that many *New York Times* readers commenting online objected to Ruiz-Camacho's depictions of Mexico as dangerous; you may need to point out that he acknowledges that he still harbors "prejudices about [his] own country" (paragraph 15), and that wrestling with those lingering stereotypes is part of his purpose for writing. You might also encourage students unfamiliar with current affairs in Mexico to look into the violence and kidnappings Ruiz-Camacho mentions; see the fourth writing topic following the essay.

Content Quiz

1. Where did Ruiz-Camacho grow up?
   [Toluca, Mexico, a suburb of Mexico City.]

2. What character was depicted on the wristwatch Ruiz-Camacho purchased on his first trip to California?

[Mickey Mouse, posed as Tony Manero from *Saturday Night Fever*. (The alarm clock he purchased later featured Kermit the Frog.)]

3. Why did the author postpone taking his sons to Mexico for as long as he did?
[For "many reasons, including time, money, green-card procedures and the wave of violence that struck my home country soon after I left." The violence—particularly "the drug and extortion and kidnapping wars of recent years"—seems most pertinent to him.]

4. What did Ruiz-Camacho's sons love best about Mexico?
[The Maya pyramids.]

5. What are ocarinas?
[Traditional handcrafted Mexican wind instruments, similar to whistles, said to reproduce the sounds of figures from Aztec mythology.]

Vocabulary Quiz

1. *Aspirational* (paragraph 1) is closest in meaning to
   a. traditional   b. ambitious   c. breathless
   [b. ambitious]

2. *Alluring* (2) is closest in meaning to
   a. attractive   b. wealthy   c. kind
   [a. attractive]

3. *Memento* (5) is closest in meaning to
   a. treasure   b. mint   c. souvenir
   [c. souvenir]

4. *Expeditions* (5) is closest in meaning to
   a. journeys   b. errands   c. shortcuts
   [a. journeys]

5. *Rustic* (15) is closest in meaning to
   a. orange-colored   b. dangerous   c. unsophisticated
   [c. unsophisticated]

Answers

Meaning

1. Ruiz-Camacho comes closest to expressing his thesis in paragraph 6, where he suggests that "far-off lands" are always different and therefore "more intriguing," especially to children, but not necessarily better than one's own home.

2. The similarities and differences between the Flintstones and the Jetsons are central to Ruiz-Camacho's comparison of the past (represented for him by

Mexico) and the future (represented by the United States). Students unfamiliar with these American cultural products of the 1960s may not recognize how similar the cartoons are (both produced by Hanna-Barbera and voiced by many of the same actors, they aired during the same time period and had similar storylines, even though they take place thousands of years apart); the gloss note highlighting these points should help. Ruiz-Camacho's idea is that Mexico and the United States—for middle-class families at least—are as much alike as they are different.

3. Ruiz-Camacho was "afraid [his] kids wouldn't connect with the place [he] came from" (paragraph 9) and that they would find his home country lacking in sophistication and amenities, much as he did as a child. While they did, indeed, compare the two countries, ironically they loved Mexico more.

Purpose and Audience

1. His purpose is explanatory. Ruiz-Camacho means simply to contemplate the similarities and differences between Mexican and American middle-class cultures, and between past and future; he concludes that no one aspect of his comparison is superior to another—an idea neatly captured in the final image of a traditional Mexican handicraft juxtaposed with an e-book reader on his son's nightstand.

2. As with much of his writing, Ruiz-Camacho seems to be aiming for an international audience. Although he wrote this essay for the *New York Times*, his assumptions about readers' knowledge of ongoing unrest in Mexico suggests he expects that at least some of his readers will be intimately aware of the situation there; at the very least he assumes an educated audience up to date on current affairs.

Method and Structure

1. The essay is arranged subject-by-subject: paragraphs 1–6 examine Ruiz-Camacho's childhood vision of America; paragraphs 7–16 look at his children's experience of Mexico. The points of comparison, addressed by turn in each half of the essay, are tourist destinations (amusement parks and Los Angeles vs. the Maya pyramids and the Yucatán Peninsula), souvenirs (pop-culture timepieces vs. traditional handicrafts), and overall impressions ("otherworldly" in each case).

2. Although the author focuses on surface differences between American and Mexican cultural artifacts and tourist destinations, his overall emphasis is on the remarkable similarities between his initial reaction to California and his sons' reactions to the Yucatán Peninsula and Teotihuacán, as well as shared middle-class values. Emphasizing similarities is an appropriate choice, because readers would normally assume that the two countries are more different than they are alike.

3. The author narrates his childhood trips to the United States in paragraphs 1–5 and lists examples of the souvenirs he chose in paragraphs 4–6; he then

narrates his sons' childhood trips to Mexico in paragraphs 7–14 and gives examples of the souvenirs they chose in paragraphs 14–16. Ruiz-Camacho also uses example to consider the television shows and movies that influenced his expectations of American culture. The narratives give the essay a structure and a personal authority; the examples of artifacts from both cultures particularize the comparison, making it more immediate and convincing.

Language

1. Other images that invoke space include "light years away from any form of civilization" (paragraph 2); the example of *The Jetsons/Los Supersónicos* (2–3); "otherworldly" (2, 16); "the Millennium Falcon Spaceship from *Star Wars*" (2); "cars didn't glide along the street as I'd imagined" (3); "more intriguing and far-off lands" (6); "Back on the ground" (14); "Guillermo's Kindle" (16). The space-age metaphors emphasize how foreign and futuristic America seemed to the young Ruiz-Camacho (and, by contrast, how mythical the Aztec ruins seemed to his sons); the hyperbole underscores his sense of feeling out of place.

2. In addition to "Up North" (paragraphs 2 and 15), Ruiz-Camacho also capitalizes "Better North" (5) and "Central Mexico" (12). The capital letters impart an exaggerated sense of importance and a hint of irony.

3. In addition to space-age and futuristic words and phrases (see question 1 under "Language"), Ruiz-Camacho repeats the word "souvenir" (title, paragraph 15) and variations on it: "otherworldly toys" (2), "wristwatch" (4, 6), "memento" (5), "alarm clock" (5, 6), "keepsake" (6), and "ocarinas" (14, 16). Much as the space-age phrases invoke the future, these terms all invoke the passage of time (itself a word that appears frequently and in multiple forms throughout the essay) and memories of the past.

Barbara Lazear Ascher
The Box Man (p. 258)

Barbara Lazear Ascher's classic rumination on the quiet dignity of a homeless person has been retired from its long-running anchor position in Part One of *The Compact Reader*, but because so many teachers cite "The Box Man" as one of their favorites and find that it is still relevant to their students, we've given the essay a new home in Comparison and Contrast, where it fits quite nicely with the chapter's theme of examining stereotypes.

To engage students actively in Ascher's subject, you might ask them to do some prewriting as preparation for reading the essay. Possible questions: What's the difference between solitude and loneliness? What kind of people would you describe as lonely? solitary? Or, to move in another direction: What is your impression of the homeless? Do you think some people choose to be homeless? Can one find dignity in such a situation?

If researched writing is a component of your class, the third writing topic after Ascher's essay suggests one possible avenue of response to the problem of homelessness. For students who are interested, you might want to point out that Jarrod Ballo's research essay, "Women and Children First" (p. 407), was written as a response to that very prompt.

Content Quiz

1. To what purpose did the Box Man put the plastic milk crate he found in a doorway?
    [He used it as a sofa, with a cardboard box two feet away as a coffee table.]

2. What was Ascher's favorite book as a child?
    [*The Boxcar Children*, a story about orphaned runaways making a home in the woods.]

3. What evidence does Ascher offer to support her belief that the Box Man chooses to live on the streets?
    [The mayor of New York offered him the "alternative" of a homeless shelter, but the Box Man "backed away."]

4. Whose way of life does Ascher find preferable: that of the homeless man she describes, or that of the two older women she imagines? Why?
    [The homeless man's, because it's more dignified.]

5. Where does Ascher suggest people can best find friendship?
    ["[I]n our own voice"—that is, in chosen solitude and self-acceptance.]

Vocabulary Quiz

1. *Fervor* (paragraph 2) is closest in meaning to
    a. intensity   b. illness   c. expression
    [a. intensity]

2. *Ingenious* (10) is closest in meaning to
    a. unintelligent   b. practical   c. creative
    [c. creative]

3. *Vacancy* (14) is closest in meaning to
    a. housing   b. emptiness   c. vacation
    [b. emptiness]

4. *Plethora* (17) is closest in meaning to
    a. mythology   b. birds   c. abundance
    [c. abundance]

5. *Solace* (20) is closest in meaning to
   a. comfort   b. loneliness   c. sunshine
   [a. comfort]

Answers

Meaning

1. Although the essay focuses on the quiet dignity of one homeless man, Ascher's primary subject is solitude.

2. Ascher states her thesis near the end of her essay: "[We are] all outcasts from the dream of perfect understanding. We might as well draw the night around us and find solace there and a friend in our own voice" (paragraph 20). In choosing solitude, Ascher is saying, the Box Man confirms the essential aloneness of human beings (19) but also demonstrates that we can "find solace" within ourselves (20).

3. Ascher leads up to and supports her idea by portraying three distinct characters—the Box Man (paragraphs 1–7, 11–12) and, in contrast, two women whose loneliness seems unchosen (13–16, 17). The comparison is developed with specific details from Ascher's observations (such as the Box Man's hunched shuffle [3] and a woman's nearly empty purse [14]) and from the imagined lives these observations suggest (such as the remote, perhaps nonexistent children [14]).

4. Ascher does assume some familiarity with literature—at least with the writings of Henry David Thoreau (paragraphs 9, 11) and Cynthia Ozick (16), with the Boxcar Children books (9–10), and with the doomed heroines named in paragraph 20 (Anna Karenina, Emma Bovary, and Shakespeare's Ophelia and Juliet). Each of these works has something to say about independence or loneliness, especially for women. However, readers who do not know the literature Ascher cites are still likely to understand and appreciate her main point.

Purpose and Audience

1. Ascher seems to have written her essay for two interlocking reasons: to show and thus explain that solitude need not always be lonely and to argue gently for defeating loneliness by becoming one's own friend. In choosing the Box Man as her subject, she reveals perhaps a third purpose as well—to convince readers that a homeless person can have dignity and may achieve a measure of self-satisfaction lacking in some people who do have homes. The inferences that readers might draw from Ascher's essay depend in part on the personal store of knowledge and ideas they bring to it. A reader with firsthand experience of poverty, for instance, might take issue with the author's assumptions and conclude that some observers fail to understand the root problems of homelessness. On the other hand, a lonely older woman might read the same essay, see something of herself in it, and decide to heed Ascher's advice to "find . . . a friend in [her] own

voice" (paragraph 20). And a reader familiar with *Walden* might recognize connections between Thoreau's and Ascher's philosophies and want to investigate them further.

2. "The Box Man" appears to be written for a general audience of people who have experienced, or expect to experience, loneliness at some point in their lives. Ascher seems to assume that her readers, like her, are people with homes, people to whom the Box Man and his life might seem completely foreign: she comments on the Box Man's slow shuffle (paragraph 3); his mysterious discrimination among boxes (4); his "blistered legs" (11); how miserable his life looks; his bandages; the cold night he inhabits (12); the fearful or condescending approaches of strangers (12, 18). Building from this assumption that her readers will find the Box Man strange, Ascher takes pains to show the dignity of the Box Man—his "grand design" for furniture (5), his resemblance to commuters (6), his grandmotherly finger licking (7), his refusal of handouts (18). A few other apparent assumptions about her audience also influence Ascher's selection of details, if less significantly. Ascher seems to address women: in paragraph 20 she speaks of each person confiding in "her" friend, and she chooses only female figures from literature to illustrate "us . . . all outcasts from the dream of perfect understanding." She assumes a familiarity with literature (see question 4 under "Meaning"). Finally, Ascher seems to address people who are familiar with, if not actually residents of, New York City: she refers to a New York street address (2); alludes to a New York newspaper, the *Daily News*, and a New York subway line, the IRT Express (6); and mentions the city's mayor (12).

Method and Structure

1. In her examination of chosen and unchosen solitude, Ascher focuses on several points of comparison. The first point is where each person lives—outdoors, in the homeless man's case, and in apartments for the women. She also considers the care with which each character furnishes and decorates his or her home, showing that the homeless man puts just as much effort into making his home pleasant as the women do. She examines each character's relationships with other people, revealing that the Box Man shies away from contact with others while suggesting that the women have been shunned by their families or discarded by their coworkers. Ascher also looks at each person's way of passing the time alone: the Box Man reads the newspaper with a sense of purpose; the women eat alone, lavish attention on pets and plants, and idly watch television late into the night. Seeing dignity in the Box Man's solitude and desperation in the women's, Ascher concludes that chosen loneliness is preferable.

2. Ascher keeps her organization fairly simple. She does not begin with a formal introduction or a statement of her idea but instead starts right off with her main example, the inspiration for her idea. In the first seven paragraphs she narrates and describes the Box Man's activities. Then, in

paragraphs 8–12, she explains what appeals to her about circumstances like the Box Man's and she applies those thoughts to what she imagines are his thoughts. Still delaying a statement of her main idea, Ascher contrasts the Box Man and two other solitary people, whose lives she sees as different from his (13–17). Finally, she returns to the Box Man (18–19) and zeroes in on her main idea (19–20). Though she has withheld this idea until the end, we see that everything in the essay has been controlled by it and directed toward it.

3.   Ascher's primary support for her comparison consists of three examples—specific instances of solitary people. The method of example especially suits Ascher's subject and purpose because it allows her to show contrasting responses to solitude: one person who seems to choose it and two people who don't. She develops her examples with description, vividly portraying the Box Man and the two women, as in paragraphs 6–7, so that we see them clearly. Paragraphs 1–7 in the portrayal of the Box Man involve retelling, or narrating, his activities. Ascher uses division or analysis to tease apart the elements of her three characters' lives.

Language

1.   One reason Ascher's essay works so well is that she uses specific language to portray her three characters and to let us know what she thinks about them. For instance, the language changes markedly from the depiction of the Box Man to the next-to-last paragraph on solitude. The Box Man comes to life in warm terms: Ascher watches him with "silent fervor" (paragraph 2); he seems "dogged by luck" (5); he sits with "slow care" and opens the newspaper with "ease" (6); his page turning reminds Ascher of "grandmothers" (7); it is conceivable that, in Thoreau's word, the Box Man's imagination has "pasture" to roam, that he dreams of "heroic ages" and a "goddess trailing her garments" (11). In contrast, isolation comes across as a desperate state in paragraph 20, where Ascher uses words such as "blank stares," "strangers," "exile," "littered," and "outcasts." In describing the two solitary women—those who evidently have not found comfort in aloneness—Ascher uses words that emphasize the heaviness of time and the sterility of existence. The first woman "drags" her meal out and crumbles crackers between "dry fingers" (13), a "vacancy of expression" on her face (14). She lacks even the trinkets of attachment—a "gold charm bracelet" with "silhouettes" of grandchildren (14). A vividly imagined photograph of her ex-boss and his family (15)—the wife with "her hair in a gray page boy," "the three blond daughters"—emphasizes the probable absence of such scenes in the woman's own life. The contrast in language helps to emphasize Ascher's point about the individual's ability to find comfort in solitude.

2.   Ascher uses occasional sentence fragments to stress the accumulation of details or the quickness of her impressions. For example, in paragraph 10 the incomplete sentences beginning "To" sketch Ascher's dream. And in paragraph 18 the incomplete sentences beginning "Not" emphasize the Box Man's withdrawal. Although incomplete sentences can be unclear,

these and the others in Ascher's essay are clear: she uses them deliberately and carefully, for a purpose.

3. Both of the sets of incomplete sentences in paragraphs 10 and 18 (see the question above) gain emphasis from parallelism. The parallelism begins in the complete sentence preceding each set of incomplete sentences—for example, ". . . I long to live like a Boxcar Child, to have enough open space and freedom of movement. . . . To turn streams into iceboxes. To be ingenious with simple things. To let the imagination hold sway."

Chapter 12
Definition
Pursuing Happiness

Judy Brady
I Want a Wife (p. 276)

Brady's definition uses carefully selected examples to present an angry statement about a wife's place in the home and in society. Some students may initially misunderstand the essay and think that Brady really does want a slave of her own. Other students may see the essay as excessively hostile toward wives, husbands, and marriage. And still other students may find Brady's sense of oppression somewhat passé, not as much of an issue now as it was in the less liberated early 1970s. Class discussion may be guided by the questions under "Purpose and Audience" and by the second and third writing topics.

Content Quiz

1. With whom does the child of Brady's recently divorced male friend live?
   [The child's mother.]

2. Why does Brady want to go back to school?
   [So she can become economically independent and support herself and her family.]

3. Why should a wife go on family vacations?
   [To continue caring for her partner and for the children.]

4. According to Brady's definition, which partner in a marriage must remain sexually faithful to the other?
   [The wife.]

5. What should the first wife do if a new wife is taken?
   ["Take the children and be solely responsible for them."]

Vocabulary Quiz

1. *Nurturant* (paragraph 3) is closest in meaning to
   a. compassionate   b. gentle   c. nourishing
   [c. nourishing]

2. *Hors d'oeuvres* (6) is closest in meaning to
    a. appetizers   b. cocktails   c. napkins
    [a. appetizers]

3. *Replenished* (6) is closest in meaning to
    a. removed   b. refilled   c. rewashed
    [b. refilled]

4. *Adherence* (7) is closest in meaning to
    a. indifference   b. attachment   c. attention
    [b. attachment]

5. *Monogamy* (7) is closest in meaning to
    a. sexual faithfulness   b. equality in a marriage   c. marriage to
    only one person
    [c. marriage to only one person]

Answers
Meaning

1. A wife is a person whose entire function is the selfless serving of others, especially the husband.

2. The wife's chief responsibilities are to work when doing so is beneficial to the spouse, to care for the children, to care for the house and to cook, to meet the spouse's physical and emotional needs, and to arrange and run social events. The wife's behavior should be entirely selfless. The spouse's responsibilities are to attend school and study and eventually to support dependents "if need be" (paragraph 3) but nothing is required or contributed at home. The spouse's behavior may be entirely selfish.

Purpose and Audience

1. Brady's purpose is to attack society's—and men's—attitudes toward the role of wife. She presents a deliberately one-sided definition, exaggerating to achieve this purpose.

2. Brady seems to assume that her readers are mostly women who will understand and appreciate her anger. Her perspective seems to be that of a middle-class woman in her twenties or early thirties: the wife works to put the spouse through school; the children are relatively young; the family lives in a house; and the couple has an active social life.

3. Answers will vary widely.

Method and Structure

1. Readers may take the role of a wife as a given—or may have in 1971—but Brady sees a need to show how the wife is taken advantage of. By presenting a slanted definition, she encourages readers to see things her way.

2. The definition is highly specific and clearly distinguishes the role of a wife from, say, the role of a housekeeper or a lover. It is also thorough in that it covers a wide range of responsibilities and behaviors. But some readers may think that the omission of any positive elements in the relationship between wife and spouse—what keeps the wife at the job? love? security?—makes the definition less than complete.

3. Paragraph 1 suggests that the author is defined by society according to her role as a wife. Paragraph 2 presents a man who seems to view a wife's role just as Brady goes on to define it: he is divorced; he has left his child to his wife; and he wants "a wife"—as if anyone might do. The question at the end of the introduction leads into the definition; once the earlier question is answered, the final rhetorical question opens up the divorced man's wish and Brady's wish to everyone.

4. With classification, Brady makes the definition more manageable. She classifies the wife's responsibilities into financial support and child care (paragraph 3), housekeeping and cooking (4), emotional support (5), social organization (6), and sexual fulfillment (7). The categories are increasingly personal and intrusive, thus emphasizing the exploitation of women in marriage.

Language

1. Brady's tone is angry and contemptuous, and it is achieved largely through irony: "It may mean a small cut in my wife's income . . . , but I guess I can tolerate that" (paragraph 3); "I want a wife who will not bother me with rambling complaints about a wife's duties" but "will listen to me when I feel the need to explain a rather difficult point I have come across in my course of studies" (5).

2. The repetition portrays the spouse as childish, demanding, and selfish.

3. Use of the phrase "my wife" emphasizes the spouse's depersonalization and possession of the wife. At the same time, the phrase allows Brady to avoid expressing a wish for another woman, which might be more distracting than the occasionally awkward sentences now in the essay.

4. Such expressions underline the irony.

Augusten Burroughs
Unhappily Ever After (p. 281)

In one of the many quirky yet earnest chapters of advice in his offbeat self-help book *This Is How*, Burroughs pleas with reader to learn from his mistakes and live their lives in a better, happier way. Although his writing style is unconventional and deliberately breaks several rules of grammar (it may be worth noting that Burroughs dropped out of high school and never finished college), students should appreciate the author's message that being unhappy isn't such a bad thing; they might even take comfort in seeing that nonstandard sentences don't necessarily get in the way of effective expression.

In seemingly addressing his definition of happiness to an audience of passively unhappy women (see question 3 under "Purpose and Audience"), Burroughs offers an interesting retort to Judy Brady's complaints, in "I Want a Wife" (p. 276), that traditional gender roles are oppressive. Class discussion, then, could center on how Brady, or any other woman, might be expected to respond to Burroughs's advice, or how Burroughs's own marriage, and his expectations for it, as hinted at in paragraph 27 of his essay, compare to Brady's.

Content Quiz

1. What common phrase does Burroughs believe causes "misery and permanent unhappiness" for those who utter it?
   ["I just want to be happy."]

2. To what medical condition does Burroughs compare wanting something?
   [A mole, or a cancer that spreads.]

3. What does Burroughs say is the key to finding happiness?
   [Defining it, "precisely" and "exactly," and then making changes to achieve it.]

4. Is Burroughs a happy person?
   [No.]

5. What two states of mind does Burroughs offer as alternatives to *happy*?
   [*Interested* and *fascinated*.]

Vocabulary Quiz

1. *Guileless* (paragraph 3) is closest in meaning to
   a. young   b. innocent   c. dangerous
   [b. innocent]

2. *Bespoke* (12) is closest in meaning to
   a. custom-made   b. out loud   c. secretive
   [a. custom-made]

3. *Melancholy* (22) is closest in meaning to
   a. angry   b. hopeful   c. sad
   [c. sad]

4. *Friskiness* (22) is closest in meaning to
   a. playfulness   b. cleanliness   c. fanciness
   [a. playfulness]

5. *Spectrum* (29) is closest in meaning to
    a. rainbow   b. range   c. body
    [b. range]

Answers
Meaning

1. The problem, according to Burroughs, is that expressing a desire for happiness implies a lack of same, which in turn becomes a self-fulfilling prophecy. Or in other words, "I just want to be happy" fuels a general dissatisfaction with life and distracts a person from pursuing actions that could lead to happiness, or at least some kind of contentment.

2. The "standard" definition of happiness that Burroughs cites is similar to that put forth by Carlin Flora in her paragraph from *Psychology Today* (see p. 270 of the text): a general satisfaction with life punctuated with joy. In place of such a vague and impossible standard, Burroughs would like for readers to define their own versions of happiness with sets of "concrete" (paragraph 11), "specific" (15), and "possible" (15) personal goals, and then to adjust their actions accordingly.

3. "Unhappily ever after" is an allusion to a common final line of fairy tales and children's stories: "And they lived happily ever after." Burroughs is suggesting that stating a desire to be happy reveals unrealistic expectations that amount to childish fantasies—and will also lead to disappointment.

Purpose and Audience

1. Burroughs addresses his advice to those who, like him, are not happy. This is evident in his use of the second-person *you* throughout the essay, and in his use of the imperative mood to encourage readers to rethink assumptions and change behaviors so that "maybe you could be mostly content" (paragraph 14).

2. Most obviously, Burroughs assumes that his readers are unhappy but want to be happy. He seems also to assume an audience composed primarily of relatively affluent women, as evident in his examples, such as "Honey, I'm in love with your youngest sister and she's agreed to marry me so I'd like a divorce" (paragraph 2); "the dark-haired boyfriend . . . since the blond musicians haven't worked out so well" (9); "breast implants" (9); "your own online jewelry business" (15). Burroughs is openly gay, and the happy people he uses as examples in paragraphs 27 and 28 are men (the first one his husband), so it's possible he means for all of his examples to apply regardless of gender. All the same, the overall effect is that he's talking to women.

3. Responses will vary. Students may agree or disagree with Burroughs, but they should do so on the basis of their own close analysis of his definition.

Method and Structure

1.   The synonyms Burroughs uses include "like" (paragraphs 9, 15), "well-being" (13), "contentment"/"content" (13, 14, 21), "joy" (13, 14, 20), "love" (15, 28), "interesting"/"interested" (15, 22, 31), "tenderness" (22), "friskiness" (22), "focus" (28), and "fascinated" (31). Notice that the "standard" synonyms suggest passive experience but Burroughs's synonyms are more active and deliberate. Students' proposed synonyms will vary.

2.   The crux of Burroughs's definition is a paradox: he argues that although wishing for happiness can reinforce a person's feelings of misery, unhappiness itself is not necessarily the opposite of happiness, nor is it necessarily a bad state of being. Some people, he says, are just not happy, but that "does not mean [they] must be sad or dark" (paragraph 31). As long as they can develop their own personal definitions of happiness, as Burroughs has done, they'll be fine.

3.   Most of Burroughs's *This Is How*, like "Unhappily Ever After," is written in short, staccato paragraphs, often only one sentence (or one sentence fragment) long. The style is deliberate and journalistic; it lends a clipped sense of urgency to the author's tone. Students may find, however, that combining some of the paragraphs—a revision that seems most appropriate for paragraphs 12–14 and 20–24—does improve coherence and enhance readability.

4.   For one thing, they're both men. But more relevant to Burroughs's purpose and thesis, they're not *trying* to be happy or wishing they were happy; quiet satisfaction, intelligence, and finding pleasure in work are simply natural to their temperaments.

Language

1.   Probably most striking of Burroughs's metaphors are "a hole cut out of the floor and covered with a rug" (paragraph 5) and "The 'I just want to be happy' bear trap" (10)—both kinds of snares—as well as the "mole behind your ear" (8–9), a characterization of desire as a kind of cancer. Additional metaphors include "a blueprint for what happiness is" (16), "This recipe of defining what happiness means to you" (17), "just a shell of words" (25), and "Happiness is a treadmill of a goal for people who are not happy by nature" (30).

2.   Students are often told to avoid the first person and indefinite use of the second person in their writing, but these points of view are essential to achieving Burroughs's purpose of engaging readers so that he can offer them advice. Notice that he relies more on the second person in the beginning of the essay, as he establishes background and explains his position, then shifts point of view in paragraph 18, when he switches the focus to his own experience for evidence. If he were to have stuck with the more

objective, academic third person for the essay, it would have lost its intimacy and his definition would have turned into an abstraction—a pitfall Burroughs specifically advises readers to avoid.

3. Although readers may reasonably object to Burroughs's casual way with his sentences and argue that the grammar flaws weaken his credibility as a writer, he is using fragments, comma splices, and vague pronouns to approximate a spoken voice. The author is trying to establish a connection with his readers by assuming a conversational style, encouraging readers to imagine that he is talking with them in an intimate, personal way.

Jessica Sayuri Boissy
One Cup at a Time (p. 287)

In explaining why Boissy's essay on the Japanese concept of *ichigo ichie*—or "one encounter, one chance"—was selected as a *Prized Writing* winner, UC Davis teacher Karma Waltonen writes,

> the beauty of Jessica's essay was immediately apparent, as it commented on both the word and its cultural signifiers and integrated the Zen spirit of the phrase into the style of writing itself. . . . [We should] hope to hold the lesson here, that although "the water in the kettle eventually boils," we should not take any thing or any moment for granted.

We would add that "One Cup at a Time" also offers an excellent example of using a visual element for a purpose. Far from mere decoration, the Japanese calligraphy Boissy includes with her essay is essential to her definition of *ichigo ichie*. As such, she takes care to explain the nuances of philosophy the image reveals, analyzing the *kanji* to interpret their meaning visually, while pointing out to readers their different and repeated elements to express both their interrelationship and their contribution to her extended definition.

Boissy's essay deals with the topic of changing relationships, a concept that arouses an immediate and profound emotional response in most students. She uses the method of definition to help her account for the complexity of experiences that we share with all those whom we regard as friends—as well as relatives, other students, teachers, and colleagues. Class discussion could begin by eliciting information about students' friends and proceed to differentiate the varying relationships that develop among individuals and groups.

Content Quiz

1. What is the literal English translation of the Japanese phrase *ichigo ichie*? ["One encounter, one chance."]

2. Why, according to Boissy, are English interpretations of *ichigo ichie* inadequate?
   [They're too wordy and complicated, and they "lack the Zen spirit that permeates this phrase."]

3. What are *kanji*?
   [Japanese characters used for writing.]

4. How did Boissy first experience *ichigo ichie* for herself?
   [By attending a *chado*, or Japanese tea ceremony, when she was in middle school.]

5. Why does Boissy urge readers to treasure every encounter with another person, even if the meeting seems routine?
   [Because life is a series of changes and therefore every encounter is unique, never to be experienced in the same way again—"living fully in the present" is her way of enjoying "life . . . to its fullest."]

Vocabulary Quiz

1. *Aesthetic* (paragraph 1) is closest in meaning to
   a. purpose   b. pleasure   c. sporting
   [b. pleasure]

2. *Transience* (1) is closest in meaning to
   a. change   b. homelessness   c. radio
   [a. change]

3. *Impinges* (3) is closest in meaning to
   a. influences   b. interferes   c. supervises
   [b. interferes]

4. *Permeates* (5) is closest in meaning to
   a. fixes   b. creates   c. fills
   [c. fills]

5. *Serene* (6) is closest in meaning to
   a. severe   b. tasteful   c. relaxed
   [c. relaxed]

Answers
Meaning

1. The "cup" in Boissy's title refers to the tea consumed in the Japanese ceremony she describes in paragraphs 6–8. She uses it as a metaphor that reinforces the meaning of *ichigo ichie* as "one cup, one moment," or "In this context, *ichie* maintains the meaning of 'one encounter' but *ichigo* becomes 'one bowl of tea'" (6). Boissy states her thesis as it applies to this metaphor in her introduction and conclusion: "For me, this phrase has brought

awareness of the value of living each day, hour, minute, and second to the fullest and seizing each chance encounter that life unexpectedly brings" (1); "it is through these changes that *ichigo ichie* stresses the importance of treating each encounter as a once-in-a-lifetime event and focusing on the details of each occasion, the particular people and things involved daily. . . . [L]iving fully in the present—*ichigo ichie*—drinking life, and tea, to its fullest—one cup at a time" (9).

2. The *American Heritage Dictionary* tells us that *Zen* is "a school of Mahayana Buddhism that asserts that enlightenment can be attained through meditation, self-contemplation, and intuition rather than through faith and devotion." Colloquially, the term refers to simplicity and peacefulness in the pursuit of an activity. For Boissy, the "Zen spirit" (paragraph 5) also stresses the role of Japanese culture and heritage in forming a personal philosophy of life.

Purpose and Audience

1. Boissy seems to have written her essay for at least two connected reasons: to express the meaning(s) of a particular Japanese phrase that has no English equivalent and through them to persuade readers to live in the moment, never taking any encounter or relationship for granted.

2. Boissy addresses her teacher and classmates directly in her conclusion: "even if we meet each other in class every Tuesday and Thursday, I am not the same student and you are not the same teacher, because we are all participants in this inevitable change" (paragraph 9). Students' responses will vary, of course, with some perhaps finding that in attending an elite school and referring to "receiving our PhD" (9), Boissy assumes an unusually intellectual audience. Students may be expected to project their own responses onto Boissy's original UC Davis readers.

Method and Structure

1. Using definition allows Boissy to explore the nuances of meaning in a cultural concept—*ichigo ichie*—whose phrasing has no satisfactory English equivalent. As she explains the language problem, "the simplicity of meaning shatters when translated into English" (paragraph 4): translations are unnecessarily wordy, and "English equivalents lack the Zen spirit that permeates this phrase" (5).

2. As Boissy explains her reason for including the calligraphy, "the meaning of *ichigo ichie* can be comprehended visually" (paragraph 3). She nonetheless takes care to analyze the characters' meanings in paragraph 2, showing how the Japanese *kanji* symbolize the separate elements of each word, reveal their parallelism and symbolism when taken together, and emphasize the unity and coherence of the phrase as a whole, allowing each reader to "be the sole interpreter of what *ichigo ichie* means to him or her" (3).

3. Boissy is attempting through typography and punctuation to re-create the dreamlike sensations of the tea ceremony, emphasizing the "mixing of sensory impressions" (paragraph 8) and attempting to "create the feeling of *ichigo ichie*" (8).

4. The three methods are mutually dependent here: Boissy explains the Zen-like process of achieving *ichigo ichie* through the rituals of a tea ceremony by stressing the role of the five senses—sight, sound, touch, smell, and taste—in creating a sense of oneness and serenity.

Language

1. Boissy provides brief formal definitions of each of the other Japanese words that factor into her extended definition: "*kanji*, characters that embody the meanings in graphic forms" (paragraph 2); "*chado*, the Japanese tea ceremony" (6); "yakimono, *pottery streaked with ash glaze*" (7); "*monosuki, furumai*, and *chashitsu*, or things, behavior, and setting" (8). (She does not define *tatami* because the word has been adopted into the English language through regular use.) In using these additional Japanese words—which presumably translate satisfactorily—she emphasizes the sense of cultural heritage the tea ceremony and the concept of *ichigo ichie* offer her.

2. Boissy's tone captures the spirit of Zen, which she achieves through a patient, teacherly style of writing involving repetition and restatement of her main point throughout.

Chapter 13

Cause-and-Effect Analysis

Investigating the Working World

Ellen Goodman
The Company Man (p. 306)

Written as a parable, Ellen Goodman's classic essay is a warning to Type A personalities. The moral of her story is simple—don't work too hard—but her technique is complex. Goodman deftly combines irony, repetition, and *pathos* to create a portrait of a universal everyman and family made deeply unhappy by workplace success.

"The Company Man" is often anthologized, usually as a model of definition (as question 4 under "Method and Structure" suggests). As a cause-and-effect analysis, however, Goodman's essay offers an excellent opportunity to discuss the differences between immediate and remote causes: see question 1 under "Meaning." Perhaps more significant, it offers an opportunity to examine students' assumptions about what their careers might entail and to consider how they could forge a track that takes their personal values fully into account as they think about their futures.

Content Quiz

1. When did Phil die?
   ["3:00 a.m. Sunday morning."]

2. With which of his children was Phil closest?
   [His youngest son.]

3. What did Phil typically eat for lunch?
   [Egg salad sandwiches.]

4. Why did Phil's widow need to stay on good terms with the president of his company?
   [She would need him to help her with her finances.]

5. How many of Phil's employees will be considered for his job?
   [Three.]

Vocabulary Quiz

1. *Coronary* (paragraph 2) is closest in meaning to
   a. heart   b. crown   c. glow
   [a. heart]

2. *Thrombosis* (2) is closest in meaning to
   a. pulse   b. clot   c. break
   [b. clot]

3. *Conceivably* (3) is closest in meaning to
   a. hopefully   b. possibly   c. obviously
   [b. possibly]

4. *Board* (12) is closest in meaning to
   a. eat and sleep   b. plank of wood   c. lonely
   [a. eat and sleep]

5. *Discreetly* (16) is closest in meaning to
   a. brazenly   b. kindly   c. cautiously
   [c. cautiously]

Answers

Meaning

1. The obituary attributes Phil's death to an immediate cause—a "coronary thrombosis" (paragraph 2), or heart attack. But Goodman blames his death on remote causes—a lifetime of overwork, unhealthy habits, worry, and isolation.

2. Goodman's essay is a cautionary tale about working too hard. Her point, it seems, is that to sacrifice all of one's family and personal life to a job is a tragic mistake.

3. "The Company Man" is filled with numbers. Beyond those mentioned in the question, she cites "3:00 a.m. Sunday morning" (paragraphs 1, 3, 15), "one of three" who might be promoted to president (3), "six days a week, five of them until eight or nine at night" (4), "four-day week" (4), "twenty or twenty-five pounds" overweight (4), "maybe sixty" employees (6), "[t]hree of them" in line for Phil's job (6), "Helen, forty-eight years old" (7), the daughter who is "twenty-four" (10), the son who is "twenty" (11), "the last two years" of worry (11), "the sixty-year-old company president" (13), "the forty-eight-year-old widow" (13), "the fifty-one-year-old deceased" (13), "5:00 p.m. the afternoon of the funeral" (16), and "[o]ne of three men" (16) who could replace Phil. The essay reads like an actuarial table and suggests that businesses see workers as numbers, not human beings.

Purpose and Audience

1. Goodman was writing to a general national audience of newspaper readers. But this essay seems to be aimed squarely at Phil's peers: adult male workaholics who may be headed down the same path he took.

2. Goodman's purpose is to nudge readers to examine their own lives—to think for more than just "five or ten minutes about" the lessons in her parable (paragraph 2). She wants them to rethink their attitudes toward work and upward mobility and strive instead for a healthy balance between their jobs and their personal lives.

Method and Structure

1. The cause, of course, is workaholism (some students might identify it as pressure to work hard). The effects are several: social isolation (paragraph 4), poor physical health (4), estrangement from family (7–12), emotional damage to loved ones (7–12), financial damage to loved ones (7, 13), worry and stress (11, 14), and, ultimately, premature death.

2. Goodman's essay is full of strategic repetition. In addition to the opening line, which implies that Phil was working when anybody else would be asleep, she repeats variations on "the obituary didn't say that" (paragraphs 2, 6); "of course" (2, 4, 16); "coronary thrombosis" and "heart attack" (2, 14); "Type A" (2, 14); "one of three" people in line for two different promotions (3, 6, 16); and the notion that Phil will be missed (7, 8, 13). The repetitions suggest the inevitability of his early death, hint at the meaninglessness of his work, and give the essay unity.

3. Phil's job is unimportant, in both the specific and general senses: his work is meaningless to his life and to his employer, and describing it would distract from readers' understanding of the story. Other missing details include Phil's last name and his children's names, the name of the company president, where the characters live and work, what his wife's former office job entailed, and what his older son does as a "hard-working executive in a manufacturing firm down South" (paragraph 9). Goodman leaves out such details because she intends for her main character to serve as an everyman—someone in whom readers might recognize themselves or people they know.

4. A "Type A" personality is someone who is driven, aggressive, status conscious, prone to working long hours, and (according to some theories) susceptible to heart disease. Goodman clarifies the personality traits at several points in the essay. She uses synonyms to define "Type A" as "workaholic" (paragraph 2) and "heart-attack natural" (14). She stresses his position as a vice-president (3), his desire to be one of the "Important People," and his view of golf as work (4) to reveal the emphasis he put on status. She stresses his late nights and six-day workweek (4–5) to show his tendency to put in long hours. She provides examples of his two sons—the older one who seems to have inherited the personality and the younger one who caused

Phil worry because he didn't—to contrast Type A with the more easygoing Type B (9, 11). And she informs readers that Phil did, indeed, suffer a heart attack in the end (2, 14).

Language

1. Goodman's tone is distant and unemotional—and dripping in irony. The repetitions of the phrase "of course" (paragraphs 2, 4, 16) in particular lend a sense of resignation and inevitability to what is essentially Goodman's version of Phil's obituary. She achieves distance in part by using the first person only once, in an aside in the second paragraph, and by stressing numerical facts over emotional responses throughout. And she injects an ironic qualifier in nearly every sentence, such as "—on his day off—" in paragraph 3 and "during a time when his own company had begun the four-day week for everyone but the executives" in paragraph 4.

2. The quotations, too, are ironic. Those from the obituary—"extracurricular interests" (paragraph 4), "survivors" (7), and "dearly beloved" (9)—read like scare quotes and suggest how empty Phil's life turned out to be. Those from people speaking at his funeral underscore his family's emotional detachment and his employer's lack of concern.

3. Phil devoted himself to and sacrificed his life for a company that didn't care. At the same time, the conclusion implies that the man who takes his job will suffer the same fate.

Stephanie Alaimo and Mark Koester
The Backdraft of Technology (p. 311)

Students sometimes complain that writing an essay for an English class is an empty exercise because nobody but the teacher will read it and the task has no purpose beyond earning a grade. This strong student op-ed piece suggests an effective way to counter objections that writing assignments are pointless. Most school newspapers, as well as many national media outlets (National Public Radio's *This I Believe* comes to mind), encourage students to submit their essays for publication. You might consider framing at least one assignment as a newspaper or magazine submission, encouraging (or even requiring) students to send their essays to a local, regional, or national publication for consideration. Knowing that their writing will have a broad and clearly defined audience usually gives even the most reluctant student writers a real sense of purpose and seriousness.

The Compact Reader is always looking for new student essays as well. We would be thrilled if your students sent their work to Bedford/St. Martin's for possible inclusion in the next edition. Simply ask students to include their name, address, and phone number on the first page of their essay and send their finished essay(s) to *Compact Reader* Editor, Bedford/St. Martin's, 75 Arlington Street, Boston, MA 02116.

Content Quiz

1. What do the authors describe as "society's newest upgrade in not having to wait"?
   [The self-service checkout machine.]

2. What do the authors believe are the hidden costs of self-service checkouts?
   [Jobs and human interaction.]

3. Where, according to the authors, are self-checkout machines manufactured?
   [Somewhere other than the United States.]

4. Give at least two examples of the mechanization of customer service identified in the essay.
   [Self-service gas pumps, ATM machines, video rental services such as Netflix, online pizza orders.]

5. Who do the authors say gains the most from mechanizing customer service?
   [Corporations.]

Vocabulary Quiz

1. *Stockpiled* (paragraph 5) is closest in meaning to
   a. saved   b. paid   c. cut
   [a. saved]

2. *Implausible* (8) is closest in meaning to
   a. possible   b. unlikely   c. believable
   [b. unlikely]

3. *Precarious* (9) is closest in meaning to
   a. split   b. dangerous   c. scenic
   [b. dangerous]

4. *Tenuous* (9) is closest in meaning to
   a. unstable   b. promising   c. angry
   [a. unstable]

5. *Subsist* (10) is closest in meaning to
   a. employ   b. argue   c. live
   [c. live]

Answers
Meaning

1. *Backdraft* is a firefighters' term for a sudden explosion that occurs when a fire seems to be under control; it is caused by the introduction of fresh air to smoldering embers in a room that has been depleted of oxygen. (Students may have difficulty finding the word in a general or college dictionary, but explanations are easily found online. A few may recognize the concept from the 1991 Kurt Russell movie.) Using the word in the title allows Alaimo and Koester to imply something that is left unsaid in the essay itself yet informs at least part of their purpose. The idea is that even a seemingly innocuous technology has the potential to blow up in our faces.

2. Alaimo and Koester understand the tendency, as students may notice in the authors' use of "we" to implicate themselves in the behavior, as well as in their effort to acknowledge that their readers are reasonable people ("who wants to wait?" [paragraph 1]; "it seems easy enough to forget" [4]; "Sure, these new robots and computers reduce work" [7]). Ultimately, however, they condemn the unthinking preference for what's easy. They express their opinion unequivocally in paragraph 10: "To choose the self-checkout simply as a convenience cannot be morally justified unless these jobs remain."

Purpose and Audience

1. The purpose of this essay is unmistakably persuasive, as the last sentence makes clear. Alaimo and Koester urge their readers to "[s]ay 'No!' to self-checkout" (paragraph 11). In other words, they're calling for a boycott.

2. Presumably, they're addressing other students at DePaul University. You may need to point out to your students that DePaul is a large, urban Catholic university with a tradition of faith, community service, and social justice—although the authors' emphasis on morality in paragraph 10 might tip them off. Alaimo and Koester seem to believe that their readers are, like themselves, at least nominally religious and committed to social justice (which is why they don't feel a need to explain what they mean by "morally justified" [10]). They also assume that their fellow students are somewhat advantaged and have lofty aspirations for their own futures (as we can infer from their warning that "your elitist job market [could be] nuked" [8]).

Method and Structure

1. Cause-and-effect analysis enables Alaimo and Koester to explore how self-checkout came to be and explain how the convenience actually harms us. They explain that retailers like self-checkout because it lets them reduce payroll expenses. The authors further suggest that the existence of the self-checkout option is one of the reasons for long lines at registers that do have

cashiers: stores are cutting back on staffing and forcing customers to serve themselves. And the more willing we are to do the work ourselves, the less need there will be for human cashiers, ironically making the staffed lines even longer. More important, Alaimo and Koester warn, our choice of convenience over human interaction is reducing the number of jobs available for unskilled workers.

2. The scenario encourages readers to consider how the issue affects them personally, making the authors' argument more immediate and compelling.

3. Opinions will vary. Students may notice that the authors fail to provide evidence for a few questionable assertions, such as their assumptions that "self-checkout machines are probably not manufactured in the United States" (paragraph 5) and that "any job or task could become entirely technologically mechanized" (8). Students might also reasonably accuse Alaimo and Koester of oversimplifying, because they rely almost exclusively on necessary causes, identifying no one (sufficient) cause for the popularity of self-checkout or the loss of jobs (see pp. 297–98 of the text). At the same time, the authors do consider immediate, remote, major, and minor causes, lending their argument a respectable level of complexity given its length and the scope of their subject. Readers' own depth of knowledge and personal interests will affect how persuasive they deem the essay to be.

4. The examples of mechanization of customer service in paragraph 6 demonstrate that the problem is not limited to supermarket self-checkout lines, making the authors' subject more relevant for readers and suggesting the broader implications of their subject. The method of argument and persuasion, of course, pervades the essay as a whole and serves as the authors' primary reason for analyzing causes and effects in the first place.

Language

1. Although Alaimo and Koester obviously feel strongly about their message and are occasionally confrontational about it ("your elitist job market nuked" [paragraph 8]; "cannot be morally justified" [10]; "it could be you" [11]), their overall tone is probably best described as earnest. They seem honestly to believe that their essay may help people keep their jobs, if only readers will listen.

2. The authors seem to be attempting to create a friendly rapport with their readers by peppering an otherwise serious essay with slang and colloquialisms. Unfortunately, a few of the phrases are clichés, and one might go further to argue that "trapped in a precarious fork in the road" (paragraph 9) is a mixed metaphor disguised as a cliché. The casual language may cause some readers to conclude that the writing (and perhaps the thinking behind it) is unnecessarily sloppy.

Dana Thomas
The Fake Trade (p. 316)

With this compelling and alarming analysis of causes and effects, Thomas is sure to surprise readers who have never given a second thought to the cheap knockoffs and questionable merchandise we've all seen at flea markets, dollar stores, and big-box discounters. Even if students recognize a fake when they see one, most have probably not considered where counterfeit goods come from or how they might contribute to such horrors as human trafficking and slave labor.

Content Quiz

1. What kind of handbag did the little girl at the lemonade stand have?
    [An imitation Louis Vuitton Murakami pouch.]

2. What kinds of merchandise are counterfeited?
    ["Everything." Thomas gives as examples handbags, luxury cars, medicine, health and beauty aids, perfume, and brakes.]

3. Why do people buy counterfeit goods?
    [Because they believe counterfeiting is a "victimless crime."]

4. Identify at least two methods counterfeiters use to smuggle items into the United States.
    [They once packed them with legal merchandise; now they might ship raw materials for manufacturing or finishing in the United States, ship generic items and add labels when they get here, hide brand labels under generic ones, or create the appearance of legitimacy by applying for a trademark for a slightly altered logo (knowing that it will be denied but slipping past customs in the process).]

5. What major US retailer did Fendi sue in 2006 for selling counterfeits?
    [Wal-Mart Stores, Inc.]

Vocabulary Quiz

1. *Ingesting* (paragraph 6) is closest in meaning to
    a. saving   b. swallowing   c. carrying
    [b. swallowing]

2. *Syndicates* (8) is closest in meaning to
    a. organizations   b. channels   c. fakes
    [a. organizations]

3. *Clandestine* (8) is closest in meaning to
    a. flaming   b. illegal   c. hidden
    [c. hidden]

4. *Invariably* (8) is closest in meaning to
   a. angrily   b. lie   c. always
   [c. always]

5. *Pretense* (13) is closest in meaning to
   a. appearance   b. before   c. proof
   [a. appearance]

Answers

Meaning

1. Most simply, *counterfeit* means "fake" and *legitimate* means "real." But Thomas certainly intends for the words' connotations to resonate. The word *counterfeit* seems somehow less judgmental than *fake*, and it carries a sheen of objectivity that obscures the full reality of its meaning; the usage echoes consumers' misguided belief that fake goods don't hurt anybody. At the same time, the word *legitimate* conveys a much stronger sense of moral judgment than *real* does. By juxtaposing the two words so often—and by reinforcing the connotations with the synonyms *fake*, *pirated*, *real*, and *genuine*—Thomas underscores her point that counterfeit goods are not equivalent to their legitimate counterparts and that they are far from harmless, no matter what readers might think.

2. A "victimless crime" is an illegal activity that doesn't hurt anybody; some people use the concept to justify breaking laws that seem pointless or irrelevant to them. Clearly, Thomas does not believe that counterfeiting falls into this category. She mentions the idea because her purpose in writing the essay is to counter the widely held assumption that buying counterfeit products causes no harm.

3. Thomas explains that she said nothing to the girl because "[i]t wasn't her fault her family had given it to her" (paragraph 20). She doesn't want to make a child feel bad, a reasonable and compassionate decision. But students may well object that the child could have asked (even begged) for the cartoon-inspired handbag, that preteens are prime targets of fashion merchandising and can be alarmingly brand conscious, and that a girl of that age is old enough to understand what Thomas chose not to tell her.

Purpose and Audience

1. Thomas's relatively objective reportorial approach to exposing the realities of counterfeiting suggests that she wants to educate readers. At the same time, however, she clearly wants to persuade readers to stop buying fake goods. Her purpose is most evident in paragraph 8, where she outlines the horrors associated with the counterfeit market and cites other readers' and listeners' decisions to "never knowingly buy another fake good"; in paragraphs 15–19, where she explains how to recognize counterfeits; and in her conclusion, where she issues a call to action imploring readers to "spread the word" and "just stop buying the stuff" (paragraph 20).

2. Students may or may not need to be reminded that "The Fake Trade" was first published in *Harper's Bazaar*, an upscale fashion magazine for women. Thomas's use of handbags as a recurring example makes clear that her intended audience is female, and her references to luxury brand names and boutique shopping suggest that her readers are fashion conscious and relatively affluent.

Method and Structure

1. Given the author's purpose in exposing the unimagined consequences of buying counterfeit goods, cause-and-effect analysis is almost inevitable as the choice of method. The subject (global impacts of consumer behavior) lends itself to the method perfectly.

2. As Thomas explains it, the market for counterfeit goods exists because of the law of supply and demand. Consumers "keep happily buying fakes" because they're less expensive than legitimate brands and because buyers don't think they're causing any harm (paragraph 7). For counterfeit operations, the practice is enormously profitable, accounting for "approximately $600 billion annually" (5) and allowing individual counterfeiters to earn "millions" (14) at a time. The consequences of participating in this market, however, include lost business and lost jobs in the United States (5); unsafe and even deadly products (6); and support for "international crime syndicates that deal in money laundering, human trafficking, and child labor" (8).

3. As is often the case with cause-and-effect analyses, the organization of this essay is somewhat complex. Thomas opens with a narrative about an encounter with a little girl (paragraphs 1–4), and then moves to a brief overview of the counterfeit industry (6) and examples of counterfeit goods (6). She then digs in to the heart of her cause-and-effect analysis, considering why people buy fakes and what happens when they do (7–8). Next, she acknowledges that crackdowns have had some success (9), explains how the "supply chain" once worked (10), and describes current practices (11–14). She follows that with tips on how to recognize counterfeits and ensure that one's purchases are legitimate (15–19). She concludes by returning to her opening anecdote and issuing a call to action, imploring readers to share their new awareness and to "stop buying the stuff" (20). This approach allows Thomas to pull readers in, establish the significance of her subject, surprise readers with new and potentially upsetting information, explain how and why authorities are trying to stop counterfeiting, and persuade readers that they must become part of the solution.

4. The author alludes to published studies in paragraphs 5 and 6 and cites two directly in paragraph 7; she also refers to a Web resource in paragraph 18. She quotes some of the experts she interviewed—two lawyers and a law enforcement agent—in paragraphs 6, 12, 13, and 17. Her personal experience comes into play in paragraphs 1–4, 8, 9, and 20. The evidence from sources helps establish the validity of her concern, confirms that what

she says is true, and lends her an air of authority. Her personal anecdotes enliven the essay and help make the subject more concrete for readers; they also ensure that Thomas doesn't lose her voice to her sources.

5. Thomas's examples (paragraphs 6, 9) and process analyses (10–14) should shock and frighten most readers. Both strategies offer an effective way to get readers' attention and make them care about the subject.

Language

1. Because the organization of this essay is complex (see question 3 under "Method and Structure"), Thomas is careful to mark transitions among her supporting points. Paragraph transitions include "Though the fashion business has" (paragraph 5), "One of the primary reasons" (7), "But the reality is" (8), "a decade ago" (9), "As long as there is a demand, however" (10), "But as fashion companies grew wise" (11), "Another" (12, 13), "By the time the brand realizes what's going on" (14), "Well" (16), "Of course" (19), and "Most important" (20).

2. Thomas's tone is both balanced and urgent—a good choice considering her purpose. She cultivates the sense of balance by relying on quotations, facts, and examples from her sources, hovering in the background as an objective reporter through most of the essay. But at the same time, Thomas paints a disturbing picture and (toward the end) addresses readers directly, emphasizing the horrors of counterfeiting and pleading with readers to not be involved with it.

Chapter 14

Argument and Persuasion
Discussing Social Issues

Anna Quindlen
The C Word in the Hallways (p. 343)

The subject of student violence is a sensitive one, particularly for students who may have had a personal connection to a campus shooting, as well as for those who worry about the possibility of an incident on their own campus. All the same, Quindlen's essay offers an excellent opportunity to discuss the effectiveness of using emotional appeals in argument.

One way to initiate discussion might be to ask how much has changed since Quindlen wrote this essay. Teachers and administrators have indeed started paying more attention to students' mental health, but many would argue that the increased scrutiny has caused more problems than it has solved. Others might reply that mental illness is just as stigmatized—if not more so—as it was in 1999. Still others might point out that despite the media frenzies that accompany each new shooting, the problem (as devastating as it is) is neither as new nor as widespread as news reports imply.

Content Quiz

1. What is a "psychological autopsy"?
   [It's the process by which doctors try to identify the reasons for a teenager's suicide or homicide.]

2. Who were Kip Kinkel and Sam Manzie?
   [Both were seventeen-year-olds who committed murders: Kinkel killed his parents and two classmates; Manzie killed an eleven-year-old boy.]

3. What ending did film censors insist be added to the 1956 movie *The Bad Seed*?
   [They forced the producers to add a scene in which the fictional father spanked the lead character as punishment for her killing spree.]

4. With what weapon did Kip Kinkel kill his father?
   [With the same gun (a Glock) that his father bought for him as an alternative to therapy.]

5. According to Quindlen, how many mentally ill children do not get psychological treatment?
   [Two-thirds of the total, which is estimated at six million.]

Vocabulary Quiz

1. *Ludicrous* (paragraph 4) is closest in meaning to
   a. laughable   b. cautious   c. thoughtful
   [a. laughable]

2. *Loll* (7) is closest in meaning to
   a. fight   b. droop   c. enjoy
   [b. droop]

3. *Utilitarian* (7) is closest in meaning to
   a. psychological   b. practical   c. financial
   [b. practical]

4. *Derision* (9) is closest in meaning to
   a. approval   b. support   c. ridicule
   [c. ridicule]

5. *Psychotropic* (10) is closest in meaning to
   a. mind-altering   b. recreational   c. legal
   [a. mind-altering]

Answers

Meaning

1. The author's thesis is stated in the introduction: "Yet one solution continues to elude us, and that is ending the ignorance about mental health, and moving it from the margins of care and into the mainstream where it belongs. As surely as any vaccine, this would save lives" (paragraph 2). In other words, Quindlen believes that if American culture destigmatized mental illness and became more willing to treat it like any other illness, fewer troubled teenagers would kill themselves or others.

2. Quindlen focuses her essay on relatively targeted teen killings, using as her primary examples Kip Kinkel (who killed his parents and two Oregon classmates in November 1999) and Sam Manzie (who killed a young boy in his New Jersey home the same month), both of whom were sentenced to life in prison when they were seventeen years old. As she sees it, both boys were mentally ill. She further suggests that Kinkel's father aided and abetted his actions by buying him a gun and that Manzie was the victim of a pedophile.

3. Quindlen blames society for its actions, believing that these boys killed because their mental illnesses went untreated: in Kinkel's case because his father disapproved of therapy, and in Manzie's case because his parents

couldn't afford the necessary care. Ultimately, she presents Kinkel and Manzie as victims.

4. She is implying that our culture encourages boys to use violence to solve their problems, a point she reinforces later when she remarks that "talk therapy, or even heartfelt talk, is somehow sissified, weak" (paragraph 9).

Purpose and Audience

1. Quindlen makes her purpose clear in her conclusion: she wants readers not only to recognize that "mental illness is an illness, not a character flaw" (paragraph 10) but also to act on that understanding and ensure that troubled children get the treatment they need.

2. Her reference to "we parents" in paragraph 10 suggests that Quindlen is writing primarily to parents of teenagers, hoping to urge them to take their children's problems more seriously. By extension, her conclusion hints that she also imagines representatives of insurance providers, hospitals, and schools among her readers.

3. The omission will almost certainly trouble, or at least puzzle, some readers, but there are reasonable explanations for Quindlen's decision not to include the Columbine tragedy in her discussion. On the surface, her essay is a response to two very specific incidents that took place at around the same time. On a deeper level, however, it may be that the scale of Columbine is just too overwhelming to contemplate in a brief essay, that Quindlen doesn't put Harris and Klebold in the same category of untreated mental illness in which she places Kinkel and Manzie, or that she doesn't see fit to try to excuse their behavior—or to blame the massacre on society. (Such an attempt would probably have alienated readers.)

Method and Structure

1. Quindlen's argument is highly emotional. She sets the tone with her opening observation that the phrase "psychological autopsy" is "the saddest" one she's "read in a long time" (paragraph 1). Just a few examples of emotional appeal in her essay include her reference to "black-bordered photographs in yearbooks and murder suspects with acne problems" (2), her comment that "[s]o many [lives] have already been lost" (3), her depiction of Manzie's father trying to navigate the insurance system (6), her chilling allusion to lobotomies (7), her acknowledgment that her argument has an element of the "[w]arm fuzzies" to it (7), her question of "how we would respond if two-thirds of America's babies were not being immunized" (8), and the "what if" scenario of her conclusion.

2. She tackles opposing viewpoints in paragraph 4, with her reference to the "ludicrous" solution to child homicides epitomized in the movie *The Bad Seed*, and in paragraphs 5 and 6, in which she acknowledges that Kinkel and Manzie did receive mental health care (but insists that it was inadequate). Although her discussion of the boys' treatment does seem balanced

and reasonable, students may rightly object that in relying on a movie that is over fifty years old to characterize those who disagree with her perspective, Quindlen is unfairly depicting her opponents as almost comically irrational.

3. Depending on readers' knowledge of Shakespeare's play and Yeats's poem, these quick allusions pack a lot of meaning. *Romeo and Juliet,* of course, is largely a story about teenagers who get caught up in circumstances that were not of their making. "The Second Coming" describes the end of the world as the arrival of a terrible beast that destroys the innocent. Most college students (and many high school students) will have at least a passing familiarity with the play; you may want to bring a copy of the poem to class and share it with students.

4. Quindlen's examples of teenage killers (paragraph 3) and ineffective responses (4) establish the urgency of the problem and the need for a better solution. The paragraphs of comparison and contrast explaining the boys' treatment (5, 6) emphasize the inadequacy of contemporary mental health interventions. The essay as a whole could be read as a cause-and-effect analysis, but the dangerous relationship between current attitudes and teenage boys' violence is articulated most clearly in paragraphs 8 and 9.

Language

1. The "C word" refers to *crazy,* a derisive word Quindlen doesn't utter until paragraph 9. The use of the euphemism in the title, along with the whispered quality of the word itself at the end of the essay, underscores the stigma that society attaches to mental illness.

2. After asserting that "mental illness is an illness, not a character flaw" (paragraph 10), Quindlen creates an emphatic rhythm by ending three of the last four sentences with the same phrase: insurance providers, hospitals and schools, and parents "should act like it." She then uses a variation of this phrase ("will believe it") to argue that her solution will work.

3. Quindlen's tone is consistently plaintive, begging readers to take seriously the problem of mental illness. Although some readers will consider it effective, others may find it cloying.

Charlie Spence
Sixteen (p. 349)

Spence's essay is serious, and his position controversial, but his argument is relatively easy to follow. Taking as his premise the idea that juvenile offenders should be punished, he carefully establishes good reasons for his argument that trying and sentencing them as adults is both excessive and wrong: adolescents' brains aren't fully developed; therefore not only can't they comprehend the true nature of their crimes, but they also can and should be successfully rehabilitated and released back into society. At several points in his argument, Spence questions a common assumption without alienating his readers. If nothing else, he is skilled at building common ground.

What is perhaps most instructive in Spence's essay is that even a prison inmate arguing for more lenient sentencing can establish a strong ethical appeal. The author's personal story, then, might offer a good opening for class discussion (see question 1 under "Purpose and Audience" and question 2 under "Method and Structure"). How do Spence's circumstances affect his credibility? How successfully does he overcome this potential problem? How can students apply the same strategies to their own arguments?

Content Quiz

1. What is Proposition 21?
   [A California law, passed in 2000, that gives district attorneys the option of trying fourteen- to seventeen-year-old defendants as adults.]

2. How many juvenile offenders were serving life sentences in the United States and in Israel at the time this essay was written?
   [There were 2,387 in the United States; seven in Israel.]

3. What crime was committed by the fourteen-year-old Spence knew in Juvenile Hall?
   [For a reward of twenty-five cents, the boy beat up a homeless man, causing his death.]

4. At what age does a "life" sentence end in juvenile facilities?
   [Twenty-five.]

5. What did the US Supreme Court rule in its decision for *Roper v. Simmons*?
   [That executing a minor is unconstitutional. The judges cited juveniles' lack of mental and emotional development in their opinion.]

Vocabulary Quiz

1. *Discretion* (paragraph 2) is closest in meaning to
   a. permission   b. judgment   c. secret
   [b. judgment]

2. *Prodigious* (4) is closest in meaning to
   a. evil   b. huge   c. smart
   [b. huge]

3. *Subsequent* (5) is closest in meaning to
   a. later   b. violent   c. tricky
   [a. later]

4. *Inclinations* (7) is closest in meaning to
    a. tendencies   b. hills   c. errors
    [a. tendencies]

5. *Pinnacle* (8) is closest in meaning to
    a. conclusion   b. argument   c. height
    [c. height]

Answers
Meaning

1. Spence asserts his central assumption in paragraph 6. "Juvenile offenders," he says, "should be punished for serious crimes they commit." In other words, the purpose of prison is punishment. Contrary to current practice, Spence believes prison should be used as an opportunity to rehabilitate criminals, an assertion he repeats throughout the essay.

2. Spence believes that sentencing juveniles to life is immoral because children lack the neurological development "to control sudden spontaneous inclinations or urges" (paragraph 7) or to fully comprehend the consequences of their actions (3, 5, 7, 8). Spence points out that we recognize adolescents' immaturity "as a determining factor for conduct" (8) when establishing minimum ages for activities such as smoking, drinking, and voting but fail to consider their mental development when handing out sentences: "The contrast here is drastic," he says, because "by one means we are suggesting that seventeen-year-old teenagers are only entering a mature enough mental state to choose whether they wish to watch an R-rated movie, yet by another we are suggesting that they are mature enough to understand the full consequences of a crime they may commit" (7). Because their minds are not completely matured, Spence argues, we should aim to rehabilitate juvenile offenders rather than put them away for life.

3. Readers will naturally be curious to know what Spence did as a sixteen-year-old to warrant being tried as an adult and convicted to a life sentence. Many will be frustrated that he doesn't say, and some may be suspicious of his credibility as a result. We can only assume that the crime was serious, and, most likely, that Spence regrets it. In the end, however, it doesn't matter, because part of Spence's point is that people like him should not be "brand[ed] . . . for life for the worst thing he or she did as a child" (paragraph 6).

Purpose and Audience

1. It may strike some readers as a little overwrought, but Spence's opening story is meant to put the author in a sympathetic light. In addition to establishing his remorse for the crime he committed, the sense of bewilderment and confusion expressed in the narrative hints at Spence's main argument: that children can't really understand the consequences of their actions. How students respond to it will depend on their own attitudes toward

violent and juvenile offenders. Some may feel empathy for the writer; others won't have any pity for him.

2. The ideal reader would probably be lawmakers from a state with a high rate of juvenile incarceration, such as California, since Spence's purpose is to persuade readers that juvenile sentencing guidelines should be changed. Prisoners, of course, will already have a strong opinion on sentencing, and they probably don't need Spence to persuade them that imprisonment doesn't help them. But average citizens are important to Spence, too, because it was voters who passed Proposition 21 in the first place. By striving to influence public opinion, Spence could conceivably influence votes on future legislation.

Method and Structure

1. Spence's evidence is drawn partly from his experiences as an imprisoned juvenile offender but more so from academic studies and expert opinion. He provides examples of his own and a fellow prisoner's experiences, for instance, to demonstrate that children understand the consequences of their actions differently than adults do. More important, however, he draws on incarceration statistics, child psychology, and legal opinion (*Roper v. Simmons* [7]) to explain *why* children's brains aren't fully developed, to show that imprisonment is especially hard on them, and to alert readers to the fact that America is the only country that routinely sentences juvenile offenders to long prison terms. Because readers may doubt a convicted criminal's credibility, Spence needs these authoritative sources to prove the validity of his claims.

2. Most readers can be expected to doubt Spence's objectivity. After all, how seriously can we take a convicted juvenile offender's claim that life sentences for juvenile offenders are unfair? Spence's credibility is helped from the start by his willingness to acknowledge his status as a lifer. And in some ways, he turns his credibility problems to his advantage, most notably by sharing his firsthand knowledge of juvenile crime and of the effects that long sentences have on children and by using his personal experience to provide compelling examples (such as the child who killed a homeless man [paragraph 5]). He wisely uses the expert testimony of scholars (4, 5, 6), child psychologists (5), and the US Supreme Court to develop and support his claims, and he makes a point of introducing statistical and factual evidence to support individual points. Spence works to build common ground with his readers by acknowledging the validity of opposing viewpoints (see question 3, below). And by presenting his argument in a calm, rational, and thoroughly supported way, Spence presents himself as evidence that young offenders can be rehabilitated.

3. Spence anticipates that many readers will object to his argument, so he tries to build common ground. He begins paragraph 3, for instance, by stating "It is easy for me to understand the feelings of one who is opposed to my position" and conceding that "[j]uveniles do commit crimes that are serious and are considered to be 'adult crimes.'" Similarly, in paragraph 6,

he agrees that "[j]uvenile offenders should be punished for serious crimes they commit" but immediately qualifies that with "but as juveniles in juvenile facilities." The effect is a reasonable, well-considered argument that acknowledges opposing positions but calmly explains why they're wrong.

4. The United States and Israel are the only two countries that sentence juvenile offenders for life. While the United States has given nearly 2,400 life sentences to children, Israel has given only seven and none in the past six years. By highlighting the stark difference, Spence is trying to persuade readers that American sentencing practices are extreme, unparalleled, and unreasonable, perhaps even barbaric.

Language

1. Spence accepts that violent juvenile offenders should spend time behind bars, but he believes that life sentences in adult facilities are unreasonable and unproductive; he would like to see an emphasis on rehabilitation instead. Because he knows that his position will be controversial, he maintains a carefully measured tone that borders on conciliation.

2. His point is that most juvenile offenders are immature children, not hardened, calculating criminals. By repeating the words *child* and *children* as well as variations of them—*juveniles, adolescents, teenagers*—several times in his essay, he emphasizes the need to educate children and protect them from their impulses *before* they get into trouble, as well as the potential for reeducating them after they make a mistake.

Sherry Turkle
Privacy Has a Politics (p. 356)

Sherry Turkle is both a renowned scholar and an engaging storyteller. In "Privacy Has a Politics" the author's narrative skill helps support her argument that by failing to protect their privacy, Americans risk losing civil liberties.

Of the people who relinquish their privacy online, Turkle is clearly most concerned for high school and college students. It seems equally clear that she doesn't imagine those students as part of her audience. Classroom discussion might begin with how accurate your students find the author's characterization of them and their peers (see question 3 under "Language"). How much information about themselves have they revealed online? Are they comfortable with such levels of self-exposure, or have they felt twinges of worry? Why? Do they think Turkle portrays their attitudes and actions fairly? And to what extent does their assessment of the author's assumptions affect their response to her argument?

Content Quiz

1. What former presidential candidate does Turkle credit with first using the Internet to organize a political campaign?
    [Howard Dean. Barack Obama, she says, "transformed" Dean's methods into an even more powerful tool.]

2. According to Turkle, what two kinds of behavior do young people see happening online?
    [Embarrassing and political. They tend to believe that the former will be forgiven and that the latter will get a person into trouble.]

3. What does Turkle think of the notion that "if you have nothing to hide, you have nothing to fear"?
    [She not only rejects it but also finds it chilling. Such claims, she insists, are beside the point.]

4. What French philosopher wrote about prison architecture and self-policing citizens?
    [Michel Foucault.]

5. Why was it important to Turkle's grandmother that "no one can look at your mail" in America?
    [As an immigrant from Eastern Europe accustomed to government surveillance of citizens, she was grateful for the civil liberties guaranteed to Americans but worried by the political implications of the McCarthy hearings. Privacy, as she saw it, is a right worth defending.]

Vocabulary Quiz

1. *Transgression* (paragraph 2) is closest in meaning to
    a. sexuality   b. violation   c. change
    [b. violation]

2. *Luminary* (3) is closest in meaning to
    a. celebrity   b. lightbulb   c. producer
    [a. celebrity]

3. *Assent* (5) is closest in meaning to
    a. height   b. amusement   c. agreement
    [c. agreement]

4. *Relinquish* (6) is closest in meaning to
    a. surrender   b. auction   c. protect
    [a. surrender]

5. *Validation* (6) is closest in meaning to
    a. free parking   b. approval   c. lack of privacy
    [b. approval]

Answers
Meaning

1. The author cites a combination of peer pressure (paragraphs 2, 5, 8), insecurity (6), and naïveté (2, 9) to explain why high school and college students so readily expose themselves through technology. She reminds readers of the potential for embarrassment (2) and asserts the possibility for government surveillance (3–6) and loss of civil liberties (7–9) in an effort to persuade them to hold their personal information private.

2. In paragraphs 3–5, Turkle blames an Internet version of Foucault's panopticon—a sense of surveillance and potential censure intensified by the lack of privacy online—for creating "a chilling effect on political speech" (1) and a fear of engaging in "political behavior that might get you into trouble" (2). She amplifies her concern in paragraph 7, when she cautions that "the Internet has fulfilled the dream of the panopticon."

3. Turkle warns that Americans' ability to protect their rights is threatened by the political apathy stemming from a feeling of helplessness (paragraph 6) inculcated by an online culture that asserts the best response to lack of privacy "is to just be good" (7). The less privacy we have as individuals, she argues, the more we resign ourselves to government abuse.

Purpose and Audience

1. Turkle's thesis is stated most fully in paragraph 9: "In democracy, perhaps we all need to begin with the assumption that everyone has something to hide, a zone of private action and reflection, one that must be protected no matter what our techno-enthusiasms." Her purpose is to make readers rethink their positions, of course, but more so to start "a conversation" (10) by questioning assumptions.

2. Turkle's audience, while nonspecialized, is apparently educated, for her essay contains several cultural and historical references (a wiretapping scandal, Foucault's panopticon, the McCarthy era, Luddites) that young students, in particular, might not be expected to recognize.

Method and Structure

1. By acknowledging the Web's political benefits before raising concerns about its political dangers, Turkle simultaneously addresses an opposing viewpoint and enhances her ethical appeal by establishing herself as a reasonable observer.

2. Turkle's argument appeals to both reason and emotion. The closest reasoning appears in paragraphs 4–6, where the author seeks causes and forges a connection between acquiescence to expectations of self-surveillance and resignation in the face of "public exposure." She appeals to emotion throughout, but especially when discussing her teenaged informants—for instance, in paragraph 9: "I am haunted . . ."

3. Turkle says that she regards the mailbox episode as a "civics lesson." Certainly it offers a powerful reminder that the US government has been known to monitor and jail its citizens for highly questionable reasons, and could feasibly do so again. At the same time, the story allows her to reiterate her conviction that privacy is a foundational American right and to explain how it protects civil liberty.

Language

1. In its literal sense, a panopticon is an architectural design that places an observation tower at the center of a round structure. In Foucault's metaphor, it is a cultural environment that fosters a paranoid sense of constant exposure, creating a dystopia in which citizens police themselves out of fear. What troubles Turkle is not just that Foucault's vision of imposed discipline seems to have become reality online, but also that some technology advocates have misinterpreted the concept, "with no apparent irony" (paragraph 7), as a justification for giving up privacy (3).

2. The allusion is to the early nineteenth-century political movement in which textile workers, led by Ned Ludd, protested the Industrial Revolution by smashing machinery. The term *Luddite* has come to carry a negative connotation, suggesting a stubborn resistance to technological change. Turkle is insisting that despite her concerns, she doesn't mean to be destructive.

3. Although Turkle exhibits a genuine concern for young people, some students might (reasonably) find her tone patronizing or condescending.

CASEBOOK: IMMIGRATION

George F. Will's essay works with the following pieces by Marie Myung-Ok Lee and Roberto Rodríguez to form a trio of readings on a shared subject. Will and Lee take opposing positions on the question of birthright citizenship, while Rodríguez argues for the dignity of and respect for immigrants of color. Although the writers don't speak to each other directly, their arguments do.

George F. Will
Subject to Interpretation (p. 362)

Originally published in his syndicated column as "An Argument to Be Made about Immigrant Babies and Citizenship," George F. Will's case against birthright citizenship is sure to raise some students' hackles while at the same time reconfirming others' biases against illegal immigrants. We include it in the *Compact Reader* not to raise controversy or discomfort, but to model an argument based on a critical reading of sources. Will's argument relies on synthesis of ideas from government documents and an academic paper in a scholarly journal; he quotes the original author extensively, yet he manages to hold his own voice and make his own argument.

The two essays following "Subject to Interpretation," Marie Myung-Ok Lee's "I Was an Anchor Baby" and Roberto Rodríguez's "The Border on Our Backs," should offer a balm to any students offended by aspects of Will's essay. Lee makes the issue of birthright citizenship poignantly personal, while Rodríguez expresses angry indignation at the assumptions lurking beneath arguments like Will's. Class discussion might start not with where students stand on immigration reform (a question likely to lead to heated and unproductive arguments), but with the question of why immigration continues to be such a hot-button topic in America. Why do people on both sides of the issue tend to get so upset?

Content Quiz

1. What "simple reform" does Will propose? That is, what does he say is the only action necessary to "end the practice of 'birthright citizenship'" in America?
   [Reinterpret the first sentence of the Fourteenth Amendment, which Will claims has been misunderstood.]

2. On whose scholarly work does Will base his argument?
   [University of Texas law professor Lino Graglia, whose paper was published in the *Texas Review of Law and Politics*.]

3. Why, according to Will, could the authors of the Fourteenth Amendment to the US Constitution "not have intended birthright citizenship for illegal immigrants"?
   [Because at the time the document was written and ratified, there were no restrictions on immigration, and hence no illegal immigrants to be granted citizenship.]

4. Is a child born in the United States to foreign diplomats granted American citizenship at birth?
   [No.]

5. What percentage of American-born children have mothers who are in the United States illegally and therefore should not be considered citizens, as Will sees it?
   [Nearly 10% nationwide. The numbers in Los Angeles county are significantly higher (two thirds in public hospitals, one half overall).]

Vocabulary Quiz

1. *Jurisdiction* (paragraphs 2, 6, 8, 9) is closest in meaning to
   a. speech   b. authority   c. legality
   [b. authority]

2. *Conferring* (2) is closest in meaning to
   a. giving   b. meeting   c. denying
   [a. giving]

3. *Inducement* (3) is closest in meaning to
   a. barrier   b. motivation   c. suggestion
   [b. motivation]

4. *Stipulate* (6) is closest in meaning to
   a. argue   b. complain   c. specify
   [c. specify]

5. *Impediment* (10) is closest in meaning to
   a. obstruction   b. platform   c. walk
   [a. obstruction]

Answers
Meaning

1. Will establishes that his subjects are "birthright citizenship" and "misinterpretation" of the Fourteenth Amendment in the first sentence of paragraph 2. He leads up to his thesis throughout the essay and states it explicitly in his conclusion: "Graglia seems to establish that there is no constitutional impediment to Congress ending the granting of birthright citizenship to those whose presence here is 'not only without the government's consent but in violation of its law'" (10)—in other words, he argues there is no need to repeal the Fourteenth Amendment, because it already excludes the children of illegal immigrants from citizenship. His solution is for Congress to apply the Amendment as legal scholar Lino Graglia interprets it.

2. Birthright citizenship, as Will defines it, is "the practice of conferring citizenship on children born here to illegal immigrants" (paragraph 2), as well as "'the greatest possible inducement to illegal entry'" on the part of prospective parents (3)—a "reward" (5) for breaking the law. Children born to illegal immigrants are granted citizenship because, he says, policymakers have misinterpreted the Fourteenth Amendment, specifically the phrase "subject to the jurisdiction thereof" (4).

3. As Will explains it, the Civil Rights Act of 1866 and the Fourteenth Amendment, by extension, explicitly exclude American Indians from birthright citizenship because their primary loyalties are to their tribes, not the United

States government. The same principle of "divided allegiance" (paragraph 6), he argues, applies to children of parents whose legal affiliations are with another country, whether they are diplomats (7) or aliens (9). Alert students may notice that Will intends to exclude the children of "legal as well as illegal" (6) immigrants from automatic citizenship as well.

Purpose and Audience

1. It is conceivable that an opinion piece in a publication such as the *Washington Post* might play a small part in legislative change. Readers of such publications include policymakers, to be sure, but, more important, major newsmagazines influence public opinion, which in turn influences congressional opinion and action.

2. The ideal readers would probably be members of Congress, since Will's stated purpose is to effect legislation ending birthright citizenship for children of immigrants. Immigrants could be expected to object to Will's premise on a personal level. Lawyers will probably already have strong opinions on constitutional law, and their ideas are not likely to be changed by a journalist citing a legal paper in a mainstream publication. But average Americans are important to Will, because a groundswell of anti-immigration sentiment could force Congress to act.

3. Will goes out of his way to project a reasonable, considered argument grounded in legal scholarship, and he quotes expert opinion extensively, so he probably does not mean to provoke or upset his readers. At the same time, he acknowledges that immigration is a contentious issue, and he opens his essay by suggesting he has a reasonable solution, setting a tone of conciliation. Some students are likely to be offended by his position and his claims nonetheless, while others are sure to embrace it.

Method and Structure

1. A possible syllogism might be: "The Fourteenth Amendment grants citizenship to persons born in the United States and not subject to the jurisdiction of another country. Persons born to immigrants are subject to the jurisdiction of another country. Therefore, persons born to immigrants are not granted American citizenship." Some readers might accuse Will of begging the question (i.e., children of immigrants cannot be granted citizenship because they're not citizens). If they reject either his major or minor premise, they'll conclude that his argument doesn't work.

2. Will's major source is an unnamed academic paper by law professor Lino Graglia, published in the *Texas Review of Law and Politics* — a self-described conservative legal publication that prides itself on publishing work that mainstream journals avoid. He relies heavily on Graglia's expert opinion, quoting him extensively. With the exception of birth statistics presented as congressional testimony and cited in paragraph 10, most of Will's other sources — the text of the Fourteenth Amendment (2), the Civil Rights Act

of 1866 (6), the "regulations issued by the departments of Homeland Security and Justice" (6–7), the opinions of Senator Lyman Trumbull (8), and an 1884 Supreme Court decision (9)—are all indirect citations from Graglia's paper. Some students might question the accuracy of Will's birth statistics (although the data do seem to hold up to scrutiny), and others may object that Will relies too much on a single source or that he quotes more extensively than necessary, but overall the author's sources seem reliable enough given his perspective and his purpose.

3. Will does not seem to address opposing viewpoints in this essay, unless one counts the introductory acknowledgment that "immigration arguments . . . may soon again be at a roiling boil" (paragraph 1). The omission of conflicting arguments may present a problem for some readers, but the author's purpose is not so much to engage in a debate as to assert the implications of one legal scholar's interpretation of the Fourteenth Amendment.

4. As Will interprets the Amendment (through Lino Graglia), the Fourteenth Amendment grants citizenship to people born in the United States to legal American citizens—and no one else.

Language

1. Will characterizes the immigration debate as a steaming kettle on the verge of boiling over. In doing so, he acknowledges that the issue is contentious and implies that some people could be hurt; at the same time, the metaphor suggests that the situation can easily be brought under control—simply by removing the heat.

2. In arguing constitutional interpretation, Will is making a legal case for his subject. The legal terms, while technical and difficult for a lay audience, are nonetheless appropriate; they lend his argument a serious, academic weight and bolster his credibility with congressional readers. By repeating the terms *jurisdiction* and *allegiance* in particular, Will emphasizes his key points and gives his essay coherence.

3. Will throws out *welfare* in paragraph 3 and repeats *illegal* throughout the essay (1, 2, 4, 5, 6, 9, 10). For many readers, the words have highly negative, inflammatory associations that raise the specter of non-US citizens taking advantage of American jobs and benefits. Will likely intends to strengthen the force of his argument by heightening those associations for readers already inclined to distrust immigrants.

4. Despite the contentiousness of his subject and the thrust of his solution, Will establishes a dispassionate, reasoned tone for his argument—as he must to ensure that he doesn't alienate those readers not already on his side of the issue.

Marie Myung-Ok Lee

I Was an Anchor Baby (p. 368)

Writing from a calm yet earnest point of view shortly after House Republican Jon Kyle of Arizona called for a congressional hearing on the issue of birthright citizenship—and a few months after George F. Will published "Subject to Interpretation" (p. 362)—Lee provides a very personal perspective on what has become a very public and increasingly heated issue. In reminding readers of the history of immigration laws, she deftly sidesteps the more controversial elements of the debate by reframing its terms. As she puts it at the beginning of the essay, birthright citizenship does "nothing to resolve [illegal] parents' situation; if anything, it only add[s] to their stress" (paragraph 3). And in the end, she stresses, the issue is about "American family" values (15). Some students will agree wholeheartedly, of course, while others might reject Lee's angle altogether.

A good place to begin a discussion of Lee's topic would be to focus on students' own immigration histories, exploring where their families came from and sharing stories they may have heard from relatives before delving into what could easily become an unpleasant argument about immigration and legal status. Regardless of where students stand on the issue, they should come to recognize that the debate has a human component that is often overlooked.

Content Quiz

1. From what country did Lee's parents come to the United States?
   [Korea.]

2. What does Lee's father do for work?
   [He is an anesthesiologist.]

3. What two laws made Lee's parents illegal immigrants?
   [The Chinese Exclusion Act of 1882 and the Immigration and Naturalization Act of 1924.]

4. How were Lee's parents saved from deportation?
   [The residents of the author's hometown of Hibbing, Minnesota, signed a petition to allow them to stay, and the local representative in Congress granted them status as "permanent alien residents."]

5. Who signed the 1965 immigration law that enabled Lee's parents to apply for citizenship?
   [President Lyndon Johnson.]

Vocabulary Quiz

1. *Invoked* (paragraph 2) is closest in meaning to
   a. coined   b. used   c. forced
   [b. used]

2.   *Liaison* (4) is closest in meaning to
     a. soldier   b. communicator   c. offender
     [b. communicator]

3.   *Eschewed* (8) is closest in meaning to
     a. avoided   b. honored   c. coveted
     [a. avoided]

4.   *Fathom* (11) is closest in meaning to
     a. accept   b. understand   c. dispute
     [b. understand]

5.   *Entitled* (13) is closest in meaning to
     a. encouraged   b. excited   c. allowed
     [c. allowed]

Answers
Meaning

1.   Lee's purpose and main idea are evident throughout the essay, but her
     major claim is stated at the end of her introduction: "The words [anchor
     baby] suggest that having a child in America confers some kind of legal
     protection on illegal parents. . . . But in reality, merely having a baby on
     American soil doesn't change the parents' status" (paragraphs 2–3). She
     wants readers to reject arguments for repealing the Fourteenth Amend-
     ment; by extension, she also wants them to have a greater appreciation for
     the contributions immigrants make to American society, legal or not.

2.   As Lee explains, an anesthesiologist "administer[s] anesthesia" (paragraph
     4). The definition isn't especially helpful, but students should be able to
     infer that anesthesiologists are doctors who use drugs to manage patients'
     pain during surgery. Lee suggests that most doctors don't want to do the
     work because it involves "long hours," stress, and constant vigilance (5–6).

3.   Lee's parents were refugees from the Korean War (paragraphs 1, 4). They
     came to the United States at the encouragement of American doctors so
     that her father could "continue his education" (4) and overstayed their stu-
     dent visas (1). They did not apply for citizenship because they were ineli-
     gible to do so: laws banned Asian immigration (7–8). Although a town-wide
     petition succeeded in granting her parents permanent residency (12–13), it
     was only when President Johnson "signed a new immigration act" (15)
     that they were eligible to apply. They immediately did, successfully passed
     the exams, and "finally" became "an American family" (15).

Purpose and Audience

1.   Lee is writing for a general audience of *Los Angeles Times* readers, but she
     seems to direct her argument specifically at those who might be sympa-
     thetic to arguments that the Fourteenth Amendment encourages or enables
     illegal immigration. She assumes, first, that her readers value American

citizenship. Several other assumptions are apparent in the focus of her sub-claims: that readers value medical expertise and hard work (paragraphs 4–5, 14), that they respect the law (7–10), that they're unfamiliar with legal history (7–8, 15), that they mistrust immigrants (7, 11), and that they put a strong emphasis on family (1, 15) and community (12–13).

2.   Lee is sharing a personal experience, to be sure, especially with her empha-sis on her family's story. But her purpose is ultimately more serious. She wants to reveal what she sees as the misinformation and faulty assump-tions underlying arguments for amending the US Constitution, and to per-suade readers to reject "calls to repeal [the Fourteenth] Amendment" (2) on the grounds that repeal would be harmful to immigrants and citizens alike.

Method and Structure

1.   Lee draws on her family's and friends' experiences to support her argu-ment: she asserts that her parents were invited to study and work in the United States (paragraphs 4–5); that "peculiar laws rather than criminal intent . . . made [her] parents outlaws at the time of [her] birth" (7); that the families of her "immigrant and second-generation friends" had similar experiences (10); that American citizens benefit from the work she and her father have done (11–13); and that her "father worked at a job that other Americans did not want to do" (14). The argument is inductive: What was true for her parents, Lee implies, is true for most immigrant parents of American children.

2.   In addition to the personal experience and observations she uses through-out, Lee supports her argument with historical facts (paragraphs 7–8, 15), with the opinion of a "Korean American . . . academic who has written groundbreaking books and nurtured a generation of scholars" (10), pub-lished research concluding that "immigrants, legal and not, are more law-abiding than the rest of the populace, and possibly more patriotic" (10), and with the expert opinion of a president calling Asian immigration bans "'a cruel and enduring wrong in the conduct of the American nation'" (15). How convincing her evidence is will vary from student to student; some may catch that the studies Lee mentions in paragraph 10 are unattributed and therefore may question the validity of her generalization.

3.   Lee briefly describes the opposing argument in her introduction, summa-rizing the effort "to repeal [the Fourteenth] Amendment" as a mistaken belief that birthright citizenship benefits illegal immigrants and character-izing her opponents' attitudes as "pejorative" (paragraph 2). The rest of her essay presents her counterargument. While Lee certainly comes across as fair and reasonable, some readers might object that she does not fully address the arguments for repeal, focusing only on the "anchor baby" aspect and ignoring other points.

4.   Paragraphs 3–6, 9, and 12–15 narrate the family history. Lee gives exam-ples of laws banning Asian immigration in paragraphs 7–8 and 15. In para-graphs 8–10, 12–13, and 15, she details how those laws affected her family

and friends. By mixing personal examples with national trends, she emphasizes the human aspect of an issue that might otherwise seem abstract.

Language

1. An "anchor baby" is a child of non-US citizens granted American citizenship by virtue of having been born in the United States. In the minds of immigration opponents, such children provide incentive for illegal immigration by giving parents a reason to stay in the country and potential sponsorship for their own citizenship applications. To Lee, it's a racial slur. Like many members of minorities do, she reclaims the term and gives it a new, more positive definition: "we anchored my father to this place where his skills were so needed" (13).

2. The author's tone is vulnerable but calm; Lee expresses her personal feelings and pride in her father's (and her own) accomplishments to appeal to readers' emotions.

Roberto Rodríguez

The Border on Our Backs (p. 374)

Added to the tenth edition of *The Compact Reader* at the request of multiple instructors, Roberto Rodríguez's "The Border on Our Backs" is sure to get a rise out of students, as the author of the essay no doubt intends. As the last of three essays in a thematic casebook on the often uncomfortable issue of immigration, this is also the angriest and least compromising. Now a professor of Mexican American and race studies at the University of Arizona (he was a graduate student when he wrote this essay), Rodríguez holds no punches in expressing his view that efforts to reform immigration at any level reflect long-standing problems of American imperialism and the racism that plagues society and politics both.

Throughout his essay, Rodríguez poses some rather difficult—and often scathing—rhetorical questions, as indicated in question 3 under "Purpose and Audience." You might direct students' attention to these questions: what does Rodríguez hope to gain with them?

Content Quiz

1. Whom does the author blame for the poor treatment of immigrants from Mexico and Central America?
   ["Extremist" politicians, specifically Republicans.]

2. What, according to Rodríguez, is anti-immigrant "hysteria" really about?
   [He says it comes down to "race, color and dehumanization."]

3. To whom does the United States ultimately belong, as Rodríguez sees it?
   [Indigenous peoples, or Indians.]

4. What groups would Rodríguez like to see protesting on behalf of Mexican immigrants?
   [All of the other marginalized people in the United States: "African Americans, American Indians, Asians, Mexican Americans, and poor and white middle-class workers."]

5. How does Rodríguez define *apartheid*?
   [A "two-tiered society."]

Vocabulary Quiz

1. *Draconian* (paragraph 2) is closest in meaning to
   a. fresh   b. cruel   c. European
   [b. cruel]

2. *Vilification* (5) is closest in meaning to
   a. insults   b. anger   c. hatred
   [a. insults]

3. *Indigenous* (8) is closest in meaning to
   a. indignant   b. traditional   c. native
   [c. native]

4. *Obliterated* (8) is closest in meaning to
   a. transformed   b. erased   c. rejected
   [b. erased]

5. *Complicit* (9) is closest in meaning to
   a. guilty   b. difficulty   c. worried
   [a. guilty]

Answers

Meaning

1. Rodríguez is alluding to the idiomatic English phrase "you have a monkey on your back"—similar in structure, we might note, to the Mexican "tienes un nopal en la frente," or "you have a cactus on your forehead" (paragraph 9 footnote). The origin of the monkey-on-your-back idiom is uncertain, although it seems to date to at least the mid-nineteenth century and refers, variously, to a serious burden or problem that won't go away, an addiction, or a source of rage. In alluding to it in his title, Rodríguez neatly sums up the combined struggles, frustration, and anger he addresses in his essay. And by replacing the "monkey" with "the border," he effectively invokes the notion that immigration itself is a burden for migrants, as are international politics.

2. Rodríguez seems to find the whole issue of immigration reform absurd—and more to the point, racist and dehumanizing. He makes his position—equal rights for all—clear in paragraph 2, where he cites protesters' pleas "to be treated as full human beings"—and again in his conclusion, when he asserts that Mexicans and Central Americans living in the United States "are neither illegal nor even immigrants" (paragraph 14) but human members of the global population. He comes closest to stating his thesis in paragraph 11: "a society divided into legal and illegal human beings is no longer acceptable."

3. In addition to the Berlin Wall, Rodríguez mentions apartheid and ethnic cleansing campaigns (in South Africa, Africa, the Middle East, and the Balkans, although the author doesn't say so). He seems to be making several points with these examples. For one thing, that ethnic tensions over borders and citizenship are not unique to the United States and Mexico, and that they sometimes turn violent; at the same time, he implies that other political divisions have been viewed with moral outrage on a global level, and that many of them (Berlin, apartheid) have been demolished and relegated to history as a result. The same could happen here, he suggests.

4. Rodríguez is denying American sovereignty. The borders, he is saying, are artificial creations of a government that has routinely and illegally exploited and dehumanized the indigenous peoples of North America "who've been here forever" (paragraph 9). The implication is that Native Mexicans and Americans therefore have an inherent right to US citizenship.

5. Rodríguez cites "American Indians, African Americans and Asians" (paragraph 11)—as well as other Mexican Americans and "poor and white middle-class workers" (10)—as inspiration because they've struggled with the same oppressions and dehumanization currently being experienced by immigrants from Mexico and Central America. Rather than being "baited into fighting with" each other (10), he'd like to see them stand together and speak up for universal human rights.

Purpose and Audience

1. As indicated in the note preceding his essay and as implied in the author's own references to "draconian immigration bills" (paragraph 2), "flawed . . . bills" (13), and protests and rallies against them (2, 12, 14), Rodríguez is responding to the introduction of the Comprehensive Immigration Reform Act of 2006 and to the national outrage it sparked among Latino immigrants in particular. His essay is a call to arms—not literally, perhaps, but certainly Rodríguez intends to rile up his readers and make them as angry as he is. He expresses his goal very clearly toward the end of the essay in his thesis statement: he wants readers to "step forward and tell their representatives that a society divided into legal and illegal human beings is no longer acceptable" (11).

2. Rodríguez is writing primarily to an audience of Mexican and Central American immigrants living in the United States, whether they are in the country legally or not. By using the first-person point of view, he involves those readers in his argument directly and intimately and encourages them to share his perspective.

3. Most of Rodríguez's questions are rhetorical: they do not have easy answers, if they have answers at all. He includes them because they are the kinds of questions that plague and frustrate him every day. Writing the essay is a way of posing them to those who may not have thought of them and of prodding his readers to think critically about the issues he confronts; they're also in no small part confrontational, meant to provoke Caucasian readers with sarcasm.

Method and Structure

1. "The Border on Our Backs" presents a highly emotional argument, and students are likely to have an emotional response. Rodríguez supports his claims not with specific evidence but rather with generalizations and questions, such as "how and why do government agents single us out at lines, borders and internal checkpoints?" (paragraph 5). Some readers will surely object to this choice and cite the lack of specific evidence as a flaw in the argument, but given the author's purpose of provoking thought and indignation rather than of proposing a solution, the reliance on *pathos* above all else seems appropriate.

2. Rodríguez is arguing against "anti-immigrant hysteria" (paragraph 1) in general and Republican politicians in particular. He is not kind in his characterizations of his opponents, calling them "extremist" (1, 11) "draconian" (2), "anti-family" (2), "shameless" (5), and "complicit in our dehumanization" (9) — and coming just short of calling them racist.

3. Most notably, Rodríguez suggests throughout his essay that opponents to immigration, particularly to Mexican and Central American immigration, are guilty of hasty generalization and stereotype; he also implies that treating immigrants as either legal or illegal is an either-or fallacy. Readers might point to something of an ad hominem attack against Republican politicians on Rodríguez's part, to be sure, while others might object that the entire essay represents an inappropriate emotional appeal that ignores the question (immigration reform).

4. Rodríguez's definitions are dripping in irony. Obviously no political dictionary defines *Mexican* or *Central American* as the author says they do; his point is that they may as well, because that's how American society defines immigrants from south of the border. By baldly stating the negative perceptions of and hostilities toward Latinos, Rodríguez grabs readers' attention, engages them in his subject, and explicitly rejects the first five definitions he lists, finally substituting his own interpretation of his subject with two definitions of his own.

Language

1. Rodríguez is unmistakably angry and uncompromising, even militant. His tone will surely put some readers on the defensive despite his efforts to form a bond with them (see question 2 under "Purpose and Audience"). Other readers, particularly those who have had feelings similar to the author's, may feel that the tone strengthens the essay and gives it a punch it might not otherwise have.

2. Despite his angry tone (see the question above), Rodríguez infuses his argument with academic diction. Terms such as "dehumanization," "criminalization," and "exploitation," as well as "repatriations" (2), "auto–ethnic cleansing" (7), "indigenous" (8), and the like, while leaning toward race-studies jargon, help the author to come across as educated and well informed.

3. Particularly by ending his essay with an untranslated Nahuatl proverb, Rodríguez involves his Mexican and Central American readers in his essay as insiders while deliberately excluding many American readers from understanding; he also celebrates those very cultures that immigration policy devalues.

Guide to the Elements of Writing

The Compact Reader offers advice on writing from the general, such as organizing and revising, to the particular, such as tightening sentences and choosing words. Consult the page numbers here for help with your writing. To find the meaning of a particular term or concept, consult the Glossary on pages 412–26.